TECHNOLOGY, GROWTH, AND DEVELOPMENT

An Induced Innovation Perspective

Vernon W. Ruttan

New York   Oxford
OXFORD UNIVERSITY PRESS
2001

Oxford University Press

Oxford   New York
Athens   Auckland   Bangkok   Bogotá   Buenos Aires   Calcutta
Cape Town   Chennai   Dar es Salaam   Delhi   Florence   Hong Kong   Istanbul
Karachi   Kuala Lumpur   Madrid   Melbourne   Mexico City   Mumbai
Nairobi   Paris   São Paulo   Singapore   Taipei   Tokyo   Toronto   Warsaw

and associated companies in
Berlin   Ibadan

Published by Oxford University Press, Inc.
198 Madison Avenue, New York, New York 10016
http://www.oup-usa.org

Oxford is a registered trademark of Oxford University Press

Library of Congress Cataloging-in-Publication Data

Ruttan, Vernon W.
    Technology, growth, and development : an induced innovation perspective / by
Vernon W. Ruttan.
        p.   cm.
    Includes bibliographical references and index.
    ISBN 0-19-511871-5
    1. Technological innovation—Economic aspects.   2. Economic development.   I. Title.
HC79.T4.R88 2000
338'.064—dc21   00-029124

Printing (last digit): 9 8 7 6 5 4 3 2

Printed in the United States of America
on acid-free paper

Let no man look for much progress in the sciences unless natural philosophy be carried on and applied to particular arts, and the particular arts be carried back again to natural philosophy.

FRANCIS BACON (1620)

The learning of one man does not subtract from the learning of another, as if there were a limited quantity to be divided into exclusive holdings. . . . That which one man gains by discovery is a gain of other men. And these multiple gains become invested capital.

JOHN WESLEY POWELL (1886)

Brief Table of Contents

Contents

PREFACE

In 1970 I assumed responsibility for a course on "Technology and Development" in the University of Minnesota Department of Economics. The course had been pioneered by the late Jacob Smookler in the mid-1960s.

In 1973 I left the University to become president of the Agricultural Development Council. When I returned to the University in 1978 I again assumed responsibility for the course. In the early 1970s major attention was given to the reasons for the rapid spurt in productivity growth in the United States that began in the early 1940s. By the late 1970s the major challenge was to explain the productivity slowdown that began in the early 1970s.

Beginning in the late 1980s I began to make more formal notes for my classroom presentations and pass them out to my students. By the early 1990s the idea for a book that would serve the needs of my students and the broader research policy community began to take shape. Completing this book in the late 1990s, I find myself attempting to interpret the conflicting evidence on resurgent productivity growth in the U.S. economy and the sustainability of economic growth into the twenty-first century.

The coverage of this book is less than complete. My focus has been on the process of technical change in the goods-producing industries—the industries that are the source of growth in material consumption. I have not attempted to explore the process of technical change in the service industries. This is an important omission. The service industries are variously estimated to account for 60–70% of economic activity in the advanced industrial economies.

A unique feature of this book is its commitment to an endogenous or induced innovation interpretation of technical change. It is hard to imagine a more powerful set of forces acting to change the rate or direction of technical change than a change in the price of natural resources or of labor relative to capital.

A second unique feature of this book is the prominence it gives to biological technology. Biological technology has been neglected both by students of the history of technology and in science policy studies. During the last half of the twentieth century advances in biological science and technology have been associated with dramatic changes in the agricultural and health sectors. Concerns about the sustainability of economic growth have increasingly focused on the impact of the intensification of agricultural and industrial production on the ecological services of the biosphere.

This book is not written as a celebration of scientific and technical achievement in the United States. During the last half century, the capacity that the United States employed so effectively in the nineteenth century—to learn and borrow knowledge and technology from others—was allowed to atrophy. The transition to sustainable development in the twenty-first century will require the enlargement of scientific and technical capacity in presently poor countries. This should not be regarded as a burden on either the developed or less developed countries. Rather it represents an opportunity to multiply the intellectual talent necessary to navigate the sustainability transition.

I am indebted to the Sloan Foundation and the University of Minnesota Agricultural Experiment Station for support during the preparation of this book. I owe a very large debt to the numerous colleagues who have read and criticized my work. Students in my course on Technology, Growth, and Development have read and prepared written comments on part or all of the manuscript during the 3 years that I was most heavily involved in preparation of the book. I owe a particular debt to Jesse Ausubel, Zvi Griliches, Hans Binswanger, Robert Evenson, Irwin Feller, Arnulf Grübler, Yujiro Hayami, Edward Layton, Richard Nelson, and Nathan Rosenberg, whose work has informed my own over the years. Marilyn Clement, Linda Littrell, and Elizabeth Postigo have typed, and retyped, portions of the manuscript. The quality of the writing has benefitted from the editorial efforts of Mary Heather Smith.

PART ONE

PRODUCTIVITY AND ECONOMIC GROWTH

Since the time of Ricardo and Malthus, in the early decades of the nineteenth century, concern about the sustainability of economic growth have typically centered around the constraints imposed by natural resources—the availability of land to produce food for human consumption or of energy to fuel the needs of an industrial society (Chapter 1). More recently concerns have focused on the environmental damage resulting from the intensification of agricultural and industrial activity.

There has been a substantial slowing of economic growth in the advanced industrial economies since the late 1960s (Chapter 2). At the same time Japan and a number of other East Asian economies have experienced growth rates that lie outside the experience of the higher income Western economies. Other poor countries, particularly in Africa, have failed to achieve measurable growth in per capita income.

In the 1980s and 1990s there has been a renewed burst of interest by economists in understanding the sources and differences in growth experience. Among economists it has been widely assumed that economic growth rates in the advanced industrial economies converge toward a "natural" rate that depends on the rate of growth of the labor force, the savings rate, and the rate of technical change. This view has been reexamined in light of new growth theory and tested against historical experience with the aid of new and more powerful tools. The chapters in this section attempt to provide a perspective on the role of technical change in development thought and experience.

CHAPTER 1

Is Economic Growth Sustainable?

Can economic growth be sustained? Is technical change the engine of economic growth? These issues have generated intense controversy since at least the early years of the industrial revolution. They emerged with even greater intensity during the last half of the twentieth century.

Controversies about the sustainability of economic growth have typically centered on the constraints imposed by exhaustible natural resources—land to produce food for human consumption or energy to fuel the machines of industrial society.

Economists and technologists have typically taken an optimistic view toward the possibilities of sustainable growth. Ecologists and many natural scientists have often taken a more pessimistic view. This disagreement is illustrated by the running debate between ecologist Paul Ehrlich and economist Julian Simon.

DOOMSTERS AND BOOMSTERS

In *The Population Bomb* published in 1968, and in a number of subsequent books and papers, Paul Ehrlich argued that too many people consuming too many resources and disposing of too many pollutants were exhausting the world's resources and threatening to make the planet uninhabitable. He argued that present population and consumption levels were, even in the late 1960s, well beyond the globe's sustainable carrying capacity. This view was challenged by Julian Simon in an iconoclastic article published in 1980 in the prestigious journal *Science*, titled "Resources, Population, Environment: An Oversupply of False Bad News" and in several subsequent books. Simon was particularly critical of the view that population growth represents a threat to affluence. He argues that people are the ultimate resource—the sources of new ideas and new inventions.

The dispute between the Malthusian perspective of Ehrlich and the Cornucopian perspective of Simon was not confined to scholarly articles and books. It erupted onto editorial pages. Ehrlich characterized Simon as the leader of a "space age cargo cult" of economists convinced that new resources would miraculously fall like manna from the heavens.[1]

In 1980 Simon issued a challenge to all Malthusians—let anyone pick any natural resource product, such as wheat, oil, coal, timber, or metals, and select any future date at which they would become scarce. Simon argued that if a resource were to become scarcer as the world's population grew then its price should rise. He stood willing to bet that the price of any natural resource product selected would decline. Ehrlich derisively announced that he would "accept Simon's astonishing offer before other greedy people jump in." He then formed a consortium with two colleagues and selected five metals—chrome, copper, nickel, tin, and tungsten—in quantities that each cost $200 in the current market. A futures contract was drawn up obligating Simon to sell Ehrlich and his colleagues these quantities of these metals 10 years later—at 1980 prices corrected for inflation. If the combined cost turned out to be higher than $1000 Simon would pay the difference. If prices fell Ehrlich and his colleges would pay Simon the difference. With the contract signed Ehrlich and Simon returned to questioning each others credentials, credibility, and intelligence for the rest of the 1980s.

At the end of the decade, the average price of the five metals (corrected for inflation) had fallen by over 40%. Ehrlich mailed Simon a check for $576.07. But Simon was not ready to settle for a single victory. Nor was Ehrlich ready to concede that the consumption of the earth's resources and the degradation of the environment associated with population growth would not lead to disaster. He conceded only that he erred on time scale. Disaster is still inevitable! Simon, in turn, offered a new bet— let the doomsters pick any trend pertaining to human welfare and bet that conditions will get worse in terms of the measures they select—such as life expectancy, the price of a natural resource product, some measure of air or water pollution—and choose the area of the world and the future year. Ehrlich and a colleague have suggested a list of 15 indicators. At the time of Simon's death in early 1998 Simon and Ehrlich had not yet agreed on the terms of a new bet.

THE DISMAL SCIENCE

Many economists hesitate to associate themselves with Simon's extreme boomster-ism. Most would concur, however, that a combination of slowing population growth, capital accumulation, and technical change will enable the people of most countries to achieve higher levels of material consumption in the future than in the past.

Economists have not always been so optimistic. In the nineteenth century economics was considered the "dismal science." A central concern was with the pressure of population against resource supplies. Writing during the early years of the industrial

---

[1] For the Ehrlich and Simon arguments see Ehrlich (1968), Ehrlich and Ehrlich (1970), and Simon (1980, 1981). For comment in the popular press on the debate see Tierney (1990), McCoy (1995), and Ehrlich and Schneider (1995). See also Myers and Simon (1994).

revolution Thomas R. Malthus, a clergyman and professor of history and political economy at Haileyburg College, and David Ricardo, a successful stockbroker and member of the British Parliament, articulated the major elements of what came to be termed the classical model of economic development.[2] It is worth reviewing what Schumpeter termed "the magnificent dynamics" of the classical model both for the uncompromising pessimism of its vision and because many of the elements of the model continue to inform, often unknowingly, contemporary debates about the role of population, resources, and technology in the process of economic development.

There was basic agreement among the classicals that the growth of the labor force and the accumulation of capital were the fundamental sources of economic growth. There was also agreement that the possibilities of productivity growth in agriculture, from the division of labor and invention, were more limited than the possibilities in manufacturing. In manufacturing, the progress of invention might more than offset the tendency for diminishing returns. But in agriculture, and in the other natural resource sectors, it was held that the progress of invention would be incapable of offsetting the effects of diminishing returns. Finally, there was agreement that at the institutionally determined "natural" wage rate the long-run supply of labor is perfectly elastic.

The dynamics of the classical model, most fully developed by Ricardo, can be illustrated by tracing the effect of an increase in production resulting from a new invention. A similar sequence could be developed as the result of the discovery of new land or new raw materials.

- The increase in production creates a surplus over and above the amount necessary to cover the subsistence wage. This disposable surplus represents a "wages fund" that capitalists can use to hire more labor.
- The increase in the wages fund results in competition among capitalists for the inelastic (in the short run) supply of labor. The effect is a rise in the wage rate and a decline in the rate of return to capital.
- The higher wage rate induces an increase in the rate of population growth. The rise in wage rates and the increase in population generate a rise in the demand for food.
- The rise in the demand for food is met by bringing progressively lower quality land into production—land on which the marginal product of an incremental dose of capital and labor is lower than on the land already in use.
- The price of food rises in order to cover the cost of production on the marginal land. The effect of rising food prices is to reduce the real wage rate. As the wage rate approaches the subsistence level the rate of population growth declines.
- The production surplus that gave rise to the higher profits and the higher wage rates initially realized by capitalists and workers is absorbed by a combination of higher

---

[2] The classical synthesis emerged between the publication in 1776 of Adam Smith's *Wealth of Nations* (1937) and the publication in 1817 of David Ricardo's *The Principles of Political Economy and Taxation* (1911). Malthus is best known for his 1798 *An Essay on the Principle of Population* (1970). For the development of the classical synthesis see Tribe (1978:110–146).

land rents and the subsistence wages of a larger labor force. When the surplus has been fully absorbed, a new stationary equilibrium is reached at which all the surplus above the laborers' minimum subsistence is captured by landlords. A new round of growth is dependent on new inventions or new discovery.

In the classical model, diminishing returns to increments of labor and capital applied to an inelastic supply of land represented a fundamental constraint on economic growth. Ricardo's policy prescription was to repeal the tariff on grain (the Corn Laws). Liberalization of grain imports would prevent the domestic terms of trade from turning against the industrial sector. The Ricardian model provided ideological support to the economic interests of the emerging industrial capitalists in their efforts to achieve political ascendancy over the landed aristocracy.

In retrospect, it is clear that Ricardo and Malthus were overly pessimistic about the potential of technological progress in agriculture. In the presently developed countries total factor productivity (output per unit of total input) in agriculture has risen rather than declined in the process of economic development. The real price of agricultural commodities has declined since the middle of the nineteenth century in spite of the constraints on land resources. In contrast to the prediction of the Ricardian model, the share that land and other natural resource products account for in national income has also declined in the process of economic development. Technical change in agriculture, and in other raw material sectors, has released the constraints on growth implied by inelastic resource supplies.

The plausibility of concern about the sustainability of economic growth has been periodically reinforced during periods of economic crisis. In the late 1930s, toward the end of the Great Depression, Professor Alvin Hansen of Harvard University argued in a presidential address to the American Economic Association: "We are passing, so to speak, over a divide which separates the great era of growth and expansion of the nineteenth century from an era in which no man, unwilling to embark on pure conjecture can as yet characterize with clarity or precision" (Hansen, 1939:2). Hansen went on to identify the labor-saving character of technological innovation, the end of the era of expansion in land cultivation, and decline in the growth of population as the basis for his concern.

LIMITS TO GROWTH

During the years since World War II environmentalists have replaced economists as the dismal scientists. The trauma of the Great Depression and the fear of post-World War II economic instability directed economists' attention to an exploration of the conditions and the economic policies that could lead to "steady-state" sustainable economic growth. Productivity growth, resulting from technical change, was identified as a fundamental source of economic growth. Concerns about the constraints imposed by a scarcity in natural resources receded.

Beginning in the 1970s, economists' optimism about economic growth was challenged by the coincidence of a global energy crisis and the slowing of economic growth in the developed industrial economies. The Ricardo–Malthus concern with the adequacy of the natural resource base to sustain economic growth was supplemented by an intense concern about environmental degradation. These were highlighted for the general public by the press coverage given to the book *Limits to Growth* sponsored by the Club of Rome.[3]

There were three main elements in these new concerns:

- Continued concern about scarcity of food, raw materials, and energy under conditions of burgeoning population growth.
- Rising demand for environmental assimilation of residuals—the spillovers into the environment of pollutants arising as by-products from commodity production, energy production, and transportation.
- Growth in consumer demand for environmental amenities—for the direct consumption of environmental services associated with rapid growth in per capita income and high income elasticity of demand for environmental services such as freedom from pollution and congestion.

During the 1980s fears about the adequacy of material and energy resources abated. But concern about the implications of a series of environmental changes that were occurring at the global level intensified. These included the possibility that increases in the concentration of carbon dioxide (CO_2) and other "greenhouse" gasses in the atmosphere were leading to massive changes in climate and that human encroachment on the environment was leading to irreparable loss of biodiversity (Turner et al., 1990; Stern et al., 1992).

There has also emerged since the 1970s a renewed concern about the "social limits to growth." In the 1920s the German historian Oswald Spengler (1926, 1928) argued that Western "culture" had lost its dynamism and was heading toward becoming a static "civilization." In the mid-1980s Yale historian Paul Kennedy (1987) put forth the theses that strategic "overreach"—an imbalance between strategic commitment and economic capacity—had been the major source of decline in major empires in the past and had become a source of excessive burden on economic growth in the United States and U.S.S.R. since the middle of the twentieth century. At the time the book was written, however, it would have been considered excessively audacious, even in 1987, to have predicted the imminent collapse of Soviet empire.

Among its critics technical change came to be regarded as part of the problem confronting both the modern world and the poor countries that had been left behind. The view become pervasive in both popular and elite culture that modern

---

[3] See Meadows et al. (1972). For a critical review see Nordhaus (1973). For an update see Meadows et al. (1992).

technology—reflected in the cataclysm of war, the degradation of the environment, and the psychological cost of rapid social change—was dangerous to the modern world and the future of humankind (Ruttan, 1971). In a much more sophisticated exploration of the social limits to growth Fred Hirsch (1976) argued that the good things of life are restricted not only by the physical limits imposed by natural and human resources but also by the capacity to expand consumption without quality deterioration.

PRODUCTIVITY GROWTH

An important lesson from history is that sustained economic growth has been exceptional rather than typical. An important lesson from contemporary developing countries is that sustained economic growth has been exceedingly difficult to achieve.

In this section I present the results of a two sector economic growth simulation constructed in the spirit of the Ricardo–Malthus classical model. The model is excessively simple when compared to the complexity of the world in which we live. Yet even in its simplicity it has features that most of us will recognize as similar to our world. The lesson of the simulation is that if technical change falters in any sector of the economy the result will be a dampening of economic growth for the entire economy. The model differs from the Ricardo–Malthus model in that zero growth in per capita income may be unavoidable even in the absence of resource constraints!

The model economy is composed of two sectors—the automobile sector and the education sector (Table 1.1). In the automobile sector technical change generates a rate of growth in labor productivity (output per worker) of 3.0% per year. In the education sector there is no technical change. Labor productivity, the student–teacher ratio, remains unchanged. The name that I have given the two sectors is not important. I could have labeled one sector "professional sports"—the number of players on baseball and football teams has not changed in my memory. I could have labeled the other sector "everything else"—all those progressive goods and service production activities that have experienced technical change and productivity growth. I could have labeled one section the service sector and the other the material goods-producing sector.

In Table 1.1 I present two submodels. In Model I all of the gains in productivity are realized in the form of an increase in automobile consumption. None of the labor released by gains in labor productivity in the automobile sector is transferred to the education (or service) sector. It is used to produce more automobiles (or material goods). In Model II, I assume that all of the labor released by productivity in the automobile sector is transferred to the education (or service) sector. The two models can be viewed as extreme limiting cases of the same underlying model.[4]

---

[4] The inspiration for the two models in Table 1.1 is Baumol (1967). See also Baumol et al. (1989):124–126.

Table 1.1 Hypothetical Growth Paths for a Two-Sector Economy

	Automobile Sector					Education Sector				
Year	Labor Input (#)	Labor Productivity (Index)	Auto Output (Index)	Wage Rate ($/hr)	Auto Price ($/unit)	Labor Input (#)	Labor Productivity (Index)	Education Output (Index)	Wage Rate ($/hr)	Cost of Education ($/unit)
				Model I: No Reallocation of Labor						
t_0	100	100	100	1.00	1,000	100	100	100	1.00	1,000
t_{10}	100	135	135	1.35	1,000	100	100	100	1.35	1,345
t_{20}	100	181	181	1.81	1,000	100	100	100	1.81	1,805
t_{30}	100	243	243	2.43	1,000	100	100	100	2.43	2,425
				Model II: Full Reallocation of Labor						
t_0	100	100	100	1.00	1,000	100	100	100	1.00	1,000
t_{10}	74	135	100	1.35	1,000	126	100	126	1.35	1,245
t_{20}	55	181	100	1.81	1,000	145	100	145	1.81	1,805
t_{30}	41	243	100	2.43	1,000	159	100	159	2.43	2,425

Assumption: Productivity growths of 3.0% per year in the automobile sector and 0.0% in the education sector.

Source: Author's calculations.

In Model I population and labor force remain unchanged—the economy has already achieved zero population growth. Note that the number of workers in each sector remains 100 (or an index of 100) over the entire 30 years in which I let the simulation run. With labor productivity rising at 3% per year and the number of workers unchanged, labor productivity rises from an index of 100 to 243. I also assume that workers have a contract with the automobile industry that specifies that wages will increase at the same rate as labor productivity. This assumption is consistent with the overall experience in the U.S. economy for most of the post-World War II period (Figure 1.1). Thus wage rates rise to $2.43 per hour. If we had started with wages at $10.00 per hour they would have risen to $24.30 per hour. Note also that the price of automobiles remains unchanged. Because of the rise in labor productivity it was possible to hold automobile prices unchanged while increasing workers' wage rates because of productivity growth.

Now let us examine what happens in the education sector. Labor productivity does not rise but teachers' wage rates rise at the same rate as in the automobile sector. If it does not rise teachers will walk across the street and take jobs in the automobile sector. But if productivity does not rise and wages do rise, the cost of schooling (or tuition) must also rise. In the economy of Model I students (or taxpayers) are paying a lot more for education but are not consuming more education. This tendency for wages to rise in labor-intensive sectors that are not able to achieve productivity growth has been termed by Baumol "the service sector cost-disease."

The world of Model I may not look exactly like the world we live in. But most of us would agree that it has been easier to get productivity growth in the automobile sector

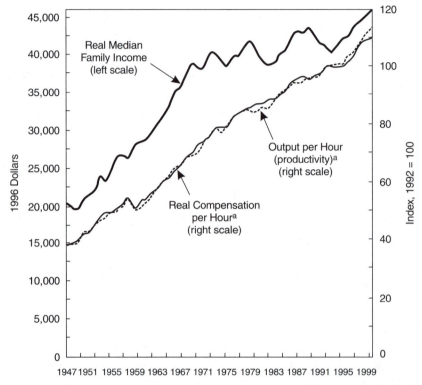

Figure 1.1 Real income, productivity, and compensation in the U.S. economy, 1947–2000.
[a] Business sector: Compensation deflated by implicit price deflator. (Adapted from Chart 1–4 of *Economic Report of the President*, 1995, p. 26. Real income data for 1994–1997, productivity data for 1994–1998, and compensation data for 1994–1998 are from *Economic Report of the President*, 1999, pp. 366 and 384. Real income data for 1998–2000, productivity data for 1999–2000, and compensation data for 1999–2000 are projected.)

than in the education sector. And most would also agree, even without looking at the numbers, that the cost of education has gone up faster than the cost of automobiles.

In Model II we take a modest step toward making the simulation more realistic. It is quite possible, even before we have two cars in every garage, that the demand for automobiles—for the material components of consumption—might begin to fall off. People get satiated. In more technical language, the income elasticity of demand for automobiles (or material consumption) declines. People would like to consume more education or other forms of "cultural consumption" (such as baseball games or symphony concerts).

It may be a bit extreme but in Model II we are going to hold automobile consumption unchanged—only one car in every garage! As productivity growth releases workers from automobile production they will be transferred to the education sector. This resembles the structural transformation that has occurred in the American economy over the last half century (Figure 1.2a and b). Consumption of agricultural commodities in the United States no longer rises as income rises. Employment in agriculture has declined from almost 50% of total employment in 1870 to less than 2% in the late 1990s. Employment in manufacturing, mining, and construction has declined from over 30% of total employment in 1950 to about 20%. Employment in the service sector (including government) accounted for over 75% of the labor force in the late 1990s.

Note that in the model economy, employment in the automobile sector has declined from 100 workers to 41 (or from 100,000 to 41,000) over the 30-year period. If the productivity growth model that has been set in motion continues to run the time will come, in the not too distant future, when there will be only one worker left in the automobile sector. Note also that in each decade the 3% annual decline in the labor force releases fewer workers to be transferred to the education sector (3% of 100 workers is three workers, 3% of 67 workers is only two workers, and 3% of 33 workers is only one worker).

As the number of workers released by productivity growth in the automobile sector declines the rate of growth of output in the education sector slows down. But the cost per unit of output in the education sector continues to rise as before. As the number of workers that can be transferred from the automobile sector declines, and the share of employment in the total economy employed in the education sector rises, the growth of the total economy grinds to a halt. Workers and consumers have higher levels of consumption than at the beginning—either in the form of more automobiles (as in Model I) or in the form of more education (as in Model II), or, under some cases intermediate to I and II, more of both. But eventually growth stops. We have backed into a no growth economy—not because of resource or environmental constraints but because of failure to achieve productivity growth in at least some service sector industries.

It appears from the simulation that if there is one sector that does not achieve productivity growth, it will eventually cause the entire economy to grind to a halt—and the larger the share of the economy that does not achieve productivity growth the more rapidly the economy will approach what the classical economists termed a "steady state."

The classicals were mistaken when they assumed productivity growth was not possible in the agricultural sector. It is also a mistake to assume that productivity growth is not possible in the service sector. Use of computers is, after some delay, contributing to productivity growth in the financial services sector. Television has made it possible for more people to watch the World Series baseball or the Metropolitan Opera. But relief from the cost disease has been only temporary. Real costs in technology-intensive transmission of television signals have declined. But the cost of labor intensive programming has risen dramaticaly (Baumol et al., 1989:137–140). It would also be possible to make the model more sophisticated, and less intelligible, by introducing more sectors and making more realistic assumptions about substitution in the material and service components of consumption. One could also

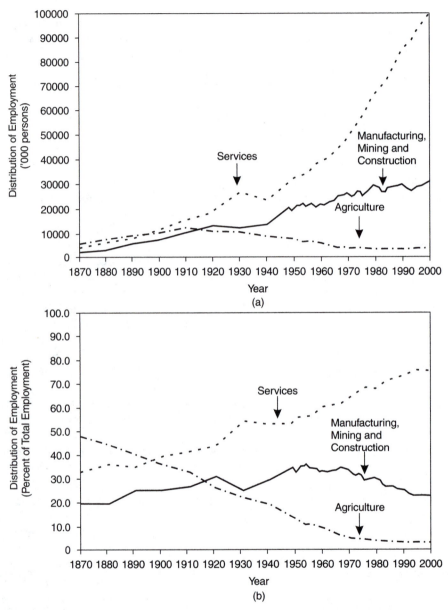

Figure 1.2 Sectoral distribution of employment in the United States, 1870–2000: (a) thousand persons; (b) percentage of total employment. (*Sources: Statistical Abstract of the United States.* Prepared by the Chief of the Bureau of Statistics, Treasury Department 1899, 1911. Bureau of the Census. *Historical Statistics of the United States*, Washington, DC: U.S. Government Printing Office, 1970. *Current Population Survey*. U.S. Department of Labor. Bureau of Labor Statistics.)

appeal to the scale economies and technological spillover employed in the "new growth theory" (Chapter 2). Even so it would not be possible to avoid a conclusion that if there are sectors in which productivity growth is not feasible, or is severely constrained, the effect would be to severely limit the possibilities for long-term sustainable economic growth.

THE BOOK PLAN

I will return again to the issues raised in this introductory chapter in subsequent chapters. In addition to this chapter the book consist of five parts.

In Part I, I examine the role of productivity change in the process of economic growth. In Part II, I explore the processes of innovation, the role of economic factors in influencing the rate and direction of institutional and technical change, and the process of diffusion of technology. In Part III I review the history of technical change in a number of important sectors and industries—agriculture, energy, chemicals, computers, and biotechnology. Part IV is devoted to a number of more general issues—the national systems of technical change, technology and the environment, and technology policy. In a final chapter I return to the theme of this chapter—the transition to sustainable development.

REFERENCES

Baumol, W. J. "Macroeconomics of Unbalanced Growth: The Anatomy of Urban Crisis." *American Economic Review* 57 (1967):415–426.

Baumol, W. J., S. A. Baty-Blackman, and E. N. Wolff. *Productivity and American Leadership: The Long View.* Cambridge, MA: MIT Press, 1989.

Ehrlich, P. R. *The Population Bomb.* New York: Ballentine Books, 1968.

Ehrlich, P. R., and A. H. Ehrlich. *Population, Resources, Environment: Issues in Human Ecology.* San Francisco, CA: W. H. Freeman, 1970.

Ehrlich, P. H., and S. H. Schneider. *Bets and Ecofantasies.* Stanford, CA: Morrison Institute for Population and Resource Studies, Paper 0060, 1995.

Hansen, A. H. "Economic Progress and Declining Population Growth." *American Economic Review* 29 (1939):1–15.

Hirsch, F. *Social Limits to Growth.* Cambridge, MA: Harvard University Press, 1976.

Kennedy, P. *The Rise and Fall of the Great Powers: Economic Change and Military Conflict from 1500–2000.* New York: Random House, 1987.

Malthus, T. R. *An Essay on the Principle of Population, as It Affects the Future Improvement of Society, with Remarks on the Speculations of Mr. Goodwin, M. Candorcet and Other Writers.* Hammondsworth, UK: Penguin Books, 1970.

McCoy, C. "When the Boomster Slams the Doomster, Bet on a New Wager." *Wall Street Journal* (June 5, 1995):A1, A9.

Meadows, D. H., D. L. Meadows, and J. Randers. *The Limits to Growth: A Report for the Club of Rome's Project on the Predicament of Mankind.* New York: Universe Books, 1972.

Meadows, D. H., D. L. Meadows, and J. Randers. *Beyond the Limits: Confronting Global Collapse, Envisioning a Sustainable Future.* Post Mills, VT: Chelsea Green Publishers, 1992.

Myers, N., and J. Simon. *Scarcity or Abundance? A Debate on the Environment.* New York: W. W. Norton, 1994.

Nordhaus, W. D. "World Dynamics: Measurement without Data." *Economic Journal* 83 (1973):1156–1183.

Ricardo, D. *The Principles of Political Economy and Taxation.* London: J. M. Dent & Sons, 1911.

Ruttan, V. W. "Technology and the Environment." *American Journal of Agricultural Economics* 53 (1971):707–717.

Simon, J. H. "Resources, Population, Environment: An Oversupply of False Bad News." *Science* 208 (1980):1431–1437.

Simon, J. H. *The Ultimate Resource.* Princeton, NJ: Princeton University Press, 1981.

Smith, A. *Wealth of Nations.* E. Cannon, ed. New York: Random House, 1937.

Spengler, O. *The Decline of the West.* New York: Alfred A. Knopf, 1926, 1928.

Stern, P. C., O. R. Young, and D. Druckman. *Global Environmental Change: Understanding the Human Dimensions.* Washington, DC: National Academy Press, 1992.

Tierney, J. "Betting the Planet." *New York Magazine* 2 (1990):52–53, 75–79.

Tribe, K. *Land, Labor and Economic Discourse.* London: Routledge and Kegan Paul, 1978.

Turner, B. L., W. C. Clark, R. W. Kates, J. F. Richards, J. T. Mathews, and W. B. Meyer, eds. *The Earth as Transformed by Human Action.* Cambridge, UK: Cambridge University Press, 1990.

CHAPTER 2

Catching Up and Falling Behind[1]

During the quarter century following World War II, the United States was clearly the world's most productive economy. The lead held by the United States in both the older mass production industries and the newer high technology industries was taken for granted both within the country and abroad. By the 1970s the United States was no longer as confident of its technical superiority. Growth of labor productivity and per capita income had slowed (Figure 1.1). Technological leadership in many industries had eroded and in some areas the United States had fallen behind. Per capita income in the other major industrial countries was rapidly converging toward that in the United States (Figure 2.1).

In the mid-1980s a major controversy emerged among students of economic growth regarding the extent and reasons for convergence. In this chapter I first review the convergence controversy. This is followed by a review of the theories of economic growth that have been advanced to interpret the role of technical change in the growth experience of the advanced industrial countries. I then discuss some of the analytical and empirical issues involved in measuring the contribution of technical change to economic growth. A final section takes a more careful look at the efforts to identify the role of technical change in the growth of the U.S. economy of the past half century.

THE CONVERGENCE CONTROVERSY

It has been widely assumed among students of economic growth that over time economic growth rates in mature economies converge toward a "natural rate" that depends on the growth rate of the labor force, the rate of investment, and the rate of technical change. Departures from this "natural rate" were regarded as temporary aberrations to be corrected by appropriate policies.

It was also generally assumed that over the long run economic forces should lead toward the convergence of economic growth rates and income levels among countries. A number of reasons have been suggested:

---

[1] I am indebted to Moses Abramovitz (1986) for both the title of this chapter and his perceptive writings about technical change and economic growth, and to Willis Peterson, Gopinath Munisamy, Terry Roe, and Tugrul Temmel for helpful comments on earlier drafts of this chapter.

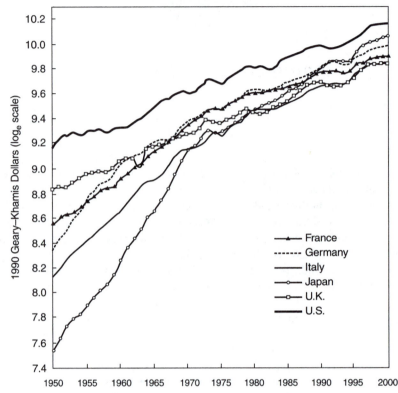

Figure 2.1 Real per capita GDP in the six largest OECD economies, 1950–2000. (*Sources:* Adapted from David Dollar and Edward N. Wolff, *Competitiveness; Convergence; and International Specialization*, Cambridge, MA: MIT Press, 1993. Data for 1950–1994 are from Angus Maddison, *Monitoring the World Economy 1820–1992*, Paris, France: Organization for Economic Cooperation and Development (OECD), 1995. Data for 1995–1997 are converted from *National Accounts: Main Aggregates 1960–1997*, 162, Paris, France: Organization for Economic Cooperation and Development (OECD), 1999. Data for 1998–2000 are projected.)

- Marginal returns to capital investment are lower in countries with high ratios of capital to labor than in countries with low ratios of capital to labor. Convergence occurs as a result of diminishing returns to reproducible capital and a slowing of growth rates in the countries in which production is characterized by the highest capital intensity.
- The cost of advancing technology is an increasing function of the level of technology. This will result in a slowing of the rate of technical change in the more advanced countries.
- The existence of a technological gap between early and late developers will enable the late developers to grow more rapidly. The relatively backward nations not only

have a pool of technical knowledge to utilize, but they can also avoid the mistakes of the leading economies.

- If institutions adapt themselves to a given technology, late developers will have an advantage over early developers because there are fewer institutional constraints on adoption of new technology. The late adopters are also freer to develop institutions that are consistent with the newer technology.

A Convergence Club?

A controversy over the convergence hypothesis was initiated in a 1986 article by William Baumol. He began by noting the wide gaps in per capita income and in labor productivity among countries that are characteristic of the modern era (Figures 2.2a and b) His reading of the fragmented evidence available on living standards in earlier periods suggested that prior to the beginning of the nineteenth century differences in productivity among countries were relatively small and differences over time were imperceptible. The technological changes that have permitted rapid growth in output per worker during the past 150 years had no earlier historical counterpart. "Living standards in Ancient Rome . . . were in many respects higher than in eighteenth century England . . . . In 1870, U.S. output per capita was comparable to 1980 output per capita in Honduras and the Philippines and slightly below that of China, Bolivia, and Egypt!" (Baumol, 1986:1073–1074).[2]

Baumol went on to argue that for several centuries before 1850 there must have been increasing divergence in the level of technology and in labor productivity and per capita income among the presently advanced countries. But since 1850 a process of convergence has been underway. For evidence Baumol drew on data assembled by Angus Maddison (1982). The countries with lowest gross domestic product (GDP) per work hour in 1870, have grown much more rapidly than the initial leaders (Figure 2.2a). The higher a country's output per worker in 1870, the more slowly the level grew over the next century. The convergence is accounted for almost entirely by a systematic tendency for the poorer countries to experience higher rates of labor productivity growth. The same relationship held for the period 1950–1979 (Figure 2.2b). The higher a country's productivity in 1950, the more slowly the level of productivity grew over the next four decades. Baumol's analysis also indicated that there had been convergence among the centrally planned economies as well as among the developed market economies. But he was skeptical that any convergence had occurred between the less developed countries and the developed market economies.

---

[2] Between 1870 and 1990 growth in real per capita gross national product (GNP) in the United States grew at 1.75% per year. "If the U.S. growth rate had been lower by just 1 percentage point per year, then U.S. real per capita GNP in 1990 would today be about the same as in Mexico and Hungary" (Barro and Sala-i-Martin, 1995:1). The importance of what might appear to be small differences in the annual rate of productivity or per capital income growth is illustrated by the increases that could be achieved in one generation (20 years) at the following growth rates: 3.5–100%, 2.7–50%, 1.1–25%, 0.5–10%.

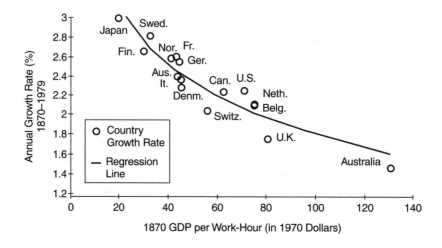

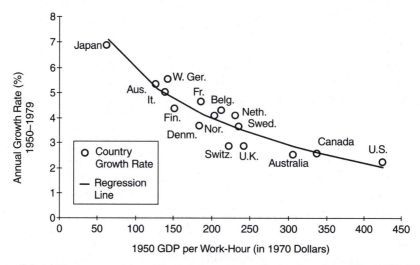

Figure 2.2 (a) Convergence in growth rates among presently developed countries, 1870-1979. (b) Convergence in growth rates among presently developed countries, 1950–1979. (*Source:* W. J. Baumol, S. A. Batey Blackman, and E. N. Wolff, *Productivity and American Leadership: The Long View*, Cambridge, MA: MIT Press, 1989:94.)

Baumol argued that the leading countries are not made worse off as a result of convergence. Productivity growth in Japan enables citizens of the United States and the United Kingdom to import automobiles, cameras, television sets, and many other items far more cheaply than if the productivity of Japan had stagnated (Baumol, 1986:1083). He could also have added that growth of agricultural productivity in the

United Sates has permitted Japan to buy feed grains and the Europeans to buy oil seeds cheaper than if U.S. agricultural productivity had stagnated.

But was Baumol right? Not everyone agreed with his analysis.

The Deck Was Stacked

The convergence thesis of Baumol was almost immediately challenged. Critics argued that Baumol had stacked the deck by picking the winners (DeLong, 1988).[3] By picking a "convergence club" of winners—the nations that have grown most rapidly—convergence is all but guaranteed! But, what should Baumol have done? DeLong argued that he should have picked all countries that were relatively rich in 1870. When he replicated the Baumol analysis, comparing the 22 "once rich countries" DeLong found little evidence of convergence. The lack of convergence was accounted for by Spain, Portugal, Ireland, Chile, and Argentina. They were counted among the rich in 1870. Why didn't they grow? DeLong finds that a variable for religion and/or democracy is important. If he had substituted a North–South geographic variable, he might have found that it worked equally as well (Sachs, 1997)!

Baumol responded to the DeLong challenge by examining the data for a broader set of countries. Using data from a study by Bairoch (1976), Baumol and Wolff (1988) examined the experience of several base period country groupings (top 8, top 9, top 10, top 11). This confirmed divergence among European countries until the latter part of the nineteenth century. However, if the number is expanded to all 19 countries studied by Bairoch (1976), divergence continued into the twentieth century. Baumol argues that this is precisely what should have been expected. "Before the Industrial Revolution, the countries of Europe (with perhaps the exception of the Dutch Republic) were relatively homogeneous in their general poverty. Then Great Britain pulled ahead, inaugurating a period of divergent growth which was intensified as a small set of European leaders—including Belgium, Switzerland, the Netherlands, France, and Germany—also jumped ahead of the others" (Baumol and Wolff, 1988:1156). Baumol and Wolff also examined the growth experience of a broader group of countries for which data on real gross domestic product had been assembled by Summers and Heston (1984) for 1950–1980. This analysis suggested divergence among the lower income countries and convergence among the higher income countries (Baumol and Wolf, 1988:1159).

From 1950 to 1980 much of the convergence among the richer countries occurred as a result of the very rapid gains in two countries—Japan and Italy. Since 1980 two other countries have undergone rapid convergence—the Republic of Korea and the Republic of China (Taiwan). As research by economic historians has extended time series data on per capita income and productivity earlier into the nineteenth century and cast their net across a wider group of countries it is clear that there

---

[3] See also Friedman (1992:2129–2132) and Quah (1993:247–443).

have been episodes of both convergence and divergence since the early nineteenth century (Figure 2.3). The large gap in levels of GDP between the countries of Western Europe and its Western offshoots (such as the United States, Canada, and Australia) occurred primarily during the first half of the twentieth century—a period in which Western Europe experienced two destructive "civil wars." During the period since World War II catch-up has characterized not only the countries of Western Europe but also Southern Europe, Eastern Europe, Latin America, and, most dramatically, East Asia. Only Africa seems not yet to have ventured fully into a modern growth path (Maddison, 1995; Williamson, 1996).

In his more recent writing Baumol and his co-authors are less secure in insisting that convergence is natural. "There are many mysteries . . . among them the curious consistency with which recent candidates for convergence have been drawn from the Far East, while those countries that seem to have lost their membership have all been in Latin America" (Baumol et al., 1989:108). They are also are a bit more concerned about the implication of convergence for the United States. They suggested that the post-World War II U.S. experience was similar to that of Great Britain during the first half of the twentieth century when that country embarked on its long period of decline. "It is clear that productivity policy remains a critically important matter for the long run economic welfare of the United States as well as that of the world" (Baumol et al., 1989:108).

Conditional Convergence

The controversy set in motion by Baumol and DeLong entered a new round in the early 1980s. Several students insisted that the convergence controversy had been cast too narrowly. A simple relationship between some beginning level of income or productivity (whether 1870 or 1950) and subsequent growth in output per capita on output per worker could not be expected to hold across all countries. A country's rate of growth could be expected to depend not only on its initial level of income or productivity but also on other critical conditions such as its rate of savings and investment, its rate of growth in population or labor force, and the level or rate of growth in the education of its working population (Dowrick and Nguyen, 1989; Mankiw et al., 1992; Williamson, 1996; Barro, 1997).

Figure 2.4, from Mankiw et al. (1992), presents a series of graphic illustrations of the effect of adding measures of the rate of accumulation of physical capital (through saving), and of the growth of the working age population (Figure 2.4b) and of the accumulation of human capital, in the form of a more highly educated labor force (Figure 2.4c) to the usual convergence diagram. Figure 2.4a presents, for 75 countries with populations of 1 million or more, a simple scatterplot of the annual growth rate of income per capita from 1960 to 1985 against the logarithm of income per capita in 1960. There is no evidence in Figure 2.4a that the countries that were poorer in 1960 grew faster. Figure 2.4b takes into account the effects of investment (as a share of GDP) and population growth. It shows that if investment and population were held

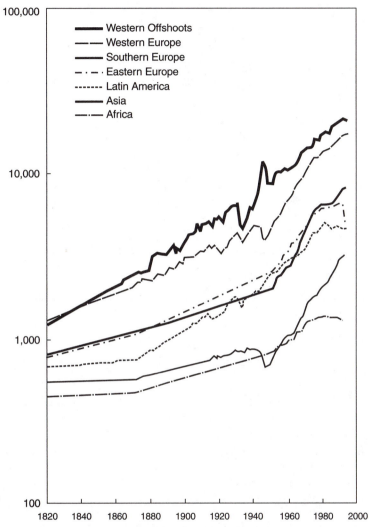

Figure 2.3 Levels of GDP per capita by region, 1820–1992. (*Source:* A. Maddison, *Monitoring the World Economy: 1820–1992*, Paris: Organization for Economic Cooperation and Development, Development Center, 1995:12.)

constant, at their 1960 level, there would have been a tendency for poor countries to grow faster than rich countries. But higher rates of investment resulted in higher rates of growth and higher rates of growth in the labor force resulted in lower rates of growth in income per working adult. Figure 2.4c indicates that when, in addition, the level of human capital, in the form of education, is held constant the tendency for convergence is further strengthened.

a. Unconditional

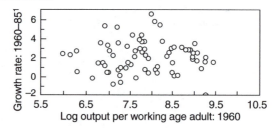

b. Conditional on investment[2] and population[3] growth

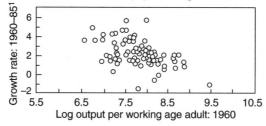

c. Conditional on investment[2] and population[3] growth and education[4]

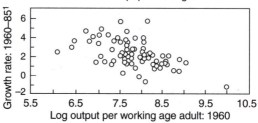

Figure 2.4 Unconditional versus conditional convergence, 1960–1985. [1]Rate of growth of output per working age adult, 1960–1985. [2]Average share of real investment in real gross domestic product. [3]Rate of growth of the working-age population (between 15 and 64 years). [4]Percentage of the working-age population in secondary school. (*Source:* Adapted from N. Gregory Mankiw, David Romer, and David N. Weil, "A Contribution to the Empirics of Economic Growth," *The Quarterly Journal of Economics* 107:2 (May 1992), pp. 407–437. © 1992 by the President and Fellows of Harvard College and the Massachusetts Institute of Technology.)

The implication the authors draw from Figure 2.4 (and the econometric analysis on which the figures are based) is that there is a "natural" tendency toward convergence. However, by increasing their capital investment, slowing the growth rate of their labor force, and investing in the education of their labor force, the richer countries have been able to increase their rates of growth of per capita income (per member of the worker age population) at approximately the same rate, on average, as the poorer countries—and hence avoid convergence. The econometric results suggest that if poor countries can raise their rates of investment in physical and human capital more rapidly than rich countries and lower their rates of population growth to approximately the same rates as richer countries it would be possible to reduce the per capita income differences by half over a period of about 35 years. This is very close to the historical experience of the newly industrializing countries (NICs) of East Asia. But it is sharply different than the experience of most developing counties. An overwhelming feature of modern economic growth has been the massive divergence of absolute and relative incomes across countries (Pritchett, 1997).[4]

What are the implications of convergence for the United States? Nelson and Wright (1992) note that arguments about the sources of convergence can be classified under three broad headings. *One* sees U.S. growth, particularly the post-World War II "spurt," as transient. It is due to the disruption of the other major industrial countries during World War II and the late start of the industrialization of the NICs and other presently poor countries. A *second* view sees not convergence but rather U.S. industry losing out in a competitive struggle with industries in other nations. In this view the United States is falling behind as England has over the last century. A *third* view posits the erosion of the economic significance of national borders. As markets and technology have become more global the network of individuals and organizations generating and improving new science-based technologies has become less national and more transnational. I will be returning to these issues in later chapters in this book.

GROWTH ECONOMICS

The preceding discussion of the convergence controversy has proceeded with relatively little attention to modern macroeconomic theories of economic growth. Modern growth theory was, however, implicit in the discussion of convergence. In this section it is made more explicit.

There have been three waves in the evolution of macroeconomic growth theory in the past half century (Box 2.1).[5] The first was stimulated by the work of Harrod (1939) and Domar (1946, 1947). The second wave began in the 1950s with the development by Solow (1956, 1957) and Swan (1956) of a neoclassical model of economic growth. The third wave was initiated in the mid-1980s by Romer (1986) and Lucas (1988).

Keynesian Growth

The following question, using somewhat different terminology, was posed by Harrod and Domar; Under what circumstances is an economy capable of achieving steady-state growth? This question had forced itself onto the economic agenda by the Great Depression of the 1930s and the expectation that the end of World War II would be

---

[4] For an exceedingly useful review of the empirics of convergence, see Temple (1999:112–156).

[5] See, for example, the collection of seminal papers in Wolff (1997). I have reviewed the evolution of growth economics and its contribution to development economics in greater detail. See Ruttan (1998).

followed by renewed instability. In the Harrod–Domar view instability in economic growth was the result of failure to equate a "warranted" and a "natural" rate of growth. The warranted rate of growth is dependent on the savings rate and on a given capital requirement per unit of output. The natural rate is the maximum long-run sustainable rate of growth. It is determined by the rate of growth of the labor force and the rate of growth of output per worker.

An attraction of the Harrod–Domar model was that it attempted to study long-run growth with the tools of Keynesian economics that had recently become familiar to economists. Use of the model diffused rapidly to the planning agencies of many newly independent countries. It seemed to confirm the widely held belief among development economists and planners that the transition from slow to rapid growth required a sustained rise in the rate of savings and investment. It provided a rationale for interventions designed to raise savings rates and encourage investment in heavy industry in order to remove the constraints on production resulting from capital equipment. It was also interpreted as consistent with the view that achieving sustained growth would be more difficult for capitalist economies than for economies in which the central planning apparatus would have more direct access to the instruments needed to force a rise in the saving rate and to allocate investment to its most productive uses.

Neoclassical Growth

Development of the neoclassical model by Solow and Swan was motivated by skepticism that a sustained rise in the savings rate is the key to the transition from a slow to a fast growth path. "The model has a constant returns to scale aggregate production function with substitution between two inputs, capital and labor. The model is completed by assuming that a constant fraction of output is invested" (Prescott, 1988:7). The model was employed in a 1957 paper in which an aggregate two factor (labor and capital) production function was used in accounting for growth in the U.S. economy. To Solow's surprise, and to the surprise of the profession generally, 80% of the growth in U.S. output per worker over the 1909–1949 period was accounted for by changes in the technology coefficient. The two papers triggered a whirlwind of theoretical and empirical research that lasted well into the 1970s.

In the initial Solow–Swan neoclassical model a country that succeeds in permanently increasing its savings (investment) rate will, after growing faster for a while, achieve a higher *level* of output than if it had not done so. The development and diffusion of a new general purpose technology could result in a temporary "spurt" in the rate of productivity and output growth and raise per capita income to a new higher level. But unless a new general purpose technology emerges the rate of growth will return to the earlier "natural" rate of growth. The country will not achieve a permanently higher *rate* of growth of output (Solow, 1988:308). This seemed to completely reverse the earlier Harrod–Domar implications. Technological change replaced growth of capital equipment as the primary source of growth. Subsequent growth-accounting exercises employing broader definitions of capital resulted in somewhat lower estimates of the contribution of technical change. But, as noted earlier in this chapter, technical change continued to outweigh growth of physical capital stock by a substantial margin in studies conducted in the United States and other presently developed countries. Research on sources of growth in poor or newly developing countries typically found that a much smaller share of economic growth was accounted for by productivity growth. This was often interpreted as an indication that inappropriate technology transferred from high-wage economies, where it had been developed, to low-wage economies failed to generate productivity gains as high in low-wage as in high-wage economies.

Endogenous Growth

The economics literature of the 1980s on endogenous growth was initially motivated by the apparent inconsistency between the implications of the neoclassical theory and (1) lack of evidence of convergence toward steady-state growth even among presently developed economies and (2) the difficulty in successfully accounting for differences in income growth rates or income levels across developed and developing countries.

In the initial endogenous growth models, long-run growth is driven primarily by the accumulation of knowledge (Romer, 1986). The production of new knowledge exhibits diminishing returns at the firm level. However, the creation of new knowledge by one firm is assumed to generate positive-external effects on the production technology of other firms. Furthermore, the production of consumption goods, which is a function of both the stock of knowledge and other inputs, exhibits increasing returns. The three elements, decreasing returns in the production of new knowledge, externalities associated with new knowledge, and increasing returns in the production of output ensure that a competitive equilibrium will exist, even in the presence of externalities.

The initial models advanced by Romer abandoned the neoclassical assumption of perfect competition and required either constant or increasing returns to capital. An important implication of the model is that the market equilibrium is suboptimal since the external effects of the accumulation of knowledge are not considered by the firm in making production decisions. Another implication is that factor shares, typically employed as the elasticity coefficients in the neoclassical production function, can no longer be used to measure the contribution of capital and labor. Romer suggests that the typical capital coefficient (0.25) severely underestimates the contribution of capital and the labor coefficient (0.75) severely overestimates the contribution of labor.

In the Lucas (1988) alternative to the neoclassical model human capital serves as the engine of economic growth. Lucas employed a two-sector model in which human capital is produced by a single input, human capital, and in which final output is produced by both human and physical capital. Two alternative human capital models were analyzed. In the first, the schooling model, the growth of human capital depends on how a worker allocates his or her time between current production and accumulation of human capital. In the second, the learning-by-doing model, the growth of human capital is a positive function of the effort devoted to the production of new goods. In 1990 Romer advanced an alternative endogenous growth model in which he followed Lucas in emphasizing the importance of human capital in the development of new knowledge and technology.

As his work continued to mature Romer has turned to the contribution of ideas as the primary source of economic growth (Romer, 1993, 1997). Romer argues that neoclassical growth theory explains growth in terms of interactions between technology and conventional inputs. In his most recent version of the new growth theory, the sources of growth are "ideas" and "things." Ideas are nonrival goods. Things are rival goods. For Romer, scale effects are important because ideas, which are nonrival goods that are not consumed in the process of use, are expensive to develop but are inexpensive to use. Their value increases with the size of the market. An implication is that new institutional arrangements will be required, beyond traditional intellectual property rights and government subsidies, to induce an appropriate level of investment in the development of ideas.

● BOX 2.1

Three Growth Models

The Keynesian (Harrod–Domar) Growth Model

In the Harrod–Domar model instability in economic growth is the result of failure to equate a "warranted" and a "natural" rate of growth. When the warranted rate is given by s/v and the natural rate by $n + m$ the equilibrium expression is

$$s/v = n + m$$

where

s is the saving rate (a fixed fraction of net output)

v is the capital requirement per unit of output

n is the rate of growth of the labor force (and population)

m is the rate of labor-saving technical change

Thus, if the savings rate were 10% of income and the capital output ratio 4, the warranted rate of growth would be 2.5%. If the labor force was growing at 1.0% and labor productivity at 1.5% per year, the warranted and natural rates would be equated.

The Neoclassical (Solow–Swan) Growth Model

The contribution of the neoclassical (Solow–Swan) growth model was to substitute a variable capital-output ratio for the fixed coefficient capital-output ratio in the Harrod–Domar model. The model has a constant returns to scale aggregate production function that permits substitution between capital and labor. It is assumed that a constant fraction of output is invested.

$$c_t + i_t = f(k_t, n_t)$$

$$k_{t+1} = k_t + i_t$$

$$i_t = \sigma f(k_t, n_t)$$

where

c is consumption

i is investment

k is capital

n is labor

σ is the fraction of output invested.

The Endogenous (Romer–Lucas) Growth Model

The "new" literature on endogenous growth was motivated by a presumed lack of evidence of convergence toward steady-state growth in the presently developed economies and by the inability to successfully account for differences in growth rates or income levels across countries. The initial models are frequently referred to as AK models after the assumed production function AK where K can be thought of as a proxy for a composite capital good that includes physical and human components.

$$Y = K^{1-\alpha}(AL_Y)^\alpha$$

$$A = \delta L_A$$

where

Y is output

A is productivity, knowledge or ideas

K is capital

δ parameterizes the efficiency of research and development (R&D). Labor is used in two activities, the production of output (L_Y) and the search for innovations (L_A) so that $L_Y + L_A = L$.

Given some level of knowledge A, doubling capital and labor input into production is sufficient to double output; doubling the stock of knowledge as well would lead to more than doubling of output.

Sources: In preparing this box, I have drawn on R. F. Harrod, "An Essay in Dynamic Theory," *Economic Journal* 49 (1939):14–33; R. F. Harrod, *Toward a Dynamic Economics*, London: MacMillan, 1948; E. Domar, "Capital Expansion, Rate of Growth and Employment," *Econometrica* 14(1946):137–147; E. Domar, "Expansion and Employment," *American Economic Review* 37 (1947):343–355; R. M. Solow, "A Contribution to the Theory of Economic Growth," *Quarterly Journal of Economics* 70 (1956):65–94; R. M., Solow, "Technical Change and the Aggregate Production Function," *Review of Economics and Statistics* 29 (1957):312–320; T. W. Swan, "Economic Growth and Capital Appreciation," *Economic Record* 32 (1956):343–361; P. M. Romer, "Increasing Returns and Long Run Growth," *Journal of Political Economy* 94 (1986):1002–1037; P. M. Romer, "The Origins of Endogenous Growth," *Journal of Economic Perspectives* 8 (1994):3–22; R. E. Lucas, Jr., "On the Mechanics of Economic Development," *Journal of Monetary Economics* 22 (1988):3–42; R. E. Lucas, Jr., "Making a Miracle," *Econometrica* 61 (1993):3–42; E. C. Prescott, "Robert M. Solow's Neoclassical Growth Model: An Influential Contribution to Economics," *Scandinavian Journal of Economics* 90 (1):7–12; V. W. Ruttan, "The New Growth Theory and Development Economics: A Survey," *Journal of Development Studies* 35 (1998):1–26; C. I. Jones, *Introduction to Economic Growth*, New York: W. W. Norton, 1998.

The most important implication of the Romer–Lucas-inspired endogenous growth literature for economic development has been the endogenization of human capital formation. This led to an important analytical result: when investment takes place in an economic environment with increasing returns to scale the marginal product of capital need not, as in the neoclassical model, decline over time to the level of the discount rate. Thus, at least in the model, the incentive to enhance the quality of human and physical capital may permanently raise the long-run rate of growth in per capita income. This makes it possible for government to permanently increase the rate of economic growth, and not just the level of per capita income, by pursuing an active technology policy (Verspagen, 1992:659).

The new growth literature debate has also helped to clarify the puzzle discussed at the beginning of this chapter. Why have some poor countries, over a period of as little as two generations, been able to achieve levels of productivity and income roughly comparable to the levels achieved by the older developed countries? A poor country that is able to raise its rate of investment in physical and human capital, take advantage of the opportunities for transfer of knowledge and technology, and lower its rate of population growth has an opportunity to experience a period of exceptionally rapid growth. Italy, Japan, Korea, and Taiwan are recent examples. However, as these opportunities are exhausted, the growth rates of the newly rich countries will decline, as implied in neoclassical growth theory, toward the rates of the older rich countries, unless they develop endogenous capacity to generate new knowledge and new technology (Basu and Weil, 1998).[6]

---

[6] By the mid-1990s the Romer–Lucas "new growth theory" had stimulated a massive empirical literature designed to test the endogenous growth hypothesis. Some of this literature is reviewed in the previous section. For a review, see Temple (1999). The Romer–Lucas work has also stimulated the preparation of

Neither the old nor the new growth models adequately address the constraints on growth discussed in the two classical models discussed in Chapter 1. The existence of an inelastic supply of natural resources (or the services of nature) or failure to achieve productivity growth in an important sector of the economy would substantially constrain the capacity to generate long-term sustainable growth. A second concern with both the neoclassical and the new endogenous growth theories is that they focus on the proximate sources of growth rather than the more fundamental sources.[7] Both have neglected the institutional sources of economic growth. Improvements in the quality of physical and human capital will lead to diminishing returns in the absence of productivity-enhancing and institutional innovation. And the new income streams generated by institutional innovation will atrophy in the absence of technical change. In subsequent chapters I give particular attention to the sources of both technical and institutional change and to the dialectical interactions between these two sources of growth.

ACCOUNTING FOR ECONOMIC GROWTH

In Chapter 1, and in the discussion of the convergence controversy in this chapter, I focused primarily on labor productivity as an indicator of technical change. Labor productivity—output per worker—is relatively easy to measure. Because of its historically close association with labor compensation (Figure 1.1), it has also been used as a rough measure of economic welfare. The development of the Swan–Solow neoclassical model of economic growth shifted attention to total or joint factor productivity—output per unit of total input—as an indicator of technical change and economic performance (Griliches, 1996:1324–30).

The shift from the use of partial productivity measures, such as output per unit of labor input, to output per unit of total input, such as total factor productivity (or joint factor productivity) encountered a number of difficult analytical and measurement problems. There are a number of inherent analytical problems involved in the construction of indexes of total factor productivity. These include the effects of (1) changes in relative input and product prices over time, (2) labor-saving or capital-saving bias (nonneutrality) of technical change, and (3) economies or diseconomies of scale.[8]

---

several textbooks that review and extend the work in growth economics (Barro and Sala-i-Martin, 1995; Aghion and Howitt, 1998; Jones, 1997).

[7] One major exception is the research agenda being pursued by Parente and Prescott (1994, 2000). They invoke institutional constraints on the efficient use and diffuse of technologies developed in the most advanced countries to explain the large and persistent differences in productivity and income levels among countries that cannot be explained by differences in human and physical capital. A second is the recent emphasis by Romer (1997) on the need for new institutional arrangements to induce an appropriate level of investment in the development of ideas.

[8] For the simple analytics of total factor productivity measurement see the Appendix. For a definitive treatment, see Fisher and Shell (1998).

There has also been a continuing debate about the measurement of factor inputs.[9] Beginning in the mid-1960s, Professors Jorgenson and Griliches, then at the University of Chicago, argued that if quantities of output and input were measured accurately, growth in total output would be largely explained by growth in total input. More specifically, "if changes in total factor productivity are corrected for errors in the measurement of output, capital services, and labor services the rate of growth of total factor productivity would be reduced from 1.6% per year to 0.1% per year" (Jorgenson and Griliches, 1967:249). Critics insisted that Jorgenson and Griliches obtained their low estimates of productivity growth by introducing new errors, particularly in their adjustment for use of capital and land. Edward Dennison argued that they had inappropriately counted as contributions of capital and land the gains made possible by technical change. The debate between Dennison and Jorgenson and Griliches led to substantial refinements in the methodology of productivity measurement. In the end Jorgenson and Griliches conceded that even with the appropriate refinements their initial research agenda, accounting for all of output growth by a corrected version of total inputs, could not be realized (Jorgenson et al., 1972:67; Hulten, 2000).

Comparative Productivity Growth

It is now conventional for growth accountants, working within the framework of the neoclassical model of economic growth, to include adjustments for changes in the quality of labor and quality of other factors that may bias change in total factor productivity as an indicator of technical change. The conceptual framework for such adjustments, employed by Professor Angus Maddison, a leading student of growth accounting, is presented in Box 2.2.

The estimates of long-term productivity growth constructed by Professor Maddison, joint factor productivity, augmented joint factor productivity, and residual factor productivity, growth are presented in Table 2.1. Three comparisons stand out:

- The first post-World War II quarter century does appear to be unique. Each of the countries experienced much more rapid productivity growth during 1952–1973 than during either 1913–1950 or 1973–1984. In addition, joint factor productivity growth was higher in 1973–1984 than in 1913–1950 for France, Germany, Japan, and the United Kingdom.

---

[9] For a review of the early contributions see Griliches (1996). The papers from an extended exchange between Edward Dennison and Dale Jorgenson and Zvi Griliches have been collected in a Brookings Institution reprint (Jorgenson et al., 1972). For an exceedingly thoughtful discussion, see the presidential address to the American Economic Association by Arnold C. Harberger (1998:1–32).

● BOX 2.2

ALTERNATIVE PRODUCTIVITY MEASURES

Labor Productivity	$\dot{\pi}_1 = \dot{O} - \dot{L}$
Capital Productivity	$\dot{\pi}_2 = \dot{O} - \dot{K}$
Joint Factor Productivity	$\dot{\pi}_3 - \dot{O} - a\dot{L} - (1-a)\dot{K}$
Augmented Joint Factor Productivity	$\dot{\pi}_4 = \dot{O} - a\dot{L}^* - (1-a)\dot{K}^*$
Residual Factor Productivity	$\dot{\pi}_5 = \dot{O} - a\dot{L}^* - (1-a)\dot{K}^* - \dot{S}$

where

$\dot{O}$ is rate of increase in output

$\dot{L}$ is rate of increase in labor input

$\dot{K}$ is rate of increase in capital input

$\dot{L}^*$ is rate of increase in augmented labor (Dennison)

$\dot{K}^*$ is rate of increase in augmented capital (Maddison)

$\dot{S}$ is rate of change in supplementary factors

Supplementary factors:

1. change in economic structure
2. convergence (catch up)
3. trade liberalization
4. energy price effects
5. economies of scale at the national level
6. natural resource discovery
7. government regulation and crime
8. labor hoarding/dishoarding
9. use of capacity effect

   Labor input estimates were augmented by adjustments for age, sex, and education. Capital is augmented by arbitrarily assuming a 1.5% annual improvement. Thus technical change in capital equipment is arbitrarily built into the estimates.

Source: Angus Maddison, "Growth and Slowdown in Advanced Capital Economies," *Journal of Economic Literature* 25 (June 1987):649–698.

- The United States experienced the most rapid growth in productivity in 1913–1950 but slipped behind other countries in 1950–1973 and in 1973–1984. Augmented joint factor productivity turned negative in the United States in 1973–1984.

- The augmented joint factor productivity estimates that incorporate the effects of improvement in labor and capital quality run 0.5 to 1.0 percentage points below the joint factor productivity growth rates. The same relationship holds in comparisons between 1913–1950 and 1973–1984 as in joint factor productivity.

Among the supplementary factors the following were significant:

- Structural change has been an important factor. At the early stage of industrialization, the shift of labor from agriculture to nonagricultural sectors made an important contribution to productivity growth. Among the presently industrialized countries only Japan can continue to make significant gains from this source. As the share of agriculture has declined to below 5%, transfer of labor to other sectors generates smaller increments in economic growth.

- The countries that lagged in beginning their industrial development and agricultural modernization process did experience, as argued in the convergence literature, a "catch-up bonus." Among the major industrial countries Japan has been the greatest beneficiary during the period covered by these data. The United States and Germany were important beneficiaries in the nineteenth century.

- During the interwar period (1918–1940) protectionist economic policies exerted an important dampening effect by limiting economics of scale and productivity growth. This effect has been reversed since World War II as more open trading policies have been adopted.

Productivity Trends in the United States

During the early 1980s the methods developed by scholars such as Dennison, Griliches and Jorgenson, and Maddison to separate changes in factor quality from other sources of productivity changes were being adopted by the federal agencies responsible for the construction of annual input, output and productivity measures.[10] In 1983 the Bureau of Labor Statistics (BLS) of the U.S. Department of Labor published multifactor (or joint factor) productivity estimates, extending back to 1948, for the private business and private nonfarm business sectors. The BLS estimates for 1948–1994 are summarized in Table 2.2. The BLS estimates suggest a decline from the 1948–1973 rates since 1973. The data indicate a partial recovery in multifactor productivity during the 1990s, but do not suggest a recovery to anywhere near the 1948–1973 rate. Interpretation of the data for the period beginning with 1990 is somewhat ambiguous.

---

[10] For a very useful review see Boskin and Lau (1992:32).

Table 2.1   Long-Term Productivity Growth in Advanced Industrial Countries

(a) Joint Factor Productivity, 1913–1984
(Annual Average Compound Growth Rate)[a]

	1913–1950	1950–1973	1973–1984
France	1.42	4.02	*1.84
Germany	0.86	4.32	1.55
Japan	1.10	*5.79	1.21
Netherlands	1.25	3.35	0.81
United Kingdom	1.15	2.14	1.22
United States	*1.99	1.85	0.52
Average	1.30	3.58	1.19

(b) Augmented Joint Factor Productivity, 1913–1984
(Annual Average Compound Growth Rate)[b]

	1913–1950	1950–1973	1973–1984
France	0.61	3.11	0.93
Germany	0.19	3.61	*1.13
Japan	0.04	*4.69	0.43
Netherlands	0.53	2.38	0.14
United Kingdom	0.38	1.53	0.64
United States	*1.19	1.05	−0.27
Average	0.49	2.73	0.50

(c) Residual (Unexplained) Factor Productivity Growth
(Annual Average Compound Growth Rate)[c]

	1913–1950	1950–1973	1973–1984
France	0.48	1.81	0.59
Germany	0.32	1.63	0.69
Japan	0.13	0.64	0.04
Netherlands	0.41	1.06	0.46
United Kingdom	0.38	1.06	0.49
United States	0.81	0.81	−0.01
Average	0.42	1.17	0.38

*Most rapid growth.

[a]Joint factor productivity equals GDP growth minus the contributions of labor quantity, residential capital quantity, and nonresidential capital quantity.

[b]Augmented joint factor productivity is equal to joint factor productivity minus the contributions of labor quality and capital quality.

[c]Residual factor productivity is equal to joint factor productivity minus the contribution of supplementary sources of growth in output.

Source: A. Maddison, "Growth and Slowdown in Advanced Capitalist Economies," *Journal of Economic Literature* 25 (June 1987):649–698 (Tables 11a, 11b, 20).

Table 2.2 Sources of Growth in Real Output in the Private Nonfarm Business Sector

	1948–1973	1973–1979	1979–1900	1990–1997
Real output	4.1	2.9	2.6	2.4
Contribution to output				
Total factor input	**2.2**	**2.6**	**2.7**	**2.0**
Labor Input	1.0	1.4	1.5	1.4
Hours	*0.8*	*1.4*	*1.1*	*1.0*
Employment	1.1	1.8	1.3	
Work week	−0.3	−0.4	−0.2	
Composition	*0.1*	*0.0*	*0.3*	*0.4*
Education	0.2	0.3	0.3	
Work experience	−0.1	−0.3	0.1	
Other	0.0	0.0	0.0	
Capital Input	1.2	1.2	1.2	0.6
Stock	*0.9*	*0.9*	*0.9*	
Composition	*0.3*	*0.3*	*0.3*	
Multifactor productivity	**1.9**	**0.4**	**0.0**	**0.4**
R&D	0.2	0.1	0.2	0.2
Other	1.7	0.2	−0.2	0.1

Note: May not sum to total due to rounding.

Source: Bureau of Labor statistics.

Professor Jorgenson has also continued to refine his efforts to partition the growth in total output among changes in labor quantity, labor quality, capital stock, capital quality, and total or joint factor productivity (Figure 2.5). There were substantial shifts in the share of output accounted for by the several sources of growth following the productivity slowdown of the late 1960s and early 1970s. Between 1966–1973 and 1973–1995 the share of growth accounted for by changes in labor quality declined from 13.1 to 9.8%, the share accounted for by capital quality rose from 2.1 to 8.7%, and the share accounted for by productivity declined from 32.0 to 10.2%. The rise in the share of growth accounted for by the traditional inputs, from 52.8 to 71.2%, is consistent with other evidence on the productivity slowdown in the United States since 1973.

By comparing the growth of multifactor productivity in the several sectors of the economy, and the changing relative importance of the several sectors, we can gain some insight into the sectoral sources of the slowdown in productivity (Table 2.3). The rate of multifactor productivity growth in the agricultural sector has been well above that in the rest of the economy throughout the post-World War II period (Jorgenson and Gollop, 1995:389–399). Growth in multifactor productivity in the manufacturing sector has exceeded that of the rest of the nonfarm business sector since the mid-1970s. Apparently much of the slowdown in the multifactor productivity growth is due to slow productivity growth in the service sector. What this means

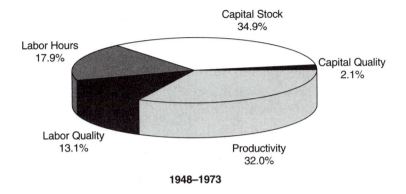

1948–1973

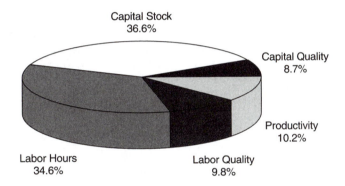

1973–1996

Figure 2.5 Sources of output growth in the United States, 1948–1973 and 1973–1996. (*Source:* D. Jorgenson and E. Yip, *Progress in Productivity Measurement: An Overview*, paper presented at a seminar in commemoration of Zvi Griliches' 20 years as Director of the NBER program on Productivity and Technological Progress, National Bureau of Economic Research, Cambridge, MA, March 5–6, 1999, appendix figures and tables.)

is somewhat ambiguous since measurement of changes in output and productivity in these sectors is less precise, and probably less accurate, than in the goods-producing sector.[11]

---

[11] Data assembled by Jorgenson et al. (1987) suggest that over the entire 1948–1979 period in the goods-producing sector the lowest rate of productivity growth has been in the extractive industries (such as natural gas, petroleum, and coal products) and in the primary metal industries. In the nonmanufacturing sector negative productivity growth rates occurred in transportation services, street railways, bus lines and taxicabs, radio broadcasting and television, and business services and institutions. The decline in several transportation sectors was apparently associated with declining demand.

Table 2.3   The Distribution of GNP by Major Industrial Sector, in Current Prices (Percentages)

Industry	1947	1959	1969	1977	1990	1997
Agriculture, forest, and fishing[a]	8.8	4.1	3.0	2.8	2.0	1.6
Mining[a]	2.9	2.5	1.8	2.7	1.8	1.5
Manufacturing[a]	28.1	28.6	26.9	23.6	18.4	17.0
Transportation and utilities[a]	8.9	9.1	8.6	9.1	8.7	8.3
Construction	3.9	4.8	5.1	4.8	4.4	4.1
Wholesale Trade	7.1	6.9	6.7	7.0	6.5	6.9
Retail Trade	11.7	9.9	9.8	9.6	9.3	8.8
Finance, insurance, and real estate	10.1	13.8	14.2	14.4	17.7	19.4
Other services	8.6	9.7	11.5	13.0	18.9	20.4
Government	8.6	10.2	12.6	12.5	12.2	12.7
"Measurable" sectors[a]	**48.**7	**44.**3	**40.**3	**38.**2	**30.**9	28.4

Note: Numbers before 1977 are not strictly comparable, since the latest revision was carried back only to 1977.

[a]Agriculture, forest and fishing, mining, manufacturing, and transportation and utilities.

Sources: Adapted from Z. Griliches, "Productivity, R&D, and the Data Constraint," *American Economic Review* 84 (1, March 1994):1–23. Data are from Tables 6.1 and 6.2 of the *National Income and Product Accounts*, 1928–1982, and *Survey of Current Business*, May 1993 and March 1999.

FALLING BEHIND

There is now almost universal agreement among students of economic growth that for more than a generation the U.S. economy has performed poorly compared to the first quarter century after World War II (Krugman, 1994:700). In this section I examine some of the explanations for the slowdown in productivity and per capita income growth.

Initially there was a tendency to attribute the slowdown to temporary effects associated with the business cycle. Productivity growth typically begins to slow as the economy returns to full employment and continues to decline into the following recession. During the latter part of a recession and during the initial recovery, productivity typically increases. A reason for this cyclical behavior is that during the beginning of a recession firms have generally been reluctant to lay off workers because they want to avoid rehiring costs when the next expansion occurs. When expansion occurs employment expands more slowly than production. But as the peak of the expansion approaches less experienced workers are drawn into the labor force and less productive facilities, that may have been idled during the recession, are also brought on line (Sbordone, 1996). The persistence of the slowdown for over two decades weakened the credibility of the business cycle explanation. It is not unusual, however, to find articles in the popular and business press, particularly during the early recovery phase of a business cycle, proclaiming that the latest data demonstrate that the U.S. economy is now back on a high productivity growth path.

If the slowdown was real what were its sources? There is yet no fully adequate explanation. But six sources appear to account for a major share of the slowdown. These include energy prices, private capital formation, public infrastructure investment, technical progress, the composition of output, and government regulation. A number of popular explanations have also been advanced for which there is little empirical support. Among such explanations are deterioration of American management, a rise in dishonesty and crime, costs of pollution abatement and safety regulations, depletion of natural resources, a reduction in the work ethic — "people just don't want to work anymore," and business school education, which has diverted management attention from technology to finance—"managers no longer understand technology."[12]

Energy and Raw Material Prices

The argument that the slowdown was due to the dramatic increases in energy, particularly petroleum, prices in 1973 and 1979 has been most vigorously advanced by Jorgenson (1986). The plausibility of the energy price explanation is largely based on the timing. The sharp decline in the role of productivity increases that began in 1974 followed the 1973 oil crisis. And the further decline in the rate of productivity increase that began in 1980 followed the 1979 oil shock. Jorgenson argued that the energy price shocks made many existing energy-intensive industrial facilities obsolete and induced the substitution of capital, materials, and labor for inputs of electricity and nonelectrical energy. Critics observed that energy prices are a small portion of total cost (1.5% in 1973 and 2.5% in 1997) and thus do not weigh heavily in calculations of productivity (Berndt, 1990). There is now broad agreement that the energy crisis of the 1970s did impose a burden on productivity growth that lasted well into the 1980s, but there remains substantial disagreement about the magnitude (Chapter 7). There is also substantial evidence that the rise in the prices of raw materials that coincided with the rise in energy prices also played an important role in damping productivity growth (Bruno, 1984).

Capital Formation

The role of capital formation as a source of the productivity slowdown has generated a great deal of controversy. Several factors have contributed to the difficulty of interpreting the evidence. Output per unit of capital did show a modest decline—by 13.5% in 1965–1973 and 12.8% in 1973–1978. However, partly as a result of greater participation in the labor force, total hours worked rose rapidly after the mid-1960s (from 0.38% in 1948–1965 to 1.44% in 1965–1973 and 1.42% per year in 1973–1978) resulting in a decline in the capital–labor ratio. Since new capital equipment is generally more productive than older capital equipment, even a modest slowdown

---

[12] In this section I draw very heavily on Dennison (1985:44–57) and Wolff (1985:29–57).

in investment contributes to slowing of productivity growth. Part of the new capital equipment that was installed after the mid-1960s was to meet new environmental and safety standards rather than to increase productivity. Wolff estimated that changes in the rate and composition of capital formation may have accounted for over half of the productivity slowdown between 1965 and 1973 and over a quarter of the productivity slowdown between 1973 and 1978.

Public Infrastructure Investment

The relationship between public infrastructure investment and productivity growth has been explored by several students of productivity growth (Aschauer, 1989; Munnell, 1990). Munnell noted that nearly two-thirds of nonmilitary public capital consists of "core infrastructure." This includes the highways, airports, and mass transit facilities that link the nation together, and the electric and gas utility plants, water supply facilities, and sewers that allow industry to operate. A second major category of nonmilitary public capital is buildings—including schools, national research laboratories, hospitals, police and fire stations, courthouses, garages, and passenger terminals—all of which contribute to an environment that facilitates private production.

The stock of public nonmilitary capital grew at a rate of 4.1% per year during 1948–1969 and only 1.6% per year during 1969–1987. As the rate of public investment declined the rate of growth in the public capital–labor ratio also declined. Aschauer estimated that the decline in investment in public capital has lowered labor productivity growth by between 0.1 and 0.2 percentage points per year from its long-term rate of growth of 1.7% annually.[13]

The Service Sector

Another important source of decline in the rate of productivity growth has been a change in the sectoral composition of output (Table 2.3). Productivity growth is influenced by shifts in the composition of output among high- and low-productivity sectors. The shift in employment from the agricultural to the manufacturing sector was, in the early post-war period, an important source of productivity growth for the U.S. economy. Growth in the relative size of the service sector became, in the 1980s and 1990s, a focus for much of the concern about the decline in the rate of productivity growth in the U.S. economy. The service sector is composed of a broad spectrum of industries, ranging from those that produce cultural amenities (symphony orchestras and baseball teams) to those such as financial services, telecommunications, and airlines. About the only thing they have in common is that what they produce is not

---

[13] Peterson (1994) has shown that the decline in public capital investment has been a response to a decline in the marginal rate of return on public capital. This conclusion is not, of course, inconsistent with the conclusion that the slower rate of public capital investment accounts for part of the productivity slow down.

a physical product. Much of the concern focused on those sectors of the service and related industries that are relatively labor intensive and for which productivity change is difficult to achieve (Chapter 1).

A more careful analysis suggests that in spite of the growth in the share of GNP and the share of the labor force employed in the service sector, if we deflate the output figures for manufacturing and services and construct estimates of their real outputs, we find that in the United States "the share of the real output of the services relative to that of manufacturing has not been rising" (Baumol et al., 1989:121). What is going on here? The growth of the share of GNP accounted for by the service sector is largely due to the rise in the price of services, particularly those that are more labor intensive, relative to manufacturing. In 1985 it was estimated that from 20 to 25% of the decline in the overall rate of productivity growth since the late 1960s was accounted for by shifts in the sectoral composition of final output toward services (Wolff, 1985:46).

Technical Change

As stated earlier, most studies that attempt to quantify the contribution of technical change to the productivity slowdown measure the effect of technical change by treating it as a residual (Box 2.1). This often leads to implausible results, particularly over short periods. Considerable attention has been given to use of more sophisticated econometric methods to capture the impact of slowdown in R&D spending on productivity growth. The results suggest that the effects have been relatively modest, accounting for something in the neighborhood of 10% of the slowdown in total factor productivity in manufacturing since the early 1970s (Wolff, 1985:42–44, 51).

The question that remains, however, is would higher investment in R&D have generated more rapid productivity growth? The United States spends a relatively small share of GNP on non-defense-related R&D—in the neighborhood of 1.0% of GNP. Critics have argued that during the Cold War the diversion of research resources allocated to defense and space exploration was a burden on technical change in the civilian economy (Chapter 13). But it is doubtful that R&D expenditures can continue to rise at a rate substantially faster than the rate of growth of GNP without encountering diminishing returns. One of the issues that very few students have been willing to face is that R&D is, in many respects, the quintessential service industry. It is highly labor intensive and hence subject to the Baumol "cost disease" (Chapter 1). In rebuttal, the endogenous growth theorists have argued that R&D is subject to increasing returns that more than offset the fact that costs rise more rapidly than the general price level.

Failure to Measure

It is possible that measurement and data problems are partially to blame for the diffi-culty that economists have experienced in explaining the United States productivity slowdown (Griliches, 1994). Our national income accounts were designed in an era when the economy was simpler—when the United States had a large agricultural sector and a growing manufacturing sector. Even then there were major sectors of the economy—such as construction, most services, government and other public institutions—in which there were no adequate output measures and relevant price deflators were inadequate.

In the early post-World War II period only about half of the overall economy was accounted for by sectors with readily measurable output. By 1990 the fraction of the economy for which reasonably accurate productivity measures are available had fallen below one-third (Table 2.3). Furthermore, the diversion of resources out of goods production to the generation of technology and to development of the skills required to use the new technology for productivity is not captured in the national income accounts (Howitt, 1998). We have simply not allocated the resources that would be required to maintain and modernize our national accounts infrastructure to the Department of Labor's Bureau of Labor Statistics (BLS) and the Department of Commerce's Bureau of Economic Analysis (BEA). In the mid-1990s arguments over the accuracy of measurement generated a major debate about the accuracy of cost of living measures (Box 2.3).

● BOX 2.3

THE GREAT COST OF LIVING INDEX DEBATE

The problems involved in measuring a cost of living index are similar to those involved in constructing productivity indexes. In 1994 Federal Reserve Board Chairman Alan Greenspan suggested, in testimony before Congress, that he thought the annual change in the Consumer Price Index (CPI) might be overstated by as much as 1.0 percentage point. An upward bias in the CPI of this magnitude would have important policy implications. Changes in income tax brackets and social security benefits are adjusted each year by the rate of inflation as measured by the CPI.

In the winter and spring of 1995 the Senate Finance Committee held hearings in which leading economists presented testimony on the accuracy of the CPI. The Committee then appointed five of the economists to an Advisory Commission, chaired by Michael Boskin, to Study the CPI. An interim report was released in September 1995 and a final report in December 1996. In its final report the Commission indicated that its best estimate was that the CPI overstated inflation by 1.1% per year. There were immediate calls for adjustment in the formula for tax bracket creep and social security payments. Reporters and legislators who ordinarily would have preferred to know as little as possible about the arcane issues of index number construction found themselves confronted with the problem of understanding and interpreting the findings of the Boskin Report.

The Boskin Commission found four major sources of bias in the CPI:

Substitution bias: Because the CPI monitors the prices in a fixed basket of goods and services, it does not take account of the extent to which consumers are able to save by switching to items that rise less rapidly in price. The Commission estimated the size of this bias as 0.4 percentage points annually. *Retail outlet substitution*: The CPI compares prices in the same stores through time. But if consumers save by switching to discount stores that charge lower prices, the CPI will overstate what shoppers are actually paying. The Commission estimated the size of this bias as 0.1 percentage points annually. *Quality bias*: The Commission argued that the CPI fails to fully account for all the quality improvements in goods and services through time. If this is the case the CPI will wrongly report that the items have risen in price when in fact consumers are paying more to get a better product. *New goods bias*: New products are not incorporated fully into the CPI immediately after they are introduced. Consequently when their price falls, as is often the case with new products such as hand calculators, the CPI will miss the price decline and thereby overstate inflation. The Commission estimated the size of the quality and new goods bias together at 0.6 percentage points annually (Baker, 1998:2–3).

The bias in the CPI also has important implications for the measurement of productivity growth. Most of the price data used by the Department of Commerce BEA to construct the consumption component of the GDP are the same prices the BLS collects to construct the CPI. Thus, to the extent that the CPI overstates inflation it understates the growth of the consumption component of the GDP. The same sorts of bias exist in the price indexes for production goods as exist for consumption goods (Baker, 1998:84).

An understatement of real GDP growth implies an understatement of the same magnitude in labor productivity growth. Labor productivity growth measures the increase in real final output in the private business sector (consumption, investment, and net exports) per hour worked (or percent of total input). Thus if the Boskin Commission is correct in its claim that the CPI has been understating inflation by 1.1% per year, productivity measurers have also been understated by a comparable amount (Baker, 1998:84–85).

Critics have argued that the understatement is substantially smaller than the estimates of the Boskin Commission. Among the criticisms is that the Commission failed to take into account measurement improvements that had already been made and fails to appreciate the extent to which the CPI already adjusts for quality changes. The critics generally agree with the Commission's technical recommendations regarding the use of alternative price indexes, such as the use of geometric weighing, to more adequately capture substitution bias.

They also support the recommendation that greater effort be made to more adequately incorporate quality changes. There is no disagreement that there is an upward bias in the CPI. I find it surprising, however, how difficult it is to find either the supporters or the critics of the Boskin Report suggesting that resources be made available to the BLS to enable it to make the recommended improvements.

The five economists were Ellen Dulberger (International Business Machines), Robert Gordon (Northwestern University), Zvi Griliches (Harvard University), Dale Jorgenson (Harvard University), and Michael Boskin (Stanford University). Boskin, who had served as head of the Council of Economic Advisers during the Bush Administration, was selected as chairman.

The Advisory Commission to Study the Consumer Price Index, *Toward a More Accurate Measure of the Cost of Living,* Washington, DC: Senate Finance Committee, December 4, 1996. The report and several criticisms are reproduced in Dean Baker, ed., *Getting Prices Right: The Debate Over the Consumer Price Index*, Armonk, NY: M. G. Sharp, 1998.

The best estimates suggest that "failure to measure" cannot account for more than 0.2 percentage points of the slowdown in productivity growth since the early 1970s. It is clear, however, that failure to measure accurately (Sichel, 1997) is responsible, to a substantial degree, for what has come to be known as the "computer paradox" (Chapter 9).

PERSPECTIVE

In spite of the optimistic implications of the new endogenous growth models it remains unclear whether the period of rapid growth in productivity that characterized the U.S. economy during the middle decades of this country—roughly from the mid-1930s to the mid-1970s—was a temporary aberration or whether it can be recovered by the pursuit of more appropriate economic policy by the early decades of the twenty-first century. It has been argued that the rapid growth experienced in the United States in the 1950s and 1960s involved little more than making up for the lost growth of the great depression of the 1930s (Figure 2.6). In this view, the United States simply resumed in the 1970s its long-term neoclassical growth path: "Either nothing in the U.S. experience since 1880 has had a large persistent effect on the growth rate or whatever persistent effects have occurred have miraculously been offsetting" (Jones, 1995:499).

The consensus view among growth economists in the late 1990s was that for the United States and other presently high-income countries, the sustainable rate of growth in per capita income is in the neighborhood of 2.0% per year. Policy failure, such as distortion of market incentives, a decline in investment in human capital,

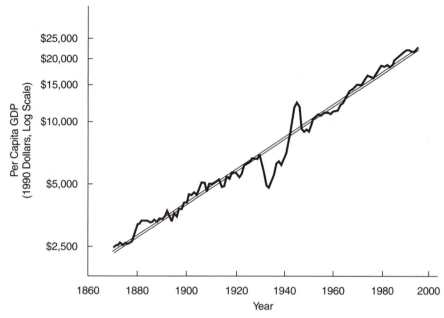

Figure 2.6 Real per capita gross domestic product in the United States, 1870–1994. (*Source:* From *Introduction to Economic Growth* by Charles I. Jones. Copyright © 1998 by W. W. Norton & Company, Inc. Used by permission of W. W. Norton & Company, Inc.)

or a decline in the advancement of new knowledge or technology, could result in a lower growth rate in per capita income. But the penalty of being rich is that even vigorous policy reform would be unlikely to push the rate of per capita income growth more than a few tenths of a percent above the 2.0% level (Barro, 1997:17). For poor countries, in a position to transfer technical and institutional knowledge from more advanced countries, as well as pursue high rate of investment in human, physical, and institutional capital, higher rates are possible, at least until they began to catch up with the leaders.

Certainly there are important sources of growth that cannot be recovered. The growth momentum associated with the rise in labor force participation, particulary of women, during the post-World War II period cannot be an important source of future economic growth. Employment in agriculture in the United States is now well below 2.0% of the U.S. labor force. The transfer of labor from agriculture in the United States can never again become a dynamic source of growth for the total economy even if growth in productivity in the agricultural sector continues to exceed the rate of growth in the rest of the economy. The momentum generated by productivity growth in the manufacturing sector also seems destined to play itself out. Employment in manufacturing declined from over 30% of the U.S. labor force in the early postwar period to less than 20% by the late 1990s (Figure 1.2). It is not difficult to anticipate a decline in employment in manufacturing to below 10% of the labor force in the early decades of the next century. Thus, even rapid productivity growth in manufacturing will exert less and less leverage on productivity growth in the total economy in the future.

This perspective is consistent with the hypothetical model developed in Chapter 1. It seems apparent that if the United States and other rich countries are to maintain even the relatively modest per capita income growth rates achieved in the 1990s it will be necessary to advance productivity growth more rapidly in those areas, other than the material goods-producing sectors, in which productivity growth has been slow, or unmeasured. As this book was being completed the argument was being advanced, particularly in the business press, that the United States was entering a new era of growth acceleration fueled by the pervasive diffusion of advances in information technology in the service industries (Madrick, 1999). If these projections are to be realized it seems apparent that the U.S. economy will have to become more effective at exploiting institutional innovations as a source of economic growth during the first half of the twenty-first century.

REFERENCES

Abramovitz, M. "Catching Up, Forging Ahead and Falling Behind." *Journal of Economic History* 46 (June 1986):385–406.

Aghion, P., and P. Howitt. *Endogenous Growth Theory.* Cambridge, MA: MIT Press, 1998.

Aschauer, D.A. "Is Public Expenditure Productive?" *Journal of Monetary Economics* 23 (1989):177–200.

Bairoch, P. "Europe's Gross National Product, 1800–1973." *Journal of European Economic History* 5 (1976):213–340.

Barro, R. J. *Determinants of Economic Growth: A Cross-Country Empirical Study.* Cambridge, MA: MIT Press, 1997.

Barro, R. J., and X. Sala-i-Martin. *Economic Growth.* New York: McGraw-Hill, 1995.

Basu, S., and D. N. Weil. "Appropriate Technology and Growth." *Quarterly Journal of Economics* 6(1998):1025–1054.

Baumol, W. J. "Productivity Growth, Convergence and Welfare: What the Long-Run Data Show." *American Economic Review* 76 (1986):1072–1085.

Baumol, W. J., and E. N. Wolff. "Productivity Growth, Convergence, and Welfare: Reply." *American Economic Review* 78 (December 1988):1155–1159.

Baumol, W. J., S. A. B. Blackman, and E. N. Wolff. *Productivity and American Leadership: The Long View.* Cambridge, MA: MIT Press, 1989.

Berndt, E. R. "Energy Use, Technical Progress and Productivity Growth: A Survey of Economics Issues." *Journal of Productivity Analysis* 2 (1990):67–83.

Boskin, M. J., and L. J. Lau. "Capital, Technology and Economic Growth." In *Technology and the Wealth of Nations*, N. Rosenberg, R. Landau, and D. C. Mowery, eds., pp. 18–55. Stanford, CA: Stanford University Press, 1992.

Bruno, M. "Raw Materials, Profits, and the Productivity Slowdown." *Quarterly Journal of Economics* 99 (1984):1–29.

DeLong, J. B. "Productivity Growth, Convergence and Welfare: Comment." *American Economic Review* 78 (December 1988):1138–1154.

Dennison, E. F. *Trends in American Economic Growth, 1929–82.* Washington, DC: The Brookings Institution Press, 1985.

Domar, E. "Capital Expansion, Rate of Growth and Employment." *Econometrica* 14 (1946): 137–147.

Domar, E. "Expansion and Employment." *American Economic Review* 37 (1947):343–355.

Dowrick, S., and Nguyen, D. "OECD Comparative Economic Growth, 1950–85: Catch-Up and Convergence." *American Economic Review* 79 (December 1989):1010–1030.

Fisher, F. M., and K. Shell. *Economic Analysis of Production Price Indexes.* Cambridge, UK: Cambridge University Press, 1998.

Friedman, M. "Do Old Fallacies Ever Die?" *Journal of Economic Literature* 30 (December 1992):2129–2132.

Griliches, Z. "Productivity and the Data Constraint." *American Economic Review* 84 (1994): 1–23.

Griliches, Z. "The Discovery of the Residual: A Historical Note." *Journal of Economic Literature* 34 (1996):1324–1330.

Harberger, Arnold C. "A Vision of the Growth Process." *American Economic Review* 88 (1998):1–32.

Harrod, R. F. "An Essay in Dynamic Theory." *Economic Journal* 49 (1939):14–33.

Howitt, P. "Measurement Obsolescence and General Purpose Technologies." In *General Purpose Technologies and Economic Growth*, E. Helpman, ed., pp. 218–251. Cambridge, MA: MIT Press, 1998.

Hulten, C. R. "Total Factor Productivity: A Short Biography." Cambridge, MA: National Bureau of Economic Research Working Paper 7471, January 2000.

Jones, C. I. "Time Series Tests of Endogenous Growth Models." *Quarterly Journal of Economics* 110 (1995):495–526.

Jones, C. I. *Introduction to Economic Growth.* New York: W. W. Norton, 1997.

Jorgenson, D. W. "The Great Transition." *Energy Journal* 7 (July 1986):1–13.

Jorgenson, D. W., and F. M Gollop. "Productivity Growth in U.S. Agriculture: A Postwar Perspective." In *Productivity, Vol. 1: Postwar U.S. Economic Growth*, D. W. Jorgenson, ed. pp. 389–399. Cambridge, MA: MIT Press, 1995.

Jorgenson, D. W., and Z. Griliches. "The Explanation of Productivity Change." *Review of Economic Studies* 34 (1967):249–282.

Jorgenson, D. W., and E. Yip. "Progress in Productivity Measurement: An Overview." Paper presented at a seminar in commemoration of Zvi Griliches' 20 years as Director of the NBER Program on Productivity and Technological Progress, Cambridge, MA, March 5 - 6, 1999.

Jorgenson, D. W., Z. Griliches, and E. F. Denison. *The Measurement of Productivity: An Exchange of Views between Dale W. Jorgenson and Zvi Griliches and Edward F. Denison.* Washington, DC: The Brookings Institution Press, reprint no. 244, 1972.

Jorgenson, D. W., F. M. Gollop, and B. M. Fraumeni. *Productivity and U.S. Economic Growth.* Cambridge, MA: Harvard University Press, 1987.

Krugman, P. *The Age of Diminished Expectations: U.S. Economic Policy in the 1990s.* Cambridge, MA: MIT Press, 1994.

Lucas, R. E., Jr. "On the Mechanics of Economic Development." *Journal of Monetary Eco-*

nomics 22 (July 1988):3–42.

Maddison, A. *Phases of Capitalist Development.* New York: Oxford University Press, 1982.

Maddison, A. "Growth and Slowdown in Advanced Capitalist Economies." *Journal of Economic Literature* 25 (June 1987):649–698.

Maddison, A. *Monitoring the World Economy: 1820–1992.* Paris: Organization for Economic Cooperation and Development (OECD), 1995.

Madrick, J. "How New is the New Economy." *New York Review* 1999 (September 23):42–50.

Mankiw, N. G., D. Romer, and D. N. Weil. "A Contribution to the Empirics of Economics Growth." *Quarterly Journal of Economics* 107 (1992):407–437.

Munnell, A. H. "Why Has Productivity Growth Declined: Productivity and Public Investment." *New England Economic Review* (January/February 1990):3–22.

Nelson, R. R., and G. Wright. "The Rise and Fall of American Technological Leadership: The Post War Era in Historical Perspective." *The Journal of Economic Literature* 23 (1992):1931–1964.

Parente, S. L., and E. C. Prescott. "Barriers to Technology Adoption and Development." *Journal of Political Economy* 102 (1994):298–321.

Parente, S. L. and E. C. Prescott. *Barriers to Riches.* Cambridge, MA: MIT Press, 2000.

Peterson, W. "Overinvestment in Public Sector Capital." *Cato Journal* 14 (1994):65–72.

Pritchett, L. "Divergence, Big Time." *Journal of Economic Perspectives* 11 (1997):3–17.

Quah, D. "Galton's Fallacy and Tests of the Convergence Hypothesis." *Scandinavian Journal of Economics* 95 (4 1993):427–443.

Romer, P. M. "Increasing Returns and Long Run Growth." *Journal of Political Economy* 94 (October 1986):1002–1037.

Romer, P. M. "Idea Gaps and Object Gaps in Economic Development." *Journal of Monetary Economics* 32 (1993):543–573.

Romer, P. M. "Beyond Market Failure." In *AAAS Science and Technology Policy Yearbook, 1996- 97,* A. H. Teich, S. D. Nelson, and C. McEnanoy, eds., pp. 143–160. Washington, DC: American Association for the Advancement of Science, 1997.

Ruttan, V. W. "The New Growth Theory and Development Economics: A Survey." *Journal of Development Studies* 35 (1998):1–26.

Sachs, J. "The Limits of Convergence: Nature, Nurture and Growth." *The Economist* (June 14, 1997):19–22.

Sbordone, A. M. "Cyclical Productivity in a Model of Labor Hoarding." *Journal of Monetary Economics* 38 (1996):331–361.

Sichel, D. E. "The Productivity Slowdown: Is a Growing Unmeasurable Sector the Culprit?" *The Review of Economics and Statistics* 779 (1997):367–370.

Solow, R. M. "A Contribution to the Theory of Economic Growth." *Quarterly Journal of Economics* 70 (February 1956):65–95.

Solow, R. M. "Technical Change and the Aggregate Production Function." *Review of Economics and Statistics* 39 (August 1957):312–320.

Solow, R. M. "Growth Theory and After." *American Economic Review* 78 (1988):307–317.

Summers, R., and A. Heston. "Improved International Comparisons of Real Product and Its Composition, 1950–1980." *Review of Income and Wealth* 30 (June 1984):207–262.

Swan, T. W. "Economic Growth and Capital Accumulation." *Economic Record* 32 (1956): 343–361.

Temple, J. "The New Growth Evidence." *Journal of Economic Literature* 37 (1999):112–156.

Verspagen, B. "Endogenous Innovation in Neo-Classical Growth Models: A Survey." *Journal of Macroeconomics* 14 (1992):631–662.

Williamson, J. G. "Globalization, Convergence and History." *Journal of Economic History* 56 (1996):277–306.

Wolff, E. N. "The Magnitude and Causes of Recent Productivity Slowdown in the United States: A Survey of Recent Studies." In *Productivity Growth and U.S. Competitiveness*, W. J. Baumol and K. McClennan, eds., pp. 29–57. New York: Oxford University Press, 1985.

Wolff, E. N., ed. *The Economics of Productivity.* Cheltenham, UK: Edward Elgar, 1997.

APPENDIX

TECHNICAL CHANGE AND PRODUCTIVITY GROWTH: SOME SIMPLE ANALYTICS

In this Appendix I present some of the simple analytical concepts that are involved in the measurement of total factor productivity (or joint factor productivity).[1] An important issue is, under what conditions is it appropriate to interpret total factor productivity as a measure of the contribution of technical change to production. Students will find the material useful in helping them understand the controversies that continue to confront those who construct and interpret productivity growth. The general reader may, however, want to skip this Appendix and proceed directly to Chapter 3.

In the first section of this Appendix, I illustrate, graphically and numerically, the index number and production function approaches to the measurement of productivity growth. In the second aprt of the Appendix, I illustrate graphically the sources of bias that are inherent in the construction of productivity measures.

INDEX NUMBERS AND PRODUCTION FUNCTIONS

Production is a process in which inputs are transformed into outputs. It involves the transformation of flows of (1) capital services, (2) labor services, (3) energy, and (4) raw materials into output. The production function specifies the quantitative relation between inputs and outputs. In Figure A2.1 the isoquant Q_0 is used to depict the input–output and factor substitution relationships between two factors (K and L).

---

[1] In preparing this Appendix I have drawn on Ruttan (1952), Solow (1957), Domar (1961), Richter (1966), Fisher and Shell (1972:739–755), Hulten (1973, 1978), Binswanger and Ruttan (1978), Allan and Diewardt (1981), Elster (1983), Haltmaier (1984), and Hsieh (1998).

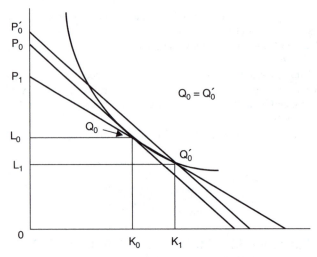

Figure A2.1 Isoquant and isocost map.

An *isoquant* is defined as the locus of factor combinations that produces the same output ($Q_0 = Q_0'$). (K_0, L_0) and (K_1, L_1) are on the same isoquant if and only if

$$Q = f(K_0, L_0) = f(K_1, L_1)$$

An *isocost line* is the locus of input combinations with the same total cost, *given* the factor prices.

$$P_0 \text{ through } Q_0 < P_0' \text{ through } Q_0'$$

The producer will choose the point on the unit isoquant that lies on the lowest isocost curve. A change in the factor price ratio, leading to a new set of isocost curves, will lead the producer to choose a new point on the isoquant to minimize cost. A shift to P_1 will result in a choice of Q_0'.

This model rests on four rather restrictive assumptions: (1) profit maximization (behavioral assumption), (2) existing technical possibilities and constraints can adequately be represented by the production function or isoquant (the state of nature), (3) all points on the unit isoquant are assumed equally accessible (technical assumption), and (4) perfect competition (institutional assumption).

Measuring Technical Change: The Index Number Approach

If we select a base year (t_0) and correct for price changes the items entering into the input and output accounts of a second year (t_1), the (percentage) difference between the (Laspeyres) input index and the (Laspeyres) output index in the second year measures the contribution that technical change has made to output between t_0 and t_1. The productivity index is the index of output per unit of total input in t_1.

$$\text{In } t_0: \quad _q p_0 Q_0 = A_0(_l p_0 L_0 + _k p_0 K_0)$$

$$\text{In } t_1: \quad _q p_0 Q_1 = A_1(_l p_0 L_1 + _k p_0 K_1)$$

$$_q p_0 = \$1.00 \quad Q_0 = 100 \quad Q_1 = 200$$

Let: $\quad _l p_0 = 0.75 \quad L_0 = 100 \quad L_1 = 133.3$

$$_k p_0 = 0.25 \quad K_0 = 100 \quad K_1 = 200$$

$$\textit{Total Productivity Index } A_1 = \frac{_q p_0 Q_1}{_l p_0 L_1 + _k p_0 K_1}(100)$$

$$A_1 = \frac{\$1.00(200)}{\left[(0.75)(133.3) + (0.25)(200)\right]}$$

$$= \frac{200}{150}(100) = 133.3$$

where

$_q p_0$ is the output price in time t_0

$_l p_0$ is the wage rate in time t_0

$_k p_0$ is the price of capital at t_0

Labor Productivity	Capital Productivity	Capital/Labor Ratio
$\frac{Q_1}{L_1}(100)$	$\frac{Q_1}{K_1}(100)$	$\frac{K_1}{L_1} = \frac{200}{133.3} = 1.50$
$\frac{200}{133.3}(100) = 150$	$\frac{200}{200}(100) = 100$	

The index number approach is illustrated graphically in Figure A2.2. In the illustration output is held constant ($Q_0 = Q_1$), capital input is held unchanged ($K_0 = K_1$), and labor input is reduced ($L_1 < L_0$).

Measuring Technical Change: The Production Function Approach

If we construct a production function for the base period (t_0) and then substitute the inputs of a second period (t_1) into the function, the contribution that technical change has made to the change in output between the two periods can be measured by the difference between the output (or the index of output) actually produced in t_1 and the output (or the index of output) estimated from the base period production function. A Cobb–Douglas (linear in logarithms) production function is employed in the following illustration.

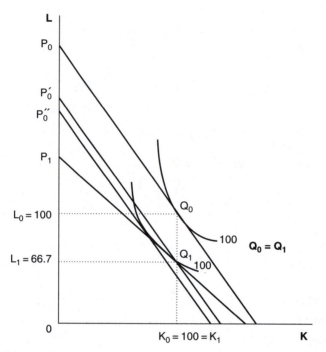

Figure A2.2 Measuring technical change.

$$\text{In} \quad t_0 : Q_0 = A_0 L_0^{l_0} K_0^{k_0}$$

$$\text{In} \quad t_1 : Q_1 = A_1 L_1^{l_0} K_1^{k_0}$$

$$Q_0 = 100 \quad Q_1 = 200$$

$$l_1 = 0.75 \quad L_0 = 100 \quad L_1 = 133.3$$

$$k_0 = 0.25 \quad K_0 = 100 \quad K_1 = 200$$

$$A_1 = \frac{Q_1}{L_1^{l_0} K_1^{k_0}}$$

$$A_1 \frac{200}{(1.333)^{0.75}(200)^{0.25}} = \frac{200}{(39.24)(3.761)} = \frac{200}{147.55}(100) = 136$$

Total Productivity Index $= 136$

Why is the productivity index obtained in the production framework approach (136) larger than the productivity index obtained with the index number approach (133)?

The answer is found in the form of aggregation. In the previous section we employed linear aggregation—no matter how much capital (K) we substituted for Labor (L) the weights ($_l p_0 = 0.75$ and $_k p_0 = 0.25$) ensured that three additional units of capital would substitute for one unit of labor. When we employ logarithmic (or exponential) aggregation we implicitly assume that the rate of substitution of capital for labor remains unchanged in percentage (rather than arithmetic) terms. Thus as labor input declines relative to capital along Q_1 it takes larger absolute amounts of capital (K) to substitute for one unit decline in labor input.

Definition of Inputs and Outputs

Should output be measured net or gross of intermediate inputs? It has been customary for growth accountants working at the macroeconomic level to employ only capital (K) and labor (L) as factors of production. This is because at the economy-wide level interfirm and intersector transfers of intermediate inputs (the output of one firm that becomes an input into production for another firm) cancel out. The comparable practice at the firm or industry level would be to measure output in terms of the "value added" to the capital (K) and labor (L) employed by the firm. Value added is obtained by substracting the cost of the intermediate inputs from the value of the firm's output.

Students of technical change working at the firm or sector level typically employ measures of total input (including intermediate inputs) and total output. This is because technical advances may be embodied in intermediate inputs as well as capital or labor. If intermediate inputs are omitted, as in value added, important sources of productivity growth may be missed. Productivity estimated will, however, differ when output is measured in terms of value added (net of intermediate inputs) and when it is measured in terms of total output (gross of intermediate inputs). The relationship between the two measures is illustrated in the following example.

Assume an economy with two sectors—agriculture and industry—in which the output of the agricultural sector is employed as an input in the industrial sector.

$$\textit{Agriculture:} \quad Q_a = a_1 L_1^{l_1} K_1^{k_1}$$

$$\textit{Industry:} \quad Q_I = a_2 L_2^{l_2} K_2^{k_2} Q_a^{q}$$

$$\textit{Economy:} \quad Q = a_1^q a_2 L_1^{l_1 q} K_1^{k_1 q} L_2^{l_2} K_2^{k_2}$$

The *indexes of technical change* are

$$\textit{Agriculture:} \quad A_a = \frac{(a_1)_1}{(a_1)_0}$$

$$\textit{Industry:} \quad A_I = \frac{(a_2)_1}{(a_1)_0}$$

$$\textit{Economy:} \quad A = \frac{(a_1^q a_2)_1}{(a_1^q a_2)_0}$$

$$
\text{Let:} \quad
\begin{array}{lll}
(a_1)_0 & = 1 & (a_2)_0 = 1 \quad q = 0.5 \\
(a_1)_1 & = 1.7 & (a_2)_1 = 1.4
\end{array}
$$

$$
\text{Then:} \quad
\begin{aligned}
A_a &= 1.7 \\
A_I &= 1.4 \\
A &= \frac{(1.7)^{0.5}(1.4)}{(1)^{0.5}(1)} = (1.3)(1.4) = 1.8
\end{aligned}
$$

A will always exceed A_I as long as industry uses any part of the output of agriculture as an intermediate input. The same principle applies for any industry that uses inputs from another industry as intermediate inputs. To understand productivity growth among sectors use total output production functions. To compare sector and total economy use value-added sector production functions or index numbers.

SOURCES OF BIAS IN PRODUCTIVITY MEASUREMENT

In the previous section the index number and production function approaches to the measurement of technical change were discussed. We established that in choosing a weighing system (arithmetic, logarithmic, or other) in the index number approach, we are making an implicit judgment about the form of the production function. We also recognized that the productivity estimates are not independent of our definition of output and input.

I would now like to consider the four major sources of bias that occur in any effort to measure productivity change over time or among countries.

- Bias resulting from change (or differences) in relative prices of factors and products.
- Bias due to nonneutral technical change.
- Bias due to changes in the degree of disequilibrium.

I will not attempt to present proofs. The objective is to provide an intuitive understanding.

Changes in Factor and Product Prices

If prices of factors do not remain unchanged relative to each other, or prices of products do not remain unchanged relative to each other, a unique measure of technical change is not possible. This is referred to as the "index number problem."

CHANGE IN FACTOR PRICES

If, in constructing the input index, inputs in both t_0 and t_1 are weighted by t_0 prices, the input index will rise if the input combination used to produce the given level of

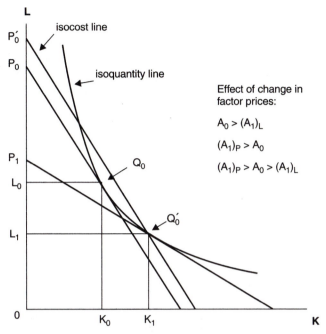

Figure A2.3 Effect of change in factor prices.

output shifts away from Q_0 to some other point $Q'_0 (Q'_0 = Q'_1)$ on the same isoquant curve (Figure A2.3).

$$period\ 0\ inputs \qquad period\ 1\ inputs$$

$$_l p_0 L_0 + _k p_0 K_0 < {}_l p_0 L_1 + _k p_0 K_1$$

$$\frac{q p_0 Q'_0}{_l p_0 L_0 + _k p_0 K_0} > \frac{q p_0 Q_1}{_l p_0 L_1 + _k p_0 K_1}$$

$$A_0 > (A_1)_L$$

Thus the results of using a base period (Laspayres) index suggest technological regression when none has occurred. If we had employed an end period (Paasche) index the results would have suggested a decline in inputs and a rise in output per unit of input when none had occurred.

$$(A_1)_P > A_0$$

The correct index of output per unit of total input ($A_0 = 1.00$) would be bracketed by the two estimates:

$$(A_1)_P \geq A_0 \geq (A_1)_L$$

CHANGES IN PRODUCE PRICES

Product prices may also change (Figure A2.4). Given the transformation or production possibility curve I (which measures the output that can be produced from a constant quantity of input), assume that the price of product X rises relative to the price of product Y. If the relative prices of X and Y are initially indicated by the slope of line p_0, the optimum output combination, X_0 and Y_0, is produced at I_0. In t_1 after the rise in the price of X relative to the price of Y, indicated by the slope of p_1, the optimum output combination, X_1 and Y_1, is produced at I_0'.

If, in constructing an output index, products are evaluated at t_0 prices in both periods, the output index falls as we move away from I_0 to any other point I_0' on the same transformation curve.

$$period\ 0\ output \qquad period\ 1\ output$$

$$(_xp_0X_0 + {_y}p_0Y_0) > (_xp_0X_1 + {_y}p_0Y_1)$$

$$\frac{_xp_0X_0 + {_y}p_0Y_0}{_ip_0I_0} > \frac{_xp_0X_1 + {_y}p_0Y_1}{_ip_0I_0'}$$

$$A_0 > (A_1)_L$$

The results, using the base period (Laspayres) output index, again suggest technological regression when none has occurred. if we had employed an end period (Paasche) index, the results would have suggested a rise in productivity.

$$(A_1)p > A_0$$

and again

$$(A_1)p \geq A_0 \geq (A_1)_L$$

The effect is to increase the bias as compared to a situation in which only factor prices have changed.

The same principles would hold if we were making comparison between two countries with different price structures. We can, however, use the "bracketing" provided by the Lapayres and Paasche indexes to determine the possible magnitude of "index number bias."

The index number bias tends to increase the longer the time period between revision in the price weights (or production function coefficients). Thus the bias can be reduced by revising the weights or coefficients more frequently. Part of the debate over the accuracy of the cost of living index (Box 2.2) was about the effects of the changes in relative prices between revisions of the base prices. The rates of change in output and input are then linked for successive periods to form continuous index numbers of output, input, and productivity.

Bias due to Nonneutrality

To this point we have assumed that shifts in the production function have been neutral. This is a rather strong assumption. Technical change may also be biased in a labor- or

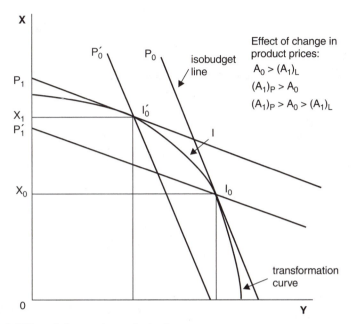

Figure A2.4 Effect of changes in product price.

capital-saving direction (Box A2.1). Figure A2.5 will be used to illustrate the effect of nonneutral technical change on the bias in use of total productivity as a measure of technical change.

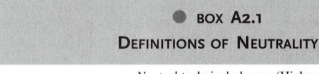

BOX A2.1

DEFINITIONS OF NEUTRALITY

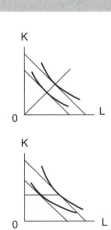

Neutral technical change (Hicks neutrality). The K/L ratio remains unchanged, with given factor prices, as the unit isoquant shifts toward the origin. With neutral technical change the marginal rate of substitution among factors remains unchanged. And with prices unchanged factor shares also remain unchanged.

Labor-saving technical change (Harrod neutral). Capital per unit of output (K/Q) remains unchanged and the capital–labor ratio (K/L) rises, with given factor prices, as the unit isoquant shifts toward the origin. Marginal productivity of capital remains constant, labor rises.

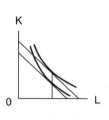

Capital-saving technical change (Solow neutral). Labor per unit of output (L/Q) remains unchanged and the capital–labor ratio (K/L) falls, with given factor prices, as the unit isoquant shifts toward the origin. Marginal productivity of labor remains constant, capital rises.

Adapted from J. Elster, *Explaining Technical Change*, Cambridge: Cambridge University Press, 1983:100. For a more complete explanation see Binswanger and Ruttan (1978:42–43).

Bias due to Changes in Relative Prices and Change in Neutrality

Suppose that in addition to changes in factor or product prices between the two periods, the production function shifts in a nonneutral manner.

1. Assume in Figure A2.5 an isoquant system that includes $X_0 X_0$ and $X_1 X_1$. Between t_0 and t_1 we have, in effect, doubled both output (from Q_0 to $\bar{Q}_1$) while increasing K(from K_0 to $\bar{K}_1$ and L from L_0 to $\bar{L}_1$). Thus, since there has been no technical change or change in factor prices:

$$\frac{{}_q p_0 Q_0}{{}_l p_0 L_0 + {}_k p_0 K_0} = \frac{{}_q p_0 \bar{Q}_1}{{}_l p_0 \bar{L}_1 + {}_k p_0 \bar{K}_1} = A_0 = 1$$

2. Let $X_1 X_0$ represent the isoquant system resulting from introduction of "labor-saving" technical change such that output level $X_1 X_1$ can now be produced along $X_1 X_0$. The optimum combination of labor and capital at p_0 prices will be L_0 and K_1—where p_0' is tangent to $X_1 X_0$ at Q_1'. At Q_1' we are using less labor and more capital than at Q_1.

$$\frac{{}_q p_0 Q'}{{}_l p_0 L_0 + {}_k p_0 K_1} > \frac{{}_q p_0 \bar{Q}_1}{{}_l p_0 \bar{L}_1 + {}_k p_0 \bar{K}_1} \quad \text{(since } p_0' \text{ is below } p_0'' \text{)}$$

$$A_1 > \bar{A}_1 = 1$$

3. If, however, the original price system had been represented by p_1, p_1', and p_1'' instead of p_0, p_0', and p_1'' (i.e., if labor had been "cheaper") the gain from the "labor-saving" technical change would have been smaller—the distance between p_1'' and p_1' (tangent to $X_1 X_1$ at $\bar{Q}_1'$ and to $X_1 X_0$ at $\bar{Q}_1''$). Thus

$$A_1 > A_1' > A_0 = 1$$

4. Earlier we showed that if technical change was Hicks neutral, changes in relative prices between t_0 and t_1, would bias the measure of technical change. *We have now shown that if technical change is nonneutral between t_0 and t_1 the measure of technical change is no longer independent of the relative prices that prevail.*

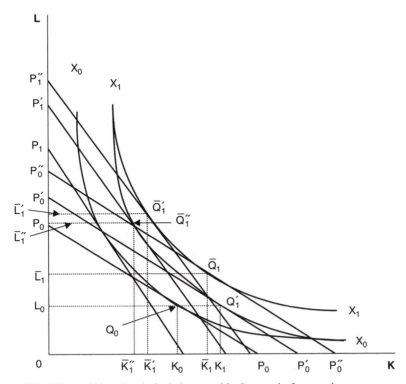

Figure A2.5 Effects of biased technical change with changes in factor prices.

An implication is that the gains from labor-saving technical change are less in a low-wage than in a high-wage economy.

What happens to index number bias when nonneutral technical change is combined with changing relative prices?

- Suppose the factor-saving and price effects both act in the same direction as when "labor-saving" technical change is combined with increases in the price of labor relative to capital? In this case the rise in the price of labor induces substitution of capital for labor and the technical change bias induces labor saving by increasing the marginal productivity of capital relative to labor. In this case he index number bias and the neutrality effect tend to be cumulative:

$$(A_1')p \geq (A_1)p \geq A_1 \geq (A_1)_L \geq (A_1')_L$$

- Suppose, however, that the factor-saving effect and the price effect act in the opposite direction (technical change is autonomous). The rise in the price of labor causes substitution of capital for labor. But the technical change bias increases the marginal productivity of labor relative to capital. In this case, if the technical change is sufficiently nonneutral, the "true" measure of technical change could fall outside of the index number "brackets."

Disequilibrium in Factor and Product Markets

Assume no change in factor prices and no change in technology between t_0 and t_1. If in Figure A2.5 t_0 factor inputs L_0 and K_0 were being used inefficiently to produce some output level

$$Q_{0i} < Q_0$$

and if in t_1 the input levels $\bar{L}_1$ and $\bar{K}_1$ in Figure A2.5 were being used to produce $\bar{Q}_1$, the result would be a measured increase in output per unit of input even though no technical change had occurred. This is the source of the typical bias in productivity measures that occurs during the recovery from a recession.

Similarly, if in period t_0 inputs L_0 and K_0 were being used to produce Q_o but in period t_1 inputs $\bar{L}_1$ and $\bar{K}_1$ were being used to produce some

$$\bar{Q}_1 < \bar{Q}_1$$

the productivity index would show a decline when there had been no technological regression. This is the source of the bias in productivity measures that typically occurs during the slowing down of economic activity during a recession when excess workers are being "hoarded" in expectation of economic recovery.

In empirical work attempts are made to determine or correct for the degree of disequilibrium between the two periods being compared.

Scale, Size, and Scope

In Figure A2.6 scale economies suggest that a move from Q_1 to Q_2 would be accompanied by a less than proportionate change in L and K. In popular discussion, and even among some economists, if is common to use the terms economies of scale and economies of size interchangeably. For analytical purposes the distinctions are important. Economies of scale reflect efficiency gains associated with proportional increases in factor inputs.

Economies of size, depicted in Figure A2.7, reflect substitutions among factors when an increase in one factor relative to other factors (such as capital relative to labor), is associated with an increase in firm size. In Figure A2.7 the change in factor ratios is entirely the result of change in factor price ratios. Labor productivity rises because of factor substitution rather than technical change.

Ecomomies of scope occur when there are complementarities, resulting in cost savings, from incorporating multiple products in the same firm (not illustrated). The source of complementarity may be technical or institutional—in research and development, in production, in distribution, or in finance.

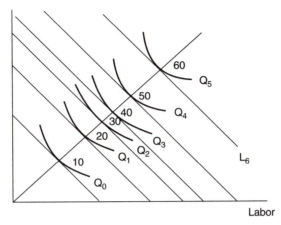

Figure A2.6 Economies and diseconomies of scale.

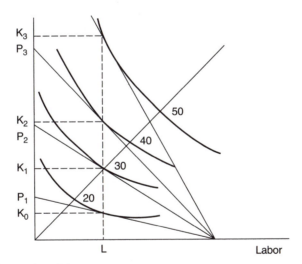

Figure A2.7 Economies of size.

It is useful, analytically, to distinguish among the productivity gains associated with economies of scale, size, and scope. But economies of scale, size, and scope may themselves occur as a result of prior technical change. It is particularly difficult, in empirical research, to partition the sources of productivity growth among technical change and scale, size, and scope economies.

REFERENCES

Allen, R. C., and W. E. Diewardt. "Direct Versus Superlative Index Number Formulae." *Review of Economics and Statistics* 63 (1981):430–435.

Binswanger, H. P., and V. W. Ruttan. *Induced Innovation: Technology, Institutions and Development.* Baltimore, MD: Johns Hopkins University Press, 1978.

Domar, E. D. "On the Measurement of Technological Change." *Economic Journal* 34 (1961): 739–755.

Elster, J. *Explaining Technical Change.* Cambridge, UK: Cambridge University Press, 1983.

Fisher, F. M., and K. Shell. *The Economic Theory of Price Indices: Two Essays on the Effects of Taste, Quality and Technical Change.* New York: Academic PRess, 1972.

Fisher, F. M., and K. Shell. *Economic Analysis of Production Price Indexes.* Cambridge, UK: Cambridge University Press, 1998.

Haltmaier, J. "Measuring Technical Change." *Economic Journal* 94 (1984):924–930.

Hsieh, C. T. "Measuring Biased Technical Change." Princeton, NJ: Princeton University Woodrow Wilson School, August 1998.

Hulten, C. "Divisia Index Numbers." *Econometrica* 41 (1973):1017–1026.

Ruttan, V. W. *Technological Progress in the Meat Packing Industry.* Chicago, IL: University of Chicago Department of Economics, Ph.D. Thesis, March 1952 (also U.S. Department of Agriculture Marketing Research Report 59, January 1954).

Solow, R. M. "Technical Change and the Aggregate Production Function." *Review of Economies and Statistics* 39 (1957):312–320.

PART TWO

SOURCES OF TECHNICAL CHANGE

The chapters in this section address the process of invention and innovation, the determinants of the rate and direction of technical change and the role of social and economic influences on the adoption, diffusion, and transfer of technology.

The rapid technical change that western society has experienced since the middle of the eighteenth century has been the result of a remarkable fusion of science and technology (Chapter 3). "The great invention of the nineteenth century was the invention of the method of invention." The institutional inventions included the agricultural experiment station, the industrial research laboratory, and the research university. As these institutions emerged the old distinctions between "doing science" and "doing technology" began to erode. Knowledge flowed from technology to science as well as from science to technology. And technology itself was advanced by the "learning by doing" and "learning by using" of the suppliers and users of technology.

Changes in the economic environment in which the public and private suppliers of new knowledge, new technology, and new institutions function powerfully influence the rate and direction of technical and institutional change (Chapter 4). In the early 1950s both technical and institutional change were treated by economists as exogenous to the economic system—as "manna from heaven." By the 1990s both technical and institutional change were seen as largely endogenous—as induced by changes (and differences) in the economic environment.

During the 1940s and 1950s a substantial tradition of research on the adoption and diffusion of technology emerged in several subfields of sociology, particularly in rural sociology and health sociology (Chapter 5). Research by economists has been stimulated by public policy interest in policies to speed the rate of adoption and diffusion of technology and the effects of transfer of technology on international development and competitiveness.

The theories and models of technical and institutional change available to us at the present time are not well articulated. In attempting to understand the generation and adoption transfer of new technology and institutions, we are confronted with a kit of loose tools and a body of historical generalizations.

CHAPTER 3

The Process of Invention and Innovation[1]

The rapid technical change that Western society has experienced since the middle of the last century has been the result of a remarkable fusion of technology and science. In the West this fusion was built on ideological foundations that, from the early Middle Ages, have valued both the improvement of material well-being and the advancement of knowledge.

But this union of science and technology did not come smoothly. Historically, the relationship between science and technology (and between scientists and engineers and agronomists) has been uneasy. Until well into the nineteenth century advances in agricultural and industrial technology evolved almost entirely from mechanical insight and husbandry practice. "Science was traditionally aristocratic, speculative, intellectual in intent; technology was lower-class, empirical action oriented" (White, 1968:79).

The purpose of this chapter is to clarify understanding of the process of technical change. Does technical change arise as a product of the occasional insight of great minds? Or is it primarily a product of incremental innovations that emerge during the process of production and practice? Is the relationship between advances in science and technology essentially linear—running from advances in science to technology development? Are advances in technology a primary source of the demand for new scientific knowledge? In the first section of this chapter I review the several perspectives on the role of skill and insight in the process of technical change. I then draw on three case studies to illustrate the complex interactions between skill and insight in the emergence of new general purpose technologies. In a third section I draw on the two earlier sections to construct a more complex interpretation of the relationship between advances in scientific and technical knowledge. I then discuss the processes that lead to the generation of new knowledge and new technology in the modern research institutions—the industrial research laboratory, the agricultural experiment station, and the research university. In a final section I assess the role of learning by doing and learning by using in realizing the productivity gains inherent in modern complex technologies.

---

[1] I am indebted to William Baldwin, Edward Layton, and Andrew Van de Ven for comments on an earlier draft of this chapter. Throughout the chapter I draw on Mokyr (1990) more than can readily be acknowledged.

INVENTION AND INNOVATION

Most social scientists would probably accept the sequence of invention, innovation, and technical change as representing a logical sequence. Invention in some manner is antecedent to innovation, and innovation is in turn antecedent to technological change. But the precise distinction between the terms is not always clear. In this section I attempt to clarify the three concepts. A comparison of Schumpeter's treatment of the role of innovation and the innovator in the process of economic development with Usher's model of the emergence of strategic inventions provides a useful focus.

Schumpeterian Innovation

The concept of innovation has traditionally played a more important role in economics than the concept of invention. It was not, however, until Schumpeter identified innovation as the essential function of the entrepreneur and then constructed a theory of economic development in which the innovator and innovation, credit, and profit maximization were the three central elements, that the concept achieved its greatest vogue.[2]

Schumpeter distinguished innovation and the innovator from invention and the inventor (Ruttan, 1959). He repeatedly emphasized the distinction: "Innovation is possible without anything we should identify as invention, and invention does not necessarily induce innovation, but produces of itself no economically relevant effect at all" (Schumpeter, 1939:84).

Schumpeter not only rejected the idea that innovation directly depends on invention, he also asserted that the process that produces innovations is distinctly different "economically and sociologically" from the process that produces inventions. Schumpeter then proceeded to defined innovation in terms of a change in the form of the production function.

"This function describes the way in which quantity of products varies if quantity of factors vary. If instead of quantities of factors we vary the form of the function, we have an innovation" (Schumpeter, 1939, I:87–88). But Schumpeter's concept of change in the production function included institutional as well as technical change: "the setting up of a new production function . . . covers the case of a new commodity as well as a new form of organization or a merger, or the opening up of new markets" (Schumpeter, 1939, I:88).

Schumpeter was primarily interested in changes in the production function of the technological leaders—the innovating firms—because of the growth forces that adoption of new methods of production set in motion. In his view innovations

---

[2] Schumpeter's discussion of the role of innovation in economic growth is developed most fully in *Business Cycles* (1939, Chapters III and IV). For an earlier and less well-developed discussion see Schumpeter (1934, Chapter 2).

always entail construction of new plants and equipment: they are introduced by new firms and are associated with the rise to leadership of new men (Schumpeter, 1939:93–96).

Since the early 1980s there has been a "neo-Schumpeterian" revival.[3] A primary focus of the leaders of the revival has been on the dynamics of the "carrying out of new combinations" of factors and products and in the resultant "creative destruction" of old products and old firms through the forces of competition. The concept of the production function itself is frequently viewed as an obstacle to understanding the process of innovation (Nelson and Winter, 1982:59–65).

It seems hard to believe, in view of the enthusiasm of the neo-Schumpeterian school, that neither *Business Cycles* nor Schumpeter's other works contain anything that can be identified as a theory of innovation. The business cycle, in Schumpeter's system, is a direct consequence of the appearance of clusters of innovations. But there is no real explanation as to why innovations seem to appear in clusters or why the clusters appear to possess particular forms of periodicity.

If Schumpeter, in spite of his emphasis on innovation, did not present a theory of innovation, where is such a theory to be found? I argue in the next section that the beginnings of such a theory were developed by Usher in his classic, *A History of Mechanical Inventions* (1929, 1954).

Sources of Invention

Although the concept of invention has traditionally occupied an important role in the historical and sociological literature on technical change, it has until recently occupied only a peripheral role in the economics literature.[4] One of the problems economists have had difficulty resolving is how to provide an acceptable analytical definition in contrast with the legal-institutional definitions employed by national patent offices.

Usher's solution to this problem was to define invention in terms of the emergence of "new things" that require an "an act of insight" going beyond the normal exercise of technical or professional skill:

> *Acts of skill* include all learned activities whether the process of learning is an achievement of an isolated adult individual or a response to instructions by other individuals. *Inventive acts of insight* are unlearned activities that result in new organizations of prior knowledge and experience. (Usher, 1955:526) . . . Such acts of insight frequently emerge in the course of performing acts of skill, though characteristically the act of insight is induced by the conscious perception of an unsatisfactory gap in knowledge or mode of action. (Usher, 1955:523)

---

[3] See, for example, Heertje and Perlman (1990), Scherer and Perlman (1992), Shionoya and Perlman (1994), and Cohen (1995).

[4] For an excellent early literature survey, see Nelson (1959:101–127).

Usher's interest in the study of inventions goes beyond definition and description to an attempt to explain the emergence of inventions in contrast with the performance of acts of skill. He identifies and considers three general approaches to this problem— the transcendentalist, the mechanistic process, and the cumulative synthesis—but ultimately rejects the first two.

The *transcendentalist approach* attributes the emergence of invention to the inspiration of an occasional genius who from time to time achieves direct knowledge of essential truths through the exercise of intuition.[5] Usher rejected this view as ahistorical. He argued that the act of insight is not a rare, spontaneous phenomenon. Rather, the act of insight that results in the perception of a new relationship requires a highly specific conditioning of the mind within the framework of the problem to be solved. The transcendentalist view is essentially supply side. It is not an accident, in other words, that a bicycle mechanic made important contributions to the development of the automobile (Chapter 11). A contemporary equivalent of the transcendentalist view is that autonomous advances in science and technology determine the rate and direction of technical change.

The *mechanistic process* theory views invention as proceeding under the stress of necessity.[6] The individual inventor is an instrument of broad historical forces: "with the progress of invention apparently a device can no longer remain unfounded when the time for it is ripe. There is no indication that any individual's genius has been necessary to any invention that was of any importance—to the historian and social scientist, the progress of invention appears to be impersonal" (Gilfillan, 1935:10). The detailed historical studies of invention by Gilfillan demonstrated, however, that the process leading to a major invention typically represents a new combination of a relatively large number of individual elements accumulated over long periods of time.

Usher argues that the mechanistic process approach tends to overlook the significant fact that the "acts of insight" required to overcome a particular discontinuity or resistance are possible for only a limited number of individuals who have both an awareness of the problem and elements of a solution within their frame of reference. Even under these conditions, it is not certain that the specific act of insight required for a solution to the problem will occur.

---

[5] This view has often been attributed to Samuel Smiles, the author of *Lives of Engineers* (1966). Smiles did view the engineers, inventors, and industrialists who transformed the British environment and society during the nineteenth century as culture heros. His writing exhibits, however, a deep appreciation of the role of skills acquired through experience and insight that lead to advances in engineering design and practice (Hughes, 1966:1–29). For a heroic view of the inventor–entrepreneur, see Hughes (1986). For a heroic view of the agronomists and plant breeders who contributed to the development of modern high-yield crop varieties see Stakeman et al. (1967).

[6] This view was advanced most vigorously by several University of Chicago sociologists (Ogburn and Thomas, 1922; Ogburn 1937; Gilfillan, 1935, 1952). For later review of the evidence and reasons for multiple discovery and independent discovery in science and technology see Merton (1973).

In formulating the *cumulative synthesis* approach, which he offers as an alternative to the transcendentalist and mechanistic process theories of invention, Usher drew on the understanding of mental and social processes provided by Gestalt psychology.[7] Within this framework major inventions emerge from the cumulative synthesis of relatively simple inventions, each of which requires an individual "act of insight."

In the case of the individual invention, four steps are outlined:

1. *Perception of the problem*, in which an incomplete or unsatisfactory pattern or method of satisfying a want is perceived. Perception of the unsatisfactory performance is often induced by changes in the external economic environment.

2. *Setting the stage*, in which the elements or data necessary for a solution are brought together through some particular configuration of events or thought. Among the elements of the solution is an individual who possesses sufficient *skill* in manipulating the other elements.

3. *The act of insight*, in which the essential solution of the problem is found. Usher stresses the fact that large elements of uncertainty surround the act of insight. It is this uncertainty that makes it impossible to predict the timing or the precise configuration of a solution in advance.

4. *Critical revision*, in which the new invention is redesigned or reengineered to meet the technical and economic requirements for successful adoption and diffusion.

A major or strategic invention represents the cumulative synthesis of many individual inventions, each of which has usually gone through all of the separate steps. Many individual inventions do no more than set the stage for a major invention, and new acts of insight are again essential when the major invention requires substantial critical revision to adapt it to particular uses. A schematic presentation of the elements of the individual act of insight and the cumulative synthesis can be found in Figures 3.1 and 3.2.

Usher's cumulative synthesis theory is appealing on grounds other than its basis in Gestalt psychology. It provides a unified theory of the social processes by which "new things" come into existence, a theory broad enough to encompass the whole range of activities characterized by the terms science, invention, and innovation. It is no longer necessary to maintain, as Schumpeter did, the increasingly artificial distinction between the processes of invention and innovation, or to explain away

---

[7] "The Gestalt analysis presents the achievements of great men as a special class of acts of insight, which involves synthesis of many items derived from other acts of insight. In its entirety, the social process of innovation thus consists of acts of insight of different degrees of importance and at many levels of perception and thought. These acts converge in the course of time toward massive synthesis. Insight is not a rare or unusual phenomenon as presented by the transcendentalists; nor is it a relatively simple response to need (as presumed by the mechanistic process theorists)" (Usher, 1954:61). Usher's emphatic insistence that the history of technical change is more than a history of inventions, that it must be understood in terms of larger social and economic forces, was anticipated by Marx (Rosenberg, 1982:34–551).

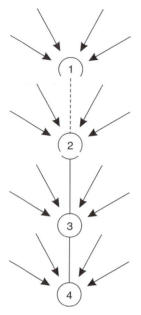

Figure 3.1 The emergence of novelty in the act of insight. Synthesis of familiar items: (1) perception of an incomplete pattern, (2) setting the stage, (3) the act of insight, and (4) critical revision and full mastery of the new pattern. (After Abbott P. Usher, *A History of Mechanical Inventions.* Copyright © 1955 by Princeton University Press. Used by permission of Princeton University Press.)

the intimate association between scientists, inventors, and entrepreneurs as "merely a chance coincidence." In spite of attempts by historians of technology to draw on other models, the Kuhn (1962) model of scientific revolutions, for example, to advance understanding of the emergence of new technology, Usher's model has retained its currency. Hughes' model of technological systems, for example, draws directly on the cumulative synthesis model (Hughes, 1978:166–182; Weingart, 1984:131–132; Chapter 7).

It is conventional in economics to reserve the term innovation for the emergence of novelty in economic organization and use invention for the emergence of novelty in technology. I see no particular point in such a distinction, and in fact see many advantages in eliminating a distinction for which there is no real conceptual basis Indeed, it would be more in line with both popular usage and the terminology of other disciplines to use the term innovation for any "new thing" in the area of science, technology, or art. When greater precision is required, innovation can be preceded by an appropriate adjective—"scientific innovation," "technical innovation," "organizational innovation," or something even more precise. Invention then becomes that special subset of technical innovation on which patents can be obtained.

Another advantage of Usher's theory is that it clarifies the points at which conscious efforts to speed the rate or alter the direction of innovation can be effective. It is at the second and fourth steps—*setting the stage* and *critical revision*—that conscious efforts will have the greatest impact. By consciously bringing together the elements of a solution—by creating the appropriate research environment—the stage can be

Figure 3.2 The process of cumulative syntheses. A full cycle of strategic invention and part of a second cycle. Roman numerals I through IV represent steps in the development of a strategic invention. Small figures represent individual elements of novelty. Arrows represent familiar elements included in the new synthesis. (After Abbott P. Usher, *A History of Mechanical Inventions*, Cambridge, MA: Harvard University Press, 1954.)

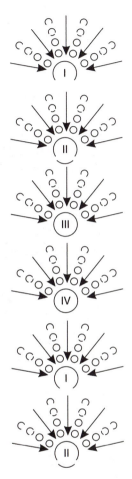

set in so that fewer elements are left to chance. It would be inaccurate to suppose that we can now, or perhaps ever, find it possible to set the stage in such a manner as to guarantee a breakthrough in any particular area. But as we learn more about the effectiveness of various research environments, the probability that breakthroughs will be achieved should be increased.

At the level of *critical revision*, we have made considerable progress in bringing economic and administrative resources to bear. This is the stage that typically absorbs the largest share of resources devoted to new product development. In the drug industry, for example, the first three stages typically absorb 10–15% and the critical revision stage 80–90% of the resources for research and development (Gambardella, 1995:20; Chapter 10). Many of the elements of critical revision require "acts of skill" in contrast to "acts of insight." The effectiveness of modern research procedures in shortening the time span from the test tube to the production line testifies to our ability to exert conscious direction at the level of applied research and technology development.[8]

CUMULATIVE SYNTHESIS: THREE CASES

In this section I present three cases that illustrate the value of the Usher cumulative synthesis approach for interpreting the process of invention and innovation. These are the development of the Watt–Boulton steam engine, of modern rice varieties, and of the microprocessor. The Watt–Boulton steam engine is a classic example of the process of innovation in the area of mechanical technology. The steam engine became the dominant general purpose technology of the nineteenth century. The development of modern varieties of rice for the tropics illustrates the role that the agricultural experiment station plays in advancing biological technology. It was advances in biological technology that enabled the world's farmers to meet the dramatic growth in demand for food associated with a more than doubling of world population in the second half of the twentieth century. The microprocessor is an example of an advance in electronic technology by a research-based entrepreneurial firm. The computer and semiconductor, to which it gave rise, became pervasive sources of technical change across both the manufacturing and service industries toward the end of the twentieth century.

The Watt–Boulton Steam Engine[9]

The steam engine was the first of the great strategic or "general purpose" mechanical technologies associated with the industrial revolution. It opened up new opportunities in mining and manufacturing that would otherwise not have become available until much later.

Steam power was first employed in the mining industries. As the demand for coal and metals expanded, efforts to obtain them from ever deeper mines intensified. Many ingenious devices were invented to rid the mines of water, but flooding remained a major problem, and the chief obstacle to further expansion of output. In 1698 Thomas Savery, a military engineer, obtained a patent for a steam pump, which he called "The Miner's Friend."

A few of Savery's pumps were erected in the first decade of the eighteenth century. Their use was restricted by the low pressure that the boilers and piping could withstand. Thomas Newcomen, a plumber, and his assistant, John Calley, improved on Savery's

---

[8] An important limitation in the Usher *cumulative synthesis* model is that it has little to say about the rate and direction of technical change. These issues are discussed in Chapter 4.

[9] In this section I draw on Ferguson (1964), Scherer (1965), Hills (1970), and Cameron (1993).

pump and developed the first piston-operating steam engine in 1712. The Newcomen engine (Figure 3.3) consisted of a cylinder fitted with a piston. Water was boiled in a boiler and the steam was fed into a cylinder. When the cylinder was filled with steam the counterweighted pump plunger moved the piston to the extreme upper end of the stroke. A spray of cold water was applied to the cylinder to cool the steam. The steam condensed, creating a vacuum. The atmospheric pressure acting on the piston caused it to move down in the cylinder, and the resulting force acting on the beam lifted the pump plunger. The invention underwent several revisions. Applying the cooling water to the exterior of a cylinder was found to be too slow, so the water was instead sprayed inside the cylinder. Another problem was that air and other noncondensable gases accumulated within the cylinder, causing the engine to stop after a few strokes. This difficulty was overcome by allowing some steam to blow out each time the cylinder was filled. The valves for admitting steam and condensing water to the cylinder were first operated by hand. Later they were operated by the motion of the engine so that after start-up the engines became self-actuating.

By the end of the century, several hundred Newcomen engines had been erected in Britain, and a number on the Continent as well. They were employed, like the Savery engines, mainly in coal mines, where fuel was cheap. However, they were large, cumbersome, expensive, and not thermally efficient. These deficiencies laid the foundation for the Watt–Boulton engine. The development of the Watt–Boulton engine can be described in terms of the stages in the Usher cumulative synthesis model.

PERCEPTION OF THE PROBLEM

The major deficiency of the Newcomen engine was its large consumption of fuel in relation to the work produced. In the early 1760s, James Watt, a "mathematical instrument maker" (laboratory technician) in the University of Glasgow, was asked to repair a small working model of a Newcomen engine used for demonstration purposes in the course on natural philosophy. Intrigued, Watt began to experiment with the engine.

SETTING THE STAGE

The stage had been set by Watts' knowledge of basic mechanical principles and his skills as a fine toolmaker. As an expert fine toolmaker, Watt was able to produce the needed parts for the engine himself. Such delicately made parts were unavailable in the market.

ACT OF INSIGHT

While walking across the Glasgow Green on a Sunday afternoon in the Summer of 1765, Watt conceived a solution. It would be to condense the steam, not in the operating cylinder, but in a separate "condenser" into which it would be drawn by a pump. Because the cylinder and piston remained at steam temperature, substantial increases in fuel efficiency could be realized (Figure 3.4).

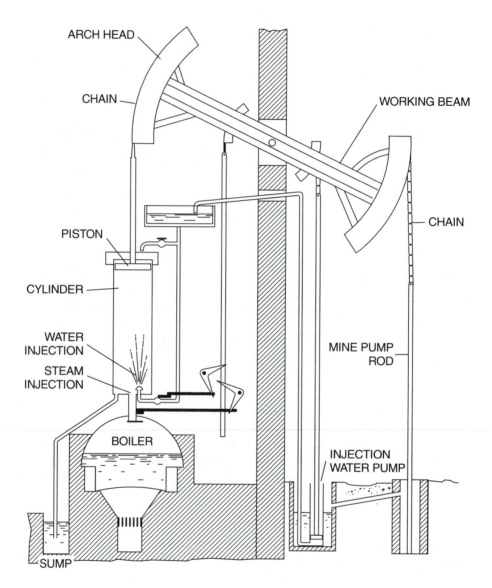

SUCCESSFUL ENGINE by Newcomen introduced steam into a cylinder that was then cooled with injection of water, creating partial vacuum. Atmospheric pressure forced piston down to achieve pumping; weight of mine-pump rod and equipment then raised piston for new cycle.

Figure 3.3 The Newcomen steam engine. (*Source:* Eugene S. Ferguson, "The Origins of the Steam Engine," *Scientific American* 211 (January 1964): 104.)

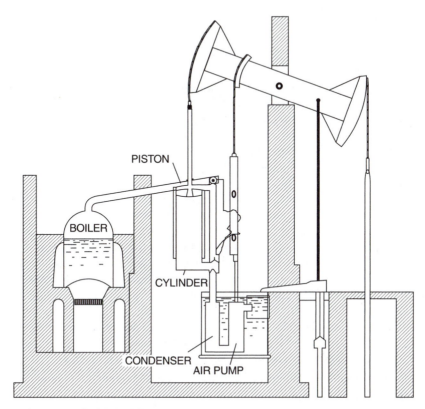

PISTON

BOILER

CYLINDER

CONDENSER

AIR PUMP

CONTRIBUTIONS BY WATT to the steam engine included the development of a separate condenser, as depicted here. Newcomen had effected the condensation in the main cylinder.

Figure 3.4 The Watt–Boulton steam engine. (*Source:* Eugene S. Ferguson, "The Origins of the Steam Engine," *Scientific American* 211 (January 1964): 104.)

CRITICAL REVISION

This stage involved an attempt to develop a commercially successful operational engine based on the principle of condensation. A number of technical obstacles, including obtaining a cylinder sufficiently smooth to prevent the steam from escaping, plagued the engine and delayed its practical use for several years (Figure 3.4).

In 1774 Watt formed a partnership with Matthew Boulton, a successful hardware manufacturer near Birmingham, who provided Watt with the time and facilities for further experimentation. At the same time, John Wilkinson, a nearby ironmaster, patented a new boring machine for making cannon barrels, which also sufficed for engine cylinders. Watt also made a number of other improvements, among them an insulated steam jacket around the cylinder, an airpump to maintain the vacuum in the steam condenser, a centrifugal governor to regulate the speed of the engine, and a device to convert the reciprocating motion of the piston to rotary motion.

In 1775 Parliament, by a special act, extended the term of Watt's patent for 25 years and the firm of Boulton and Watt- began commercial production of steam engines. One of their first customers was John Wilkinson, who used the engine to operate the bellows for his blast furnace. Most of Boulton and Watt's early engines were used for pumping water from mines, especially the tin mines of Cornwall, where coal was expensive and the savings in fuel consumption compared with the Newcomen engine were considerable. The first spinning mill to be driven directly by a steam engine began production in 1785. By 1800, when the patent expired, the Watt–Boulton partnership had built about 500 engines.

It has been argued that the patent extension, which enabled Watt and Boulton to charge an annual "premium" or a lifetime "annuity" for use of their engines, slowed its diffusion. It also impeded further innovation since Watt, concerned about safety, discouraged the development of engines with higher steam pressure. He also discouraged the installers of his machines from attempting to develop steam-driven transportation. The expiration of the patent was followed by a period of intensive innovation in the development and use of steam engines (Hills, 1970; Smil, 1994).

Watt was the classic inventor. Boulton was the classic Schumpeterian entrepreneur. Watt's early engines were characterized by many operational problems. Improvement drew on continuing interaction between the inventor and users. Boulton's successful entrepreneurship depended on an intimate association between inventor and entrepreneur.

Modern Varieties of Rice[10]

The development of high-yielding modern varieties of rice for tropical environments is a particularly important example of the contribution of plant breeding to productivity growth. It is also a useful example of the linkage between advances in biological science and advances in biological technology. The plant-breeding methods used to develop improved crop varieties and hybrids were based on advances in knowledge in biology, particularly Mendelian genetics, that had occurred during the first several decades of the twentieth century.[10]

Advances in crop and animal productivity prior to the twentieth century were not closely linked to advances in biological knowledge. Interregional diffusion of crop varieties, animal breeds, tools, and husbandry practices constituted important

---

[10] Mendel's research on the inheritance of traits in garden peas was published in 1866. It did not directly influence crop breeding until the independent rediscovery and confirmation of the laws of inheritance around 1900 (see Chapter 10).

[10] In this section I draw heavily on Stakeman et al. (1967) and on Wortman and Cummings (1978). I also draw on my own experience as a staff member of the International Rice Research Institute during 1963–1965.

sources of productivity growth in prehistory. The voyages of Columbus initiated a series of dramatic changes in agricultural production and land use in both the old and the new worlds. The advent of industrialization and lower costs of land and water transportation made possible by the steam engine also stimulated growth of agricultural production in areas characterized by abundant land and low population density.

By the 1950s, however, the possibility of expanding agricultural production by the opening up of new land or the simple transfer of technology had largely been exhausted. Since the middle of the twentieth century an increasing share of the growth in agricultural production, in both developed and developing countries, has been accounted for by increases in yield—by increases in output per hectare. In spite of limited expansion of land area, a number of developed and developing countries sustained annual growth in agricultural production of 3.0 to 5.0%, well above the 1.0 to 2.0% growth rate during much of the previous century (Chapter 6).

These higher modern growth rates are due to improved technologies for crop and animal production, which have been generated by very substantial investments in agricultural research. Initially this research was conducted primarily in public sector institutions—experiment stations and laboratories operated by ministries of agriculture or universities. Since the 1970s private sector research organizations operated by seed companies, animal breeders, and chemical companies have come to account for a larger share of agricultural research directed specifically to development of technology.

In this section I use the Usher cumulative synthesis model to interpret the stages in the development of high-yielding varieties of rice for the tropics.

PERCEPTION OF THE PROBLEM

A series of post-World War II assessments by national and international agencies led to the perception that rapid growth in food demand, rising out of population and income growth, was leading to a potentially severe food crisis in South and Southeast Asia. Rice was the basic food staple for much of the population in the region. In spite of intensive methods of cultivation yields had remained low—in the range of 1.0–2.0 metric tons per hectare since the turn of the century—while in the temperate rice-producing areas of the world—the United States, Southern Europe, and Japan—rice yields had risen substantially.

Attempts to directly transfer higher yielding temperate region varieties of rice to the tropics had failed. Japan had increased rice yields on Taiwan during the 1920s and 1930s, not by directly transferring Japanese varieties to Taiwan, but by investing in the research capacity in Taiwan necessary to develop varieties or rice that used both Japanese and Taiwanese genetic materials. The direct transfer of biological technology across agroclimatic regions was limited by biological constraints. During the 1950s it became apparent to both national governments and assistance agencies that the development of stronger agricultural research capacity in the tropical rice-producing areas of Asia would be necessary if the biological constraints that limited rice yields were to be overcome.

SETTING THE STAGE

The stage was set for the development of modern varieties of rice by the establishment of the International Rice Research Institute (IRRI) and by efforts to strengthen national rice research programs in the late 1950s and early 1960s. The process that led to the establishment of the IRRI began in 1953 when the Rockefeller Foundation sent a mission to Asia to assess whether it might be of assistance in strengthening agricultural research in the region. Consultations were held with the governments of the region and with the Ford Foundation, which had active programs in many countries of the region. The result was a decision to establish the IRRI adjacent to the College of Agriculture of the University of the Philippines at Los Banos. The Philippine Government donated the necessary land, the Ford Foundation agreed to supply funds for capital construction, and the Rockefeller Foundation assumed responsibility for operating expenses and for providing a core staff of scientists to organize and direct the research program. The agreement to establish the Institute was signed in 1959.

By 1962 the IRRI facilities had been constructed, an international interdisciplinary staff had been recruited, and the research program was initiated.[12] The facilities included laboratories, greenhouses and screenhouses, and extensive field plots. One of the most important steps in setting the stage was the initiation of a program to create a world collection of domesticated varieties of rice and their wild relatives. This was the genetic material from which it was hoped that higher yielding varieties could be designed. Under the direction of the brilliant Chinese geneticist T. T. Chang, IRRI became one of the world's premier germplasm and utilization centers. Arrangements for cooperation in the development and testing of new varieties were made with national research organizations and universities throughout the region. An intense program of seminars and research reviews was initiated to focus the efforts of the diverse research team on the central objective of the Institute—to raise rice yields in Asia.

ACT OF INSIGHT

The key act of insight emerged out of the interaction between Peter Jennings, a plant breeder from the United States, and Arkira Tanaka, a plant physiologist from Japan. In 1964 Jennings published a paper that identified what, in economists' language, might be termed a model of a biologically efficient rice plant (Jennings, 1964:13–15).

---

[12] The initial scientific staff included the following disciplines and individuals: agronomy, Moomaw, Hawaii; plant breeding and genetics, Beachell and Jennings, United States, and Chang, Taiwan; soils, Ponnamperuma, Sri Lanka; plant physiology, Tanaka, Japan, and Vergara, Philippines; plant pathology, Ou, Taiwan; entomology, Pathak, India; chemistry and biochemistry, Akazawa, Japan and Juliano, Philippines; statistics, Oñate, Philippines; agricultural economics, Ruttan, United States; agricultural engineering, Johnson, United States; communications and sociology, Byrnes, United States (Stakeman et al., 1962:298).

The proposed plant ideotype was short and stiff strawed, photoperiod insensitive, and had, under conditions of favorable nutrition and growing environment, a higher ratio of grain to straw than the taller traditional varieties (Figure 3.5).

This conceptual innovation, though somewhat controversial when first advanced, enabled rice breeders to select promising crosses much more rapidly by screening for plant type rather than for yield alone. These varieties were similar physiognomically to the Ponlai type varieties that had been developed by Japanese breeders working in Taiwan 30 years earlier (Hayami and Ruttan, 1970:563–589). But it was not until the Jennings–Tanaka collaboration that the conceptual basis for the better performance of the Ponlai varieties was understood and thus could serve as a model for breeding practice.

CRITICAL REVISION

Progress occurred much more rapidly than initially anticipated. Within 6 years after the initiation of the rice-breeding program at IRRI, a series of new varieties of rice with yield potentials 50–100% higher than traditional varieties was being released by IRRI for use by rice producers. The diffusion of the new seed-fertilizer rice production technology was so rapid that the press began referring to "green revolution" varieties of rice.

In spite of the rapid initial adoption of these varieties of rice, a process of continuous adaptation has been necessary. The initial releases tended to be susceptible to a number of diseases and insects. Pathogens and insects, which had inflicted only minor damage

Figure 3.5 Different plant types of rice. Left, tall conventional plant type. Center, improved high-yielding, high-tillering plant type. Right, proposed low-tillering ideotype with higher yield potential. (*Source:* Gurdev S. Kush, "Breeding Rice for Sustainable Agricultural Systems," *International Crop Science* I. Madison, WI: Crop Science Society of America, 1993:198.)

on the lower yielding traditional varieties, emerged as major sources of yield loss for the new higher yielding varieties. The germplasm collection was evaluated for sources of disease and insect resistance. Resistant varieties were used by the breeders to develop a series of varieties with multiple disease and insect resistance. These multiple resistance varieties have the advantage that they can be grown with lower doses, or even without synthetic pesticides. Attention was also given to developing varieties adapted to different ecosystems—rainfed (nonirrigated) lowland areas, upland (high elevation) areas, deepwater areas subject to flooding, and tidal areas with salinity, nutrient deficiency, and mineral toxicity problems.

By the early 1980s it was not uncommon for farmers using good agronomic practices in favorably endowed areas to obtain yields of 6–8 metric tons of rice per hectare. At the same time, experiment station researchers were finding it difficult to design varieties that could consistently exceed yields of 10 metric tons per hectare even under optimum conditions. It appeared that a new yield ceiling had replaced the old yield ceiling of around 2 metric tons that had characterized the traditional varieties of the 1950s. Furthermore, substantial maintenance research—the research needed to maintain existing yields in the presence of coevolution of pests and pathogens—was required.

In the mid-1980s the leader of the IRRI rice-breeding program, Gundev Kush, proposed a new ideotype to replace the Jennings–Tanaka model. The new ideotype would be characterized by an even higher ratio of grain to straw (harvest index) and significantly higher yields (Kush, 1993:189–199). The new plant type is just beginning to be tested under field conditions.

The Microprocessor[13]

The transistor (or chip) was the seminal invention in the development of the semiconductor industry. Its invention was followed by the integrated circuit, a complex chip with more than one active device on it. The invention of the microprocessor completed the inventive steps in the development of the central processing unit of computers and other microelectronic applications. It is regarded as the single most important invention leading to the development of the personal computer (Chapter 9). The invention of the microprocessor provides another illustration of the Usher cumulative synthesis model.

The microprocessor was invented by Marcian (Ted) Hoff of Intel in 1969–1970. The *perception of the problem* began when a Japanese hand-held calculator company, Busicom, requested that Intel provide it with wired logic circuits that would perform the calculator's functions. The *stage was set* by Intel's prior experience as a leading producer of memory devices and by Ted Hoff's previous experience with general purpose computers.

---

[13] This case is based largely on Fransman (1995:168–169) and Moore (1996:55–80). See also Chapter 9.

The *act of insight* occurred when Hoff perceived that a general purpose computer architecture could be used to meet Busicom's requirements less expensively. He suggested that a processor, if designed to use transistors efficiently, could be built on a single chip with about the same complexity as other Intel memory chips. "He envisioned a central processor chip, which combined with a chip containing program memory storage in a fixed memory called Read Only Memory (ROM) and a read/write memory (RAM) of the kind that we were developing, would make a complete computing system that could be used to make any of the Busicom calculators, changing only the stored program" (Moore, 1996:70). Hoff's insight made it possible to meet Busicom's needs, cutting the development effort from 13 complex chips to one (plus two memory chips), and at the same time have a product of far greater general applicability.

Critical revision was necessary to realize the full potential of the microprocessor. The first microprocessor had such limited processing capacity that Intel thought its use would be restricted to applications such as calculators and traffic lights. This seemed to be confirmed by the more powerful processors also being developed in the early 1970s for military application. Beginning in 1979, however, when Intel introduced a new family of microprocessors (the X86 family), performance increased by multiples of four or five every 3 years. This technological trajectory has been termed "Moore's Law" after Gordon Moore, one of the founders of Intel. By the mid-1990s single microprocessors were able to perform the functions that required large mainframe computers a decade earlier.

A point that should be reemphasized is that in each of these cases many more resources were brought to bear at the critical revision than at earlier stages. Chip-manufacturing processes had also become much more complex. With each succeeding generation of semiconductor process technology, the costs of designing new chips was rising even more rapidly than the increase in chip capacity. By the late 1980s, factories designed to produce the most advanced chip required an investment of over $2 billion.

LINKAGES BETWEEN SCIENCE AND TECHNOLOGY

The Usher cumulative synthesis model is incomplete in its representation of the linkages between science and technology.[14] Usher used the model to clarify the relationship between skill and insight in the process of technical innovation. The model is a reasonable representation of the innovation process in an area such as mechanical technology, in which advances in technology have often preceded or not been intimately linked with advances in science. It is also an accurate representation of the stages in Edison's invention of the high-resistance incandescent electric lamp filament at his Menlo Park laboratory (Chapter 7). But it is less adequate as a

---

[14] In this section I draw on Thirtle and Ruttan (1987:2–11) and Ruttan (1982:56–60).

description of the innovation process in which there is an intimate relationship, for example, between advances in biological science and agricultural technology or between advances in chemistry and in chemical engineering.

In the nineteenth century there was a remarkable fusion of theoretical and empirical inquiry. By the middle of the twentieth century a new orthodoxy had emerged to the effect that modern technology was simply applied science. In this linear or "assembly line" model, basic science developed theory and understanding; applied science took that knowledge and used it in the design of new technology. In the United States this new orthodoxy was reinforced by the success of World War II science-based military technology. It found its most influential expression in the report by Vannevar Bush on postwar scientific research. "Basic research leads to new knowledge. It provides scientific capital. It creates the fund from which the practical applications of knowledge must be drawn. Today it is truer than ever that basic research is the pacemaker of technological progress" (Bush, 1945:19). It was argued further in the Bush report that new product and new processes are founded on new principles and new conceptions, which in turn are developed by research in the purest realms of science, and that basic research is performed without thought of private ends. The Bush report became the charter for United States postwar science and technology policy. The linear or assembly line science-based technology model tended to dominate postwar R&D management, science, and technology policy, and many of the early postwar studies of invention and innovation.[15]

In practice the interactions between advances in science and technology tend to be much more complex (Figure 3.6). Instead of a single path running from scientific discovery or innovation through applied research to development, it is more accurate to think of science-oriented and technology-oriented research as two interacting paths that both lead from, and feed back into, a common pool of scientific and technical knowledge (Layton, 1974:31–41). In some cases the path leads from technical change back to science. The invention of the steam engine preceeded and contributed to advances in knowledge in metallurgy and thermodynamics. The Wright brothers developed the first airplane without an understanding of aerodynamic theory. Their invention induced advances in aerodynamic theory and materials science.

The link to the common pool of existing knowledge, however, is not the only channel of interaction. In many instances, there are direct linkages or interactions that occur at the leading edge of both paths. The linkage between science and technology varies greatly among fields. The division between leading-edge biotechnology and modern biological science has almost completely disappeared. Biotechnology both

---

[15] The Bush report was the product of a small committee made up largely of leaders in academic science. It is apparent, in retrospect, that Bush, drawing on his experience in early computer development and in the creation of the electronics company Raytheon, and with military research and development during World War II, held a more complex view of the relations between science and technology and had hoped for a report that would place greater emphasis on support for pioneering technical research (Wise, 1985:231). For the intellectual and institutional history of the linear model of the relationship between science and technology, see Stokes (1997:26–57).

The Linear Model

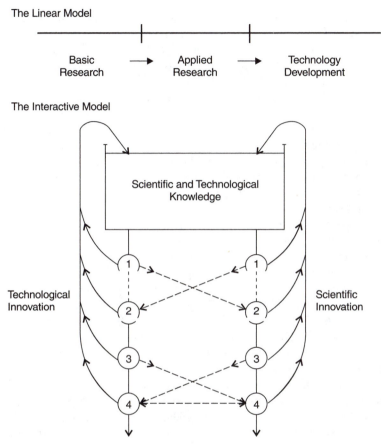

Figure 3.6 Relations between advances in scientific and technical knowledge. (Adapted from Vernon W. Ruttan, *Agricultural Research Policy*, Minneapolis, MN: University of Minnesota Press, 1982:57; Donald E. Stokes, *Pasteur's Quadrant: Basic Science and Technological Innovation*, Washington, DC: The Brookings Institution Press, 1997:10.)

draws on and contributes to new science. In contrast the chemical technology subfield of organic compounds draws on relatively old science (Navin and Olivastro, 1992). In some cases, a single individual or research team may occupy a leading position in advancing knowledge along both scientific and technical paths. Examples include scientist–engineers such as Irving Langmuir who carried out fundamental research in electrochemistry and played an active role in the development of improved filaments for electric light bulbs and in the development of radio vacuum tubes at the General Electric Research Laboratory (Reich, 1983:199–221) and William Shockley, who as head of the solid-state research group at the Bell Laboratories, both advanced the theory of semiconductors and made the initial advances in transistor technology

(Chapter 9). The process outlined in Figure 3.6 is also descriptive of the interactions between George H. Schull of the Carnegie Institution and Donald Jones of the Connecticut Agricultural Experiment Station in the development and extension of the theory of hybrid vigor and the invention of the double-cross method of hybrid corn (maize) seed production.

It is also a valid representation of the interrelationship between scientific and technological advances in genetics and genetic engineering. Maureen KcKelvey has described the process of advances in science and technology in terms that are consistent with Figure 3.6. Early uses of genetic engineering developed along a different trajectory from that of science. The firms R&D activities stressed improvements in reliability, level of gene expression, purity, ease of processing, and other factors that would enable the new pharmaceutical products to compete technically and economically. In contrast scientists working in molecular biology and related fields attempted to advance knowledge about the human genome. These two separate but interacting trajectories developed because of the different social and economic forces operating on the two scientific communities (Chapter 10).

Layton has described this intimate linkage between advances in science and technology, in which there is both a flow of technology into science and a flow of scientific knowledge into engineering, by the metaphor of "mirror-image twins" (Layton, 1971:562–581). Price has suggested that science and technology, although independent, are related like a pair of dancers and that what keeps them linked is "the music of instrumentalities." "The history of the craft of experimental science is the missing link between the history of technology and that of science. It is now recognized that the ancient craft of the clockmaker runs side by side with that of scientific instrument making and that those twin crafts contained much of the repertoire of fine metal work which made possible the Industrial Revolution" (Price, 1984:110). Price goes on to argue that the most common source of shifts in scientific paradigms are changes in technology that demand an interpretation.

This interrelated model of science and technology makes clear the central role of the modern research institution in the process of scientific and technical innovation.

THE RESEARCH INSTITUTION

"The greatest invention of the 19th century was the invention of the method of invention" (Whitehead, 1925:98). The industrial research laboratory, agricultural experiment station, and research university emerged in the last half of the nineteenth century. They institutionalized the process of transforming intellectual and physical capital into new knowledge and new technology (Mowery, 1990).

Our understanding of the internal processes that condition the productivity of a research organization, and of the relation of these internal processes to the external environment, is surprisingly weak. The literature tends to fall into two categories. There is an historical literature that draws primarily on the notebooks and reflections of participants in the research process. There is a research management literature that draws from both psychology and sociology (Van de Ven et al., 1989). And there is a newer "ethnographic" literature based largely on participant observation of laboratory life by sociologists and anthropologists.[16]

In Box 3.1, "The First American Industrial Laboratory," I describe the laboratory that Thomas A. Edison established in Menlo Park, New Jersey in 1888. Edison established his laboratory to be an "invention factory." Edison's description of the inventive process at his Menlo Park laboratory is remarkably similar to the Usher stages. As an inventor–entrepreneur Edison was extremely sensitive to the external economic environment, as well as to the scientific and technical opportunities, in organizing his research program. Figure 3.7 is a somewhat stylized model of the research institute.[17] In the figure the internal production processes are related to the external environment in which it operates. A research institute's production processes involve the transformation of the stock and flow of human and material resources into intermediate products. These products are, in turn, transformed into outputs. The outputs can be categorized under three headings—information, capacity, and influence.

● BOX 3.1

THE FIRST AMERICAN INDUSTRIAL LABORATORY

The first American industrial research laboratory in the modern sense was established by Thomas A. Edison at Menlo Park, New Jersey in 1876. The invention of the high-resistance incandescent lamp and the development of a system for the generation and distribution of electric power by Edison and his research team at Menlo Park established the foundation for the electric utility industry.

Prior to establishing his Menlo Park laboratory Edison had been responsible for a number of important inventions, the most important being in the area of telegraphy. In 1869 he was attracted to New York where he worked as an independent inventor with support from the Western Union Company.

---

[16] The classic ethnographic study is Latour and Woolgar (1979). For a collection of useful papers see MacKenzie and Wajcman (1985). For reviews see Woolgar (1982) and Law (1987). Woolgar classifies the ethnographic literature under two headings, instrumental and reflexive. The burden of the ethnographic literature is to deconstruct the mystery of scientific activity to show that doing science is very much like doing most other kinds of work. The reflexive literature is more concerned with the logic of the thought processes of the inhabitants of research laboratories.

[17] In this section I draw on the organization of the Edison Laboratory in Menlo Park (Box 3.1), on the early history of research at General Electric and American Telegraph and Telephone (Reich, 1985); on discussions of the relationship between advances in science and technology by Dasgupta and David (1994), and on my own experience at the International Rice Research Institute.

In the early 1870s Edison established a factory in Newark, New Jersey to manufacture telegraphic equipment for Western Union. At Newark Edison began to assemble the research and development team that would become the core group for his Menlo Park laboratory (Reich, 1985:42–45).

Edison's inventive and manufacturing efforts for Western Union in Newark were sufficiently profitable to enable him to establish the Menlo Park laboratory. He visualized the Menlo Park facility as an "invention factory"—capable of turning out "a minor invention every ten days and a big thing every six months or so." He chose the Menlo Park location because it would provide insulation from the distractions of the Newark urban environment. Edison was a compulsive worker who often worked and slept in his laboratory for several days at a time, and he expected the same dedication from his staff.

The staff that Edison attracted to Menlo Park included Charles Batchelor, a master craftsman, who had come from England to install textile machinery and had joined Edison in Newark; John Kreusi, trained in Switzerland as a master mechanic, who transferred from Newark to take charge of the Menlo Park machine shop; Hermon Claudius, who had a Ph.D. degree in electrical engineering and experience as a system designer in the Austria telegraph system; and Francis Upton, a Princeton graduate who had spent a postgraduate year studying the mathematics of electrodynamics with Herman von Helmholtz at the University of Berlin. The Menlo Park laboratory complex also evolved by a broad array of expensive machine tools, chemical apparatuses, library resources, scientific instruments, and electrical equipment to support the inventive efforts of the staff.

In 1878, 2 years after moving to Menlo Park, Edison began to focus his efforts on the development and introduction of a system of electric lighting. On October 20, 1878 he announced in the *New York Sun* a plan for underground distribution of electricity from centrally located generators. At the time of his announcement Edison had no generator, no promising incandescent lamp, and no system of distribution.

> I have the right principle and am on the right track, but time, hard work and some good luck are necessary, too. It has been just so in all of my inventions. The first step is an intuition, and comes with a burst, the difficulties arise—something gives out and then . . . little faults and difficulties . . . show themselves and months of intense watching, study and labor are requisite before commercial success or failure is finally reached. (quoted by Hughes, 1979, from a letter from Edison to Theodore Puskas, November 13, 1887)

A major problem that had to be solved was the invention and development of a high-resistance filament for the incandescent light. On the basis of careful economic calculations Edison determined that a high-resistance lamp filament, in contrast to the low-resistance one tried by earlier inventors of incandescent lamps, should be necessary to compete economically with gas lights. These calculations did not, however, lead directly to a selection of an appropriate filament. Edison and his assistants found it necessary to test over 3000 different materials, including platinum and bamboo, before finally settling on carbonized cotton thread. Hughes notes that "Edison's method of invention and development in the case of the electric light system was a blend of economics, technology (especially experimentation), and science. In his notebooks pages of economic calculations are mixed with pages reporting experimental data . . . and hypothesis formulation based on science" (Hughes, 1979:135).

Hughes goes on to note:

> The analysis of the Edison method as revealed in the invention of the high-resistance filament . . . cuts close to the core of his creativity. As he declared, there was an abundance of patient hunt and try, and even his most superficial biographers grasp this. Furthermore, those who want to discount the Edisonian method, as compared to the so-called scientific method of the laboratory scientists who followed him, choose to stress his empirical approach. This superficiality and distortion are regrettable as one more of many instances of the obfuscation of the value of creativity. What should be stressed are the flashes of insight within a context of ordered desiderata. By ordering priorities, Edison defined the problem and insisted, as many other inventors, engineers and scientists have, that to define the problem is to take the major step toward its solution. The prime desideration was an incandescent light economically competitive with gas; the major flash of insight was realizing that Ohm's and Joule's laws defined the relationship between the technical variables in his system and allowed their manipulation to achieve the desired economy. (Hughes, 1979:138)

In October 1879, the same month in which he identified the first practical filament, Edison announced the generator for his system. The Pearl Street central station began to supply light for the Wall Street district in September 1882. The age of central-station incandescent lighting had begun.

Sources: Adapted primarily from Thomas P. Hughes, "The Electrification of America: The System Builders," *Technology and Culture* 20 (1979):124–161; Thomas P. Hughes, *Networks of Power: Electrification in Western Society, 1880–1930,* Baltimore: The Johns Hopkins University Press, 1983; Leonard S. Reich, *The Making of Industrial Research: Science and Business at GE and Bell, 1876–1926,* Cambridge, MA: Cambridge University Press, 1985. I have also drawn on the revisionist biography by David E. Nye, *The Invented Self: An Autobiography from Documents of Thomas Edison,* Odense: Odense University Press, 1983; and the popular account by Neil Baldwin, *Edison: Inventing the Century,* New York: Hyperion, 1995.

Research Output

The most important and visible output of a research laboratory is the *information,* in the form of new knowledge or new technology. At the more fundamental or basic end

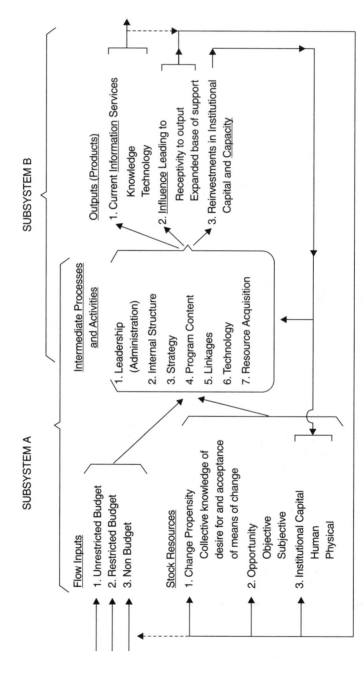

Figure 3.7 Stylized model of a research institute. (Adapted from Melvin G. Blase and Arnold Paulson, "The Agricultural Experiment Station: An Institution Development Perspective," *Agricultural Science Review* 10 (Second Quarter, 1972):11–16.)

of the research spectrum, the new knowledge may be embodied in published research papers. At the technology development end of the spectrum the research may result in patent applications. The ultimate test, however, is whether the new knowledge is embodied in a new product or a new practice. In biomedical research this may mean a new vaccine or a new drug. In agriculture it may mean a higher yielding or pest-resistant crop variety (cultivar). If a research institution or system is to achieve economic viability, the flow of new knowledge and technology that it generates must in turn generate new income streams. These new income streams may accrue largely to the sponsoring organization in the case of privately funded research, or to society more broadly in the case of publicly funded research.

If a research system is to remain a valuable private or social asset, it must also devote resources to reinvestment in institutional *capacity*—to the enlargement of its own physical and intellectual capital. This means diverting some resources to the production of information that does not have immediate application. This also means expanding the capacity of its scientific staff through time devoted to graduate education, study leaves, and supporting or basic research. The facilities, administrative structure, and ideology that serve as a rationale for the research program must also be continuously updated in response to new scientific and technical opportunities, changes in the market environment, or changes in social priorities (Dresch, 1995:179–183). The end of the Cold War has, for example, resulted in major reordering of demand for the defense-oriented research at Department of Energy national laboratories such as Oak Ridge and Lawrence Livermore.

The frequent arguments about the relative emphasis that should be devoted to "basic" and "applied" research in a research organization often reflect a deeper disagreement concerning the relative emphasis that should be given to the production of immediately useful knowledge and technology relative to the expansion of capacity—particularly to the capacity embodied in the professional staff of the organization. They may also reflect the fact that there are very large spillover effects resulting from investment in intellectual capacity. In general, only a small part of the benefits of basic research accrues to the benefit of the firm, the university, or even the nation that supports the research. There also is often a substantial spillover from generic applied research and development. External recognition of the contributions of creative scientists and engineers enhances their ability to capture the "rents" from their capacities by moving to other research organizations or to attract the resources needed for the commercial exploitation of their skills.

Research institutions typically devote significant resources to increasing their *influence* (Mukerji, 1989). To establish a successful claim on current and future resources, a research institution usually finds it necessary to maintain effective relationships with funding agencies, legislative bodies, government agencies, and private foundations. The institution may also find it useful to devote resources to building a positive image as a valuable public resource. Although the resources devoted to the production of influence may have little direct value to society, such activities are essential to obtaining the grant or institutional support necessary for the maintenance and continuity of both public and private research institutions. Institutions that have outlived their social function as producers of information and technology frequently devote excessive amounts of resources to organizational maintenance activities.

Intermediate Processes

The intermediate or transactive processes and activities identified in Figure 3.7 are for internal use. They have little direct value to society; their value is derived from their contribution to the output of the research institution. But they are indispensable to the productivity of the research institution itself. They represent the "engine" or the "production function" that determines the efficiency with which the research system makes use of the resources available to it. By and large, these intermediate services must be produced by the research institution itself rather than purchased from external sources.

LEADERSHIP

Leadership, or perhaps more appropriately research entrepreneurship, is an extremely important intermediate product. The idea that all a research director needs to do is to hire good people and let them "do their own thing" has only minimal relevance at a time when the solution to many significant technical and social problems requires concerted research effort. Leadership must be sensitive to changing social goals. It must have the perspective that enables it to effectively transmit the broader goals of the research program to the scientific and technical staff and to the external agencies (corporate officers, government agencies, foundations).

INSTITUTIONAL STRATEGY

Strategy or doctrine is reflected in the articulation of institutional goals and philosophy and in operating style of an institution. For example, during the 1960s the traditional production-oriented doctrine of the U.S. state and federal agricultural research system experienced severe stress under increasing pressure to place greater emphasis on studying the environmental spillover effects of technical change in agriculture, the problems of human capital formation, and the socioeconomic dimensions of community development.

LINKAGE

The linkage or networking services include the contacts and networking relationships with individuals and institutions outside the research station or laboratory—those with other scientists and laboratories, the clients who use the services of the laboratory, and sources of support. The linkages, sometimes referred to as "invisible or virtual colleges," carry messages in both directions. It is through the linkages with the outside that a research institution is influenced by the external changes in science and technology and in the economic and social environment. In the United States, the state agricultural experiment stations have traditionally been characterized by an exceedingly complex set of linkages with the external environment—with private sector research organizations, state crop improvement associations, the agricultural extension service and community and regional development councils, producer- and consumer-interest groups, and the entire hierarchy of local, state, and federal administrative and political institutions.[18]

RESEARCH TECHNOLOGY

The technology or the methodology of research is in continuous flux. The research program must be organized in such a way that the research staff is aware of, and contributes to, the advances in its own and closely related fields. Resources devoted to the production of research technology represent a capital investment in the capacity of the individual research worker. Research organizations that devote a relatively high proportion of their efforts to "frontier" research are often able to pay lower salaries to comparable scientific personnel than organizations devoted primarily to technology development because staff members are willing to accept part of their "pay" in the form of investment in their own capacity.

INTERNAL STRUCTURE

Program specifications often imply drastic modifications in the internal structures of a research organization. Basic research, generic research, and technology development often are located in large central laboratories. Research is carried out by teams involving scientists, engineers, and technicians. Problem-oriented interdisciplinary "centers" or "teams" erode the decision-making authority of discipline- or commodity-oriented departments. During periods of stress, the reformulation of doctrine, the redirection of programs, and the reorganization of internal structure may absorb substantial resources and seriously compete with the production of information. These efforts must be justified primarily in terms of their impact on the future research productivity and economic viability of the research organization.

LEARNING BY DOING AND USING

Research conducted within the confines of the industrial research laboratory, the agricultural experiment station, and the research university is characteristic of the

---

[18] Freeman and Soete (1997:225) note that the typical pattern of networking is shifting from in-house corporate R&D departments with good external communications to a pattern of networking collaborative innovation. This changing pattern is characteristic of industries undergoing rapid science-based technical change such as the pharmaceutical and biotechnology industries (see Chapter 10).

way new knowledge and new technology are generated in the chemical, electronic, biomedical, and several other science-based industries. It is not, however, the only, and in some sectors of the economy not even the major source of invention. Many preindustrial societies experienced a slow but continuous development of agricultural technology. The presently irrigated wet rice systems of East Asia evolved as a result of a gradual transition from a shifting cultivation to multicropping systems in which the same plot yields two or more crops per year (Boserup, 1965). In many industries the individual inventor remains, as in the time of Watt, an important source of invention. As late as 1950 less than half of all the patented inventions in the United States were made by technicians, engineers, and scientists employed as full-time researchers or inventors (Schmookler, 1957). In areas in which advances in science and advances in technology are not tightly linked, in many areas of mechanical technology for example, individual inventors continue to account for a large share of inventions. In disparate areas such as agricultural machinery and scientific instruments, a very high proportion of innovations is made by users. Many of the improvements leading to increases in productivity are made by production workers, technologists, or managers who are engaged directly in the production process, or by users of newly introduced technologies or products. Computer software is a particularly dramatic example of an industry in which users of the technology account for a large share of innovations. Yet it is only recently that learning by doing and learning by using have come to be recognized as important sources of technical change and productivity growth.

Learning by doing is a form of learning that takes place after a technical innovation has been adopted. It may involve "doing more" or "doing it longer" or some combination of the two. It involves acquisition of new skills, process technology inventions, and improvements in the organization of production. Only those workers, technicians, and managers who are intimately familiar with the minutiae of production are in a position, in Usher's terminology, to perceive the problem and have the insight to conceive a solution.[19]

Learning by using is a closely related concept. It occurs during the utilization of a product. Designers of major new technologies, or even improvements in well-known technologies, are rarely able to anticipate all of the problems that will occur in actual use. Nor are they able to anticipate the many new opportunities that users often find for even relatively simple technologies. Farmers adapted the early automobile to uses completely unanticipated by the manufacturers—as tractors, snowmobiles, and as sources of stationary power for cutting wood or chopping silage (Kline and Pinch, 1996:763–795). In the case of new aircraft or automobile designs, safety defects are often revealed only after extended use. The environmental effects of "first-generation" pesticides, such as DDT, became apparent only many years after use in public health and agricultural insect control applications. The designers and managers involved in

---

[19] An alternative approach to learning by doing is that learning is a function of cumulative gross investment rather than cumulative production (Sheshinski, 1967). In this section attention is focused primarily on the effects of experience.

each new generation of computers consistently failed to anticipate the uses that would be found for their machines.

Liberty Ships

The importance of learning by doing was first noted by engineers working in industries such as aircraft and shipbuilding. In the 1930s Wright (1936) observed that the direct labor cost of producing an airframe declined with the number of airframes produced. A particularly dramatic example of learning by doing was the decline in man-hours required to produce Liberty Ships and other vessels during World War II (Figure 3.8).

"In all yards for which data were obtainable, a given percentage increase in output tended to result in a constant percentage decrease in labor requirements. Average declines of 16 to 22 percent in the number of man hours required per ship accompanied each doubling of output in representative yards building Liberty ships, Victory ships, tankers and standard cargo vessels" (Searle, 1945:1132). What made the results particularly striking is that the gains in productivity did not reflect changes in design. From December 1941 through December 1944, a total of 2456 Liberty ships, all with the same standardized design, were produced.

Such observations, along with the new data produced by Solow and others in the 1950s showing that productivity growth was accounting for a large share of growth in output per worker, led to a formalization, by Kenneth Arrow, of the learning-by-doing hypothesis (Arrow, 1962). More recently the concept has been extended, by Nathan Rosenberg (1982), to the process of learning by using. In spite of the growing body of empirical research the learning-by-doing and learning-by-using literature has, until

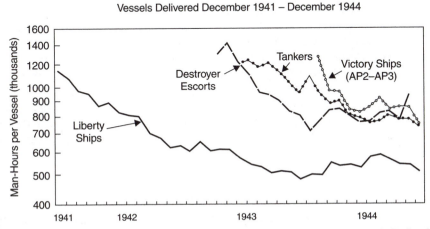

Figure 3.8 Man-hour requirements for selected shipbuilding programs. (*Source:* A. D. Searle, "Productivity Changes in Selected Wartime Shipbuilding Programs," *Monthly Labor Review* 61 (December 1945);1136.)

recently, been regarded as a somewhat embarrassing stepchild in the literature on technical change. In preparing this book, for example, I had a good deal of difficulty in deciding whether it should be discussed in this chapter or in the chapter on diffusion of technology.

Although the Arrow and the Rosenberg insights received general assent, they remained neglected as a research agenda until the late 1980s. In Arrow's model the productivity of a given firm is assumed to be an increasing function of cumulative aggregate output for the industry. Increasing returns arise because new knowledge is discovered in the process of investment and production. This generates external economies because the new knowledge becomes public knowledge.

The attempt to develop a new approach to the theory of economic growth, in which technical change is treated as endogenous rather than exogenous to the economic system, has focused increasing attention on learning by doing and learning by using (Romer, 1986, 1987; Lucas, 1988, 1993; Stokey, 1988; Grossman and Helpman, 1992). Lucas, in particular, draws direct inspiration from the work of Searle (Figure 3.8). He notes, however, that there is considerable ambiguity in the sources of the productivity growth attributed to learning by doing. "Is it the individual worker who is doing the learning? The managers? The organization as a whole? Are the skills being learned specific to the production process on which the learning takes place or more general? Does learning accrue solely to the individual worker, manager, or organization that does the producing, or is some of it readily appropriable by outside observers?" (Lucas, 1993:282).

Lucas goes on to develop a model in which economic growth is generated only by learning by doing. Growth can be sustained, however, only by the continuous introduction of new goods. But he cautions that in spite of the attractive features of the model, it must be regarded as "a purely fictional world" (Lucas, 1993:271). Lucas does insist that the main engine of economic growth is the accumulation of human capital—of knowledge. Accumulation of human capital takes place in schools, in research organizations, and in the course of producing goods. But little is known about the relative importance of these different modes of accumulation (Lucas, 1993:271). Lucas generalizes, however, that for understanding periods of very rapid growth in a single economy, in Taiwan and Korea during 1960–1980 for example, learning on the job seems to be the most central. An implicit assumption is that learning in the production of specific products, whether Liberty ships or computer chips, must spill over through moving up the "quality ladder" for any particular product, and to the production of related products.

Semiconductors

Irwin and Klenow (1994) have attempted to answer several of the questions raised by Lucas, using the semiconductor industry as a case. Their objective was to determine whether the benefits of learning by doing remain solely within the originating firm or whether there are significant spillovers to other firms nationally or internationally.

Irwin and Klenow note:

> The most prominent "stylized fact" about the semiconductor industry is that unit
> costs fall significantly as production experience (cumulative output) rises. Because
> semiconductors can be produced only with exacting standards of precision and
> cleanliness, the production process can be fine-tuned with the information gathered
> from successive production runs. Specifically, learning-by-doing takes the form of
> ever increasing "yields," that is, ever increasing percentage of usable semiconductor
> chips, as cumulative output rises. For example, early in the product cycle of a
> semiconductor, as much as 90 percent of output is flawed or nonfunctioning and must
> be discarded; once greater production experience has been acquired, this failure rate
> can fall under 10 percent. (Irwin and Klenow, 1994:1203)

Early observers suggested that early generation high-volume commodity chips
such as dynamic random-access memories (DRAMs) become "technology drivers"
that speed the learning process in subsequent generations of memory chips. It was
generally believed that a large portion of the benefit accrues to the firms doing the
learning and only limited benefits spill over to other firms. It has also been argued
that the flow is only in one direction—Japanese firms learn from U.S. firms but U.S.
firms do not learn from Japanese firms.

Irwin and Klenow employed a series of carefully designed econometric tests of the
several generalizations. They used quarterly data on average industry selling price and
on shipments by each producing merchant firm (32 firms in all, with an average of 18
firms producing each type of chip) for 1974 through 1992 for each of seven successive
generations of DRAMs (4K, 16K, 64K, 256K, 1M, 4M, and 16M). Average prices
for several generations are plotted in Figure 3.9. Irwin and Klenow summarize their
results as follows:

- Learning rates, as measured by change in productivity, average 20% per year.
- Firms learn three times more from an additional unit of their own cumulative
  production than from an additional unit of another firm's cumulative production.
- Learning spills over just as much among firms in different countries as among firms
  in a given country.
- Japanese firms are indistinguishable from others in learning speeds.
- Spillovers from one generation of chips to the next are weak.

They conclude that "the significant learning rates that we find strengthen the case
that learning contributes to economic growth, but the absence of strong support for intergenerational learning spillovers weakens the case" (Irwin and Klenow, 1994:1224).

As evidence on learning by doing has accumulated, it has become clear that there
are substantial differences both among plants in the same firm producing the same
product and among competing firms producing the same product. From a management
point of view it is important to understand whether the knowledge involved in learning

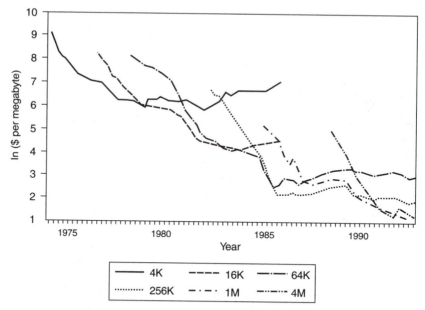

Figure 3.9 Dynamic Random Access Memory (DRAM) prices. (*Source:* Douglas A. Irwin and Peter J. Klenow, "Learning-by-Doing Spillovers in the Semiconductor Industry," *Journal of Political Economy* 102 (1994):1211.)

by doing resides primarily with the workers or the managers. A number of factors that influence differences in learning over time or among plants have been identified (Argote and Epple, 1990; Epple et al., 1996). Among the more interesting findings is that the largely "tacit" knowledge—knowledge that is not verbalized—acquired through learning by doing depreciates with lack of use. Among the factors accounting for depreciation are large fluctuations in production (as in military aircraft), turnover of skilled workers and engineers associated with downsizing, and prolonged strikes. The tacit knowledge that is internalized by workers and managers intimately involved in production has made it exceedingly difficult to design programs to enhance learning by doing.

In spite of the many remaining ambiguities in our understanding of learning-by-doing it seems useful to resist the temptation to extend the concept to the entire invention–innovation process. It is most useful to think of learning by doing in Usher's framework, as the critical revision necessary to realize the full potential of an innovation.[20] Thus productivity improvements by workers and managers that

---

[20] In this I am following William Fellner, "Learning by doing will here be interpreted . . . as cost-saving achieved in circumstances in which the productive facilities and the product remain unchanged (except that initial deficiencies become eliminated). The alternative would be to broaden the concept so as to include the bulk of all innovating activity" (Fellner, 1969:119).

improve the yield rate in the production of a single generation of memory chips is appropriately identified as learning by doing. The development of a new generation of memory chips is, in contrast, appropriately identified as a new invention or innovation even though the engineers who develop the new generation have presumably learned from the development of the previous generation. Learning by doing and learning by using thus exhibit diminishing returns in the production of any specific good. Thus over the long run, productivity growth requires continuous advances in technology.

The learning-by-using model has not yet given rise to a significant body of empirical research. The same limits would, however, seem to apply. Both learning by doing and learning by using are appropriately viewed as methods of realizing the potential productivity gains inherent in an invention or an innovation. Failure to exploit these potential gains can dampen economic growth. But in the absence of new strategic inventions most of the opportunities for productivity gains would be exhausted over a relatively short time.

PERSPECTIVE

Three broad themes run through this chapter. The first is that the stages in the process of innovations are similar in both science and technology. The Usher cumulative synthesis model, with the stages running from perception of the problem, setting the stage, act of insight, and critical revision, is consistent with the process of how "new things" emerge in both science and technology. Furthermore, a very large share of the resources invested in both advancing knowledge and technology is devoted to the last stage—to critical revision.

A second is that the flow of knowledge in the process of advancing technology runs both from science to technology and from technology to science. The flow from science to technology is strongest and most immediate in those fields in which the underlying science is youngest—in chemistry, electronics, and biology. The link between advances in science and technology has been less immediate in those areas such as mechanics and metallurgy in which the science has often following the technology.

A third is that both learning by doing and learning by using are important sources of productivity growth. But the processes by which tacit knowledge is acquired and applied by workers and consumers are not well understood. It seems apparent, however, that both acts of insight and critical revision, as described in the Usher model, play important roles.

REFERENCES

Argote, L., and D. Epple. "Learning Curves in Manufacturing." *Science* 247 (23 February 1990):920–924.

Arrow, K. J. "The Economic Implications of Learning by Doing." *Review of Economic Studies* 29 (1962):155–173.

Blase, M. G., and A. Paulson. "The Agricultural Experiment Station: An Institutional Development Perspective." *Agricultural Science Review* 10 (Second Quarter 1972):11–16.

Boserup, E. *The Conditions of Agricultural Growth: The Economics of Agrarian Change under Population Pressure.* Chicago: Aldine, 1965.

Bush, V. *Science: The Endless Frontier.* Washington, DC: Office of Scientific Research and Development, 1945.

Cameron, R. *A Concise Economic History of the World.* New York: Oxford University Press, 1993.

Cohen, W. "Empirical Studies of Innovative Activity." *Handbook of the Economics of Innovation and Technological Change,* P. Stoneman, ed., pp. 182–264. Oxford, UK: Basil Blackwell, 1995.

Dasgupta, P., and P. A. David. "Toward a New Economics of Science." *Research Policy* 23 (1994):487–521.

Dresch, S. P. "The Economics of Fundamental Research." In *The Academy in Crisis: The Political Economy of Higher Education,* J. W. Sommer, ed., pp. 171–196. New Brunswick, NJ: Transaction Publishers, 1995.

Epple, D., L. Argote, and K. Murphy. "An Empirical Investigation of the Microstructure of Knowledge Acquisition and Transfer through Learning by Doing." *Operations Research* 44 (1996):77–86.

Fellner, W. "Specific Interpretations of Learning by Doing." *Journal of Economic Theory* 1 (1969):119–140.

Ferguson, E. S. "The Origins of the Steam Engine." *Scientific American* (1964):98–107.

Fransman, M. *Japanese Computer and Communications Industry: The Evolution of Industrial Giants and Global Competitiveness.* Oxford, UK: Oxford University Press, 1995.

Freeman, C. and Luc Soete. *The Economics of Industrial Innovation,* 3rd ed. Cambridge, MA: MIT Press, 1997.

Gambardella, A. *Science and Innovation: The U.S. Pharmaceutical Industry during the 1980s.* Cambridge, MA: Cambridge University Press, 1995.

Gilfillan, S. C. *The Sociology of Invention.* Chicago, IL: Follet, 1935.

Gilfillan, S. C. "Prediction of Technical Change." *The Review of Economies and Statistics* 34 (1952):368–385.

Hayami, Y., and V. W. Ruttan. "Korean Rice, Taiwan Rice and Japanese Agricultural Stagnation: An Economic Consequence of Colonialism." *Quarterly Journal of Economics* 89 (1970):563–589.

Heertje, A., and M. Perlman, eds. *Evolving Technology and Market Structure: Studies in Schumpeterian Economics.* Ann Arbor, MI: University of Michigan Press, 1990.

Hills, R. L. *Power in the Industrial Revolution.* Manchester, UK: Manchester University Press, 1970.

Hughes, J. *The Vital Few: The Entrepreneur and American Economic Progress,* 2nd ed. New York: Oxford University Press, 1986.

Hughes, T. P. "Introduction." In *Selections from Lives of the Engineers with an Account of Their Principal Works by Samuel Smiles,* Thomas P. Hughes, ed., pp. 1–30. Cambridge, MA: MIT Press, 1966.

Hughes, T. P. "Inventors: The Problems They Choose, the Ideas They Have and the Inventions

They Make." In *Technological Innovation: A Critical Review of Current Knowledge,* Patrick Kelly and Melvin Kranzberg, eds., pp. 166–182. San Francisco, CA: San Francisco University Press, 1978.

Hughes, T. P. "The Electrification of America: The System Builders." *Technology and Culture* 20 (1979):124–161.

Irwin, D. A., and P. W. Klenow. "Learning-by-Doing Spillovers in the Semiconductor Industry." *Journal of Political Economy* 102 (1994):1200–1227.

Jennings, P. R. "Plant Type as a Breeding Objective." *Crop Science* 4 (1964):13–15.

Kline, R., and T. Pinch. "Users as Agents of Technological Change: The Social Construction of the Automobile on the Rural United States." *Technology and Culture* 37 (1996):763–795.

Kuhn, T. *The Structure of Scientific Revolutions.* Chicago, IL: University of Chicago Press, 1962.

Kush, G. S. "Breeding Rice for Sustainable Agricultural Systems." *International Crop Science* I. Madison, WI: Crop Science Society of America, 1993.

Latour, B., and S. Woolgar. *Laboratory Life: The Social Construction of Scientific Facts.* London and Beverly Hills, CA: Sage, 1979.

Law, J. "The Structure of Sociotechnical Engineering—A Review of the New Sociology of Technology." *Sociological Review* 35 (1987):404–425.

Layton, E. "Mirror Image Twins: The Communities of Science and Technology in 19th Century America." *Technology and Culture* 12 (1971):562–580.

Layton, E. "Technology as Knowledge." *Technology and Culture* 15 (1974):31–41.

Lucas, R. "On the Mechanics of Economic Development." *Journal of Monetary Economics* 22 (1988):3–42.

Lucas, R. "Making a Miracle." *Econometrica* 61 (1993):251–272.

MacKenzie, D., and J. Wajcman, eds. *The Social Shaping of Technology: How the Refrigerator Got Its Hum.* Philadelphia, PA: Open University Press, 1985.

Merton, R. K. "Priorties in Scientific Discovery." In *The Sociology of Science: Theoretical and Empirical Investigations.* R. K. Marton, ed. Chicago, IL: University of Chicago Press, 1973:286–324.

Mokyr, J. *The Lever of Riches: Technological Creativity and Economic Progress.* New York: Oxford University Press, 1990.

Moore, G. E. "Intel-Memories and the Microprocessor." *Daedalus* (1996):55–80.

Mowery, D. C. "The Development of Industrial Research in U.S. Manufacturing." *American Economic Review* 80 (1990):345–347.

Mukerji, C. *A Fragile Power: Scientists and the State.* Princeton, NJ: Princeton University Press, 1989.

Navin, F. and D. Olivastro. "Status Report: Linkages between Technology and Science." *Research Policy* 21 (1992):237–279.

Nelson, R. R. "The Economics of Invention: A Survey of the Literature." *Journal of Business* 32 (1959):101–127.

Nelson, R. R., and S. G. Winter. *An Evolutionary Theory of Economic Change.* Cambridge, MA: Harvard University Press, 1982.

Ogburn, W. F. *Technological Trends in National Policy.* Washington DC: U.S. Government Printing Office, 1937.

Ogburn, W. F., and D. S. Thomas. "Are Inventions Inevitable?" *Political Science Quarterly* 37 (1922):83–98.

Price, D. J. de Solla. "Is Technology Historically Independent of Science? A Study in Statistical Historiography." *Technology and Culture* 6 (1965):553–568.

Price, D. J. de Solla. "Notes Toward a Philosophy of the Science/Technology Interaction." In *The Nature of Knowledge: Are Models of Scientific Change Relevant?* Rachel Laudan, ed., pp. 105–114. Dordrecht: Kluwer Academic Publishers, 1984.

Reich, L. S. "Irving Langmuir and the Pursuit of Science and Technology in the Corporate Environment." *Technology and Culture* 24 (1983):199–221.

Reich, L. S. *The Making of American Industrial Research: Science and Business at G.E. and Bell, 1876–1926.* Cambridge, UK: Cambridge University Press, 1985.

Romer, P. M. "Increasing Returns and Long Run Growth." *Journal of Political Economy* 94 (1986):1002–1037.

Romer, P. M. "Growth Based on Increasing Returns Due to Specialization." *American Economic Review* 77 (1987):56–62.

Rosenberg, N. *Inside the Black Box: Technology and Economics.* Cambridge, UK: Cambridge University Press, 1982.

Ruttan, V. W. "Usher and Schumpeter on Invention, Innovation and Technological Change." *Quarterly Journal of Economics* 73 (1959):596–606.

Ruttan, V. W. *Agricultural Research Policy.* Minneapolis, MN: University of Minnesota Press, 1982.

Searle, A. D. "Productivity Changes in Selected Wartime Shipping Programs." *Monthly Labor Review* 61 (1945):1132–1147.

Scherer, F. M. "Invention and Innovation in the Watt-Boulton Steam Engine Venture." *Technology and Culture* 6 (1965):165–187.

Scherer, F. M., and M. Perlman, eds. *Entrepreneurship, Technological Innovation and Economic Growth: Studies in the Schumpeterian Tradition.* Ann Arbor, MI: University of Michigan Press, 1992.

Schmookler, J. "Inventors Past and Present." *Review of Economics and Statistics* 39 (1957): 321–333.

Schumpeter, J. A. *The Theory of Economic Development.* Cambridge, MA: Harvard University Press, 1934.

Schumpeter, J. A. *Business Cycles*, 2 Vols. New York: McGraw-Hill, 1939.

Sheshinski, E. "Tests of the 'Learning by Doing' Hypothesis." *Review of Economics and Statistics* 49 (1967):568–578.

Shionoya, Y., and M. Perlman, eds. *Innovation in Technology Industries, and Institutions: Studies in Schumpeterian Perspectives.* Ann Arbor, MI: University of Michigan Press, 1994.

Smil, V. *Energy in World History.* Boulder, CO: Westview Press, 1994.

Smiles, S. *Selections from Lives of the Engineers, with an Account of Their Principle Works.* Edited and with an Introduction by T. P. Hughes. Cambridge, MA: MIT Press, 1966.

Stakeman, E. C., R. Bradfield, and P. C. Mangelsdorf. *Campaigns Against Hunger.* Cambridge, MA: Harvard University Press, 1967.

Stokes, D. E. *Pasteur's Quadrant: Basic Science and Technological Innovation.* Washington, DC: The Brookings Institution Press, 1997.

"The New Encyclopedia Britannica." *Macropaedia* Vol. 17, pp. 624–625. Chicago, 1974.

Thirtle, C. G., and V. W. Ruttan. *The Role of Demand and Supply in the Generation and Diffusion of Technical Change.* London: Harwood Academic Publishers, 1987.

Usher, A. P. *History of Mechanical Inventions,* 2nd ed. Cambridge, MA: Harvard University Press, 1954. (First edition, 1929.)

Usher, A. P. "Technical Change and Capital Formation." In Universities-National Bureau Committee for Economic Growth, *Capital Formation and Economic Growth,* pp. 423–550. Princeton, NJ: Princeton University Press, 1955.

Van de Ven, A. H., H. L. Angle, and M. S. Poole. *Research on the Management of Innovation: The Minnesota Studies*. New York: Harper and Row, 1989.

Weingart, P. "The Structure of Technological Change: Reflections on a Sociological Analysis of Technology." In *The Nature of Technological Knowledge: Are Models of Scientific Change Relevant?* Rachel Laudan, ed., pp. 115–142. Dordrecht: Kluwer Academic Publishers, 1984.

White, L., Jr. *Machines Ex Deo: Essays in the Dynamism of Western Culture*. Cambridge, MA: MIT Press, 1968.

Whitehead, A. N. *Science and the Modern World*. New York: Macmillan, 1925.

Wise, G. "Science and Technology." *Osiris* 1, 2nd series (1985):229–246.

Woolgar, S. "Laboratory Studies: A Comment on the State of the Art." *Social Studies of Science* 12 (1982):481–498.

Wortman, S., and R. W. Cummings, Jr. *To Feed This World: The Challenge and the Strategy*. Baltimore, MD: Johns Hopkins University Press, 1978.

Wright, T. P. "Factors Affecting the Cost of Airplanes." *Journal of Aeronautical Sciences* 3 (1936):122–128.

CHAPTER 4

Technical and Institutional Innovation

I n this chapter I attempt to clarify the role of economic factors in inducing changes in technology and institutions. Technical change is a powerful force in inducing institutional change. Similarly, the process of technical change depends on the institutions that generate new knowledge and new technology. The information and incentives transmitted by markets, one of the more pervasive institutions in modern society, are particularly powerful in inducing changes in both technology and institutions.

In the first section of this chapter I discuss the sources of technical change. In the second section I discuss the sources of institutional change. In the final section I discuss the elements of a more complete model of technical and institutional innovation. Both technical and institutional change are important and interdependent sources of economic growth. Technical change is a source of demand for institutional change and institutional change opens up new technical opportunities. Among critical factors that induce technical and institutional innovation are changes in the environments external to institutions, organizations, and agents. Agents respond to these changes in their environment by actions that generate technical and institutional change. The analytical framework outlined in this chapter will be used in later chapters to interpret technical and institutional changes in the agricultural, electric power, chemical, computer, and biotechnology industries.

SOURCES OF TECHNICAL CHANGE

The 1960s through the 1980s was a very productive period for new theory and empirical insight into the process of technical change.[1] In the 1960s and 1970s

---

[1] I am indebted to Esben Sloth-Anderson, W. Brian Arthur, Erhard Bruderer, Jason E. Christian, Paul A. David, Jerry Donato, Giovanni Dosi, Laura McCann, Richard Nelson, Nathan Rosenberg, Tugrul Temel, Michael A. Trueblood, Andrew Van de Ven, and Sidney Winter for comments on an earlier draft of this section. I have explored the issues discussed in this section in two articles (Ruttan, 1996, 1997). The section on induced technical changes was initially developed jointly with Yujiro Hayami (1970, 1971, 1985). For criticism, see Dosi (1997) and Wright (1997) and several of the papers in Koppel (1995). For comprehensive reviews of the economics of technical change, see Kennedy and Thirwal (1972); Thirtle and Ruttan (1987); and Freeman (1994).

attention focused on the importance of changes in demand and in relative factor prices. In the late 1970s and early 1980s attention shifted to evolutionary models inspired by revived interest in Schumpeter's work on the sources of economic development. Since the early 1980s these evolutionary models have been complemented by the development of historically grounded "path-dependent" models of technical change. Each of these models has contributed substantial insight into the generation and choice of new technology. In this chapter I argue that the three models—induced, evolutionary, and path dependent—represent complementary elements of a yet to be developed more general theory.

Induced Technical Change

At least three major traditions of research have attempted to analyze the impact of change in the economic environment on the rate and direction of technical change. The *demand pull* perspective has emphasized the relative importance of market demand growth on the supply of knowledge and technology. A second *macroeconomic* or *growth theory* approach arose out of attempts to explain the apparent stability of factor shares to labor in the presence of rapidly rising wage rates. The third *microeconomic* model was built directly on early observations by Sir John Hicks that a change in the relative price of factors of production is itself a spur to innovation and to invention of a particular kind—directed at economizing the use of a factor that has become relatively expensive (Hicks, 1932:125–151). This third tradition has resulted in substantial effort by economic historians and agricultural and resource economists to understand the role of differences and changes in relative *factor endowments* on the direction of technical change.

DEMAND PULL AND THE RATE OF TECHNICAL CHANGE

In his now classic study of the invention and diffusion of hybrid maize, Zvi Griliches demonstrated the role of demand in determining the timing and location of invention (Griliches, 1957). Jacob Schmookler, in a massive study of patent statistics, showed that when investment rose, capital goods inventions also rose; when investment fell, the flow of patent applications also declined. He concluded that demand was more important in stimulating inventive activity than advances in the state of knowledge (Schmookler, 1962, 1966). In the mid-1960s, Raymond Vernon (1966, 1979) introduced a demand pull model to interpret the initial invention and diffusion of consumer durable technologies—such as automobiles, television, refrigerators, and washing machines—in the United States rather than in other developed countries (Chapter 5).

Arguments about the relative importance of demand-side forces and supply-side forces, such as advances in knowledge, intensified in the late 1960s. A study conducted by the Office of the Director of Defense Research and Engineering purported to show that the significant "research events" contributing to the development of 20 major weapons systems were predominantly motivated by military need rather than disinterested scientific inquiry. This view was challenged in studies commissioned by the National Science Foundation that, not unexpectedly, found science events of much greater importance as a source of technical change (Thirtle and Ruttan, 1987:6–11).

Careful industry studies suggest that both "supply and demand factors play an important role in innovation and in the life cycles of industries, but the relationship between the two varies with time and the maturity of the industrial sector concerned" (Walsh, 1984:233). One need not insist that basic research is the cornucopia from which all inventive activity flows to conclude that investment in the generation of scientific and technical knowledge can open up new possibilities for technical change. Nor should it be necessary to demonstrate that advances in knowledge, inventive activity and technical change flow automatically from changes in demand to conclude that changes in demand represent a powerful inducement for the allocation of research resources (Scherer, 1982).

FACTOR ENDOWMENTS AND THE DIRECTION OF TECHNICAL CHANGE

Modern interest in the effect of factor endowments on the direction of technical change dates to the early 1960s. John R. Hicks had earlier suggested: "The real reason for the predominance of labor saving inventions is surely that . . . a change in the relative prices of the factors of production is itself a spur to innovation and to inventions of a particular kind—directed at economizing the use of a factor which has become relatively expensive" (Hicks, 1932:124–125). Following Hicks' suggestion, William Fellner argued that firms with some degree of monopsony power had an incentive to make "improvements" that economized on the progressively more expensive factors of production, and that expectations of future changes in relative factor prices would induce even firms operating in a purely competitive environment to seek improvements that would save the more expensive factors (Fellner, 1956:220–222; see also Fellner, 1961, 1972).

An intense dialogue around the issue of induced innovation in the 1960s and early 1970s was triggered by W. E. G. Salters' explicit criticism of Hicks' induced technical change hypothesis: "At competitive equilibrium each factor is being paid its marginal value product; therefore all factors are equally expensive to firms" (Salter, 1960:16). He went on to argue that "the entrepreneur is interested in reducing costs in total, not particular costs. . . . When labor costs rise any advance that reduces total cost is welcome, and whether this is achieved by saving labor or saving capital is irrelevant" (Salter, 1960: 43–44; see also Blaug, 1963). It is difficult to understand why Salters' criticism of Hicks' induced technical change theory attracted so much attention except that students of economic growth were increasingly puzzled about why, in the presence of substantial deepening of capital in the U.S. economy, factor shares to labor and capital had appeared to remain relatively stable. The differential growth rates of labor and capital in the U.S. economy were regarded as too large to be explained by simple substitution.

The Growth-Theoretic Model. The debates about induced technical change centered on two alternative models—one a growth-theoretic approach and the second a microeconomic version. The most formally developed version was the growth-theoretic approach introduced by Kennedy (1964, 1966, 1967) and Samuelson (1965, 1966). In the Kennedy model the initial conditions included (1) given factor prices, (2) an exogenously given budget for research and development, and (3) a fundamental trade-off (a transformation function) between the reduction in labor requirements and the reduction of capital requirements. The model assumes a production function with factor-augmenting technical change. Kennedy cast his analysis in terms of changes in relative factor shares rather than changes in relative factor prices because of the growth theory implications.

The following example represents an intuitive interpretation of the Kennedy model.

> Suppose it is equally expensive to develop either a new technology that will reduce labor requirements by 10 percent or one that will reduce capital requirements by 10 percent. If the capital share is equal to the labor share, entrepreneurs will be indifferent between the two courses of action. . . . The outcomes of both choices will be neutral technical change. If, however, the labor share is 60 percent, all entrepreneurs will choose the labor reducing version. If the elasticity of substitution is less than one, this will go on until the labor and capital shares again become equal, provided the induced bias in technical change does not alter the (fundamental) trade-off relationship between technical changes that reduce labor requirements on the one hand, or capital requirements on the other. (Binswanger, 1978a:32)

By the early 1970s the growth-theoretic approach to induced technical change was under severe attack (Nordhaus, 1969:93–115; Nordhaus, 1973; David, 1975:44–57). Nordhaus notes that in the Kennedy model, no resources are allocated to inventive activity. A valid theory "of induced innovation requires at least two productive activities; production and invention. If there is no invention then the theory of induced innovation is just a disguised case of growth theory with exogenous technological change" (Nordhaus, 1973:210). Furthermore, as technological change accumulates there is no effect on the trade-off between labor and capital augmenting technological change (Nordhaus, 1973:215). He insisted that the model is "too defective to be used in serious economic analysis." (Nordhaus, 1973:208). The growth-theoretic version of induced innovation has never recovered from the criticism of its inadequate microeconomic foundation.[2]

The Microeconomic Model. A second approach to induced innovation, built directly on Hicksian microeconomic foundations, was developed by Syed Ahmad (1966,

---

[2] Zvi Griliches has recently pointed out to me (in conversation) that another reason for the decline in interest among economic theorists was the difficulty, pointed out by Diamond et al. (1978:125–147), in simultaneously measuring the bias of technical change and the elasticity of substitution between factors. This problem had, however, already been solved (Binswanger, 1974a, 1974b; Binswanger and Ruttan, 1978:73–80, 215–242). For a more recent discussion see Haltmaier (1986).

1967a, 1967b). In his model, Ahmad employed the concept of a historic *innovation possibility curve* (IPC). At a given time there exists a set of potential production processes, determined by the basic state of knowledge, available to be developed. Each process in the set is characterized by an isoquant with rather narrow possibilities for substitution. Each process in the set requires that resources be devoted to research and development before the process can actually be employed in production. The IPC is the envelope of all unit isoquants of the subset of those potential processes that the entrepreneur might develop with a given amount of research and development expenditure.

● BOX 4.1

THE HICKS–AHMAD MODEL OF INDUCED TECHNICAL CHANGE

Assume that I_t is the unit isoquant describing a technological process available in time t and that IPC_t is the corresponding IPC (Figure 4.1). Given the relative factor prices described by line $P_t P_t$, I_t is the cost-minimizing technology. Once I_t is developed, the remainder of the IPC becomes irrelevant because, for period $t + 1$, the IPC shifts inward to some IPC_{t+1}. This occurs because it would take the same R&D resources to go from I_t to any other technique on IPC_t as to go from I_t to any technique on IPC_{t+1}. If factor prices remain unchanged and technical change is neutral, the new unit isoquant will

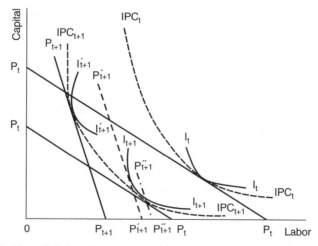

Figure 4.1 Ahmad's induced innovation model. (Adapted from Syed Ahmad, "On The Theory of Induced Invention," *Economic Journal* 76 (1966), © The Royal Economic Society, Figure 1 amended.)

be I_{t+1} on IPC_{t+1}. If, however, factor prices change to $P_{t+1}P_{t+1}$, then it is no longer optimal to develop I_{t+1}. Instead, a technological process corresponding to some I'_{t+1} becomes optimal. In the graph, $P_{t+1}P_{t+1}$ corresponds to a rise in the relative price of labor. If the IPC has shifted neutrally, I'_{t+1} will be relatively labor saving in comparison to I_t.

Ahmad's graphic exposition is useful as an illustration of the induced innovation process of a one period microeconomic model in which a firm or a research institute has a fixed exogenous budget constraint. When research budgets are no longer fixed, a mathematical exposition is more convenient (Binswanger, 1978a:26–27). In a multiperiod model the shift from I_t to I'_{t+1} would occur in a series of steps in response to incremental shifts from P_t to P_{t+1}. One way of thinking about this process would be to appeal to "learning-by-doing" and "learning-by-using" concepts (Arrow, 1962; Rosenberg, 1982a, Chapter 5).

DIALOGUE WITH DATA

The initial dialogues about the logic of the Kennedy–Samuelson growth-theoretic and the Hicks–Ahmad microeconomic approaches to induced technical change were conducted within the confines of the standard two-factor (labor and capital) neoclassical model. Among economic historians there has been a continuing debate about the role of land abundance on the direction of technical change in the industrial sector. Among agricultural economists there has emerged a large literature on the bias of technical change along mechanical (labor-saving) and biological (land-saving) directions.

Habakkuk (1962) argued that the ratio of land to labor, which was higher in the United States than in Great Britain, raised real wages in American agriculture and thereby increased the cost of labor to manufacturers. He argued, in effect, that in the nineteenth century, the higher U.S. wage rates resulted not only in the substitution of capital for labor (more capital) but induced technical changes (better capital) biased in a labor-saving direction (James and Skinner, 1985).

The issue became controversial among economic historians. The criticisms of the labor-scarcity theses focused primarily on the issue of the impact of land abundance on the substitution of capital for labor—the "more capital" rather than the "better capital" part of the thesis (Fogel, 1967; Ames and Rosenberg 1968; David, 1973, 1975:24–30). David argued that economic historians "steered away from serious re-evaluation of the proposition about the rate and bias of innovation, precisely because standard economic analysis was thought to offer less reliable guidance there than on questions of the choice of alternative known techniques of production" (David, 1975:31).

David also insisted that the argument could not be resolved without a more intensive mining of the historical evidence. But recourse to measurement could not be expected to get very far without a theoretically grounded definition of an operational concept that distinguishes between choice of technology and technical change and between bias in the direction of technical change and the rate of technical change. David argued that can this can be done by embracing "the concept of a concave, downward sloping 'innovation-possibility frontier' " (David, 1975:32). He then went on to argue along the same lines as Nordhaus (1973) that the particular pattern of changes in macroproduction relationships observed in the United States could not be rationalized within the framework of a *stable* innovation-possibility frontier (David, 1975:33).

David also insisted that bias in the direction of technical change could be understood only by building a theory of induced innovation on microeconomic foundations consistent with engineering and agronomic practice. This also meant abandoning both neoclassical growth theory and the neoclassical theory of the firm. Furthermore, it would be necessary to incorporate the intimate evolutionary connection "between factor prices, the choice of technique and the rate and direction of global technical change" (David, 1975:61). He differentiated his approach from neoclassical production theory by suggesting that substitution may involve an element of innovation. This is similar to the mechanism that Ahmad (1966) and Hayami and Ruttan (1970) had earlier employed to account for the shift in the IPC (or, in David's terms, the FPF). It should be viewed as an extension rather than an alternative to the neoclassical model.

When he turned to the technical relationships among natural resources, labor, and capital, David argued, drawing on the work of Ames and Rosenberg (1968) and his own earlier work (David, 1966), that in the mid-nineteenth century mechanical technology and land were complements—"The relevant fundamental production functions for the various branches of industry and in agriculture did not possess the property of being separable in the raw materials and natural resource inputs; instead the relative capital intensive techniques . . . were also relatively resource using" (David, 1975:88). Greater availability of natural resources facilitates the substitution of capital for labor. The formal introduction of the role of relative resource abundance (or scarcity) clearly represents an important extension as compared to the traditional two-factor (labor and capital) neoclassical models. But the primary significance is that David opened the door, and identified most of the elements, of what has since become known as the path-dependent model of technical change (David, 1975:65, 66).

There are substantial differences in the extent to which the several induced technical change models have been tested against empirical data. The demand-induced model was developed in close association with empirical studies and was not subjected to formal modeling or theoretical critique until fairly late (Lucas, 1967; Mowery and Rosenberg, 1979). The growth-theoretic version of factor-induced technical change has been peculiarly unproductive of empirical research. The microeconomic version of factor-induced technical change has, in contrast, been highly productive in stimulating a wide body of applied research. The first formal test based directly on microeconomic foundations was the Hayami–Ruttan test against the historical experience of agricultural development in the United States and Japan (Hayami and Ruttan, 1970).[3] It seemed apparent that neither the enormous differences in land–labor

---

[3] At the time the article was written Hayami and Ruttan were familiar with the growth-theoretic literature by Fellner, Kennedy, and Samuelson but not with the Ahmad article and his subsequent exchange with Fellner

ratios between the two countries nor the changes in each country over time could be explained by simple factor substitution. Hayami and Ruttan employed a four-factor model in which (1) land and mechanical power were regarded as complements and land and labor as substitutes, and (2) fertilizer and land infrastructure were regarded as complements and fertilizer and land as substitutes.

BOX 4.2
THE HAYAMI–RUTTAN MODEL OF
INDUCED TECHNICAL CHANGE

The process of advance in mechanical technology in the Hayami–Ruttan model is illustrated in the left-hand panel of Figure 4.2. I_0^* represents the innovation possibility curve (IPC) in time zero; it is the envelope of less elastic unit isoquants corresponding, for example, to different types of harvesting

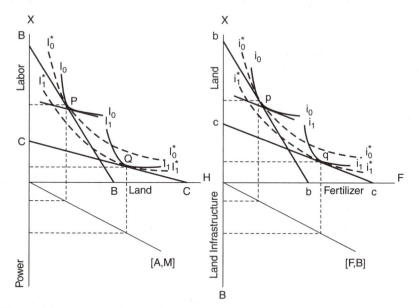

Figure 4.2 Induced technical change in agriculture. (*Source:* Yujiro Hayami and Vernon W. Ruttan, *Agricultural Development: An International Perspective*, Baltimore: Johns Hopkins University Press, 1985:91.)

and Kennedy. The inspiration for the 1970 Hayami–Ruttan paper was the historical observations about the development of British and American technology by Habakkuk (1967). See Ruttan and Hayami (1994).

machinery. The relationship between land and power is complementary. Land-cum-power is substituted for labor in response to a change in the wage rate relative to an index of land and power prices. The change in the price ratio from BB to CC induces the invention of labor-saving machinery—say a combine for a reaper.

The process of advance in biological technology is illustrated in the right-hand panel of Figure 4.2. Here i_0^* represents an IPC that is an envelope of relatively inelastic land–fertilizer isoquants such as L_0. When the fertilizer–land price ratio declines from bb to cc a new technology—a more fertilizer-responsive crop variety—represented by C_1 is developed along i_0^*. Since the substitution of fertilizer for land is facilitated by investment in land and water development, the relationship between new fertilizer-responsive varieties and land infrastructure is complementary.

In Figure 4.2 the impact of advances in mechanical and biological technology on factor ratios is treated as if they are completely separable. This is clearly an oversimplification. It is not essential to the Hayami–Ruttan-induced technical change model that changes in the land–labor ratio be a direct response to the price of land relative to the wage rate (Thirtle and Ruttan, 1987:30, 31).

The econometric tests conducted by Hayami and Ruttan suggested that the enormous change in factor proportions that occurred during the process of agricultural development in the two countries "represents a process of dynamic factor substitutions accompanying changes in the production function induced by changes in relative factor prices" (Hayami and Ruttan, 1970:1135). Their work was followed by a large number of empirical tests of the microeconomic version of the induced technical change hypothesis in the agricultural and natural resource sector. Within the industrial sector the evidence has been strongest in the natural resource- and raw material-using industries (Jorgenson and Fraumeni, 1981; Wright, 1990; Jorgenson and Wilcoxen, 1993). As of the mid-1980s the tests in agriculture, both in the United States and abroad, provided conclusive evidence that changes (and sometimes differences) in relative factor endowments and prices exert a pervasive impact on the direction of technical change.[4]

---

[4] Olmstead and Rhode (1993) have criticized the Hayami and Ruttan work on both conceptual and empirical grounds. At the conceptual level they find confusion between the relative factor "change variant," which is used in explaining productivity growth over time within a given country, and the "level variant" of the model, which is used in analysis of international productivity differences. They also argue, on the basis of regional tests of the induced technical change hypothesis in U.S. agriculture, that the induced technical change model holds only for the central grain-growing regions. In a later paper using state level data, Ohmstead and Rhode (1995) found somewhat stronger support for the induced technical change hypothesis. For further criticism and a defense see Koppel (1994).

Evolutionary Theory

The modern revival of interest in an evolutionary theory of technical change derives largely from work by Richard R. Nelson and Sidney G. Winter in the mid-1970s (Nelson and Winter, 1973, 1974, 1975, 1977; Nelson et al., 1975).[5] These articles in turn served as a basis for the highly acclaimed book, *Evolutionary Theory of Economic Change* (Nelson and Winter, 1982). The theory advanced by Nelson and Winter has been identified by the authors as "Schumpeterian" in its interpretation of the process of economic change.[6] The second cornerstone of the Nelson–Winter model is the behavioral theory of the firm in which profit-maximizing behavior is replaced by decision rules that are applied routinely over an extended period of time (Simon, 1955, 1959; Cyert and March, 1963).

The Nelson–Winter evolutionary model jettisons much of what they consider to be the excess baggage of the neoclassical microeconomic model—"the global objective function, the well defined choice set, and the maximizing choice rationalization of firm's actions. And we see 'decision rules' as very close conceptual relatives of production 'techniques' whereas orthodoxy sees these things as very different" (Nelson and Winter, 1982:14). The production function and all other regular and predictable behavior patterns of the firm are replaced by the concept of "routine"—"a term that includes characteristics that range from well-specified technical routines for producing things, procedures for hiring and firing, ordering new inventory, or stepping up production of items in high demand to policies regarding investment, research and development (R&D), or advertising, and business strategies about product diversification and overseas investment" (Nelson and Winter, 1982:14). The distinction between factor substitution and shifts in the production function is also abandoned. The two fundamental mechanisms in the Nelson–Winter models are the *search* for better techniques and the *selection* of firms by the market (Elster, 1983:14). In their models the microeconomics of innovation is represented as "a stochastic process dependent on the search routines of individual firms" (Dosi et al., 1992:10). The learning activities leading to technical changes are characterized by (1) local

---

[5] Nelson and Winter identify Alchian (1950) and Penrose (1952) as representing direct intellectual antecedents of their work. For the theoretical foundations of the Nelson–Winter collaboration, see Winter (1971). For the historical and philosophical foundations see Elster (1983:131–158) and Langolis and Everett (1994). Ulrich Witt (1993) has assembled many of the most important articles in the field of evolutionary economics in a collection of readings, *Evolutionary Economics*. For a review of recent evolutionary thought about economic change see Nelson (1995:48–90).

[6] The Nelson–Winter model departs from Schumpeter in its treatment of the linkage between invention and innovation. For Schumpeter there was no necessary link between invention and innovation (Chapter 3). Nelson and Winter employ the term evolutionary metaphorically—"We emphatically disavow any intention to pursue biological analogies for their own sake" (1982:11). However, they regard their approach as closer to Lamankianism than Mendelianism. Yet their description of the evolutionary process of firm behavior and technical change as a Markov process, and their use of the Markov mechanism in their simulation, is analogous to the Mendelian model.

search for technical innovations, (2) imitation of the practices of other firms, and (3) satisfying economic behavior.

● BOX 4.3
THE NELSON–WINTER EVOLUTIONARY MODEL

In initial Nelson–Winter models, search by the firm for new technology, whether generated internally by R&D or transferred from suppliers or competitors, is set in motion when profits fall below a certain threshold. The models assume that in this search the firms draw samples from a distribution of input–output coefficients (Figure 4.3). If A is the present input combination, then potential input–output coefficients are distributed around it such that there is a much greater probability of finding a point close to A then of finding one far away. Search is local. Once the firm finds a point B it makes a profitability check. If costs are lower at B than at A, the firm adopts the point B and stops searching. Otherwise, search continues. Thus, the technology described by the point $\mathring{B}$ input–output and factor ratios will be accepted if labor is relatively inexpensive, that is, if relative prices are described by line CD. But if labor is relatively expensive, as described by $C'D'$, the firm will reject the $\mathring{B}$ technology and continue to search for another technology until it finds another point, say $\mathring{B}'$. The technology at point $\mathring{B}'$ will be labor saving relative to that at $\mathring{B}$.

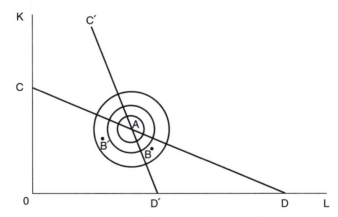

Figure 4.3 Sampling and selection of new input–output coefficients. (Adapted from Richard R. Nelson and Sidney G. Winter, "Factor Price Change and Factor Substitution in an Evolutionary Model," *Bell Journal of Economics* 6 (1975):472. Copyright © 1975. Reprinted by permission of RAND.)

> The stochastic technology search process is built into a model with many competing firms. All profits above a "normal" dividend—investors are satisfizers rather than optimizers—are reinvested so that successful firms grow faster than unsuccessful ones. The capital stock of the economy is determined by the total investment by all firms. Labor supply is elastic to the firm.

Simulation runs rather than formal analysis or tests against historical experience are employed to demonstrate the plausibility of the models. The simulations start from an initial point at which all firms are equal. The model determines endogenously the output of the economy, the wage–rental rate, and the capital accumulation rates. Nelson and Winter have used a series of variations in their basic model to explain how changes in market structure influence the rate of technical change, the direction of technical change, and the importance of imitation and innovation.

When firms check the profitability of alternative techniques uncovered by their search processes, a higher wage rate will cause certain techniques to fail the profitability tests they would have passed at a lower wage rate, and enable others to pass the tests they would have failed at a lower wage rate. The latter will be capital intensive relative to the former. Thus a higher wage rate nudges firms to move in a more capital-intensive direction. Also, the effect of a higher wage rate is to make all technologies less profitable (assuming, as in their model, a constant cost of capital) but the cost increase is proportionately greatest for those that involve a low capital–labor ratio. Since firms with high capital–labor ratios are less adversely affected by high wage rates then firms with low capital–labor ratios, capital intensive firms will tend to expand relatively to labor-intensive ones. For both of these reasons a higher wage rate will tend to increase capital intensity (Nelson and Winter, 1974:900). The responsiveness of the capital labor ratio to changes in relative factor prices is rather striking because, except for the profitability check, search (or research) outcomes are random (Nelson and Winter, 1982:175–184), and the inducement mechanism comes about through competition, survival, and growth rather than through efforts to maximize profits.

The early Nelson–Winter models were criticized for the "dumb manager" assumption in which the search (or research) process is triggered only when profits fall below a threshold level. An implication is that an increase in demand for a product can lead to a reduction in research effort. This was hardly consistent with either historical evidence or with a Schumpeterian perspective. The restriction was relaxed in the second round of Nelson and Winter models by the explicit introduction of directed research. As the wage–rental ratio rises research effort is allocated to sampling the spectrum of capital-intensive techniques (Nelson and Winter, 1975, 1977).

Winter has devoted considerable attention to extensions of the initial Nelson–Winter models. In a 1984 article, for example, Winter abandons the assumption of the level playing field in which the initial conditions were the same for all firms. The basic model is augmented to include entirely new firms. Winter uses this expanded model to explore the growth path of two industrial regimes. One is an "entrepreneurial regime" that he identifies with the early Schumpeter of *The Theory of Economic Development* (1934). The second is a "routinized regime" that he identifies with the Schumpeter of *Capitalism, Socialism and Democracy* (1950). The entrepreneurial regime model is designed so that innovations are primarily associated with the entry of new firms. In the routinized regime innovations are primarily the result of internal R&D by established firms. Several suggestions have been made for further extension of the Nelson and Winter models to include the creation of new industries, interaction among industries, and product innovation and imitation, for example (Andersen, 1994:118–131).

It is important to clarify the role of historical process in the Nelson–Winter evolutionary models. The condition of the industry in each time period shapes its condition in the following period. "Some economic processes are conceived as working very fast, driving some of the model variables to (temporary) equilibrium values within a single period (or in a continuous time model, instantaneously). In both the entrepreneurial and routinized Schumpeterian models, for example a short-run equilibrium price of output is established in every time period. Slower working processes of investment and of technological and organizational change operate to modify the data of the short-run equilibrium system from period to period (or from instant to instant)" (Winter, 1984:290).

Two issues that I find difficult to resolve are why there have been so few efforts by other scholars to (1) advance the Nelson–Winter methodology[7] or (2) to test the correspondence between the plausible results of the Nelson–Winter simulations and the historical experience of particular firms or industries.[8] Simulation is capable of generating a wide range of plausible behavior, but the hypotheses generated by the simulations have seldom been subjected to rigorous empirical tests. The closest they or others come to empirical testing is the demonstration that it is possible to generate plausible economy-wide growth paths or changes in marketshare.

Path Dependence

The argument that technical change is "path dependent" was vigorously advanced, by W. Bryan Arthur and several colleagues in the late 1970s and early 1980s (Arthur,

---

[7] For a useful interpretation and extension see Anderson (1944). Anderson's work is particularly helpful in clarifying the "poorly documented" computational steps of the Nelson–Winter models. Anderson supplements the mathematical notation employed by Nelson and Winter by an algorithmically oriented programming notation. An appendix, "Algorithmic Nelson and Winter Models" (pp. 198–219) is particularly useful.

[8] Since the mid-1970s there has emerged a large body of empirical research on technical change that can be categorized as broadly Schumpeterian or evolutionary in inspiration (see the review by Freeman, 1994). The point I am making, however, is quite different. There has been very little effort to use the simulation models to generate hypothesis about the process of technology development and then to either identify historical counterparts or to test the outcomes against historical experience in a rigorous manner. The one exception with which I am familiar is the Evenson–Kislev (1975:140–155) stochastic model of technological discovery. The model was used to interpret the stages in sugar cane varietal development (Box 6.1). The Evenson–Kislev model did not, however, draw directly on the Nelson–Winter stochastic model.

1983; Arthur et al., 1983; see also Arthur, 1989, 1990, 1994).[9] In the mid and late 1980s Paul David presented the results of a series of historical studies—of the typewriter keyboard, the electric light and power supply industries, and others—that served to buttress the plausibility of the path dependence perspective (David, 1985, 1986, 1993; David and Bunn, 1988). The effect of the work by Arthur and his colleagues has been to emphasize the importance of increasing returns to scale as a source of technological "lock-in." In some nonlinear dynamic systems positive feedbacks (Polya processes) may cause certain patterns or structures that emerge to be self-reinforcing: such systems tend to be sensitive to early dynamic fluctuations. "Often there is a multiplicity of patterns that are candidates for long-term self-reinforcement; the accumulation of small events early on 'pushes' the dynamics of technical choice into the orbit of one of these and thus 'selects' the structure that the system eventually locks into" (Arthur et al., 1987:294).

The authors provide an intuitive example: Think of an urn of an infinite capacity.

> Starting with one red and one white ball in the urn, add a ball each time, indefinitely, according to the following rule. Choose a ball in the urn at random and replace it; if it is red, add a red; if it is white, add a white. Obviously this process has increments that are path dependent—at any time the probabilities that the next ball added is red exactly equals the proportion red. . . . Polya proved in 1931 that in a scheme like this, the proportion of red balls does tend to a limit X_1 and with probability one. But X is a random variable uniformly distributed between 0 and 1. (Arthur et al., 1987:259)

Thus, by analogy, in an industry characterized by increasing returns small historical or chance events that give one of several technologies an initial advantage can (but need not) "drive the adoption process into developing a technology that has inferior long-run potential" (Arthur, 1989:117).

Arthur employs a series of progressively complex models to simulate situations in which several technologies compete for adoption by a large number of economic agents. Agents have full knowledge of the technology and returns functions but not of the events that determine entry and choice of technology by other agents. His analyses are carried out for three technological regimes (constant, increasing, and diminishing returns) with respect to four properties of the paths of technical change (predictable, flexible, ergodic, path efficient).[10] The only unknown is the set of historical events

---

[9] Arthur encountered unusual delay before his work was accepted in a leading economics journal. His 1986 *Economic Journal* paper was initially submitted to the *American Economic Review* in 1983. It was rejected by the *American Economic Review* twice and by the *Quarterly Journal of Economics* twice and accepted by the *Economic Journal* only after an appeal. By the time the paper was finally accepted in the *Economic Journal* referees were noting that the path dependence idea was already recognized in the literature (Gans and Shepherd, 1994:173).

[10] "A process *predictable* if the small degree of uncertainty built in 'averages away' so that the observer has enough knowledge to pre-determine market shares accurately in the long run; *flexible* if a subsidy or tax adjustment to one of the technologies' returns can always influence future market choice; *ergodic* (not path dependent) if different sequences of historical events lead to the same market outcome with probability one; . . . and *path efficient* if at all times equal development (equal adoption) of the technology that is behind in adoption would not have paid off better" (Arthur, 1989:118, 199).

that determines the sequence in which the agents make their choices. The question he attempts to answer is whether the fluctuations in the order of choice will make a difference in final adoption shares.

Arthur's simulations reinforce the importance of increasing returns as a necessary condition for technological lock-in.

> Under constant and diminishing returns the evolution of the market reflects only *a priori* endowments, preferences, and transformation possibilities; small events cannot sway the outcome. . . . Under increasing returns, by contrast, many outcomes are possible. Insignificant circumstances become magnified by positive feedbacks to 'tip' the system into the actual outcome 'selected.' The small events in history become important. The early, almost accidental, dominance of personal computer software by Microsoft is a frequently cited example (Chapter 9). (Arthur, 1989:127)

In *Technical Choice*, David characterizes his work as an evolutionary alternative to neoclassical theory. As noted earlier he explicitly rejected the Fellner and Kennedy versions of the induced technical change approach to the analysis of factor bias. He also rejected the early work of Nelson and Winter as being "fundamentally neo-classical-inspired" (David, 1975:76). But he shares the view of Nelson and Winter that the neoclassical model is excessively restrictive since factor substitution typically involves not simply a movement along a given production function but an element of innovation leading to a shift in the function itself. He does assume that the firm has knowledge of available (or potentially available) alternative technologies and chooses rationally among them.

In research conducted in the mid and late 1980s, David employs a series of technical changes—the typewriter keyboard, the electric light and power supply industries—to buttress the plausibility of the path dependence perspective. His already classic paper on the economics of QWERTY (the first six letters on the left of the topmost row of letters on the typewriter and now the computer keyboard) explored why an inefficient (from today's perspective) typewriter keyboard was introduced and why it has persisted.[11] David's answer is that an innovation in typing method, touch typing, gave rise to three features that were crucially important in causing QWERTY to become "locked in" as the dominant keyboard arrangement. These features were *technical interrelatedness*, *economics of scale*, and *quasiirreversibility* of investment (David, 1985:334). Technical interrelatedness refers to the need for system compatibility—in this case the linkage between the design of the typewriter keyboard and typists' memory of a particular keyboard arrangement. Economics of scale refers to the decline in user cost of the QWERTY system (or any other system) as it gains in acceptance relative to other systems. The quasiirreversibility

---

[11] Liebowitz and Margolis (1990, 1994, 1995) disagree with David's interpretation of the market's rejection of the supposedly more efficient Dvorak keyboard. In their view, given the available knowledge and experience at the time, QWERTY represented a rational choice of technology. For a response to the Liebowitz and Margolis criticism, see David (1997).

of investments is the result of the acquisition of specific touch typing skills (the "software"). These characteristics are sometimes bundled under the rubric of positive "network externalities." Another example of network externalities is found in the rapidly expanding communications industry. It is better to be connected to a big network than a small one. With computers and telephones, for example, the more people who are on your network the more people you are connected with—and at lower costs. There are decreasing returns once the production and distribution system has been established. Network externalities seem to be more characteristic of the service industries than of the agriculture or manufacturing industries.

This kind of path-dependent technical change is an apt paradigm for the history of technology at a time when the impact of scale economies on productivity growth has been rediscovered and embodied in a "new growth economics" literature (Romer, 1986; Lucas, 1988; Barro and Sala-i Martin, 1995: Chapter 2). But Arthur's results suggest some caution. "Increasing returns, if they are bounded, are in general not sufficient to guarantee eventual monopoly by a single technology" (Arthur, 1989:126). And there is substantial empirical evidence that scale economies, which often depend on prior technical change, are typically bounded by the state of technology (Levin, 1977:208–21).[12]

A technology policy conclusion that might be drawn is that intervention by a central authority to ensure that sufficient resources are devoted to the exploration of alternative technologies could reduce the probability of lock-in of an inferior technology. But even this may not be sufficient to eliminate the possibility of selecting an inferior technology. The development of nuclear power is a case in point. In the early 1950s, the U.S. Atomic Energy Commission initiated a program to support and evaluate alternative nuclear reactor designs. Before this evaluation was completed, three events intervened that led to selection of the light water reactor for commercial development. One was the U.S. navy's choice of the light water design for its submarine program. A second was the desire, following the successful development of the Soviet nuclear bomb in 1949, for an early construction of a nuclear power-generating station to demonstrate peaceful use of nuclear energy by the United States. A third was subsidies for building turn-key light water reactors in Europe by the U.S. government and by General Electric and Westinghouse to preempt other technical alternatives. In retrospect, it is quite clear that chance events, originating largely in the political–bureaucratic structure, had the effect of directing the development of atomic power along an inferior trajectory (Cowan, 1990:565–566, Chapter 7).

Both induced innovation and evolutionary theory suggest that as scale economies are exhausted (and profits decline) the pressure of growth in demand will focus

---

[12] Scale economies have become the new "black box" of new growth economics (Chapter 2). It is hard to believe that much of the productivity growth that is presumably accounted for by scale economies is not the disequilibrium effect of prior technical change (Landau and Rosenberg, 1992:93; Liebowitz and Margolis, 1994:139).

scientific and technical effort on breaking the new technological barriers that lock technology into inferior or obsolete trajectories. Superior technologies that have lost out as a result of chance events in the first round of technical competition have frequently turned out to be successful as the industry developed.[13] And induced technical change theory suggests that research effort will be directed to removing the constraints on growth resulting from technological constraints or inelastic (or scarce) factor supplies.[14]

The transition from coal to petroleum-based feedstocks in the heavy organic chemical industry is a particularly dramatic example (Chapter 8). From the 1870s through the 1930s, German leadership in the organic chemical industry was based on coal-based technology. Beginning in the 1920s with the rapid growth in demand for gasoline for automobiles and trucks in the United States, a large and inexpensive supply of olefins became available as a by-product of petroleum refining. By the end of World War II, the U.S. chemical industry had shifted rapidly to petroleum-based feedstocks. In Germany this transition—impeded by skills, education, and attitudes that had been developed under a coal-based industrial regime—was delayed by more than a decade (Grant et al., 1988; Stokes, 1994; Chapter 8).

Toward a More General Theory?

Each of the three models of technical innovation—induced, evolutionary, and path dependent—has both strengths and limitations. One common theme is disagreement with the assumption in neoclassical growth models that a common production function is available to all countries regardless of human capital, resource, or institutional endowments. It should by now be obvious that differences in productivity levels and rates of growth cannot be overcome by the simple transfer of capital and technology. The asymmetries between firms and countries in resource endowments and in scientific and technological capabilities are not easily overcome. The technologies that are capable of becoming the most productive sources of growth are often location specific. A second common theme is an emphasis on microfoundations. This emphasis

---

[13] See, for example, the exceedingly careful study of technological substitution in the case of cochlear implants by Van de Ven and Garud (1993) and Garud and Rappa (1994). The cochlear implant is a biomedical invention that enables hearing by profoundly deaf people. The early technology was characterized by the conditions that David and Arthur identify with technological lock-in. Yet in spite of initial commercial dominance the "single-channel" technology was completely replaced by the "multiple channel" technology. For other cases see Foray and Grubler (1990), Cheng and Van de Ven (1994), and Liebowitz and Margolis (1992, 1995).

[14] The development of semiconductor technology as a replacement for vacuum tubes for amplifying, rectifying, and modulating electrical signals is an example of a shift in technological trajectories induced by technological constraints (Dosi, 1984:26–45). The development of fertilizer-responsive crop varieties represents an example of a shift in technological trajectories induced by changes in resource endowments (Hayami and Ruttan, 1985:163–198). The emergence of the gas turbine from a niche technology to an important source of electric power generation since the early 1980s was induced, in part, by the exhaustion of scale in steam turbine generation (Islas, 1997:49–66; Chapter 7).

on microfoundations is common to the approaches that have abandoned neoclassical microeconomics as well as to those that have attempted to extend neoclassical theory.

The major limitation of the growth-theoretic version of the induced innovation model is the implausibility of the innovation possibility function (IPF). The shape of the IPF is independent of the bias in the path of technical change. As technical change progresses there is no effect on the "fundamental" trade-off between labor and capital augmenting technical change. Thus, as Nordhaus notes, the growth theoretic approach to induced innovation fails to rescue growth theory from treating technical change as exogenous. It has been unproductive of empirical research and is no longer viewed as an important contribution to growth theory.

The major limitation of the microeconomic version is that its internal mechanism— the learning, search, and formal R & D processes—remains inside a black box. The model is driven by exogenous changes in the economic environment in which the firm (or public research agency) finds itself. The microeconomic model has, nevertheless, been productive of a substantial body of empirical research and has helped to clarify the historical process of technical change, particularly at the industry and sector level both within and across countries.

The strength of the evolutionary model is precisely in the area where the microeconomic-induced innovation model is weakest. It builds on the behavioral theory of the firm in an attempt to provide a more realistic description of the internal workings of the black box. The Nelson and Winter evolutionary approach has not, however, become a productive source of empirical research. The results of the various simulations are defended as plausible in terms of the stylized facts of industrial organization and of firm, sector, and macroeconomic growth. The lack of empirical testing may be because the simulation methodology lends itself to the easy proliferation of plausible results. At present the evolutionary approach must be regarded as a "point of view" rather than as a theory (Arrow, 1995).

The strengths of the path dependence model lies in the insistence of its practitioners on the importance of the sequence of specific microlevel historical events. In this view current choices of techniques became the link through which prevailing economic conditions may influence the future dimensions of technology and knowledge (David, 1975:39, 57). However, the concept of technological lock-in, at least in the hands of its more rigorous practitioners, applies only to network technologies characterized by increasing returns to scale. In industries with constant or decreasing returns to scale historical lock-in does not apply.

There can be no question that technical change is path dependent in the sense that it evolves from earlier technological development. In spite of somewhat similar motivation, the path dependent literature has not consciously drawn on the Nelson–Winter work for inspiration.[15] It is necessary to go beyond the present

---

[15] For an important attempt to integrate the evolutionary and path-dependent approaches, see Garud and Rappa (1994).

path-dependent models, however, to examine the forces responsible for changes in the rate and direction of technical change. But there is little discussion of how firms or industries escape from lock-in. What happens when the scale economies resulting from an earlier change in technology have been exhausted and the industry enters a constant or decreasing returns stage? At this point it seems apparent that changes in relative factor prices would, with some lag, have the effect of bending or biasing the path of technical change along the lines suggested by the theory of induced technical change. Similarly a new radical innovation may, at this stage, both increase the rate and modify the direction of technical change.

The study of technical change in the semiconductor industry by Dosi (1984) represents a useful illustration of the potential value of a more general model. The Dosi study is particularly rich in its depth of technical insight. At a rhetorical level, Dosi identifies his methodology with the Nelson–Winter evolutionary approach. In his empirical research, however, he utilizes an eclectic combination of induced innovation, evolutionary, and path dependence interpretations of the process of semiconductor technology development. A more rigorous approach to the development of a general theory of the sources of technical change will be required to bridge the three "island empires."[16]

SOURCES OF INSTITUTIONAL INNOVATION

Technical change is increasingly generated by activities carried out in institutions that have become pervasive during the last century—the industrial research laboratory, the agricultural experiment station, and the research university (Chapter 3).[17] Changes in resource endowments, cultural endowments, and technology have been an important source of institutional change (Figure 4.4). It is important, therefore, even in a book with a primary emphasis on technical change, that attention be given to the process of institutional innovation. I will be drawing on the concepts discussed in this section in later chapters. In attempting to understand historical and institutional change, I employ a model that is similar to the model of induced technical change discussed earlier in

---

[16] I would like to make clear to the reader my particular historical and epistemological bias: Departures from neoclassical microeconomic theory, when successful, are eventually seen as extensions and become incorporated into neoclassical theory. Thus, for example, the microeconomic version of induced technical change can now be viewed as an extension of, rather than a departure from, the neoclassical theory of the firm. Nelson and Winter attempt to confront this problem by arguing that there are two alternative views of neoclassical theory. One is the more rigorous "literal" view. The other is termed the "tendency" view. Applied economists with a primary interest in interpreting economic history or behavior tend to employ the tendency view. They identify evolutionary theory with the tendency view (Nelson and Winter, 1975:467).

[17] This section draws heavily on Ruttan (1978, 1997) and on my earlier work with Yujiro Hayami. See particularly Ruttan and Hayami (1984) and Hayami and Ruttan (1985). For a very useful review, see Lin and Nugent (1995).

this chapter. Institutional change is viewed as largely endogenous—as induced by changes in physical, social, and economic environments.[18]

The purpose of this section is not to understand how institutions evolve from a primitive institutional "state of nature." Rather it is to better understand how agents, acting individually and collectively, redesign existing institutions, such as land tenure or labor relations, or design new institutions, such as constructed markets to manage atmospheric pollution, that have a reasonable chance of success. Successful institutional design or redesign cannot simply be the product of the designers' objective function or negotiations among interested groups and representative bodies. If institutional design or redesign is to be successful, it must respond to the changes occurring in the environment in which it will exist—such as increases in the price of labor relative to land or a rise in the relative value of open access environmental relative to other factors.

In this section I elaborate a theory of institutional innovation in which shifts in the demand for institutional innovation are induced by changes in relative resource endowments and by technical change. The impact of advances in social science knowledge and of cultural endowments on the supply of institutional change will also be considered. Finally, after examining the forces that act to shift the demand and supply of institutional innovation, elements of a more general model of technical and institutional change will be presented.

What Is Institutional Innovation?

Institutions are the social rules that facilitate coordination among people by helping them form expectations for dealing with each other. They reflect the conventions that have evolved in different societies regarding the behavior of individuals and groups.[19]

---

[18] Schotter (1981:3–4) notes that in economics, there have been, historically, two distinct interpretations of the rise of social institutions—"collectivist" and "organic." He identifies the collectivist view with the work of Commons and the organic view with that of Menger and Hayek. What Schotter terms the organic view is similar to the endogenous or induced innovation view employed in this section. What he terms the collectivist view is similar to what Hurwicz (1972, 1998) terms the "designer" perspective. I employ a design perspective, informed by the induced innovation perspective, in my discussion of institution design and redesign. Thus, I reject the need to choose between these two perspectives. They are complementary rather than competitive. Further, the objective of the approach that I employ is not to "liberate" economics from its fixation on the market (Schotter, 1981:1). Rather, my perspective is to apply the tools of neoclassical microeconomics to the analysis and design of institutional change.

[19] There is considerable disagreement regarding the meaning of the term *institution*. A distinction is often made between the concepts of institution and organization. The broad view, which includes both concepts, is most useful for our purpose and is consistent with the view expressed by both Commons (1950:24) and Knight (1952:5). This definition also encompasses the classification employed by Davis and North (1971:8, 9). The more inclusive definition is employed so as to be able to consider changes in the rules or conventions that govern behavior (1) within economic units such as families, firms, and bureaucracies, (2) among economic units as in the cases of the rules that govern market relationships, and (3) between economic units and their environment, as in the case of the relationship between a firm and a regulatory agency. Thus, organizations are defined as a subset of institutions involving deliberate coordination (Vanberg, 1994).

In the area of economic relations they have a crucial role in establishing expectations about the rights to use resources in economic activities and about the partitioning of the income streams resulting from economic activity (Runge, 1981a; Schotter, 1981:11).

To perform their essential role, institutions must be stable for an extended time period. But institutions, like technology, must also change if development is to occur. Anticipation of the latent gains to be realized by overcoming the disequilibria resulting from changes in factor endowments, product demand, and technical change is a powerful inducement to institutional innovation.[20] Institutions that have been efficient in generating growth in the past may, over time, come to direct their efforts primarily to protecting vested interests and thus become obstacles to further economic development.[21] The growing disequilibria in resource allocation create opportunities for political entrepreneurs or leaders to organize collective action and bring about institutional changes.

This perspective on the sources of *demand* for institutional change bears some similarity to the traditional Marxian view.[22] Marx considered technological change as the primary source of institutional change. The view expressed here is somewhat more complex in that it considers changes in factor endowments and product demand as equally important sources of institutional change. This definition of institutional change is not limited to the dramatic or revolutionary changes of the type anticipated by Marx. Rather, I share with Lance Davis and Douglass North the view that basic institutions such as property rights and markets are more typically altered through the accumulation of incremental or evolutionary institutional changes such as modifications in contractual relations or shifts in the boundaries between market and nonmarket activities (Davis and North, 1971:9). Very substantial shifts in the demand for institutional services may be required to overcome the transaction costs involved in negotiating changes in institutional arrangements and in overcoming resistance in implementing new institutional arrangements (Williamson, 1985:15–42).

There is a *supply* dimension as well as a demand dimension in institutional change. Collective action leading to changes in the supply of institutional innovations often involves intense conflict among interest groups. Clearly, the process is much more complex than the two-class conflict between the property owners

---

[20] See North and Thomas (1970:1–17, 1973) and Schultz (1975:827–846).

[21] The role of special interest "distributional coalitions" in slowing society's capacity to adopt new technology and reallocate resources in response to changing conditions is a central theme in Olson (1965, 1982).

[22] "At a certain stage of their development, the material forces of production in society come in conflict with the existing relations of production, or—what is but a legal expression for the same thing—with the property relations within which they had been at work before. From forms of development of the forces of production these relations turn into their fetters. Then comes the period of social revolution. With the change of the economic foundation the entire immense superstructure is more or less rapidly transformed" Marx (1913:11–12). For a discussion of the role of technology in Marxian thought, see Rosenberg (1982b:34–51).

and the propertyless assumed by Marx. In this view, the supply of institutional innovations is strongly influenced by the cost of achieving social consensus. The cost of institutional innovation depends on the power structure of vested interest groups. It also depends critically on cultural traditions and ideologies, such as nationalism or religion, that make certain institutional arrangements more easily accepted than others.

Advances in knowledge in the social sciences (and in related professions such as law, administration, planning, and social service) can shift the supply and hence reduce the cost of institutional innovation in a manner somewhat similar to the way advances in the natural sciences reduce the cost of technical change. Advances in game theory have, during the past several decades, enabled economists and political scientists to bring an increasingly powerful set of tools to bear on their interpretation of institutional and technical change (Schotter, 1981; Ostrom, 1990; Aoki, 1996). In spite of the power of these new tools, application of standard neoclassical microeconomic models involving shifts in the demand for and supply of institutional change remains exceedingly useful.[23]

Insistence that the processes of institutional innovation and diffusion can be understood by treating institutional change as endogenous to the economic system represents a clear departure from the tradition of modern analytical economics.[24] This does not mean that it is necessary to abandon analytical economics. On the contrary, I try to expand the scope of modern analytical economics by treating institutional change as endogenous.

Demand for Institutional Innovation: Property Rights and Market Institutions

In some cases the demand for institutional innovation can be satisfied by the development of new forms of property rights, more efficient market institutions, or

---

[23] The microeconomic approach to understanding the process of institutional change is similar to that employed by Becker in analyzing institutions such as the family (Becker, 1991, 1993). A major difference is that I focus on the effects of changes in the environment, such as changes in relative factor and product prices, that are exogenous to the institution being studied, that induce institutional change over time.

[24] The orthodox view was expressed by Samuelson (1948): "The auxiliary [institutional] constraints imposed upon the variables are not themselves the proper subject of welfare economics but must be taken as given" (221–222). Contrast this with the more recent statement by Schotter: "We view welfare economics as a study . . . that ranks the system of rules which dictate social behavior" (1981:6). There are now five fairly well-defined "political economy" traditions that have attempted to break out of the constraints imposed by traditional welfare economics and treat institutional change as endogenous. These include (1) the theory of property rights, (2) the theory of economic regulation, (3) the theory of interest group rent seeking, (4) the liberal-pluralist theories of government, and (5) the neo-Marxian theories of the state. In the property rights theories government plays a relatively passive role; the economic theory of regulation focuses on the electoral process; the rent-seeking and liberal-pluralist theories concentrate on both electoral and bureaucratic choice processes; and the theory of the state attempts to incorporate electoral, legislative choice, and bureaucratic choice processes. For a review and criticism, see Rausser et al. (1982:547–614).

evolutionary changes arising out of direct contracting by individuals at the level of the community or the firm (Coase, 1960). In this section I draw on agricultural history for examples.

The English agricultural revolution was associated with the enclosure of open fields and the replacement of small peasant cultivators, who held their land from manorial lords, with a system in which large farmers used hired labor to farm the land they leased from the landlords. The First Enclosure Movement, in the fifteenth and sixteenth centuries, resulted in the conversion of open arable fields and commons to private pasture in areas suitable for grazing. It was induced by expansion in the export demand for wool. The Second Enclosure Movement in the eighteenth century involved conversion of communally managed arable land into privately operated units. It is now generally agreed that it was largely induced by the growing disequilibrium between the fixed institutional rent that landlords received under copyhold tenures (with lifetime contracts) and the higher economic rents expected from adoption of new technology, which became more profitable as a consequence of higher grain prices and lower wages. Enclosure was followed by substantial increases in land and labor productivity and by a redistribution of income from farmers to landowners.[25]

In another example, opening up nineteenth-century Thailand for international trade and the reduction in shipping rates to Europe resulted in a sharp increase in the demand for rice. The land available for rice production, which had been abundant, became more scarce. Investment in land development for rice production became profitable. The response was a major transformation of property rights. In the half century after 1850, rights in human property (corvée and slavery) were largely replaced by more precise private property rights in land (Feeney, 1982, 1988).[26]

The decollectivization of agriculture in China, beginning in 1979, provides a dramatic contemporary example of the impact of the transformation of property rights (Lin, 1987, 1988; Fan, 1991). The changes were induced by a disequilibrium between productivity, in the range of 30% between crop yields under the collective system and technology frontier yields. A transition to the household system was initiated spontaneously by peasant households, in spite of official sanctions, in a number of collectives in Sichwan Province in 1978. By the early 1980s the transition had extended to other provinces and to small-scale industrial and commercial activities at the township level and by the mid-1980s to broad sectors of the national economy. In Box 4.1 I discuss a contemporary Philippine case. The case is particularly interesting

---

[25] There has been a continuing debate among students of English agricultural history about whether the higher rents that landowners received after enclosure were because (1) enclosed farming was more efficient than open-field farming, or (2) enclosures redistributed income from farmers to landowners. See Chambers and Mingay (1966), Dahlman (1980), Allen (1982:937–953), and Overton (1996).

[26] For a similar interpretation of the evolution of property rights in precolonial Hawaii, see Roumasset and La Croix (1988).

because it is based on the interaction between technical and institutional changes in a carefully researched Philippine village.

● BOX 4.4

A PHILIPPINE CASE STUDY OF INSTITUTIONAL INNOVATION

Research conducted by Yujiro Hayami and Masao Kikuchi in a Philippine village, beginning in the late 1970s, has enabled us to examine in some detail a contemporary example of the interrelated effects of changes in resource endowments and technical change on the demand for institutional change in land tenure and labor relations. The case is particularly interesting because the institutional innovations occurred as a result of private contracting among individuals. The study is unique in that it is based on a rigorous analysis of microeconomic data for East Laguna Village over a period of several decades.

Changes in Technology and Resource Endowments

Between 1956 and 1976, rice production per hectare in the study village rose dramatically, from 2.5 to 6.7 metric tons per hectare per year. This increase resulted from two technical innovations. In 1958, the national irrigation system, which permitted double-cropping to replace single-cropping, was extended to the village. The second major technical change was the introduction in the late 1960s of high-yielding varieties of rice. The diffusion of modern varieties was accompanied by increased use of fertilizer and pesticides and by the adoption of improved cultivation practices such as straight-row planting and intensive weeding.

Population growth in the village was rapid. Between 1966 and 1976 the number of households rose from 66 to 109 and the population rose from 383 to 464, while the cultivated area remained virtually constant. The number of landless laborer households increased from 20 to 54. In 1976 half of the households in the village had no land to cultivate. The average farm size declined from 2.3 to 2.0 hectares. The land was farmed primarily by tenants. Traditionally, share tenancy was the most common form of tenure. In both 1956 and 1966, 70% of the land was farmed under share tenure arrangements. In 1963, an agricultural land reform code was passed that was designed to break the political power of the traditional landed elite and to provide greater incentives to peasant producers of basic food crops. A major feature of the new legislation was an arrangement that permitted tenants to initiate a shift from share tenure to leasehold, with rent under the leasehold set at 25% of the average yield for the previous 3 years. Implementation of the code between the mid-1960s and the mid-1970s resulted in a decline in land farmed under share tenure to 30%.

Induced Institutional Innovation

The shift from share tenure to lease tenure was not, however, the only change in tenure relationships that occurred between 1966 and 1976. There was a sharp increase in the number of plots under subtenancy arrangements. (The number increased from one in 1956 to five in 1966, and to 16 in 1976.) Subtenancy was illegal under the land reform code; the subtenancy arrangements were usually made without formal consent of the landowner. The most common subtenancy arrangement was fifty–fifty sharing of costs and output between subtenant and operator. Hayami and Kituchi hypothesized that the incentive for the emergence of the subtenancy institution was disequilibrium between the rent paid to landlords under the leasehold arrangement and the equilibrium rent—the level that would reflect both the higher yields of rice obtained with the new technology and the lower wage rates implied by the increase in population pressure against the land.

To test this hypothesis, market prices were used to compute the value of the unpaid factor inputs (family labor and capital) for different tenure arrangements during the 1976 wet season. The results indicate that the share to land was lowest and the operators' surplus was highest for the land under leasehold tenancy. In contrast, the share to land was highest and no surplus was left for the operator who cultivated the land under the subtenancy arrangement (Table 4.1). Indeed, the share to land when the land was farmed under subtenancy was very close to the sum of the share to land plus the operators' surplus under the other tenure arrangement. The results are consistent with the hypothesis. A substantial portion of the economic rent was captured by the leasehold tenants in the form of operators' surplus. On the land farmed under a subtenancy arrangement, the rent was shared between the leaseholder and the landlord.

A second institutional change, induced by higher yields and the increase in population pressure, has been the emergence of a new pattern of labor relationship between farm operators and landless workers. According to the traditional system called *hunusan,* laborers who participated in the harvesting and threshing activity received one-sixth of the harvest. By 1976, most of the farmers (83%) adopted a system called *gamma,* in which participation in the harvesting operation was limited to workers who had performed the weeding operation without receiving wages. The emergence of the *gamma* system can be interpreted as an institutional innovation induced by the disequilibrium between the institutionally determined wage rate and the market rate. In the

Table 4.1 Factor Shares of Rice Output Per Hectare, Wet Season 1976

| | | | | Factor shares[a] | | | | | | |
| | | | | | Land | | | | | |
	Number of Plots	Area (ha)	Rice Output[b]	Current Inputs[b]	Landowner[b]	Sublessor[b]	Total[b]	Labor[b]	Capital[b,c]	Operator's Surplus[b]
Leasehold land	44	67.7	2889 (100.0)	657 (22.7)	567 (19.6)	0 (0)	567 (19.6)	918 (31.8)	337 (11.7)	410 (14.2)
Share tenancy land	30	29.7	2749 (100.0)	697 (25.3)	698 (25.3)	0 (0)	698 (25.4)	850 (30.9)	288 (10.5)	216 (7.9)
Subtenancy land	16	9.1	3447 (100.0)	801 (23.2)	504 (14.6)	801[d] (23.2)	1305 (37.8)	1008 (29.3)	346 (10.1)	−13 (−0.4)

[a] Percentage shares are shown in parentheses.

[b] Kilogram per hectare.

[c] Sum of irrigation fee and paid and/or imputed rentals of carabao, tractor, and other machines.

[d] Rents to subleasors in the case of pledged plots are imputed by applying the interest rate of 40% crop season (a mode in the interest rate distribution in the village).

Source: Yujiro Hayami and Masao Kikuchi, *Asian Village Economy at the Crossroads: An Economic Approach to Institutional Change,* Tokyo: University of Tokyo Press, 1981, and Baltimore: Johns Hopkins University Press, 1982:111–113.

1950s, when the rice yield per hectare was low and labor was less abundant, the one-sixth share may have approximated an equilibrium wage level. With the higher yields and more abundant supply of labor, the one-sixth share became larger than the marginal product of labor in the harvesting operation.

To test the hypothesis that the *gamma* system permitted farm operators to equate the harvesters' share of output to the marginal productivity of labor, imputed wage costs were compared with the actual harvesters' shares (Table 4.2). The results indicate that a substantial gap existed between the imputed wage for the harvesters' labor alone and the actual harvesters' shares. This gap was eliminated if the imputed wages for harvesting and weeding labor were added. Those results are consistent with the hypothesis that the changes in institutional arrangements governing the use of production factors were induced when disequilibria between the marginal returns and the marginal costs of factor inputs occurred as a result of changes in factor endowments and technical change. Institutional change, therefore, was directed toward the establishment of a new equilibrium in factor markets.

A second round of technical and institutional changes has occurred since the completion of the changes described in this section. Nonfarm employment opportunities have expanded as a result of better transport to the metropolitan Manila area and the location of a small metal craft industry in the village; wage rates have risen and small portable threshing machines have largely replaced

Table 4.2 Comparison between the Imputed Value of Harvesters' Share and the Imputed Cost of *Gamma* Labor

	Based on Employers' Data	Based on Employees' Data
Number of working days of *gamma* labor (days/ha)[a]		
Weeding	20.9	18.3
Harvesting/threshing	33.6	33.6
Imputed cost of *gamma* labor (P/ha)[b]		
Weeding	167.2	146.4
Harvesting/threshing	369.6	369.6
Total	536.8	516.0
Actual share of harvesters:		
In kind (kg/ha)[c]	504.0	549.0
Imputed value (P/ha)[d]	504.0	549.0
Imputed value minus total	−32.8	33.0

[a] Includes labor of family members who worked as *gamma* laborers.

[b] Imputation using market wage rates (daily wage = P8.0 for weeding, P11.0 for harvesting).

[c] One-sixth of output per hectare.

[d] Imputation using market prices (1 kg = P1).

Source: Yujiro Hayami and Masao Kikuchi, *Asian Village Economy at the Crossroads: An Economic Approach to Institutional Change,* Tokyo: University of Tokyo Press, 1981, and Baltimore, MD: Johns Hopkins University Press, 1982:121.

manual threshing. The labor share for harvesting has declined and a new form of labor contract, referred to as *new hunusan*, has emerged. As a result of nonfarm employment, incomes of former farm labor households have risen.

In the Philippine village case reviewed here the induced innovation process leading toward the establishment of equilibrium in factor markets occurred very rapidly, even though many of the transactions between landlords, tenants, and laborers were less than fully monetized. Informal contractual arrangements or agreements were used. The subleasing and the *gamma* labor contract evolved without the mobilization of substantial political activity or bureaucratic effort. Indeed, the subleasing arrangement evolved in spite of legal prohibition.

Sources: In this box I draw primarily on and Y. Hayami and M. Kikuchi, *Asian Village Economy at the Crossroads: An Economic Approach to Institutional Change,* Tokyo: University of Tokyo Press, 1981, and Baltimore, MD: Johns Hopkins University Press, 1982; M. Kikuchi and Y. Hayami, "Inducements to Institutional Innovations in an Agrarian Community," *Economic Development and Cultural Change* 29 (1980):21–36; M. Kikuchi and Y. Hayami, "Technology, Markets, and Community in Contract Choice: Rice Harvesting in the Philippines," *Economic Development and Cultural Change* 47 (1999):371–386; and Y. Hayami and M. Kikuchi, *A Rice Village Saga: The Three Decades of Green Revolution in the Philippines* (London, UK: Macmillan Press, 2000).

The major conclusion I draw from the English enclosure movement, the evolution of Thai property rights, and the Philippines subtenancy case is that disequilibrium between institutional rents and economic rents represents a powerful source of demand for institutional change.

The Demand for Institutional Innovation–Nonmarket Institutions for the Supply of Public Goods

The examples of institutional change advanced in the previous section, such as the enclosure in England and the evolution of private property rights in land in Thailand and the Philippines, have contributed to the development of a more efficient market system. Institutional changes of this type are profitable for society only if the costs involved in the assignment and protection of rights are smaller than the gains from better resource allocation. If those costs are very high, it may be necessary to design nonmarket institutions to achieve more efficient resource allocation.[27]

---

[27] Harold Demsetz has pointed out that the relative costs of using market and political institutions are rarely given explicit consideration in the literature on market failure. An appropriate way of interpreting the "public goods" versus "private goods" issue is to ask whether the costs of providing a market are too high relative to the cost of nonmarket alternatives (Demsetz 1964:11–26). A similar point is made by Hurwicz (1972:37–44).

In Japan, for example, although the system of private property rights was developed on cropland during the premodern period, communal ownership at the village level permitted open access to large areas of wild and forest land that were used for the collection of firewood, leaves, and wild grasses to fertilize rice fields. Over time, detailed common property rules evolved to govern the use of communal land so as to prevent resource exhaustion.[28] Detailed stipulations of the time and place of use of communal land as well as rules for mobilizing village labor to maintain communal property (such as applying fire to regenerate pasture) were often enforced with religious taboos and rituals. Those communal village institutions remained viable because it was quite costly to demarcate and partition wild and forest land and to enforce exclusive use.[29] Group action to supply public goods, such as the maintenance of communal land or water resources, may work effectively if the group involved is small (Ostrum, 1990; Ostrom et al., 1999). If a large number of people are involved in the use of a public good, however, as in the case of marine fisheries, it is more difficult to respond to the demand for more effective resource management by means of voluntary agreements.[30] Action by a higher authority with coercive power, such as government, may be required to limit free riding.

The "socialization" of agricultural research, as discussed earlier in this chapter, is common, not only in socialist economies but also in market economies. New information or knowledge resulting from research is typically endowed with the attributes of a public good characterized by *nonrivalness* or jointness in supply and use and *nonexcludability* or external economies.[31] The first attribute implies that the

---

[28] For the distinction between open access and common property, see Ciriacy-Wantrup and Bishop (1975:713–727). In the case of open access, use rights have not been fully established. In the case of common property, rules have been established that govern joint use. Common property is therefore a form of land use that lies between the extremes of open access and fully exclusive private rights. The problem of resource exhaustion in open access properties was elaborated in Demsetz (1967) and Alchian and Demsetz (1973). These issues are discussed more completely in Chapter 12.

[29] The term *public economies* has been used "to describe collective consumption units that provide services by arranging for the production, regulation, access, patterns of use, and appropriation of collective good" (Ostrom, 1998:6–7).

[30] Olson (1965). Several students of institutional change have emphasized that coordinated or common expectations, resulting from the assurance provided by traditional institutions or common assumptions about equity or ideology, have permitted much larger groups to engage in either implicit or explicit voluntary cooperation than is implied by Olson's model. See Runge (1981a:189–199). North (1981:54) notes that "the premium necessary to induce people to become free riders is positively correlated with the perceived legitimacy of the existing institution."

[31] For a characterization of the nonrivalness and nonexcludability attributes of public goods, see Samuelson (1954:387–389, 1955:350–356, 1958:332–338). Nonrivalness is an essential attribute of information. The use of information about a new farming practice (contour plowing, for example) by a farmer is not hindered by the adoption of the same practice by other farmers. Nonexcludability, in contrast, is not a natural attribute of information but rather is determined by institutional arrangements. In fact, patent laws are an institutional arrangement that makes a certain form of information (called an "invention") excludable, thereby creating profit incentives for private creative activities. Retention of trade secrets is another legally sanctioned method of retaining control over inventions or other forms of new technical knowledge. These

good is equally available to all. The second implies that it is impossible for private producers to appropriate through market pricing the full social benefits arising directly from the production (and consumption) of the good—it is difficult to exclude from the use of the good those who do not pay for it. A socially optimal level of supply of such a good cannot be expected if its supply is left to private firms. Because present institutional arrangements are such that much information resulting from basic research is nonexcludable, it has been necessary to establish nonprofit institutions to advance basic scientific knowledge.[32]

A unique aspect of agricultural research in the past, particularly that directed to advancing biological technology, was that many of the products of research—even in the applied area—were characterized by nonexcludability. Protection by patent laws was either unavailable or inadequate. The nature of agricultural production made it difficult to restrict information about new technology or practices. Furthermore, even the largest farms were relatively small units and were not able to capture more than a small share of the gains from inventive activity. Private research activities in agriculture have been, until fairly recently, directed primarily toward developing mechanical technology for which patent protection has long been established.[33]

The public-good attributes of the research product together with the stochastic nature of the research production function have made public support of agricultural research socially desirable. It does not necessarily follow, however, that agricultural research should be conducted exclusively in government institutions financed by tax revenue. The social benefit produced by agricultural research can be measured as the sum of increases in consumers' and producers' surpluses resulting from the downward shift in the supply function of agricultural commodities. If the benefit consists primarily of producers' surplus, agricultural research may be left to the self-organizing activities of agricultural producers (that is, institutions such as agricultural commodity organizations and cooperatives). Research on a number of tropical export crops grown under plantation conditions, such as sugar, bananas, and rubber, is often organized in this manner.

If agricultural research were left entirely to the private sector, however, the result would be serious bias in the allocation of research resources. Resources would flow primarily to areas of technology that are adequately protected by variety registration, patents, or trade secrets(such as the inbred lines used in the production of

---

arrangements are designed to promote more efficient resource allocation through market arrangements, as discussed in the previous section (Chapter 14).

[32] For a history of the establishment of public sector agricultural research systems in a number of developed and developing countries, see Ruttan (1983); also see Chapters 6 and 13.

[33] In a number of countries "breeders' rights" and "petty patent" legislation have induced rapid growth in private sector research and development in agriculture (Ruttan, 1982; Evenson and Evenson, 1983). Advances in biotechnology have been associated with rapid extension of intellectual property rights (Chapter 10).

hybrid corn seed). Other areas, such as research on open-pollinated seed varieties, biological control of insects and pathogens, and improvements in farming practices and management, would be neglected. The socialization of agricultural research or the predominance of public institutions in agricultural research, especially in the biological sciences, can be considered a major institutional innovation designed to respond to demand for more profitable technology that could not be embodied in proprietary products. Since the mid-1990s the traditional margin between public and private goods in biological technology has undergone a substantial shift as the result of further institutional innovation—the extension of patent protection for the development of new life forms (Chapter 10).

The Supply of Institutional Innovation

The disequilibria in economic relationships associated with economic growth, such as technical change leading to the generation of new income streams, and changes in relative factor endowments, have been identified as important sources of demand for institutional change. Institutional innovations are demanded because they enhance the welfare of rational actors. But why are the institutional innovations supplied? The sources of the supply of institutional innovations have largely been ignored in the economics literature. There is little literature, for example, on how economic knowledge, or more broadly social science knowledge, influences economic or social policy.

From the perspective of the theory of the state, as developed in political science, the supply of major institutional innovations necessarily involves the mobilization of substantial political resources by political entrepreneurs and innovators. It is useful to think of a supply schedule of institutional innovation that is determined by the marginal cost schedule facing political entrepreneurs as they attempt to design new institutions and resolve the conflicts among various interest groups (or suppression of opposition when necessary). Institutional innovations will be supplied if the expected return from the innovation that can be captured by the political entrepreneurs exceeds the marginal cost of mobilizing the resources necessary to introduce the innovation. To the extent that the private return to the political entrepreneurs is different from the social return, the institutional innovation will not be supplied at a socially optimal level (Frohlich et al., 1971; Guttman, 1982).

Thus the supply of institutional innovation depends critically on the power structure or balance among interest groups in a society. If the power balance is such that the political entrepreneurs' efforts to introduce an institutional innovation with a high rate of social return are adequately rewarded by greater prestige and stronger political support, a socially desirable institutional innovation may occur. But if the institutional innovation is expected to result in a loss to a dominant political block, the innovation may not be forthcoming, even if it is expected to produce a large net gain to society as a whole.

It is also possible that socially undesirable institutional innovations may occur if the returns to the entrepreneur or the interest group exceed the gains to society. For example, it is common to observe that government market interventions such as licenses, quotas, rationing, and price controls are promoted by interest groups seeking "institutional rents" or monopoly profits. Rent seeking by interest groups does not contribute to the creation of new income streams in society, but it does entail social costs. These costs result in losses in market efficiency that government interventions produce and the waste of resources used to obtain them, such as lobbying and bribery.[34]

The failure of many developing countries to institutionalize the agricultural research capacity needed to take advantage of the large gains from relatively modest investments in technical change may be caused, in part, by the divergence between social returns and private returns to political entrepreneurs. In the mid-1920s, for example, agricultural development in Argentina appeared to be proceeding along a path roughly comparable to that of the United States. Mechanization of crop production lagged slightly behind that in the United States. Grain yields per hectare averaged slightly higher. In contrast to the United States, however, output and productivity in Argentine agriculture remained relatively stagnant between the mid-1920s and the mid-1970s. It was not until the late 1970s that Argentina began to realize significant gains in agricultural productivity. One reason for this lag in Argentine agricultural development was the disruption of export markets in the 1930s and 1940s. Students of Argentine development have suggested that other reasons were the political dominance of the landed aristocracy and the rising tensions between urban and rural interests (de Janvry, 1973; Smith, 1969; Cavallo and Mundlak, 1982). In the Argentine case, the bias in the distribution of political and economic resources apparently imposed exceptionally costly delays in the institutional innovations needed to take advantage of the relatively inexpensive sources of growth that technical change in agriculture could have made available. Our understanding of how individuals "self organize" to bring about small scale institutional innovations is even less adequate than the larger scale innovation involving action by governments (Ostrom, 1990:42–45).[35]

Cultural endowments, including religion and ideology, exert a strong influence on the supply of institutional innovation. They make some forms of institutional change less costly to establish and impose severe costs on others. For example, the traditional moral obligation in the Japanese village community to cooperate in the maintenance of communal infrastructure has made it less costly to implement rural development programs in Japan than in societies lacking such traditions. These activities had their

---

[34] For the seminal work on rent seeking, see Tullock (1967). Other major works include Stigler (1971) and Krueger (1974). For a useful collection of the emerging literature on rent seeking see Buchanan et al. (1980). For a literature review see Tollison (1982).

[35] For the most successful effort to develop a framework for the analysis of the supply of institutional innovation by small-scale self-organized groups, see Ostrom (1990). See particularly the series of case studies in Chapters 3–5.

origin in the feudal organization of rural communities in the pre-Meiji period. But practices such as maintenance of village and agricultural roads and of irrigation and drainage ditches through joint activities in which all families contribute labor were still practiced in well over half of the hamlets in Japan as recently as 1970 (Ishakawa, 1981:325–347). The traditional patterns of cooperation have represented an important cultural resource on which to erect modern forms of cooperative marketing and joint farming activities. Similar cultural resources are not available in South Asian villages, where, for example, the caste structure inhibits cooperation and encourages specialization.

Likewise, ideology may reduce the cost to political entrepreneurs of mobilizing collective action for institutional change. In the United States, for example, the Jeffersonian concept of agrarian democracy provided ideological support for the series of land ordinances culminating in the Homestead Act of 1862, which established the legal framework that encouraged an owner–operator system of agriculture in the American West (Cochrane, 1979:41–47, 179–188). Strong nationalist sentiment in Meiji Japan, reflected in slogans such as "A Wealthy Nation and Strong Army" (Fukoku Kyohei), helped mobilize the resources needed for the establishment of vocational schools and agricultural and industrial experiment stations (Hayami et al., 1975). In China, communist ideology, reinforced by the lessons learned during the guerrilla period in Yenan, inspired the mobilization of communal resources to build irrigation systems and other forms of social overhead capital (Schran, 1975:379–402). Thus ideology can be a critical resource for political entrepreneurs and an important factor affecting the supply of institutional innovations.

Social Science Knowledge

Advances in social science knowledge can lead to institutional innovations that generate new income streams or that reduce the cost of conflict resolution and thus shift the supply of institutional change to the right. Throughout history, improvements in institutional performance have occurred primarily through the slow accumulation of successful precedents or as by-products of expertise and experience. Institutional change was generated through the process of trial and error, much in the same manner that technical change was generated before the invention of the research university, the agricultural experiment station, or the industrial research laboratory. The institutionalization of research in the social sciences and related professions has opened up the possibility that institutional innovation can proceed much more efficiently and that it will be increasingly possible to substitute social science knowledge and analytical skill for the more expensive process of learning by trial and error.

The research that advanced our understanding of the production and consumption of rural households in less developed countries demonstrates how advances in knowledge increase the supply of more efficient institutions (Schultz, 1968; Nerlove, 1974). In a number of countries this research has led to the abandonment of policies that viewed peasant households as unresponsive to economic incentives. And it has led to the design of policies and institutions that make more productive technologies available to peasant producers and to the design of more efficient price policies for factors and products.

In the examples of the demand for and supply of institutional innovation discussed in the previous sections, there has been little attempt to consider the interaction between the supply and demand for institutional innovation. There is, however, a modest literature that has employed the "political market" metaphor to discuss the market for votes within legislative bodies, the market for the distribution of wealth among constituencies, and exchanges between legislators and bureaucrats and constituencies and interest groups (Keohane et al., 1998). In Chapter 12 I present a case study of how shifts in both supply and demand for sulfur dioxide (SO_2) pollution control led to the design of a "constructed market" for tradable air pollution permits. Constituents and environmental interest groups were the source of the increase in demand for the regulation of SO_2 emissions. Advances in economic knowledge led to an understanding of the very large cost reductions that could be achieved by utilizing a "constructed market" rather than traditional "command and control" methods to reduce SO_2 emissions. Resource economists, the federal bureaucracy, and Congress responded by supplying a constructed market in tradable emission permits.

Models that have been most widely employed in recent institutional analysis, such as the tragedy of the commons, the logic of collective action, the prisoner's dilemma game, and mechanism design, are profoundly pessimistic about the ability of individuals, acting alone or in cooperation, to achieve common action. The problem of optimal institutional design has not been solved even at the most abstract theoretical level (Hurwicz, 1972, 1998). Producers or consumers, or both, will have an incentive to deviate from the formal rules of the allocation mechanism (a failure of "incentive compatibility"), and they are able to do so by misrepresenting facts about which (because of "information decentralization") they have unique, privileged informa- tion (producers about their production functions, consumers about the preferences) (Goodin, 1996:32). The research on institutional innovation by Hayami and Ruttan, by Ostrom (1990), and by Keohane et al., (1998) is much more optimistic. But it is possible to be optimistic only if the objective is to design better rather than optimal institutions. In the next section I discuss some of the elements of a more complete model of institutional innovation.

A PATTERN MODEL OF INDUCED INNOVATION

The elements of a model that maps the relationships among resource endowments, cultural endowments, technology, and institutions is presented in Figure 4.4.[36] The

---

[36] Fusfeld uses the terms *pattern* or *Gestalt* model to describe a form of analysis that links the elements of a general pattern together by logical connections. The recursive multicausal relationships of the pattern model imply that the model is always "open"—"it can never include all of the relevant variables and

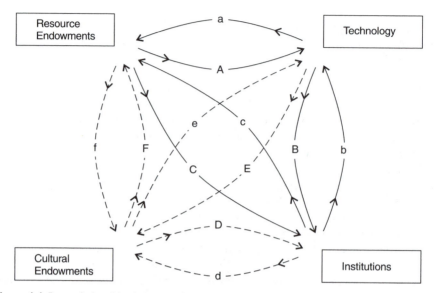

Figure 4.4 Interrelationships between changes in resource endowments, cultural endowments, technology, and institutions. (*Source:* Reprinted from Daniel R Fusfeld, "The Conceptual Framework of Modern Economics," *Journal of Economic Issues* 14 (March, 1980):1–52, by special permission of the copyright holder, the Association for Evolutionary Economics.)

model goes beyond the conventional general equilibrium model in which resource endowments, technologies, institutions, and culture (conventionally designated as tastes) are given.[37] In the study of long-term social and economic change the relationships among the several variables must be treated as dialectical or recursive.

   The changes in the Japanese and U.S. industrial technology and organization since World War II illustrate the dialectical or recursive interaction between technical and institutional change. The early postwar productivity gap in automobile assembly induced innovations in inventory control, assembly methods, and vehicle quality in Japan. These in turn induced the development of "lean production" in the U.S. automobile industry. U.S. innovations in information and communication technology

---

relationships necessary for a full understanding of the phenomena under investigation" (Fusfeld, 1980:33). Ostrom (1990) uses the term *framework* rather than *pattern model*. "The framework for analyzing problems of institutional choice illustrates the complex configuration of variables when individuals . . . attempt to fashion rules to improve their individual and joint outcomes. The reason for presenting this complex array of variables as a framework rather than a model is precisely because one cannot encompass the degree of complexity within a single model" (214).

[37] In economics, the concept of cultural endowments is usually subsumed under the concept of tastes, which are regarded as given, that is, not subject to economic analysis. I use the term *cultural endowments* to capture those dimensions of culture that have been transmitted from the past. Contemporary changes in resource endowments, technology, and institutions can be expected to result in changes in cultural endowments (Ruttan, 1988).

led to institutional changes in the form of network-based coordination beyond the boundaries of the traditional firm in the Unitd States. Japanese firms responded by adapting similar institutional arrangements in an attempt to overcome the U.S. lead in high technology sectors such as biotechnology (Aoki, 1996:17; Chapter 11).

The formal economic models that are employed to analyze the supply and demand for technical and institutional change can be thought of as "nested" within the general equilibrium framework of Figure 4.4. One advantage of the "pattern model" outlined in Figure 4.4 is that it helps to identify areas of ignorance. Our capacity to model and test the relationships between resource endowments and technical change is relatively strong. Our capacity to model and test the relationships between cultural endowments and either technical or institutional change is relatively weak. A second advantage of the model is its usefulness in identifying the components that enter into other attempts to account for secular economic and social change. Failure to analyze historical change in a general equilibrium context tends to result in a unidimensional perspective on the relationships bearing on technical and institutional change.

For example, historians working within the Marxist tradition often tend to view technical change as dominating both institutional and cultural change. In his book *Oriental Despotism,* Wittfogel (1957) views the irrigation technology used in wet rice cultivation in East Asia as determining political organization. As it applies to Figure 4.4, his primary emphasis was on the impact of resources and technology on institutions (B) and (C). A serious misunderstanding can be observed in neo-Marxian critiques of agricultural developments associated with the "green revolution." These criticisms have focused attention almost entirely on the impact of technical change on labor and land tenure relations. In terms of Figure 4.4, both the radical and populist critics have emphasized relation (B), but they have tended to ignore relationships (A) and (C).[38] This bias has led to repeated failure to identify effectively the separate effects of population growth and technical change on the growth and distribution of income. The analytical power of the more complete induced innovation model was illustrated in the work discussed earlier in this chapter concerning the impact of both technical change and population growth on changes in land tenure and labor market relationships in the Philippines.

Alchian and Demsetz (1973) identify a primary function of property rights as guiding incentives to achieve greater internalization of externalities. They consider that the clear specification of property rights reduces transaction costs in the face of growing competition for the use of scarce resources. North and Thomas (1970, 1973), building on the Alchian–Demsetz paradigm, have attempted to interpret the economic growth of Western Europe between 900 and 1700 primarily in terms of

---

[38] A major limitation of the Marxian model is the emphatic rejection of a causal link between demographic change and technical and institutional change (North, 1981:60, 61). This blindness to the role of demographic factors, and to the impact of relative resource endowments, originated in the debates between Marx and Malthus. An attempt to correct this deficiency represents the major innovation of the "cultural materialism" school of anthropology (Harris, 1979).

changes in property institutions.[39] During the eleventh and thirteenth centuries the pressure of population against increasingly scarce land resources induced innovations in property rights that in turn created profitable opportunities for the generation and adoption of labor-intensive technical changes in agriculture. The population decline in the fourteenth and fifteenth centuries was viewed as a primary factor leading to the demise of feudalism and the rise of the national state (line *C*). These institutional changes in turn opened up new possibilities for economies of scale in nonagricultural production and in trade (line *b*).

The proliferation of institutions has been identified by Mancur Olson (1952) as a source of economic decline. He also regards broad-based encompassing organizations as having incentives to generate growth and redistribute incomes to their members with little excess burden. For example, a broadly based coalition that encompasses the majority of agricultural producers is likely to exert political pressure for growth-oriented policies that will enable its members to obtain a larger share of a larger national product. A smaller organization that represents the interests of the producers of a single commodity is more likely to pursue the interests of its members at the expense of the welfare of other producers and the general public. In contrast, an even more broadly based farmer–labor coalition would be more concerned with promoting economic growth than would an organization representing a single sector. But large groups, in Olson's view, are inherently unstable because rational individuals will not incur the costs of contributing to the realization of the large group program—they have strong incentives to act as free riders. As a result, organizational "space" in a stable society will be increasingly occupied by special interest "distributional coalitions." These distributional coalitions make political life divisive. They slow down the adoption of new technologies (line *b*) and limit the capacity to reallocate resources (line *c*). The effect is to slow down economic growth or in some cases initiate a period of economic decline.[40]

The relationships in the lower left-hand corner of Figure 4.1 (dashed lines) have received relatively little attention from economists. An important exception is the analysis by Avner Greif of how the differential impact of the collectivist cultural endowments of Maghrebi traders and the individualistic cultural endowments of Genoese traders (*D*) influenced the development of commercial institutions in the Mediterranean region in the eleventh and twelfth centuries (Greif, 1994:912–950).

What are the implications of the theory of induced innovation outlined in this chapter for the research agenda on the economics of institutional change? It has been possible to advance our knowledge about the rate and direction of technical change significantly by treating it as endogenous—as induced primarily by changes in relative resource endowments and the growth of demand. A beginning has been

---

[39] For a critical perspective on the North-Thomas model see Field (1981:174–198). Field is critical of the attempt by North and Thomas to treat institutional change as endogenous.

[40] Olson (1982). For a critical review of the Olson work, see North (1983:163, 164).

made in developing a theory of induced institutional innovation in which institutional innovation is treated as endogenous. There is now a significant body of evidence suggesting that substantial new insights on institutional innovation and diffusion can be obtained by treating institutional change as an economic response to changes in resource endowments and technical change.

Changes in cultural endowments, including the factors that economists typically conceal under the rubric of tastes and that political scientists include under ideology, are important sources of both technical and institutional change. But our capacity to develop rigorous empirical tests capable of identifying the relative significance of the relationships between cultural endowments and the other elements of the model outlined in Figure 4.4 remains unsatisfactory. Until colleagues in the other social sciences provide more helpful analytical tools, economists will be forced to adhere to a strategy that focuses primarily on the interactions between resource endowments, technical change, and institutional change.

Throughout this book the theory of induced innovation is employed as a primary organizing concept for interpreting the processes leading to changes in the rate and direction of technical and institutional change. This does not mean that I insist that either the rate or direction of either technical or institutional change is entirely endogenous. There is an autonomous element in advances in knowledge and in technical and institutional change. Neither economic nor political markets behave with textbook precision. Yet it will become increasingly clear in the later chapters that changes in the relative endowments and prices of land, raw materials, energy resources, capital, and labor have had pervasive impacts on both technical and institutional change.

REFERENCES

Ahmad, S. "On the Theory of Induced Innovation." *Economic Journal* 76 (1966):344–357.

Ahmad, S. "Reply to Professor Fellner." *Economic Journal* 77 (1967a):662–664.

Ahmad, S. "A Rejoinder to Professor Kennedy." *Economic Journal* 77 (1967b):960–963.

Alchian, A. A. "Uncertainty, Evolution and Economic Theory." *Journal of Political Economy* 58 (1950):211–222.

Alchian, A.A., and H. Demsetz. "The Property Right Paradigm." *Journal of Economic History* 33 (1973):16–27.

Allen, R. C. "The Efficiency and Distributional Consequences of Eighteenth Century Enclosures." *Economic Journal* 92 (1982):937–953.

Ames, E., and N. Rosenberg. "The Enfield Arsenal in Theory and History." *Economic Journal* 78 (1968):730–733

Anderson, E. S. *Evolutionary Economics: Post-Schumpeterian Contributions.* London: Pinter, 1994.

Antonelli, C. *The Economics of Localized Technological Changes and Industrial Dynamics.* Dordrecht: Kluwer Academic Publishers, 1995.

Aoki, M. "Toward Comparative Institutional Analysis: Motivations and Some Tentative Theorizing." *Japanese Economic Review* 47 (1996):1–19.

Arrow, K. "The Economic Implications of Learning by Doing." *Review of Economic Studies* 29 (1962):155–173.

Arrow, K. "Viewpoint." *Science* 267 (March 17, 1995):1617.

Arthur, W. B. "On Competing Technologies and Historical Small Events: The Dynamics of Choice Under Increasing Returns." International Institute for Applied Systems Analysis Paper WP, 83–90, Laxenburg, Austria, 1983.

Arthur, W. B. "Competing Technologies, Increasing Returns, and Lock-In by Historical Events." *The Economic Journal* 99 (March 1989):116–131.

Arthur, W. B. "Positive Feedbacks in the Economy." *Scientific American* 262 (February 1990):92–99.

Arthur, W. B. *Increasing Returns and Path Dependence in the Economy.* Ann Arbor, MI: The University of Michigan Press, 1994.

Arthur, W. B, Y. M. Ermoliev, and Y. M. Kaniovski. "Path Dependence Processes and the Emergence of Macro-structure." *European Journal of Operational Research* 30 (June 1987):294–303.

Barro, R. J., and X. Sala-i-Martin. *Economic Growth.* New York: McGraw-Hill, 1995.

Becker, G. S. *A Treatise on the Family.* Cambridge, MA: Harvard University Press, 1991.

Becker, G. S. "The Economic Way of Looking at Behavior." *Journal of Political Economy* 101 (1993):385–409.

Binswanger, H. P. "A Cost Function Approach to the Measurement of Elasticities of Factor Demand and Elasticities of Substitution." *American Journal of Agricultural Economics* 56 (1974a):377–386.

Binswanger, H. P. "The Measurement of Technical Change Biases with Many Factors of Production." *American Economic Review* 64 (1974b):964–976.

Binswanger, H. P. "Induced Technical Change: Evolution of Thought."In *Induced Innovation: Technology, Institutions and Development,* H. P. Binswanger, and V.W. Ruttan, eds., pp. 13–43. Baltimore, MD: Johns Hopkins University Press, 1978a.

Binswanger, H. P. "The Micro Economics of Induced Technical Change." In *Induced Innovation: Technology, Institutions and Development*, H. P. Binswanger and V. W. Ruttan, eds., pp. 91–127. Baltimore, MD: Johns Hopkins University Press, 1978b.

Binswanger, H. P., and V. W. Ruttan, eds. *Induced Innovation: Technology, Institutions and Development.* Baltimore, MD: Johns Hopkins University Press, 1978.

Blaug, M. "A Survey of the Theory of Process-Innovation." *Economica* 63 (1963):13–32.

Buchanan, J. M., R. D. Tollison, and G. Tullock. *Toward a Theory of the Rent-Seeking Society.* College Station, TX: Texas A&M University Press, 1980.

Cavallo, D. and Y. Mundlak. "Agriculture and Economic Growth in an Open Economy: The Case of Argentina." Washington, DC: International Food Policy Research Institute, Research Report 36, December 1982.

Chambers, J. D., and G. E. Mingay. *The Agricultural Revolution*, 1750–1880. London: B. T. Batsford and New York: Schocken Books, 1966.

Cheng, Y .T., and A. H. Van de Ven. "Learning the Innovation Journey: Order Out of Chaos?" Minneapolis, MN: University of Minnesota Strategic Management Center, Discussion Paper 208, October 1994.

Ciriacy-Wantrup, S. V., and R. C. Bishop. " 'Common Property' as a Concept in Natural Resource Policy." *Natural Resources Journal* 79 (October 1975):713–727.

Coase, R. H. "The Problem of Social Cost." *Journal of Law and Ecomomics* 3 (1960):1–44.

Cochrane, W. W. *The Development of American Agriculture: A Historical Analysis*. Minneapolis, MN: University of Minnesota Press, 1979.

Commons, J. R. *The Economics of Collective Action*. New York: Macmillan, 1950.

Cowan, R. "Nuclear Power Reactors: A Study in Technological Lock-In." *Journal of Economic History* 50 (1990):801–814.

Cyert, R.M., and J. G. March. *A Behavioral Theory of the Firm*. Englewood Cliffs, NJ: Prentice Hall, 1963.

Dahlman, C. J. *The Open Field System and Beyond: A Property Rights Analysis of an Economic Institution*. Cambridge, UK: Cambridge University Press, 1980.

David, P. A. "Mechanization of Reaping in the Ante-Bellum Midwest." In *Industrialization in Two Systems: Essays in Honor of Alexander Gerscherkron*, H. Rosovsky, ed., pp. 3–39. New York: John Wiley, 1966.

David, P. A. "Labor Scarcity and the Problem of Technological Practice and Progress in the Nineteenth Century." Cambridge, MA: Harvard Institute of Economic Research, Research Paper 297, May 1973.

David, P. A. *Technical Choice, Innovation and Economic Growth*. Cambridge: Cambridge University Press, 1975.

David, P. A. "Clio and the Economics of QWERTY." *American Economic Review* 76 (1985): 332–337.

David, P. A. "Understanding the Economics of QWERTY: The Necessity of History." In *Economic History and the Modern Economist*, W. N. Parker, ed., pp. 30–49. New York: Basil Blackwell, 1986.

David, P. A. "Path Dependence and Predictability in Dynamic Systems with Local Network Externalities: A Paradigm for Historical Economics." In *Technology and the Wealth of Nations: the Dynamics of Contracted Advantage*, D. Foray and C. Freeman, eds., pp. 208–231. London: Pinter, 1993.

David, P. A. "Path Dependence and the Quest for Historical Economics: One More Chorus of the Ballad of QWERTY." Oxford, UK: Oxford University, All Souls College, November 1997 (mimeo).

David, P. A., and J. A. Bunn. "The Economics of Gateway Technologies and Network Evolution: Lessons From Electricity Supply History." *Information Economics and Policy* 3 (1988):165–202.

Davis, L. E., and D. C. North. *Institutional Change and American Economic Growth*. Cambridge, UK: Cambridge University Press, 1971.

de Janvry, A. "A Socioeconomic Model of Induced Innovations for Argentine Agricultural Development." *Quarterly Journal of Economics* 87 (August 1973):410–435.

Demsetz, H. "The Exchange and Enforcement of Property Rights." *Journal of Law and Economics* 7 (October 1964):11–26.

Demsetz, H. "Toward a Theory of Property Rights." *American Economic Review* 57 (May 1967):347–359.

Diamond, P., D. McFadden, and M. Rodriguez. "Measurement of Factor Substitution and Bias of Technological Change." In *Production Economics: A Dual Approach to Theory and Applications*, M. Fuss and D. McFadden, eds., Vol. 2, pp. 125–147. Amsterdam: North Holland, 1978.

Dosi, G. *Technical Change and Industrial Transformation*. New York: St. Martins Press, 1984.

Dosi, G. "Sources, Procedures, and Microeconomic Effects of Innovation." *Journal of Economic Literature* 26 (1988):1120–1071.

Dosi, G. "Opportunities, Incentives and the Collective Patterns of Technological Change." *Economic Journal* 107 (1997):1530–1547.

Dosi, G., K. Pavitt, and L. Soete. *The Economics of Technological Change and International Trade*. New York: New York University Press, 1990.

Dosi, G., R. Giannetti, and P. A. Toninelli, eds. *Technology and Enterprise in a Historical Perspective*. Oxford, UK: Oxford University Press, 1992.

Dosi, G., C. Marengo, and G. Fagiolo. *Learning in Evolutionary Environments*. Laxenburg, Austria: International Institute for Applied Systems Analysis, WP-96–124, 1996.

Elster, J. *Explaining Technical Change*. Cambridge: Cambridge University Press, 1983.

Evenson, D. D., and R. E. Evenson. "Legal Systems and Private Sector Incentives for the Invention of Agricultural Technology in Latin America." In *Technical Change and Social Conflict in Agriculture: Latin American Perspectives*, M.E. Piñeiro and E. J. Trigo, eds., pp. 189–216. Boulder, CO: Westview Press, 1983.

Evenson, R. E., and Y. Kislev. *Agricultural Research and Productivity*. New Haven, CT: Yale University Press, 1975.

Fan, S. "Effects of Technological Change and Institutional Reform on Production and Growth in Chinese Agriculture." *American Journal of Agricultural Economics* 73 (May 1991):266–275.

Feeny, D. *The Political Economy of Productivity: Thai Agricultural Development, 1880–1975*. Vancouver: University of British Columbia Press, 1982.

Feeny, D. "The Demand and Supply of Institutional Arrangements." In *Rethinking Institutional Analysis and Development*. V. Ostrom, D. Feeny, and H. Picht, eds., pp. 159–209. San Francisco, CA: International Center for Economic Growth, 1988.

Fellner, W. *Trends and Cycles in Economic Activity*. New York: Henry Holt, 1956.

Fellner, W. "Two Propositions in the Theory of Induced Invention." *Economic Journal*. 71 (1961):305–308.

Fellner, W. "Emperical Support for the Theory of Induced Innovation." *Quarterly Journal of Economics* 85 (1971):580–604.

Field, A. J. "The Problem with Neoclassical Institutional Economics: A Critique with Special Reference to the North/Thomas Model of Pre-1500 Europe." *Explorations in Economic History* 18 (1981):174–198.

Fogel, R. W. "The Specification Problem in Economic History." *Journal of Economic History* 27 (1967):283–308.

Foray, D., and A. Grubler. "Morphological Analysis, Diffusion and Lock-out of Technologies: Ferrous Casting in France and the FRG." *Research Policy* 19 (1990):535–550.

Freeman, C. *The Economics of Industrial Innovation*, 2nd ed. Cambridge, MA: MIT Press, 1982.

Freeman, C. "The Economics of Technical Change." *Cambridge Journal of Economics* 18 (1994):463–514.

Frohlich, N., J. A. Oppenheimer, and O. R. Young. *Political Leadership and Collective Goods*. Princeton, NJ: Princeton University Press, 1971.

Fusfeld, D. R. "The Conceptual Framework of Modern Economics." *Journal of Economic Issues* 14 (1980):1–52.

Gans, J. S., and G. B. Shepherd. "How Are the Mighty Fallen: Rejected Classic Articles by Leading Economists." *Journal of Economic Perspectives* 8 (1994):165–179.

Garud, R., and M.A. Rappa. "A Socio-cognitive Model of Technology Evolution: The Case of Cochlear Implants." *Organization Science* 5 (1994):344–362.

Goodin, R. E. "Institutions and Their Design." In *The Theory of Institutional Design,* R. E. Goodin, ed., pp. 1–53. Cambridge, UK: Cambridge University Press, 1996.

Grant, W., W. Patterson, and C. Whitston. *Government and the Chemical Industry: A Comparative Study of Britain and West Germany.* Oxford, UK: Oxford University Press, 1988.

Greif, A. "Cultural Beliefs and the Organization of Society: A Historical and Theoretical Reflection on Collectivist and Individualist Societies." *Journal of Political Economy* 102 (1994):912–950.

Griliches, Z. "Hybrid Corn: An Exploration in the Economics of Technological Change." *Econometrica* 25 (1957):501–522.

Grubler, A. and N. Nakicenovic. "The Dynamic Evolution of Methane Technologies." In *The Methane Age*, T. H. Lee, H. R. Linden, D. A. Dryfus, and T. Vasco, eds., pp. 13–44. Dordrecht: Kluwer Academic Publishers, 1988.

Guttman, J. M. "Can Political Entrepreneurs Solve the Free Rider Problem?" *Journal of Economic Behavior and Organization* 3 (1982):1–10.

Habakkuk, H. J. *American and British Technology in the Nineteenth Century.* Cambridge, UK: Cambridge University Press, 1962.

Haltmaier, J. "Induced Innovation and Productivity Growth: An Empirical Analysis." Washington, DC: Federal Reserve Board Special Studies Paper 220, February 1986.

Harris, M. *Cultural Materialism: The Struggle for a Science of Culture.* New York: Random House, 1979.

Hayami, Y., M. Akino, M. Shintani, and S. Yamada. *A Century of Agricultural Growth in Japan.* Minneapolis, MN: University of Minnesota Press, 1975.

Hayami, Y., and M. Kikuchi. *Asian Village Economy at the Crossroads: An Economic Approach to Institutional Change.* Tokyo: University of Tokyo Press, 1981 and Baltimore, MD: Johns Hopkins University Press, 1982.

Hayami, Y., and M. Kikuchi. *A Rice Village Saga: The Three Decades of Green Revolution in the Philippines* London, UK: MacMillan Press, 2000.

Hayami, Y., and K. Otsuka. *The Economics of Contract Choice: An Agrarian Perspective.* Oxford, UK: Oxford University Press, 1993.

Hayami, Y., and V. W. Ruttan. "Factor Prices and Technical Change in Agricultural Development: The United States and Japan, 1880–1960." *Journal of Political Economy* 78 (1970):1115–1141.

Hayami, Y., and V. W. Ruttan. *Agricultural Development: An International Perspective.* Baltimore, MD: Johns Hopkins University Press, 1985. (First edition, 1971.)

Hayami, Y., and S. Yamada. "Agricultural Research Organization in Economic Development: A Review of the Japanese Experience." In *Agriculture in Development Theory*, L.G. Reynolds, ed., pp. 224–249. New Haven, CT: Yale University Press, 1975.

Hicks, J. *The Theory of Wages.* London: Macmillan, 1963. (First edition, 1932.)

Hurwicz, L. "Organized Structures for Joint Decision Making: A Designer's Point of View." In *Interorganizational Decision Making*, M. Tiute, R. Chisholm, and M. Radnor, eds., pp. 37–44. Chicago, IL: Aldine, 1972.

Hurwicz, L. "Issues in the Design of Mechanisms and Institutions." In *Designing Institutions for Environmental and Resource Management,* E. T. Loehman and D. M. Kilgour, eds., pp. 29–56. Cheltenham, UK: Edward Elgar, 1998.

Ishikawa, S. *Essays on Technology, Employment and Institutions in Economic Development*

Comparative Asian Experience. Tokyo: Kinokuniya, 1981.

Islas, J. "Getting Round the Lock-in in Electricity Generating Systems: The Examples of the Gas Turbine." *Research Policy* 26 (1997):49–66.

James, J. A., and J. S. Skinner. "Resolution of the Labor-Scarcity Paradox." *Journal of Economic History* 45 (1985):513–539.

Jorgenson, D. W., and B.M. Fraumeni. "Relative Prices and Technical Change." In *Modeling and Measuring National Resource Substitution*, E. R. Bendt and B. Fields, eds., pp. 17–47. Cambridge, MA: MIT Press, 1981.

Jorgenson, D. W., and P. J. Wilcoxen. "Energy, the Environment, and Economic Growth." In *Handbook of Resource and Energy Economics,* A. V. Kneese and J. L. Sweeney, eds., Vol. III, pp. 1267–1349. Amsterdam: Elsevier Science Publishers, 1993.

Kamien, M. I., and N. L. Schwartz. "Optimal Induced Technical Change." *Econometrica* 36 (1969):1–17.

Kennedy, C. "Induced Bias in Innovation and the Theory of Distribution." *The Economic Journal* 75 (1964):541–547.

Kennedy, C. "Samuelson on Induced Innovation." *Review of Economics and Statistics* 48 (1966):442–444.

Kennedy, C. "On the Theory of Induced Innovation—A Reply." *Economic Journal* 77 (1967): 958–960.

Kennedy, C., and A. Thirwal. "Technical Progress: A Survey." *Economic Journal* 82 (1972): 11–72.

Keohane, N. O., R. L. Revesz, and R. N. Stavins. "The Positive Political Economy of Instrumental Choice in Environmental Policy." *Harvard Environmental Law Review* 22 (1998):313–367.

Khan, A. R. *Growth and Inequality in the Philippines: Poverty and Landlessness in Rural Asia.* Geneva: International Labour Office, 1977.

Kikuchi, M., and Y. Hayami. "Inducements to Institutional Innovations in an Agrarian Community." *Economic Development and Cultural Change* 29 (1980):21–36.

Knight, F. H. "Institutionalism and Empiricism in Economics." *American Economic Review* 43 (1952):51.

Koppel, B., ed. *Induced Innovation Theory and International Agricultural Development: A Reassessment.* Baltimore, MD: Johns Hopkins University Press, 1995.

Krueger, A.O. "The Political Economy of the Rent-Seeking Society." *American Economic Review* 64 (1974):291–303.

Landau, R., and N. Rosenberg. "Successful Commercialization in the Chemical Process Industries." In *Technology and the Wealth of Nations*, N. Rosenberg, R. Landau, and D. C. Mowery, eds., pp. 73–119. Stanford, CA: Stanford University Press, 1992.

Landes, D. S. "What Room for Accident in History?: Explaining Big Changes by Small Events." *Economic History Review* 47 (1994):637–656.

Langolis, R. N. and M. J. Everett. "What is Evolutionary Economics?" In *Evolutionary and Neo-Schumpeterian Approaches to Economics*, L. Magnusson, ed., pp. 11–47. Dordrecht: Kluwer, 1994.

Levin, R. C. "Technical Change and Optimal Scale: Some Evidence and Implications." *Southern Economic Journal* 44 (1977):208–221.

Liebowitz, S. J., and S. E. Margolis. "The Fable of the Keys." *Journal of Law and Economics* 33 (1990):1–25.

Liebowitz, S. J., and S. E. Margolis. "Market Processes and the Selection of Standards."

University of Texas at Dallas School of Management Working Paper, March 1992.

Liebowitz, S. J., and S. E. Margolis. "Network Externality: An Uncommon Tragedy." *Journal of Economic Perspectives* 8:2 (1994):133–150.

Liebowitz, S. J., and S. E. Margolis. "Path Dependence, Lock In, and History." *Journal of Law Economics and Organization* 11 (1995):205–226.

Lin, J. Y. "The Household Responsibility System Reform in China: A Peasants' Institutional Choice." *American Journal of Agricultural Economics* 69 (1987):410–425.

Lin, J. Y. The Household Responsibility System in China's Agricultural Reform." *Economic Development and Cultural Change* 36 (1998):S199–S224.

Lin, J. Y. and J. B. Nugent. "Institutions and Economic Development." In *Handbook of Development Economics,* J. Behrman and T. N. Srinavasan, eds., Vol. IIIA, pp. 2301–2369. Amsterdam, Netherlands: Elsevier Science, B. V., 1995.

Loehman, E. T., and D. M. Kilgour, eds. *Designing Institutions for Environmental and Resource Management.* Cheltenham, UK: Edward Elgar, 1998.

Lucas, R. E., Jr. "Tests of a Capital-Theoretic Model of Technological Change." *Review of Economic Studies* 34 (1967):175–180.

Lucas, R. E., Jr. "On the Mechanics of Economic Development." *Journal of Monetary Economics* 22 (1988):3–42.

Marx, K. *A Contribution to the Critique of Political Economy.* Chicago, IL: Charles H. Kerr, 1913.

Mowery, D. C., and N. Rosenberg. "The Influence of Market Demand Upon Innovation: A Critical Review of Some Recent Empirical Studies." *Research Policy* 8 (1979):103–153.

Nelson, R. R. "The Simple Economics of Basic Scientific Research." *Journal of Political Economy* 67 (1959):304.

Nelson, R. R. "Recent Evolutionary Theorizing About Economic Change." *Journal of Economic Literature* 33 (March 1995):48–90.

Nelson, R. R., and S. G. Winter. "Toward an Evolutionary Theory of Economic Capabilities." *American Economic Review* 63 (1973):440–449.

Nelson, R. R., and S. G. Winter. "Neoclassical vs. Evolutionary Theories of Economic Growth: Critique and Prospects." *Economic Journal* 84 (1974):886–905.

Nelson, R. R., and S. G. Winter. "Factor Price Changes and Factor Substitution in an Evolutionary Model." *Bell Journal of Economics* 6 (1975):466–486.

Nelson, R. R., and S. G. Winter. "Simulation of Schumpeterian Competition." *American Economic Review* 67 (1977):271–276.

Nelson, R. R., and S. G. Winter. *An Evolutionary Theory of Economic Change.* Cambridge, MA: Harvard University Press, 1982.

Nelson, R. R., S. G. Winter, and H. L. Schuette. "Technical Change in an Evolutionary Model." *Quarterly Journal of Economics* 40 (1976):90–118.

Nerlove, M. "Household and Economy: Toward a New Theory of Population and Economic Growth." *Journal of Political Economy* 82 (1974), Part 2:S200–S218.

Nordhaus, W. D. *Invention, Growth and Welfare: A Theoretical Treatment of Technical Change.* Cambridge, MA: MIT Press, 1969.

Nordhaus, W. D. "Some Skeptical Thoughts on the Theory of Induced Innovation." *Quarterly Journal of Economics* 87 (1973):208–219.

North, D. C. *Structure and Change in Economic History.* New York: W. W. Norton, 1981.

North, D. C. "Ideology and the Free Rider Problem." *Structure and Change in Economic History.* New York: W. W. Norton, 1981.

North, D. C. "A Theory of Economic Change." *Science* 219 (1983):163, 164.

North, D. C., and R. P. Thomas. "An Economic Theory of the Growth of the Western World." *Economic History Review* 23 (1970):1–17.

North, D. C., and R. P. Thomas. *The Rise of the Western World.* London, UK: Cambridge University Press, 1973.

Olmstead, A. L., and P. Rhode. "Induced Innovation in American Agricultures: A Reconsideration." *Journal of Political Economy* 101 (1993):100–118.

Olmstead, A. L., and P. Rhode. "Induced Innovation in American Agriculture: An Econometric Analysis." Institute of Government Affairs, University of California, Davis, CA, 1995 (mimeo).

Olson, M., Jr. *The Logic of Collective Action: Public Goods and the Theory of Groups.* Cambridge, MA: Harvard University Press, 1965.

Olson, M. *The Rise and Decline of Nations: Economic Growth, Stagflation, and Social Rigidities.* New Haven, CT: Yale University Press, 1982.

Ostrom, E. *Governing the Commons: The Evolution of Institutions for Collective Action.* Cambridge, UK: Cambridge University Press, 1990.

Ostrom, E. *The Comparative Study of Public Economics.* Memphis, TN: P. K. Seidman Foundation, 1998.

Ostrom, E., J. Barger, C. B. Field, R. B. Norgaard, and D. Policansky. "Revisiting the Commons: Local Lessons, Global Challenges." *Science* 284 (1999):278–282.

Overton, M. *Agricultural Revolution in England: The Transformation of the Agrarian Economy: 1500–1850.* Cambridge, UK: Cambridge University Press, 1996.

Penrose, E. T. "Biological Analogies to the Theory of the Firm." *American Economic Review* 42 (1952):804–819.

Rausser, G. C., E. Lichtenberg, and R. Lattimore. "Developments in Theory and Empirical Applications of Endogenous Governmental Behavior." In *New Directions in Econometric Modeling and Forecasting in U.S. Agriculture*, G. C. Rausser, ed., pp. 547–614. New York: Elsevier, 1982.

Romer, P. M. "Increasing Returns and Long-run Growth." *Journal of Political Economy* 94 (1986):1002–1037.

Rosenberg, N. "Science, Invention and Economic Growth." *Economic Journal* 84 (1974):90–108.

Rosenberg, N. "Learning by Using." In *Inside the Black Box: Technology and Economics*, N. Rosenberg, ed., pp. 120–140. Cambridge: Cambridge University Press, 1982.

Rosenberg, N. *Inside the Black Box: Technology and Economics.* New York: Cambridge University Press, 1982b.

Roumasset, J., and S. J. La Croix. "The Coevolution of Property Rights and Political Order: An Illustration from Nineteenth Century Hawaii." In *Rethinking Institutional Analyses and Development: Issues, Alternatives, and Choices,* V. Ostrom, D. Feeny, and H. Picht, eds., pp. 315–336. San Francisco, CA: International Center for Economic Growth, 1988.

Runge, C. F. *Institutions and Common Property Externalities: The Assurance Problem in Economic Development.* Ph.D. dissertation, University of Wisconsin–Madison, 1981a:xvi.

Runge, C. F. "Common Property Externalities: Isolation, Assurance, and Resource Depletion in a Traditional Grazing Context.*" American Journal of Agricultural Economics* 63 (1981b):595–606.

Ruttan, V. W. "Induced Institutional Change." In *Induced Innovation: Technology, Institutions and Development*, H. P. Binswanger and V.W. Ruttan, eds., pp. 327–357. Baltimore, MD: Johns Hopkins University Press, 1978.

Ruttan, V. W. "Changing Roles of Public and Private Sectors in Agricultural Research." *Science* 216 (April 2, 1982):23–29.

Ruttan, V. W. *Agricultural Research Policy*. Minneapolis, MN: University of Minnesota Press, 1983.

Ruttan, V. W. "Cultural Endowments and Economic Development: What Can Economists Learn from Anthropology?" *Economic Development and Cultural Change* 36 (1988):S247–271.

Ruttan, V. W. "Induced Innovation and Path Dependence: A Reassessment with Respect to Agricultural Development and the Environment." *Technological Forecasting and Social Change* 53 (1996):41–60.

Ruttan, V. W. "Induced Innovation, Evolutionary Theory and Path Dependence: Sources of Technical Change." *Economic Journal* 107 (1997):1520–1529.

Ruttan, V. W., and Y. Hayami. "Toward a Theory of Induced Institutional Change." *Journal of Development Studies* 20 (1984):203–223.

Ruttan, V. W., and Y. Hayami. "Induced Innovation Theory and Agricultural Development: A Personal Account." In *Induced Innovation Theory and International Agricultural Development: A Reassessment*, B. Koppel, ed., pp. 22–36. Baltimore, MD: Johns Hopkins University Press, 1994.

Salter, W. E. G. *Productivity and Technical Change*, 1st ed. Cambridge: Cambridge University Press, 1960.

Samuelson, P. A. *Foundations of Economic Analysis*. Cambridge, MA: Harvard University Press, 1948.

Samuelson, P A. "The Pure Theory of Public Expenditure." *Review of Economics and Statistics* 36 (1954):387–389.

Samuelson, P. A. "Diagrammatic Exposition of a Theory of Public Expenditure." *Review of Economics and Statistics* 37 (1955):350–356.

Samuelson, P. A. "Aspects of Public Expenditure Theories." *Review of Economics and Statistics* 40 (1958):332–338.

Samuelson, P. A. "A Theory of Induced Innovation along Kennedy-Weizsacker Lines." *Review of Economics and Statistics* 47 (1965):343–356.

Samuelson, P. A. "Rejoinder: Agreements, Disagreements, Doubts and the Case of Induced Harrod-Neutral Technical Change." *Review of Economics and Statistics* 48 (1966):444–448.

Scherer, F. M. "Demand Pull and Technological Inventions: Schmookler Revisited." *Journal of Industrial Economics* 30 (1982):225–237.

Schmookler, J. "Changes in Industry and in the State of Knowledge as Determinants of Industrial Invention." In *The Rate and Direction of Inventive Activity: Economic and Social Factors*, R. R. Nelson, ed., pp. 195–232. Princeton, NJ: Princeton University Press, 1962.

Schmookler, J. *Invention and Economic Growth*. Cambridge, MA: Harvard University Press, 1966.

Schotter, A. *The Economic Theory of Social Institutions*. Cambridge, MA: Cambridge University Press, 1981.

Schran, P. "On the Yenan Origins of Current Economic Policies." In *China's Modern Economy in Historical Perspective,* D. H. Perkins, ed., pp. 279–302. Stanford, CA: Stanford

University Press, 1975.

Schultz, M . W. "The Value of the Ability to Deal with Disequilibria." *Journal of Economic Literature* 13 (1975):827–846.

Schultz, T. W. "Institutions and the Rising Economic Value of Man." *American Journal of Agricultural Economics* 50 (1968):1113–1122.

Schumpeter, J. A. *The Theory of Economic Development.* Cambridge, MA: Harvard University Press, 1934.

Schumpeter, J. A. *Capitalism, Socialism and Democracy.* New York: Harper, 1950.

Simon, H. A. "A Behavioral Model of Rational Choice." *Quarterly Journal of Economics* 69 (1955):1–18.

Simon, H. A. "Theories of Decision Making in Economics." *American Economic Review* 49 (1959):258–283.

Smith, P. H. *Politics and Beef in Argentina: Patterns of Conflict and Change.* New York: Columbia University Press, 1969.

Stigler, G. J. "The Theory of Economic Regulation." *Bell Journal of Economics and Management Science,* 2 (Spring 1971):3–12.

Stokes, R. G. *Opting for Oil: The Political Economy of Technical Change in the West German Chemical Industry, 1945–61.* Cambridge, UK: Cambridge University Press, 1994.

Thirtle, C. G., and V.W. Ruttan. *The Role of Demand and Supply in the Generation and Diffusion of Technical Change.* London, UK: Harwood Academic Publishers, 1987.

Tollison, R. "Rent Seeking: A Survey." *Kyklos* 35 (1982):575–602.

Tullock, G. "The Welfare Costs of Tariffs, Monopolies and Theft." *Western Economic Journal* 5 (June 1967):224–232.

Vanberg, V. *Rules and Choice in Economics.* London, UK: Routledge, 1994.

Van de Ven, A., and R. Garud. "Innovation and Industry Development: The Case of Cochlear Implants." In *Research on Technological Innovation, Management and Policy,* R. Burgelman and R. Rosenbloom, eds., Vol. 5, pp. 1–46. Greenwich, CT: JAI Press, 1993.

Vernon, R. "International Investment and International Trade in the Product Cycle." *Quarterly Journal of Economics* 80 (1966):190–207.

Vernon, R. "The Product Cycle Hypothesis in a New International Environment." *Oxford Bulletin of Economics and Statistics* 40 (1979):255–267.

Walsh, V. "Invention and Innovation in the Chemical Industry: Demand-Pull or Discovery-Push?" *Research Policy* 13 (1984):211–234.

Williamson, O. E. *The Economic Institutions of Capitalism: Firms, Markets, Relational Contracting.* New York: Collier Macmillan, 1985.

Winter, S. G. "Satisficing, Selection and the Innovating Remnant." *Quarterly Journal of Economics* 85 (May 1971):237–261.

Winter, S. G. "Schumpeterian Competition in Alternative Technological Regimes." *Journal of Economic Behavior and Organization* 5 (1984):287–320.

Witt, U. *Evolutionary Economics.* Aldershot, UK: Edward Elgar Publishing, 1993.

Wittfogel, K. A. *Oriental Despotism: A Comparative Study of Total Power.* New Haven, CT: Yale University Press, 1957.

Wright, G. "The Origins of American Industrial Success, 1889–1940." *The American Economic Review* 80 (1990):651–667.

Wright, G. "Toward a Historical Approach to Technological Change." *Economic Journal* 107 (1997):1560–1566.

CHAPTER 5

Technology Adoption, Diffusion, and Transfer[1]

T he fundamental significance of technical change in the process of economic growth has been established in previous chapters. Its significance can be described in several ways: (1) it permits the substitution of knowledge for resources, (2) it facilitates the substitution of less expensive and more abundant resources for more expensive resources, (3) it releases the constraints on growth imposed by inelastic resource supplies, or (4) it is the source of the new income streams that are captured in our measures of economic growth.

The economic and social impacts of new knowledge and new technology are realized, however, only with its adoption and utilization. There are substantial gaps in income and productivity even among the most advanced countries (Chapter 2). The enormous differences in productivity and income between developed and developing countries suggest that substantial gains can be realized by the transfer of technology from the most advanced to the least developed countries.

Serious study of the process of diffusion and adoption of technology by economists began only in the 1950s. Much of the early research by both sociologists and economists on adoption and diffusion of technology draw on experience in agriculture. The theory and method developed in these early studies were adopted in the early studies of the diffusion of industrial technology. In this chapter I first discuss the sociological origin of diffusion research and the two early studies of the diffusion of hybrid corn that became the source of the theory and method employed in later studies. I then turn to studies of the diffusion of technology within and among industrial firms. The final sections of the chapter are directed to international technology transfer.[2]

---

[1] In this chapter I draw on several earlier studies (Hayami and Ruttan, 1985:255–298; Thirtle and Ruttan, 1987:77–129; Ruttan, 1996).

[2] I have not attempted in this chapter to deal with the economic or political factors that influence the process of transfer of defense-related technology.

CONVERGENCE OF TRADITIONS

Well-developed research traditions on diffusion emerged during the early decades of the century in anthropology and in sociology.[3] A large body of research on the diffusion of educational innovations was conducted by Paul Mort of the Columbia University Teachers College in the 1920s and 1930s. By the end of the 1950s, strong traditions of diffusion research had emerged in rural sociology and in medical sociology. During the late 1950s and the 1960s these fields were joined by communications, geography, marketing, and economics.

Prior to the mid-1960s each diffusion tradition had developed as a relatively self-contained intellectual enclave. These enclaves began to converge with the publication of a series of papers in the early 1960s by Elihu Katz and several colleagues (Katz, 1960; Katz et al., 1963). In a 1960 paper, Katz noted that researchers in the field of communications had only recently became aware of and begun to draw on the studies of the diffusion of new ideas and technology in rural sociology.

Katz argued that what the study of mass communications had learned after three decades of research is that the mass media were far less potent than had been expected. This led to a search for sources of resistance to change, which in turn led to an emphasis on the importance of interpersonal relations. This was followed by three developments in communications research on diffusion: (1) studies were designed to characterize individuals by their relationships to others as well as their individual attributes; (2) small group studies linked research on the mass media with interpersonal communications; and (3) research focused on attempts to introduce change from outside a social system. "Here the work of the rural sociologists is of major importance. For the last two decades the latter have been inquiring into the effectiveness of campaigns to gain acceptance of new farm practices in rural communities while taking explicit account of the relevant channels of communication both outside and inside the community" (Katz, 1960:437). Katz attributed the delay in recognition of the role of interpersonal communication on the part of the mass communication research community to the fact that it drew its intellectual inspiration primarily from psychology rather than from sociology.

This was followed by the publication in 1963 of a paper in which Katz and several colleagues attempted to integrate the conceptual frameworks that had emerged in the several traditions that had, it appeared, been "independently invented" and "scarcely knew of each others existence" (Katz et al., 1963:240). A definitive effort to catalogue the literature and to synthesize and evaluate the theories and research finding on the diffusion of technical innovations was made by Everett M. Rogers in his now classical book, *Diffusion of Innovations* (first published in 1962 and updated in 1971, 1983, and 1995).

---

[3] The development of adoption–diffusion research has been tracked very carefully in a series of books by one of the early students in the field (Rogers, 1962, 1983, 1995; Rogers with Shoemaker, 1971). Its early development has been the subject of an important sociology of science case study by Diane Crane (1972).

THE DIFFUSION OF AGRICULTURAL TECHNOLOGY

Hybrid corn (maize) was released to farmers by the Iowa State Agricultural Experiment Station in 1928 and promoted by the Iowa Agricultural Extension Service and by the commercial seed companies that marketed the seed. It had a yield advantage relative to open pollinated corn in the 15–20% range. By 1940 it had been adopted by most Iowa corn growers.

In 1941 Bruce Ryan, a professor of rural sociology at Iowa State University, obtained funding from the Iowa Agricultural Experiment Station to conduct a study of the spread of hybrid seed among Iowa farmers. Sponsorship by the Iowa Agricultural Experiment Station was based on the presumption that a better understanding of the diffusion process of hybrid corn would be useful in designing more effective efforts to diffuse other innovations developed by the station. The study involved interviews with 259 farmers living in two small communities in central Iowa. The study by Ryan and Gross (1943, 1950) of the diffusion of hybrid-seed corn "more than any other study, influenced the methodology, theoretical framework, and interpretations of later students in the rural sociology tradition, and in other research traditions as well" (Rogers, 1983:54).

The Ryan–Gross Study attempted to answer a series of questions that have dominated most subsequent research on diffusion until well into the 1970s. "What variables are related to innovativeness? What is the rate of adoption of an innovation, and what factors explain this rate? What role do different communication channels play at various stages in the innovations-decision process?" (Rogers, 1983:56). The pattern of diffusion that they observed was the now classic sigmoid or "S-shaped" adoption curve and the symmetric bell-shaped curve describing the distribution of adopters over time (Figure 5.1).

Ryan and Gross interpreted the slope of the diffusion curve as a consequence of the interpersonal network of information exchanges between those individuals who had already adopted the innovation and those who would be influenced to do so. The sociopsychological research paradigm created by the Ryan and Gross investigation became the academic template that was to be adopted first by other rural sociologists in agricultural diffusion research and then by almost all other research traditions on diffusion. In her study of the "invisible college" of rural sociologists investigating diffusion as of the mid-1960s, Diana Crane credits Ryan and Gross with 15 of the 18 most widely used innovations in the field (Crane, 1972:74).

One of the remarkable aspects of the technology diffusion studies by rural sociologists was how rapidly the results were utilized by practitioners. Agricultural extension workers and other change agents found the diffusion model, particularly the five-stage categorization of the distribution of adopters over time—(1) innovators, (2) early adopters, (3) early majority, (4) late majority, and (5) laggard—and the social–psychological and communication characteristics associated with each category, exceedingly useful in their educational programs with farmers. During the late 1950s Professors George M. Beal and Joe M. Bohlen of the Department of Rural

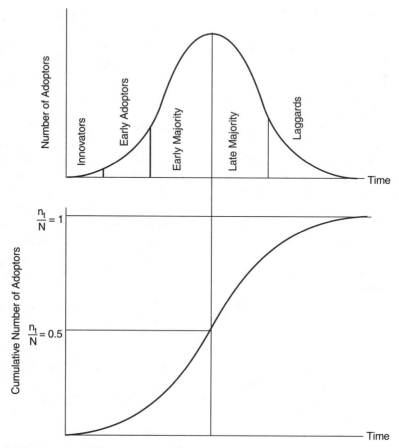

Figure 5.1 The epidemic model—the process of diffusion of technical change viewed as similar to spread of infectious disease. (*Source:* Colin G. Thirtle and Vernon W. Ruttan, *The Role of Demand and Supply in the Generation and Diffusion of Technical Change*, London: Harwood Academic Publishers, 1987:81.)

Sociology at Iowa State University utilized a visual presentation illustrating diffusion processes and concepts in over 160 meetings with change agents including extension workers, advertising agency personnel, sales workers, and industrial managers (Beal and Bohlen, 1957). It was this immediate operational value of the insight gained from diffusion research for health campaigns, technical assistance programs, and other areas that led to the rapid growth of support for diffusion research in fields other than rural sociology.

During the 1960s an attempt was made to locate diffusion research within the broader field of communications research. This was a major thrust in the second edition of Rogers book on diffusion of innovations (retitled *Communication of*

Innovations, 1969). The learning behavior of individuals was identified as the underlying source of the symmetry of the diffusion process. The elementary S–M–C–R communication model in which a source (S) sends a message (M) via certain channels (C) to receiving individuals (R) had, however, been implicit in much of the early diffusion research. Diffusion research in turn, by tracing communication patterns over time, enriched the understanding of communications researchers in the dynamics of the communication process and of the differential impact of the several channels of communication at different stages of the communications process (Rogers with Shoemaker, 1971:250–266).[4]

A second study that played a seminal role in diffusion studies was by Zvi Griliches of the diffusion of hybrid corn both within and across regions.[5] The Griliches study has occupied a role in subsequent studies by economists similar to that of Ryan and Gross in sociology. Griliches set for himself a larger research agenda than Ryan and Gross. His objective was to simultaneously explain the rate of diffusion within areas—the "acceptance problem"—and the timing of the development of hybrid corn for specific areas—the "availability problem." This was important because

> Hybrid corn was the invention of a method of inventing, a method of breeding superior corn for specific localities. It was not a single invention immediately available everywhere. The actual breeding of adoptable hybrids had to be done separately for each area. Hence besides the difference in the rate of adoption by farmers . . . we have also to explain the lag in the development of adaptable hybrids for specific areas. (Griliches, 1957:502)

The procedure employed by Griliches was to summarize the diffusion path in each hybrid corn maturity zone by fitting an S-shaped logistical trend function to data on the percentage of corn area planted with hybrid seed (Figure 5.2). The logistic trend function is described by three parameters—an origin, a slope, and a ceiling. Griliches used differences in the *slope*, which indicates the rate of acceptance, and the *ceiling*, which measures the percentage of acceptance at which the use of hybrid seed tended to stabilize, of the S-shaped logistic curve to measure changes in the acceptance or demand for hybrid maize seed. He interpreted his results as indicating that differences among regions in the rate (slope) and level (ceiling) of acceptance are both functions of the profitability of a shift from open-pollinated to hybrid corn.

For operational purposes Griliches identified the date of *origin* as the date at which a region began to plant 10% of its ceiling acreage to hybrid corn as an indicator of commercial availability or viability. The 10% level was chosen as the origin to indicate that the development had passed through the experimental stage and that superior hybrids were available to farmers in commercial quantities. The average

---

[4] For further review of the sociological tradition of adoption–diffusion research see Ruttan (1996).

[5] Griliches' study of the diffusion of hybrid corn (maize) was carried out as a Ph.D. thesis research study at the University of Chicago (Griliches, 1957, 1958).

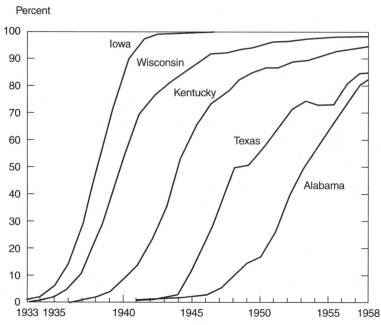

Percent

Figure 5.2 Percentage of all corn acreage planted to hybrid seed. (*Source:* Reprinted with permission from Zvi Griliches, "Hybrid Corn and Economics of Innovation, *Science* 132 (July 29, 1960):275–280. Copyright © 1960 American Association for the Advancement of Science.)

lag between technical availability, when hybrid seed was placed on the market, and commercial availability, using the 10% definition, was approximately 2 years. He attempted to explain variations in the date of origin or of commercial availability by the size and density of the hybrid seed market, estimated from the density of corn production in the region.

From this analysis Griliches concluded that the suppliers of the new hybrid seed technology, both public sector agricultural experiment stations and commercial seed companies, were guided by the expected returns to their investments in the research, development, and production of the hybrid seed. In spite of the lack of a direct market test of the returns to research and development, in the case of the publicly (USDA and state) supported experiment stations the "contribution of the various experiment stations is strongly related to the importance of corn in the area. In the 'good' corn areas the stations did a lot of work on hybrids and in the marginal areas, less" (Griliches, 1957:511).[6] The approach employed by Griliches was clearly consistent with the Usher cumulative synthesis model of research and development leading to a major

---

[6] The Griliches study triggered an extended debate about the relative significance of "sociological" and "economic" variables in the diffusion process. See Bradner and Straus (1959), Griliches (1960), Rogers and Haven (1962), Griliches (1962), Babcock (1962), and Klonglan and Coward (1970). Arrow (1969:33)

invention outlined in Chapter 3. The results were also consistent with the induced technical change model outlined in Chapter 5. Both growth of demand and changes in factor endowments acted to induce the invention and development of hybrid corn.

During the first third of the twentieth century U.S. agriculture was clearly experiencing diminishing returns to incremental "doses" of labor and capital applied to land. In an era in which animals, primarily horses, were the basic motive power for American agriculture corn and other feed grains were a primary source of energy in U.S. agriculture. Productivity growth in corn production was stymied until hybrid corn was invented. Between 1880 and the mid-1920s corn yields had remained essentially unchanged at approximately 27 bushels per acre. Corn prices rose sharply relative to the general price level between 1900 and 1920 (Hayami and Ruttan, 1985:214–219).

The stage was set by these economic changes to induce the research and development that led to the commercial availability of hybrid corn and to the adoption of hybrid corn by farmers. By the mid-1920s the constraints on growth of agricultural production imposed by an inelastic supply of land and relative stagnation in the production of feed and food grains in U.S. agriculture were being released by the invention of hybrid corn and improved varieties of other grain crops, the mechanization of motive power, and the sharply declining real costs of fertilizer.

DIFFUSION OF INDUSTRIAL TECHNOLOGY

A major program of research on the economics of industrial research and technical innovation was initiated by Edwin Mansfield in the early 1960s.[7] Both the conceptual framework and methodology employed by Mansfield were substantially influenced by the earlier research by the rural sociologists and Griliches in the diffusion of hybrid corn.

Mansfield's research was distinguished from that of Griliches, however, in that he considered the factors that influenced both interfirm and intrafirm rates of diffusion.[8] He initially examined the interfirm rates of adoption of 12 innovations in four industries—bituminous coal, iron and steel, brewing, and railroads. The innovations were the shuttle car, trackless mobile loader, and continuous mining machine in bituminous coal; the by-product coke oven, continuous wide-strip mill, and continuous annealing line for tin plate in iron and steel; the pallet-loading machine, tin container,

---

noted that "the economists are studying the demand for information by potential innovators and sociologists the problem of the supply of communication channels."

[7] Mansfield's research on diffusion of technology has been reported in a series of journal articles (Mansfield, 1961, 1963a, 1963b). For a definitive report see Mansfield (1968). For later work in the Griliches–Mansfield tradition see Nasbeth and Roy (1974), Davies (1979), and Stoneman (1983). The studies by Davies and Stoneman present highly formalized interpretations of the adoption–diffusion model.

[8] A second important distinction is that in the studies by Mansfield, and in most subsequent studies of industrial diffusion, the public sector was not an active participant in the diffusion process. More recently there has been renewed interest in the role of the public sector in the diffusion of industrial technology (Chapter 14), environmental technology (Kemp, 1997), and defense technology (Sidel, 1995).

and high-speed bottle filler in brewing; and the diesel locomotive, centralized traffic control, and car retarders in railroads.

The effect of these studies was to confirm, for the industries studied, the importance of the variables that accounted for adoption of hybrid corn—profitability and the proportion of firms already using the new technique. Mansfield's study also identified the size of the investment required (relative to the size of the firm) and the difference in industrial structure as influencing the rate of adoption (Mansfield, 1961).

Mansfield insisted that to understand how rapidly a new industrial technique displaces an old one it was important to understand not only the factors that determine the initial adoption decision but also the factors that influence the rate of intrafirm adoption. Because of its importance as a model for later studies of intrafirm diffusion, I present his study of the diffusion of the diesel locomotive in some detail.

Diffusion of the Diesel Locomotive

The first operational diesel locomotive made in the United States involved a joint effort by Ingersoll-Rand (which built the engine), General Electric (which made the components), and American Locomotive (which built the structure). It was introduced for demonstration purposes in 1924—11 years after the first diesel engine was introduced in Europe.

"The early diesel locomotives were heavy, slow and without much power. . . . They were usually adopted for use where there was a smoke nuisance or fire hazard. In 1933, General Motors came out with an improved locomotive that was smaller, faster and more powerful than previous types and in 1934 the era of diesel "streamliners" began. By 1935, 50 percent of the major American railroads had begun to use diesel locomotives" (Mansfield, 1968:174, 175). The innovators tended to be the larger rail lines. They tended to haul little coal. The "coal roads" were reluctant to adopt diesel locomotives partially because coal was relatively cheap for them and partially because they did not want to alienate their major customers.

By 1940 the diesel locomotive was widely used for switching purposes. There were, however, still questions regarding its maintenance costs and other factors governing its profitability. Adoption was delayed during World War II because of material shortages. By the end of the war diesels consisted of almost 10% of the total locomotive stock. Acceptance was widespread, but few firms expected diesels to completely displace the steam locomotives.

Mansfield notes, however, that

> several developments helped make the advantage of complete dieselization more obvious. *First,* further refinements were made in diesel design, and the price per horsepower of the diesel locomotive continued to decline relative to steam. *Second,* it became obvious that large savings could be effected by completely eliminating the facilities needed to service and repair steam locomotives. *Third,* the remaining uncertainties regarding the diesel locomotives performance and maintenance

were largely dispelled and the problems of training crews and ancillary personnel were met with the assistance of the locomotive manufacturers. (Mansfield,
1968:177)

The rates of replacement of steam by diesel locomotives varied widely among
different railroads. Among a group of 30 randomly selected Class I railroads an
average of 9 years was required to make the transition from 10% to 90% replacement
of steam by diesel. However, 20% of the firms made the transition from 10% to 90%
dieselization in 3 to 4 years. In contrast, 10% required 14 or more years to make the
transition (Table 5.1).

From his econometric analysis Mansfield concluded that a substantial part of the
variation in the intrafirm rate of diffusion was accounted for by "differences in the
profitability of investing in the diesel locomotive, interfirm differences in size and
liquidity, and interfirm differences in the date when the process of dieselization began.
Increases in each of these factors (other than firm size) resulted in increases in the
intrafirm rate of diffusion" (Mansfield, 1968:205).

In spite of the early contributions by Griliches and Mansfield, interest by economists
on research in diffusion of technology did not "take off" until well into the 1970s.
By the early 1980s, at the time when research on technology diffusion by sociologists had fallen off, research on diffusion by agricultural, industrial, and marketing
economists and by technologists began to experience explosive growth.[9] The research
by agricultural and other economists on diffusion of technology drew substantial
inspiration, at least initially, from the diffusion research by the rural sociologists.
Research by technologists was, however, much less self-conscious about drawing

Table 5.1   Time Interval for Rate of Replacement by Diesel Locomotives[a]

Time Interval (years)	Number of Firms[a]	Percentage of Firms
14 or more	3	10
11 to 13	7	23
8 to 10	11	37
5 to 7	3	10
3 to 4	6	20
Total	30	100

[a] Time interval between date when diesel locomotives were 10% of all locomotives and date when they were 90% of all
locomotives: 30 randomly chosen Class I railroads.

Source: Edwin Mansfield, *Industrial Research and Technological Innovation: An Econometric Analysis*, New York: W.
W. Norton, 1968:178. (After Interstate Commerce Commission, *Statistics of Railways*, 1925:61.) Copyright © 1968 by
W. W. Norton & Company, Inc. Reprinted by permission of W. W. Norton & Company, Inc.

---

[9] For reviews by economists see Gold (1981), Feder et al. (1985), Thirtle and Ruttan (1987), Metcalf
(1982), Soete (1985), and Karshenas and Stonesman (1995). For reviews by technologists, see Grübler
(1991a, 1991b, 1998).

on the earlier sociological literature. By the mid-1980s, an increasing share of the literature on diffusion was being produced in Western Europe at institutions such as the Science Policy Research Unit (SPRU) at Sussex in the United Kingdom, the International Institute for Applied Systems Analysis (IIASA) in Austria, and the Maastricht Economic Research Institute on Innovation and Policy (MERIT) in the Netherlands. Just as sociologists have been little influenced by the research on diffusion by economists, recent research by economists and technologists has progressed with little reference to the earlier research by sociologists.

Diffusion was first viewed as a *unary* process—that is describing the diffusion of an innovation only by isolated measures such as the number of adopters. In a next step, studies analyzed diffusion as a *binary* process of substitution for other processes or products available on the market. Finally, studies analyzed diffusion as a *multivariate phenomenon* involving a number of competing alternatives with changing relative market shares.

The early studies on hybrid corn reviewed previously in this chapter treated what was essentially a binary process (replacement of open-pollinated by hybrid corn) as a unary process—the adoption and diffusion of a superior technology. The replacement of the steam by the diesel locomotive was, however, analyzed as a binary process. The replacement of draft animals by automobiles in the United States is another example of a largely binary process (Figure 5.3). The environment in which diffusion phenomena are embedded is only rarely so simple as to allow for a unary or a binary view of the diffusion process. Most major changes in technology are characterized by a sequence of introduction, diffusion, and in turn replacement of a number of innovations, several of which compete simultaneously on the market. The multivariate diffusion process is illustrated in Figure 5.4. Four different steel technologies, with decreasing and increasing market shares, were competing for market shares over long periods of time. Note that although adoption externalities allow for an initial rapid expansion of market share below the 10% threshold, there is an inverse phenomenon at the end of the life cycle of a technology. Old technologies appear—after a period of steady (logistical) decline in market share—to retreat at a slower rate from the last few percent market shares. In the following section I discuss the introduction and diffusion of the basic oxygen steel process in greater detail.

The Basic Oxygen Steel Case[10]

After World War II, engineers at the Linz steel complex in Austria began a series of experiments concerning the use of oxygen in steel production. The basic idea behind these experiments dates back to Bessemer's work in the mid-nineteenth century. But because low-cost oxygen was not available (and for other reasons), this idea was

---

[10] In this section I draw on Ray (1969); Oster (1982), and Grübler (1991a).

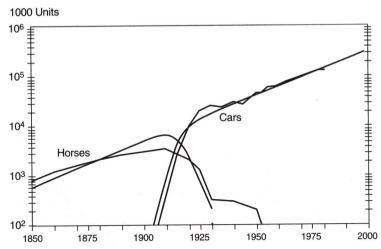

Figure 5.3 Number of horses and cars in the United States. (*Source:* Reprinted from *Technological Forecasting and Social Change,* 39, Arnulf Grübler, "Diffusion: Long-Term Patterns and Discontinuties," p. 162. Copyright © 1991, with permission from Elsevier Science.)

not applied widely until after World War II. After a series of unsuccessful attempts, Austrian engineers were able in 1949 to produce good quality steel without damaging the vessel or destroying the lance. In 1952, they went from a 2-ton vessel to a 35-ton vessel, and in 1953 they established a second plant at Donawitz. From Linz–Donawitz, the procedure acquired it name—the LD process. After the advent of the 35-ton oxygen converter, numerous improvements and extensions were carried out, particularly to widen the product mix and to make the process suitable for high phosphorus ores.

The LD oxygen converter must be charged with hot metal, and thus must be located near a blast furnace. Scrap is charged first, after which the molten ore is poured in. The vessel is then put back in an upright position, and the lance is lowered until it is 4–8 feet above the metal. The lance, a tube about 50 feet long and 10 inches in diameter, is water cooled to withstand the furnace heat. It injects oxygen of 99.5% purity, which results in oxidation burning of part of the iron and nearly all of the carbon, manganese, phosphorus, and silicon impurities. When the carbon is gone, the fire burns out. Oxygen converters must have a charge made up of 70–75% or more of hot metal, which means that a maximum of 30% can be scrap. This was in contrast to the current practice of using 50% scrap in open-hearth furnaces and up to 90% in electric furnaces.

The oxygen process is frequently, but not always, cheaper than open-hearth or electric furnaces. An important point in its favor is that the capital cost of an oxygen converter is only about one-half of the capital cost of an open hearth. However, if a blast furnace is not already nearby, this cost advantage may be offset. Moreover,

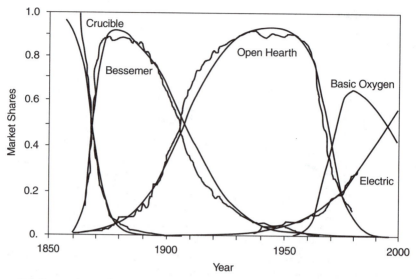

Figure 5.4 Successive replacements of process technologies for raw steel production in the United States (in factional share of raw tonnage of steel produced). (*Source:* Reprinted from *Technological Forecasting and Social Change,* 39, Arnulf Grübler, "Diffusion: Long-Term Patterns and Discontinuities," Copyright © 1991, with permission from Elsevier Science.)

the capital cost of an electric furnace can, under some circumstances, be lower than either oxygen converters or open hearths. Nonetheless, the lower capital cost of the oxygen process has been an important factor in its displacement of the open hearth. For example, in the late 1950s, it was estimated that the capital cost of the basic oxygen process was about $15 per ton, as compared with about $40 per ton for an open hearth.

Another factor affecting the profitability of the oxygen process is the price of scrap. As noted above, oxygen converters use less scrap than open hearths and electric furnaces. Thus, a higher relative price of scrap will raise the cost of production of open hearths relative to that of oxygen converters. At low scrap prices, electric furnaces may have lower production costs than oxygen converters, particularly if the scale of operations is small. But if the scale is large, oxygen converters seem to have lower costs than open-hearth or electric furnaces, even if scrap prices are relatively low. The total cost of producing 1.5 million tons of ingot per year was about 11% lower for the basic oxygen process than for an open hearth in 1962.

Figure 5.4 indicates that the oxygen process accounted for less than 5% of U.S. steel production before 1960 and close to 60% by 1980. Clearly, the oxygen process steadily displaced earlier steel-making techniques in the United States. Whether this diffusion process has occurred as rapidly as it should is a matter of controversy. Some observers have insisted that the American steel industry was relatively slow in introducing the oxygen process. However, the steel producers have denied this charge. And a study by Tsao and Day (1971) concluded that the diffusion rate was close to optimal.

Patterns of diffusion of basic oxygen steel in 11 countries from 1956 to 1968 is shown in Figure 5.5. The percentage of total steel output produced by the oxygen process in 1969 was highest in Austria, Japan, and the Netherlands, and lowest in France, the United Kingdom, and Italy. Relative to this group of countries, the U.S. percentage was about in the middle. Of course, one reason for the rapid rate of acceptance in Austria was the fact that the process originated there. In Japan and the Netherlands, the relatively quick transition to the oxygen process was due in part to the fact that the Japanese and Dutch steel industries were expanding more rapidly than the steel industries in the other counties during this period. They could add oxygen converters to expand their capacity, whereas in other countries oxygen converters were more likely used to replace existing capacity.

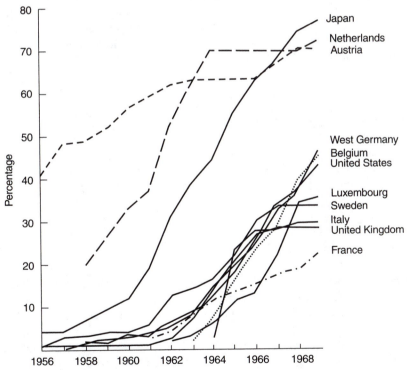

Figure 5.5 Shares of basic oxygen steel in total crude steel output. (*Source:* L. Nasbeth and G. F. Roy, *The Diffusion of New Industrial Process: An International Study*, Cambridge: Cambridge University Press, 1974:153. Reprinted with the permission of Cambridge University Press.)

NEW THEORY AND NEW METHOD

As research on diffusion evolved the economists became engaged in an increasingly intensive theoretical and methodological dialogue. Explicit attention was given to recent theoretical developments and to the formalization of production, human capital, market, and spatial relationships. Attention was also given to the issues of congruence between the implications of the formal theory and the statistical or econometric models used for testing and estimation (Feder et al., 1985; Silverberg, 1991). Economists also became concerned with additional dimensions of adoption such as intensity of use and complementarity among closely related innovations (Smale et al., 1995). They extended the reinvention concept to include the continuous flow of improvements by the suppliers of technology and to the development of unified models of the invention–diffusion process (Thirtle and Ruttan, 1987; Knudson and Ruttan, 1988). Economists also began to give increasing attention to the international diffusion of technology (Vernon, 1966, 1979; Hayami and Ruttan, 1985; Soete, 1985).

Since the late 1970s there has emerged a "second generation" of diffusion research by economists and technologists that departs substantially from the initial Griliches–Mansfield approach. This research falls into two broad classes: (1) research that employs conventional microeconomic equilibrium models and (2) research that employs a newer set of evolutionary models (Thirtle and Ruttan, 1987:108–124; Lissoni and Metcalf, 1994; Karshenas and Stoneman, 1995).

Equilibrium Models

In the "equilibrium models" diffusion is seen as a transition between equilibria levels, defined by changing economic attributes (e.g., costs, prices), and a changing environment (e.g., differences in market structure). Diffusion is interpreted less as a learning phenomenon than as a result of the interaction of changes in the innovation and adoption environment (i.e., the interaction between suppliers and customers of an innovation) (Grübler, 1991:26).

An important second-stage innovation has been the further adaptation of the sociological diffusion models by marketing economists to forecast consumer demand. Demand for consumer durables was modeled and estimated as a function of (1) a coefficient of innovation, which measures the number of initial innovators buying a product, (2) a coefficient of imitation, which is intended to capture the behavior of the population assumed to be imitating the behavior of the rest of the population, and (3) an index of market potential to reflect the ceiling on market penetration. Individuals adopting the new product because of mass media are concentrated in the early postintroduction period (Bass, 1969, 1980; Rogers, 1995:79–83).[11] Recent studies by agricultural economists working in developing countries have given increased

---

[11] For an exceedingly useful review of diffusion research in marketing, building on the initial research by Bass, see Mahajan et al. (1990).

attention to subjective food quality preferences by producers in the adoption of new technology. Adesina and Baidu-Forson (1995) found that adoption of improved sorghum varieties in Burkina Faso was influenced by perception of quality for making a local porridge and of improved varieties in Guinea by perception of ease of cooking.

Another important innovation within the equilibrium tradition has been the conceptualization by technologists of the process of technological change as a substitution rather than a diffusion phenomenal. The focus in this research has been on the changing relative share of competing technologies. In models in which several technologies are competing, each technology undergoes three distinct phases in terms of market share—logistic growth, nonlogistic saturation, and logistic decline. Substitution models have been developed most fully and applied most extensively by Nakićenović and several colleagues at the International Institute for Applied Systems Analysis (IIASA).[12] A primary motivation has been the use of such models in technology assessment and forecasting.

The more radical applications of the equilibrium approach completely abandon the communication model. Diffusion takes time not because information is imperfect (or because contigation takes time) but because the new technology is initially not superior to existing technology for some potential adopters or uses. Firms are assumed to behave optimally. Thus firms that have not adopted the new technology are not ill informed or behaving irrationally but are simply waiting for the optimal timing of adoption (Lissoni and Metcalf, 1994; Chari and Hopenhayen, 1991). Intellectual links with the sociological origins of diffusion research were completely severed.

In spite of substantial advances in both the theoretical and methodological sophistication, Grübler notes that the equilibrium models continue to be criticized on several counts: (1) the mathematical properties and economic rationale for the application of the logistic model to the diffusion process; (2) the binary nature of most diffusion models and the static assumption on size of potential adopters; and (3) a narrow definition of the group of influencing variables (Grübler, 1991:14). It is rather striking that Grübler's criticisms of the diffusion research by industrial economists and technologists as well as the earlier criticism of diffusion research by agricultural economists by Feder et al. (1985) are remarkably similar to the early criticisms by rural sociologists of the methodological limitations of the early sociological literature (Lionberger, 1960). It is also significant that in spite of the criticisms that use of the S-shaped logistic curve lacks adequate grounding in either microeconomic or communication theory, efforts to dislodge it have been unsuccessful. It has remained remarkably robust as a description of both the diffusion and the substitution processes. Attention continues to be focused, as in the early Griliches study, on explaining the parameters of the diffusion curve.

---

[12] Substitution models for two technologies (old and new) were developed by Fisher and Prey (1971). For an extension of the Fisher–Prey model to incorporate multiple substitution, see Marchette and Nakiénović (1979).

Evolutionary Models

The evolutionary models attempt to remedy a number of the perceived limitations of the equilibrium models. They describe diffusion as an evolutionary process under conditions of uncertainty, diversity of economic agents, and disequilibrium dynamics. And they try to model the complex feedback mechanisms at work at the microlevel among economic agents. In these models, the structural changes induced by the diffusion of an innovation are influenced by changing technological and behavioral diversity, learning, and selection mechanisms. These, together with their interrelated feedbacks, generate continuous adjustment processes to a changing technological environment and result in ordered evolutionary paths at the macro (industry) level. The basic task in the development of an evolutionary or, more appropriately, a self-organizing model consists in representing the feedback loops between the structure of an industry, the behavior of firms, and the evolution of the industry (Grübler, 1991:8, 29; Lissoni and Metcalf, 1994:120–126; Katz and Shapiro, 1986; Arthur and Lane, 1994; Dosi et al., 1986; Silverberg et al., 1988).

Giovanni Dosi and his colleagues at IIASA have outlined an exceedingly ambitious agenda for the evolutionary modeling of the innovation–imitation–diffusion process. They accept the challenge that earlier research had given inadequate attention to the interactions among technology development and diffusion. A fully developed evolutionary model should be capable of incorporating the characteristics of each technology (sources of basic knowledge; degrees of appropriability and tacitness of innovation, complexity of research, production, and products; and the existence and role of various forms of economies of scale and cumulativeness of technological learning). It should also be able to incorporate the degrees and forms of diversity between economic agents (including their technological capabilities and variety of search procedures and behavioral rules) and the endogenous evolution of incentives, constraints, and selection mechanisms (including the evolution of relative profitabilities of different technologies, firm sizes, cash flows, and market shares) (Dosi et al., 1986:8, 9).

In practice substantial compromise, when compared with the above objectives, has been necessary. Nevertheless, Dosi and his colleagues have been able to develop simulation models incorporating capital stock innovations that generate industry-level diffusion curves similar to those that describe historical industry diffusion patterns. They have also been able to clarify the implications of firm-level differential adoption strategies under alternative assumptions about appropriability of outcomes such as market share and firm survival and about how firm-level behavior generates this industry-level diffusion curves.

In his evaluation of recent progress in the development of evolutionary models, which he regards as more promising than the equilibrium models, Grübler notes that the outcome of a simulation run is the result of the particular technological, market, and behavioral variables assumed. He argues that it is premature to discuss the results of a simulation in terms of how well it represents reality. Instead the model demonstrates only the dynamic behavior of such an evolutionary self-organizing system. The main lesson to be learned is that the dynamic interaction between the macrolevel and microlevel in such a system leads to the emergence of spatial and temporal patterns that are driven, rather than dissipated, by microlevel diversity. From this perspective, regularity in evolutionary paths at the macrolevel is not a contradiction but rather a consequence of the diversity of technological expectations, designs, dynamic appropriability, and behavior of economic agents (Grübler, 1991:37, 38). Chari and Hopenhayen (1991) suggested that the next step in the development of equilibrium models should be a model in which technical innovation and adoption are jointly and endogenously determined. My sense is that the development of such a model would eliminate most of the defining distinctions between the equilibrium and evolutionary models.

THE PRODUCT CYCLE AND INTERNATIONAL TRADE

By the mid-1960s increasing attention was being given to attempts to understand the role of the "technology factor" in international trade.[13] Economists initially attempted to understand the reasons leading to the transfer of technology by U.S.-based multinational firms to their foreign subsidiaries. Later this interest was extended to attempts to understand the growth of exports from other high-income countries of products originally developed in the United States, both by the subsidiaries of U.S. multinational firms and by national firms located in other countries. During the 1990s, advances in endogenous growth theory stimulated a renewed interest in the relationships between international trade and the diffusion of technology (Grossman and Helpman, 1991; Chapter 2).

In 1966 Raymond Vernon of the Harvard Business School proposed a "product cycle" model to explain why new products tended to be first invented and produced in the United States, why foreign production facilities were established by the innovating firms, and why this was followed by exports back to the United States (Vernon, 1966). Vernon argued that the United States market offered unique opportunities for the new consumer durables.

The United States market consisted of a large number of consumers with incomes higher than in any other national market. In the mid-1960s U.S. average per capita incomes were twice as high as in Western Europe. Thus, the United States offered a unique market opportunity for products responsive to the wants of high-income consumers. The United States was characterized by high (and rising) labor costs, abundant capital, and highly developed capital markets. This provided an opportunity for the development of both labor-saving consumer durables (such as washing machines and dish washers) and producer durables (such as fork lift trucks and automatic control systems).

---

[13] The seminal contribution was Vernon (1966). See also Gruber and Marquis (1969), and Vernon (1970).

Vernon noted that although these two factors help explain why new products designed for high-income consumers or to save labor were initially invented in the United States, they did not explain why the new products were first produced in the United States rather than in a lower wage location. His explanation is in terms of the evolution of product technology and design during its early stages of the product cycle.

> The product itself may be quite unstandardized for a time; its inputs, its processing, and its final specifications may cover a wide range. Contrast the great variety of automobiles produced and marketed before 1910 with the thoroughly standardized product of the 1930s, or the variegated radio designs of the 1920s with the uniform models of the 1930s. (Vernon, 1966:195)

During the initial stage in the product cycle feedback from the market with respect to consumer preferences is exceedingly important. Engineers highly skilled in product design and a labor force that can efficiently implement the new production technology are also important. These considerations argue for a location in which communication between all those involved in the success of the new product—engineers, research and development personnel, suppliers, financial institutions, and consumers—is rapid and effective.

As demand for a product expands, a "technological trajectory" becomes established, designs become standardized, the need for flexibility declines, mass production becomes feasible, and concerns about cost of production, particularly labor costs, become more important. If the product has a high-income elasticity of demand or is an effective substitute for labor, demand will grow in other countries in which income is converging toward U.S. levels (Chapter 2). This demand from abroad will first be met by exporting from the United States and later, as demand continues to grow, by establishing subsidiaries or by entering into joint venture arrangements with firms in other advanced countries. As production expands, in Western Europe or Japan, for example, it may become advantageous to service third world country markets from the new location. If labor costs are low enough the next stage will be to export the products, transistor radios and hand calculators, for example, back to the United States. A third stage occurs when production capacity is established in low-income countries to take advantage of even lower costs. Production in the low-income countries may initially include only labor-intensive components. But the establishment of such capacity often involves substantial human capital investment and a "learning-by-doing" element that leads to the establishment of firms that are able to compete with producers in the innovating countries. The transfer of memory chip technology from the United States to Japan and later to Korea is an example (Chapter 10). The stages of product development and trade are outlined in Figure 5.6.

Within a decade serious questions were being raised about the relevance of the product cycle model.[14] The income gap between the United States and other devel-

---

[14] See, for example, Giddy (1978). For a response see Vernon (1979).

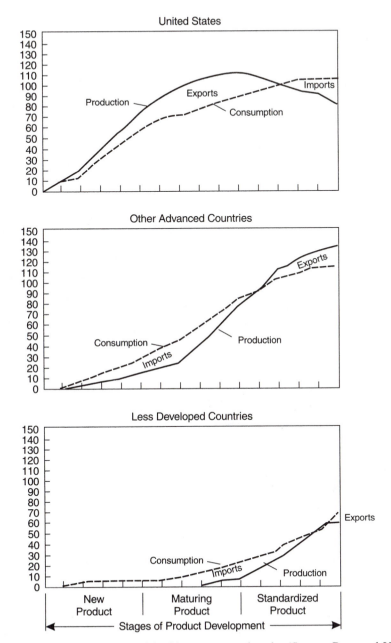

Figure 5.6 The product cycle model of investment and trade. (*Source:* Raymond Vernon, "International Investment and International Trade in the Product Cycle," *Quarterly Journal of Economics* 80 (May 1966):19.)

oping countries had narrowed or disappeared. The economic environment in these countries was as conducive as in the United States to the development of high-income elasticity of demand consumer goods and labor-saving producers equipment. Some of the consumer goods also found markets among the new middle classes in the developing countries and the cost savings of some labor-saving and information equipment are so large that they respond to an almost homogeneous world market. Examples include automobiles, aircraft, computers, and pharmaceuticals. Such firms, producing for a global market,

> can be exported to maintain the central core of their innovative activities close to headquarters where complex face-to-face consultation among key personnel will be possible; in this respect such firms are likely to perform in a manner consistent with the product cycle pattern. Firms in this category, in response to the pressures of host governments, are commonly prepared to establish carefully selected development activities in countries in which they hope to do business. (Vernon, 1979:262, 263)

The product cycle model has also been modified to interpret the "product life cycle." Initially, product innovations are designed to expand the market by attracting new buyers. As product designs stabilize the number of firms in the industry declines, firm size grows, and market share stabilizes. The ability to profit from cost-reducing process innovations increases as firm size increases. At this stage the firm may also find it profitable to transfer operations to developing countries characterized by lower labor or material costs (Klepper, 1996).

ENDOGENOUS GROWTH AND TECHNOLOGY TRANSFER

One of the most important spillover effects of the endogenous growth literature of the 1990s was an attempt to explore the relationships between trade and growth. Technology transfer plays an important role in this literature (Grossman and Helpman, 1991; Coe et al., 1997:134–149; and Parente and Prescott, 2000). In their several works Grossman and Helpman abandon the assumption, employed in neoclassical growth theory, that technological opportunities are the same throughout the world. They insist that the process of assimilating existing technologies in the less developed countries is not unlike that of creating entirely new technologies in the developed world. Countries in which technological research is carried out acquire a comparative advantage in the form of human capital endowments.

Starting from these more realistic assumptions, Grossman and Helpman proceed to show how external relationships affect a country's growth performance: (1) international exchange opens channels of communication that facilitate the transmission of technical information; (2) international competition encourages entrepreneurs in trading countries to pursue new ideas and new technology; (3) international integration enlarges the size of the market in which innovative firms operate; and (4) international trade induces a reallocation of resources. In this process countries can lose as well as gain from trade. Countries with a large high technology sector (and labor with a high human capital component) may experience long-term gains relative to countries with abundant supplies of raw labor (Grossman and Helpman, 1991:237–238).

In a world in which the Grossman–Helpman assumptions hold, there can be a substantial role for technology policy (Chapter 13). A favorable intellectual property regime can encourage the transfer of technology by multinational firms. Strategic investments in education and in R&D can be used to create an institutional infrastructure that encourages technology transfer (Box 8.1).

THE COSTS OF TECHNOLOGY TRANSFER

A clear implication of the endogenous growth literature is, however, that technology transfer and adoption are not costless. Transfer of agricultural technology or the technology required to exploit natural resources often requires substantial adaptation reinvention to become economically viable. Just as new corn hybrids had to be developed for different agroclimatic zones in the United States, the new hybrids or new varieties had to be developed for specific agroclimatic zones in other countries. Similarly, as implied by the induced technical change model, the transfer of industrial technology often has to be reengineered to take advantage of lower cost labor or local raw materials in order to be economically viable. In many cases international transfer of technology requires the development of research and development capacity and the transfer of scientists, engineers, and agronomists before the new technology can be developed or adopted to become economically viable in a host country.

The industrial technology transfer process involves a number of cost elements over and above the direct cost of the capital equipment. These include (1) preengineering technological negotiation and exchange, (2) engineering costs associated with the transfer of process design and engineering, (3) exchanges of research and development personnel, and (4) pre-start-up training and debugging costs. Each of these cost categories reflects intensive inputs of human capital. Several institutional characteristics influence the cost and success of the transfer: (1) the extent to which the technology is completely understood by the transfer personnel of the firm that is the source of the technology; (2) the age of the technology and the extent to which it has stabilized; (3) the extent of experience with the technology by different firms and under different economic environments; and (4) the level or interest of research and development of physical and institutional infrastructures in the host country (Teece, 1977; Reddy and Zhao, 1990; Leonard-Benton, 1995).

In considering costs, it is useful to distinguish among three types of technology transfer: (1) material transfer, (2) design transfer, and (3) capacity transfer (Hayami and Ruttan, 1985:260–262). Material transfer is characterized by the simple import of materials such as seeds, machines, and entire "turn-key" factories. Local adaptation or reengineering of the borrowed technology is not attempted. The second type is the transfer of technology primarily through the transfer of designs in the form of blueprints, formulas, handbooks, and others. Exotic plant material or foreign equipment may be imported primarily for purposes of reverse engineering. This typically requires engineering capacity more advanced than simple material transfer.

The third type of technology transfer involves the transfer of scientific knowledge and technical capacity or capability.[15] The development of technological capacity often requires not only the strengthening of national education facilities that provide the trained labor force required for technology transfer but also the strengthening of the scientific and technical capacity necessary to adapt the technology for use of local material resources and to the local economic environment. As technology becomes more sophisticated, firms are better able to absorb advanced technology, adapt it to local factor endowments, and realize higher levels of productivity, if they have already acquired internal R&D capacity (Cohen and Leventhal, 1989). All three levels of transfer may be involved as a foreign subsidiary develops over time (Box 5.1 and Box 8.1).

In many academic discussions of technology transfer it is often assumed that more open global markets, more rapid transportation, and almost instant communication have conspired to make technical knowledge and capability freely available on a global basis. Yet there continues to be substantial clustering of industrial innovation and location based on endowments of human capital and technical and institutional infrastructure (Porter, 1998). An example is the cluster of high fashion leather goods firms in Northern Italy. The industry is supported by sophisticated design capability; by suppliers of material, components, and equipment; and by marketing and media services. In the United States examples of such clusters include the concentration of the medical devices industry in Minnesota, the household furniture industry in North Carolina, and biotechnology firms in the San Francisco area. The dominance of such clusters is reinforced by the diffusion of tacit technical knowledge within the cluster areas. Although world scientific knowledge has the characteristic of a public good, the tacit character of much technical knowledge can represent a major obstacle to the rapid interregional or international transfer of technical capability. This point has been made more sharply by Ronald Findlay (1978:1), "While the book of blueprints, in some abstract sense, may be open to the world as a whole, one may have to pay a stiff price to look at some of the pages."

---

[15] Technological capacity or capability includes the stock of skills and competencies necessary to evaluate and utilize scientific and technical information. This includes the tacit knowledge about production processes that cannot be transferred in the form of capital equipment or designs (Arora, 1992:23–28).

● BOX 5.1
HEWLETT-PACKARD IN SINGAPORE

The Early Days

In the late 1960s, a high-level team of managers from Hewlett-Packard (HP) investigated potential manufacturing sites in Asia. According to trip leader John Doyle, Singapore appealed to the team because "the government was stable, understanding, responsive, reliable, and honest. Potential employees seemed to be energetic, educated, honest, creative—and they spoke English, which would help build team cohesion." To take advantage of the low cost of labor in the region, HP started operations with the extremely labor-intensive stringing of computer core memories. In 1973, the company switched Singapore operations to the assembly of the HP-35 calculators, and by 1977, the facility was also producing computer keyboards, solid-state displays, integrated circuits, and isolators. All of these products were designed, developed, and initially manufactured in the United States before being transferred to Singapore for production.

The 1980s

In 1981, when Hewlett-Packard moved some production of the sophisticated HP41C handheld programmable calculators to Computer Products Singapore (CPS), CPS proposed conducting a cost-reduction program. Since one of the opportunities for lowering cost involved reducing the number of integrated circuits, CPS set up a center to work on designing application-specific integrated circuits (ASICs). As a Chinese manager recalled, "Without the design capability and the ability to do chip integration, whatever cost-reduction plan we had might not have happened." A group of 20 CPS engineers and technicians went to the United States for more than a year to learn ASIC design. On their return, they succeeded in reducing the number of integrated circuits in the calculator.

In 1983, production of HP's first ink-jet printer (the "ThinkJet") was transferred to Singapore. When it was manufactured in the United States, 80% of the parts came from U.S. or European vendors. After transfer to Singapore, 80% were sourced in Asia. The assembly was highly automated. Engineering Manager Lim Kok Khoon recalled, "Line processes now became critical. Before, when we produced at low volume, stopping the line was no big deal. But now inventory would pile up fast. Quality became a significant issue, and logistics were critical." CPS implemented statistical quality control and went to a just-in-time inventory system. In the period from 1984 to 1985, the manufacturing costs for the ThinkJet declined by 30%. One-third of the savings was attributable to line efficiencies and the rest to lower Singapore overhead, quality improvements, and lower-cost materials sourcing.

Source: Adapted from Dorothy Leonard-Barton, *Wellsprings of Knowledge: Building and Sustaining the Sources of Innovation,* Boston, MA: Harvard Business School, 1995:224, 230–231.

RESISTANCE TO TECHNOLOGY

Much of the technology adoption–diffusion research reviewed in this chapter has employed an implicit assumption that new technology will be adopted if it passes the market test of profitability. Delays in diffusion, captured in the S-shaped adoption curve, are assumed to be the result of psychological, sociological, and structural factors that may delay, but not prevent, the diffusion of profitable technology. Much of diffusion research has been conducted with the objective of loosening the constraints that dampen the rate of diffusion.

There has also been a smaller literature dealing with resistance or barriers to the diffusion of technology.[16] A continuing theme in economic history has been the large and persistent differences in output per worker among countries in the textile industry, even when using identical technology (Clark, 1987:141–173). One motivation for resistance has been the economic interest of workers in protecting their jobs or the conditions of employment and of industry for protection against the "creative destruction" of technological competition. There is a tradition running back to the early days of the industrial revolution of resistance to labor-saving technology on the part of workers who feared their jobs would be displaced by machines (Randall, 1991). Protest by workers against the introduction of textile machines and low wages in Britain between 1811 and 1816 gave rise to the term Luddite, after the legendary leader of the protests, as a generic term of denigration for antitechnology protests.

A second motivation has been criticism or resistance by intellectuals fearful of the impact of technical change on social organization, civic culture, and human and natural environments. Throughout most of U.S. history technical change was viewed by both the general public and by intellectuals as an instrument not only of economic progress but of social and cultural development. Monumental public works such as Hoover Dan, the great skyscrapers that punctured the sky in our large cities, and the electricity-driven machinery in our factories were viewed both as aesthetically pleasing and as a sign of the vitality of U.S. culture. This optimism began to undergo a radical change

---

[16] This literature has been reviewed by Mokyr (1994, 1998). See also Bauer (1995). For an attempt to explain differences in levels of per capita income among countries in terms of barriers to trade enacted by interest groups and government see Parente and Prescott (2000).

in the first decades after World War II.[17] A perspective emerged among intellectuals that technology dehumanizes the link between labor and production, that increased specialization and professionalism are responsible for deepening class divisions and inequality, that technology is responsible for the increasing cataclysm of war, that the transfer of technology from advanced to poor countries will be accompanied by political domination, that technical change is destructive of cultural values and communal relations, and that technological change results in negative environmental externalities.

Over the long term resistance to technology has seldom been successful. The Luddites have usually lost! Nuclear power is one of the few modern examples of a major on-line technology that has been successfully challenged by protest movements (Rucht, 1995:277–291). But even unsuccessful protest movements have led to important social reforms. Among the more important have been labor market reforms, regulation of food and drugs, and legislation designed to limit the negative environmental spillover effects of agricultural and industrial intensification. When protests have been successful in bringing about reform it is generally because they have been able to mobilize substantial political resources. In later chapters these issues are discussed with specific reference to agriculture (Chapter 6), energy (Chapter 7), biotechnology (Chapter 10), and the environment (Chapter 12).

PERSPECTIVE

Substantial progress has been made in our understanding of technology adoption, diffusion, and transfer. Yet the S-shaped logistic diffusion curve has remained re-markably robust as a description of the technology diffusion and the substitution processes.[18]

Advances in theory and method have contributed to improvements in our understanding of the timing of initial adoption, the rate of diffusion, and the limits (or ceiling) to adoption or replacement. In the early studies of adoption and diffusion by sociologists considerable attention was given to the personality characteristics of the firm operator or manager. The studies of economists have traditionally focused primarily on the impersonal forces of the market. More recent studies in the new

---

[17] For a dramatic example of this change in perspective, it is useful to compare the early and later work of Lewis Mumford. His writing of the 1920s, exemplified by *Technics and Civilization* (1934), presents an optimistic view of the impact of technical change. His later work, exemplified by *The Pentagon of Power* (1964), was deeply pessimistic about social, cultural, and political effects of technical change (Hughes and Hughes, 1990).

[18] There is also a small literature that suggests that the diffusion of institutional innovations, including the diffusion of diffusion studies, follows an S-shaped time path similar to the path followed by the diffusion of technology (Nakićenović and Grübler, 1991; Rogers, 1995:45; Grübler, 1998:56–58). It is somewhat surprising that sociologists, who have contributed so much to our understanding of the diffusion of technology, have contributed so little to knowledge about the diffusion of social institutions.

age of mergers and takeovers give renewed attention to "corporate culture," tacit knowledge, and the idiosyncratic behavior of corporate management.

The product cycle clearly provided very powerful insight into the process of international diffusion of technology and the composition of foreign direct investment during the first two decades after World War II. But the United States no longer plays as dominant a role in the generation of income elastic consumer goods or labor-saving technical change as in the past. New products and new processes are transformed more rapidly than in the past among firms and across national borders. But if the product cycle is extended to include the entire "convergence club" of developed nations (Chapter 2), the model still provides powerful insight into the international transfer of technology.

In spite of advances in theory and methodology the effectiveness of communication networks and profitability continue to be recognized as primary factors affecting adoption, diffusion, and transfer. International technology transfer is limited or enhanced by the extent to which markets are open or by the extent of market intervention by governments. There is, however, increasing awareness of the constraints imposed on technology transfer by the importance of tacit knowledge in technical capability.

REFERENCES

Adesina, A. A., and J. Baidu-Forson. "Farmers Perception and Adoption of New Agricultural Technology: Evidence from Analyses in Burkina Faso and Guinea, West Africa." *Agricultural Economics* 13 (1995):1–9.

Arora, A. *Tacit Knowledge, Technology Licensing, and the Acquisition of Technological Capability*. Stanford, CA: Stanford University Ph.D. Thesis, 1992.

Arrow, K. J. "Classification Notes on the Production and Transmission of Technological Knowledge." *American Economic Review* 59 (1969):29–35.

Arthur, W.B., and D.A. Lane. "Information Contigation." In *Increasing Returns and Path Dependence in the Economy,* W. B. Arthur, ed., pp. 69–97. Ann Arbor, MI: University of Michigan Press, 1994.

Babcock, J. M. "Adoption of Hybrid Corn: A Comment." *Rural Sociology* 27 (1962):332–338.

Bass, F. M. "A New Product Growth Model of Consumer Durables." *Management Science* 5 (1969):215–227.

Bass, F. M. "The Relationship Between Diffusion Rates, Experience Curves and Demand Elasticities for Consumer Durable Technological Innovations." *Journal of Business* 53 (1980):51–67.

Bauer, M., ed. *Resistance to New Technology.* Cambridge: Cambridge University Press, 1995.

Beal, G. M., and J. M. Bohlen. *The Diffusion Process.* Ames, IA: Iowa State Agricultural Experiment Station, Special Report, 1957.

Bradner, L., and M. A. Straus. "Congruence Versus Profitability in the Diffusion of Hybrid Sorghum." *Rural Sociology* 24 (1959):381–383.

Chari, V. V., and H. Hopenhayen. "Vintage Human Capital, Growth and the Diffusion of New Technology." *Journal of Political Economy* 99 (1991):1142–1165.

Clark, G. "Why Isn't the Whole World Developed? Lessons from the Cotton Mills." *Journal of Economic History* 67 (1987):141–173.

Coe, D., E. Helpman, and A. W. Hoffmaister. "North South R&D Spillovers." *The Economic Journal* 107 (1997):134–149.

Cohen, W. M., and D. A. Leventhal. "Innovation and Learning: The Two Faces of R&D." *Economic Journal* 99 (1989):569–596.

Crane, D. *Invisible Colleges: Diffusion of Knowledge in Scientific Communities.* Chicago, IL: University of Chicago Press, 1972.

Davies, S. *The Diffusion of Process Innovations.* Cambridge, UK: Cambridge University Press, 1979.

Dosi, G., L. Orsenigo, and G. Silverberg. *Innovation Diversity and Diffusion: A Self-Organization Model.* Sussex, UK: University of Sussex Science Policy Research Unit, 1986.

Feder, G., R. E. Just, and D. Zilberman. "Adoption of Agricultural Innovations in Developing Countries: A Survey." *Economic Development and Cultural Change* 33 (1985):255–298.

Findlay, R. "Relative Backwardness, Direct Foreign Investment, and the Transfer of Technology: A Simple Dynamic Model." *Quarterly Journal of Economics* 42 (1978):1–16.

Fisher, J. C., and R. H. Prey. "A Simple Substitution Model of Technological Change." *Technological Forecasting and Social Change* 3 (1971):75–88.

Giddy, I. H. "The Demise of the Product Cycle Model." *International Business Theory* 7 (1978):90–97.

Gold, B. "Technological Diffusion in Industry: Research Needs and Shortcomings." *Journal of Industrial Economics* 29 (1981):247–269.

Griliches, Z. "Hybrid Corn: An Exploration of the Economics of Technical Change." *Econometrica* 25 (1957):501–522.

Griliches, Z. "Research Costs and Social Returns: Hybrid Corn and Related Innovations." *Journal of Political Economy* 66 (1958):419–431.

Griliches, Z. "Congruence Versus Profitability: A False Dichotomy." *Rural Sociology* 25 (1960):354–356.

Griliches, Z. "Profitability Versus Interaction: Another False Dichotomy." *Rural Sociology* 27 (1962):327–330.

Grossman, G. M., and E. Helpman. *Innovation and Growth in the Global Economy.* Cambridge, MA: MIT Press, 1991.

Gruber, W. H., and D. G. Marquis, eds. *Factors in the Transfer of Technology.* Cambridge: MIT Press, 1969.

Grübler, A. "Diffusion: Long Term Patterns and Discontinuities." *Technological Forecasting and Social Change* 39 (1991a):159–180.

Grübler, A. "Introduction to Diffusion Theory." In *Computer Integrated Manufacturing*, Vol. 3. *Models, Case Studies and Forecasts of Diffusion*, R. Clyres, W. Haywood, and I. Tohijou, eds., pp. 3–53. London, UK: Chapman and Hall, 1991b.

Grübler, A. *Technology and Global Change.* Cambridge, UK: Cambridge University Press, (1998).

Hayami, Y., and V. W. Ruttan. *Agricultural Development: An International Perspective,* 2nd ed. Baltimore, MD: Johns Hopkins University Press, 1985.

Hughes, T. P., and A. C. Hughes (eds.). *Lewis Mumford: Public Intellectual.* Oxford: Oxford University Press, 1990.

Katz, E. "Communication Research and the Image of Society: Convergence of Two Traditions." *American Journal of Sociology* 65 (1960):435–440.

Katz, E., and C. Shapiro. "Technology Adoption in the Presence of Network Externalities." *Journal of Political Economy* 94 (1986):722–841.

Katz, E., H. Hamilton, and M. L. Levin. "Traditions of Research on the Diffusion of Innovation." *American Sociological Review* 28 (1963):237–252.

Kemp, R. *Environmental Policy and Technical Change: A Comparison of the Technological Impact of Policy Instruments*. Cheltenham, UK: Edward Elgar, 1997.

Klepper, S. "Entry, Exist, Growth and Innovation over the Product Life Cycle." *The American Economic Review* 86 (1996):562–583.

Klonglan, G. E., and E. W. Coward, Jr. "The Concept of Symbolic Adoption: A Suggested Interpretation." *Rural Sociology* 35 (1970):77–83.

Knudson, M. K., and V. W. Ruttan. "Research and Development of a Biological Innovation: Commercial Hybrid Wheat." *Food Research Institute Studies* 21 (1988):45–68.

Leonard-Benton, D. *Wellsprings of Knowledge: Building and Sustaining the Sources of Innovation*. Boston, MA: Harvard Business School Press, 1995.

Lionberger, H. L. *Adoption of New Ideas and Practices: A Summary of Research Dealing with the Acceptance of Technological Change in Agriculture with Implications in Facilitating Social Change*. Ames, IA: Iowa State University Press, 1960.

Lissoni, F., and J. S. Metcalf. "Diffusion of Innovation: Ancient and Modern: A Review of the Moen Themes." In *Industrial Innovation*, M. Dodgeson and R. Rothwell, eds., pp. 106–141. Aldershot, UK: Edgar Elgar, 1994.

Mahajan, V., E. Muller, and F. Bass. "New Product Diffusion Models in Marketing: A Review and Directions for Research." *Journal of Marketing* 54 (1990):1–26.

Mansfield, E. "Technological Change and the Rate of Imitation." *Econometrica* 29 (1961):741–766.

Mansfield, E. "Intrafirm Rates of Diffusion of an Innovation." *Review of Economics and Statistics* 45 (1963a):348–354.

Mansfield, E. "The Speed of Response of Firms to New Techniques." *Quarterly Journal of Economics* 77 (1963b):290–311.

Mansfield, E. *Industrial Research and Technological Innovation: An Econometric Analysis*. New York: W. W. Norton, 1968.

Marchette, C., and N. Nakićenović. *The Dynamics of Energy Systems and the Logistical Substitution Model*. Laxenburg, Austria: International Institute for Applied Systems Analyses RR 79–13, 1979.

Metcalf, J. S. "The Diffusion of Invention: An Interpretive Survey." In *Technical Change and Economic Theory*, G. Dosi, C. Freeman, R. Nelson, G. S. Silverberg, and L. Soete, eds. New York: Pinter, 1988.

Mokyr, J. "Progress and Inertia in Technological Change." In *Capitalism in Context: Essays in Honor of R. M. Hartwell*, J. James and M. Thomas, eds., pp. 230–254. Chicago, IL: University of Chicago Press, 1994.

Mokyr, J. "Innovation and Its Enemies: The Economic and Political Roots of Technological Inertia." In *A Not So Dismal Science*, M. Olson and S. Kahhöner, eds., pp. 67–104. Oxford, UK: Oxford University Press, 1998.

Mumford, L. *Technics and Civilization*. New York: Harcourt Brace, 1934.

Mumford, L. *The Pentagon of Power*. New York: Harcourt, Brace Jovanovich, 1964.

Nakićenović, N., and A. Grübler, eds. *Diffusion of Technologies and Social Behavior*. Berlin: Springer-Verlag, 1991.

Nasbeth, L., and G. F. Roy. *The Diffusion of New Industrial Process: An International Study*. Cambridge, UK: Cambridge University Press, 1974.

Oster, S. "The Diffusion of Innovation Among Steel Firms: The Basic Oxygen Furnace." *Bell Journal of Economics* 13 (1982):45–56.

Parente, S. L. and E. C. Prescott. *Barriers to Riches*. Cambridge, MA: MIT Press, 2000.

Porter, M. F. "Clusters and the New Economics of Competition." *Harvard Business Review* (November/December, 1998):77–90.

Randall, A. *Before the Luddites*. Cambridge, UK: Cambridge University Press, 1991.

Ray, G. F. "The Diffusion of New Technology: A Study of Ten Processes in Nine Industries." *National Institute Economic Review* 48 (1969):40–83.

Reddy, N. M., and L. Zhao. "International Technology Transfer: A Review." *Research Policy* 19 (1990):285–307.

Rogers, E. M. *Diffusion of Innovations*. New York: Free Press of Glencoe, 1962.

Rogers, E. M. *Diffusion of Innovations,* 3rd ed. New York: The Free Press, 1983.

Rogers, E. M. *Diffusion of Innovations,* 4th ed. New York: The Free Press, 1995.

Rogers, E. M. and A. E. Haven. "Adoption of Hybrid Corn: A Comment." *Rural Sociology* 27 (1962):327–330.

Rogers, E. M., with F. F. Shoemaker. *Communication of Innovations: A Cross Cultural Approach*. New York: Free Press, 1971.

Rogers, E. M., with L. Svenning. *Modernization Among Peasants: The Impact of Communication*. New York: Holt, Rinehart & Winston, 1969.

Rucht, D. "The Impact of Anti-Nuclear Power Movements in International Comparison." In *Resistance to New Technology: Nuclear Power, Information Technology and Biotechnology*, M. Bauer, ed., pp. 277–291. Cambridge, UK: Cambridge University Press, 1995.

Ruttan, V. W. "What Happened to Diffusion Research? *Sociologia Ruralis* 36 (1996):51–73.

Ryan, B., and N. C. Gross. "The Diffusion of Hybrid Seed Corn in Two Iowa Communities." *Rural Sociology* 8 (1943):14–24.

Ryan, B., and N. C. Gross. *Acceptance and Diffusion of Hybrid Corn Seed in Two Iowa Communities*. Ames, IA: Iowa Agricultural Experiment Station Research Bulletin 372-RS, 1950.

Sidel, R. W. *Technology Transfer: Half-Way Houses*. Los Alamos, NM: Los Alamos National Laboratory Center for National Security Studies, Report No. 17, May 1995.

Silverberg, G. "Adoption and Diffusion of Technology as a Collective Evolutionary Process." *Technological Forecasting and Social Change* 39 (1991):67–80.

Silverberg, G., G. Dosi, and L. Orsenigo. "Innovation, Diversity and Diffusion: A Self Organization Model." *The Economic Journal* 98 (1988):1032–1054.

Smale, M., P. Heisey, and H. Leathers. "Maize of the Ancestors and Modern Varieties: The Microeconomics of High-Yielding Variety Adoption in Malawi." *Economic Development and Cultural Change* 43 (1995):351–368.

Soete, L. "International Diffusion of Technology, Industrial Development and Technological Leapfrogging." *World Development* 13 (1985):409–422.

Stoneman, P. *The Economic Analysis of Technological Change*. Oxford, UK: Oxford University Press, 1983.

Teece, D. J. "Technology Transfer by Multinational Firms: The Resource Cost of Transferring Technological Know-How." *Economic Journal* 77 (1977):49–57.

Thirtle, C. G., and V. W. Ruttan. *The Role of Demand and Supply in the Generation and Diffusion of Technical Change*. London: Horwood Academic Publishers, 1987.

Tsao, C. S., and R. H. Day. "A Process Analysis Model of the U.S. Steel Industry." *Management Science* June (1971):B588–B608.

Vernon, R. "International Investment and International Trade in the Product Cycle." *Quarterly Journal of Economics* 80 (1966):190–207.

Vernon, R., ed. *The Technology Factor in International Trade*. New York: Columbia University Press, 1970.

Vernon, R. "The Product Cycle Hypothesis in a New International Environment." *Oxford Bulletin of Economics and Statistics* 41 (1979):255–267.

PART III

TECHNICAL INNOVATION AND INDUSTRIAL CHANGE

The chapters in this section focus on the development of a series of strategic or general purpose technologies. These technologies have had a pervasive impact on economic growth that extends well beyond the industries in which they originated. They have changed the course of world history.

The origins of agriculture (Chapter 6) extend back more than 10,000 years. But it is only in the last century and a half that society has begun to provide farm people with the knowledge and technology that have enabled them to respond to the demands of rapidly growing urban–industrial societies. Yet in many poor countries farm people do not yet have access to the knowledge and the technology needed to meet the demands their societies are placing on them.

Prior to the nineteenth century the primary sources of energy were animal and human power, fuel wood and agricultural wastes, and wind and water power (Chapter 7). The industrial revolution has been associated with dramatic changes in primary energy sources. Beginning a series of strategic inventions in the 1870s and 1880s, electricity has risen to account for an increasing share of energy consumption in factories, offices, and homes.

The chemical industry was the first science-based industry (Chapter 8). It was the primary vehicle of Germany's drive to catch up with the United Kingdom in the nineteenth century. The focus of technical effort in the chemical industry has been to transform low-value raw materials into useful intermediate and consumer products. It has had a pervasive impact on technical change in other industries ranging from agriculture and textiles to automobiles.

The computer is regarded by some as the most significant technical development of the second half of the twentieth century. The modern computer was in turn dependent on the development of the transistor, a truly revolutionary invention that drew directly on scientific research in solid-state physics (Chapter 9). Although use of the computer has become pervasive in commerce, in industry, and in the home, its economic impact is still being debated.

Advances in biotechnology have been even more closely linked to advances in basic science than advances in the chemical and computer industries (Chapter 10). Although based on scientific advances that occurred in the early 1950s, it became a source of technical change, primarily in the agricultural and pharmaceutical industries, only in the 1990s. Biotechnology has been widely hailed as the general purpose technology that will dominate the first half of the twenty-first century.

In these chapters I provide considerable detail on technical change in these industries. This reflects a view that it is important to link general principles with specific experience. Considerable attention is also given to the early or "heroic" stages of invention and innovation. In part this is because in the early stages, it is often fairly easy to identify the roles that particular individuals have played. It is also because inventors and innovators have played particularly creative roles in the emergence of new technologies and new industries. Understanding the role that such individuals have played in particular settings, and the economic and social forces operating on such individuals, provides insight into the institutional changes out of which "new things" continue to emerge. As industries mature less attention is given to the role of individual inventors and innovators. This is because during the more mature stages of scientific and technical change advances tend to occur incrementally rather than in rapid spurts.

CHAPTER 6

Technical Change and
Agricultural Development[1]

Prior to the beginning of the twentieth century, almost all increases in crop and animal production occurred as a result of increases in the area cultivated. By the early years of the twenty-first century, almost all increases must come from increases in land productivity—in output per acre or per hectare. This is an exceedingly short period to make the transition from a resource-based to a science-based system of production. In the presently developed countries the beginning of this transition began in the latter half of the nineteenth century. In many developing countries the transition did not begin until well into the second half of the twentieth century.

During the second half of the twentieth century, the demands placed on worldwide agricultural production more than doubled due to growth in population and income. These demands are likely to double again by the middle of the twenty-first century. Very substantial scientific and technical effort will be required, particularly in the world's poorest countries, to complete the transition to a sustainable system of agricultural production if the challenge is to be met.

There has been a sharp increase in our understanding of the role of agriculture in the process of economic development since the 1950s. In the early post-World War II literature, agriculture, along with other natural resource-based industries, was viewed as a sector from which resources could be extracted to fund development in the industrial sector. Growth in agricultural production was viewed as an essential condition, or even a precondition, for growth in the rest of the economy. But the processes by which agricultural growth was generated remained outside the concern of most development economists.[2]

---

[1] I am indebted to Randolph Barker, Pierre Crosson, Carl K. Eicher, Wallace Huffman, Yujiro Hayami, and Philip G. Pardey for comments on an earlier draft of this chapter.

[2] See particularly Lewis (1954:139–191), Rostow (1956:25–48), and Ranis and Fei (1961:533–565). For a review of the history of thought on the contribution of agriculture to economic development see Hayami and Ruttan (1985:11–40). The massive literature on agricultural development has been reviewed by Eicher and Barker (Africa), Mellor and Mohander (Asia), and Schuh and Brandão (Latin American) in Martin (1992).

In this chapter, I first review the several models of agricultural development by which different societies have, over time, achieved growth in agricultural production. I then discuss the necessary transition to sustainable growth and the various constraints on that transition. Throughout the chapter I give particular attention to the experience of the United States and Japan, two countries in which agricultural development has occurred under extremely different resource endowments.

MODELS OF AGRICULTURAL DEVELOPMENT

A first step in any attempt to understand the process of agricultural development is to abandon the view, expressed by many early development economists, of agriculture in premodern or traditional societies as essentially static. Sustained rates of growth in agricultural output in the 0.5 to 1.0% per year range were feasible over extended periods in many preindustrial societies.[3] With the advent of industrialization, the growth of agricultural output shifted upward to the range of 1.5 to 2.5% per year.

During the Industrial Revolution, rates of growth in this range occurred over relatively long periods in Western Europe, North America, and Japan. Since the middle of the twentieth century, the growth rate has again shifted upward to over 3%, primarily in newly developing countries such as Mexico, Brazil, and the Peoples' Republic of China. Viewed in historical context, the problem of agricultural development is not that of transforming a static agricultural sector into a modern dynamic sector, but of responding to the growth of demand in a modernizing society.

In this section, I review the several models of agricultural development that Yujiro Hayami and I distilled from the natural and social science literature (Hayami and Ruttan, 1971:26–63, 1985:45–72). The models, although presented sequentially, should not be interpreted as stages in the process of agricultural development. Even the most highly developed country's agricultural development, in some regions or in some commodity sectors, is best understood in terms of several of the models. Each model continues to serve as a source for ideas that influence current thought about agricultural development.

The Resource Exploitation Model

Throughout history, expansion of the area cultivated or grazed has been the main means of increasing agricultural production. The most dramatic example in western history was the opening up of new continents—North and South America and Australia—to European settlement during the eighteenth and nineteenth centuries (Crosby, 1972; Turner, 1995). With the advent of cheap transport, associated with

---

[3] For a useful collection of papers on technical change in prehistoric agriculture see Struever (1971). For Western Europe see van Bath (1963); for East Asia see Ishikawa (1967). See also Boserup (1981) and Cohen (1995:32–45).

the introduction and diffusion of the steamship and the railroad during the latter half of the nineteenth century, the countries of the new continents became increasingly important sources of food and agricultural raw materials for the metropolitan countries of Western Europe—thus releasing the constraints on growth imposed by land quality in the classical model (Chapter 1).

In earlier times, similar processes of bringing new land into cultivation had proceeded, though at a less dramatic pace, in the village economies of Europe, Asia, and Africa. The first millennium A.D. saw the agricultural colonization of Europe north of the Alps, the Chinese settlement of the lands south of the Yangtze, and the Bantu occupation of Africa south of the tropical forest belts. Population pressure, resulting in intensified land use in existing villages, was followed by pioneer settlement, the establishing of new villages, and the opening up of forest or jungle to cultivation. In Western Europe, agricultural practices evolved from neolithic forest fallow to systems of shifting bush and grassland cultivation, followed by short fallow systems and later by annual cropping. This process is still underway in tropical forest areas in Southeast Asia, Latin America, and Africa (Pingali et al., 1987).

The classical resource exploitation model (Chapter 1) was based on an oversimplified understanding of the history of agricultural development. The history of land use, both in temperate and tropical environments, indicates that the supply of land services has been much more elastic than implied by the static view of land as either the "original and indestructible power of the soil" or a natural agent of production. The most extreme challenge to the classical position has been suggested by Ester Boserup (1965). In a survey of historical patterns of land use under preindustrial conditions in both temperate and tropical regions, Boserup suggests a pattern of continuous development from extensive to more intensive systems. In her work, the sharp distinction between cultivated and uncultivated land is replaced by increasing frequency of cultivation, ranging from forest and bush fallow to multicropping systems in which the same plot bears two or more crops per year. In this view, soil fertility becomes a dependent variable responding to the intensity of land use, rather than a determinant of the intensity of land use.

Another weakness of the resource exploitation model is its lack of insight into the problem of generating growth in land and labor productivity when the slack resulting from underutilized natural resources has been exhausted. Agricultural growth based on the resource exploitation model is not sustainable over the long run. Rather it is necessary to make a transition from exploiting the services provided by nature to (1) developing resource-conserving or -enhancing technologies that involve more intensive land and water management, such as crop rotation, manuring, and irrigation; and (2) substituting modern industrial inputs such as fertilizer for natural soil fertility, using chemical and biological pest management agents, and developing modern fertilizer-responsive varieties of crops. To gain access to these new sources of growth, a society must invest in the land and water infrastructure, the industrial capacity needed to produce modern inputs, and the scientific research and human capital needed to develop new technology and use it effectively.

The Conservation Model

The conservation model of agricultural development evolved from the advances in crop and livestock husbandry associated with the English agricultural revolution. The English agricultural revolution involved the development of an intensive, integrated, crop–livestock husbandry system.[4] New forage and green manure crops were introduced, and animal manures became more available. This "new husbandry" permitted intensified crop–livestock production through the recycling of plant nutrients, in the form of animal manures, to maintain or enhance soil fertility. The advances in technology were accompanied by the consolidation and enclosure of farms and by investments in land development such as the drainage of wetlands. The Norfolk crop-rotation system replaced the open-three-field system in which arable land was allocated between permanent crop land and permanent pasture. The effect was a substantial growth in both total agricultural output and output per acre. The inputs used in the conservation system were largely supplied within the agricultural sector. It provided the technical basis for English "high farming" as it evolved in 1850–1870, following the repeal of the Corn Laws.

English "new husbandry" principles were transplanted to Germany where they complemented the doctrine of soil exhaustion emerging in the new field of soil science. This doctrine held that any permanent system of agriculture must provide for the complete restoration to the soil of all elements removed in crop production. "The doctrine of soil exhaustion first took shape in the later part of the eighteenth century, when the humus theory of plant nutrition was dominant. It was then supposed that plants derived their food from the organic matter in the soil, collectively designated as humus" (Usher, 1923:385–411). With the demonstration of the relation of soil minerals to plant growth by Justus von Liebig and others during the second quarter of the nineteenth century, the soil exhaustion doctrine was extended to include the maintenance of the mineral content of the soil.

Beginning in the mid-1920s economists attempted to "rationalize" the theory of conservation and to explore more formally the economic significance of conservation principles, particularly in the field of fertility maintenance, used in agricultural practice. By the early 1950s a new body of literature, embracing both technical (soil science, plant nutrition, agronomic practice, and conservation engineering) and economic knowledge was leading to a more rational view of both the farm management and public policy aspects of soil fertility and of the role of land in agricultural development (Ise, 1925:284–291; Ciriacy-Wantrup, 1938:86–101; Bunce, 1942).

---

[4] Agricultural historians have stressed the "evolutionary" in contrast to the "revolutionary" aspects of these changes. The improved methods were the result of the accumulation of a very large number of small adaptations, only a few of which—advances in cattle breeding, the substitution of turnips and cultivated forages for fallow—were new. For the new husbandry, see Timmer (1969:375–395). For a survey of perspectives on the English agricultural revolution, see Grigg (1982), and Allen (1992). Allen shows that there were two agricultural revolutions in English history—the yeoman's and the landlord's. He attributes most of the gains in land productivity to the yeoman's revolution.

In the United States, and in many other countries, however, the rationalization of conservation practice was under continuous pressure as a result of the international economic stagnation during the 1930s, the resource drains on agriculture during World War II, and the rapid growth in demand for agricultural commodities arising out of global population and income growth.

Agricultural development based on indigenous knowledge of conservation practices and technical change induced by population growth has been capable, in many parts of the world, of sustaining production growth over long periods of time (Boserup, 1965; Ishikawa, 1967; Bray, 1986). The East Asian wet rice cultivation system differs from the Western European conservation model in that it was a monoculture rather than a polyculture system. The most serious effort in recent history to develop agriculture within the conservation model framework was made by the People's Republic of China during its experiment with communal farming (1958–1978). But an agricultural strategy based on recycling of plant, animal, and human manures was unable to achieve a rate of growth in production compatible with China's rate of growth in the demand for agricultural commodities.[5]

A more modest role for development within the framework of the conservation model is appropriate in both developing and developed economies. The energy crises of the 1970s redirected the attention of plant and soil scientists and agricultural planners toward greater reliance on biological sources of plant nutrition and energy-saving methods of cultivation. The conservation model, sometimes called the low-input sustainable agriculture (LISA) model, can continue to make an important contribution to growth of agricultural production in developing countries (Ruttan, 1994a; Reardon, 1998). And in the developed countries it will remain a source of inspiration to the organic and other alternative farming system movements (Bunch and López, 1995).

The Diffusion Model

The diffusion of knowledge, technology, and institutions has, throughout history, been an important source of economic development (Chapter 5). Diffusion of better husbandry practices and of crop and livestock varieties and breeds has been a major source of productivity growth in agriculture since prehistoric times. The classical studies by Vavilov (1949–50) and Sauer (1969) initiated a research agenda that has led to a better understanding of the extensive diffusion of cultivated plants and domestic animals in prehistory and in the classical civilizations. By the last half of the nineteenth century, the process of plant exploration and discovery had become highly institutionalized. In the British Empire, the effort was organized through a system of botanic gardens developed to facilitate the transfer, testing, and introduction of plant materials (Brockway, 1979). In the United States crop exploration and introduction became a

---

[5] For a useful assessment of the role of indigenous knowledge in modern economic development, see Agrawal (1995).

major activity of the Department of Agriculture (Klose, 1950). Similar programs became an integral part of all leading national agricultural research programs.

Beginning in the late 1930s research on the diffusion of agricultural technology became a major focus of research by rural sociologists, first in the United States and then abroad (Chapter 5). The insights this research provided contributed to the effectiveness of agricultural extension services and strengthened the confidence of agricultural administrators and policymakers in the validity of the diffusion model. The pervasive acceptance of this model, coupled with the wide gaps in national agricultural productivity and the firm presumption of inefficient resource allocation among "irrational tradition-bound" peasants, produced an extension or technology transfer bias in agricultural development strategy during the 1950s. These programs were expected to transform tradition-bound peasant producers into "economic agents," who would respond more rationally to the technical opportunities available to them and reallocate resources more efficiently in response to economic incentives.

The limitations of the diffusion model as a foundation for agricultural development policies became increasingly apparent as technical assistance and community development programs, based explicitly or implicitly on the diffusion model, failed to generate either rapid modernization of traditional farms or rapid growth in agricultural production. The inadequacy of policies based on a combination of the land exploitation, conservation, location, and diffusion models led, in the 1960s, to a reexamination of two assumptions: (1) that agricultural technology could readily be diffused from the high-productivity to the low-productivity countries and (2) that the transfer of knowledge from progressive to lagging farmers within an economy could become an important source of productivity growth. Effective technology transfer became increasingly dependent on the transfer of research capacity. This advance in understanding did not, however, prevent international development assistance agencies, particularly the World Bank, from supporting the development of large agricultural extension bureaucracies in countries that had not yet acquired the research capacity to generate new knowledge or new technology.

● BOX 6.1
International Diffusion of Sugarcane

Sugarcane represents a classic example of the international diffusion and transfer of an agricultural technology. It is of interest because the process has evolved from simple transfer of biological materials to the transfer of capacity to develop new sugarcane technology. There have been four stages in the transfer and development of sugarcane.

Stage I. Natural Selection and Diffusion of Wild Canes

Sugarcane was cultivated in India as early as 400 B.C. Sugarcane and the art of sugar making were diffused from India to China, to Arabia, and to the Mediterranean region very early. Shortly after 1400 A.D. sugarcane was introduced on Madeira and in the Azores. Columbus took it with him to Hispaniola on his second voyage to the New World in 1493. From there it was carried to Cuba and Puerto Rico, and later to Mexico, Peru, and Brazil. Throughout this period the cane used in commercial cultivation was one of two closely related thin-stemmed varieties. In 1791 Captain Bligh (of *Mutiny on the Bounty* notoriety) collected and introduced a thick-stemmed variety that rapidly replaced the thin-stemmed forms within a few years.

Stage II. Sexual Reproduction

In nature the sugarcane plant produces only asexually. Until methods of sexual reproduction were discovered this limited the selection of superior clones from indigenous cultivated or wild forms. Procedures for the sexual reproduction of sugarcane were discovered at a Dutch research station in Java (in 1887) and at a British research station in Barbados (in 1888). By 1920 commercial varieties developed at experiment stations in Java, Barbados, India, and Hawaii had been transferred to most of the sugar-growing areas of the world. Only simple tests and demonstrations were required for recipient countries to propagate and diffuse the varieties locally.

Stage III. Interspecific Hybridization

Breeding for disease resistance became an important concern since many of the new varieties were found to be susceptible to local diseases and pests. Disease-resistant varieties were developed by crossing a wild thin-stemmed variety with a high-yielding thick-stemmed variety. Through a series of crosses and back crosses, new interspecific hybrids were developed that incorporated the hardiness and disease resistance of the wild species with the desirable characteristics of cultivated varieties. Later the Coimbatore station in India developed a series of trihybrid disease-resistant varieties that were transferred to every sugar cane-producing country in the world. Although this transmission was widespread, it was highly dependent on local experiment station capacity for adaptation.

Stage IV. Location-Specific Breeding

The Coimbatore (India) station set the stage for modern sugar cane variety development research, which emphasizes the development of varieties suited to specific soil, climate, disease, and management requirements. More than 100 experiment stations around the world are now engaged in the development of locally adapted sugarcane varieties. Very few varieties are transferred internationally for cultivation, although genetic material for use in local development programs and sugarcane-breeding knowledge and technology do continue to be transferred. Meetings of sugarcane research scientists and international consultancies represent an important institution for transferring new scientific and technical knowledge.

An important lesson from the history of sugarcane research is the significant role of advances in fundamental knowledge in the productivity of applied research. Each advance in knowledge—sexual reproduction, interspecific hybridization, and location-specific breeding—led to new breeding technology and to rapid development of new varieties. But over time the gains that could be realized from exploiting the most recent advance in breeding technology declined and the scientific and technical effort, and cost, of developing new varieties rose.

Sources: R. E. Evenson, J. P. Houck, and V. W. Ruttan, "Technical Change and Agricultural Trade: Three Examples—Sugar Cane, Bananas and Rice." In *The Technology Factor in International Trade*, R. Vernon, ed., New York: NY, Columbia University Press, 1970:415–480; R. E. Evenson and V. Kislev, *Agricultural Research and Productivity*, New Haven, CT: Yale University Press, 1975:140–155.

The High-Payoff Input Model

By the early 1960s a new perspective, more fully informed by both agricultural science and economics, was beginning to emerge. It had become increasingly clear, because of agroenvironmental constraints, that much of agricultural technology was "location specific." Techniques developed in advanced countries are not generally directly transferable to less developed countries with different climates and different resource endowments. Evidence had also accumulated that only limited productivity gains were to be had by the reallocation of resources in traditional peasant agriculture. Economic relationships in peasant society had traditionally been viewed as organized by considerations of dependency and reciprocity rather than by market relationships. Schultz (1964) insisted that peasants in traditional agrarian societies are rational resource allocators and that they remained poor because most poor countries provided them with only limited technical and economic opportunities to which they could respond—they were "poor but efficient."

The key to transforming a traditional agricultural sector into a productive source of economic growth was, in Schultz's view, the public and private investment to make modern high-payoff technical inputs available to farmers in poor countries:

The principal sources of high productivity in modern agriculture are reproducible sources. They consist of particular material inputs and of skills and other capabilities required to use such inputs successfully. . . . But these modern inputs are seldom ready-made. . . . In general what is available is a body of knowledge which has made it possible for the advanced countries to produce for their own use factors that are technically superior to those employed elsewhere. This body of knowledge can be used to develop similar, and as a rule superior, new factors appropriate to the biological and other conditions that are specific to the agriculture of poor countries." (Schultz, 1964:145–47)

This implies three types of relatively high-productivity investments for agricultural development: (1) in the capacity of agricultural research institutions to generate new location-specific technical knowledge, (2) in the capacity of the industrial sector to develop, produce, and market new technical inputs, and (3) in the schooling and nonformal (extension) education of rural people to enable them to use the new knowledge and technology effectively.

The enthusiasm with which this high-payoff input model was accepted and translated into doctrine was due at least as much to the success of plant breeders and agronomists in developing high-yielding modern grain varieties for the tropics as in the power of Schultz's ideas.[6] High-yielding wheat and maize varieties were developed in Mexico, beginning in the 1950s, and high-yielding rice varieties in the Philippines beginning in the 1960s (Chapter 3). These varieties were highly responsive to industrial inputs, such as fertilizer and other chemicals, and to more effective soil and water management. The high returns associated with the adoption of the new varieties and associated technical inputs and management practices led to rapid diffusion of the new varieties among farmers in a number of countries in Asia, Latin America, and Africa. The impact on farm production was sufficiently dramatic to be heralded as a "green revolution." The significance of the high-payoff input model is that policies based on the model have resulted in growth in agricultural production consistent with the demands being placed on the agricultural sector in a number of developing countries that were experiencing exceedingly high rates of both population and income growth.

The high-payoff input model remains incomplete, however, even as a model of technical change in agriculture. It does not attempt to explain how economic conditions induce an efficient path of technical change for the agricultural sector of a particular society. Nor does the high-payoff input model attempt to explain how economic conditions induce the development of new institutions, such as agricultural experiment stations, that become suppliers of new knowledge and new technology.

---

[6] The Schultz "poor but efficient" hypothesis represented a direct rejection of the traditional Marxian view that the role of the peasantry in economic development was to serve as a "reserve army" that would be a source of low cost supply of labor to a growing urban-industrial sector (Hayami, 1996). It was received skeptically by most development economists. See, for example, Lipton (1968). For a particularly vicious review of *Transforming Traditional Agriculture* see Balough (1964). For an appreciative retrospective evaluation see Ball and Pounder (1996:735–760). Schultz was a recipient of the 1979 Nobel award in economics, along with W. Arthur Lewis, for his contributions to development economics.

INDUCED TECHNICAL CHANGE IN AGRICULTURE

Beginning in the early 1970s Hayami and Ruttan (1971, 1985) and Binswanger and Ruttan (1978) formulated a model of agricultural development in which both technical and institutional change were treated as endogenous to the economic system.[7] Development of the model started with the recognition that there are multiple paths of technological development (Figure 6.1). Alternative technological trajectories have been developed to facilitate the substitution of relatively abundant (hence cheap) factors for relatively scarce (hence expensive) factors (Chapter 4). In agriculture it is useful, consistent with the terminology of Hicks, to term techniques designed to facilitate the substitution of other inputs for labor "labor saving," and techniques designed to facilitate the substitution of other inputs for land "land saving" (Chapter 4). Two kinds of technology generally correspond to this taxonomy: mechanical technology to "labor saving" and biological (and chemical) technology to "land saving."[8] The former is designed to substitute power and machinery for labor. The latter, biological technology, is designed to substitute intensive production practices or industrial inputs for land. This substitution may be accomplished through increased recycling of animal (including human) and green manures, through use of chemical fertilizers, and through husbandry practices, management systems, and other technical inputs such as pesticides, or pest- and pathogen-resistant crop varieties that enhance yield.

The distinction between mechanical and biological technology may be somewhat overdrawn, of course. All mechanical innovations are not necessarily motivated by incentives to save labor, nor are all biological innovations necessarily motivated by incentives to save land. For example, in Japan horse plowing was initially introduced in order to cultivate more deeply, so as to increase yield per hectare. In the United States tomatoes have been developed that have a sturdier skin and ripen at the same time to facilitate mechanical harvesting. At the most sophisticated level, technological progress in agriculture often depends on a complex of simultaneous advances in both biological and mechanical technology (Chapter 10).

Mechanical Processes

The mechanization of farming has been intimately associated with the industrial revolution (Habakkuk, 1962; Rosenberg, 1976:32–49, 108–125, 249–259). Although progress of agricultural and industrial mechanization represents a response to the same set of fundamental economic forces, the mechanization of agriculture cannot be treated as simply the adaptation of industrial methods of production to agriculture. The

---

[7] For a discussion of the process of technical change induced by population growth in preindustrial societies, see Boserup (1965) and Geertz (1966). For an argument that technical change in agriculture was induced by national security consideration, see Perkins (1997).

[8] This distinction was first employed by Heady (1949:293–316). It is similar to the distinction between "laboresque" and "landesque" capital suggested by Sen (1959:279–285).

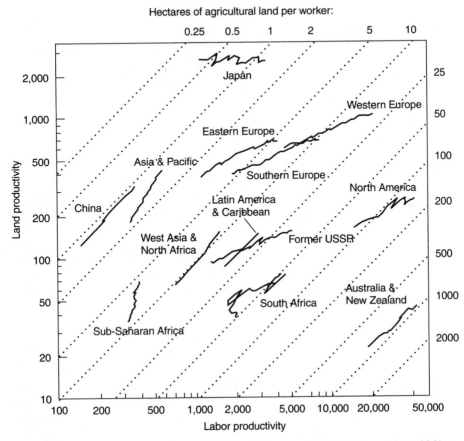

Figure 6.1 International comparison of land and labor productivities by region: 1961 to 1990. *Note:* AgGDP in nominal local currency units was first deflated to base year 1980 using country-specific AgGDP deflators and then converted to U.S. dollars using agricultural output PPPs. The number of countries on which the regional (weighted averages) area is based is as follows: sub-Saharan Africa (17), Asia and the Pacific (11), Latin America and the Caribbean (18), West Asia and North Africa (9), Europe (13), and North America (2). Hectares of agricultural land per economically active member of the agricultural population includes arable plus permanently cropped and permanently pastured land. "Agricultural workers" is here defined as economically active in agricultural production. (*Source:* B. J. Craig, P. G. Pardey, and J. Roseboom, "International Productivity Patterns: Accounting for Input Quality, Infrastructure and Research," *American Journal of Agricultural Economics*, 79 (1997):1066.)

spatial nature of crop production results in significant differences between agriculture and industry in the pattern of machinery use (Brewster, 1950:69–81; Johnson and Ruttan, 1994). The spatial dimension of crop production requires that the machines suitable for agricultural mechanization must be mobile—they must move across or through materials that are immobile, in contrast to moving materials through stationary machines, as in most industrial process.

In the industrial sector, the replacement of handicraft methods of production with machine methods was associated with a factory system of organization in which the individual worker becomes specialized in one particular operation. In farming, the sequence of operations from preplanting to postharvesting remains as widely separated by time intervals after mechanization as before. The seasonal characteristic of agricultural production requires a series of specialized machines—for land preparation, planting, pest and pathogen control, and harvesting—specifically designed for sequential operations, each of which is carried out only for a few days or weeks in each season. This also means that it is no more feasible for workers to specialize in one operation in mechanized agriculture than in premechanized agriculture. In addition, in a "fully mechanized" agricultural system, because of the mobility and specialization characteristics, investment per worker is generally much higher than that in industry.

It is clear, regardless of the impact of the economic organization of agriculture, that a major economic force, leading to the greater use of mechanical equipment in both crop and animal production, has been the growth in demand for labor in the urban–industrial sector. The effect was to induce the development and adoption of labor-saving mechanical technology. The major consequence is a rise in labor productivity—output per worker or per labor hour. In economies in which the price of labor is low and where the price of material goods—of machinery—is high, there is little incentive to mechanize either field or material-handling operations. As the value of labor rises, either as a result of rising demand for labor in the urban–industrial sector or as a result of greater demand for agricultural commodities, mechanization is typically adopted first for those activities in which stationary power sources can be used—for pumping water and threshing grain, for example. Mechanization of machines that must move across the landscape typically represents a later stage.[9]

Biological and Chemical Processes

In agriculture, biological and chemical technology and processes are more fundamental than mechanization or machine processes. Until the 1960s "green revolution"—the development and diffusion of modern high-yielding varieties of wheat, maize, and rice—a typical treatise on economic development passed over innovation in biological technology with a quick reference to the need for better seeds and improved methods of cultivation. The technical changes associated with mechanization seemed to imply a sharp break with the past and the prospect of instant modernization. In

[9] The pace of mechanization may also be influenced by soil and topography. For a discussion of the constraints on mechanization during the transition from shifting cultivation to intensive agriculture, see Pingali et al. (1987). For a discussion of the transition from land-saving to labor-saving technology in rice production in Southeast Asia, see Pingali et al. (1997:40–61).

contrast, the advances in biological technology, at least until the recent advances in biotechnology (Chapter 10), seemed to pose neither the threat nor the promise of a radical reorganization of agrarian structure.

Advances in biological and chemical technology have been introduced primarily by a desire to increase crop output per unit of land area or to improve the yield of animal products per unit of feed or of breeding stock. In crop production, these advances have typically involved one or more of the following three elements: (1) land and water resource development to provide a more satisfactory environment for plant growth; (2) modification of the environment by the addition of organic and inorganic sources of plant nutrition to the soil to stimulate plant growth and the use of biological and chemical means to protect plants from pests and disease; and (3) selection and breeding of new biologically efficient crop varieties specifically adapted to respond to those elements in the environment that are subject to human control. Similar processes are characteristic of advances in livestock agriculture.

Taiwan represents a particularly illuminating case of biological technology transforming agriculture (Hayami and Ruttan, 1971:198–212). By the mid-1920s, under Japanese administration, Taiwan had acquired the essential elements for rapid growth of its rice economy: (1) irrigation systems capable of delivering water to much of the rice land throughout the year, (2) technical inputs, such as chemical fertilizers, acquired through integration with the Japanese economy, and (3) improved rice varieties, initially achieved through selection of the best local varieties and later through a program of crossbreeding designed to adapt fertilizer-responsive Japanese varieties to local conditions. In addition, economic integration also resulted in rapid development of the local transportation and marketing systems, opening up the Japanese market and creating incentives to increase the marketable surplus of rice in Taiwan.

The Japanese administration found it necessary to invest in agricultural research since Japanese varieties of rice could not be directly transferred to Taiwan. The varieties of rice developed by Japanese rice breeders in Taiwan, referred to as Ponlai varieties, first became available in the mid-1920s. By 1940 Ponlai varieties were planted on half of the total area devoted to rice. The new varieties, combined with the development of the irrigation system, created an opportunity for growth in the use of commercial fertilizer in order to realize the higher yield potential. The new technology, along with improvement in cultural practices, resulted in rapid increases in yield per hectare until the late 1930s, when the Japanese military effort began to divert resources away from development objectives.

The "green revolution" has, since its initial development and adoption in South and Southeast Asia in the late 1960s, been the subject of substantial controversy. It has been described, mistakenly, as a Western technology inappropriately introduced into South and Southeast Asia. It is more correctly described as an East Asian technology adapted to South and Southeast Asia. The initial criticisms suggested that the new technology would widen inequities in income distribution and social polarization in rural communities. Careful studies conducted in the late 1970s and early 1980s indicated that these concerns have been overblown (Hayami and Ruttan, 1985:336–

345; David and Otsuka, 1988:441–450).[10] More recent criticisms have focused on the environmental effects of the intensification of agricultural production (Conway and Pretty, 1991; Conway, 1997; Pingali et al., 1997:91–125). Even the most severe critics concede that the "green revolution" technology has substantially enhanced the rate of growth in agricultural production.[11]

The Metaproduction Function

A requisite for growth in agricultural productivity is the capacity to respond to changes in factor and product prices. In the case of factor prices the capacity to respond involves not only the movement along a fixed production surface (factor substitution) but also the creation of new production surfaces appropriate for the new set of prices (Figure 6.2). For example, even if fertilizer prices decline relative to the prices of land and farm products, increases in the use of fertilizer may be limited unless new crop varieties are developed that are responsive to higher levels of fertilizer inputs.

For illustrative purposes the relationship between fertilizer use and yield may be drawn as in Figure 6.2, letting u_0 and u_1 represent the fertilizer–response curves of older and improved varieties, respectively. For farmers facing u_0, a decline in the fertilizer price relative to the product price from p_0 to p_1 would not be expected to result in much increase in fertilizer application or in yield. The full impact of a decline in fertilizer price on use and output can be fully realized only if u_1 is made available to farmers through the development of more responsive varieties. Conceptually, it is possible to draw a curve such as U in Figure 6.2 that is the envelope of many individual response curves, each representing an individual variety of a particular crop such as rice or wheat. This curve may be termed a "metaproduction function."[12]

The metaproduction function can be regarded as the envelope of the neoclassical production function. In the *short run*, in which substitution among inputs is circumscribed by the rigidity of existing capital and equipment, production relationships can best be described by an activity with fixed factor–factor and factor–product ratios. In the *long run*, in which the constraints exercised by existing capital disappear and are replaced by the fund of available technical knowledge, including all alternative factor–

---

[10] Critics of the "green revolution" have often failed to distinguish between technical and institutional bias. Although biological technology is generally neutral with respect to scale, the institutional environment into which the new technology is introduced—including tenure arrangement, factor and product markets, and credit institutions—is often biased against small producers. It is important, for purposes of policy reform, to correctly identify whether the source of the bias is technical or institutional (Hayami and Ruttan, 1985:336–345).

[11] The empirical grounding of a number of the critical studies has been so weak that it is hard to avoid the conclusion that it has been ideologically motivated. For two of the more egregious examples, see Pearse (1980) and Shiva (1991).

[12] See Chapter 4 for a more general discussion of the process of induced technical change. The term "metaproduction function" was first introduced by Hayami and Ruttan (1970:895–911). See also Lau and Yotopoulos (1989:241–269).

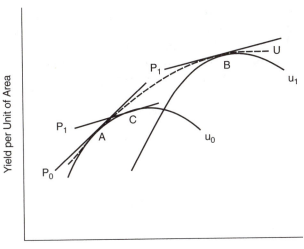

Figure 6.2 Shift in fertilizer response curve along the metaresponse curve. (*Source:* Y. Hayami and V. W. Ruttan, *Agricultural Development: An International Perspective*, Baltimore, MD: Johns Hopkins University Press, 1985:134.)

factor and factor–product combinations, production relationships can be described by the neoclassical production function. In the *secular period* of production, in which the constraints given by the available fund of technical knowledge are further relaxed to admit all potentially discoverable technical possibilities, given the state of scientific knowledge, production relationships can be described by the metaproduction function that describes all conceivable technical alternatives that might be discovered. The metaproduction function may also be considered as an operational representation of the innovation possibility curve (Figure 4.2)—operational in the sense that it can be identified at the laboratory or field plot level or even in the fields of farmers operating at the technical frontier. The metaproduction function does not remain fixed over time. It shifts in response to the accumulation of scientific knowledge.

The theory of induced technical change suggests that countries with different resource endowment will follow different paths or trajectories in technological development. This is clearly true in the case of countries characterized by extreme differences in factor endowments such as Japan and the United States. The historical relationship between use of fertilizer per hectare of arable land and the fertilizer–land price ratio for Japan and the United States is shown in Figure 6.3. The relationship between farm draft power per worker and the power–labor price ratio is shown in Figure 6.4. The data presented in these two figures can be interpreted as representing a dynamic factor-substitution process. Factors have been substituted for each other as the metaproduction function has itself shifted in response to changes in long-run factor prices. Each point on the metaproduction function surface is characterized by a technology that can be described in terms of specific power, types of machinery, crop varieties, and animal breeds. Changes of the magnitudes represented in Figures 6.3 and 6.4 could occur only as a result of technical change. They are too large to have occurred as a result of simple factor substitution along a neoclassical production function. They were induced to a significant extent by the long-term trends in relative factor prices.[13]

Data on land and labor productivity across and over time for a broad group of countries and major geographic regions are also broadly consistent with the induced technical change model (Hayami and Ruttan 1985:118–133; Craig et al., 1991b:182–

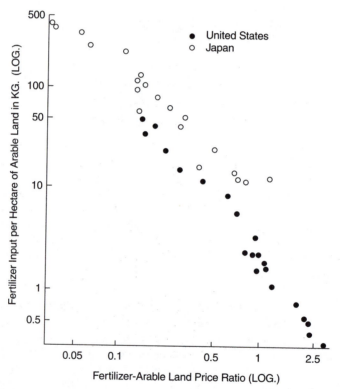

Figure 6.3 Relation between fertilizer input per hectare of arable land and the fertilizer-arable land price ratio. (hectares of arable land that can be purchased by one ton of N + P_2O_5 + K_2O contained in commercial fertilizers), the United States and Japan: quinquennial observations for 1880–1980. (*Source:* Y. Hayami and V. W. Ruttan, *Agricultural Development: An International Perspective,* Baltimore, MD: Johns Hopkins University Press, 1985:179.)

---

[13] For a more rigorous test of the induced technical change hypothesis against Japanese and U.S. agricultural history see Hayami and Ruttan (1985:178–204). See also Binswanger and Ruttan (1978).

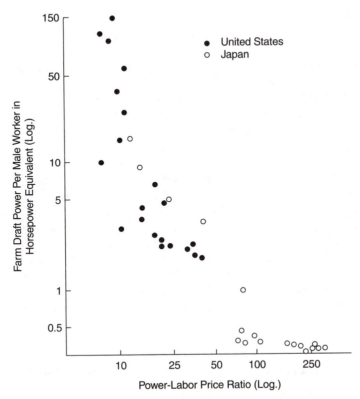

Figure 6.4 Relation between farm draft power per male worker and power–labor price ratio (hectares of work days that can be purchased by one horsepower of tractor or draft animal), the United States and Japan: quinquennial observations for 1880–1980. (*Source:* Y. Hayami and V. W. Ruttan, *Agricultural Development: An International Perspective*, Baltimore, MD: Johns Hopkins University Press, 1985:179.)

185, 1997:1064–1076). Figure 6.1 shows output per hectare (vertical axis) and output per male worker (horizontal axis) for major geographic regions.[14] Regions characterized by low land per worker ratios have tended to follow a biological technology trajectory similar to the earlier Japanese path. Regions characterized by high land per worker ratios have tended to follow a mechanical technology trajectory. Countries with intermediate land–labor ratios have followed an intermediate trajectory. Note particularly that technical change in Japanese agriculture, which had earlier followed a biological technology trajectory, has been induced by rising wage rates in the industrial sector to shift toward a mechanical technology trajectory during the post-World War II

[14] For a similar figure showing longer term (1880–1979) trajectories for a number of presently developed countries, see Hayami and Ruttan (1985:131). For a test of the induced technical change hypothesis against the experience of the former centrally planned economies, see Fan and Ruttan (1992).

period. Since the initial studies by Hayami and Ruttan the induced technical change model has been tested against the experience of a large number of developed and developing countries (Thirtle and Ruttan, 1987).[15]

The exceedingly wide differences in output per hectare for any given level of output per worker and the exceedingly wide differences in output per worker for any given level of output per hectare is rather encouraging in terms of the prospect for agricultural development in countries with low land and/or labor productivity (Figure 6.1). Growth-accounting exercises, using cross-country production functions, suggest that in the poorest less developed countries (LDCs), output per worker could be increased by several multiples with adequate investments in research, education, and technical inputs, even if land area per worker continues to decline because of growing population pressure in rural areas. With a modest reduction in labor intensity, accompanied by rapid advances in yield-increasing technology, the low-income LDCs should be able to achieve levels of labor productivity roughly comparable to the levels achieved in the older developed countries of Western Europe in the 1960s and 1970s. Achievement of labor productivity levels comparable to present levels in the developed countries would, however, require both advances in yield-increasing biological technology and the substitution of mechanical technology for labor associated with substantial reduction in the agricultural labor force (Hayami and Ruttan, 1985:150–157).

SCIENTIFIC AND TECHNICAL CONSTRAINTS

As noted, prior to the beginning of the twentieth century almost all increases in agricultural production occurred as a result of the extension of cultivated area.[16] There were, of course, important exceptions to this generalization, particularly in Western Europe and in East Asia. In the half century since World War II there have been unprecedented rates of growth in population, in per capita income, and in agricultural production. World population increased from 2.5 billion in 1950 to approximately 6 billion in 2000. Population growth, though slower than during 1950–2000, will likely add upward of 3 to 5 billion people to the world population by 2050. In addition, the very poor often spend as much as half of any increase in per capita income on food. The most rapid growth in demand for agricultural commodities is likely to

---

[15] For a theoretical critique see Grabowski (1995). Archibald and Brandt (1991:127–145) found that although technical change over the period 1886–1940 in Japan was consistent with relative price changes, advances in biological technology have, at time, been labor saving as well as land saving. Olmstead and Rhode (1993:100–118) found that in the United States technical change was consistent with the induced technical change model only in the important grain-producing areas of the Midwest. See also the several papers in Koppel (1995).

[16] In this and the following section I draw heavily on Ruttan (1999a). Many of the issues discussed in this section are treated in a more general context in Chapters 12 and 14.

come in the early decades of the twenty-first century when population growth rates in the poorest countries will remain high and income growth will generate substantial additional demand (Rosegrant et al., 1995). It would be unwise to assume that the rate of growth in demand for agricultural commodities, arising out of population and income growth, will be much slower over the period 2000–2050 than over the past half century.[17]

The challenge facing world agriculture and the agricultural research community over the next half century will be to make a transition to a sustainable system of agricultural production or what Gordon Conway (1997) has termed a "doubly green revolution." Some critics of the "green revolution," or what is often termed "the in-dustrial approach" to agricultural development, argue that the gains from agricultural intensification have come at too high a cost in terms of energy consumption and depletion of natural resource stocks, and that the gains of the past half century are not sustainable (Naylor, 1996:99–123; Ruttan, 1994a:209–219).

In the 1950s and 1960s it was not to difficult to anticipate the sources of increase in agricultural production over the next several decades. Advances in crop production would come from expansion in irrigated area, from more intensive application of fertilizer, from use of crop protection chemicals, and from the development of crop varieties that were more responsive to inputs and management.[18]

It was anticipated that advances in animal production would come from genetic improvement and advances in animal nutrition (Chapter 3). At a more fundamental level, increase in grain yields would occur primarily as a result of changes in plant architecture that would enable plants to capture more solar energy and an increased ratio of grain to total dry matter in individual plants. Increases in production of animals and animal products would come about largely by decreasing the proportion of feed consumed that is devoted to animal maintenance and increasing the proportion used to produce usable animal products.[19]

It is much more difficult to anticipate the sources of increases in production over the next half century. There are severe physiological constraints on further increasing the grain-to-dry matter ratio in plants, or further reducing the percentage of animal feed

---

[17] There is a long tradition of attempting to project the human-carrying capacity of the earth. Most of these studies have assumed that per capita food production is the ultimate constraint on human-carrying capacity. For a review, see Cohen (1995:161–236, 402–418). I share Cohen's skepticism about such estimates. Furthermore, I would view it as disastrous if the world is ever forced to discover its human-carrying capacity.

[18] A major puzzle has been why fertilizer has not yet become a major source of growth in agricultural production in sub-Saharan Africa (SSA). In the mid-1990s, fertilizer use averaged less than 10 kg per hectare in SSA compared to 65 kg per hectare in Latin America, 77 kg per hectare in South Asia, and over 200 kg per hectare in East Asia. High fertilizer prices and lack of yield response to fertilizer have been advanced as reasons for low levels of fertilizer use (Yanggen et al., 1998).

[19] In this section, and throughout this chapter, I have focused more heavily on technical change in crop agriculture than in animal agriculture. For useful reviews of the organization and economics of animal research, see Johnson and Ruttan (1997) and Fuglie et al. (1999).

devoted to animal maintenance (Cassman, 1999; Sinclair, 1999). These constraints can be expected to impinge most severely in those areas that have already achieved the highest levels of output per hectare or per animal unit—as in Western Europe, North America, and East Asia. During the 1990s, there was a slowing of yield increases in those areas that had achieved the most rapid yield increases in the 1970s and 1980s— rice yields in Asia and maize yields in the United States, for example (Pingali et al., 1997:62–90).

There are also preliminary indications of declines in agricultural research productivity. As average grain yields, under favorable conditions, have risen from the 1–2 to the 6–8 metric ton per hectare range, the share of research budgets devoted to maintenance research—the research needed to maintain existing crop and animal productivity levels—has risen as a proportion of the total research budget (Plucknett and Smith, 1986:40–45). As a result, the scientist-years required to achieve incremental yield increases in wheat and maize have been rising more rapidly than the yield increases (Maredia and Eicher, 1995:402, 410). And the cost per scientist-year has been rising more rapidly than the general price level (Pardey et al., 1989:289a–296; Huffman and Evenson, 1993:236–237). It is difficult to escape a conclusion that those regions of the world that have achieved the most rapid gains in productivity over the past half century—such as the great plains and delta regions of North America— have begun to experience diminishing returns to conventional plant breeding and agronomic research.

The good news is that evidence is accumulating that investment in agricultural research in many less favored areas—such as the rainfed semiarid areas, upland and mountain areas, and areas in which soils have been depleted or degraded, as in much of Africa—is now beginning to realize relatively high rates of return. These higher rates of return often depend on the use of technology and practices to enhance soil productivity, such as use of nitrogen-fixing green manures, and improvements in the physical and institutional infrastructures in these neglected areas (Fan and Hazel, 1999). It is possible that genetic engineering methods will, in the next several decades, also become a source of technical change and productivity growth in these previously neglected areas. In the meantime, the older methods based on the technologies originally pioneered by Liebig, Mendel, and Pasteur will have to serve as the scientific foundation on which technology development must be constructed (Chapter 10).[20]

The capacity to respond to the scientific and technical constraints that impinge on agricultural production differs widely among countries. There is a group of high-income, primarily OECD countries, for which neither population nor income growth will impose significant demands on growth in agricultural production. Most of these countries have completed the demographic transition. Growth in per capita income

---

[20] Several students have presented more optimistic scenarios based on projection of historical productivity trends. See particularly Waggoner (1997). For attempts to assess the contribution of biotechnology to yield increases, see Evenson (1998).

no longer is an important source of growth in demand for food or other agricultural commodities. The agricultural sector in these countries will be able to respond to the constraints imposed by environmental concerns by reducing demands on land and water resources without seriously depressing growth in agricultural production. Productivity growth in excess of the slow growth in domestic demand will enable some countries in this group to expand agricultural exports. They will also expand their imports of beverages, fruits, vegetables, and other commodities produced in low-income tropical countries (Islam, 1990).

A second group of middle-income countries, with per capita incomes in the U.S. $1,000–10,000 range, is generally well advanced toward the demographic transition and is experiencing moderate to high rates of income growth. Many have achieved substantial agricultural research and technology development capacity and moderately strong capacity in some other areas of science and technology. A combination of moderate population growth and rapid income growth will continue to impose substantial demands on their farmers, at least in the early decades of the next century. Most countries in this group will need to strengthen both their agricultural research and technology development capacity and their broader scientific base if they are to provide their farmers with the knowledge and technology needed to respond to the growth of domestic demand. Some, however, particularly in Latin America, Eastern Europe, and the former Soviet Union, continue to be, or will become, important exporters of agricultural commodities. At present, most of these countries have only weak scientific, technical, and institutional capacity to respond to growing environmental concerns.

A third group of low-income countries, mostly in sub-Saharan Africa, is only beginning to enter the demographic transition. Per capita incomes are growing slowly, or even declining. As incomes start to rise in these countries, a combination of high income growth and continued rapid population growth will result in rapid growth in the demand for food and other agricultural commodities, well into the second quarter of the twenty-first century. These countries have limited financial resources to import agricultural commodities. They have exceedingly weak agricultural research and technology development capacity, and even weaker capacity to meet the demands of their societies for agricultural production, environmental quality, and improvement in health.

RESOURCE AND ENVIRONMENTAL CONSTRAINTS

Resource and environmental constraints represent a second set of constraints on growth in agricultural production. One type of environmental constraint is the impact of agricultural intensification on agricultural production itself. This includes the degradation and loss of soil resources due to erosion, the water logging and salinity associated with irrigation, the coevolution of pests and pathogens associated with use of chemical controls, and the impact of global climate change.

Soil

Soil erosion and degradation have been widely regarded as major threats to sustainable growth in agricultural production both in developed and developing countries (Bennett, 1931; Kellogg, 1948; Pimentel et al., 1976)[21] and have been projected to become even more severe constraints in the future (Pimentel et al., 1995a). It has been suggested, for example, that by 2050 it may be necessary to feed "twice as many people with half as much topsoil" (Harris, 1990:118).[22]

Attempts to assess the implications of erosion on agricultural production confront serious difficulties. Water and wind erosion estimates are measures of the amount of soil moved from one place to another rather than the soil lost to agricultural production. Most studies do not provide the information necessary to estimate yield loss from erosion and degradation. Even in the United States credible national soil erosion estimates are available for only three years (1982, 1987, and 1992). These studies indicated that the rate of soil erosion had declined by 24% between 1982 and 1992, presumably because some 30 to 35 million acres of highly erosive cropland were put in the Conservation Reserve. Only the 1982 studies included estimates of the yield loss from erosion. The estimates indicated that if the 1982 erosion rates continued for 100 years, the yield loss at the end of the period would amount to only about 2 to 3% (Crosson, 1995a, 1995b; Alt et al., 1989).

The extent of soil degradation and loss and its impact on crop production in developing countries are even less well understood than in the United States. The estimates of severe degradation that appear in the literature are typically based on expert opinion rather than carefully designed and adequately monitored experiments. Reliable information on the productivity effects of soil erosion in most developing countries is not available for major soils and crops (Lal, 1984:70; Anderson and Thompapillia, 1990). There is, however, reliable data on long-term soil loss for China and Indonesia. These studies indicate, somewhat surprisingly, that although there has been some decline in soil organic matter and nitrogen, there has been little or no loss of topsoil or productive capacity over more than half a century (Lindert, 1998, 1999).

The fact that the data are so limited should not be taken to suggest that soil erosion and degradation may not be a serious problem. But it should indicate some caution in accepting some of the more dramatic pronouncements about the inability of soil resources to sustain agricultural production (National Research Council, 1993:54–57; Scherr, 1999). The impact of human-induced soil degradation and loss is not evenly distributed across agroclimatic regions, either in developed or developing countries. The impact on the resource base and on regional economies is primarily local rather

---

[21] Land degradation is a broader concept than erosion. It includes "the sum of areas affected by soil degradation, drylands with vegetation degradation but no soil degradation, and degraded moist tropical forest lands" (Daily et al., 1997).

[22] For a very useful introduction to the issues discussed in this section see the exchange in *Science* between Crosson (1995b) and Pimentel et al. (1995b).

than global. Where soil erosion does represent a significant threat to the resource and the economic base of an area, the gains from implementation of the technical and institutional changes necessary to reclaim degraded soil resources, or at least to prevent further degradation, can even in very poor countries often be sufficient to induce adoption of soil-conserving technology (Sanders et al., 1996:72–114; Smale and Ruttan, 1997).

Water

During the last half century, water has become a resource of high and increasing value. In the arid and semiarid areas of the world, water scarcity is becoming an increasingly serious constraint of growth of agricultural production.[23] The change in the economic value of water results from very large increases in withdrawal of water for domestic, industrial, environmental, and, most importantly, irrigation. The International Water Management Institute (IWMI) estimates that slightly more than one billion people live in arid regions that will force *absolute* water scarcity by 2025. IWMI projects a decline in withdrawals of water for irrigation in almost all of these areas between 1990 and 2025.[24]

During the past half century irrigated areas in developing countries more than doubled, from less than 100 million to almost 200 million hectares. About half of developing country cereal production is grown on irrigated land (Alexandratos, 1995:58–63). The issue of the relationship between water scarcity and food production has generated a substantial debate. It has been suggested that impending water shortages in North China will be so severe by 2025 that China will need to import upward of 210 million metric tons of grain per year to meet the demand arising out of population and income growth (Brown and Halweil, 1998). The IWMI study, though somewhat less alarmist, indicates that although South China will have surplus water, North China will experience absolute water scarcity (Seckler et al., 1999).

Much of public sector irrigation investment has been devoted to the development (and rehabilitation) of gravity irrigation systems. In most arid regions, the topography that is best suited to the development of large-scale irrigation systems has already been exploited. Investment costs of adding surface irrigation capacity have risen by several

---

[23] For an useful review, see Seckler et al. (1999). See also Food and Agriculture Organization (1995), Rosegrant (1997), and Raskin et al. (1998). The study by Raskin et al. gives more explicit attention to withdrawals for domestic, industrial, and environmental purposes. In developed countries, the use of water to protect in-stream environmental values is increasingly in competition with withdrawals for irrigation.

[24] Countries characterized by *absolute* water scarcity do not have sufficient water resources to maintain 1990 levels of per capita food production from irrigated agriculture, even at high levels of irrigation efficiency, and also meet reasonable water needs for domestic, industrial, and environmental purposes by 2025. Countries characterized by *severe* water scarcity have potential water resources sufficient to meet reasonable water needs by 2025, but only if they make very substantial improvements in water efficiency and investments in water development. The IWMI study assumes that when withdrawal exceed 50% of annual water resource flows the cost of further water resource development is likely to be prohibitive (Seckler et al., 1999:47)

multiples during the past half century. It is unlikely that there will be substantial new investment in large-scale gravity irrigation systems in the foreseeable future unless food prices rise significantly above the levels of the late 1990s.

In spite of the large public investment in gravity irrigation systems, the area irrigated using tube wells to pump groundwater has expanded even more rapidly. In many respects pump irrigation from aquifers is an ideal form of irrigation. The water is stored underground with no loss from evaporation. Water is generally available during the dry season even during drought years when reservoirs for surface irrigation may be dry. Economic incentives for efficient water use operate more effectively since access to water is under the control of individual producers rather than an inefficient, and often corrupt, irrigation bureaucracy. But expansion of groundwater exploitation also faces difficult problems in many areas. One is that withdrawals from groundwater aquifers greatly exceed recharge rates in many areas. A second is the intrusion of saline and polluted water into groundwater aquifers.

There are substantial negative spillover effects or externalities in both surface and groundwater systems that impact directly on agricultural production. One of the most common problems of gravity systems is water logging and salinity resulting from excessive water use and poorly designed drainage systems. In Pakistan, for example, water logging and salinity have resulted in loss of irrigated acreage sufficient to offset the new areas added to the irrigation system. In the Aral Sea basin in Central Asia, excessive water withdrawal has resulted in contraction of the Aral Sea and water logging and salinity in irrigated areass, and threatens the economic viability of the region.[25] The extraction of groundwater from aquifers in excess of recharge lowers the groundwater level and raises pumping costs. In some countries these spillover effects are sufficient to offset the contribution of expansion of irrigated areas to agricultural production.

The institutional arrangements under which producers obtain access to water contribute to inefficient water use. These institutional arrangements are an important source of negative spillover effects. In addition, they have failed to provide the incentives to induce the development and adoption of technology that would lead to growth of water productivity—agricultural output per acre foot or per cubic meter—comparable to the increases that have occurred in land or labor productivity (Mellor, 1996). But designing institutional arrangements to induce improvements in water efficiency and productivity will not be easy. The reforms that are typically suggested involve (1) clarification and security of water rights, (2) design of water markets and implementation of pricing policies, (3) quotas, charges, and taxes on groundwater withdrawals, and (4) greater local control over the management of public irrigation systems (National Research Council, 1992; Easter et al., 1998). It is possible to identify some successes from such efforts, but, in general, it has been difficult to design reforms

---

[25] One of the most comprehensive efforts to identify the world's threatened regions was organized by a group of scholars from the Department of Geography at Clark University (Kasperson et al., 1995). For the Aral Sea Basin study, see Glazovsky (1995:92–140).

that are both economically and politically viable. Transaction costs in water markets are often high. And water use involves a wide variety of public values that involve third parties in addition to the principals. It seems clear, however, that the rising economic value of water and the anticipated constraints on water withdrawals can be expected to induce the institutional reforms necessary to achieve integrated surface and groundwater and water quality and quantity management.

Pest Control

Pest control has become an increasingly serious constraint on agricultural production in spite of dramatic advances in pest control technology over the past half century. Prior to the latter decades of the nineteenth century, farmers relied almost exclusively on cultural methods such as crop rotation to control pests. Chemical control began in the 1870s with the development of arsenical and copper-based insecticides. Biological control dates from the late 1880s with the introduction of the vedelia beetle (from Australia) to control a California citrus pest, the cottony cushion scale. Efforts were also made to identify and develop pest-resistant crop and animal varieties and breeds.[26]

Pest control strategies changed dramatically with the development of dichlorodiphenyltrichloroethane (DDT) in the late 1930s and its use, during World War II, to protect American troops against malaria and other insect-born diseases. Early tests found DDT to be effective against almost all insect species and relatively harmless to humans, animals, and plants. It was effective at low application levels and relatively inexpensive. DDT's success directed economic entomologists and funding agencies away from fundamental research on insect biology, physiology, and ecology, as well as from alternative methods of insect pest control. Chemical companies rapidly expanded their research on synthetic organic insecticides as well as chemical approaches to the control of pathogens and weeds.

Problems of negative externalities were encountered shortly after the introduction of DDT. When DDT was introduced in California to control the cottony cushion scale, the scale's introduced predator, the vedalia beetle, turned out to be more susceptible to DDT than the scale itself. In 1947, just 1 year after its introduction, citrus growers, confronted with a resurgence of the scale population, were forced to restrict the use of DDT. In Peru, the cotton boll worm quickly built up resistance to DDT and other chlorinated hydrocarbon pesticides. Producers then turned to the more recently developed, and much more toxic, organophosphate insecticides, which again selected for resistant strains of the boll worm. In the meantime, natural predators were almost completely exterminated. Cotton production in Peru collapsed and was revived only after a program to regulate insecticide use was implemented (Palladino, 1996:36–41).

During the 1950s, an increasing body of evidence suggested that the benefits of the pesticides introduced in the 1940s and early 1950s were obtained at a substantial

---

[26] The best single review of pest control issues is the National Research Council (1996b). See also Ruttan (1982:200–210); Palladino (1996b:1–46); Fernandez-Cornejo and Jans (1999).

cost. The costs included not only the loss of resistance in target populations and the destruction of beneficial insects, but also the direct and indirect effects on wildlife populations and on human health. In the early 1960s, public concern about these effects was galvanized by dramatic revelations of the health and environmental effects of the new insecticides (Carson, 1962). These concerns initially emerged in the United States and other developed countries, but at about the same time, the adoption of the high-yielding "green revolution" cereal varieties in developing countries was associated with rapid growth in pesticide use. When yields were low there had been little benefit from pest control. As yields rose, the economic incentive to adopt chemical pest control technologies also rose.

The solution to the pesticide crisis offered by the entomology community was integrated pest management (IPM). IPM involved the integrated use of cultural control, biological control, chemical control, and pest-resistant crop varieties. It is more complex for the producer to implement than spraying by the calendar. It requires skill in pest monitoring and understanding of insect ecology. And it often involves cooperation among producers for effective implementation.[27] At the time IPM began to be promoted as a pest control strategy in the 1960s, there was very little IPM technology available. IPM represented little more than a rhetorical device to paper over the differences between economic and ecological entomologists. But by the 1970s, sufficient research had been conducted to successfully implement a number of important IPM programs (Conway and Pretty, 1991:578–580). However, exaggerated expectations about the possibility of large reductions in pesticide use that could be achieved without significant decline in crop yields were not realized.[28]

Integrated approaches to weed management (IWM) evolved later than IPM, in part because resistance to chemical herbicides occurred much more slowly than resistance to insecticides. Rising real wage rates in developed and even some developing countries induced replacement of labor-intensive hand and mechanical weeding by chemical weed control (Naylor, 1996). By the mid-1990s, however, the development of genetically engineered herbicide-resistant crop varieties resulted in a new set of concerns (Paolatti and Pimentel, 1995). In some cases, herbicide-resistant crops may have beneficial effects on the environment—for example, when a single broad-spectrum herbicide that breaks down rapidly in the environment is substituted for several applications of a herbicide that is more persistent in the environment. When a

---

[27] The elements of the very successful program to control cotton pests (boll weevil, pink bollworm, and tobacco budworm) in Texas included (1) establishment of a uniform planting period and adoption of short duration varieties, (2) irrigation prior to planting, (3) application of insecticide only in areas in which high bollworm populations are expected, (4) selective application of an organophosphate insecticide during harvest, (5) defoliation of mature crops (so all bolls open at the same time), (6) use of mechanical strippers (to kill larvae) in harvesting, (7) shredding of stalks and plow down immediately after harvest, and (8) imposition of fines on uncooperative producers. Implementation of the program involved organizing pest control districts with responsibility for enforcement (Conway and Petty, 1991:578–580).

[28] See, for example, Curtis et al. (1991) and Pimentel et al. (1991). For a critique, see Gianessi (1991).

single herbicide is used repeatedly, however, it does pose the danger of selecting for herbicide-resistant weeds (Powles et al., 1997; Snow and Palma, 1997). Like IPM, exaggerated expectations that IWM would result in a large reduction of herbicide use remain unrealized. The impact of agricultural intensification and the coevolution of pathogens, insect pests, and weeds in response to control efforts will continue to represent a major factor in directing the allocation of agricultural research resources to maintenance research.

Health

Illness is a significant constraint on labor productivity in agriculture in many developing countries. Farm workers are often incapacitated—too ill to work—for 15–20 days each year. And even when they are at work, productivity may be severely constrained by a combination of malnutrition and parasitic and infectious disease.[29] Since the mid-1960s, a number of commonly used health indicators, such as life expectancy and infant mortality, have shown substantial improvement in almost all developing countries. Most developing countries, except a few of the very poorest, have begun the epidemiological transition from early death from infectious and parasitic disease toward late death by cancer, heart attack, and stroke. Yet there are important reasons for concern about the possible reversal of recent progress. Dramatic progress has been made in the reduction of infectious diseases and the control of diarrheal diseases. However, (1) the reemergence of a number of infectious and parasitic diseases, such as tuberculosis and malaria, (2) the diffusion of parasitic diseases such as schistosomiasis and of bacterial diseases such as cholera, and (3) the emergence of new infectious diseases such as AIDS, Ebola, and Lyme disease have generated serious concern among both health professionals and the general public.[30]

A second set of health concerns has emerged out of the environmental consequences of agricultural and industrial production. The health effects of agricultural intensification include the direct effects of intensive use of insecticides and herbicides.[31] Industrial intensification has, in some areas, resulted in soil degradation by heavy metals. The effects of disease are often compounded by malnutrition. Calorie intake per capita has been declining for as much as two decades in a number of sub-Saharan African countries. If a number of these health threats emerge simultaneously, it is not too difficult to construct scenarios in which there are sufficient numbers of sick people in some villages to become a serious constraint on food production.

---

[29] For a comprehensive treatment, see Dasgupta (1993:401–523). For a very careful analysis of the interactions among soil erosion, pesticide exposure and health, see Pingali et al. (1997:91–125).

[30] Lederberg (1996) lists the reemergence or diffusion of three viral, eight parasitic, and nine bacterial diseases, and the emergence or first recognition of 29 other diseases between 1973 and 1985.

[31] See, for example, Antle and Pingali (1994), Pingali et al. (1994), Pingali and Roger (1995), Crissman et al. (1998).

Climate Change

In the late 1950s, measurements taken in Hawaii indicated that carbon dioxide (CO_2) was increasing in the atmosphere. Beginning in the late 1960s, computer model simulations indicated possible changes in temperature and precipitation that could occur due to human-induced emission of carbon dioxide (CO_2), nitrous oxide (N_2O), and other "greenhouse gases" into the atmosphere. By the early 1980s, a fairly broad consensus had emerged in the climate change research community that greenhouse gas emissions could, by 2050, result in a doubling of the atmospheric concentration of CO_2 from preindustrial levels, a rise in global average temperature by 1.5 to 4.5°C (about 2.7 to 8.0°F), and a complex pattern of worldwide climate changes. Since the beginning of the 1980s, a succession of studies have attempted to assess how an increase in the atmospheric concentration of greenhouse gasses could affect agricultural production (Parry, 1990; Fischer et al., 1995:115–159; Bruce et al., 1996; Grübler, 1998; Rosenzweig and Hillel, 1998).[32]

There are three ways in which increases in atmospheric CO_2 concentrations may affect agricultural production. First, increased CO_2 concentrations in the atmosphere may have a positive effect on the growth rates of crop plants (and weeds) through the CO_2 "fertilization effect" and by decreasing the rate of transpiration. The magnitude of the CO_2 fertilization effect remains highly uncertain. It has not yet been possible to separate the effects of the increase in CO_2 concentrations over the past half century from other factors that have contributed to higher yields. A second way that agricultural production could be impacted is that higher temperatures could result in a rise in the sea level, resulting in inundation of coastal areas and the intrusion of salt water into groundwater aquifers and surface waters. Low-lying island and coastal agricultural areas—in Bangladesh, for example—could be impacted very severely. The largest impact on agricultural production will be due to the effects of greenhouse gas-induced changes in temperature, rainfall, and sunlight. Greenhouse gas-induced warming is expected to be greatest in mid- and high-latitude (above 45°) regions. Subtropical and tropical regions will experience less extreme temperature changes. Monsoon rains are likely to penetrate further northward. Northern areas in which production is presently constrained by length of the growing season, such as the northern fringes of the Canadian prairie, might expect both higher yields and an expansion of area devoted to cereals and forage plants. But at an aggregate level, food supply does not appear to be seriously threatened by global climate change over the next half century (Fischer et al., 1995:155; Reilly et al., 1999).

---

[32] See Chapter 12 for a more complete discussion of the sources of greenhouse gas emissions, the potential impact of global climate change, and global climate change policy. Because CO_2 accounts for over half of greenhouse gas, climate changes forcing the increase in greenhouse gas emissions are usually reported in terms of CO_2 equivalent. Fossil fuel consumption is the major source of CO_2 emissions. NO_2 accounts for approximately one-quarter of greenhouse gas climate forcing. Since nitrogen is the most rapidly growing chemical fertilizer, there is an inherent conflict between food production and the control of NO_2 emissions (Frink et al., 1999; Socolow, 1999).

What inferences do I draw from this review of resource and environmental constraints on the transition to agricultural sustainability? It is unlikely that soil loss and degradation will represent a serious constraint on global agricultural production in the foreseeable future. But soil loss or degradation could become a serious local or regional constraint in a number of fragile resource areas. It is also unlikely that lack of water resources will become a severe constraint on global agricultural production in the foreseeable future. But in 40 to 50 of the world's most arid countries, plus major regions in several other countries, competition from household, industrial, and environmental demands will result in a reallocation of water away from irrigation. In the more arid regions of the world, water scarcity is becoming the "single greatest threat to food security, human health and natural ecosystems"(Seckler et al., 1999:1).

The problem of pest and pathogen control will have increasingly serious implications for sustainable growth in agricultural production in both developed and developing countries. Both resistant crop varieties and chemical methods of control tend to induce target pest resistance. New pest control technologies must constantly be replaced by a succession of resistant varieties and chemical (or biochemical) agents. Health constraints, combined with nutritional deficiency, could become a serious constraint on agricultural production in villages in some of the world's poorest countries. Nature is not a passive actor in the battle to protect humans, nonhuman animals, and plants from pests and pathogens. Nature fights back!

Recent projections of the impact of global climate change on agricultural production are much more optimistic than projections made a decade ago (Adams et al., 1999). The scientific and empirical basis for the more optimistic projections is, however, much too fragile to serve as a secure foundation for policy. There is great uncertainty about the rate of climate change that can be expected over the next half century. Few of the models have give adequate attention to the synergistic interactions among climate change, soil loss and degradation, ground and surface water storage, and the incidence of pests and pathogens. Actions taken to mitigate global climate change, such as land-intensive approaches to carbon sequestering, substitution of fuels based on agricultural raw materials for petroleum-based fuels, and efforts to control carbon, nitrous oxide, and methane emissions, could have a larger negative effect on crop and animal production than the direct effects of climate change. These interactive effects could add up to a significantly larger burden on sustainable growth in production than the relatively small effects of each constraint considered separately. A clear implication is that the "island empires" of agricultural, health, and environmental research will have to build much more effective bridges among the several disciplines to enable a successful navigation of the transition to sustainable agriculture.

AGRICULTURAL RESEARCH SYSTEMS

The agricultural sector of the presently developed countries have, during the twentieth century, been remarkably successful in overcoming the constraints on agricultural production resulting from the exhaustion of the land frontier. Since the middle of the twentieth century, these countries have been joined in making the transition from growth based on the resource exploitation model to growth based on the higher payoff input model. This transition has been made possible by a remarkable institutional innovation—the development of public sector agricultural research systems.[33]

At the beginning of the nineteenth century, Great Britain was regarded by those interested in agricultural improvement as the "school for agriculture."[34] Agricultural research was initiated by private individuals, usually innovative farmers or owners of large estates. In 1843 Sir John Bennet Lawes established on his ancestral estate the Rothamsted Agricultural Experiment Station, now the oldest continuously operated agricultural experimentation in the world. Shortly before his death, Lawes endowed the station through the Lawes Agricultural Trust. As the research program expanded and became more costly, government funds were increasingly sought and obtained until the research program at Rothamsted became almost wholly funded by the British government through the Agricultural Research Council.

By the end of the nineteenth century, leadership in agricultural research had passed to Germany (Grantham, 1984:191–214). The German approach to the development and application of science and technology is illustrated by von Liebig's research in the field of agricultural chemistry and by the establishment of publicly supported agricultural experiment stations. The publication of *Organic Chemistry in its Relation to Agriculture and Physiology* (1840) by Justus von Liebig is regarded by many as the dividing line in the evolution of agricultural research—a major step toward the development of a science-based agricultural technology. Von Liebig's great accomplishment was "to bring together and interpret the very considerable mass of chemical and related data pertaining to plants and soils that had accumulated up to that time" (Salman and Hanson, 1964:22). His refutation of the prevailing humus theory of plant nutrition and his proposed mineral theory represented a major success of his approach.

Von Liebig's greatest achievement as a teacher was the introduction, at Giessen, of the laboratory method for training research students in organic chemistry. It was the first laboratory of its kind. Students from all over the world were attracted to it. The demonstration of the power and value of von Liebig's approach to the organization of scientific research led directly to the establishment of specialized agricultural research laboratories and experiment stations. The first publically supported agricultural exper-

---

[33] I do not, in this chapter, discuss a number of other important institutional innovations that have contributed to growth in agricultural production in a number of developed and developing countries, such as the reform of land tenure, and market institutions. For an induced innovation interpretation of a number of these institutional changes in developing countries, see Hayami and Ruttan, 1971, 1985:388–415). For an induced institutional interpretation of U.S. agricultural commodity policy, see Ruttan (1984:549–559).

[34] For greater detail on the development of national agricultural research systems, see Ruttan (1982) and Alston et al. (1999). For an evaluation of donor assistance for the development of national agricultural research systems, see Purcell and Anderson (1997:107–174).

iment station in Germany was organized at Mockern, Saxony in 1852. During the next 25 years, 74 publicly supported agricultural experiment stations were established in Germany. The German model of public sector agricultural research became the model for agricultural research in the United States and in most other presently developed countries.

The U.S. System

The institutional patten that emerged for the organization of U.S. agricultural research drew heavily on the German system for its model of institutional organization and in its training of young scientists. A number of the "science entrepreneurs" who were responsible for the establishment of U.S. agricultural research stations had studied in Germany. Institutionalization of agricultural research in the United States involved the creation of a dual federal–state system. The federal system developed more rapidly than the state system. Yet it was not until the closing years of the nineteenth century that either the state or the federal system acquired any significant capacity to respond to the rising demand for scientific and technical knowledge.

The emergence, toward the end of the century, of a viable pattern of organization for agricultural research in the federal Department of Agriculture involved breaking away from a discipline-oriented structure and organizing scientific bureaus focusing on a particular set of problems or commodities. By the early 1900s, the scientific bureaus of the United States Department of Agriculture (USDA) included the Bureau of Plant Industry, the Bureau of Entomology, the Bureau of Soils, the Bureau of Biological Survey, and the Weather Bureau. The Office of Experiment Stations maintained liaison with state agricultural experiment stations (SAESs) and handled the transmission of federal funds appropriated for use by the state stations (Dupree, 1957:165; Huffman and Evenson, 1993:31–34).

The capacity of the state Land-Grant (public) universities to provide new scientific and technical knowledge of agricultural development was even more limited than that of the Department of Agriculture. The key federal legislation establishing the USDA–SAES research–teaching–extension system included the act establishing the USDA in 1862, the Morrill or Land-Grant College Act of 1862, the Hatch Act, providing for state agricultural experimentation research support in 1887, and the Smith–Lever Act, providing federal support for the state agricultural extension program in 1914.[35] The first state experiment station, the Connecticut State Agricultural Experiment station, was not established until 1877. And it was not until the early 1920s that it was possible to claim, with some degree of confidence, that a national agricultural research

---

[35] Huffman and Evenson (1993:3) note: "These legislative acts and the institutions developed and supported by them were major institutional innovations The institutions, as embodied in these legislative acts, were not simply the product of exceptional 'inspiration' . . . of legislators and policy makers of the day. By the time each of these major pieces of legislation was passed considerable institutional development and experience with earlier institutions had been realized."

and extension system had been effectively institutionalized at both the federal and state levels.[36]

The structure of the U.S. agricultural research system remained essentially unchanged between the mid-1920s and the mid-1960s. It became an increasingly important source of new knowledge and new technology. Its contribution to the development and diffusion of hybrid corn was a particularly dramatic example (Chapter 5). Since the mid-1960s, the federal–state agricultural research system has undergone a series of external and internal challenges from a variety of scientific, populist, and ideological perspectives. The external challenges included populist criticisms of the narrow focus of agricultural research, typified by two seminal publications: Rachel Carson's *Silent Spring* (1962) and Jim Hightower's *Hard Tomatoes, Hard Times* (1973). Carson's book drew attention to the environmental effects of intensive use of agricultural pesticides. Hightower's book criticized the public agricultural research system for subverting the interests of farmers and consumers in favor of agricultural business interests. Although both books contained a frustrating melange of errors and half-truths, along with valid criticisms, they did serve to dramatize the major limitation of the U.S. agricultural research system—that it was too narrowly focused on plants, animals, and soils (Fitzgerald, 1991).

A second, and opposing criticism emerged from within the agricultural research community itself. In 1972 a committee of the National Research Council severely criticized the quality of research being conducted by the USDA and the state agricultural experiment stations as outmoded, pedestrian, and inefficient (National Research Council, 1972). It was also critical of the formula-funding mechanism the federal government used to support state agricultural research and the limited role of peer evaluation in the allocation of research resources. Thus, although the populist critics were criticizing agricultural research for its narrow focus on productivity-enhancing technical change, the internal criticism objected to excessive focus on technology development and the neglect of basic science. An important consequence of the internal criticism was the passage of the National Agricultural Research, Extension, and Teaching Policy Act of 1977, which authorized a USDA competitive research program for plant science and for nutrition research that would be open to all scientists in either public or private institutions.

While attempting to respond to these external and internal criticisms, both the federal and state systems have been subject to substantial budget stringency (Figure 6.5).

---

[36] The structure of the U.S. federal–state agricultural research system differs substantially from that in most other developed countries. In the United States between two-thirds and three-fourths of public sector agricultural research has been conducted at the state agricultural experiment stations operated by the state Land Grant universities. In other OECD countries, less than one-fourth of public agricultural research has been conducted at universities (Alston et al., 1998, Table 2). In the Japanese system a relative high percentage of agricultural research is funded by prefectural governments and conducted at prefectural experiment stations. Hayami and Ruttan have argued that the decentralized funding and governance of agricultural research in the United States and Japan has made public sector agricultural research in the two countries particularly responsive to market forces and the needs of farmers in each state or prefecture (Hayami and Ruttan, 1985:251).

Between 1890 and 1980, resources available to the U.S. public agricultural research system had grown at a real rate of over 4% per year. Since 1980 the resources available to the federal system have remained essentially unchanged in real terms while support at the state level has grown more slowly than in the past. Meanwhile private agricultural research has continued to grow rapidly (Huffman and Evenson, 1993:95, 96; Fuglie et al., 1996:9–18). By the early 1970s expenditures for private sector agricultural research began to exceed the level for public sector agricultural research. In 1996 USDA research expenditures were $936 million, SAES expenditures were approximately $2.2 billion, and private sector expenditures were approximately $3.9 billion (Figure 6.6). As private sector agricultural research has grown there has also been a shift in its composition. Research on postharvest technology has risen relative to production-oriented research. And within production-oriented research the share directed to research on mechanical technology has declined while the share directed to advancing biological and chemical technology has risen. Public sector agricultural research is concentrated even more heavily than private sector agricultural research on advancing biological technology (Huffman and Evenson, 1993:93–127).[37]

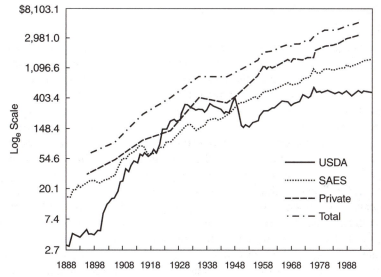

Figure 6.5 Expenditures on state agricultural experiment station (SAES), U.S. Department of Agriculture (USDA), and U.S. private agricultural research, fiscal years 1888–1997 (millions of 1984 dollars). (Adapted from W. E. Huffman and R. E. Everson, *Science for Agriculture: A Long-Term Perspective*, Ames IA: Iowa State University Press, 1993:94. Data for 1991–1997 from J. M. Alston, J. E. Christian, and P. G. Pardey, *Agricultural R&D Investments and Institutions in the United States*, Paying for Agricultural Productivity, Chapter 4, Baltimore, MD: Johns Hopkins University Press, 1999.)

---

[37] For a comparison with recent trends in other developed countries see Alston, Pardey, and Smith (1998d).

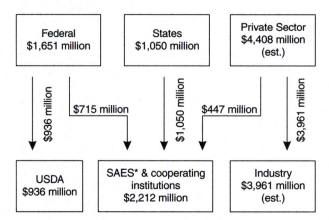

Figure 6.6 Sources and flows of funding for agricultural research in 1996. *SAES are the State Agricultural Experiment Stations; cooperating institutions include the 1890 forestry and veterinary schools. (*Source:* Federal and state research expenditures from *Inventory of Current Research*, USDA. Private sector/industry expenditures based on Fuglie et al., 1996, p. 9.)

There has been continuous pressure during the 1980s and 1990s to reevaluate the appropriate role of public and private sector agricultural research.[38] The primary rationale for commodity-oriented public sector investment in agricultural research has been that in many areas incentives for private sector research have not been adequate to induce an optimum level of research investment—that the social rate of return exceeds the private rate of return because a large share of the gains from private sector agricultural research is captured by other firms, by farmers, and by consumers, rather than by the firm that develops the technology. This is particularly true when the new knowledge or technology generated by research is not protected by patents or trade secrets. There is little incentive for a private firm to invest in research if the results cannot be embodied in a proprietary product. Private and social rates of return to agricultural research suggest that both the public and private sectors in the United States are underinvesting in agricultural research. Marginal social rates of return to private sector agricultural research have been estimated at upward of 40%—well above the 15–20% normally regarded as sufficient to induce private sector investment. This suggests that a substantial share of the benefits of private sector agricultural research spills over to other firms, producers, and consumers. Marginal social rates of return to public sector agricultural research have been even higher—upward of 70%

---

[38] For a recent evaluation, see the Committee on the Future of the Colleges of Agriculture in the Land Grant University System (National Research Council, 1996a). The committee attempted to assess the strengths and weaknesses of the colleges of agriculture and to suggest reforms that would more effectively position the system for the twenty-first century.

(Huffman and Evenson, 1993:243–248; Alston and Pardey, 1996:203–207; Fuglie et al., 1996:24–33).[39]

Traditionally it has been more difficult for the private sector to capture the benefits from advances in biological technology than the benefits from advances in mechanical technology. Patent protection of mechanical (and chemical) inventions has been more highly developed than protection of advances in biological technology. But this is changing. Intellectual property rights in the development of hybrid corn and sorghum have been protected by trade secrets in the form of proprietary inbred lines (Chapter 4). The Plant Variety Protection Act of 1970 provided stronger property rights to breeders of open-pollinated crop varieties. In 1980 the Supreme Court established a framework for patenting genetically altered living organisms. In 1985 the U.S. patent office ruled that a genetically altered corn plant was patentable (Huffman and Evenson, 1993:248–250). These changes have greatly enhanced private sector incentives for investment in both the old biological technology and the newer biotechnologies related to agriculture, even in some areas of generic or basic science that were regarded as the natural province of the public sector (Figure 6.5).

The implications of these developments for the allocation of research resources between the public and private sector can be illustrated by the case of hybrid corn. The early hybrid corn companies engaged primarily in reproduction and marketing of hybrids developed by public sector breeders. The larger companies, such as Pioneer and DeKalb, quickly developed their own breeding programs. During the 1980s, the share of public inbred lines used as parents for commercial hybrids declined dramatically. Public sector corn-breeding research has been refocused toward basic genomic investigation and genetic engineering. In the late 1990s substantial resources were devoted to genomic research (Chapter 10). This research, like the initial public sector investment in hybrid corn development and the production of public inbred lines, meets the criteria for public sector research funding set out at the beginning of this section. Not even the largest private seed company is able to capture more than a small share of the benefits of its own genomic research.

A second major criterion for public sector investment in agricultural research has been its complementarity with education. There is a strong synergistic interaction between research and education. This relationship is so strong that in many fields, particularly at the most advanced levels, research carries a strong penalty when conducted apart from graduate education or postdoctoral research. And graduate education can hardly be effective if both students and teachers are not engaged in research. As the public sector continues to shift its research resources away from

---

[39] Alston et al. (1998a) have shown that estimated rates of return to research are dependent on the lag structure employed in making the estimates. They argue that the use of inappropriate lag structures has resulted in an upward bias in most reported rate of return studies. Estimates of high rates of return to agricultural research have been controversial beginning with the hybrid corn studies by Griliches (1958:419–431). See, for example, Wise (1975:246–261) and Fox (1985). The criticisms have contributed to the refinement of the methodology used in estimating rates of return but have not seriously damaged the credibility of the estimates (Alston et al., 1998c; Evenson and Kislev, 1999).

technology development to pretechnology and even more basic research, new methods will have to be developed to finance the training of those who will conduct plant-breeding research and development in the private sector.

A third consideration relevant to the role of public and private sector agricultural research is related to the externalities or spillover effects of agricultural production. As noted above, the intensification of agricultural production has had important negative feedback effects that contribute to the degradation of the agricultural resource base and of natural environments. Those costs have not been included in the rate of return estimates referred to above. There are few incentives to induce the private sector investment needed to identify the resource and environmental impacts or to develop the knowledge and technology needed to respond to the negative resource and environmental impacts. Substantial expansion and reallocation of public sector agricultural research resources will be required if these issues are to be adequately addressed.

The International Agricultural Research System

Substantial progress was made in the first several decades of the twentieth century in initiating agricultural research capacity in Latin America and in the colonial economies of Asia and Africa. These efforts were typically focused on tropical export crops such as sugar (Box 6.1), rubber, cotton, banana, coffee, and tea. The disruption of international trade during the great depression of the 1930s and during World War II, followed by the break-up of colonial empires, aborted or severely weakened many of these efforts. Some, however, such as the Rubber Research Institute of Malaya (now Malaysia), achieved world class capacity and continued to function as effective sources of new technology into the post-World War II era (Brockway, 1979).[40]

For the architects of the post-World War II set of global institutions, meeting world food needs and reducing poverty in rural areas were essential elements in their vision of a world community. In the immediate postwar years much of the responsibility for assisting developing countries in achieving these objectives fell on the United Nations Food and Agriculture Organization (FAO). But John Boyd Orr, the first director general of the FAO, burdened with the memory of the agricultural surpluses of the 1930s, was highly critical of the view that knowledge and technology represented a serious constraint on agricultural production capacity. "No research was needed to find out that half the people in the world lacked sufficient food for health, or that with modern engineering and agricultural science the world food supply could easily be increased to meet human needs" (Boyd Orr, 1966:160).

Assistance for agricultural development in the poor countries was conducted largely along the lines implied by the technology transfer model of agricultural

---

[40] In this section I draw heavily on Ruttan (1982:90–115, 1986; Hayami and Ruttan, 1985:264–274; Pardy, Roseboom, and Anderson, 1989; Bell et al., 1994; Anderson and Dalrymple, 1999; Alston, Craig, and Roseboom, 1998b; and Alston and Pardey, 1999).

development. By the early 1960s, however, it was becoming apparent that the gains in production from simple technology transfer had largely played themselves out. The inadequacies of policies based on the technology transfer or extension model led to a reexamination of the assumptions about diffusing agricultural technology from high-productivity to low-productivity countries or regions. As noted above, the result was the emergence of a new perspective: that agricultural technology, particularly yield-enhancing biological technology, was highly "location specific." Evidence was also accumulated that only limited productivity gains could be achieved by the reallocation or more efficient uses of the resources available to peasant producers in poor countries. The stage had been set for the design of policies consistent with the high-payoff and induced technical change models. These insights, from experience and analysis, shaped the responses to the world's food crises of the 1960s and 1970s. The immediate response was the transfer of large resources, including food aid, to the food-deficit countries (Ruttan, 1996:149–202). The longer term response was the mobilization of resources to develop a system of international agricultural research institutes and to strengthen national agricultural research systems in less developed countries.

In the late 1950s the Ford and Rockefeller Foundations collaborated in establishing an International Rice Research Institute (IRRI) in the Philippines. This was followed by the establishment of the International Center for the Improvement of Maize and Wheat (CIMMYT) in Mexico, the International Institute of Tropical Agriculture (IITA) in Nigeria, and the International Center for Tropical Agriculture (CIAT) in Colombia. It became apparent by the late 1960s that the financial requirements needed to maintain the research and development programs of the four institutes were stretching the capacity of the two foundations. In 1971 the Ford and Rockefeller Foundations, the World Bank, the FAO, the United Nations Development Program (UNDP), and several bilateral donor agencies organized a Consultative Group on International Agricultural Research (CGIAR).

The initial centers focused their research mainly on the major food crops grown in developing countries—rice, wheat, maize, potatoes, and cassava. These were joined in the 1970s by centers focusing on livestock production and animal disease, on arid and semiarid areas, on food policy, and on the conservation of genetic resources, and in the 1990s by the addition of new centers on banana and plantain, forestry, soils, irrigation, and agroforestry (Table 6.1). The expansion of the CGIAR system was not accompanied by a comparable increase in the resources available to the system. Donor contributions, which amounted to $335–340 million in current dollars in 1998, had declined in real terms from the levels achieved a decade earlier. A larger share of the resources available to the system was earmarked by donors for specific projects, often involving donor country scientists. In addition, research effort was reallocated away from productivity-enhancing research to broader issues of rural development and the environmental impacts of the intensification of agricultural production.

The crisis facing the system was not only financial. A number of the CGIAR centers have experienced the difficulties associated with organizational maturity. There is

Table 6.1 The CGIAR Centers: 1997

Center	Date of Joining CG	Date of Foundation	Headquarters Location	Main Areas of Focus		1997 Budget (million US$)
				Commodity/Activity	Region/Agroecological Zone	
IRRI, International Rice Research Institute	1971	1960	Los Baños, Philippines	Rice, rice-based ecosystems	World Asia	35.0
CIMMYT, Centro Internacional de Mejoramiento de Maiz y Trigo	1971	1966	El Batan, Mexico	Wheat, maize	World	30.4
CIAT, Centro Internacional de Agricultura Tropical	1971	1966	Cali, Colombia	Phaseolus bean, cassava, rice, tropical pastures	World Latin America Latin America/lowland tropics	33.3
IITA, International Institute of Tropical Agriculture	1971	1967	Ibadan, Nigeria	Farming systems, rice, maize, cassava, cocoyams, soybeans	Humid and subhumid tropics World	31.9
ICRISAT, International Crops Research Institute for the Semi-Arid Tropics	1972	1972	Patancheru, India	Farming systems, sorghum, millet, pigeonpeas, chickpeas, groundnuts	Semiarid tropics (Asia, Africa) World	27.5
CIP, Centro Internacional de la Papa	1972	1970	Lima, Peru	Potato, sweet potato, other root crops	World	25.5
ILRAD, International Laboratory for Research on Animal Diseases	1973	1973	Nairobi, Kenya	See ILRI		NA
ILCA, International Livestock Center for Africa	1974	1974	Addis Ababa, Ethiopia	See ILRI		NA
IPGRI, International Plant Genetic Resources Institute[a]	1974	1974	Rome, Italy	Promote activities to further collection, conservation, evolution, and utilization of germplasm	World	19.6
WARDA, West Africa Rice Development Association	1974	1970	Bouaké, Côte d'Ivoire	Rice	West Africa	9.2
ICARDA, International Center for Agricultural Research in the Dry Areas	1976	1976	Aleppo, Syria	Farming systems, barley, lentils, faba beans, wheat, kabali chickpeas	North Africa/Near East World North Africa/Near East	27.6
ISNAR, International Service for National Agricultural Research	1979	1979	The Hague, The Netherlands	Strengthen national agricultural research systems	World	10.4

IFPRI, International Food Policy Research Institute	1980	Washington DC, United States	Identify and analyze national and international strategies and policies for reducing hunger and malnutrition	World, with primary emphasis on low-income countries and groups	18.1
ICRAF, International Centre for Research in Agro-forestry	1991	Nairobi, Kenya	Agroforestry, multi-purpose trees	World	22.2
IWMI, International Water Management Institute[b]	1991	Colombo, Sri Lanka	Water and Irrigation management	World	10.1
ICLARM, International Centre for Living Aquatic Research Management	1992	Metro Manila, Philippines	Sustainable aquatic resource management	World	8.5
CIFOR, Center for International Forestry Research	1993	Bogor, Indonesia	Sustainable forestry management	World	10.6
ILRI, International Livestock Research Institute[c]	1995	Nairobi, Kenya, and Addis Ababa, Ethiopia	Livestock production and animal health	World	26.7

Note: NA indicates not applicable.

[a]IPGRI was first established in 1974 as the International Board of Plant Genetic Resources (IBPGR). The Board was funded as a CG Center but operated under the administration of FAO and was located at FAO headquarters in Rome, Italy. In 1993 IBPGR changes its name to IPGRI, and was established as a self-administering CG Center in its own headquarters building in Rome. An International Network for the Improvement of Banana and Plantain (INIBAP) was established in Montpellier, France in 1984. In 1992 INIBAP became a CG Center but in 1994 INIBAP's functions were placed under the adminstration of IPGRI but INIBAP continues to maintain its own board.

[b]Until 1998, the International Irrigation Management Institute (IIMI).

[c]ILRI became operational in January 1995 through a merge of the International Laboratory for Research and Animal Diseases (ILRAD) and the International Livestock Center for Africa (ILCA). ILRAD research focused on livestock diseases (world) and tickbone disease and typsanomiasis (sub-Saharan Africa). ILCA did research on aminal feed and production systems for cattle, sheep, and goats for sub-Saharan Africa.

Source: J. M. Alston and P. G. Pardey, *International Approaches to Agricultural R&D: The CGIAR.* Washington, DC: International Food Policy Research Institute (paper prepared for U.S. Office of Science and Technology Policy, Executive Office of the President), February 1999 (mimeo).

a natural life cycle sequence in the history of research organizations and research programs (Ruttan, 1982:132). When they are initially organized they tend to attract vigorous and creative individuals. As these individuals interact across disciplines and problem areas, the organization often experiences a period of great productivity. As the research organization matures, however, it often tends to settle into filling in the gaps in knowledge and technology rather than achieving creative solutions to scientific and technical problems. Since the mid-1980s the managers of several of the CGIAR institutes have been forced to confront the problem of how to revitalize a mature research organization during a period when it was necessary to make substantial cuts in research and support staff in response to budget reductions. The rapid changes in the technology of crop variety improvement associated with the advances in molecular biology and genetic engineering combined with recent institutional innovation leading to stronger private property rights in genetic materials represent a particularly difficult challenge to the ability of the CGIAR system to continue to make advances in biological technology available to the national agricultural research systems of the developing countries (see Chapter 10).[41]

Strengthening National Research Systems

As the new seed-fertilizer technology generated at the CGIAR centers, particularly for rice and wheat, began to come on-stream in the late 1960s, some donors assumed that the CGIAR centers could bypass the more difficult and often frustrating efforts to strengthen national agricultural research systems.[42] But experience confirmed that strong national research centers were essential if the prototype technology that might be developed at the international centers was to be broadly transferred, adapted, and made available to local producers. The location-specific nature of biological technology meant that the prototype technologies developed at the international centers could become available to producers in the wide range of agroclimatic regions and social and economic environments in which the commodities were being produced only if regional or local capacity to modify, adapt, and reinvent the technology was available. It became clear that the challenge of constructing a global agricultural research system capable of sustaining growth in agricultural production required the development of research capacity for each commodity of economic significance in each agroclimatic region.

But what does it mean to establish adequate research capacity to sustain agricultural development? One answer, built around a careful analysis of sources and communication of scientific and technical knowledge, is illustrated in Table 6.2.

---

[41] For a more detailed discussion of the program and financial problems facing the international agricultural research system, see CGIAR System Review Secretariat (1998).

[42] There is now an extensive literature on the development of national agricultural research systems in developing countries. For a comprehensive reviews, see Pardey et al. (1991) and Byerlee and Alex (1998). For useful case studies, see Tendler (1994, 146–180) and Eicher (1997).

The system includes six simultaneous levels of activity with both vertical (upstream and downstream) and horizontal feedbacks and linkages (Huffman, 1999:19–21). The system is similar in concept to that depicted in Figure 3.6 (Chapter 3). Level I identifies the final users of new technology, who are also a source of information about technology needs and problems. Level II is the public and private information system—extension, marketing, and distribution—that links upstream sources to final users and the public and private information systems. Level III refers to the commercialized technology and knowledge that are the product of applied research. Level IV, technology invention, identifies the engineering and applied science fields that generate new technology. Level V, pretechnology research, is directed specifically toward producing discoveries that advance the knowledge needed to design new technology and institutions. It is linked upstream to Level VI, to the fundamental basic or core sciences. A distinction between Level V and VI is that research in the Level V fields tends to be demand driven and in Level VI research tends to be supply driven.

In a further attempt to classify developing countries according to their research capacities, Evenson (1996:12–14) found only 20 developing countries that had achieved substantial capacity for agricultural technology invention (Level III). Roughly 75 developing countries with a total population of over one billion people still have very limited capacity to design and develop new agricultural technology. These countries remain substantially dependent on the CGIAR international agricultural research institutes and on the agricultural aid programs of bilateral donors for assistance in the transfer and adaptation of agricultural technology. It has been estimated that for any but the very smallest countries, such as those with less than 10 million population, a minimum public national agricultural research extension education regulatory system, primarily focused at Levels II–III, would require involvement in the neighborhood of 250 scientists, agronomists, and engineers trained at the Master's and Ph.D. levels (Ruttan, 1986).

Between the early 1960s and the early 1980s, agricultural research budgets and research personnel in developing countries grew rapidly. The global share of agricultural researchers in less developed countries increased from 33 to 58%. China alone accounted for 24% in 1981–1985. But by the late 1980s, many national research systems, particularly in Latin America and the Caribbean, were like the international system, experiencing increasing budget stringency.[43] Preliminary indications are that the rate of growth has slowed even further or, in some countries, actually declined in the 1990s. Agricultural research capacity in Russia and the other countries of the former Soviet Union had eroded badly since the mid-1980s. The effect has been to prompt a reexamination of the organization and funding of national agricultural research systems.

---

[43] The first comprehensive set of data on agricultural research expenditures and personnel in developing countries was assembled by Pardey and Roseboom (1989). The data have been more completely analyzed in Pardey et al. (1991:197–265); and Alston et al. (1998).

Table 6.2 Science and Technology in the Agricultural Research and Development System

Layer/Activity	User and Use Types		
	Producers	Governments	Consumers
I Final users/source of clientele problems	⇔		⇔
II Extension (public and private)	Resources and environment ⇌ Commodity oriented	Management and marketing ⇌ Public policy	⇌ Family and human resources
	⇔	⇔	⇔

Major Areas of Science and Technology for Agriculture

Layer/Activity	Mathematical Sciences	Physical Sciences	Biological Sciences	Biological Sciences	Social Sciences
III Products from innovation (agriindustrial development)	Farm machinery and equipment; Farm buildings; Computer equipment/software	Commercial fertilizers; Agricultural chemicals; Irrigation systems; Pest control systems	Crop/plant varieties; Horticultural/nursery species; Livestock feed	Animal breeds; Animal health products; Food products	Management systems; Marketing systems; Institutional innovations; Health care; Child care
IV Technology invention (public and private research)	Agricultural engineering and design; Mechanics; Computer design	Agricultural chemistry; Soils and soil sciences; Irrigation and water methods	Agronomy; Horticulture; Plant breeding; Applied plant pathology	Animal and poultry science; Animal breeding; Animal and human nutrition; Veterinary medicine	Farm management and marketing; Resource economics; Rural sociology; Public policy studies; Human ecology

		Integrated Pest Management			
	⇄			⇄	⇔
V Pretechnology sciences (university and public agency research primarily)	Applied math Applied physics Engineering Computer science	Climatology Soil physics and chemistry Hydrology and water resources	Plant physiology Plant genetics Phytopathology	Animal and human physiology Animal and human genetics Animal pathology Nutrition	Applied economics Statistics and econometrics Political science Sociology

		Environmental Sciences			
	⇄			⇄	⇔
VI General or core sciences (university and public agency research primarily)	Mathematics Probability and statistics	Atmospherical and meteorological sciences Chemistry Geological sciences Physics	Bacteriology Biochemistry Botany Ecology	Genetics Microbiology Molecular biology Zoology	Economics Psychology

[a] Arrows indicate the direction of linkages, upstream, downstream, or horizontal.

Source: Wallace and W. E. Huffman, "Finance, Organization and Impact of U.S. Agricultural Research: Future Prospects," Ames, IA: Dept. of Economics, Iowa State University, Staff Paper #314, March 1999. Adapted from W. E. Huffman and R. E. Evenson, *Science for Agriculture: A Long-term Perspective*. Ames IA: Iowa State University Press, 1993:43.

Both the international donor community and national governments, particularly in countries that became independent in the 1950s and 1960s, have severely underestimated the sustained commitment that would be required to build scientifically and economically viable agricultural education and research systems (Pardey et al., 1997). Beginning in the mid-1950s, Kenya developed a highly productive maize research program. But in spite of substantial external assistance, Kenya has not been able to sustain its initial success. In most developing countries there are only weak links between ministry of agriculture research organizations and universities. Research funds flow mainly to ministry research laboratories. In Nigeria, for example, the 53% of agricultural scientists in the universities received 7% of the funding for research, whereas the 47% of the scientists in government institutes had access to 93% of the funding. Furthermore, the proportion of university scientists who had received training at the Ph.D. level rather than at the Master's level was much higher in the universities. In the few countries with significant private sector agricultural research there are typically only weak links with either ministry or university research (Eicher, 1998).

By the mid-1990s, a new and more sophisticated perspective was emerging on the possibilities of transfer of agricultural technologies across agroclimatic zones. Analysis of wheat breeding indicates very substantial spillovers. Direct spillovers (varieties developed through the CIMMYT–NARS collaborative research network) accounted for more than 40% of the 1300 wheat varieties released in developing countries between 1966 and 1990. In addition, indirect transfers (varieties developed by using CIMMYT–NARS germplasm as parents in adaptive breeding programs) accounted for about 25% of all released varieties in developing countries (Byerlee and Moya, 1993). Thus, about two-thirds of all wheat varieties released in developing countries during 1966–1990 were directly or indirectly based on germplasm developed by the CIMMYT–NARS network. The share of these varieties in developing countries has increased to over 80% in the past decade. Furthermore, varieties containing CIMMYT-based genetic material had a significant yield advantage relative to varieties containing only locally based genetic material.

This experience opens up the possibility of rationalizing the international wheat-breeding system within the CGIAR–NAR system (Maredia and Eicher, 1995). Smaller countries, or countries in which only a small area is devoted to wheat production, should confine their efforts to screening varieties developed at international centers or other NARs, and then release for local adoption the varieties that are best adapted to local environments. Large countries with substantial wheat acreage, such as India, China, Brazil, Argentina, and Turkey, should have research capacity, at both the pretechnology and technology development levels, capable of taking advantage of spilling from the international system, and other NARS, and contributing to the global stock of knowledge and technology.

A new perspective was also beginning to emerge on the appropriate organization, funding, and conducting of research in national agricultural research systems. The funding and conducting of research began to be viewed as separate functions. It was suggested that a separate funding body could use a combination of institutional and competitive grant funding to achieve more effective priority setting and performance incentives. Systems became more open to greater diversity in governance, funding, and conduct of research. Public sector funding from ministries of science and technology and environment was sought and nongovenmental organizations (NGOs) either demanded, or were encouraged, to play a larger role in the allocation of research resources and the conducting of research (White and Eicher, 1999).

As private sector research by seed, agrochemical, farm machinery, and food companies expanded and became recognized as essential to national or international research, development, and technology dissemination systems, efforts have been sought to achieve a more productive balance between public and private sector research resource allocation. The emergence of a private sector biotechnology industry in a number of the more advanced developing countries such as China, India, Malaysia, and Brazil and the emergence of new forms of intellectual property protection for biological technology mean that the private sector has become engaged in areas of pretechnology and basic research that in the past have been almost the exclusive province of the public sector. Private sector research in most developing countries continues, however, to rely heavily on the public sector for the development of new varieties and hybrids.[44] The successes of public sector research, such as the international wheat-breeding system, should be interpreted as powerful evidence of the productivity of publicly supported national and international research. The international community should continue to invest enough resources in the international system to ensure that it continues to achieve a high rate of return on its provision of global public goods. If the CGIAR system had not already been invented, it would be necessary to do so!

An Incomplete System

The vision of the global agricultural research system that will be needed to sustain growth in agricultural production into the twenty-first century is reasonably clear. But the system itself is still incomplete. When it is completed, it will include a strong set of national research institutions capable of working effectively with the international system and with other national systems. These will be complemented by a private technology supply industry composed of both multinational and national firms. There continue to be several limitations in the present system, including the weak national systems in many developing countries. There has been an erosion of public sector agricultural research capacity in a number of developed countries and in the member states of the former Soviet Union.[45] Relatively few developing countries in which

---

[44] The most complete body of research on private sector agricultural research in developing countries has been a series of articles and reports by Carl Pray (1987:411–431; Pray and Echeverria, 1988:366–374; Pray and Umali-Deininger, 1998:1127–1148).

[45] I do not, in this chapter, attempt to address the problems of transition to sustainable systems of agricultural production in the formerly centrally planned economies of eastern Europe and the former U.S.S.R. Prior to

national systems exist have achieved the capacity to make effective use of the advances in knowledge and technology that could be made available to them through the international system or through collaboration with the stronger national systems. The private sector agricultural technology supply industry, although growing rapidly, still remains poorly represented in most developing countries. Although the infrastructure of the international agricultural research system remains incomplete, it is far more highly developed than the international infrastructure for health, environmental, or industrial research (Bell et al., 1994:358–380).

LESSONS FROM EXPERIENCE

In this concluding section I turn again to the experience of the United States and Japan—two countries that, in spite of extreme differences in resource endowments, have achieved comparable rates of sustained agricultural growth for over a century. Both countries were successful in generating technical change adapted to their very different and changing resource endowments. Resources saved as a result of productivity growth in agriculture were employed to generate growth in the nonagricultural sector in various forms, such as lower prices of agricultural commodities, foreign exchange earnings from agricultural commodity exports, and the transfer of labor from agricultural to industrial employment. In both countries, agriculture can be considered a mature industry. Yet in the United States, rapid productivity growth and declining real costs of production have enabled agriculture to remain a leading export industry. The small-scale labor-intensive system of agriculture practiced in Japan has enabled the agricultural sector to remain an important source of employment during the structural transformation of the Japanese economy.

The most important lesson that can be drawn from the historical experience of U.S. and Japanese agricultural development is the process by which institutional innovations were developed that facilitated the technological innovations necessary to sustain growth of agricultural productivity. The major institutional innovation responsible for the success in generating technological innovations was the development of publically supported decentralized agricultural research and education systems. Both the U.S. and the Japanese experiences are consistent with the view that the public sector must play an important role in the advancement of biological technology. Failure of contemporary developing countries to develop effective public sector agricultural science research and technology capacity has been associated with a serious distortion of the pattern of technological and resource use and vulnerability to inappropriate transfers of technology.

Both developed and developing countries will face new challenges as they attempt to make the transition to sustainable economic growth during the next half century

---

1980, the absence of effective markets had resulted in a technological trajectory that was less efficient than if relative factor–factor and factor–product prices had more accurately reflected relations factor endowment and market demand (Fan and Ruttan, 1992).

in order to meet the agricultural commodity production challenge arising out of population and income growth. New and more effective institutions will have to be developed to respond to the environmental challenges associated with regional, national, and transnational environmental change and to respond to the challenges to human health and environmental quality involving competition for water among irrigation, industrial, household, and environmental demands; control of pests and pathogens, defense against infectious and parasitic disease, and the health effects of agricultural and industrial intensification; and transnational environmental changes such as global climate change and protection of biological diversity. The design of these institutional changes will impose much broader demands for knowledge about fundamental physical and biological relationships than in the past. More secure bridges must be built among the "island empires" of agricultural, environmental, and health research.

If the world fails to make the transition to sustainable growth in agricultural production, the failure will be at least as much in the area of institutional innovation as in the area of technical change. This is not an optimistic conclusion. The design of institutions capable of achieving compatibility between individual, organizational, and social objectives remains an art rather than a science. The incentive compatibility problem has not been solved analytically, even at the most abstract theoretical level (Hurwicz, 1973; 1998). At our present stage of knowledge, institutional design is analogous to driving down a four-lane highway looking out of the rear view mirror. We are better at making course corrections when we start to run off the highway than at using foresight to navigate the transition to sustainability.

REFERENCES

Adams, R. M., B. Hurd, S. Lenhart, and N. Leary. "The Effects of Global Warming on Agriculture: An Interpretative Review." *Journal of Climate Research* (forthcoming 1999).

Agrawal, A. "Dismantling the Divide between Indigenous and Scientific Knowledge." *Development and Change* 26 (1995):413–439.

Alexandratos, N., ed. *World Agriculture Toward 2010: An FAO Study*. Rome, Italy: Food and Agricultural Organization, 1995.

Allen, R. C. *Enclosure and the Yeoman*. New York: Oxford University Press, 1992.

Alston, J. M., and P. G. Pardey. *Making Science Pay: The Economics of Agricultural R&D Policy*. Washington, DC: AEI Press, 1996.

Alston, J. M., and P. G. Pardey. *International Approaches to Agricultural R&D: The CGIAR*. Washington, DC, International Food Policy Research Institute (paper prepared for U.S. Office of Science and Technology Policy, Executive Office of the President), February 1999 (mimeo).

Alston, J. M., B. J. Craig, and P. G. Pardey. *Dynamics of the Creation and Depreciation of Knowledge, and the Returns to Research*. Washington DC: International Food Policy Research Institute, EPTD Discussion Paper No. 35, August 1998a.

Alston, J. M., B. J. Craig, and J. Roseboom. "Financing Agricultural Research: International

Investment Patterns and Policy Perspectives." *World Development* 26 (1998b):1057–1071.

Alston, J. M., M. C. Marra, P. G. Pardey, and T. G. Wyatt. *Research Returns Redux: A Meta-Analysis of the Returns to Agricultural R & D.* International Food Policy Research Institute, EPTD Discussion Paper No. 38, November 1998c.

Alston, J. M., P. G. Pardey, and V. H. Smith. "Financing Agricultural R&D in Rich Countries: What's Happening and Why." *Australian Journal of Agricultural and Resource Economics* 51 (1998d):51–82.

Alston, J. M, P. G. Pardey, and V. H. Smith, eds. *Paying for Agricultural Productivity.* Baltimore, MD: The Johns Hopkins University Press, 1999 (in press).

Alt, C., T. Osborn, and D. Colacicco. *Soil Erosion: What Effect on Agricultural Productivity?* Washington, DC: United States Department of Agriculture, Economic Research Service Information Bulletin 556, 1989.

Anderson, J. R., and D. G. Dalrymple. *The World Bank, the Grant Program and the CGIAR: A Retrospective Review.* Washington, DC: The World Bank, OED Working Paper Series #1, March 1999.

Anderson, J. R., and J. Thompapillia. *Soil Conservation in Developing Countries: Project and Policy Interaction.* Washington, DC: The World Bank, 1990.

Antle, J. M., and P. L. Pingali. "Pesticide Productivity and Farmer Health: A Philippines Case Study." *American Journal of Agricultural Economics* 76 (1994):418–430.

Archibald, S. O., and L. Brandt. "A Flexible Model of Factor Biased Technological Change: An Application to Japanese Agriculture." *Journal of Development Economics* 35 (1991):127–145.

Ball, R., and L. Pounder. " 'Efficient but Poor' Revisited." *Economic Development and Cultural Change* 44 (1996):735–760.

Balough, T. "Review of *Transforming Traditional Agriculture*." *Economic Journal* 74 (1964): 986–999.

Bell, D. E., W. C. Clark, and V. W. Ruttan. "Global Research Systems for Sustainable Development: Agriculture, Health and Environment." In *Agriculture, Environment and Health: Sustainable Development in the 21st Century.* V. W. Ruttan, ed., pp. 358–380. Minneapolis, MN: University of Minnesota Press, 1994.

Bennett, H. H. "The Problem of Soil Erosion in the United States." *Annals of the Association of American Geographers* 21 (1931):147–170.

Binswanger, H. P., and V. W. Ruttan, eds. *Induced Innovation: Technology, Institutions and Development.* Baltimore, MD: Johns Hopkins University Press, 1978.

Boserup, E. *The Conditions of Agricultural Growth: The Economics of Agrarian Change Under Population Pressure.* Chicago, IL: Aldine, 1965.

Boserup, E. *Population and Technical Change.* Chicago, IL: University of Chicago Press, 1981.

Bray, F. *The Rice Economies: Technology and Development in Asian Societies.* Oxford, UK: Basil Blackwell, 1986.

Brewster, J. M. "The Machine Process in Agriculture and Industry." *Journal of Farm Economics* 32 (1950):69–81.

Brockway, L. H. *Science and Colonial Expansion: The Role of the British Royal Botanic Gardens.* New York: Academic Press, 1979.

Brown, L., and B. Halweil . "China's Water Shortage Could Shake World Food Security." *World Watch* 11 (July/August, 1998):10–21.

Bruce, J. P., H. Lee, and E. F. Hartes, eds. *Climate Change, 1995: Economic and Social Dimensions of Climate Change.* Contribution of Working Group III to the Second Assessment Report of the Intergovernmental Panel on Climate Change. New York: Cambridge University Press, 1996.

Bunce, A. C. *The Economics of Soil Conservation.* Ames, IA: Iowa State College Press, 1942.

Bunch, R. and G. López. *Soil Recuperation in Central America: Sustaining Innovation after Intervention.* London, UK: International Institute for Environmental Development, 1995.

Byerlee, D., and G. Alex. *Strengthening National Agricultural Research Systems: Policy Issues and Good Practice.* Washington, DC: World Bank, 1998.

Byerlee, D., and C. K. Eicher. *Africa's Emerging Maize Revolution.* Boulder, CO: Lynne Rienner, 1997.

Byerlee, D., and P. Moya. *Impacts of International Wheat Breeding Research in the Developing World, 1966–90.* Mexico, DF: CIMMYT, 1993.

Carson, R. *Silent Spring.* New York: Fawcett, 1962.

Cassman, K. G. "Ecological Intensification of Cereal Production Systems Yield Potential, Soil Quality and Precision Agriculture." *Proceedings of the National Academy of Sciences U.S.A.* 96 (1999):5952–5959.

CGIAR Systems Review Secretariat. *The International Research Partnership for Food Security and Sustainable Agriculture: Third System Review of the Consultation Group on International Agricultural Research.* Washington, DC: CGIAR, October 8, 1998.

Ciriacy-Wantrup, S. "Soil Conservation in European Farm Management." *Journal of Farm Economics* 20 (1938):86–101.

Cohen, J. E. *How Many People Can the Earth Support?* New York: W. W. Norton, 1995.

Conway, G. R. *The Doubly Green Revolution: Food for All in the 21st Century.* London, UK: Penguin Books, 1997.

Conway, G. R., and J. Pretty. *Unwelcome Harvest: Agriculture and Pollution.* London, UK: Earthscan Publications, 1991.

Craig, B. J., P. G. Pardey, and J. Roseboom. "Patterns of Agricultural Growth and Economic Development." In *Agricultural Research Policy: International Quantitative Perspectives,* P. G. Pardey, J. Roseboom, and J. R. Anderson, eds., pp. 131–172. Cambridge, UK: Cambridge University Press, 1991a.

Craig, B. J., P. G. Pardey, and J. Roseboom. "Internationally Comparable Growth, Development, and Research Measures." In *Agricultural Research Policy: International Quantitative Perspectives,* P. G. Pardey, J. Roseboom, and J. R. Anderson, eds., pp. 172–193. Cambridge, UK: Cambridge University Press, 1991b.

Craig, B. J., P. G. Pardey, and J. Roseboom. "International Productivity Patterns: Accounting for Input Quality, Infrastructure and Research." *American Journal of Agricultural Economics* 79 (1997):1064–1076.

Crissman, C. C., J. M. Antle, and S. M. Capalbo, eds. *Ecological, Environmental and Health Tradeoffs in Agriculture: Pesticides and Sustainability in Andean Potato Production.* Boston, MA: Kluwer Academic Publisher, 1998.

Crosby, A. W., Jr. *The Columbian Exchange: Biological and Cultural Consequences of 1492.* Westport, CN: Greenwood Publishing Co., 1972.

Crosson, P. "Soil Erosion and Its On-Farm Productivity Consequences: What Do We Know?" Washington, DC: Resources for the Future Discussion Paper 95–29, 1995a.

Crosson, P. "Soil Erosion Estimates and Costs." *Science* 269 (1995b):461–463.

Curtis, J., L. Mott, and T. Kuhnle. *Harvest of Hope: The Potential for Alternative Agriculture to Reduce Pesticide Use.* Washington, DC: Natural Resources Defense Council, 1991.

Daily, G. C., P. A. Matson, and P. M. Vitaesek. "Ecosystem Services Supplied by Soil." In *Nature's Services: Societal Dependence on Natural Ecosystems,* G. C. Daily, ed., pp. 113–132. Washington, DC: Island Press, 1997.

Dasgupta, P. *An Inquiry into Well-being and Destitution.* Oxford, UK: Clarendon Press, 1993.

David, C. C., and K. Otsuka. *Modern Rice Technology and Income Distribution in Asia.* Boulder, CO: Lynne Rienner, 1988.

Dupree, A. H. *Science in the Federal Government: A History of Policies and Activities to 1940.* Cambridge, MA: Harvard University Press, 1957.

Easter, K. W., M. W. Rosegrant, and A. Dinar, eds. *Markets for Water: Potential and Performance.* Dordrecht, Netherlands: Kluwer Academic Publishers, 1998.

Eicher, C. K. Personal Communication. December 31, 1998.

Ehrlich, P. R. *The Population Bomb.* New York: Ballantine Books, 1968.

Evenson, R. E. "Science for Agriculture: International Perspective." *Asian Journal of Agricultural Economics* 2 (1996):11–38.

Evenson, R. E. "Biotechnology and Genetic Resources." In *Agricultural Values of Plant Genetic Resources,* R. E. Evenson, D. Gollin, and V. Santaniello, eds., pp. 261–277. New York: CABI Publishing, 1998.

Evenson, R. E., and Y. Kislev. *Agricultural Research and Productivity.* New Haven, CT: Yale University Press, 1975.

Evenson, R.E., and Y. Kislev. "Research for Agriculture: Economic Evaluations." Cambridge MA: National Bureau of Economic Research, March 5 and 6, 1999 (Conference in commemoration of Zvi Griliches' 20 years as director of the NBER Program on Productivity and Technological Progress).

Evenson, R. E., J. P. Houck, and V. W. Ruttan. "Technical Change and Agricultural Trade: Three Examples—Sugarcane, Bananas and Rice." In *The Technology Factor in International Trade,* R. Vernon, ed., pp. 415–480. New York: Colombia University Press, 1970.

Fan, S., and P. Hazel. "Should Developing Countries Invest More in Less-favored Areas? An Empirical Analysis of Rural India." Washington, DC: International Food Policy Research Institute, April 1999 (mimeo).

Fan, S., and V. W. Ruttan. "Induced Technical Change in Centrally Planned Economies." *Agricultural Economics* 6 (1992):301–314.

Fernandez-Cornejo J., and S. Jans. *Pest Management in U.S. Agriculture.* Washington, DC: United States Department of Agriculture, Agricultural Handbook 717, August 1999.

Fischer, G., K. Frohberg, M. L. Parry, and C. Rosenzweig. "Impacts of Potential Climate Change on Global and Regional Food Production and Vulnerability." In *Climate Change and World Food Security,* T. E. Dowling, ed., pp. 115–160. Berlin, Germany: Springer, 1995.

Fitzgerald, D. "Beyond Tractors: The History of Technology in American Agriculture." *Technology and Culture* 32 (1991):114–124.

Food and Agriculture Organization (FAO). *Water Development for Food Security.* Rome, Italy: FAO WFS/TEC #12, March 1995.

Fox, G. C. "Is the United States Really Underinvesting in Agricultural Research?" *American Journal of Agricultural Economics* 62 (1985):806–812.

Frink, C. R., P. E. Waggoner, and J. H. Ausubel. "Nitrogen Fertilizer: Retrospect and Prospect." *Proceedings of the National Academy of Sciences U.S.A.* (forthcoming, 1999).

Fuglie, K., N. Ballenger, K. Day, C. Klotz, M. Ollinger, J. Reilly, U. Vasavada, and J. Yee. *Agricultural Research and Development: Public and Private Investment under Alternative Markets and Institutions.* Washington, DC: USDA Economic Research Service Report AE735, May 1996.

Fuglie, K., C. Narrod, and C. Neumeyer. "Public and Private Investments in Animal Research." In *Collaboration in Agricultural Research,* K. Fuglie and D. Schimmelpfennig, eds. Ames, IA: Iowa State University Press, forthcoming, 1999.

Geertz, C. *Agricultural Involution: The Process of Ecological Change in Indonesia.* Berkeley, CA : University of California Press, 1966.

Gianessi, L. P. "Reducing Pesticide Use with No Loss in Yields? A Critique of a Recent Cornell Report." Washington, DC: Resources for the Future Discussion Paper QE91–16, 1991.

Glazovsky, N. F. "The Aral Sea Basin." In *Regions at Risk: Comparisons of Threatened Environments,* J. X. Kasperson, R. E. Kasperson, and B. L. Turner, II, eds., pp. 92–139. New York: United Nations University Press, 1995.

Grabowski, R. "Induced Innovation: A Critical Perspective." In *Induced Innovation Theory and International Agricultural Development: A Reassessment,* B. M. Koppel, ed., pp. 73–93. Baltimore, MD: The Johns Hopkins University Press, 1995.

Grantham, G. "The Shifting Locus of Agricultural Innovation in Nineteenth Century Europe: The Case of the Agricultural Experiment Stations." *Research in Economic History* 3 (1984):191–214.

Grigg, D. B. *The Dynamics of Agricultural Change.* New York: St. Martins Press, 1982.

Griliches, Z. "Research Costs and Social Returns: Hybrid Corn and Related Innovations." *Journal of Political Economy* 66 (1958):419–431.

Grübler, A. *Technology and Global Change.* Cambridge, UK: Cambridge University Press, 1998.

Habakkuk, H. J. *American and British Technology in the Nineteenth Century: The Search for Labor Saving Inventions.* Cambridge, MA: Cambridge University Press, 1962.

Harris, J. M. *World Agriculture and the Environment.* New York: Garland Publishers, 1990.

Hayami, Y. "The Peasant and Economic Modernization." *American Journal of Agricultural Economics* 78 (1996):1157–1167.

Hayami, Y., and V. W. Ruttan. "Agricultural Productivity Differences among Countries." *American Economic Review* 60 (1970):895–911.

Hayami, Y., and V. W. Ruttan. *Agricultural Development: An International Perspective.* Baltimore, MD: Johns Hopkins University Press, 1st ed. 1971, 2nd ed. 1985.

Heady, E. O. "Basic Economic and Welfare Aspects of Farm Technological Advance." *Journal of Farm Economics* 31(1949):293–316.

Hightower, J. *Hard Tomatoes, Hard Times.* Cambridge, MA: Schenkman, 1973.

Huffman, W. E. "Finance, Organization and Impact of U.S. Agricultural Research: Future Prospects." Ames, IA: Dept. of Economics, Iowa State University, Staff Paper 314, March 1999.

Huffman, W. E., and R. E. Evenson. *Science for Agriculture: A Long-Term Perspective.* Ames, IA: Iowa State University Press, 1993.

Hurwicz, L. "The Design of Mechanisms for Resource Allocation." *American Economic Review* 63 (1973):1–30.

Hurwicz, L. "Issues in the Design of Mechanisms and Institutions." In *Designing Institutions for Environmental and Resource Management*, E. T. Loehman and D. M. Kilgour, eds., pp. 29–56. Cheltenham, UK: Edward Elgar, 1998.

Ise, J. "The Theory of Value as Applied to Natural Resources." *American Economic Review* 15 (1925):284–295.

Islam, N. *Horticultural Exports of Developing Countries: Past Performance, Future Prospects and Policy Issues*. Washington, DC: International Food Policy Research Institute, Research Report 80, April 1990.

Ishikawa, S. *Economic Development in Asian Perspective*. Tokyo, Japan: Kinokuniya Bookstore Co., 1967.

Johnson, N. L., and V. W. Ruttan. "The Diffusion of Livestock Breeding Technology in the U.S.: Observations on the Relationship Between Technical Change and Industry Structure." *Journal of Agribusiness* 15 (1997):19-35.

Johnson, D. G. "The Growth of Demand Will Limit Output Growth for Food over the Next Quarter Century." *Proceedings of the National Academy of Sciences U.S.A.* 96 (1999):5915–5920.

Johnson, N., and V. W. Ruttan. "Why Are Farms So Small?" *World Development* 22 (1994): 691–706.

Kasperson, J. X., R. E. Kasperson, and B. L. Turner, II. *Regions at Risk: Comparisons of Threatened Environments*. New York: United Nations University Press, 1995.

Kellogg, C. E. "Conflicting Doctrines about Soils." *Scientific Monthly* 66 (1948):475–485.

Klose, N. *America's Crop Heritage: The History of Foreign Plant Introduction by the Federal Government*. Ames, IA: Iowa State College Press, 1950.

Koppel, B. M., ed. *Induced Innovation Theory and International Agricultural Development: A Reassessment*. Baltimore, MD: Johns Hopkins University Press, 1995.

Lal, R. "Productivity of Tropical Soils and the Effect of Erosion." In *Quantification of the Effect of Erosion on Soil Productivity in an International Context*, F. Rijsberman and M. Wolman, eds., pp. 70–94. Delft, The Netherlands: Delft Hydraulics Laboratory, 1984.

Lau, L., and P. Yotopoulos. "The Meta-Production Function Approach to Technological Change in World Agriculture." *Journal of Development Economics* 31 (1989):241–269.

Lederberg, J. "Infectious Disease: A Threat to Global Health and Security." *Journal of the American Medical Association* 276 (1996):417–419.

Lewis, W. A. "Economic Development with Unlimited Supplies of Labor." *Manchester School of Economics and Social Studies* 22 (1954):139–91.

Lindert, P. H. *Shifting Ground: The Changing Agricultural Soils of China and Indonesia*. Davis, CA: University of California–Davis, Department of Economics, 1998 (mimeo, draft).

Lindert, P. H. "The Bad Earth? Chinese Agricultural Soils Since the 1930s." *Economic Development and Cultural Change* 48 47 (1999):701–736.

Lipton, M. "The Theory of the Optimizing Peasant." *Journal of Development Studies* 4 (1968):327–351.

Maredia, M. K., and C. K. Eicher. "The Economics of Wheat Research in Developing Countries: The One Hundred Million Dollar Puzzle." *World Development* 23 (1995):401–412.

Martin, L. R., ed. *A Survey of Agricultural Economics Literature, Vol. 4. Agriculture in Economic Development, 1940s to 1990s*. Minneapolis, MN: University of Minnesota Press, 1992.

Mellor, J. W. "Accelerating Agricultural Growth—Is Irrigation Institutional Reform Necessary?" *The Pakistan Development Review* 35 (1996):399–417.

Moore, M. R., R. Gardner, and J. M. Walker. "Groundwater Institutions: Models and Experiments." In *Designing Institutions for Environmental and Resource Management,* E. T. Loehman and D. M. Kilgour, eds., pp. 321–338. Cheltenham, UK: Edward Elgar, 1998.

National Research Council. *Report of the Committee on Research Advisory to the U.S. Department of Agriculture* (The Pound Report). Springfield, VA: National Technical Information Service, 1972.

National Research Council. *Water Transfers in the West: Efficiency, Equity and the Environment.* Washington, DC: National Academy Press, 1992.

National Research Council. *Colleges of Agriculture at the Land Grant Universities: Public Service and Public Policy.* Washington, DC: National Academy Press, 1996a.

National Research Council. *Sustainable Agriculture and the Environment in the Humid Tropics.* Washington, DC: National Academy Press, 1993.

National Research Council. *Biologically Based Pest Management: New Solutions for a New Century.* Washington, DC: National Academy Press, 1996b.

Naylor, R. L. *Herbicides in Asian Rice: Transitions in Weed Management.* Manila, Philippines: International Rice Research Institute, 1996.

Naylor, R. L. "Energy and Resource Constraints on Intensive Agricultural Production." *Annual Review of Energy and the Environment* 21 (1996):99–123.

Olmstead, A. L. and P. W. Rhode. "Induced Innovation in American Agriculture: Regional Perspectives Since 1880." *Journal of Political Economy* 101 (1993):100–118.

Orr, J. B. *As I Recall.* London, UK: MacGibbon and Kee, 1966.

Palladino, P. *Entomology, Ecology and Agriculture: The Making of Scientific Careers in North America, 1885–1985.* Amsterdam, The Netherlands: Harwood Academic Publishers, 1996.

Paoletti, M. G., and D. Pimentel. "Environmental and Economic Costs of Herbicide Resistance and Host-Plant Resistance to Plant Pathogens and Insects." *Technological Forecasting and Social Change* 50 (1995):9–23.

Pardey, P. J., B. J. Craig, and M. J. Hallaway. "U.S. Agricultural Research Deflators: 1890–1985." *Research Policy* 18 (1989a):289–296.

Pardey, P., J. Roseboom, and J. R. Anderson. *Agricultural Research Policy: International Quantitative Perspectives.* Cambridge, UK: Cambridge University Press, 1989b.

Pardey, P., J. Roseboom, and J. R. Anderson, eds. *Agricultural Research Policy: International Quantitative Perspectives.* New York: Cambridge University Press, 1991.

Pardey, P., J. Roseboom, and N.M. Beintema. "Investments in African Agricultural Research." *World Development* 25 (1997):409–423.

Parry, M. L. *Climate Change and World Agriculture.* London: Earthscan Publications, 1990.

Pearse, A. *Seeds of Plenty, Seeds of Want: Social and Economic Implications of the Green Revolution.* Oxford, UK: Clarenden Press, 1980.

Perkins, J. H. *Geopolitics and the Green Revolution.* Oxford, UK: Oxford University Press, 1997.

Pimentel, D., et al. "Land Degradation: Effects on Food and Energy Resources." *Science* 194 (1976):149–154.

Pimentel, D., et al. "Environmental and Economic Impacts of Reducing U.S. Agricultural

Pesticide Use." In *Handbook of Pest Management in Agriculture*, 2nd ed., D. Pimentel, ed., pp. 679–718. CRC Press, 1991.

Pimentel, D., et al. "Environmental and Economic Costs of Soil Erosion and Conservation Benefits." *Science* 267 (1995a):1117–1123.

Pimentel, D., et al. "Response (to Crosson)." *Science* 269 (1995b):464–465.

Pingali, P., Y. Bigot, and H. P. Binswanger. *Agricultural Mechanization and the Evolution of Farming Systems in Africa.* Baltimore, MD: Johns Hopkins University Press, 1987.

Pingali, P. L., C.B. Marquez, and F.G. Palis. "Pesticides and Philippine Rice Farmer Health: A Medical and Economic Analysis." *American Journal of Agricultural Economics* 76 (1994):587–592.

Pingali, P. L., and P. A. Roger, eds. *Impact of Pesticides on Farmer Health and the Rice Environment.* Boston, MA: Kluwer Academic Publishers, 1995.

Pingali, P. L., M. Hossain, and R. V. Gerpacio. *Asian Rice Bowls: The Returning Crisis.* New York: CAB International, 1997.

Plucknett, D. L., and N. J. H. Smith. "Sustaining Agricultural Yields." *BioScience* 36 (1986):40–45.

Powles, S. B., C. Preston, I. B. Bryon, and A. R. Jutsum. "Herbicide Resistance: Impact and Management." *Advances in Agronomy* 58 (1997):57–93.

Pray, C. E. "Private Sector Research in Asia." In *Policy for Agricultural* Research, V. W. Ruttan and C. E. Pray, eds., pp. 411–432. Boulder, CO: Westview Press, 1987.

Pray, C. E., and R. G. Echeverria. "Transferring Hybrid Maize Technology: The Role of the Private Sector." *Food Policy* 13 (1988):366–374.

Pray, C. E., and D. Umali-Deininger. "The Private Sector in Agricultural Research Systems: Will It Fill the Gap?" *World Development* 26 (1998):1127–1148.

Purcell, D. L., and J. R. Anderson. *Agricultural Extension and Research Achievements and Problems in National Systems.* Washington, DC: The World Bank, 1997.

Ranis, G., and J. C. H. Fei. "A Theory of Economic Development." *American Economic Review* 51 (1961):533–565.

Raskin, P., M. Chadwick, T. Jackson, and G. Leach. *The Sustainability Transition: Beyond Conventional Development.* Stockholm, Sweden: Stockholm Environment Institute, 1997.

Raskin, P., P. Gleick, P. Kirshin, G. Pontius, and K. Strzepek. *Comprehensive Assessment of the Freshwater Resources of the World.* Stockholm, Sweden: Stockholm Environment Institute, 1998.

Reardon, T. "African Agriculture: Productivity and Sustainability Issues." In *International Agricultural Development*, 3rd ed., C. K. Eicher and J. M. Statz, eds., pp. 444–457. Baltimore, MD: Johns Hopkins University Press, 1998.

Reilly, J., D. Schimmelpfennig, and L. Lewandrowski. "The Future for Global and Regional Food Production in a Changing Environment." In *Climate Change and Global Crop Productivity,* K. R. Reddy and H. F. Hodgest, eds. Oxon, UK: CAB International, 1999 (in press).

Rosegrant, M. *Water Resources in the 21st Century: Challenges and Implications for Action.* Washington, DC: International Food Policy Research Institute, 1997.

Rosegrant, M. W., M. Agacaoili-Sombilla, and N. D. Perez. *Global Food Projections to 2020.* Washington, DC: International Food Policy Research Institute, 1995.

Rosenberg, N. *Perspectives on Technology.* Cambridge, UK: Cambridge University Press, 1976.

Rosenzweig, C., and D. Hillel. *Climate Change and the Global Harvest*. New York: Oxford University Press, 1998.

Rostow, W. W. "The Take-off Into Self-sustained Growth." *Economic Journal* 66 (1956):25–48.

Ruttan, V. W. *Agricultural Research Policy*. Minneapolis, MN: University of Minnesota Press, 1982.

Ruttan, V. W. "Social Science Knowledge and Institutional Change." *American Journal of Agricultural Economics* 66 (1984):549–559.

Ruttan, V. W. "Toward a Global Agricultural Research System: A Personal View." *Research Policy* 15 (1986):307–327.

Ruttan, V. W. "Constraints on the Design of Sustainable Systems of Agricultural Development." *Ecological Economics* 12 (1994a):209–219.

Ruttan, V. W. *Health and Sustainable Agricultural Development*. Boulder, CO: Westview Press, 1994b.

Ruttan, V. W. *Agriculture, Environment, and Health: Sustainable Development in the 21st Century*. Minneapolis, MN: University of Minnesota Press, 1994c.

Ruttan, V. W. *United States Development Assistance Policy: The Domestic Politics of Foreign Economic Aid*. Baltimore, MD: Johns Hopkins University Press, 1996.

Ruttan, V. W. "The Transition to Agricultural Sustainability." *Proceedings of the National Academy of Sciences U.S.A.* 96 (1999):5960–5967.

Ruttan, V. W. "Biotechnology and Agriculture: A Skeptical Perspective." *AgBio Forum* (http://www.agbioforum.missouri.edu/AgBioForum/General/archives.html), 1999b.

Salman, S. C., and A. A. Hanson. *The Principles and Practice of Agricultural Research*. London: Leonard Hill, 1964.

Sanders, J. H., B. I. Shapiro, and S. Ramaswamy. *The Economics of Agricultural Technology in Semi-arid Sub-Saharan Africa*. Baltimore, MD: Johns Hopkins University Press, 1996.

Sauer, C. O. *Agricultural Origins and Dispersals: The Domestication of Animals and Food-stuffs,* 2nd ed. Cambridge, MA: MIT Press, 1969.

Scherr, S. D. *Soil Degradation: A Threat to Developing Country Food Security by 2020?* Washington, DC: International Food Policy Research Institute, FAE Discussion Paper 27, February 1999.

Seckler, D., D. Molden, and R. Barker. "Water Scarcity in the Twenty-First Century." *International Journal of Water Resources Development* (forthcoming 1999).

Sen, A. K. "The Choice of Agricultural Techniques in Underdeveloped Countries." *Economic Development and Cultural Change* 7 (1959):279–285.

Shiva, V. *The Violence of the Green Revolution: Third World Agriculture, Ecology and Politics*. London: Zed Books, 1991.

Smale, M., and V. Ruttan. "Social Capital and Technical Change: The *Groupments Nam* of Burkina Faso." In *Institution and Economic Development: Growth and Governance in Less Developed and Post-Socialist Countries*, pp. 183–499. Baltimore, MD: Johns Hopkins University Press, 1997.

Snow, A. A., and P. M. Palma. "Commercialization of Transgenic Plants: Potential Ecological Risks." *BioScience* 47 (1997):86–96.

Socolow, R. H. "Nitrogen Management and the Future of Food: Lessons from the Management of Energy and Carbon." *Proceedings of the National Academy of Sciences U.S.A.* 96 (1999):6001–6008.

Struever, S., ed. *Prehistoric Agriculture*. Garden City, NY: The Natural History Press, 1971.

Tendler, J. "Tales of Dissemination in Agriculture." In *Agriculture, Environment and Health: Sustainable Development in the 21st Century*, V. W. Ruttan, ed., pp. 146–180. Minneapolis, MN: University of Minnesota Press, 1994.

Thirtle, C. G., and V. W. Ruttan. *The Role of Demand and Supply in the Generation and Diffusion of Technical Change*. London: Harwood Academic Publishers, 1987.

Timmer, C. P. "The Turnip, the New Husbandry, and the English Agricultural Revolution." *Quarterly Journal of Economics* 83 (1969) 375–395.

Turner, B. L. *Global Land Use Change: A Perspective from the Colombian Encounter*. Madrid, Spain: Consejo Superior de Investigaciones Científicas, 1995.

Usher, A. P. "Soil Fertility, Soil Exhaustion, and Their Historical Significance." *Quarterly Journal of Economics* 37 (1923):385–411.

van Bath, S. H. S. *The Agrarian History of Western Europe, A.D. 500–1850*. London: Edward Arnold, 1963.

Vavilov, N. I. *The Origin, Variation, Immunity and Breeding of Cultivated Plants*. K. S. Chester, trans. *Chronica Botanica*, Vol. 13, Nos. 1–6, 1949–50.

Waggoner, P. E. "How Much Land Can Ten Billion People Spare for Nature?" In *Technical Trajectories and the Human Environment*, J. H. Ausubel and H. D. Langford, eds., pp. 56–73. Washington, DC: National Academy Press, 1997.

White, R., and C. K. Eicher. *NGO's and the African Farmer: A Skeptical Perspective*. East Lansing, MI: Michigan State University Department of Agricultural Economics, Staff Paper 99–01, 1999.

Wise, W. S. "The Role of Cost Benefit Analysis in Planning Agricultural R&D Programs." *Research Policy* 4 (1975):246–261.

Yanggen, D., V. Keel, T. Reardon and A. Naseem. *Incentives for Fertilizer Use in Sub-Saharan Africa: A Review of Empirical Evidence on Fertilizer Response and Profitability*. East Lansing, MI: Michigan State University Department of Agricultural Economics International Development Working Paper No. 70, 1998.

CHAPTER 7

Light, Power, and Energy[1]

Prior to the nineteenth century, the primary sources of energy were animal and human power, fuel wood and agricultural wastes, and wind and water power. In developing countries, wood and other biomass sources continues to account for over one-third of total energy use. The Industrial Revolution has been associated with two major transitions in energy use. The first was made possible by the steam engine, the first technology for the direct conversion of fossil energy resources into work. The second was associated with the introduction of electricity, the first energy carrier that could be converted to light, heat, or work at the point at which it is used (Grübler, 1998:249–251). These technical changes have been associated with dramatic changes in the relative importance of the several sources of energy (Figures 7.1, 7.2, and 7.3). In the nineteenth century, with the expansion of railroads, the growth of the steel industry, and the application of steam power, the share of energy use accounted for by coal rose dramatically. Oil and gas were introduced in the 1870s. Their use has been closely associated with the growth of the internal combustion engine and the petrochemical industry. By the 1970s, each accounted for a larger share of energy use than coal. Nuclear power use, which experienced exceptionally rapid growth after its introduction in the late 1950s, has declined since the early 1980s.

A primary purpose of this chapter is to illustrate the role of the electric power industry as a pervasive source of growth across a broad industrial front. I first discuss the strategic inventions, and their inventors, that led to the substitution of electric energy for primary energy sources such as wood, coal, oil, and gas in the lighting and powering of homes, offices, and factories. In a following section, I trace the productivity implications of electric power in loosening the linkage between the location of the primary sources of energy and the location of industrial activity. In a third section, I address the question of the impact of the two great oil shocks of the 1970s on technical change and on economic growth. In a final section I argue that the electric power industry can never again exert a pervasive impact on economic growth, at least in the presently industrialized countries, as it has in the past. A

[1] I am indebted to Dean Abrahamson, Steve Corneli, Keith Fuglie, Arnulf Grübler, Richard Hirsh, Thomas P. Hughes, Dale W. Jorgenson, Kenneth H. Keller, Alfred A. Marcus, Victor Matheson, David C. Popp, and Sam H. Schurr for comments on an earlier draft of this chapter.

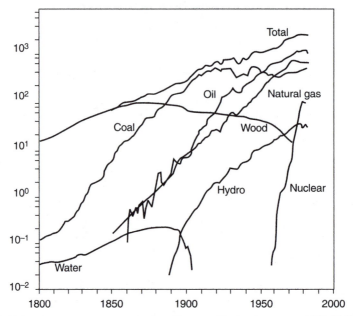

Figure 7.1 U.S. primary energy consumption. (*Source: The Methane Age,* 1988, T. H. Lee, ed., "The Dynamic Evolution of Methane Technologies," Arnulf Grubler and Nebojsa Nakicenovic, Copyright © 1988 by International Institute for Applied Systems Analysis, with kind permission from Kluwer Academic Publishers.)

discussion of the environmental implications of alternative energy futures is reserved for a later chapter.[2]

THE BATTLE OF THE SYSTEMS[3]

"The steam engine was . . . the first practical, economic and reliable machine that could convert coal's chemical energy into mechanical energy" (Smil, 1994:161). The expiration of Watt's patent on the separate condenser engine in 1800 initiated an intense period of innovation that made steam engines both more efficient and more versatile (Chapter 3). Higher pressure boilers were introduced in England in 1804 and in the United States in 1805. New engine types extended the use of the steam engine to a large variety of stationary and mobile applications.

---

[2] I do not, in this chapter, present a comprehensive treatment of the energy industries. For a useful study, see Peirce (1996).

[3] In writing this section I have drawn more than it is possible to acknowledge on Hughes (1979:124–161, 1983). I have also drawn heavily on David and Bunn (1988), David (1989, 1990, 1991), and Friedel et al. (1986).

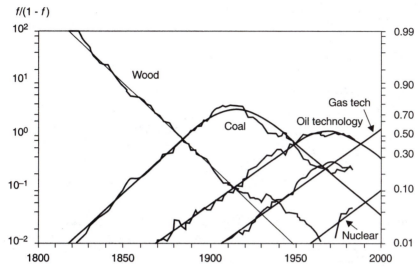

Figure 7.2 U.S. energy substitution and gas technologies. The evolution of primary energy is shown on a logarithmic scale as fractional market shares of the five primary energy sources. The fractional shares (f) are not plotted directly but rather as the ratio of the market share accounted for by a given energy source over the sum of the market shares of all other competing energy sources. This form of presentation reveals the logistic substitution path as an almost linear secular trend with small annual perturbations. Gas produced in association with oil production is allocated to oil technology. Gas production not associated with oil production is identified as gas technology. Saturation intervals between coal, oil, and gas are separated by about 50 years. (*Source: The Methane Age,* 1988, T. H. Lee, ed., "The Dynamic Evolution of Methane Technologies," Arnulf Grubler and Nebojsa Nakicenovic, Copyright © 1988 by International Institute for Applied Systems Analysis, with kind permission from Kluwer Academic Publishers.)

By the 1890s the largest steam engines in use were 30 times more powerful than the largest engines a hundred years earlier. They were also substantially more fuel efficient. But by the end of the century, steam engines were also being rapidly adapted to generate electricity that would in turn power electric motors, rather than used as a direct source of power for machine operation. The initial application of electricity, however, was the replacement of gas in the lighting of businesses, public facilities, and homes.

Edison's Direct Current System

Electrical technology was the first modern technology that was derived directly from prior scientific research. "The lexicon of electricity—ohms, amperes, galvanometers, hertz, volts—is a gallery of great scientists of the eighteenth and nineteenth centuries" (Ausubel and Marchetti, 1977:111). The first industrial research laboratory devoted

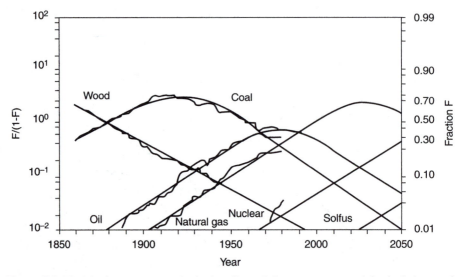

Figure 7.3 World primary energy substitution. Smooth lines represent model calculations and jagged lines are historical data. "Solfus" is a term employed to describe a major new energy technology, e.g., solar or fusion. The evolution of primary energy is shown on a logarithmic scale as fractional market shares of the five primary energy sources. The fractional shares (f) are not plotted directly but rather as the ratio of the market share accounted for by a given energy source over the sum of the market shares of all other competing energy sources. This form of presentation reveals the logistic substitution path as an almost linear secular trend with small annual perturbations. Gas produced in association with oil production is allocated to oil technology. Gas production not associated with oil production is identified as gas technology. Saturation intervals between coal, oil, and gas are separated by about 50 years. (*Source: The Methane Age*, 1988, T. H. Lee, ed., "The Dynamic Evolution of Methane Technologies," Arnulf Grubler and Nebojsa Nakicenovic, Copyright © 1988 by International Institute for Applied Systems Analysis, with kind permission from Kluwer Academic Publishers.)

to research and development was established by Thomas A. Edison in Menlo Park, New Jersey, in 1876 (see Box 3.1).

Beginning in 1878, the major focus of Edison and his Menlo Park laboratory was the development and introduction of a system of electric lighting as discussed in Chapter 4. Edison had assembled a team of electricians, mechanics, engineers, and scientists and had established effective working relationships with members of the financial and political communities in New York. On October 20, 1878 he announced a plan to introduce a system of incandescent lighting in New York. At the time of this announcement he had not yet invented either an economically viable incandescent light or a suitable system for generating and distributing electricity. Four years later, in 1882, Edison electric power stations and lighting systems were placed in operation in New York and London.

Edison was not the first to invent an incandescent lamp (Friedel et al., 1986:115–117). As early as 1859 Moses Farmer lit his house in Salem, Massachusetts, by battery-powered electric lamps that contained a glowing platinum wire. Joseph Swan introduced a carbon filament incandescent lamp at about the time when Edison was working with carbon filaments. Edison's unique contribution was in the way he brought together a blend of science, technology, and economics in the development of the incandescent lamp (see Box 3.1).

The cost of delivering electricity by expensive copper wire depended on both the distance of delivery and the thickness of the wire. To limit the length of the wire, Edison needed to locate his transmission system in an area of high-density demand. To keep the wire's cross-sectional area small and limit energy loss in transmission, he needed to keep the current low. But to turn most of the current (wattage) into light, rather than losses in the transmission wires, the resistance in the lamp filament had to be higher than the resistance in the transmission wire. This required an extremely thin filament. Edison had initially considered using a platinum filament because of its durability. Analysis of system costs directed his attention to a combination of durability and high resistance. In the fall of 1879 Edison finally settled on a carbon filament as having the right combination of resistance and durability. He also developed a system of parallel circuitry so that all the lights would not be extinguished when one was not in operation (or when one light failed).[4]

While Edison was devoting most of his attention to the incandescent lamp, Upton and several other members of the Menlo Park laboratory were simultaneously working on the design and construction of an appropriate generator. Electric power is generated by rotating a magnet inside a coil of copper wire. The generators on the market in the 1870s were high-resistance generators designed for arc lights wired in a series. On October 1, 1879 at about the same time that Edison succeeded in obtaining a filament with high resistance and durability, Upton published an article in *Scientific American* announcing a successful low internal resistance generator designed for a system of incandescent lamps connected in parallel (Hughes, 1983:36, 37).

As the designs of the incandescent light and the generator were being completed attention focused on scaling up the laboratory models of the system. A small pilot scale system for lighting Menlo Park was constructed at the same time a number of companies were being incorporated to exploit the Edison inventions. A lobbying effort was organized to obtain a franchise, opposed by the gas companies and lamplighters, allowing the Edison Electric Illuminating Company (EEIC) to establish a distribution system in New York. Edison himself personally supervised the design and construction of the central generating station, located on Pearl Street near the financial district, and the underground distribution system.

On September 4, 1882, an Edison electrician threw the switch that fed current from a Jumbo generator in the Pearl Street station to the lamps in the Wall Street district.

---

[4] The mathematical modeling of the system was done by Edison's associate, Francis Upton. "Wanting to reduce the current in order to lower conductor losses they realized that they could compensate and maintain the level of energy transfer to the lamps by raising the voltage proportionality . . . it was the eureka moment, for they realized that by increasing the resistance of the incandescent lamp filament they would raise the voltage in relationship to the current (Hughes, 1983:30).

In a gesture illustrating the interdependence of technological invention and financial backing, Edison then switched on the lamps in the offices of Drexel, Morgan and Company (Hughes, 1983:42, 43). From 1888 to 1890 the EEIC was plagued with financial difficulties. Support by the Drexel Morgan syndicate, however, permitted the system to expand. Its continued operation stimulated the sale of franchises by its parent company and the sale of equipment by the Edison manufacturing companies to electric utility supply companies.

The Alternating Current Challenge

The major problem with the direct current systems that Edison failed to resolve was the cost of transmission beyond a radius of several miles. The *technical problem* of long distance transmission was resolved by the invention of the transformer and the polyphase motor.

Numerous inventors contributed to the development of the transformer. Credit for the solution of the critical problem was due primarily to the French inventor Lucian Gaulard and his English business partner, John D. Gibbs (Hughes, 1983:86–105). At the Westminster Aquarium exhibition in 1883 they demonstrated that by using alternating current and transformers, high voltage could be employed for the economic transmission of electricity and that it could be then transformed to low voltage at the point of consumption. Gaulard's work on the development of the transformer was motivated in part by a provision of the British Electric Lighting Act of 1882 that prevented the suppliers of electricity from prescribing the voltage or other components of electric lights. In September 1884, at an international exhibition in Turin, Italy, Gaulard and Gibbs placed their transformers on a 20-mile circuit to light the exhibition buildings.

Major improvements were made in 1885 by three Hungarian engineers (Otto Bathy, Charles Zipernowski, and Max Déri) who were employed by Ganz and Company in Budapest. Ganz had already adopted alternating current (a.c.) in its entire system, which included arc and incandescent lamps, generators, and other components. By 1890 Ganz had nearly 70 central stations using alternating current generators and transformers in operation throughout Austria and Hungary. In the same year, Sebastian Ziani de Ferranti, a brilliant Italian engineer, installed an a.c. lighting system with transformers wired in parallel in London's Grosvenor Gallery (David, 1991:80).

In the United States, critical roles in the development of the alternating current system were played by the inventor William Stanley and the industrialist George West-inghouse. Westinghouse owned two railway equipment companies, Westinghouse Air Brake Company and Union Switch and Signal Company. After working with the U.S. Electric Lighting Company, Edison's major competitor for the incandescent lighting market in New York, and the Swan Electric Company in Boston, Stanley established his own laboratory to experiment with electrochemistry, incandescent lamps, and storage batteries in Englewood, New Jersey in 1883. In 1884 he entered into an agreement to move to Pittsburgh and assign his future inventions to Westinghouse. In 1885, Westinghouse ordered several transformers and secured an option on the American patent rights from Gaulard and Gibbs.

In 1885, after working out a new arrangement with Westinghouse, Stanley moved his laboratory to Great Barrington, Massachusetts, where he designed and developed an improved transformer. On March 6, 1886 lamps and transformers were installed in businesses and houses in Great Barrington and the alternating current technology system began operating on a regular basis. Stanley's alternating current transformer central station system used a 25-hp steam engine, transformers supplying either 25 or 50 incandescent lamps, and wires strung on insulators attached to the "grand old elms" that lined the village streets (Hughes, 1983:103).

In 1886 four generic difficulties still remained to be resolved: (1) The early Westinghouse and Thomson–Houston alternators (the equivalent of dynamo generators) were less energy efficient than direct current (d.c.) dynamos, especially the large "Jumbo" design introduced by Edison. (2) The d.c. system was able to provide metered electric supply, whereas no a.c. meter had yet been developed. (3) The ability to connect dynamos in parallel rather than in series meant that d.c. generators could be disconnected and reconnected to the mains in response to varying load and could be shut down for repair and maintenance—or might even break down without disrupting the entire system. (4) At a time when central stations employing the Edison system were beginning to spread fixed generating costs by supplying electricity for streetcar traction and power as well as lighting, the a.c. system's ability to compete in urban markets was restricted by the lack of any satisfactory secondary motor available to be used with alternating current (David, 1991:83, 84).

A practical motor was the most important invention needed to ensure domination of the alternating current system. The availability of alternating current and the publicity surrounding its development stimulated a burst of inventive activity devoted to the development of alternating current motors. Manufacturers loaned or gave alternating equipment to engineering schools for use in research that might advance its applications.

Nikola Tesla was the most widely acclaimed inventor of alternating current motors. While a student at Graz Polytechnic in Austria in 1877, at age 21, Tesla became aware of the limitations of the d.c. motor. He recalled that in 1882, after puzzling about possible solutions many times, he acquired the critical insight for a solution while reciting a passage from Goethe during a walk in a park with a friend. "In an instant I saw it all, and I drew with a stick on the sand the diagrams which were illustrated in my fundamental patents of May 1888" (quoted from Hughes, 1983:113). Hughes (1983:113) comments, somewhat facetiously, "Inasmuch as five fundamental, related patents were issued to Tesla in May 1888, the detail of his insight must have been remarkable!"

Tesla visualized a motor without brushes and commutator. An entirely new system with a polyphase generator would be required. His vision persisted while employed by the Austro-Hungarian State telephone system, the French Edison Electric Company, and the Edison Machine Works in New York. In 1884, he found the financial backing to establish the Tesla Electric Light and Manufacturing Company in Rahway, New Jersey. In October 1887 he filed his first two patent applications for an alternating current motor. Five more patents were filed in November and December and issued in May 1888. "The patents issued on 1 May 1888 described a system for the conversion, transmission, and utilization of energy. Essentially the system involved a generator for converting mechanical to electrical energy and a motor to convert the electrical energy once again to mechanical power. . . . The system would use high voltage . . . for transmission, and a motor would provide uniformity of speed regardless of load" (Hughes, 1983:115).

There are a plethora of conflicting claims about priority in the invention of the polyphase motor. In retrospect, it appears that Farranti substantiated his claim for priority in demonstrating the idea underlying the invention of a rotating-magnetic field system, that Tesla made the first successful patent application, that Farranti first publicly announced (by lecture) the invention or discovery, and that Haselwander and Bradley built the first full-scale polyphase generators (Hughes, 1983:118).

The manufacturer most responsible for taking the lead in developing the system in Europe was the Allgemene Elekrizitäts-Gesellchaft of Berlin and, in the United States, the Westinghouse Company. In July 1888 Westinghouse obtained an option to purchase the Tesla patent. Tesla worked in Pittsburgh for a year with Westinghouse engineers to develop a marketable motor and system. Like Stanley, he found relations with the Westinghouse engineering staff unsatisfactory and returned to his independent inventive endeavors.

Conflict

By the end of the 1880s the direct current systems developed by Edison faced substantial competition from the alternating current system, even in the central cities in which the direct current systems had a clear technological advantage. The single-phase alternating current system provided a solution to the high cost of long distance transmission. But its dominance was not ensured until the development of the polyphase motor and the rotary converter. These two inventions set the stage for the transition of the industry from an electric light industry to an electric light and power industry.

Initially, Edison appeared relatively unconcerned with the emergence of the alternating current technology. He was more concerned about competing with gas than with rival electric lighting systems. Beginning in 1885, however, Edison's concern and the concern of his financial backers increased. These concerns "took the form of court room struggles over patent rights, attempts to pass anti-competitive legislation, and public relations schemes aimed at discrediting the opposition and frightening its customers" (David, 1991:86).

The most bizarre episode was an effort made by Edison and some of his close associates to convince the public that alternating current was an unsafe basis for an electric supply system. In July 1888 Harold Brown, a former Edison Laboratory assistant, put on a demonstration of the harmful effects of alternating current that featured the electrocution of a large dog. Brown also successfully persuaded the New York state legislature to adopt alternating current for the electrocution of condemned prisoners. The Edison interests were, however, unsuccessful in their efforts to obtain legislation that would outlaw alternating current or limit its transmission to uneconomically low voltages (David, 1981:88; Hughes, 1983:107–108).

Historians have often portrayed Edison as economically irrational in stubbornly championing the direct current system, and unscientific in his dogmatic public opposition to the rival alternating current technology (David, 1991:90). David argues, however, that Edison's actions can more appropriately be viewed as "an economically rational response on the part of an inventor-entrepreneur whose long term plan to be the sole sponsor of a 'universal' electric supply system suddenly had gone awry" (David, 1983:91). Edison's intent was to slow the pace of the advance of the direct current system long enough to allow him to recover his investment and maintain his laboratory. Edison made a successful exit from the electricity industry in January 1889. He received $1,750,000 in cash, 10% of the shares, and a position on the board when his interests were merged into the Edison General Electric Company. This permitted him to turn his attention to alternative interests, including the improvement of the phonograph, the motion picture, and mining technology.

Even as the technical advantages of alternating current systems were increasingly recognized, however, existing direct current systems were not immediately replaced. Existing direct current utilities in densely populated areas continued to expand to meet load increases. Their unamortized investment in direct current was so large that it discouraged replacement with a polyphase system. If the utilities supplemented the existing direct current system with an additional and unconnected polyphase system they would lose the advantage of a single system. Furthermore, General Electric, Siemens, HEG, and the smaller British equipment manufacturing companies remained partially committed to direct current through capital investments in patents, equipment, and operating facilities as well as in experience and expertise. In addition to the Edison interests, other engineers, managers, and skilled laborers were also biased toward the older system (Hughes, 1983:120).

Hughes argues that the "the battle of the systems" had become far more complicated than a technical problem amenable to a simple technical solution. "The conflict was resolved . . . by a combination of coupling and merging. The coupling took place on the technical level; the merging on the institutional level" (Hughes, 1983:121). It involved increasingly complex relations between technical and institutional innovation.

Resolution

One example of technical coupling was the development of converters, which enabled older direct current systems to be linked directly with the newer alternating current system. The rotary converter was developed for changing direct current into polyphase and vice versa, as well as for frequency and phase conversion. Conversion was also achieved by using motors driven by one kind of current to drive a generator that produced another kind. At the Chicago Exposition of 1893 Westinghouse displayed a unified system that could handle generators and loads of varying characteristics. "The system was capable of supplying incandescent lamps, arc lights, direct current motors for both stationary and traction purposes, single phase alternating current motors, polyphase motors, and energy for thermo-electrical and electrochemical uses from a common transmissions line or ring fed by centralized, large scale generators" (Hughes, 1983:122).

The struggle between the two systems also required an institutional resolution of the conflicts in equipment manufacturing and in distribution. In the United States, an important step toward institutional resolution was Thomas Edison's relinquishing control of the Edison enterprises. In his absence, Edison General Electric's dogmatic opposition to alternating current eroded. In 1892, Edison General Electric merged with the Thomson–Houston Company, a leading manufacturer of electrical machinery that produced both direct and alternating current equipment. In 1896, General Electric, now unburdened of both Edison's influence and his name, reached a patent exchange agreement with Westinghouse that removed many of the constraints to further system development for both companies. This agreement, combined with an incandescent lighting arrangement between General Electric, Westinghouse, and several smaller manufacturers, ushered in a period of greater stability in the electrical industry (Reich, 1985:52).

The development of a coherent scheme to tap the energy potential of Niagara Falls represented a dramatic symbol of the resolution of the "battles of the currents." The Niagara power station went into service in August 1895. Westinghouse built the first two generators, the switches, and auxiliary powerhouse equipment; General Electric constructed the transformer, the transmission line to Buffalo, and the Buffalo substation. Transmission began in 1896. The consumption at the rapidly expanding industrial complex at Niagara quickly exceeded the power transmission to Buffalo (Hughes, 1983:139).[5]

These developments also signaled the end of the "heroic period" of technical innovation and development in the electric power industry. The focus of technical development shifted to process innovation and incremental product innovation. These improvements were increasingly produced by engineers employed by the major firms both in the United States and in Europe. Major deviations from established product lines typically awaited developments outside the firm. Access to the new technology was acquired through licensing rather than "in-house" inventions.

---

[5] The commercial success of the alternating current did not fully resolve the question of its technical superiority. Inventors and engineers continued to make improvements in the generators, motors, and other components of the direct current system. As late as the first decade of the twentieth century, some leading engineers still argued that direct current was more appropriate in urban areas than alternating current in terms of efficiency, reliability, and profitability (Hughes, 1983:81).

Institutional Innovation

Even more substantial institutional innovations were required to realize the economic gains made possible by the advances in technology and the integration of equipment manufacturers into coherent electric supply (utility) industries. In the United States, the manager–entrepreneur, Samuel Insull, became a pivotal figure in the evolution of the electric supply industry.

Samuel Insull began his apprenticeship in the electric power industry as a private secretary in Edison's London office. In 1880, he emigrated to America to become Edison's secretary and personal representative. In this role he was intimately involved "when Edison presided over the construction and early operation of New York's Pearl Street station; he took part in the establishment of the manufacturing facility that ultimately became General Electric; he participated in the major events involving inventors, engineers, entrepreneurs, mechanics, financiers, managers, electricians and others who made the history of the electrical industry" (Hughes, 1979:140).

In 1892, Insull moved to Schenectady to become manager of the Edison General Electric plant. Following the merger that formed the General Electric Company he moved to Chicago, at age 32, to become president of the Chicago Edison company. At the time, the Chicago Edison Company was but one of more than 20 small electric light utilities in the Chicago region. However, "within two decades Insull and his associates had created a single, mass-producing, monopolistic, technologically efficient, and economically operated company for all Chicago" (Hughes, 1979:141). The system that Insull created in Chicago became the model for other urban utilities. In presiding over the growth of the Chicago system, named the Commonwealth Edison Company in 1907 following completion of the merger, Insull demonstrated how the newer technology—the rotary converter, the frequency changer, and the steam turbine— could be coupled with the older direct current central stations to build an integrated system. These technical changes resulted in an disequilibrium between the economics of electricity production and distribution that induced the institutional changes which led to the development of integrated systems. As the small inefficient companies were absorbed, their generating plants were transformed into substations. The linkage of the technology into an integrated system "made possible the supply of incandescent light load, stationary motor load, and street car-elevated railroad load" (Hughes, 1979:146).

An early innovation was the 1903 establishment of the load dispatcher as the control center of the system. A primary responsibility of the load dispatcher was to see that each station carried a reasonable share of the system load. When a generator failed or had to be taken off load for repair, the load dispatcher reallocated load among generators and substations. The office of the load dispatcher became the source of statistical information on demand patterns of different customers. This information facilitated a responsive system design that could achieve maximum load factor. (Load factor is the ratio of the average load to the maximal load for a customer, group of customers, or the entire system during a specified period.) Insull recognized early that maximization of load factor was a central design principle. He sought customers who had both favorable and diverse load factors in order to fill in the "valleys" between peak load periods.

In the 1920s, Insull reached out beyond Chicago and connected the Chicago system with companies in the suburbs and in neighboring municipalities. Further expansion resulted in a regional system, the Public Services Company of Illinois, and a national holding company, Middle West Utilities Company. In Chicago, politics had become an essential component of Insull's system. Methods were found by which politicians "obtained wealth from political power without having to steal public money" (Hughes, 1983:206). In the 1920s Insull was able to successfully organize the state legislature to support state rather than local regulation of rates and service.

The utility industry has interpreted such developments, in Illinois and elsewhere, as part of the process of establishing an implicit social contract in which the utilities undertook to provide reliable and affordable electricity in exchange for a socially determined rate of return. This social contract did not extend, however, to providing uniform service throughout their service area. While urban life was being electrified America's farms remained without electric light or power until the establishment of the Tennessee Valley Authority and the Rural Electrification Administration in the 1930s.

Insull's holding company collapsed during the Great Depression of the 1930s. In 1934 he was accused in federal court of using the mails to defraud in connection with his bankrupt holding company. Insull was acquitted. But as Hughes notes: "History has not dealt generously with Insull. . . . For newspapers, politicians, and former competitors, Insull was a depression scapegoat; decades of complex system building were easier to ignore or forget—they involved difficult concepts, esoteric technology, uncommon economics, and sophisticated management" (Hughes, 1979:141).

Insull did not invent the Chicago system in the same sense that Edison invented the Pearl Street System. Insull was, however, a systems conceptualizer.

> Edison, though deeply aware of the seamless fabric of economics and technology, was relatively naive about the long-term economic and social factors making up the environment within which his system functioned. . . . Insull, by contrast, analyzed and articulated concepts that guided policy not only in Chicago but in other utilities as well. His conceptual synthesis involved social and marketing needs, financial trends, political (especially regulatory) policies, economic principles, technological innovations, engineering design, and managerial techniques. (Hughes, 1979:148)

The Insull integrated power system was composed of a closely articulated electric utility industry capable of using multiple sources of power, practicing effective load management, and planning for long-term growth in demand. This system was closely articulated with a technically progressive equipment manufacturing industry and with a supportive regulatory environment. It came to be viewed as a well-regulated natural monopoly that extended near-universal service at steadily declining real prices. High-voltage electric power lines marching across the countryside came to stand as the symbols of a modern, progressive urban–industrial society. The system remained unchallenged until the 1970s when it was confronted by a maturing technology, rising costs of primary energy, and the emergence of an aggressive environmental movement (Hirsh and Serchuk, 1996; Kellow, 1966). I return to this issue in a later section of this chapter.

THE TRANSFORMATION OF INDUSTRIAL ENERGY USE

Edison perceived the impact of electric power mainly in terms of the illumination of homes, offices, and factories. He did not anticipate its impact on the location and efficiency of industrial production, or its role in the development of new household technologies or entirely new industries. The substitution of electric power for prime movers such as the water wheel and the steam engine represented a major source of technical change in manufacturing during the first half of the twentieth century. Water power could not be transported long distances. It required the construction of dams, channels, and spillways. Mills had to be located adjacent to the source of power and materials transported to the mill. "Within the mill the energy had to be transmitted by gears, belts and pulleys, which lost power at every turn. In an economy based on such power transmission the factory reached an absolute limit on its size beyond which inefficiencies were too great" (Nye, 1990:193, 194).

After 1850, steam engines rapidly supplanted water power as the chief energy source in U.S. manufacturing. Steam-driven mills released the location constraint imposed by water power. But the energy was still transmitted by the same system of gears, shafts, and belts. In spite of these inefficiencies, steam engines provided about 80% of mechanical drive capacity in U.S. factories in 1900. "By 1920, however, electricity had replaced steam as the major source of motive power, and in 1929— just 45 years after their first use in a factory—electric motors represented 78 percent of total capacity for driving machines" (Divine, 1983:349).

Electrification of Mechanical Drive[6]

The electrification of mechanical drive was an important source of efficiency in energy use. It proceeded in three stages. In the first stage large electric motors simply replaced water power or steam engines in turning long line shafts. In the second stage machines were divided into groups and each group was powered by a separate smaller motor. In the third stage shafting was eliminated and each machine was run by its own electric motor (Figure 7.4).

The "direct drive" system of distributing mechanical power involved the transmission of power from a single centrally located prime mover, such as a water wheel or

---

[6] In this section I draw heavily on Divine (1982, 1983). I do not, in this section, discuss the social and cultural significance of electricity or its role in transportation and household technology. For the growth of household electric power use, see Mowery and Rosenberg (1998:105–109). For a social constructionist perspective, see Nye (1990). For an attempt to estimate the dramatic improvements in lighting efficiency, see Nordhaus (1997).

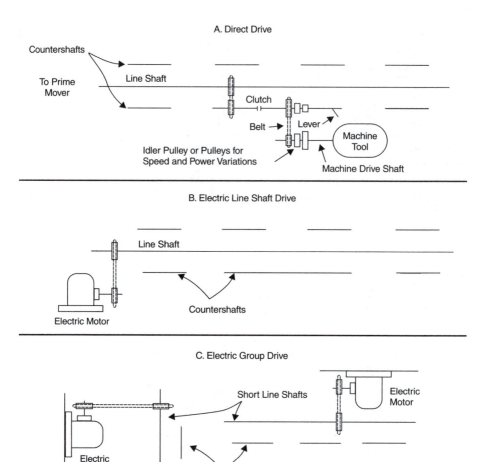

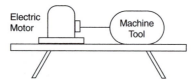

Figure 7.4 Evolution of power distribution in manufacturing. From shafts to wires. (*Source: Warner D. Devine, Jr. "From Shafts to Wires: Historical Perspective on Electrification." Journal of Economic History* 43 (June 1983):353.)

steam engine, via pulleys and leather belts to iron or steel "line shafts." The line shafts, suspended from the ceiling, typically ran the entire length of the factory. The line shafts in turn drove shorter ceiling-mounted "counter shafts." Production machinery was connected to the counter shafts by leather belts. To activate a particular machine the operator shifted a belt from an idler pulley to a drive pulley using a lever attached to the countershaft. Considerable effort was involved in belt maintenance and tightening. "The entire network of line shafts and counter shafts rotated continuously from the time the steam engine was started in the morning until it was shut down at night— no matter how many machines were actually being used. If a line shaft, or the steam engine, broke down production ceased in a whole room of machines or even the entire factory until repairs were made" (Devine, 1982:18).

The second stage, electric line shaft drive, involved little more than replacing the water or steam prime mover with an electric motor. The only difference between direct drive and the earliest electric drive systems was the type of machine used to turn the line shafts. When only small amounts of power were required it was usually cheaper to use electricity rather than steam. Electric drive also had other advantages such as cleanliness and ease of control. Perhaps most importantly, the source of electric power, unlike water or steam, did not have to be located in proximity to the factory. In the 1880s and 1890s, however, it generally continued to be cheaper to drive machinery with steam engines than with electric motors when large amounts of power were required.

In the third stage, electric group drive was used to replace the long line shafts with short line shafts, each driven by its own electric motor. This arrangement reduced the friction losses from operating the long line shafts and permitted small groups of machines to be run independently from the rest of the factory. In 1894 General Electric made the first major installations of electric motors in a factory. An a.c. system with 17 65-hp motors, mounted on the ceiling where they would be out of the way of machinery and workmen, was installed in a new textile mill in South Carolina. GE also constructed a hydroelectric station at a nearby river to transmit the power required for mill operation (Reich, 1985:52). An even larger scale group drive system was installed in the General Electric Company plant in Schenectady, New York. Forty-three direct current motors, located in 40 different shops or departments, turned a total of 5260 feet of shafts.

As early as the 1890s a number of engineers anticipated the time when each machine would be driven by its own electric motor. The fourth stage, electric unit drive, did not, however, become a dominant system until after World War I. Adoption of the unit drive resulted in direct savings in energy. There were also additional indirect savings. In the short run, gains were realized from the reduction in labor for oiling and maintenance of the old belt line equipment. Over the longer run the replacement of belts and pulleys led to the reconfiguration of plant design to facilitate more efficient flow of materials. In addition, factories were lighter, cleaner, and safer. In Box 7.1 I present an induced technical change interpretation of the electrification of factory motive power.

The Steam Turbine

A revolution in electrical-generating equipment was also occurring concomitantly with the technical changes in energy transformation. By 1900 it was becoming apparent that the reciprocating steam engines used to power electric generators were reaching a size limitation at around 5000 kilowatts (kW). In 1884 Charles A. Parsons, an English engineer, developed an engine that operated on radically different principles. Instead of cyclic motion, the steam turbines produced rotary motion as high-pressure steam pushed against blades attached to a shaft, which was connected to a generator. The machine occupied about one-tenth of the space, weighed one-eighth as much, and cost one-third as much as a reciprocating engine of equivalent power (Hirsh, 1989:20–21).

● **BOX 7.1**

AN INDUCED TECHNICAL CHANGE INTERPRETATION OF THE ELECTRIFICATION OF FACTORY MOTIVE POWER

The induced technical change model discussed in Chapter 5 can be used to present an analytical interpretation of the development and impact of the transition from steam-powered line drive to electric unit drive. The model presented in Figure 7.5 incorporates both factor substitution between capital and labor and complementarity between capital and energy.

Assume that in time t_0 energy is supplied to the textile industry by a Watt–Boulton type steam engine and is conveyed to the machines in the textile factory by belts and line shafts (Chapter 4). IPC_0 represents the innovation possibility curve in textile spinning and weaving at time t_0 technology. P_0 is the isocost line. Labor is cheap and capital is expensive. The minimum cost or equilibrium point at A identifies the optimum combination of labor (L_0), capital (K_0), and energy (E_0). Assume that between t_0 and t_1 the price of labor rises relative to the price of capital. The isocost line in t_1 is P_1.

As the price of labor continues to rise relative to capital, there will be an incentive to develop less labor-intensive technology to supply power to the textile industry and less labor-intensive technology in the textile industry. The steam turbine electric-generating technology represented such an advance in the power supply industry. Reductions in the cost of electricity in turn induced the development of electric motors, which replaced the of transmission of power to the textile machinery by belts and line shafts. The potential efficiency gains from use of electric motors also has the effect of

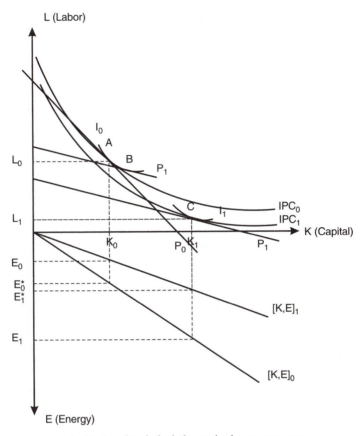

Figure 7.5 A model of induced technical change in the energy sector.

changing the complementary relationship between capital and energy from $[K, E]_0$ to $[K, E]_1$.

We can think of this development as a two-stage process. The initial effect is a shift in the unit isoquant from I_0 on IPC_0 to I_1 on IPC_1. This shift is associated with a decline in labor input (from L_0 to L_1), a rise in capital input (from K_0 to K_1), and a rise in energy input (from E_0 to E_1). The rise in output per unit of total input is associated with a rise in output per unit of labor input, a decline in output per unit of capital, and a decline in output per unit of energy.

The second stage involved the diffusion of electric motors—replacing belts and line shafts. This shift to electric motors in driving textile machinery results in a shift in the line reflecting the complementarity between capital and energy from $[K, E]_0$ to $[K, E]_1$. As a result, energy use declined further, from E_1 to E_1^*.

> The total effect of the factor price-induced technical change in energy production and utilization has been to increase output per worker, decrease output per unit of capital, and increase output per unit of energy. If the increase in output per worker is more rapid than the increase in output per unit of energy then the energy–labor ratio will rise (as it has historically). The shift from IPC_0 to IPC_1 indicates a change in total factor productivity (a decline in real cost per unit of output). Thus, the shift in factor use will not return to the original levels even if the price of energy should rise relative to the price of labor.

Parson's invention was followed by a number of small steam turbine installations. In 1900, a major central station installation was completed by Allgemene Elektrizitäts-Gesellschaft. In the United States, Samuel Insull played a major role in forcing the introduction of larger steam turbines. In 1901, against the advice of his own engineering staff, he overcame General Electric's resistance to building a 5000 kW turbine for his Chicago Fisk Street Station by threatening to contract with European manufacturers. General Electric was so unsure of its capacity to build the large turbine that it would take on the manufacturing risk only if "Chicago Edison would assume the expense of installation whether it succeeded or failed" (Hughes, 1983:211). As more turbines were installed, it became apparent that not only were they less expensive for a given capacity than the reciprocating engines, their unit cost also decreased more rapidly with size, thus permitting an accelerated decline in the cost of electricity. By 1910 steam turbines were rapidly replacing steam engines in driving electric generators.

In spite of the efficiency gains associated with the transition from prime mover direct drive to unit drive and the replacement of reciprocating engines by steam turbines, measured gains in aggregate productivity were slow to come. Part of the explanation was that it was often not profitable to immediately replace old equipment that was still operating effectively. Even when new equipment was adopted, the old equipment often remained in place to serve as "back up." A third factor was the failure to capture quality changes, such as more effective lighting and enhanced product quality, in the productivity accounts (David, 1989:15–29; Nordhaus, 1997).

David has also suggested that in the United States the General Electric–Westinghouse duopoly was able to prevent their equipment's gains in efficiency from being passed on to industrial users until well into the first decade of the twentieth century, thus slowing adoption rates. Furthermore, the indirect gains referred to above, which resulted from learning by using, occurred only with a substantial lag after initial adoption. By the 1920s, however, productivity in U.S. manufacturing was experiencing rapid growth. David argues, drawing on the epidemic diffusion model (see Chapter 5), that "there is a tendency for the productivity growth rate to reach its maximum only after the inflection point of a classic, logistic diffusion path has been passed" (David, 1989:16). He also draws a parallel with the lag in productivity impact of other technologies characterized by scale effects and network externalities, such as the computer (see Chapter 9).

Electric Power and Productivity Growth

The definitive effort, prior to the oil price shocks of the 1970s, to interpret the relationship between electrification and productivity growth in the United States was Sam Schurr and Bruce Netschert's now classic book, *Energy and the American Economy* (1960). The most dramatic result from this study was their discovery that although energy intensity in the U. S. economy, measured by the consumption of energy relative to GNP, had more than doubled between 1880 and 1910, it declined consistently after World War I (Table 7.1).[7]

Schurr and his colleagues identified three factors that accounted for the transition from increasing to decreasing energy intensity. These included (1) the changing composition of national output toward lighter manufacturing and services, (2) improvements in the thermal efficiency of energy conversion in electrical generation and railroad transportation, and (3) changes in the composition of the energy supply, particularly the growing importance of electricity and fluid fuels (primarily petroleum) relative to solid fuels (primarily coal) in manufacturing and transportation.

In a 1984 update of the 1960 analysis, Schurr (1984:140) insisted that electricity, in spite of its small share of total costs, was strategically important because it made possible the redesign of entire systems of manufacturing technology. Schurr also called attention to the relationship between the rise in energy prices after 1973 and acceleration in the decline in energy intensity (Table 7.2).

THE GREAT OIL SHOCK

Prior to the early 1970s it was conventional, in spite of the findings by Schurr and his associates, to assume that per capita income and labor productivity were closely associated with growth in energy consumption. And even Schurr and his colleagues had overlooked the effects of differential change in fuel and nonfuel raw material prices on energy–labor, energy–capital, and energy–output ratios. Electric utility companies employed projections of population and per capita income growth as the dominant variables in estimating the growth of service demand. Traditional views about the linear relationship between energy consumption and economic growth were severely challenged by the two "oil shocks" of the 1970s. The first oil price shock

---

[7] For an early exploration of the Schurr hypotheses see Richard B. DuBoff (1966:426–431). The article draws on DuBoff's 1964 Ph.D. theses (reprinted in 1979). DuBoff is particularly concerned to explain the change in the output–capital ratio, which began to decline in the United States around World War I. His interpretation was that "power capital was substituted in large measure for non-power capital requirements. Most of such power capital was in the form of electric motors and equipment. Consequently, less capital was needed per unit of output as more capital became electrified" (1966:428).

Table 7.1 U.S. Energy Consumption and Gross National Product, 1890–2000

Year	GNP [Billions of Chained (1992) Dollars]	Energy Consumption (Quadrillions of British Thermal Units)	Energy/GNP [Thousand British Thermal Units (1992) Dollars]
1890	238.6	4.497	18.84
1895	283.5	5.355	18.89
1900	348.1	7.572	21.75
1905	436.0	11.369	26.08
1910	556.2	14.800	26.61
1915	578.9	16.076	27.77
1920	640.8	19.768	30.85
1925	825.4	20.878	25.30
1930	854.1	22.253	26.06
1935	777.5	19.059	24.51
1940	1029.0	23.877	23.20
1945	1675.8	31.439	18.76
1950	1599.3	33.078	20.68
1955	1966.2	38.821	19.74
1960	2276.0	43.802	19.25
1965	2901.4	52.684	18.16
1970	3417.1	66.431	19.44
1975	3903.3	70.546	18.07
1980	4670.8	75.955	16.26
1985	5346.7	73.981	13.84
1990	6157.0	81.283	13.20
1995	6779.5	87.205	12.86
2000	8015.1	93.872	11.71

Source: Adapted from Warren D. Devine Jr., "From Shafts to Wires: Historical Perspective on Electrification," *Journal of Economic History* 43 (June 1983):347–362. For 1985–1995, GNP data are from U.S. Bureau of Economic Analysis, *Survey of Current Business* (April 1999): Table C.1, and energy consumption data are from U.S. Energy Information Administration. *Monthly Energy Review* (March 1999):25. Data for 2000 are projected.

occurred in 1973–1974 and the second in 1979–1980. Each shock resulted in a more than doubling of the real (inflation adjusted) price of oil (Figure 7.6). Prices of other primary energy sources also rose, but less dramatically.

The U.S. government responded to the energy shocks by instituting a complex and often contradictory set of interventions in energy, research, development, and conservation. These interventions tried simultaneously to shield consumers from higher energy prices and encourage energy conservation. In 1977 the Congress approved a cabinet level Department of Energy (DOE) to combine its diverse energy programs within a single agency. Greater intervention in energy markets in the 1970s was followed by steps toward decontrol and deregulation as energy price declined in the early 1980s (Marcus, 1992:35–54).

Many analysts initially interpreted the oil shocks as evidence of a fundamental transition from an environment of energy abundance and declining world prices to

Table 7.2   Average Annual Percentage Rates of Change in Total Output, Multifactor Productivity, Energy Intensity, and Relative Power Cost in the Private Domestic Business Economy, 1899–1981

	Total Output (1)	Multifactor Productivity (2)	Energy Intensity[a]			Relative Fuel and Power Cost (6)	Electric Power Share of Total Installed Power in Manufacturing[b] (7)
			Per Unit of Output (3)	Per Worker (4)	Per Unit Capital (5)		
Increase in national energy intensity, 1899–1920	3.4	1.0	1.5	2.8	2	—	4.8
Persistent decline in national energy intensity, 1920–1953	3.1	2.1	-1.2	1.1	0.5	-1	59.1
Comparative stability in national energy intensity, 1953–1973	3.7	2.3	-0.1	3.5	1.3	-0.3	84.7
Postembargo period of decline in national energy intensity							
With rising fuel and power cost, 1973–1982	1.7	-0.5	-2.7	-1.6	-5.5	8.5	
With declining fuel and power cost, 1982–1986	5.1	2.2	-3.7	-1.3	-2.0	-8.6	
Return to comparative stability in national energy intensity, 1986–1994	2.5	0.2	0.2	-0.7	0.2	-1.0	

[a]Energy is measured as Btu's of mineral fuels plus hydropower (excluding wood); relative fuel and power costs are defined as the fuel and power wholesale price index relative to the wholesale price index of all commodities.

[b]Electric power share of total installed power in manufacturing in 1899, 1920, 1953, and 1973.

Sources: 1899–1973: Adapted from Sam H. Schurr, "Energy Use Technological Change, and Productive Efficiency: An Economic-Historical Interpretation," *Annual Review of Energy* 9(1984):409–425. 1973–1994: Column (1): *Economic Report of the President*, February 1996. Column (2): Bureau of Labor Statistics, *Monthly Labor Review*, September 1996. Columns (3)–(5): Calculated from Energy Information Administration, *Monthly Energy Review*, November 1996, and Bureau of Labor Statistics, *Monthly Labor Review*, November 1996.

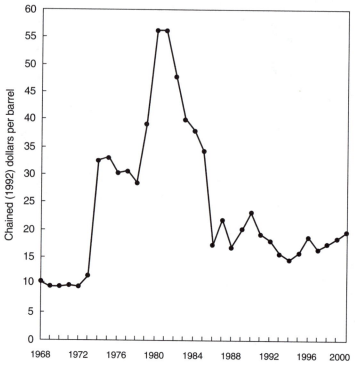

Figure 7.6 International crude oil price (the refiner acquisition cost of imported crude oil in the United States), 1968–2000. (*Source:* Adapted from J. Goldenberg, T. B. Johanson, A. K. N. Reddy, and R. H. Williams, *Energy for a Sustainable World*, Washington, DC: World Resources Institute, September 1987. Data for 1985–1997 are from U.S. Energy Information Administration, *Annual Energy Review 1997*, July 1998, p. 155. Data for 1998–2000 are projected.)

an environment of energy scarcity and longer term price increases. A perspective emerged by the early 1970s that the dominant role of energy in the economies of developed countries had locked the world into a series of self-perpetuating cycles of energy prices and economic growth. In this cycle economic growth would generate rising demand for petroleum. Upward pressure on prices would result in a sharp rise in oil prices, which in turn would generate a world recession and declining demand for oil and other forms of energy. The cycle would be completed by falling oil prices and economic recovery. Renewed upward pressure on world oil prices would then initiate a new cycle.

Even in the late 1970s and early 1980s, when the consensus that petroleum and other primary energy prices would continue to rise, or at least remain at the high levels of the early 1980s, was at its strongest, a few "contrarian" analysts resisted the weight of conventional opinion and insisted that petroleum prices again would decline toward the levels of the early 1970s. They argued that the higher prices did not signal a transition to a regime of energy scarcity. Rather, they demonstrated the power of a cartel of petroleum exporters, the Organization of Petroleum Exporting Countries (OPEC), to manage the flow of petroleum into world markets. These analysts drew on economic theory and the history of cartel arrangements to argue that such arrangements were inherently unstable.[8] By the mid-1980s the contrarians had been vindicated! Petroleum prices had fallen to near the levels of a decade and a half earlier (Figure 7.6).

The petroleum price shocks induced a massive outpouring of analysis and opinion. Concern about the impact of the oil price shocks on output and employment was initially stimulated by the coincidence of a decline in both GNP and employment in major industrial countries—in Germany, the United Kingdom, and Japan, as well as the United States. Attention was focused on the longer run implications for economic growth as it became apparent that both labor productivity and multifactor productivity growth had declined sharply in a number of industrial countries, beginning at about the time of the first oil shock, and that the lower rate of productivity growth was persisting into the 1980s (see Chapter 2).

Output and Employment[9]

The short-run implications of a large increase in petroleum prices on economic activity seem quite clear. A rise in the price of petroleum could be expected to have an immediate impact on the cost of production. The petroleum-intensive industries would experience the largest cost increases. As producers sought alternatives to petroleum, the prices of both primary energy sources, such as coal and natural gas, and of electricity could be expected to rise. Resources that are complements with primary energy, particularly capital equipment used in energy-intensive industries, would experience a decline in demand and some combination of decline in price and use. Resources that are substitutes for energy, such as labor, would experience an increase in demand and this, in turn, would result in some combination of increase in wages and employment.

This is very close to what actually happened. A decade after the first oil shock energy consumption in the United States had fallen below its 1972 level, and petroleum consumption had declined even more dramatically than total energy consumption. Jorgenson (1986:277) noted: "Among energy analysts the great discovery from the first oil crisis was the price elasticity of demand for energy." At the industry level, the impact of higher energy prices on costs was felt more severely in the production of more energy-intensive commodities. In most industries energy and capital were on

---

[8] See, for example, the collection of papers covering the period 1962–1993 by Adelman (1993).

[9] In this section I draw particularly on Jorgenson (1986) and Bohi (1989). See also the collection of papers edited by Feldman (1996).

the borderline between substitution and complementarity, so that increases in energy prices left the demand for capital largely unaffected. However, energy and labor proved to be highly substitutable, so that demand for labor rose with the increase in energy prices. In Europe this resulted in an increase in real wages, since the labor supply was inelastic with respect to wages. In the United States, where the labor supply was more elastic, the increase in labor demand led to growth in employment rather than increases in wage rates (Jorgenson, 1986:278). The effects of the increase in petroleum prices, and the associated increases in other energy prices, also had important demand side effects. For example, demand for large "gas-guzzling" U.S.-made automobiles declined. At the same time the demand for smaller, more energy-efficient automobiles from Japan rose.

Clearly the oil price shocks had an important impact on patterns of production and consumption. But were the oil price shocks responsible for the global recessions of 1974–1975 and 1979–1980? This question is more difficult because the answer depends, at least in part, on the monetary policies pursued by individual countries. The petroleum price shocks occurred during periods of global inflation. The increase in energy prices added to inflationary expectations. The 1974–1975 and 1979–1980 recessions were much larger than could be accounted for by the rise in petroleum and energy prices. The recessions were primarily a consequence of the policies adopted to control inflation. Japan, in contrast to the United States, Germany, and Great Britain, responded to the second oil crisis with a combination of wage stabilization and an expansionary monetary and fiscal policy that permitted it to avoid the recession experienced by the other three countries. My own sense is that the oil price shocks, because of their high visibility at the gasoline pump and elsewhere, helped create a political environment that was conducive to antiinflationary policy. Thus, the oil shocks contributed to the weak performance of the U.S. economy in the 1970s through both their modest direct inflationary impact and their indirect impact on strengthening the forces leading to deflationary economic policy.

Growth and Productivity

The conclusion that the energy shocks of the 1970s played a contributing but not a decisive role in the recessions of 1974–1975 and 1979–1980 did not resolve the question of their longer term productivity and growth effects. Skeptics pointed to the fact that the energy cost share in the U.S. business sector was too small for the price shocks of the 1970s to have much effect. The energy share amounted to 4.5% in 1973 (rising to 6.5% in 1974) and 7.0% in 1979 (rising to 8.5% in 1980).

The first definitive analysis of the productivity and growth effects of the rise in energy prices is the research by Jorgenson and Fraumeni (1981:17–47; Jorgenson, 1986:1–13). In his work with Fraumeni, and in related research, Jorgenson rejects the traditional macroeconomic two-factor (labor and capital) model. The linkages between energy and the economy are too complex to be captured in models that do not include energy as an intermediate input. In the Jorgenson–Fraumeni model, output is a function of the inputs of four primary factors of production—capital, labor services, energy, and materials. Time is employed as an index of the level of technology.

From their model Jorgenson and Fraumeni calculate "biases" in the rate of productivity growth for each input in each of 35 industries. Energy-using productivity growth would, for example, imply that an increase in the price of energy would slow the rate of productivity growth. Of the 35 industries in Jorgenson's study, all but six show an energy-using bias in productivity growth. From this analysis Jorgenson and Fraumeni infer that rising energy prices were an important source of the decline in productivity growth across the industrial sector and in overall economic growth in the United States during the 1970s and into the 1980s. Jorgenson and Fraumeni also found that energy and capital are on the borderline between being substitutes and complements. This appears to reflect the fact that their analysis is largely based on the years before the energy crisis when both capital and energy inputs were growing rapidly.[10]

My only qualification of the Jorgenson–Fraumeni model is that it does not enable them to fully capture the effects of the technical change induced by the rise in energy prices. In the Jorgenson–Fraumeni model the bias in technical change in each industry is constant over the period of analysis, whereas the rate of technical change in each industry is endogenous. In an induced innovation model the bias in technical change (reflected in the elasticity of output with respect to factor inputs) also would be endogenous. It is reasonable to assume that the biases in technical change captured in the Jorgenson and Fraumeni analysis, based on 1958–1974 data, were induced by the long decline in the price of electrical energy that had extended from the early 1900s to the early 1970s. When energy prices rose in the 1970s firms in energy-intensive industries began to replace capital equipment with less energy-intensive equipment and suppliers of capital equipment invested in the development of less energy-intensive, but often more capital-intensive, technologies (Berndt, 1984:325–334).

In later work Jorgenson and Wilcoxen (1990, 1993) implemented a model that incorporates both the short-run substitution effects and the longer run induced technical change effects at the industry level of energy price changes. These results indicate very large price induced technical changes in response to the higher energy prices of the 1970s and early 1980s. The Jorgenson–Wilcoxen findings of energy price-induced technical change has been confirmed by several other studies. Lichtenberg (1986:67–75) found that the 1973 oil price shocks had a substantial effect on industrial R&D expenditures. Although industrial R&D intensity was generally declining, during the 1970s and early 1980s it declined least in those industries most affected by the energy price increases. Furthermore, the share of company-financed R&D devoted to energy

---

[10] Several other studies based on data prior to the 1973 energy shock suggest that energy and capital were complements. See Berndt and Wood (1975) and the literature reviewed by Berndt (1978). Later work, drawing on the experience of the 1970s and 1980s, has confirmed that capital and labor exhibit substantial substitutability when adequate time is allowed to replace capital equipment with newer equipment designed with more expensive energy in mind (Moroney, 1992:363–380).

conservation and utilization rose during the same period. In a later paper Lichtenberg (1986:154–159) also found that the rate of investment in R&D was an increasing function of the relative price of energy. David Popp (1996) found that during 1970–1994 changes in energy prices had a strong effect on innovation (as measured by patents) in 19-energy supply and energy-using industries. The response to prices was particularly rapid in the energy-supply technologies.[11]

It is hard to avoid a conclusion, based on the evidence reviewed in this section, that the long-term decline in real energy prices prior to the early 1970s had the effect of both speeding the rate of technical change in the energy-using industries and biasing the direction of technical change in an energy-using direction. Similarly, the rise in energy prices associated with the oil shocks of the 1970s had the effect of both slowing the rate of technical change and biasing technical change in an energy-saving direction from the time of the first oil shock of 1973 until well into the 1980s. The momentum of price-induced technical change was lost when petroleum prices declined in the mid-1980s. Most of the efficiency gains induced by the higher prices during the previous decade were, however, maintained. For example, between the mid-1980s and mid-1990s, the automobile industry devoted substantial technical effort to achieving higher gasoline mileage without reducing engine power. After the decline in petroleum prices in the mid-1980s, technical effort shifted to the development of higher powered engines, while maintaining the fuel efficiencies achieved in the previous decade.

THE EXHAUSTION OF SCALE[12]

For at least a century prior to the oil shocks of the 1970s, declining real prices of energy represented a powerful engine of economic growth in the presently developed countries. The lower costs of energy extraction and the substitution of newer sources of energy for traditional sources spurred economic growth (Figures 7.1, 7.2, and 7.3). Economic growth was impacted even more strongly by the substitution of electric power for primary energy sources. The combined effect of electricity's declining real price and its flexibility in use was to induce dramatic change in both household and industrial technology.

Two effects of the oil price shocks of the 1970s were, at least temporarily, to slow economic growth and to induce the development of less energy-intensive technology. Since the mid-1980s petroleum prices have returned to near the real levels that prevailed prior to the early 1970s (Figure 7.6). Electricity prices, which rose more slowly than petroleum prices in the 1970s, did not decline to their pre-1970 levels but

---

[11] Popp also found that during 1970–1994, federal R&D had a significant supply-side effect in technical opportunities (as measured by patents) for 13 energy industries he studied. The supply-side effects were, however, smaller than the demand-side price effects.

[12] In this section I draw heavily on Hirsh (1989) and Gordon (1992).

continued to rise into the 1990s. Furthermore, output per worker in the electric power industry, which grew at almost triple the rate for the economy as a whole from 1899 to 1948, and more than double the rate from 1948 to 1973, slowed dramatically. Since the early 1970s productivity growth in the electric utility industry has approximated the slow growth of the economy as a whole (Table 7.3).

The induced innovation model suggests that the decline in electricity's real price prior to the early 1970s was an important source of technical change and productivity growth in the economy as a whole. It is important, therefore, to attempt to understand the reasons for the slowdown and reversal of productivity growth in the electric utility industry.

The Technology of Electricity Generation

Until well into the 1970s, most sources of increased productivity in electric power generation would have been familiar to Watt or Edison. Each power generation "unit," called a "boiler-turbogenerator" (BTG) unit, operated independently of other units at a given plant location. It consisted of (1) a boiler to burn the fuel and to generate and expand the steam and (2) a turbogenerator to convert high-pressure steam into electric energy through the rotary motion of a turbine shaft. A condenser converted the steam into water to complete the cycle. Until the late 1960s, technical change in the design of BTG units was aimed primarily at (1) increasing the size of generators and boilers and (2) improving the thermal efficiency of the generating cycle.

The technical design frontier was limited by the ability of the boilers to withstand high-temperatures and pressure. The frontier was pushed out by incremental advances, particularly those in metallurgy involving the development of high-temperature steel

Table 7.3   Average Percentage Rates of Change in Output per Hour Nonfarm Business and Electric Utilities, and Real Price of Electricity, Various Intervals, 1890–2000

Interval	Output per Hour Nonfarm Business (1)	Output per Hour Electric Utilities (2)	Real Price of Electricity (3)
1899–1923	2.1	5.7	−7.4
1923–1948	2.1	6.0	−6.7
1948–1963	2.6	6.8	−1.3
1963–1973	2.2	5.5	−2.6
1973–1988	1.1	1.1	1.9
1988–1998	1.2	4.3[a]	−2.1

[a]Average percentage change for 1988–1996.

Sources: Adapted from Robert J. Gordon, *Forward into the Past: Productivity Retrogression in the Electric Generating Industry*, Cambridge, MA: National Bureau of Economic Research Working Paper 3988, 1992. (1) For 1973–1998 is from *Economic Report of the President* (1999):385. (2) For 1973–1996 is from U.S. Bureau of Labor Statistics, *Monthly Labor Review* (February 1999):121. (3) For 1973–1997 is from U.S. Energy Information Administration, *Annual Energy Review 1997* (1998):233. (3) For 1998 is from U.S. Energy Information Administration, *Monthly Energy Review* (March 1999): 122, converted to real price using gross domestic product implicit price deflator for 1998, 1.127.

alloys. Much of the shift to higher temperatures and to reheat cycles was completed during the 1948–1957 decade. The increase in pressure rating continued until the late 1960s. The average size of BTG units also increased: in 1948 over half of all new units were rated below 50 (MW); in 1987, 60% of new units were above 500 MW and some were above 1000 MW.[13]

Prior to World War II engineers had employed a "design-by-experience" approach, in which each step to a new technological plateau was followed by a period of debugging before the next advance. In the postwar period, spurred by the rapidly growing demand for electricity, equipment manufacturers shifted to the more aggressive "design-by-extrapolation" approach, in which the next advance was planned before operating experience had occurred with the previous advance.

As this process continued it ran into a series of technological barriers. (1) As the level of 40% thermal efficiency was approached, the marginal cost of improving efficiency through use of exotic and expensive steels began to exceed the value of the thermal efficiency gains. (2) The increases in pressure and temperature (from 280 to 500°C) between the early 1950s and the late 1960s led to increases in corrosion activity and corrosion cracking. This in turn led to increased downtime and lower utilization rates due to higher maintenance requirements. (3) Increases in boiler and generator size also led to greater maintenance problems. Downtime was five times greater for units above 600 MW than for units in the 100 MW range. Until well into the 1980s, electricity production in plants using fossil fuels continued to be based largely on technical changes that emerged by the early 1950s. Economy of scale effects had apparently been exhausted, leading to a backing off from the largest sizes (supercritical boiler size) in the late 1970s and 1980s. Labor productivity in the largest units continued to decline, primarily because of the large maintenance costs incurred as a result of the unanticipated problems.

What Happened to Nuclear Power[14]

In the period immediately after World War II it was anticipated that nuclear energy would largely replace fossil fuels as the primary fuel source in the generation of electricity. The prospect of developing a peaceful use for nuclear energy generated considerable enthusiasm in both the scientific community and the general public. It was asserted that nuclear energy would make electricity so inexpensive that it would be "too cheap to meter" (Pool, 1997: 71). Even then the prospect was highly controversial within the scientific community. Some members of the Manhattan Project, who had

---

[13] One kilowatt (kW) is 1000 watts (W). One megawatt (MW) is 1000 kW or 1,000,000 W. One gigawatt (GW) is 1000 MW or 1,000,000,000 W. One terawatt (TW) is 1000 GW or 1,000,000,000,000 W. The large 1000-MW (1-GW) plants constructed in the early 1980s were 100,000 times larger than Edison's 10-kW Jumbo generator of 100 years earlier (Ausubel, 1997:115, 132).

[14] This section draws heavily on Cowan (1990), MacKerron (1994), World Energy Council (1993), Hill et al. (1995), Tester et al. (1991), and Pool (1997).

been involved in developing the atomic bomb, regard the commercial development of atomic energy as neither economically sound nor advisable.

The United States Atomic Energy Commission (AEC), established by the Atomic Energy Act of 1946, was given the authority to promote and regulate the development of nuclear technology for both military and nonmilitary purposes. In 1951 the AEC set out to test a number of reactor designs for nuclear power plants. However, President Eisenhower's "atoms for peace" program launched in 1954 resulted in a more intensive and less deliberative effort to develop a civilian nuclear power program.[15] The Atomic Energy Act of 1954 provided a statutory basis for the private sector development of nuclear power and for cooperation in the development of "peaceful uses" of nuclear technology with other countries (Hewlett and Hall, 1989).

Enrico Fermi demonstrated the feasibility of controlled nuclear fission at the University of Chicago's Stag Field laboratories on December 2, 1942. A decade and a half later the first commercial nuclear reactors (at Calder Hill in the United Kingdom in 1956, and at Shipping Port New York in 1957) came on line. It took another 30 years for nuclear reactors to account for 20% of electricity generated in the United States. In the United States, the earliest nuclear plants developed to produce electricity were reactors designed for use in submarines. In the United States, and later in Germany and Japan, large public R&D programs were complemented by substantial private research investment by firms such as Westinghouse, General Electric, Babcox and Wilcox, Siemens, AEG, and Mitsubishi. In the United Kingdom, France, and the U.S.S.R., the research was conducted almost exclusively by the public sector. Nowhere were the electric utility firms heavily involved in nuclear research. They assumed that replacing a fossil fuel-fired boiler with a nuclear reactor to produce steam would be a relatively simple process—"a nuclear reactor was just another way to boil water."

A number of different reactor designs were advanced in the late 1950s and early 1960s.[16] The U.S. designs used light-water cooling and enriched uranium. The British and French initially used a gas graphite reactor. Canada, the only country whose reactor design did not derive from prior miliary programs, used heavy water and natural uranium. By the mid-1960s all of the major industrial countries—the United States, Canada, the United Kingdom, the U.S.S.R., France, Germany, Sweden, and Japan—were making significant investments in nuclear plants. Construction

---

[15] The Eisenhower speech in December 1953 was a response to progress in the development of the nuclear-powered submarine under the direction of Hyman Rickover, who headed the Naval Reactors Branch of the AEC. In this effort Rickover brought together the design for a pressurized water reactor, developed under the direction of Alvin Weinberg at the Oak Ridge AEC Laboratory, with engineering capacity from the Westinghouse Corporation (Marcus, 1992:104).

[16] "Nuclear reactors are classified by two of the materials used in their construction: the coolant used to transfer heat from the reactor core; and the moderator used to control the energy level of the neutrons in the reactor core. In a light water reactor both coolant and moderator are light water—H_2O. In a heavy water reactor both are heavy water—D_2O. In a graphite reactor the coolant is a gas, usually helium or carbon dioxide, and the moderator is graphite" (Cowan, 1990:545).

experience led to improved reactor designs, which locked the industry into the light-water path of technology development. Whether other designs would in fact have been superior in the long run is open to question, although some of the engineering literature suggests that high-temperature gas-cooled reactors would have been superior. Brian Arthur (1990:99) and Robin Cowan (1990:541–567) have interpreted this history as an example of "path dependence"—light-water advanced rapidly along its learning curve and by the time other technologies were ready to compete it was too late.[17]

Cost estimates by the AEC in the 1960s indicated that nuclear power plant capital costs would be substantially greater than those of electricity generated by large coal-fired plants. It was expected, however, that this would be compensated for by low operating costs due to the limited quantities of uranium fuel required (Weinberg, 1972:28). In the 1950s and 1960s nuclear power was regarded as the only long-term solution to the energy shortage. Thus, for 20 years, from the early 1950s to the early 1970s, national energy research in the United States and in other advanced countries focused almost exclusively on nuclear power.

The anticipated economies of scale and cost reductions from "learning by doing" and "learning by using" were not realized, however. They were more than offset by increases in the complexity of reactors, due partly to initial design errors, but largely to increasingly stringent safety standards. In many cases, final costs exceeded initial estimates by 100%.[18] It became apparent by the mid-1970s that the simple and comparatively inexpensive light-water reactors of the late 1960s were, partly on engineering grounds and partly due to safety concerns, no longer commercially viable (MacKerron, 1992).

Beginning in the 1970s, safety requirements for nuclear power plants in the United States have been continually tightened by the Nuclear Regulatory Commission (successor to the Atomic Energy Commission) in response to public risk perception. Although it is not clear that changes in these requirements resulted in substantial safety improvements, the frequent design changes in the course of construction did result in higher construction costs. During the 1980s, average construction time in the United States rose to over 10 years. The costs of new nuclear plants of comparable size, corrected for inflation, quadrupled in little more than a decade. These higher capital costs pushed the cost of producing electricity from nuclear-fueled plants even higher relative to coal-burning plants. As electrical shortages began to emerge in the 1980s, utilities increasingly turned to natural gas as a source of primary energy because plants

---

[17] In retrospect the "path dependence" was forced by strategic rather than economic considerations. Pool argues that without an atomic weapons program no country would have built uranium-enrichment facilities: "without the enriched uranium supplied by the post-war bomb building program, it is unlikely that the light water reactor would have been a serious contender much less the design of choice" (Pool, 1997: 43).

[18] A rapid surge in new construction of nuclear plants in the 1960s has sometimes been interpreted as induced by the 1973 oil price shock. Damian (1992:600) argues, however, that the difficulties encountered by nuclear power were at least partially responsible for the timing of the oil price shocks of 1973 and 1978.

could be brought on line relatively quickly, even though cost per kilowatt hour might be higher than for either nuclear power or coal.

A Faustian Bargain?

In an important paper published in 1972 Alvin M. Weinberg, a leading atomic scientist and director of the Oak Ridge National Laboratory, anticipated many of the problems that have constrained the development of the nuclear power industry. "We nuclear people have made a Faustian bargain with society. On the one hand we offer the catalytic nuclear burner—an inexhaustible source of energy. Even in the short range, when we use ordinary reactors, we offer energy that is cheaper than fossil fuel. Moreover, this source of fuel, when properly handled, is almost nonpolluting. But the price we demand of society for this manageable energy source is both a vigilance and a longevity in our social institutions that we are quite unaccustomed to" (Weinberg, 1972:33). Weinberg went on to emphasize that the problems of reactor safety, transport of radioactive materials, and disposal of fuel rods and other high-level radioactive waste could be managed only by the commitment of an exceptional level of technical and scientific competence. He advocated that nuclear power production and waste storage be located at a limited number of sites where the technical and scientific skills and the social arrangements necessary for the management of a nuclear industry could be ensured.

Society has not yet demonstrated a willingness to pay the price of Weinberg's Faustian bargain. In the United States, satisfactory technology and sites for the disposal of spent fuel rods and other radioactive materials have not yet been ensured. The catastrophic meltdown of a nuclear reactor and the release of radiation from a plant in Chernobyl, Ukraine, in 1986 seemed to illustrate the vulnerability of nuclear power to economic and policy disintegration.

In the United States no new plants have been ordered since 1978 and energy plants ordered after 1974 were canceled. The path followed by France has been quite different.[19] At the time of the first oil crisis in 1973, imported oil accounted for over two-thirds of French energy consumption. Following the oil embargo, the French government committed itself to the construction of six 900-MW reactors per year. The rationale for the program was that nuclear energy was the only form of power that could be developed based on French resources. The French developed capabilities in all areas of the nuclear power cycle, from reactor design and construction to fuel supplies and waste treatment.

By the late 1990s almost 70% of French electric power production was based on nuclear power. Average plant construction time was a little under 6 years, compared to nearly 12 years in the United States. French electric rates were among the lowest in Europe and France was exporting electricity to nearly all of its neighbors. French success can be attributed, in part, to the large government subsidies to nuclear power

---

[19] This and the next paragraph draw heavily on Marcus (1993:394–395.)

research and development. It can also be attributed to a variety of other factors, including standardized design and construction of nuclear plants, greater sensitivity to the issue of oil dependence, and the competence and sophistication needed to manage a technology with high-risk potential. This success also reflects a political system in which important technical decisions are made by a bureaucratic–technical elite and the public is excluded from effective participation in such decisions.

Substantial new nuclear power construction is underway in East Asia. As of late 1996, Japan had announced plans to add 40 new nuclear reactors, and generate 42% of its electricity from nuclear reactors by 2010. South Korea had 11 nuclear reactors in operation and 19 more under construction or authorized in 1996. Expansion of nuclear power was also underway in the People's Republic of China , India, and Indonesia (Abelson, 1996:463, 465). It seems clear that strategic considerations continue to weigh heavily in decisions to maintain or expand nuclear power capacity. The experience in developing countries suggests that nuclear power programs have typically absorbed a far larger share of resources than could be justified in terms of potential economic benefits (Solingen, 1996:188). It also seems clear that few societies in which nuclear power production is continuing to expand have yet faced up to the price they will have to pay to satisfy the conditions of Weinberg's Faustian bargain.[20]

Power based on nuclear fission is still viewed by many scientists and engineers as a potentially environmentally benign technology capable of replacing the fossil fuels on a large-scale basis. Physicists and engineers have also been intrigued by the possibility of producing controlled fusion reactions in a power plant to capture the huge amounts of energy that are theoretically available. Fusion has two potentially important advantages. The first is that the fuel, hydrogen and its isotopes, is much less expensive and more abundant than the heavy metals, such as uranium, used in fission. The second is that although the fusion process would create some radioactive waste, due to irradiation of the plant construction materials, it does not create the huge amount of waste produced by fission. Fusion's major disadvantage, even should it become technically feasible, is one it shares with existing nuclear fission plants—high capital investment requirements will remain an obstacle to economic viability. It is possible of course that new strategic considerations, the threat of global warming, for example, could again shift priorities to favor nuclear power.

INSTITUTIONAL INNOVATION

Concern about the environmental and health implications of fossil fuel and nuclear power, combined with the oil shocks of the 1970s, induced an intense debate about

---

[20] Rhoades and Beller (2000) have argued that improvements in the safety and efficiency of nuclear technology underway in the late 1990s will lead to an increasing share of electrical energy being generated by nuclear fuels.

energy futures (see Chapter 12). Prior to the early 1970s, U.S. energy research and development had focused primarily on the development of nuclear energy. In 1973, for example, 67% of federal energy R&D expenditures were on nuclear power—42% on the liquid metal fast breeder reactor alone. Smaller amounts were spent on coal, petroleum, and natural gas. Renewable energy sources and conservation were largely ignored (Tilton, 1974:8–15). By the mid-1970s, it became widely believed that energy conservation could slow the rate of growth in energy use and that renewable energy sources could account for a substantial share of incremental growth in energy production. It was recognized, however, that the substitution of renewable energy sources for fossil fuel and nuclear sources and the slowing of energy use could be achieved only by changes in the technology of electric power generation and by incentives to both producers and consumers of electric power.[21]

There have been a series of government interventions, beginning with the Clean Air Act of 1970, designed to address the environmental and health implications of electric power production. There has also been a second set of interventions designed to encourage the development and adoption of renewable energy technologies. A third set of interventions was directed toward the development and adoption of energy-conserving technologies and practices. By the mid-1990s it was clear that the changes in technology and organization were quite different than the changes that had been anticipated by the reform advocates in the 1970s and 1980s.

Clean Air Policy

The objective of the 1970 Clear Air Act was to "protect and enhance the quality of the nation's air." "Healthy air" was to be achieved by 1975 by reducing concentrations of pollutants such as particulate matter, sulfur dioxide, carbon monoxide, photo-chemical oxidants, and nitrogen oxides.[22] Three months after the law was passed the Environmental Protection Agency set national standards for these pollutants. States were mandated to develop implementation plans that would reduce emissions from industrial sources to meet the EPA ambient air quality goals. But when progress was reviewed in 1975, the Council on Environmental Quality found that the mandated standards had not been met in most urban regions.

The Congressional response was to pass, in 1977, Amendments to the Clean Air Act that gave industry more time to comply. These amendments also expanded the authority of the EPA to control hazardous air pollutants. A major element of the 1997 amendments was the change in the technology to control sulfur dioxide (SO_2) emissions. Under the 1970 Act, the EPA had set standards for new generating plants

---

[21] I do not, in this chapter, consider programs for energy-conserving technology development in other areas such as transportation (see the National Research Council, 1992). Nor do I consider a number of other programs that were initiated in response to the oil shocks of the 1970s, such as the synthetic fuels program (see Cohen and Noll, 1991).

[22] In this section I draw heavily on Marcus and Geffen (1996).

at no more than 1.2 lb of SO_2 per million British thermal units (Mbtu) of coal burned. This measure encouraged utilities to build new plants to use low sulfur coal. It also favored western coal over higher sulfur eastern and Midwestern coal. Environmental advocacy groups and high sulfur coal producers urged Congress to allow utilities to continue to use high sulfur coal if they attached scrubbers to remove excess SO_2. This "end of the pipe" technology was less effective in reducing pollutants. It was also more expensive because of the capital cost of the scrubbing equipment. Nevertheless, Congress mandated a sliding scale in which plants using coal had to install scrubbers capable of removing 70–90% of SO_2, depending on the sulfur content.

The effect of the 1977 Amendments was a substantial improvement in air quality. But most urban regions still failed to meet federal standards at some time during a typical year. In 1990 Congress, increasingly concerned about the "acid rain" problem, passed the *1990 Amendment to the Clean Air Act* designed to sharply reduce SO_2 emissions. The 1990 Act established a fixed overall emission goal of 8.95 million tons of SO_2 per year by January 1995. Congress also introduced an innovative market-like pollution trading system. Generators that cut emissions more than the required amount earned pollution rights that they could sell or use themselves in case they expanded their own generating capacity. Additional credit was earned from installing scrubbers. The purpose was to achieve greater efficiency in SO_2 reduction in an air quality district by providing an incentive for those generators who could reduce SO_2 emission at the lowest cost (see Chapter 12).

Renewable Energy Policy

A second body of legislation provided incentives to generate electricity from renewable energy sources. The Public Utilities Regulatory Policies Act (PURPA), passed as part of President Jimmy Carter's National Energy Plan in 1978, was the most important piece of this legislation. PURPA required utilities to purchase power produced at or below the utilities' "avoided cost"—what it would have cost utilities to generate or purchase the additional electricity. Qualifying firms included both cogenerator firms that produce electricity as a by-product of other industrial processes, and small power producers that use a renewable resource such as water, solar, or biomass to generate electricity.

The rising price of natural gas and oil in the late 1970s and in the early 1980s encouraged a surge in the construction of generators using renewable technologies. As oil and natural gas prices declined in the 1990s, however, state regulators started lowering the "avoided cost" levels. As a result, growth in generating capacity that relied on renewable resources declined sharply. The Energy Policy Act of 1993 did, however, provide some new incentives. It provided a 10% energy tax credit for solar and gas thermal projects. It also established a 1.5 cent/kilowatt hour 10-year tax credit for electricity generated using new wind facilities and by some biomass technologies. Over half of this credit was accounted for by natural gas.

By creating a class of independent generators (qualifying facilities) and guaranteeing them a market, PURPA set in motion a process that is leading toward the deregulation of the electric utility industry. But by the mid 1980s, a number of the nonrenewable energy projects established under PURPA were experiencing technical and financial difficulties (Bailey, 1995; Kerber, 1996). Part of their difficulties were due to the expiration of legislation favoring independent producers that had acted as a stimulation to deregulation.

Deregulation[23]

In the United States, a third wave of institutional innovations and a change in the trajectory of technical change were initiated by passage of the Energy Policy Act of 1992. The Act permits wholesale purchasers of electricity, such as municipal utilities or energy-intensive firms, to choose their suppliers. The Act also obligates utilities to "wheel" power across their territories to accommodate supplier choice. The Federal Energy Regulatory Commission is not authorized to mandate retail wheeling.

Efforts to reform the structure of the electric utility industry are based on the fact that it is technically possible and economically advantageous to separate electric energy production, transmission, and distribution. Three alternatives to the existing monopoly model, in which a single company has the monopoly of producing electricity and delivering it over the transmissions network to distribution companies, or final consumers, have been proposed (Hunt and Shuttleworth, 1996:21–24).

- In the *purchasing agent* model a single buyer acquires power from a number of different generators. The effect is to encourage competition in generation. Transmission remains a monopoly. This is the model that the PURPA legislation of 1978 was intended to encourage.
- In the *wholesale competition* model retail companies buy electricity directly from a producer and deliver it over a transmission network. There is open access to both generators and transmission lines but retailers maintain monopoly service to final customers. This is the model adopted by Great Britain when it began the privatization of its electric power system in 1990. It is also the model envisaged in the U.S. Energy Act of 1992. In practice there is a tendency to combine the purchasing agent and the wholesale competition models.
- In the *retail competition* model all customers would be free to choose their supplier. There would be open access to transmission and distribution wires by alternative providers. Retail activity would be completely separate from wholesale transmission.

A precipitating event in the movement toward restructuring along the lines of the retail competition model was the publication of a White Paper on privatization of

---

[23] In this section I draw heavily on Brennan et al. (1996).

the electric utility industry by the British government in 1988. The White Paper recommended that electricity privatization should include breaking up the Central Electricity Generating Board, the nationalized industry that owned all the generating plants and transmission lines. Distribution, controlled by 12 separate publicly owned companies, was already separate from generation and transmission. "Existing plants would be divided between two generating companies; new entry of competing independent generators would be encouraged; a separate transmission company would be established; the distribution companies would provide local transport and customers would choose their suppliers, to encourage competition" (Hunt and Shuttleworth, 1996:5). The new system was implemented, following intense negotiation and several false starts, in March 1990.[24]

In the United States, the state of California has moved most rapidly toward restructuring and implementing the retail competition model. Several other states have passed legislation mandating implementation of the retail competition model. Before the model is finally implemented, however, a number of technical and institutional issues will have to be resolved. Decisions will have to be made on how to deal with "stranded costs." Will generating companies or consumers have to absorb the stranded costs if unamortized nuclear plants are forced to shut down? How will the transmission industry be regulated when transmission is separated from generation and retailing?

The 1978 PURPA created a guaranteed market for independent producers of renewable and nonrenewable energy. The Clean Air Act amendments of 1990 unleashed competition among suppliers of coal, the developers of natural gas systems, and the provider of air pollution control technologies. The Energy Policy Act of 1992 required that the Federal Energy Regulatory Commission force transmission-owning utilities to "wheel" power from generators to other utilities and electric wholesalers across their lines at reasonable, nondiscriminatory rates (FERC Order 888, April 1996). The effect was to induce the deconstruction of the integrated system that Samuel Insull and other leaders of the electrical power industry had erected in the 1920s (Kench, 2000).

WHAT HAPPENED TO ALTERNATIVE ENERGY?

At the time of the energy crisis in the early 1970s, coal, petroleum, and natural gas had largely replaced the older traditional energy sources—wood, wind, and water. And coal was rapidly being displaced by petroleum and natural gas (Figures 7.1 and 7.2). Plants using nuclear reactors to produce heat to make the steam to power the turbines and generators to produce electric power were just coming on stream. The reforms discussed in the previous section, particularly the PURPA Act of 1987, encouraged the expansion and development of power production from renewable resources. It

---

[24] Newbery (1997) notes that the most disappointing result of U.K. privatization was the continued power of the fossil generators. The substantial cost reductions associated with privatization were not translated into a corresponding fall in prices.

will be difficult to evaluate the longer run economic viability of these sources of electric power until the implications of the move toward the disarticulation of the power generation, power distribution, and power retailing functions become more fully apparent.[25]

Electricity can be generated from a large variety of renewable energy sources.[26] These include hydroelectric, geothermal, biomass, wind, solar-thermal, and photovoltaic. The petroleum crisis of the 1970s induced intense interest in alternative sources of primary energy as fuels for transportation and heating and for electric power generation. Environmental and health concerns associated with the use of coal and nuclear energy resulted in substantial technical effort to develop renewable energy sources. Some of the important characteristics of these renewable energy sources are summarized in Table 7.4.

In addition to the economic and environmental factors, some of the interest in renewable energy sources and in energy conservation was motivated by cultural considerations. Even before the rise in petroleum prices in 1973, small-scale "soft" renewable energy was being advocated by a counterculture movement that advocated "unplugging" society from centralized power sources. Renewable sources were advocated because they would contribute to eroding the power of giant public utilities and encourage individuals and communities to take charge of their own energy decisions.[27]

Increased expenditures on energy R&D represented a significant component of the federal response to the oil shocks of the 1970s. Since the early 1980s, however, both public and private sector investment in energy R&D declined consistently. During the 1980s the decline was associated with declining real prices of energy. During the 1990s the restructuring of the natural gas and electric utility industries contributed to the reduction of incentives for investment in energy R&D, particularly by the private sector (Dooley, 1998; Margolis and Kammen, 1999). The sharpest reductions were for R&D on renewable energy sources and conservation.

Energy Conservation

A combination of the energy crisis of the 1970s and concern with the impact of energy use on the environment induced an intense focus on the issue of efficiency

---

[25] I do not in this section discuss the use of renewable energy or other alternatives to petroleum fuels in the transportation sector. World petroleum production has recovered and oil prices have declined since the early 1980s (Figure 7.6). Current forecasts based on the Hubbard model suggest a decline in conventional global oil production around 2010. In the past projections based on the Hubbard model have been quite accurate (Campbell, 1997; Campbell and Laherrére, 1998). There are a number of back-up technologies that could make liquid fuel substitutes for oil available at near or slightly above the price of oil. It does not appear unreasonable, however, to anticipate some worsening of the terms at which liquid fuels become available to the transportation industry by 2020. The best single analysis of energy futures is Nakićenović et al. (1998).

[26] In this section I draw heavily on World Energy Council (1993, 1994, 1995), Tester et al. (1991), Johansson et al. (1993), Jackson (1993), and Ahmed (1994). For an earlier review see *Economist* (1991).

[27] See, for example, the very influential article by Amory B. Lovins (1976) in *Foreign Affairs*. For compilations of papers on the soft energy options, see Nash (1979) and Jackson (1993).

Table 7.4 Summary of Important Characteristics of New Renewable Energy Sources

	Solar	Wind	Geothermal	Biomass	Small Hydroelectric
Resource					
Magnitude Distribution	Extremely large Worldwide	Large Coastal, mountains, plains	Very large Tectonic boundaries	Very large Worldwide	Large Worldwide, mountains
Variation	Daily, seasonal, weather dependent	Highly variable	Constant	Seasonal, climate dependent	Seasonal
Intensity	Low, 1 kW/m² peak	Low average, 0.8 MW/km²	Low average, up to 600°C	Moderate to low	Moderate to low
Technology Options	Low to high temperature thermal systems, photovoltaics, passive systems, bioconversion	Horizontal and vertical-axis wind turbines, wind pumps, sail power	Steam and binary thermodynamic cycles, total flow turbines, geopressured, magma	Combustion, fermentation, digestion, gasification, liquefaction	Low to high head turbines and dams and turbines
Status	Developmental, some commercial	Many commercial, more developmental	Many commercial, some developmental	Some commercial, more developmental	Mostly commercial
Capacity factor	<25% without storage, intermediate	Variable, most 15–30%	High, base load	As needed with short-term storage	Intermittent to base load
Key improvements	Materials, cost, efficiency, resource data	Materials, design, siting, resource data	Exploration, extraction, hot dry rock use	Technology, agriculture and forestry management	Turbines, cost, design, resource data
Environmental characteristics	Very clean, visual impact, local climate, PV manufacturing	Very clean, visual, impact, noise, bird mortality	Clean, dissolved gases, brine disposal	Clean, impacts on fauna and other flora, toxic residues	Very clean, impact on local aquatic environment, land use

Source: World Energy Council, *New Renewable Energy Resources: A Guide to the Future,* London: Kogan Page, 1994:30.

in energy production and use. Energy accountants and conservationists identified the very substantial savings that could be realized by changes in power production, in manufacturing, in transportation, and in household heating, cooling, and lighting. Energy activists insisted that conservation measures could reduce electric energy consumption by upward of 30% by the year 2010 without major changes in behavior or life-style (Lovins, 1976). Attention was focused on the substitution of flourescent for incandescent lights; improvements in home refrigeration; more efficient heating of homes, offices, and factories; and changes in process technology such as electrically adjustable speed for machine drives.

Initially, substantial changes were induced as noted earlier by rising primary energy prices and electric power rates. For example, "the average new refrigerator in 1971 used 1,726 kWh per year, a new one produced in 1980 used only 1,280 kWh. By 1992 a new refrigerator's average consumption had declined to about 690 kWh" (Hirsh and Serchuk, 1996:299).

In the early 1980s, utility commissions played an active role in reinforcing market forces. Utility companies were prodded into introducing conservation programs, termed "demand-side management," that focused on reducing consumer use of energy services rather than on promoting demand growth. Until well into the mid-1980s most utility managers were still resisting implementation of energy-efficiency efforts. Burdened by excess generating capacity, and with access to fossil fuels at lower prices, they saw conservation efforts as eroding profitability—they were in the business of selling megawatts, not "negawatts." These views were reinforced by the sharp reduction in Energy Department research support for energy conservation.

By the early 1990s the utilities were beginning to take a more positive attitude toward demand-side management, in response to both regulatory initiatives and economic forces. In Massachusetts, for example, the Conservation Law Foundation, the New England Electric System, and three New England regulating agencies worked to develop a comprehensive program that allowed the utility to retain a portion of savings realized by customers who took advantage of energy-saving opportunities.

Some utility company executives also became convinced that energy conservation would enable them to avoid expanding capacity at a time when the cost of adding incremental capacity was substantially higher than could be profitably borne by existing rate structures. In 1990, for example, Pacific Gas and Electric announced an energy-conservation effort designed to sharply reduce planned capacity expansion in the 1990s (Hirsh and Serchuk, 1996).

Very large gains in energy efficiency have been realized. Between 1973 and 1986 the energy conversion improved by 26%—an annual average decline of 2.2%. The rate of decline in energy intensity has slowed, however, since 1986—to 0.45% per year. The source of the gains in the efficiency of energy use is not entirely clear. It has been estimated that about three-quarters of the decline in the energy/GNP ratio (Table 7.1) was the result of improved energy efficiency, with structural change and interfuel substitution accounting for the remainder.

The response of both industry and consumers to conservation opportunities remains somewhat of a puzzle. To some economists the failure of firms and consumers to take advantage of the savings implies that the savings are not there—"if there were a $20 note on the sidewalk, someone would have already picked it up!" There is a tendency for firms to require a much shorter payback on energy-savings investment than on capacity-expanding investment. Consumers often want to realize the benefits in a few months. More careful studies of the diffusion factors affecting the adoption and diffusion of energy-saving technology will be required to more adequately understand the private role of market forces and regulatory action in inducing adoption of more energy-efficient technology at both the firm and the household level. It seems apparent that in the future gains in energy efficiency, if they are achieved, will require greater precision in the use of policy instruments and will impinge more seriously on life-style choices.

Renewable Energy Sources

In this section I review the status of the major renewable primary energy sources.[28]

HYDROPOWER

Hydropower is the only renewable primary energy resource presently used on a large scale. In the mid-1990s it contributed about 5% of the electricity generated in the United States and 15% electricity generated in the world. Under favorable conditions it can be the lowest cost source of electrical energy. The world's long-term economically viable hydropower potential is estimated at 6000–9000 TWh, of which only about 2000 TWh have been developed. Most of the underdeveloped potential lies in the former Soviet Union, Canada, China, and Brazil.

Technologies for dam construction and power generation tend to be relatively mature. It is possible, however, to improve the efficiency of some older facilities. Large hydroelectric dams tend to be very capital intensive, with operating costs low relative to capital costs. Capital costs vary greatly, however, depending on site characteristics, size, time to completion, and interest rates. Technical advances in small generating equipment have made smaller facilities more competitive. The smaller plants require less land for impoundment and facilities or may, in the case of "run-of-the-river" facilities, not require impoundment.

Although hydropower avoids the environmental effects of sulfur dioxide (SO_2) and carbon dioxide (CO_2) emissions associated with use of coal as a primary energy source, hydroelectric dams often inundate large areas and thus have serious ecological and social impacts. The large capital costs and potential social and environmental impact have made projects such as Aswan (Egypt), Sadar Sarovar (India), and Three Gorges (China) very controversial. For many developing countries, however, hydropower represents a promising source of renewable technology in the immediate

---

[28] For a more detailed overview see Ahmed (1994).

future. In Ghana, electricity generated by the Volta River Authority accounts for over 90% of the electricity produced.

GEOTHERMAL

Geothermal is also more environmentally benign than fossil fuels. The main impediments to plant operation are (1) the limited number of locations in which geothermal resources make it cost effective, and (2) corrosion caused by the chemicals, particularly chloride and hydrogen sulfide, in the steam. The United States, the Philippines, Italy, and Mexico account for almost three-fourths of installed geothermal capacity. Geothermal is the largest energy source in Iceland, and there are a number of other small countries with substantial geothermal resources, including several in Central America and East Africa, where a relatively high share of electric-generating capacity could be accounted for by thermal power. Even an optimistic projection suggests, however, that geothermal power is unlikely to ever account for even 1% of world electric capacity.

BIOMASS

Biomass is the most important traditional source of energy. Although it accounts for less than 3% of primary energy used in developed countries, it still accounts for more than a third of the primary energy used in developing countries (Williams, 1994:201). The use of biomass residues from agriculture and forestry is generally limited by existing use of residues, the need to maintain soil fertility, and the high cost of assembling and transporting residues. To achieve economic viability on a large scale the cost of biomass must be low enough so that it can compete with coal and other fossil fuels as an energy feedstock. At the same time, the financial returns to biomass production must be high enough to allow biomass producers to attract the wood (and land) away from alternative uses, particularly away from other industrial uses such as wood pulp.

The most promising biomass option is the development of plantations on deforested or degraded lands in the tropics or semitropics dedicated to energy production. Improvement in technology, such as biomass gasification, promises to make biomass from plantation production more competitive with electricity produced from fossil fuels (Williams, 1994). Over the longer term, however, the use of land for food production or for the production of other biomass products, such as pulp for paper, may become a more serious constraint on use of biomass to produce electricity. Any substantial increase in the use of biomass-based fuels based on economic considerations will depend on how their contribution to greenhouse gas abatement is valued. A carbon tax on fossil fuels would enhance the competitive position of biomass fuels (Lunnan, 1997; Sedjo, 1997).

WIND

Since the early 1970s substantial progress has been made in the technology used to convert wind to electrical energy. More than 15,000 wind turbines in California and

2000 in Denmark have been integrated into existing utility grids. Further technical changes, particularly the introduction of advanced materials for airfoils and better control technologies, are expected to result in lower capital and operating costs.

Wind resources are sufficient to sustain wind-power-generating capacity several times the present world electricity consumption. A major limitation on the development of wind power is the intermittent power supplied by wind turbines; because of this the value of wind-generated electricity decreases as the share of utility requirements supplied by wind turbines rises. Nevertheless, in some areas electricity generated by wind power is approaching a cost comparable to electricity generated by coal-fired generating stations.

Solar-Thermal

Solar-thermal electric technologies are designed to concentrate large amounts of sunlight onto a small area to facilitate the buildup of heat, which can be converted into electricity in a conventional heat engine. Three major designs have been developed: (1) the parabolic-trough system, which concentrates solar energy onto a receiver located along the focal line of a trough collector; (2) the central-receiver system, which uses sun tracking mirrors to reflect solar energy onto a heat exchanger; and (3) the parabolic-dish system, which uses a tracking dish reflector to concentrate sunlight onto either a receiver engine or a receiver heat/exchanger mounted at the focal point of the dish.

All three technologies have achieved technically successful pilot plant operations. By the mid-1980s nine commercial parabolic-trough power plants had been constructed in the Mojave Desert in California. They were developed as solar–natural gas hybrid systems because cost-effective thermal storage had not yet been developed. Although these plants appeared to be commercially viable at the energy prices of the late 1970s and early 1980s, new commercial plants have not been constructed since prices for petroleum and other fossil fuel began to decline in the early 1980s. As a result of a number of factors, including loss of federal and state tax credits and a sales price linked to the price of natural gas, the California plant was forced into bankruptcy and suspended operations between 1991 and 1994 (Ahmed, 1994:43–114).

Photovoltaic

In contrast to heat engines used in other modes of electricity generation, photovoltaics are solid-state devices that convert sunlight into electricity with no moving parts. Hydrogen-bearing gases are converted into electricity without combustion. They operate quietly without emissions, are long lived, and require little maintenance. Photovoltaics consist of two basic elements: (1) the photovoltaic module and (2) a mounting structure that provides support for the module. A module consists of the photosensitive cells and encapsulating materials that protect the cells from the environment. Some modules are designed to include mirrors or lenses that focus light on the photovoltaic cells. Most applications also require inverters to convert the direct current produced by the cells to alternating current. Photovoltaics can be built in almost any size—from rooftop installations to utility scale. Because of technical advances, the cost of producing electricity with photovoltaic equipment has declined rapidly since the early 1970s, when photovoltaic devices were adopted by the U.S. space program. Although costs have continued to decline, photovoltaic electricity remained several time as costly as electricity generated by large, coal-fired plants in the mid-1990s.

Despite their high costs, photovoltaics have found a number of commercial applications. These include providing electricity for facilities in remote locations, lighting street lights and highway signs, communications, water pumping, warning signals, and others (Ahmed, 1994:48). Broader application of photovoltaic technology has been limited by a number of unresolved technical difficulties. Photovoltaic power is intermittent, because electricity can be generated only when the sun is shining. It can be an economically competitive source of peaking power, however, in periods of high electricity demand in areas such as the Southwest, where air-conditioning systems create peak demands during summer days. Another potential advantage of photovoltaic systems is that units can be located at dispersed sites throughout a utility system, thus contributing to lower transmission distribution costs and to system reliability. Projections made in the mid-1990s suggest that continued progress in the efficiency of cells and modules, combined with efficiency gains in manufacturing, may make electricity generated with photovoltaics cost competitive with electricity from conventional sources within the next several decades.

Chakravarty et al. (1997) have projected, in a simulation exercise, that if the historical rates of cost reduction in the production of solar energy can be maintained, the world will be able to move from predominant reliance on coal, oil, and natural gas by the middle of the twenty-first century. Under their most optimistic energy transition scenario, global temperatures will rise by 1.5 to 2°C by 2050 and then decline toward preindustrial levels even without imposition of carbon taxes as solar energy replaces coal, petroleum, and natural gas. Under a more conservative estimate of the rate of technological change, their model implies a maximum global temperature rise of about 2.3°C toward the end of the twenty-first century, followed by a slow decline. Even under the conservative technical change scenario, a carbon tax of $100 per ton would generate a global warming profile similar to the optimistic scenario They suggest that a U.S. carbon tax of only $5 per ton (equivalent to $0.65 per barrel of petroleum) would be more than sufficient to finance the necessary R&D to support the more optimistic scenario. And they regard photovoltaic technology as the most promising of the solar technologies (see Chapter 12).[29]

---

[29] The simulation of Chakravarty et al. (1997) incorporates (1) estimated reserves, (2) extraction costs for coal, oil, and natural gas, (3) the multiple energy demands for transportation and residential and commercial heating and cooling, and (4) price-induced endogenous technical change. They developed a disaggregated model that takes into account the possibility that energy consumers could convert to alternative fuel-using processes. The model simultaneously solves for efficiency prices of different energy sources and their respective scarcity rents. On the prospects for continued progress in photovoltaic technology, see also Watanabe (1995).

If renewable sources of primary energy are to become widely adopted over the next quarter century, it seems clear that substantial public intervention will be required (Grubb, 1993; World Energy Council, 1994:48–52). The limited commercial success that renewable sources such as biomass, wind, solar-thermal, and photovoltaic have achieved has largely been due to the limited public support for research and development of these technologies and to changes in regulatory regimes. A number of potential benefits not captured by conventional project investment criteria have been advanced in favor of renewable energy sources. These include (1) reduced air pollution, (2) abatement of global warming, (3) diversity of fuel supply, (4) reduction in the risks of nuclear proliferation, (5) restoration of degraded lands, and (6) contribution to decentralized regional development (Johansson et al., 1993:4). If electricity based on renewable resources is preferred because of these environmental and related benefits, the policy interventions required will include (1) reduction or removal of subsidies to artificially lower the costs of fossil and nuclear fuels, (2) design of policy instruments that ensure that environmental and other external costs are more adequately reflected in energy prices, and (3) stronger public support for research and demonstration of renewable energy technologies. As of the late 1990s support for such policy intervention in most major industrial countries had declined compared to a decade earlier (Dooley, 1998).

Small Is Beautiful

The impact of the legislation designed to lower SO_2 emissions and the legislation designed to open up energy markets to renewable energy has been very different than anticipated. Very few coal-fired generating facilities switched to "end of the pipe" flue gas desulfurization facilities. Manufacturers developed a strong market for scrubbers in Europe and East Asia but not in the United States. In the United States many coal-fired plants switched to cleaner low sulfur coal. The trend in construction of new facilities was toward natural gas. By the mid-1990s almost all new units scheduled to come on-line were gas fired.

The shift to gas was the result of both institutional and technical innovation. Deregulation of the natural gas industry resulted in a more reliable supply of natural gas and in lower prices. The lower fuel prices induced more rapid innovation in gas turbine technology for generating electricity.[30] The initial single gas turbine (GT) technology for burning natural gas was developed by several American and British firms that had been engaged during World War II in the development of military jet engines. The early models ranged in power up to 40 MW. Later, models in the 150–250 MW range, with thermal efficiencies in the 40% range, were introduced. They were initially used by electric utilities as a backup technology to meet peak load demands. Combined cycle gas turbine systems (CCGT), consisting of a gas

---

[30] The single best discussion of the gas turbine development is Islas (1977). See also Lee (1988).

turbine unit of 100–150 MW, plus heat recovery steam and steam turbine generators of 100–150 MW, were introduced in the early 1990s. They were able to attain thermal efficiency in the 55–58% range. These systems were able to meet extremely stringent new source performance standards for nitrous oxides (NO_x). Because of their high thermal efficiency they were suitable for meeting base load requirements. They could be added in modular units by utilities that preferred to respond to new capacity demands incrementally. A 250-MW CCGT unit could be installed in less than 2 years, as compared to 4 to 6 years for a coal-fired facility or 8 to 10 years for a nuclear facility.

Because of its experience in both jet engine technology and power production systems, General Electric was able to take an early lead in gas turbine-generating technology. However, GE was very quickly confronted with strong competition from Westinghouse, Siemens, and Asea Brown Boveri. Each established partnerships with other jet engine suppliers. GE has, however, managed to maintain technical leadership. In 1995 it introduced a CCGT generator that is able to achieve 60% thermal efficiency (Marcus and Geffen, 1996:21).

Initially, independent power producers providing natural gas-generated power in small, modular units played an important role in the market share achieved by gas turbine generators. By the mid-1990s, orders for gas turbines (single cycle, cogeneration, and combined cycle) accounted for more than 50% of the world market for new thermal-generating plants. The emergence of natural gas as the low-cost source of fuel for the generation of electricity was associated with a remarkable change in the optimum size of a generating unit. In the half century between 1930 and 1980, the optimum size of a generating unit had risen from the 100 MW range to the 1000 MW range. By the 1990s, as a result of combined cycle technology, the optimum size was again in the 100 MW range (Hunt and Shuttleworth, 1996).

In the 1990s natural gas was capturing the market share that the reformers of the 1970s and 1980s had anticipated would be captured by renewable energy sources. The energy policy reforms had opened the door to independent producers. But the development of the gas turbine enabled producers using natural gas as a primary energy source to walk through the door that energy activists thought they had opened for renewable energy.

PERSPECTIVE

In the 1990s the beginning of a major transition in the technology and organization of the power–energy complex occurred. Electric power has, in the past, been regarded as a classic example of a system characterized by technological lock-in (Hughes, 1979, 1983). The success of alternating current technology and the integration of generation, transmission, and distribution appeared to lock the industry into a system of steam power technology in power production, and into vertical integration of power production, transmission, and distribution. The innovations in regulatory regimes in the 1970s and 1980s, though, began to erode the institutional structure designed by Insull in the 1920s. In the 1970s and 1980s the stagnant technology of fossil fuel and nuclear steam power generation, and the challenge posed by environmental concerns, opened the door to gas turbine technology. It is possible that in the next several decades there may be a transition from gas turbine to solar technology in electrical power generation.

For at least the past century, primary energy substitution (Figures 7.1–7.3) has been associated with a trend toward energy sources with lower carbon content. This trend toward decarbonization has been even more pronounced in final energy consumption than in primary energy use. Both economic and environmental considerations seem likely to continue to induce technical change along this trajectory. If decarbonization is to continue into the middle of the twenty-first century and beyond, it will probably require a transition to the use of pure hydrogen as a fuel. This will require the development of an economically viable technology for splitting water (Ausubel, 1991; Grübler and Nakiéenović, 1988, 1996). Water (H_2O) can be split into hydrogen and oxygen by passing an electric current through it. In the 1950s and 1970s it was anticipated that the cost of electricity produced from nuclear power would be low enough to make electrolytic hydrogen production economically viable. In the late 1980s and early 1990s, developments in photovoltaic cells again created the possibility that hydrogen would become an economically viable fuel (Ogden and Williams, 1989).

The transition to lower carbon fuels has followed a different trajectory than anticipated a generation ago. Nuclear power has made a much less significant impact on the structure of global energy supply than anticipated. The promise of renewable energy sources lies at least a generation into the future. This is, in part, because the ratio of proven reserves to production has risen for petroleum and natural gas, rather than declining. The transition has also been due to technical advances in the conversion of fossil fuels to electricity. Design improvements have led to rapid improvements in conversion efficiency of gas turbines for the generation of electricity and to a rapid increase in the use of natural gas as a primary energy source for the production of electricity (Martin, 1996).

Attempts to forecast technological and economic futures for alternative energy sources have, however, been notoriously unreliable. It is necessary only to review the history of the nuclear power industry or the petroleum price projections of the 1980s to be reminded of these difficulties. There is a tendency by technologists to implicitly assume a model of path dependence—that available technologies will evolve over time exogenously in a manner that is independent of underlying economic forces or policies. Economists typically assume that the rate and direction of technical change will be induced by the growth of demand and by changes in relative prices with little attention to the evolution of scientific knowledge and technology.

Looking toward the middle of the twenty-first century, it is not too difficult to anticipate that technical effort in electric power generation will be directed to further reduction of carbon and other greenhouse gas emissions. There is much greater uncertainty about how rapidly solar, or other renewable, energy sources will displace nonrenewable sources. And there is even greater uncertainty about the relative contributions that can be expected from the several renewable sources.

For the immediate future it seems apparent that the long-term trend toward electricity accounting for a higher share of the energy embodied in intermediate and consumer goods will continue. Only the transportation sector has been resistant to this trend. In the low- and middle-income countries rapid growth of the electric power industry will continue to play a fundamental role in efforts to achieve industrial development and enhance the quality of life well into the twenty-first century. However, in the United States and in other developed countries it is unlikely, in spite of incremental technical improvements, that decline in the real price of electric power can be an important source of inducement for productivity growth for the U.S. economy as it was between 1870 and 1970.

REFERENCES

Abelson, P. H. "Nuclear Power in East Asia." *Science* 272 (April 26, 1996):465.

Adelman, M. A. *The Economics of Petroleum Supply: Papers by M. A. Adelman, 1962–1993.* Cambridge, MA: MIT Press, 1993.

Ahmed, K. (with an overview by D. Anderson and K. Ahmed). *Renewable Energy Technologies: A Review of Status and Costs of Selected Technologies.* Washington, DC: The World Bank, 1994.

Arthur, W. Brian. "Positive Feedback in the Economy." *Scientific American* (Feb. 1990):92–99.

Ausubel, J. H. "Energy and the Environment: The Light Path." *Energy Systems and Policy* 15 (1991):181–188.

Ausubel, J. H., and C. Marchetti. "Elektron: Electrical Systems in Retrospect and Prospect." In *Technological Trajectories and the Human Environment*, J. H. Ausubel and H. D. Langford., eds., pp. 110–134. Washington, DC: National Academy Press, 1997.

Bailey, J. "Carter Era Law Keeps Price of Electricity Up in Spite of a Surplus." *Wall Street Journal* (May 17, 1995):A1+.

Berndt, E. R. "Aggregate Energy, Efficiency, and Productivity Measurement." *Annual Review of Energy* 3 (1978):225–273.

Berndt, E. R. "The Role of Energy in Productivity Growth: Comment." In *International Comparisons of Productivity and Causes of the Slowdown*, J. W. Kendrick, ed., pp. 325–334. Cambridge, MA: M. A. Ballinger, 1984.

Berndt, E. R., and M. S. Khaled. "Energy Prices, Economies of Scale and Productivity Gains in U.S. Manufacturing, 1947–81." Vancouver: University of British Columbia, Department of Economics Discussion Paper 77–23, 1977.

Berndt, E. R., and D. O. Wood. "Technology, Prices and the Derived Demand for Energy." *The Review of Economics and Statistics* 57 (August 1975):259–326.

Bohi, D. R. *Energy Price Shocks and Macroeconomic Performance.* Washington, DC: Resources for the Future, 1989.

Brennan, T. J., K. L. Palmer, R. J. Kopp, A. J. Krupnick, and D. Burtraw. *A Shock to the System: Restructuring America's Electricity Industry.* Washington, DC: Resources for the Future, 1996.

Campbell, C. J., and J. H. Laherrére. "The End of Cheap Oil!" *Scientific American* 278 (March 1998):78–83.

Chakravarty, U., J. Roumasset, and K. Tse. "Endogenous Substitution among Energy Resources and Global Warming." *Journal of Political Economy* 6 (1997):1201–1234.

Cohen, L. R., and R. G. Noll, eds. *The Technology Pork Barrel*. Washington, DC: Brookings Institution, 1991.

Cowan, R. "Nuclear Power Reactors: A Study in Technological Lock-in." *Journal of Economic History* 50 (September 1990):541–567.

Damian, M. "Nuclear Power: The Ambiguous Lessons of History." *Energy Policy* (July 1992):596–607.

David, P. A. "Computer and Dynamo: The Modern Productivity Paradox in a Not-Too Distant Mirror." Stanford University: Stanford Center for Economic Policy Research, 172 (July 1989).

David, P. A. "The Dynamo and the Computer: An Historical Perspective on the Modern Productivity Paradox." *American Economic Review* 80/2 (May 1990):355–361.

David, P. A. "The Hero and the Herd in Technological History: Reflections on Thomas Edison and the Battle of the Systems." In *Favorites of Fortune: Technology, Growth and Development Since the Industrial Revolution,* P. Higonnet, D. S. Landes, and H. Rosovsky, eds., pp. 72–119. Cambridge, MA: Harvard University Press, 1991.

David, P. A., and J. A. Bunn. "The Economics of Gateway Technologies and Network Evolution: Lessons From Electricity Supply History." *Information Economics and Policy* 3 (1988):165–202.

Devine, W. D., Jr. *An Historical Perspective on the Value of Electricity in American Manufacturing*. Oak Ridge Associate Universities, Institute for Energy Analysis, 82–8 (M). Springfield, VA: National Technical Information Service, 1982.

Devine, W. D., Jr. "From Shafts to Wires: Historical Perspectives on Electrification." *The Journal of Economic History* 43 (June 1983):347–362.

Dooley, J. J. "Unintended Consequences: Energy R&D in a Deregulated Energy Market." *Energy Policy* 26 (1998):547-555.

DuBoff, R. B. "Electrification and Capital Productivity: A Suggested Approach." *Review of Economics and Statistics* 48 (4, 1966):426–431.

DuBoff, R. B. *Electric Power in American Manufacturing, 1889–1958*. New York: Arno Press, 1979.

Economist. "Energy and the Environment: A Power for Good, a Power for Ill." (August 31, 1991):3–30.

Feldman, D. L., ed. *The Energy Crisis: Unresolved Issues and Enduring Legacies*. Baltimore: The Johns Hopkins University Press, 1996.

Friedel, R., P. Israel, and B. S. Finn. *Edison's Electric Light: Biography of an Invention*. New Brunswick: Rutgers University Press, 1986.

Gordon, R. J. *Forward into the Past: Productivity and Retrogression in the Electric Generating Industry.* Cambridge, MA: National Bureau of Economic Research, 1992.

Grubb, M. "The Cinderella Options: A Study of Modernized Renewable Energy Technologies." In *Renewable Energy: Prospects for Implementation,* T. Jackson, ed., pp. 15–32, 239–254. Oxford, UK: Butterworth-Heinemann, 1993.

Grübler, A. *Technology and Global Change*. Cambridge, UK: Cambridge University Press, 1998.

Grübler, A., and N. Nakićenović. "The Dynamic Evolution of Methane Technologies." In *The Methane Age*, T. H. Lee, H. R. Linden, D. A. Dreyfus, and T. Vasko, eds., pp. 13–44. Dordrecht: Kluwer Academic Publishers, 1988.

Grübler, A., and N. Nakićenović. "Decarbonizing the Global Energy System." *Technological Forecasting and Social Change* 53 (September 1996):97–110.

Hewlett, R. G., and J. W. Hall. *Atoms for Peace and War, 1953–1961*. Berkeley, CA: University of California Press, 1989.

Hill, R., P. O'Keefe, and C. Snape. *The Future of Energy Use*. New York: St. Martin's Press, 1995.

Hirsh, R. F. *Technology and Transformation in the American Electric Utility Industry*. Cambridge, UK: Cambridge University Press, 1989.

Hirsh, R. F., and A. H. Serchuk. "Momentum Shifts in the American Electric Utility System: Catastrophic Change—or No Change at All?" *Technology and Culture* 37 (April 1996):280–311.

Hughes, T. P. "The Electrification of America: The System Builders." *Technology and Culture*. 20 (January 1979):124–161.

Hughes, T. P. *Networks of Power: Electrification in Western Society, 1880–1930*. Baltimore, MD: Johns Hopkins University Press, 1983.

Hunt, S., and G. Shuttleworth. "Unlocking the Grid." *IEEE Spectrum* (July 1996):20–25.

Islas, J. "Getting Round the Lock-in in Electricity Generating Systems: The Example of the Gas Turbine." *Research Policy* 26(1977):49–66.

Jackson, T. *Renewable Energy: Prospects for Implementation*. Oxford, UK: Butterworth-Heinemann, 1993.

Johansson, T. B., H. Kelly, A. K. N. Reddy, and R. H. Williams, eds. *Renewable Energy Sources for Fuels and Electricity*. Washington, DC: Island Press, 1993.

Jorgenson, D. W. "The Great Transition: Energy and Economic Change." *The Economic Journal* 7 (1986):1–13.

Jorgenson, D. W., and B. M. Fraumeni. "Relative Prices and Technical Change." In *Modeling and Measuring Natural Resources Substitution*, E. R. Berndt and B. Field, eds., pp. 17–47. Cambridge, MA: MIT Press, 1981.

Jorgenson, D. W., and P. J. Wilcoxen. "Environmental Regulation and U.S. Economic Growth." *The Rand Journal of Economics* 21 (No. 2, Summer 1990): 314–340.

Jorgenson, D. W., and P. J. Wilcoxen. "Energy, the Environment and Economic Growth." In *Handbook of Natural Resources and Energy Economics*, Vol. III, A. V. Kneese and J. L. Sweeney, eds., pp. 1267–1349. Amsterdam, Netherlands: Elsevier, 1993.

Kellow, A. *Transforming Power: The Politics of Electricity Planning*. Cambridge, UK: Cambridge University Press, 1996.

Kench, B. T. "Induced Regulatory Changes in the Electric Power Industry." Storrs, CT: University of Connecticut Department of Economics, October 1999.

Kerber, R. "Independent Electric Producers Losing Power Struggle." *Wall Street Journal* (August 7, 1996):B3.

Lee, T. H. "Combined Cycle Systems: Technology Implication." In *The Methane Age*, T. H. Lee, H. R. Linden, D. A. Dreyfus, and T. Vasko, eds., pp. 131–144. Dordrecht: Kluwer Academic Publishers, 1988.

Lichtenberg, F. R. "Energy Prices and Induced Innovation." *Research Policy* 15 (1986): 67–75.

Lovins, A. B. "Energy Strategy: The Road Not Taken?" *Foreign Affairs* 55 (October 1976):64–96.

Lunnan, A. "Agricultural-Based Biomass Energy Supply: A Survey of Economic Issues." *Energy Policy* 25 (6, 1997):573–582.

MacKerron, G. "Nuclear Costs: Why Do They Keep on Rising?" *Energy Policy* (July 1992): 641–652.

MacKerron, G. "Innovation in Energy Supply: The Case of Electricity." In *The Handbook of Industrial Innovation*, Mark Dodgson and Roy Rothwell, eds., pp. 182–190. Aldershot, UK: Edward Elgar, 1994.

Marcus, A. A. *Controversial Issues in Energy Policy*. Newbury Park, CA: Sage Publications, 1992.

Marcus, A. A. *Business and Society: Ethics, Government and the World Economy*. Homewood, IL: Irwin, 1993

Marcus, A., and D. Geffen. "The Dialectics of Competency Acquisition: Pollution Prevention in Electric Generation." Minneapolis: University of Minnesota Strategic Management Research Center Discussion Paper 220, October 1996.

Margolis, R. M., and D. M. Kammen. "Underinvestment: The Energy Technology and R&D Policy Challenge." *Science* 285 (1999):690–692.

Martin, J.-M. "Energy Technologies: Systemic Aspects, Technological Trajectories, and Institutional Frameworks." *Technological Forecasting and Social Change* 53 (September 1996):81–95.

Moroney, J. R. "Energy Capital, and Technological Change in the United States." *Resources and Energy* 14(1992):363–380.

Mowery, D. Z., and N. Rosenberg. *Paths of Innovation: Technological Change in 20th-Century America*. Cambridge, UK: Cambridge University Press, 1998.

Nakićenović, N. *Growth in Limits: Long Waves and the Dynamics of Technology*. Vienna: University of Vienna, 1984.

Nakćenović, N., A. Grübler, and A. McDonald, eds. *Global Energy Perspectives*. Cambridge, UK: Cambridge University Press, 1998.

Nash, H., ed. *The Energy Controversy: Soft Path Question and Answers*. San Francisco, CA: Friends of the Earth, 1979.

National Research Council Energy Engineering Board, Committee on Automobile and Light Track Fuel Economy (NRC). *Automotive Fuel Economy: How Far Should We Go?* Washington, DC: National Academy Press, 1992.

Newbery, D. M. "Privatization and Liberalization of Network Utilities." *European Economic Review* 41 (1997):357–383.

Nordhaus, W. D. "Traditional Productivity Estimates Are Asleep at the Switch." *Economic Journal* 107 (1997):1548–1559.

Nye, D. E. *Electrifying America: Social Meanings of a New Technology, 1880–1940*. Cambridge, MA: MIT Press, 1990.

Ogden, J. M., and R. H. Williams. *Solar Hydrogen: Moving Beyond Fossil Fuels*. Washington, DC: World Resources Institute, 1989.

Peirce, W. S. *The Economics of Energy Industries*. Westport, CN: Praeger, 1996.

Pool, R. *Beyond Engineering: How Society Shapes Technology*. New York: Oxford University Press, 1997.

Popp, D. *Induced Innovation, Energy Prices and the Environment.* Ph.D. Dissertation, New Haven, CT: Yale University Graduate School, 1996.

President's Committee of Advisers on Science and Technology. *Federal Energy Research and Development for the Challenges of the Twenty-First Century.* Washington, DC: President's Committee of Advisors on Science and Technology (PCAST), November 1997.

Reich, L. S. *The Making of American Industrial Research: Science and Business at GE and Bell, 1876–1926.* Cambridge, UK: Cambridge University Press, 1985.

Rhodes, R., and D. Beller, "The Need for Nuclear Power." *Foreign Affairs* 79 (January/February 2000):30–44.

Schurr, S. H. "Energy, Technological Change, and Productive Efficiency: An Economic-Historical Interpretation." *Annual Review of Energy* 9 (1984):409–425.

Schurr, S. H., and B. C. Netschert (with V. E. Eliasberg, J. Lerner, and H. H. Landsberg). *Energy in the American Economy, 1850–1975.* Baltimore, MD: Johns Hopkins University Press, 1960.

Sedjo, R. A. "The Economics of Forest-Based Biomass Supply." *Energy Policy* 25 (1997):559–566.

Smil, V. *Energy in World History.* Boulder, CO: Westview Press, 1994.

Solingen, E. *Industrial Policy, Technology, and International Bargaining: Designing Nuclear Industries in Argentina and Brazil.* Stanford, CA: Stanford University Press, 1996.

Tester, J. W., D. O. Wood, and N. A. Ferrari, eds. *Energy and the Environment in the 21st Century.* Cambridge, MA: MIT Press, 1991.

Tilton, J. E. *U.S. Energy R&D Policy.* Washington, DC: Resources for the Future, 1974.

Watanabe, C. "Identification of the Role of Renewable Energy." *Renewable Energy* 6 (3, 1995):237–274.

Weinberg, A. M. "Social Institutions and Nuclear Energy." *Science* 177 (July 7, 1972):27–34.

Williams, R. "Roles for Biomass Energy in Sustainable Development." In *Industrial Ecology and Global Change,* R. Socolow, C. Andrews, F. Berkhout, and V. Thomas, eds., pp. 199–225. New York: Cambridge University Press, 1994.

World Energy Council. *Energy for Tomorrow's World: The Realities, the Real Options, and the Agenda for Achievement.* New York: St. Martin's Press, 1993.

World Energy Council. *New Renewable Energy Resources: A Guide to the Future.* London: Kogan Page Limited, 1994.

World Energy Council. *Global Energy Perspectives to 2050 and Beyond.* Luxemburg, Austria: International Institute for Applied Systems Analysis, 1995.

CHAPTER 8

Technical Change in the Chemical Industry[1]

The history of the chemical industry is particularly important in any effort to understand the role of technology in economic development. The chemical industry was one of the first modern industries in which technical change depended on prior scientific research performed at the laboratory level. This linkage has remained central. In the United States, and in most other countries, the chemical and allied products industry has been one of the most research-intensive sectors of the economy. Advances in basic chemistry and in chemical engineering, a discipline that owes it origins to advances in basic chemistry, remain more closely linked than advances in most other fields of science and engineering. The commercial success of radical innovations has been a dominant factor accounting for company growth and profitability. And unlike most other fields, the engineers associated with the development of radical innovations have consistently risen to corporate leadership positions.

Governments have played a particularly important role in the development and diffusion of the chemical industry. Germany was the first nation to adopt a policy of deliberately encouraging science and technology as a stimulus to industrialization. The chemical industry was viewed as of strategic importance both economically and militarily. It was the means whereby Germany hoped to overcome resource limitations. Investment in the training of large numbers of scientists and the establishment of new scientific institutions led directly to Germany's domination of the world chemical market by the end of the nineteenth century. Governments also played an active role after both World War I and World War II in the transfer of German scientific and technical knowledge to the United Kingdom and United States (Spitz, 1988; Borkin, 1978).

The primary focus of the chemical industry is the transformation of natural materials into useful intermediate and consumer products. These products are numerous and highly varied—ranging from basic inorganic chemicals such as sulfuric acid and

---

[1] I am indebted to Ashish Arora, Rutherford Aris, John L. Enos, Edwin T. Layton, and Nathan Rosenberg for comments on an earlier draft of this chapter. Many of the issues discussed in this chapter are covered in the very useful book edited by Arora et al. (1998) and Arora et al. (1999). Se also Arora and Gambardella (1998, 1999).

ammonia, to the organic petrochemicals that serve as a basis for synthetic rubber, plastics, and fibers, to the highly specialized ingredients for pharmaceuticals and agrochemicals. The industry has tended to become increasingly diversified over time as a result of the development of new processes and products. Because of this diversity it is not possible to trace, in a single chapter, a comprehensive history of technical change in the chemical industry (Figure 8.1). In this chapter I first discuss three important inventions—synthetic dyestuffs, synthetic nitrates, and synthetic fibers—that gave rise to the modern chemical industry. I then turn to the development of the petrochemical industry in the United States and to the international transfer of the industry.[2]

It is particularly interesting to trace the relative importance of the several sources of technological change in the chemical industry. The development of the chemical industry has been characterized by both autonomous advances in scientific and technical knowledge and advances induced by growth in demand and by factor endowments. Path dependence, initially induced by resource scarcity or abundance, has at times had the effect of locking sectors of the industry into a path of development that became a barrier to adjustment at a later stage in development.

INVENTORS, INVENTIONS, AND TECHNICAL CHANGE

During the early stages in the development of the chemical industry a series of radical inventions set the direction for technical change. These inventions were generally made by bench scientists who often became entrepreneurs. In this section I discuss three such cases: (1) the development of synthetic dyestuffs, (2) the synthesis of ammonia, and (3) the invention of nylon.

Synthetic Dyestuffs

The synthetic organic chemical industry owes its origin to the discovery of coal tar-based synthetic organic dyestuffs and to the cotton textile industry's demand for better and less expensive dyes. The origins of coal tar-based synthetic dyes can be traced to Justus von Leibig's chemistry laboratory at the University of Giessen established in the early 1800s. The laboratory-based teaching method introduced by Leibig became the model for chemical instruction first in Germany and later in other countries.[3] It enabled Germany to establish leadership in chemical research. Among the topics that Leibig addressed in research of his laboratory was how to make use of the tars and other by-products resulting from the conversion of coal to coke.

---

[2] For the fertilizer industry, see Hignett (1985); for the pesticide industry, see Achilladelis et al. (1987:175–212).

[3] For an excellent biography of Leibig, and an account of the contribution of Leibig to the shaping of the discipline of chemistry, see Brock (1997).

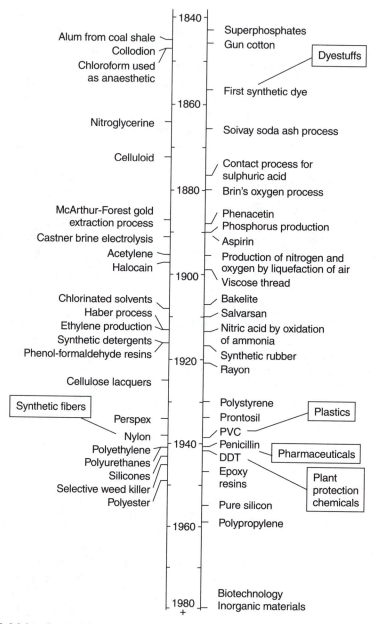

Figure 8.1 Major chemical innovations, 1840–1960. (*Source:* Margaret Sharp. "Innovations in the Chemicals Industry." In *The Handbook of Industrial Innovation*, Mark Dodgson and Roy Rothwell, eds. Aldershot, England: Edward Elgar, 1994:170.)

One of Leibig's students, August von Hoffman, was appointed the first director of the newly established Royal College of Chemistry in London in 1845. In 1856, William Perkins, an 18-year-old student studying with Hoffman, was engaged in research with the objective of synthesizing quinine. While conducting his research he accidentally discovered mauve, which became the first synthetic dyestuff. Mauve, or aniline purple, was produced by adding potassium dichromate, an oxidizing agent, to a solution of aniline in a dilute sulfuric acid. A black precipitate was formed that, after being boiled in coal tar naphtha to remove impurities, was dissolved in alcohol in which it formed a rich purple-colored solution. Use of other oxidizing agents led to the discovery of other synthetic dyes (Tilden, 1936:310–33).

In 1856 Perkins obtained a patent for the manufacture of aniline purple. The following year, with the assistance of his family, he established a manufacturing plant. In 1874 he withdrew from the manufacture of dyestuffs to again devote himself to research. Dyestuff production expanded rapidly in England in the latter part of the nineteenth century. By 1880, however, the English industry was rapidly losing its dominance to German manufacturers. Perkins attributed the loss of English leadership, during a period of rapid market expansion, to lack of training in organic chemistry in English universities and neglect of research by English dyestuff manufacturers (Tilden, 1936:317). In contrast, the rapid pace of discovery in Germany was stimulated by the establishment of industrial research laboratories and by the close collaboration between the dye companies and German universities and polytechnics.

The development of the synthetic dye industry was induced by forces operating on both the demand and supply side. Growth in demand for dyestuffs was stimulated by the rapid growth of cotton textile production in England. The supply of dyestuffs was constrained by the availability and high cost of natural materials (indigo in the case of blue dyes). The stage was set by (1) the availability of coal tar, an abundant raw material generated as a by-product of coal gas production,[4] and (2) advances in knowledge in coal tar chemistry and the establishment of laboratories for the study of natural dyestuffs. Perkins' accidental discovery of mauve represented the act of insight (Figure 3.1).

It was the development of organic chemistry, particularly the elucidation of molecular structures, that made it possible for the German dye industry to replace empirical investigation with a more scientifically grounded approach to the invention and improvement of dyestuffs. This approach permitted the expansion of the organic chemical industry from dyes to drugs and a whole host of other products as well as the dominance of world markets by the German chemical industry for the first several decades of the twentieth century (Walsh, 1984:211–234).[5]

---

[4] The development of coal tar chemistry represents an early example of a successful effort to convert a serious pollutant into a valued resource (Ayres, 1989).

[5] During the 1880s dystaffs and other organic chemicals were discovered to have medicinal effects. German and Swiss chemical companies such as Bayer and Hoescht and Cibia and Sandoz began to manufacture

The Haber–Bosch Process

Interest in the development of synthetic nitrogen in Germany was induced by the rapid growth of demand for nitrogen fertilizer, which, by the early 1900s, appeared to be rapidly outrunning the supply of Chilean sodium nitrate. The impetus was strengthened when Germany was cut off from Chilean supplies during World War I. In response, the German physical chemist, Fritz Haber, developed a process of directly synthesizing ammonia from hydrogen and nitrogen. By 1909 Haber had established the optimum conditions for the large-scale synthesis of ammonia. Commercial development was undertaken by a team of mechanical engineers, lead by Carl Bosch, of the Badische Anilin and Soda-Fabrik (BASF). The first successful direct synthesis of ammonia on a commercial scale was carried out by BASF in 1913.[6] Bosch rose to head BASF and led the effort to cartelize the German chemical industry.

The Haber–Bosch process was clearly induced by resource limitations (Hohenberg, 1967:44). It was "a supreme instance of a country developing a new technology that enabled it to overcome the shortage of a critical input-chemically bound nitrogen" (Landau and Rosenberg, 1992:96). The development of synthetic nitrogen had implications for other industries. It initiated technical developments that led to a long-term continuing decline in the price of nitrogen fertilizer, which, in turn, induced geneticists and plant breeders to develop higher yielding fertilizer-responsive crop varieties (Chapter 6).

The Haber–Bosch process was the first industrial chemical process to use very high pressure for a chemical reaction. This innovative process led directly to two other important inventions based on hydrogenation by German chemists—a coal-based synthetic gasoline in 1925 and synthetic wood alcohol (methanol) in 1933 (Hughes, 1969:106–132). It also led to inventions in the production of munitions, synthetic fibers, the synthesis of drugs and vitamins, petroleum refining, and in many other sectors of the chemical and allied products industries.

The relationship between Haber and Bosch illustrates the close relationship among science, industry, and government that has characterized advances in chemistry and in chemical engineering. Haber was a strong advocate of such collaboration both

---

drugs based on synthetic dyes. One of the most important was aspirin (salicyclic acid), first produced by Bayer in 1883 (Cockburn et al., 1999).

[6] Two other successful processes for the fixation of atmospheric nitrogen were also developed in the early 1900s. In 1903 the electric arc process was developed in Norway. Nitrogen and oxygen were combined to form nitric oxide (NO) at a very high temperature (about 3250°C) in an electric arc; at lower temperatures the nitric oxide reacted with more oxygen to form nitrogen dioxide (NO_2), which was hydrated in the presence of an electric arc to form nitric acid. The nitric acid was converted to the end product, calcium nitrate, by reaction with limestone. At about the same time the calcium cyanamide process was perfected. Calcium carbide, produced by the reaction of lime with coke in an electric furnace, was converted to calcium cyanamide ($CaCN_2$) by reaction with pure nitrogen extracted from the air. The product could be used directly as fertilizer, or it could be hydrolyzed to form ammonia (Hignett, 1985:5). Both the arc and the cyanamide processes depend on low-cost electricity and have generally not been economically viable.

in his early work and later as Director of the Kaiser Wilhelm Institute for Physical Chemistry in Berlin. Haber was also a committed German nationalist. During World War I he headed the chemistry section in the War Department for Raw Materials. In that capacity he supervised the development and first use of chlorine gas in chemical warfare. Haber received the Nobel Prize for Chemistry in 1918 for the research that led to the development of the Haber–Bosch process. Bosch received a Nobel Prize in 1931 (jointly with Frederich Bergius) for his research on high-pressure chemical processes.[7]

The Invention of Nylon

Nylon ranks as one of the outstanding accomplishments of modern organic chemistry and of private industry-sponsored basic research.[8] In 1927 E.I. DuPont de Nemours and Company set up a new laboratory under the direction of Charles Stine, dedicated to filling in the gaps of knowledge affecting important chemical processes, which might be of value for future applied research. In 1928 William H. Carothers, who had earlier taught and conducted research at the University of Illinois and at Harvard University, was appointed Director of Research in Organic Chemistry at DuPont's fundamental research laboratory in Wilmington, Delaware. At DuPont, he continued work that he had begun at Harvard on the structure of substances of high molecular weight and their formation by polymerization. His initial work on polymerization, how and why small molecules unite to form giant molecules, was regarded as an important contribution to fundamental knowledge but of little commercial significance (Spitz, 1988:271–301).

The potential commercial significance of his work was recognized when a member of Carothers' research group, attempting to produce longer polymer chains, discovered a synthetic fiber. In a somewhat anecdotal account, DuPont President (and former director of the Chemical Department) Crawford H. Greenewalt recalled that "one of Carother's associates was cleaning out a reaction vessel in which he had been making one of those polymers, and he discovered in pulling a stirring rod out of the reaction vessel that he pulled out a fiber; and he discovered its unusual flexibility, strength and the remarkable ability of this polymer to cold draw" (Mueller, 1962:335). This discovery was, however, the product of a substantial commitment to a program of fundamental research on monomers and systematic studies of the properties of various polyamides.

The discovery had obvious commercial implications for DuPont. The company, already in the textile business as a producer of rayon, was anxious to develop a synthetic fiber that would extend its mature market for rayon. A decision was made in

---

[7] Haber was forced to resign his post and fled Germany as a result of the anti-Semitic policy of the Hitler regime. For a discussion of the contribution of the German chemical industry to the German military capacity, see Grant et al. (1988:34–36) and Borkin (1978).

[8] The definitive reference is Hounshell and Smith (1988); see particularly pp. 119–326.

July 1935 to proceed with the commercial development of nylon. The development occurred in three stages. During the first year work centered on determining whether commercial production might actually be *feasible*. The next step was to determine if there were *practicable* commercial possibilities. A decision was initially made to focus on full fashioned hosiery yarn. By late 1937 DuPont succeeded in producing yarns that when knitted into nylon hosiery, compared favorably with silk. The final step involved making a *reproducible* yarn on a large scale. It took several more years to develop first a laboratory-scale manufacturing process and then a large-scale plant (Hounshell and Smith, 1988:262–273). The first DuPont plant to produce nylon began operations in late 1939. Initially planned with a capacity of 3 million pounds, before the plant was even completed DuPont decided to increase its capacity to 8 million pounds.

During the 1940s, DuPont developed or acquired a series of other polymer-based products. Teflon, a heat-resistant material, was discovered accidentally by Dr. Roy Plunkett in 1943 while doing research on fluorocarbon refrigerants; orlon, a quick-drying material with wool-like properties, was put on the market in 1947; dacron, a polyethylene-based material, was acquired from Imperial Chemical Industries (Taylor and Sudnik, 1984:150–155).

Nylon was only the second major success story in which the scientific discovery, the inventive activity, and the product development were the result of research and development conducted primarily within DuPont.[9] For most of its history, prior to 1920, DuPont had been a manufacturer solely of explosives and related products. Beginning in the early 1900s, it took steps to become a diversified chemical firm. Most of its initial chemical products (such as viscose rayon, tetraethyl lead, cellophane, and synthetic ammonia) were developed by other firms, which then sold patents or the rights to produce to DuPont. Mueller, in his 1955 analysis of DuPont's major innovations, interpreted this as indicating that "DuPont has been more successful in making product and process improvements than in discovering new products" (Mueller, 1962:344).

In the case of viscose rayon, for example, DuPont first conducted research to develop a nitrocellulose process for making artificial silk (later called rayon). When this attempt failed, it entered into negotiations to purchase the American Viscose Company, the only viscose rayon producer in the United States, but withdrew because it considered the price too high. In 1919 it entered into an agreement with a French firm, Comptior des Textiles Artificiels, for the exclusive rights to its viscose rayon technology, which was assigned to the jointly-owned (DuPont, 60%; Comptior, 40%) DuPont Fibersilk Company. In 1929 DuPont was able to enter the acetate rayon

---

[9] The first was the adaptation in 1923 of Duco lacquer, initially developed for painting fabric airplane wings during Wold War I, for use as a color finish for automobiles produced by General Motors, in which DuPont had a large financial interest. It reduced the time required to finish a car from days to hours (Mueller, 1962:326–327).

industry by acquiring manufacturing and sales rights from Societé Chimique Usines du Dhône and Société-Rhodiacete (Mueller, 1962:326, 332).

In 1923 DuPont acquired rights to manufacture cellophane in North and Central America from one of Comptior's affiliates, LaCellophane Société Anonyme. By the late 1940s, these three products, viscose rayon, acetate rayon, and cellophane, accounted for over 20% of DuPont sales. DuPont was still, however, more successful in improving its acquired technology than in initial development. For example, in 1927 it developed a method for moisture proofing cellophane and in 1934 it developed a high-strength rayon for use as tire cord. By the late 1940s, these and other synthetic fiber products accounted for approximately 40% of DuPont's sales. At that time, nylon remained the most important commercial product to come out of DuPont's own laboratories.

The DuPont experience is particularly interesting in terms of technology transfer. During its initial efforts to diversify away from the manufacture of explosives it was frequently frustrated in attempts to develop its own technology and typically resorted to acquisition of product rights from other U.S. and European chemical companies. As DuPont grew, and its product lines became more diverse, its development work become more successful and it began investing more in generic and basic research because of its ability to take advantage of serendipitous developments.

DuPont did not grow big because of its inventive superiority. It supported research and development, first because of an effort to diversify its production, and later because it was big and could internalize the gains from invention activity. Traditionally most chemical companies have specialized in a few related products, focusing either on costly and technically complex materials such as dyes or drugs or on producing large quantities of easily processed materials such as acids or ammonia. At the beginning of World War II the world chemical market was dominated by DuPont, Imperial Chemical Industries, I.G. Farben, and Solvay. These firms had developed a size of operations, of scientific and technical capacity and of access to financial resources that enabled them to diversify over a broad range of chemical products (Sudnik).[10]

In this section I have focused on three radical innovations in order to provide insight into the process of innovation in the early years of the chemical industry. Radical innovations in the chemical industry have been dominated by a relatively few large firms over large periods of time. Ten companies accounted for 44% of new products, and 50% of those that experienced greatest market success, between 1950 and 1980. This process of firm-specific "technological accumulation" outlived the

---

[10] I.G. Farben Industries AG was formed in 1925 by a merger of BASF and seven other chemical companies. The formation of Imperial Chemical Industries (ICI) was the culmination of a consolidation drive that began after World War I. Although DuPont was, by the end of the 1920s, the most diversified U.S. chemical company, American antitrust policy prevented consolidation of the U.S. chemical industry to the extent that occurred in Germany and Great Britain.

scientific and business entrepreneurs that were initially associated with the firms' rise to prominence (Freeman, 1990:74–91).

CHEMICAL ENGINEERING AND THE PETROCHEMICAL REVOLUTION

There were three prerequisites for the petrochemical revolution: "an understanding of the nature of high polymers; a source of cheap olefins and aromatics; and the development of the chemical engineering skills necessary for large scale chemical industry" (Wittcoff and Reuben, 1980:243). In the United States, expanded output of gasoline to meet the needs of the growing number of automobiles on U.S. roads led to an increase in the availability of olefins, which were by-products of the refining process. The organic chemicals are largely intermediate products that have a vast array of end uses (Figure 8.2). By the end of World War II the heavy organic chemical industry had become the most dynamic sector of the chemical and allied products industry.[11]

Chemical engineering had begun to emerge as a separate discipline by World War I. As noted in the last section, scientific understanding of polymers structure had advanced rapidly in the decade prior to World War II. In the United States, in the first two decades after World War II, the application of chemical engineering skills in petroleum refining created both an inexpensive supply of raw materials and the ability to transform the production of industrial organic chemicals from a batch process to a continuous process and to enhance the size of operation.

Chemical Engineering

The emergence of chemical engineering as a separate discipline was a distinctly American phenomenon in which a single institution, the Massachusetts Institute of Technology (MIT), played a dominant role.[12] In the later part of the nineteenth century, as noted earlier, Germany had established a tradition of chemical research with strong linkages between academic research and industrial technology development. In Germany separate roles were maintained, however, for the chemist and the engineer.

---

[11] "The chemical industry isolates and synthesizes chemicals, whereas the allied products industries modify, formulate and package products based on those chemicals" [Wittcoff and Reuben (I), 1988:12]. There are three major branches of the chemical industry—a heavy inorganic branch, a heavy organic branch, and a fine chemical branch. The heavy organic chemicals include, for example, synthetic rubber, plastics, synthetic fibers, and many other products based on petrochemicals. The primary materials used in heavy organic chemicals are the olefins (ethylene, propylene, and the butylenes), the aromatics (benzene, toluene, xylene), and methane. The olefins are made from petroleum and natural gas, the aromatics from petroleum and, to a lesser extent, from coal, and methane from natural gas.

[12] Rosenberg (1998a:193–230, 1998b:167–192). For a personal history of the development of chemical engineering, see Scriven (1991) and Futer (1980).

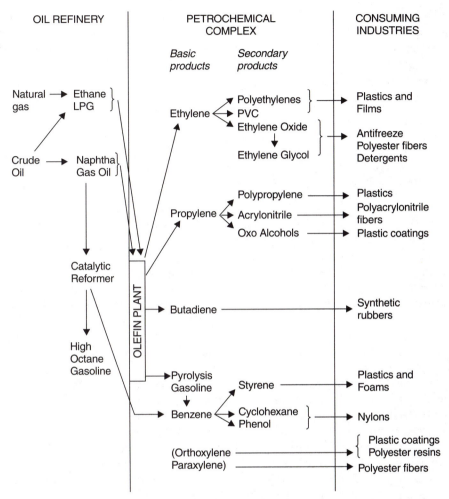

Figure 8.2 Petrochemicals: the production pathway from basic feedstock. (*Source:* Margaret Sharp. "Innovations in the Chemicals Industry." In *The Handbook of Industrial Innovation*, Mark Dodgson and Roy Rothwell, eds. Aldershot, England: Edward Elgar, 1994:171.)

In contrast, these roles were merged in the United States. Concerns about the role and status of the chemical engineer, as distinct from the role of analytical chemists and mechanical engineers, contributed to the formation of a separate professional identity for chemists employed as plant superintendents and managers and in chemical plant design and construction (Reynolds, 1991:343–365).

The first curriculum with the title of Chemical Engineering was organized by Professor Lewis Norton at MIT in 1888 (Houghton, 1972; Servos, 1980). In 1905, Professor William H. Walker, professor of industrial chemistry, and Arthur H. Noyes, professor of physical chemistry, collaborated to reorganize the program in industrial chemistry from Norton's heterogeneous collection of courses in chemistry and mechanical engineering into a more integrated program of study. By 1915 the central integrating concept had become the study of unit operations first developed by Arthur D. Little in his consulting practice.

> The central idea was to reduce the vast number of industrial chemical processes into a few basic steps such as distillation, absorption, heat transfer, filtration, evaporation, reaction and the like. Walker and Little were developing their own scientific analysis of the principles of chemical engineering based on unit operations . . . (that) involved new conceptual frameworks not used or needed by chemists . . . because chemists did not concern themselves with how one designs industrial size plants and equipment. (Landau and Rosenberg, 1992:88)

In 1916 MIT established a free-standing School of Chemical Engineering Practice, an industry–academic cooperative master's course taught at an advanced applied level. But the founders did not agree on the proper direction for this discipline. After a bitter clash between Noyes and Walker, which led to Noyes' resignation, an autonomous Department of Chemical Engineering, separate from both the Chemistry Department and the School of Chemical Engineering Practice, was established in 1921. Its first chairman was Warren K. Lewis. Although Lewis was a protégée of Walker, his emphasis on the use of mathematically sophisticated theoretical tools to predict the performance of chemical processing equipment brought him into conflict with Walker.

A second major advance in the development of the discipline of chemical engineering centered around attempts in the 1950s to incorporate more adequate scientific understanding of the basic molecular fluid mechanics and transport phenomena underlying most chemical reactions (Layton, 1988). Phenomena such as turbulence and friction, which did not lend themselves easily to theoretical treatment, had been ignored by physicists. But they could not be ignored by chemical engineers who wanted to design chemical reaction vessels. The gap between physical theory and engineering practice gave rise to efforts by chemical engineers to fill this gap in knowledge. The key to success lay in the development of appropriate dimensionless parameters. Dimensional analysis provided a theoretical basis for the development of parameters linking small bench-scale experiments with plant-scale design.

As a result of these advances, chemical engineering became more closely linked to advances in basic knowledge in chemistry. To establish chemical engineering as a separate discipline, Walker had found it necessary to break the institutional linages with chemistry at MIT. By the late 1940s a new generation of chemical engineers was reestablishing the linkages that had been severed in the 1920s. As these linkages were reestablished under the rubric of engineering science, engineering schools were again warned that "industry needs scientific engineers, not engineering scientists."

Petrochemicals

The transition from batch to continuous process in the petroleum industry began after the break-up of Standard Oil Company into a group of competitors as a result of a 1911 antitrust judgment. The two largest successor companies, Standard Oil Company of Indiana (now Amoco) and Standard Oil Company of New Jersey (now Exxon), recognized that the available technology was inadequate to meet the growing demand for gasoline resulting from the rapid adoption of the automobile.[13]

As early as 1890 the Standard Oil Indiana subsidiary established a testing laboratory at its Whiting (Indiana) refinery under the direction of William M. Burton, who had received a Ph.D. degree in chemistry from Johns Hopkins the previous year. After developing a process to eliminate undesirable sulfur compounds from refinery products, Burton was promoted to assistant superintendent of the Whiting refinery in 1892, and to superintendent in 1896. He used his authority to bring two more Johns Hopkins chemistry Ph.D.s, George Gray and Robert Humphreys, to the Whiting laboratory. In 1909 Burton and his colleagues initiated a research and development program to increase the yield of gasoline from crude oil. The process that they invented involved the development of high-pressure technology for "cracking" heavy petroleum fractions to yield gasoline.[14]

Initially, Burton's proposal to develop a high-pressure technology was rejected by the Standard Oil board, who feared that Burton would "blow the whole State of Indiana into Lake Michigan." After the 1911 divestiture Standard Oil of Indiana, with Burton serving on its board of directors, took a more positive attitude toward his proposal. The Burton process was introduced commercially in 1913. It doubled the yield of gasoline from crude oil and within a few years was a major source of Standard of Indiana's profits. The introduction of the Burton process had the effect of changing the petroleum-refining industry into a chemical-processing industry.

A main drawback of the Burton process was that the cracking was carried out in batches. Edward M. Clark, the manager of the Standard of Indiana refinery at Wood River (Illinois), after spending a summer at Whiting, initiated a program to develop a continuous process system. By 1914 he had succeeded in developing a continuous

---

[13] I do not, in this chapter, attempt to review the early history of technical change in the petroleum industry. The definitive works are Williamson and Daum (1959), Williamson et al. (1961), and Enos (1962).

[14] Early research at Standard Oil of Indiana is described in greater detail by Enos (1962:1–19). Enos employs an induced technical change framework in his discussion of the economic factors leading to the search for a technology that would increase the yield of gasoline. "There were two ways in which a shortage of crude oil could be averted; first, more could be discovered, and secondly, the existing supply could be better utilized so as to yield a larger fraction of the products which were in greater demand. In different areas of the country, depending on local conditions, emphasis was placed on one or the other. In California and Texas, which had access to excellent sources of crude oil, and the East Coast, where there was a good market for heavy residual fuels, the emphasis lay upon finding more crude oil. In the Midwest, because of diminishing local supplies and the high cost of transportation from distant fields, the emphasis lay on altering the yield structure of the petroleum products" (p. 2).

process "tube cracking still." In April 1915 the first 20 Burton–Clark units began operating at the Wood River refinery.

Later, in 1919, Standard of New Jersey established a Development Department (later the Standard Oil Development Company) headed by Frank A. Howard. It was the industry's first attempt to effectively institutionalize innovation.[15] Howard brought in Edgar Clark from Standard of Indiana and engaged MIT's Warren K. Lewis as a consultant. A research center was established at Baton Rouge under the direction of Robert Haslam, an associate of Lewis at MIT. Haslam formed a team of 15 MIT staffers and graduates to set up the research organization and in 1927 left MIT to become Vice President of the Exxon Development Department. Howard entered into a series of agreements with I. G. Farben in the late 1920s for access to the work on hydrogenation and synthetic substitutes for oil and rubber from coal. Access to continuous process technology was enhanced by the formation in the late 1930s of Catalytic Research Associates, an international research consortium that included the M.W. Kellogg Company, I.G. Farben, Jersey Standard, Indiana Standard, Imperial Chemical Industries, Royal Dutch Shell, the Texas Company, and Universal Oil Products.

By the early 1940s, the techniques and skills developed for the petroleum industry were becoming available for use in the chemical industry. Petroleum-based feedstocks began to replace coal-based feedstocks in the production of a wide range of chemical products (Figure 8.2). This was not, however, a simple process of technology transfer. Large-scale chemical manufacturing required very substantial technical innovation in order to deal with the challenges posed by complex product separation, corrosion, toxic hazards and wastes, diversified markets, and others.[16]

The process of transition to petroleum feedstocks occurred much more slowly in Europe than in the United States. In the absence of a domestic petroleum industry and strong protectionist economic policies, the European industrial organic chemical industry continued to rely more heavily on coal as a basic raw material. Even after World War II the transition to petroleum feedstocks and larger scale production was impeded by skills, attitudes, and education that had been developed under a coal-based industrial regime.[17] Thus, technical change, induced by favorable resource

---

[15] For greater detail on the development of the research program at Standard Oil of New Jersey, see Enos (1962:97–130).

[16] It had been understood in the United States that petroleum would be a better feedstock than coal since the hydrocarbons are available in a liquid form whereas coal must be converted to a liquid or gas before it can be subjected to chemical processing. As a result of the invention of the Burton and Dubbs crackers, refiners had the means, by the mid-1920s, to "crack" heavier crude oil fractions to obtain higher yields of gasoline while at the same time producing off gases that contained olefins that could be used as chemical feedstocks (Spitz, 1988:65).

[17] "Producing petrochemicals would require that German chemists and industrialists begin to think in ways completely different than they had before. There were differences, for example, in terms of the optimum scale for an industrial plant, with the petrochemical plants generally being much larger than coal-chemical facilities. . . . Design traditions had to change because the new technology required that German designers,

endowments, clearly gave the U.S. industrial organic chemical industry a substantial initial advantage relative to the European industry.

In the first two decades after World War II there was explosive growth in the demand for petrochemicals, particularly vinyl chloride, ammonia, ethylene, polypropylene resins, and noncellulosic fibers. The rapid growth in demand for these relatively homogeneous bulk intermediate chemicals created opportunities for scaling up chemical production processes. Initially, large plants were built by simply duplicating the equipment of smaller plants—such as by building two reaction "trains" instead of one. The mere duplication of the internal equipment of a plant did not, however, result in any significant lowering of costs. Reduction of costs was achieved with the design of a single "train" reaction system with the capacity of several smaller "trains." After the single "train" equipment design was first applied to the production of ethylene and ammonia, plant size experienced dramatic increases (Spitz, 1988:418–461). The size of new ammonia plants rose from 300 tons per day in the first single train unit designed by Kellogg in the early 1950s to 600–1000 tons per day in the late 1960s. Between the early 1950s and the mid-1970s, the size of the new ethylene plants rose from less than 40,000 to 400,000–600,000 metric tons per year. By the early 1970s, however, cost reductions from increases in plant size, often in the 0.2–0.3 cents per pound range, were beginning to be offset by increases in other elements of operating costs (Spitz, 1988:418–461).

An important technical change, introduced from outside the field of chemical engineering, was the adoption of computerized control systems. These systems, which drew on the new field of optimum control theory, were used in plant design and to monitor operations, collect inorganic data, and evaluate results. Software programs were developed to enable the system to automatically make start-up and shut-down decisions and to change raw material and product mixes.

The opportunities for substantial efficiency gains from new process technologies were associated with a change in the organization of the suppliers of the new technology. Specialized engineering firms (SEFs) entered the market and began to replace "in-house" chemical engineering staff (Freeman, 1968:29–57).[18] The large

---

who were trained primarily as chemists—abandon their traditional regard for 'elegance'. It took time to alter habits that had led to such success from the 1860s through the 1940s" (Stokes, 1994:5, 6).

[18] One of the most successful of these firms, formed for the purpose of developing and licensing petrochemical technology, was Scientific Design Company (later Halcon International). It was founded in 1946 by Ralph Landau and Harry Rehnberg. Both were graduates in chemical engineering from MIT and both had worked in the Manhattan Project during World War II. SD began its research in an office building in Manhattan and then moved to a warehouse building in New Jersey (Spitz, 1982:317–331; Landau, 1996:19–37). Specialized engineering firms had earlier played an important role in the development of the petroleum-refining industry. The earliest was the Universal Oil Products Company (UOP) formed in 1914. UOP was financed by J. Ogden Armour to exploit the development of a "clean circulation" cracking process based on research by Jesse A. and Caros P. Dubbs. The first prototype plant was completed in 1921. UOP stood ready to license the Dubbs process to any petroleum refinery firm, to provide the licensee with all the technical know-how surrounding the process, and to offer protection against suits brought by owners of competitive processes (Enos, 1962:60–96).

chemical companies continued to focus their efforts on product innovation and development while leaving process design and development to the specialized firms. These firms could acquire much broader experience across the entire chemical industry. As they worked for different clients they were able to take advantage of the tacit knowledge and of "learning by doing" acquired from the design and operation of plants producing a variety of products under different conditions. Technology rights and license agreements were traded for the feedback of know-how that could then be sold and licensed to other firms. Such access and experience were simply not available to an "in-house" chemical engineering staff. Between 1960 and 1990 nearly three-quarters of the major new plants were engineered, procured, and constructed by specialist firms (Freeman, 1968:30; Arora and Gambardella, 1998).

Building larger plants involved more than a simple process of "scaling up."[19] Landau and Rosenberg insist that the economies realized from larger size plants should not be confused with economies of scale.

> Building larger chemical processing plants is . . . much more than merely having assurance of access to sufficiently large markets. Such larger plants are necessarily also a product of technological innovations that make them feasible. In this respect it is much more common than it ought to be to assume that the exploitation of the benefits of large scale production is a separate phenomenon independent of technological change. In fact, larger plants typically incorporate a number of technological improvements, based on the wealth of experience and insight into better plant design, that could be accumulated only through prolonged exposure to the problems involved in the operation of somewhat smaller plants. The building of larger plants must, as a result, often await advances in the technological capabilities in plant design, equipment manufacture, and process operation. Thus, the benefits of scale cannot be attained until certain facilitating technological conditions have been fulfilled. (Landau and Rosenberg, 1992:93)

INTERNATIONAL DIFFUSION

Prior to World War I technological leadership in the chemical industry was dominated by firms located in Germany.[20] During the period between the two wars, the American and British chemical industries made rapid strides in their efforts to catch up with the

---

[19] An overly simplified view of scale economics is due, in part, to the fact that in addition to advances in technology economics of scale in the chemical industry can arise "from purely geometric factors. The capacity of a great deal of chemical equipment varies with its volume, that is with the cube of its linear dimensions. The costs on the other hand, is the cost of a surface to enclose the volume and varies with the square of linear dimensions. . . . This is called the square-cube law. It does not apply to all equipment. The capacity of a heat exchange depends on its surface area, so cost is proportional to capacity and there are no economies of scale. Control systems, in contrast, are not affected by capacity at all" (Wittcoff and Reuben, 1980:25).

[20] In this section, I draw very heavily on Spitz (1988), Sagers and Shabad (1990), and Enos and Park (1988).

German industry. By the early 1940s, U.S. and German chemical technology enjoyed a rough parity. And by the early 1950s, U.S. petrochemical technology was well ahead of that in Germany.

There have been two major stages in the diffusion of petrochemical technology since the end of World War II. The first involved the transfer of technology from the United States to Western Europe and Japan. The second involved the establishment of petrochemical capacity in the Union of Soviet Socialist Republics (U.S.S.R.) and in a number of developing countries.

Western Europe

As exports to Europe expanded, American companies, particularly the international oil companies, took the lead in establishing a European petrochemical industry by locating petrochemical facilities in Europe. In the mid-1950s, for example, Standard Oil of New Jersey (now Exxon) built petrochemical production centers next to its previously established oil refineries in England, France, and Germany. Demonstration of the superior economics of producing chemicals and other products from petroleum-based feed stocks—with the use of newly developed American technology—led, by the late 1950s, to the conversion of a number of European installations from coal to hydrocarbons. By the early 1960s, American chemical companies such as Dow, Union Carbide, DuPont, and others, had established wholly owned manufacturing plants or joint ventures in Europe. The emergence of SEFs also played an important role in transferring American technology to European firms. One of the first such collaborations occurred when Naphtachimie (a joint venture of Pechiney and Kulmann) decided to use a Scientific Design Company (SD) process in a new ethylene oxide and ethylene glycol plant in France. By 1960, Deutsche Shell had became a major competitor with SD. This led to vigorous competition between SD and Shell not only in Europe but all over the world.

As noted earlier, American leadership was initially based on its lead in making the transition from coal-based to petroleum- and natural-based feedstocks. Even after the war this transition was delayed in Europe since it was not a producer, in any substantial quantities, of either oil or gas. European firms were slow to abandon use of locally available coal and agriculturally derived feedstocks (such as ethyl alcohol). A second obstacle was the small size of European national markets. Chemical firms often found it difficult to build a plant large enough to be economically viable without developing substantial export markets. Markets in other European countries were often closed by protectionist policies and American firms were often in a better position to supply Third World markets. From the late 1940s through the 1950s, U.S. exports of petrochemicals (such as carbon black, synthetic phenol, ethylene glycol, butanol, vinyl resins, and polystyrene resins) to the European market expanded rapidly. Research by SD and other SEFs also contributed to the diffusion of technology for the production of chlorinated solvents, maleic anhydride, terephthalic acid, and other petrochemical technologies. By 1960, however, the Western European chemical industry was fully committed to petrochemical technology. This also meant that it became dependent on the Middle East for raw materials and on an integrated European and an open global market for an outlet for its expanding petrochemical industry (Stokes, 1994:234).

Japan and U.S.S.R.

The development of the petrochemical industry in Japan lagged almost a decade behind that of Western Europe.[21] Considerable progress had been made before World War I in the development of the explosives and fertilizer industries. The chemical industry, based on products such as rayon, synthetic ammonia, and coal-based chemicals, grew rapidly during the interwar period. Growth of the chemical industry immediately after World War II was, however, constrained by several handicaps. Bombing raids toward the end of the war had destroyed substantial capacity. The country was almost completely dependent on imported raw materials.

The period from the early 1950s to the early 1970s was a period of rapid catch-up for the Japanese chemical industry (Hinko et al., 1998:122–130). As in the case of Germany, it was necessary to shift from coal to petroleum as the key raw material. In 1950 the Ministry of International Trade and Industry (MITI) established rigorous criteria for investment incentives in the chemical industry. The objective of MITI support was to supply basic petrochemical products to domestic users at internationally competitive prices. Although the basic focus was on the domestic market, the government insisted on reliance on international prices as a test for efficiency and competitiveness. This was in sharp contrast to the import substitution policies followed in by most countries.

> The MITI plan specified three directions for the development of petrochemical capacity: (1) to secure basic domestic supplies of benzol, organic acids, and acetone for immediate needs in the plastics and synthetic fibers industries; (2) to introduce the domestic manufacture of ethylene and derivatives; and (3) to achieve low cost production of basic petrochemicals to raise the international competitiveness of chemical and related industries. (Hinko et al., 1998:126)

The first petrochemical complex was launched in 1957 when Nippon Petrochemicals constructed an ethylene-producing facility near Yokohama. This was followed by three more centers—Mitsui Petrochemicals, Sumito Chemicals, and Mitsubishi Chemicals in 1958 and 1959. The success of these initial incentives led to a new round of capacity expansion in the late 1960s and early 1970s. By 1980 Japan had overtaken Germany as the second largest producer of chemicals.

---

[21] For a more complete discussion of the development of the Japanese chemical industry, see Hinko et al. (1998:103–135).

In the early 1970s, however, the Japanese chemical industry was forced to confront a number of serious difficulties. Expansion in capacity continued even as the import substitution phase was being completed and as domestic demand by downstream industries was slowing. The Japanese industry was confronted with substantial excess capacity. The oil price shocks of 1973 and 1979 drove up the price of the key raw material and exacerbated the problem of excess capacity. The strategy followed by the Japanese chemical industry in response to these difficulties involved a combination of restructuring and rationalization of petrochemical facilities, expansion into overseas markets, and diversification into fine and specialty chemical and pharmaceuticals. Although expansion into international markets, particularly in Asia, was quite successful, consolidation and diversification occurred slowly and with considerable difficulty.

A major institutional constraint has been the diversified business groups (keiretsu) that link financial institutions and enterprises connected through long-term transactional relationships (such as petroleum, chemicals, fibers paper, and glass). These groups, which were a source of strength during the rapid expansion phase, became an obstacle to rapid structural change during the 1980s and 1990s. A major technological constraint on the effort to diversify was that during its rapid growth, Japanese firms had adopted a strategy of importing American and European chemical technology. Specialized engineering firms such as Stone and Weber and Scientific Design played a leading role in technology transfer. Japanese firms developed substantial capacity for making improvements in process and product technology. Although these capacities enabled Japanese firms to compete effectively in international markets in the basic heavy chemicals, it did not provide them with the capacities needed to make a rapid transition into new areas such as pharmaceuticals and biotechnology (Chapter 10).

In spite of these difficulties the Japanese chemical industry must be judged an enormous success. It is the second largest Japanese manufacturing industry (ranking just below electrical machinery). It has provided the chemical inputs that have allowed downstream industries such as synthetic fibers, plastics, automobile, and electronics industries to flourish. It is a major force in international markets. But by the 1990s it was no longer a dynamic source of growth in the Japanese economy.

The chemical industry in the U.S.S.R. had been forced to play a continuous catch-up game with the chemical industry of the West. During the 1930s, the importation of western equipment and technology resulting in rapid progress. But by end of World War II the "polymer revolution" had again opened up a wide technological gap between the West and the U.S.S.R. Synthetic rubber represented a major exception to this general pattern. Butadiene had been identified in France in the 1860s but experiments by the Russian chemist Sergoy V. Lebedev around 1910 first demonstrated its ability to be polymerized into a rubber material. Initially the butadiene for Buna rubber was derived from ethyl alcohol (ethanol) obtained by the fermentation of potatoes and other starchy agricultural raw materials. Beginning in the 1950s the ethyl alcohol for butadiene began to be derived synthetically from petroleum. By the early 1960s a new class of synthetic rubber, Isoprene, began to take the place of Buna rubber, not only in the U.S.S.R. but also in the West. As of the late 1980s the U.S.S.R. continued to be the world's leading producer of synthetic rubber.[22]

During the 1950s expansion of the chemical industry in the Soviet Union, including both the conversion of existing chemical plants from coal tar to hydrocarbon feedstocks and the building of new chemical plants, was slowed more by financial constraints than by engineering capacity. Beginning in the mid-1960s imports of capital equipment from the West began to expand rapidly. A number of European and Japanese engineering firms arranged "compensation deals" that called for payment of services in the form of exports of the chemicals that would be produced in the new plants. In 1978 *European Chemical News* listed over 100 such deals. During the 1980s, however, these compensation deals declined because of the reduction in market opportunities in the West. Most of the chemical equipment obtained from the West consisted of installations and assemblies rather than turn-key plants. Soviet contracts with Western firms generally covered process design engineering, equipment, procurement, and start-up assistance, but not complete construction. By the 1980s the trend was more toward the purchase of individual pieces of equipment to augment domestic supplies.

Research by East German and Russian chemical engineers was, at the same time, beginning to make substantial contributions to Western chemical technology. Development work by Halcon (formerly Scientific Design) on the use of borate esters for production of nylon intermediates from cyclohexane was inspired by Russian research. Russian research was at times used by U.S. companies to get into the production of chemicals where a license from a Western country was unavailable or too expensive. Despite this advanced research, the status of the Russian chemical industry as a whole remained technically backward. A survey conducted in 1986 indicated that only 16% of machines and equipment in the chemical industry met world standards and 31% even failed to meet domestic standards.

Developing Countries

As early as the 1950s a number of developing countries began to view the petrochemical industry as strategic for their own economic development.[23] Successful transfer of the petrochemical industry to the developing world has been conditioned by economic policy, market size, and petroleum resource endowments. In the 1960s and 1970s the governments of many developing countries, particularly in Latin America, employed import substitution policies to force petrochemical development. In most countries the size of the domestic market was too small to permit the development of economically viable facilities unless they were protected by high tariffs or import

---

[22] For the development of the synthetic rubber industry in the U.S., see Solo (1980) and Mowery and Rosenberg (1998:89–92).

[23] In this section I draw heavily on Chapman (1991), Enos and Park (1988), Fayad and Motamen (1986), and Saramma (1984).

quotas. Even Brazil, where the large size of the domestic market provided substantial leverage in dealing with foreign multinationals, found it necessary to depend on a state sector and substantial protection against imports until the 1990s in order to achieve economic viability. Korea, in contrast, employed a sophisticated combination of import substitution and export promotion to rapidly establish an economically viable petrochemical industry (Box 8.1).

The developing oil-producing countries have typically viewed petrochemical industry development as an opportunity to add value to raw material exports rather than in terms of import substitution.[24] Even before the first oil price shock of 1973 several of the larger oil producing countries such as Mexico, India and Iran had initiated petrochemical developments, with state ownership or substantial state intervention, and several West Asia producers had initiated nitrogen fertilizer projects. The multinational petroleum and chemical companies were, however, typically hostile or reluctant participants. With the oil price increases of 1973 and 1979 raw material costs assumed much greater significance in location decision—they "fundamentally changed the pattern of international comparative advantage in basic petrochemicals in favor of the oil and gas producers" (Chapman, 1991:152).

● BOX 8.1

TRANSFER OF PETROCHEMICAL TECHNOLOGY TO KOREA

Official support for the development of South Korea's petrochemical industry was formally announced with the publication by the Blue House on January 30, 1973 of a *Declaration of Heavy and Chemical Industrialization.* Although this declaration initiated stronger government support for the chemical industry, efforts to promote the industry began in the 1960s.

The successful transfer of petrochemical technology to Korea began with the establishment of the first modern chemical plant operated by the Chungju Fertilizer Company in 1960. Financial and technical assistance was provided by the U.S. Agency for International Development (USAID). Its staffing absorbed most of Korea's university-trained chemical engineers and in turn became an important on-the-job training center for the next generation of engineers who staffed Korea's modern chemical industry.

---

[24] In many of the Middle East and North African countries natural gas had almost zero opportunity cost. "It has been estimated that the volume of gas wastefully flared in Saudi Arabia in 1982 incorporated ethylene feedstocks equivalent to the requirements of 13 ethylene plants each producing 500,000 tons per year" (Chapman, 1991:154). Ethylene is unique as a petrochemical feedstock in that it is expensive to transport and has no alternative use other than as a fuel near the point of production.

A second foundation was laid with the establishment of Korea's first oil refinery by the Korea Oil Corporation (KOCO) at Ulsan in southeastern Korea in 1967. This was followed by a feasibility study, also financed by USAID and carried out by two U.S. consulting firms—Arthur D. Little (marketing) and Fluor (engineering). The Arthur D. Little report cautioned that the domestic market was too small to support plants capable of producing at low unit costs. Demand forecasts by the Korean government were, however, more optimistic. A decision was made to construct a facility that would produce low-density polyethylene (for synthetic fibers) and vinyl chloride (for plastics).

After a competitive bidding process Dow Chemical Company was selected as a 50–50 joint venture partner. This also meant that Dow's technology was selected. Managers and engineers from the Chungju Fertilizer Company, the only Korean source of the chemical engineering knowledge, played a major role in the negotiations with Dow. Particular attention was given to requirements for the transfer and the training of Korean engineers in the Dow technology. Dow agreed to (1) reveal all of its own designs and "know-how" to its Korean employees, (2) train the Korean engineers in all aspects of current Dow technology, and (3) replace Dow with Korean engineers as quickly as possible. The joint venture was incorporated as the Korea Pacific Chemical Corporation (later the Hanyang Chemical Corporation).

In design and operation, the Ulsan plant was initially identical to Dow plants in the United States. But by 1976, less than 4 years after start-up, Korean engineers had completely replaced foreign engineers. Korean engineers responded to the energy shortage of the 1970s by developing a number of material and energy-saving technical improvements.

The maintenance department took advantage of the low-cost technical skills of Korean workers by rebuilding or refurbishing worn parts and equipment rather than replacing them with new imported parts and equipment.

Planning for a second petrochemical complex, also established as a joint venture with Dow, began in 1977. Operations in the new plant, located at Yeochen and largely staffed with engineers from Ulsan, began in 1981. It took the Yeochen plant longer than the Ulsan plant to begin operating above the design capacity range because of weak demand at the time the plant came on stream. Performance of the Hanyang plants at Ulson and Yeochen exceed that of similar Dow plants in Canada, Spain, Hong Kong, and Chile, which depended more heavily on expatriate engineers.

During the global recession of the early 1980s Dow, squeezed between high prices for petroleum raw materials and reduced demand for petrochemical products, disposed of its interests in joint ventures in Japan, Saudi Arabia, Spain, and Korea. After lengthy negotiations Hanyang Chemical Company became a wholly owned and managed Korean company.

Why was petrochemical technology absorbed in Korea so successfully? There are several closely related reasons. One was the prior development of chemical engineering operating experience in the fertilizer industry. Another was the foresight of the government in stressing technical and engineering education and training. There was also the rigorous planning and implementation for the transfer of technology. Finally there was the careful exploration of forward and backward linkages—upstream to oil refining and downstream to the textile industry. Many observers have also insisted that cultural factors were involved. Korean engineers exhibited an exceptionally urgent desire to master the technology.

How important has the development of the petrochemical industry been for Korea's economic development? This has been a controversial issue. Proponents have emphasized the forward linkages of the industry into the textile and plastics industries, the transfer of technical skill and knowledge to other industries, and the rapid gains in efficiency in the industry. Critics have emphasized that the capital intensity of the petrochemical complex imposed high opportunity cost. The resources devoted to the petrochemical sector were not available for other investments in even more promising ventures. They also point to even higher rates of gains in multifactor productivity in the less capital-intensive sector than in petrochemicals.

Sources: Adapted from J. L. Enos and W. H. Park, *The Adoption and Diffusion of Imported Technology: The Case of Korea*, London: Croom Helm, 1988. The Enos–Park study also includes an excellent study of the adoption, absorption, and diffusion of synthetic fiber technology in Korea. For the broader political and economic context, see J. J. Stern, J. Kim, D. H. Perkins, and J.-H. Yoo, *Industrialization and the State: The Korean Heavy and Chemical Industry Drive*, Cambridge, MA: Harvard University Press, 1995.

In addition to the advantages of raw material location, the oil price increases generated both the economic and the political resources necessary to achieve cooperation from the multinational oil and petrochemical firms. By the late 1970s the growth of specialized engineering firms made it possible for almost any new producer in an oil-producing country to obtain access to the most modern petrochemical production technologies (Arora et al., 1998, 1999). The effect of the shift in location advantage and the availability of technology and financing was rapid growth of capacity in the petrochemical industry in developing countries, particularly in East Asia and North Africa in the early 1980s (Table 8.1, Figure 8.3). Substantial investment also took place in several new developed-country petroleum exporters such as Norway and Alberta (Canada).

By 1990 the developing petroleum-exporting countries were accounting for approximately 10% of petrochemical production and an even larger share of exports. By the mid-1990s almost all new investment in petrochemical development was located in the oil- and gas-exporting countries. There were, in contrast, almost no economically

Table 8.1 Major Chemical Plants Completed in Developing Countries, 1980–1986

Plant and Country	Operators	Output (kte/year)
	Ethylene	
Al Jubail, Saudi Arabia	Sabic/Shell	656
Al Jubail, Saudi Arabia	Sabic	500
Mexico	Pernex	500
Yanbu, Saudi Arabia	Sabic/Modil	450
Triunto, Brazil	Copesui	420
Taiwan	CPC	385
Yeochun, South Korea	—	350
Arun, Indonesia	Perramina	330
Pulau Ayer, Singapore	PCS	300
Aliaga, Turkey	Perkim	300
Ras Lanuf, Libya	National Oil Corp.	300
Umm Said, Qatar	Qatar Petroleum/Cdf Chimie	280
	LDPE	
Al Jubail, Saudi Arabia (LLDPE)	Exxon/Sabic	130
Yanbu, Saudi Arabia (LLDPE)	Mobil/Sabic	200
Aliaga, Turkey	Perkim	150
	HDPE	
Yanbu, Saudi Arabia	Sabic/Mobil	90
	PVC	
Ameriya, Eqypt	EPC	80
Al Jubail, Saudi Arabia	Sabic/Lucky	200

Sources: The data in this table has been brought together from a variety of sources on developments in the global petrochemical industry. Principal sources include stockbrokers' reports and data; data supplied by companies and industry associations; and reports in trade journals.

viable opportunities for petrochemical investment in the non-oil- and gas-producing developing countries.

TOWARD MATURITY

The growth of the petrochemical industry in the United States and other developed countries has slowed substantially since the early 1970s. In 1989 the authors of the MIT Commission on Industrial Productivity report noted that

> High oil prices, fluctuations in foreign exchange rates, environmental regulations, excess capacity, and a cyclical downturn in the early 1980s created a financial squeeze on American chemical firms. Part of their response was to retreat from markets in the rest of the world and to sell assets, but they also reduced R&D expenditures as a

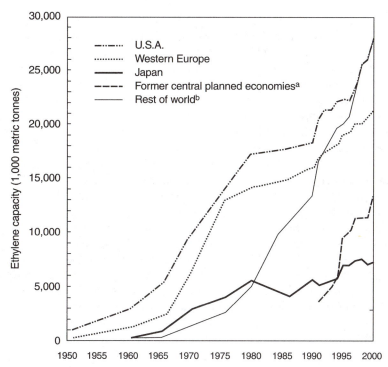

Figure 8.3 Ethylene capacity by world region, 1950–2000. [a] Former central planed economies here include Eastern Europe including F. S. U., China, and North Korea. [b] Rest of world data for 1950–1990 exclude data for former central planed economies. (*Source:* Adapted from Keith Chapman. *The International Petrochemical Industry: Evolution and Location*, Oxford: Blackwell, 1991:16. Data for 1991–1999 are from *The Oil and Gas Journal*, Tulsa, various issues. Data for 2000 are projected.)

fraction of sales even as sales declined. They cut back on basic research to focus on near term, incremental product or process improvements to improve profitability. The firms survived the financial crisis, but in the long-run no company can compete in this industry unless it is competitive in the science underlying the industry. (Dertouzos et al., 1989:15)

In retrospect it seems apparent that the slowdown in the growth of the chemical industries since the early 1970s in the United States and in Western Europe was due to factors more fundamental than the "oil shocks" of 1973 and 1979 or the global depression of the early 1980s. The MIT Commission identified several factors operating at the global level.

An important factor on the demand side was a slowing of opportunities for the substitution of plastics, polymers, and similar products for natural materials in consumer markets, at least in the advanced industrial countries. On the supply side an important factor was that by the 1970s the chemical industry, particularly the petrochemical sector of the industry, had largely become a commodity business. Process technology was roughly comparable worldwide. Development of state-of-the-art petrochemical production capacity in countries that had advantages in terms of both feedstock availability and cost contributed to declining profitability for U.S. and Western European companies. New entrants into the market, particularly the large oil companies, sharpened price competition and further reduced profit margins.

The MIT Commission also argued that the increasing reliance on specialized engineering firms for research and development, and on engineering contracting firms for plant construction, although contributing to the rapid diffusion of technology, had the effect of reducing incentives for R&D. In addition the American chemical industry was confronted by the cost of responding to increased government regulation in the areas of toxic chemicals and pollution control.

An indicator of technical maturity was a dramatic slowdown in innovation in products, processes, and equipment beginning in the 1960s. According to Dertouzos et al. (1989:192) "there were 63 major advances in the chemical industry between 1930 and the early 1980s, including major plastics and fibers and such products as fiberglass, herbicides, flame retardants, epoxy adhesives, high nitrogen fertilizers and catalytic convertors for automobiles. Of these 63 advances, 40 came in the 1930s and 1940s. Twenty emerged in the 1950s and 1960s, and only 3 in the 1970s and early 1980s." This slowdown in technical advance, combined with a slowing of growth in demand, was accompanied by a slowing of growth in labor productivity in the U.S. organic chemicals industry: from 6.6% per year in 1963–1974 to 3.2% per year in 1976–1979 and 1.0% per year in 1979–1985 (Huffstutler and Bingham, 1988).

In addition to these forces operating at the global level, the U.S. chemical industry faced several particular problems. One is the resurgence of the European chemical industry. By the early 1990s the four largest chemical companies in the world were ICI in Great Britain and the three IG Farben successor companies in Germany—Bayer, Hoechst, and BASF (Table 8.2). Each was substantially larger than IG Farben prior to its post-World War II dissolution and larger than DuPont, the largest U.S. company. Furthermore, the European companies, reversing the early post-World War II trend, have penetrated the U.S. market—six ranked among the 20 largest U.S. chemical companies in the early 1990s. Although the U.S. chemical industry remains competitive on a world scale its share of the world chemical market has declined substantially from close to fifty percent of OECD production in the late 1950s to approximately one-quarter in the late 1990s (Arora and Gambardella, 1998).

How has the chemical industry in the United States and other industrial nations responded to market and technological maturity? One response has been to restructure out of the more competitive heavy chemicals commodity sector. The effect has been further consolidation of the commodity chemicals into the hands of the major oil companies. A second response was to redirect research effort away from new and improved processes in the heavy chemical sector and toward new and improved specialty chemicals and into the pharmaceutical and biotechnology industries. By the

Table 8.2   Principal Chemical Manufacturers by Chemical Sales and R&D, 1996

Rank[a]	Manufacturer and Country	Chemical Sales (millions of dollars)	R&D as percentage of Chemical Sales
1	BASF (Germany)	26,519.3	4.9
2	Hoechst (Germany)	19,545.3	3.0
3	Bayer (Germany)	19,543.3	4.9
4	Dow Chemical (United States)	18,988.0	4.0
5	Dupont (United States)	18,044.0	na
6	Shell (Great Britain / Netherlands)	14,631.3	na
7	Novartis (Switzerland)	13,111.3	6.5
8	ICI (Great Britain)	12,629.7	na
9	Exxon (United States)	11,430.0	na
10	Elf Aquitaine (France)	10,501.0	3.0
11	Rhone–Poulenc (France)	9,117.2	3.1
12	Dainippon Ink & Chemicals (Japan)	8,696.2	na
13	Toray Industries (Japan)	7,860.4	na
14	Mitsubishi Chemical (Japan)	7,797.7	na
15	Monsanto (United States)	7,267.0	na

Note: Excluded where possible are formulated products such as pharmaceuticals and cosmetics, specialty equipment energy, and other nonchemical operations. NA, not available.

[a]Ranking based on chemical sales only.

Source: Adapted from Margaret Sharp, "Innovation in the Chemicals Industry." In *The Handbook of Industrial Innovation.* Mark Dodgson and Roy Rothwell, eds. Aldershot, England: Elgar Elgar, 1994:172. Data are from Patricia L.Layman, "Slowdown for Global Top 50," *Chemical Engineering News* 75 (29) (July 21, 1997):15–17.

late 1980s, commodity chemicals accounted for a much smaller share of total sales for chemical companies. At Dow Chemicals, for example, the proportion dropped from 63 to 35% and at Monsanto from 61 to 35% between the mid- and late-1980s (Dertouzos et al., 1989:197; U.S. International Trade Commission, 1985). By the late 1980s almost three-quarters of Monsanto's sales were accounted for by pharmaceuticals, herbicides, and agricultural biotechnology.

The European petrochemical industry has also been forced into substantial restructuring. Adjustments had been delayed by an initial effort to expand capacity to compete with the emergence of increased production of petrochemicals in the petroleum-exporting countries. Adjustment was also slowed by the fact that in Western Europe 40% of the petrochemical capacity was accounted for by state-owned or state-influenced companies. Since the mid-1980s, however, there has been substantial restructuring and downsizing in the European industry (Grant et al., 1988:202–211). The industry has shifted substantial production capacity to the United States and Asia. There has, as with U.S. chemical firms, been a redirection of scientific and technical effort into areas such as pharmaceuticals and biotechnology.[25] In 1998 a merger

---

[25] For a more detailed discussion of the restructuring of the chemical industry since 1980 see Arora and Gambardella (1998). For the diversification into biotechnology, see Chapter 10.

between Hoechst (Germany) and Rhone-Poulenc (France) created a new firm that is the leading producer of pharmaceuticals, veterinary medicine, and agrochemicals worldwide. Consolidation has continued through the 1990's.

As the chemical industry has matured it has also come into increasing conflict with the rising demands, particularly in the more developed countries, for improvements in environmental quality (Chapter 12). The chemical industry slogan of the 1950s "better living through chemistry" has been reversed. During the 1970s and 1980s the chemical industry came to be regarded as one of the dominant sources of hazardous industrial waste. It is being forced to meet the challenge of designing cleaner technologies—processes and product technologies that generate less waste and emissions. Pollution-control capital and operating expenditures in the chemical industry have risen substantially (Esteghamat, 1998). This demand has also led to the rise of a new field of industrial engineering termed "industrial ecology," which is concerned with the recycling of industrial by-products and waste materials (Allen, 1995:233–276; Chapter 12).[26]

PERSPECTIVE

What conclusions can be drawn about sources of technical change from the history of the chemical industry? In the early history of the industry resource endowments or relative factor endowments, such as the availability or lack of agricultural raw materials, coal, petroleum, and natural gas, played an important role in inducing technical change. Both the successful exploitation of abundant resources and the overcoming of the constraints imposed by resource scarcity have been highly dependent on the development of substantial scientific and technical capacity. The development of the human capacity to advance and manage development has enabled resource-poor countries such as Japan and Korea to develop internationally competitive chemical industries. The failure to develop such capacity has continued to limit the ability of resource-rich countries, such as the former U.S.S.R. and the Gulf oil producers, from taking full advantage of their resource endowments.

The chemical industry has also had important spillover impacts on technology development in related industries. It was one of the first to generate demand in the industrial sector for chemists and chemical engineers. It became, in many countries, a "school" for the training and transfer of technical skills and knowledge to other sectors. The products made available by the chemical industry, particularly as they became available at lower cost, induced further technical change in industries such as textiles, agriculture, and pharmaceuticals.

As it enters the twenty-first century the chemical industry is facing the classical problems of technological maturity. Technological progress in both process and product technology has become increasingly dependent on basic research, but

---

[26] The environmental effects of materials production are discussed in more detail in Chapter 12.

individual firms have reduced their R&D budgets, particularly in the more basic areas. Increasingly, solutions are being sought in R&D cooperation and in mergers and consolidation. It is doubtful that the chemical industry can ever again play the dynamic role in economic growth in the presently developed countries that it played between the mid-1870s and the mid-1970s.

REFERENCES

Achilladelis, B., A. Schwarzkopf, and M. Cines. "A Study of Innovation in the Pesticide Industry: Analysis of the Innovation Record of an Industrial Sector." *Research Policy* 16 (1987):175–212.

Achilladelis, B., A. Schwarzkopf, and M. Cines. "The Dynamic of Technological Innovation: The Case of the Chemical Industry." *Research Policy* 19 (1990):1–34.

Allen, D. "The Chemical Industry: Process Changes and the Search for Cleaner Technologies." In *Reducing Toxics: A New Approach to Policy and Industrial Decision Making*, Robert Gottlieb, ed., pp. 233–276. Washington, DC: Island Press, 1995.

Arora, A., and A. Gambardella. "Evolution of Industry Structure in the Chemical Industry." In *Chemical and Long-Term Economic Growth: Insights from the Chemical Industry*, A. Arora, R. Landau, and N. Rosenberg, eds., pp. 379–414. New York: John Wiley and Sons, 1998.

Arora, A., and A. Gambardella. "Chemicals." In *U.S. Industry in 2000: Studies in Competitive Performance*. D. E. Mowery, ed., pp. 363–398. Washington, DC: National Academy Press, 1999.

Arora, A., R. Landau, and N. Rosenberg. *Chemicals and Long-Term Economic Growth: Insight from the Chemical Industry.* New York: John Wiley and Sons, 1998.

Arora, A., R. Landau, and N. Rosenberg. "Dynamics of Comparative Advantage in the Chemical Industry." In *The Sources of Industrial Leadership*, D. Mowery and R. Nelson, eds., pp. 217–267. Cambridge, UK: Cambridge University Press, 1999.

Ayres, R. U. "Industrial Metabolism." In *Technology and Environment,* J. H. Ausubel, R. A. Frosch, and R. Herman, eds., pp. 23–49. Washington, DC: National Academy Press, 1989.

Borkin, J. *The Crime and Punishment of I. G. Farben.* New York: The Free Press, 1978.

Brock, W. H. *Justus von Liebig: The Chemical Gatekeeper.* Cambridge, UK: Cambridge University Press, 1997.

Chapman, K. *The International Petrochemical Industry: Evolution and Location.* Oxford, UK: Basil Blackwell, 1991.

Cockburn, I., R. Henderson, L. Orsenigo, and G. P. Pisano. "Pharmaceuticals and Biotechnology." In *U.S. Industry in 2000: Studies in Competitive Performance.* D. E. Mowery, ed., pp. 363–398. Washington, DC: National Academy Press. 1999.

Dertouzos, M. L., R. K. Lester, R. M. Solow, and The MIT Commission on Industrial Productivity. *Made in America: Regaining the Productive Edge.* Cambridge, MA: MIT Press, 1989.

Enos, J. L. *Petroleum Progress and Profits: A History of Process Innovation.* Cambridge, MA: The MIT Press, 1962.

Enos, J. L., and W. H. Park. *The Adoption and Diffusion of Imported Technology: The Case of Korea.* London: Croom Helm, 1988.

Esteghamat, E. "Structure and Performance of the Chemical Industry under Regulation." In *Chemical and Long-Term Economic Growth: Insights from the Chemical Industry,* A. Arora, R. Landau, and N. Rosenberg, eds., pp. 341–372. New York: John Wiley and Sons, 1998.

Freeman, C. "Chemical Process Plant: Innovation and the World Market." *National Institute of Economic Review* 45 (1968):29–57.

Freeman, C., ed. *The Economics of Innovation.* Aldershot, UK: Edward Elgar, 1990.

Futer, W. F. *History of Chemical Engineering.* Washington, DC: American Chemical Society, 1980.

Grant, W., W. Paterson, and C. Whitston. *Government and the Chemical Industry: A Comparative Study of Britain and West Germany.* Oxford, UK: Oxford University Press, 1988.

Hignett, T. P. *Fertilizer Manual.* Dordrecht: Kluwer Academic Publisher, 1985.

Hikino, T., T. Harada, Y. Tokuhisa, and J. A. Yoshida. "The Japanese Puzzle: Rapid Catch-Up and Long Struggle." In *Chemicals and Long-Term Economic Growth: Insights from the Chemical Industry,* A. Arora, R. Landau, and N. Rosenberg, eds., pp. 103–136. New York: John Wiley and Sons, 1998.

Hohenberg, P. H. *Chemicals in Western Europe: 1850–1914—An Economic Study of Technological Change.* Chicago, IL: Rand McNally, 1967.

Houghton, O. A. "Seven Decades of Chemical Engineering." *Chemical Engineering Progress* 73/1 (1972):89–104.

Hounshell, D. A., and J. K. Smith, Jr. *Science and Corporate Strategy: DuPont R&D, 1902–1980.* Cambridge, UK: Cambridge University Press, 1988.

Huffstutler, C., and B. Bingham. "Productivity Slows in the Organic Chemical Industry." *Monthly Labor Review* 11/3 (June 1988):44–51.

Hughes, T. P. "Technological Momentum in History: Hydrogenation in Germany, 1898–1933." *Past and Present* (August 1969):106–132.

Landau, R. "Entrepreneurs, Managers and the Importance of Finance." *Daedalus* 125 (1996): 19–37.

Landau, R., and N. Rosenberg. "Successful Commercialization in the Chemical Process Industries." In *Technology and the Wealth of Nations,* N. Rosenberg, R. Landau, and D. C. Mowery, eds., pp. 73–119. Stanford, CA: Stanford University Press, 1992.

Layton, E. T., Jr. "The Dimensional Revolution: The New Relations between Theory and Experiment in Engineering in the Age of Michelson." In *The Michelson Era in American Science, 1870–1930,* S. Goldberg and R. H. Stuewer, eds., pp. 23–38. New York: American Institute of Physics, 1988.

Mowery, D. C., and N. Rosenberg. *Paths of Innovation: Technical Change in 20th Century America.* Cambridge, UK: Cambridge University Press, 1998.

Mueller, W. F. "The Origins of the Basic Inventions Underlying DuPont's Major Product and Process Innovations, 1920 to 1950." In *The Rate and Direction of Inventive Activity: Economic and Social Factors,* Richard R. Nelson, ed., pp. 323–346. Princeton, NJ: Princeton University Press, 1962.

Reynolds, T. S. "Defining Professional Boundaries: Chemical Engineering in the Early 20th Century." In *The Engineer in America,* T. S. Reynolds, ed., pp. 343–365. Chicago, IL: University of Chicago Press, 1991.

Rosenberg, N. "Technical Change in Chemicals: The Role of University-Industry Relations." In *Chemical and Long-Term Economic Growth: Insights from the Chemical Industry,*

A. Arora, R. Landau, and N. Rosenberg, eds., pp. 193–230. New York: John Wiley and Sons, 1998a.

Rosenberg, N. "Chemical Engineering as a General Purpose Technology." In *General Purpose Technology and Economic Growth,* E. Helpman, ed., pp. 167–192. Cambridge, MA: MIT Press, 1998b.

Sagers, M. J., and T. Shabad. *The Chemical Industry in the USSR: An Economic Geography.* Boulder, CO: Westview Press, 1990.

Saramma, A. D. *Petroleum Industry: A Study of Its Spread Effects.* New Delhi: Deep and Deep Publications, 1984.

Scriven, L. E. "On the Emergence and Evolution of Chemical Engineering." In *Perspectives in Chemical Engineering: Research and Education*, Clark K. Colton, ed., *Advances in Chemical Engineering*, Vol. 16. New York: Academic Press, 1991.

Servos, J. W. "The Industrial Relations of Science: Chemical Engineering at MIT, 1900–1939." *ISIS* 71 (1980):531–549.

Solo, R. *Across the High Technology Threshold: The Case of Synthetic Rubber.* Norwood, PA: Norwood Editions, 1980.

Spitz, P. H. *Petrochemicals: The Rise of an Industry.* New York: John Wiley & Sons, 1988.

Stokes, R. G. *Opting for Oil: The Political Economy of Technological Change in the West German Chemical Industry, 1945–1961.* Cambridge, UK: Cambridge University Press, 1994.

Taylor, G. D., and P. E. Sudnik. *DuPont and the International Chemical Industry.* Boston, MA: Twayne Publishers, 1984.

Tilden, W. A. *Chemical Discovery and Invention in the Twentieth Century.* New York: E. P. Dutton, 1936.

United States International Trade Commission. *The Shift from U.S. Production of Commodity Petrochemicals to Value-Added Specialty Chemical Products and the Possible Impact on U.S. Trade.* Washington, DC: United States International Trade Commission, 1985.

Walsh, V. "Invention and Innovation in the Chemical Industry: Demand-Pull or Discovery-Push?" *Research Policy* 13/4 (1984):211–234.

Williamson, H. F., and A. R. Daum. *The American Petroleum Industry. Vol. I: The Age of Illumination.* Evanston, IL: Northwestern University Press, 1959.

Williamson, H. F., R. L. Andreano, A. R. Daum, and G. C. Klose. *The American Petroleum Industry. Vol. II: The Age of Energy, 1900–1959.* Evanston, IL: Northwestern University Press, 1961.

Wittcoff, H. A., and B. G. Reuben. *Industrial Organic Chemicals in Perspective. Part I: Raw Materials and Manufacture; Part II: Technology, Formulation and Use.* New York: John Wiley & Sons, 1980.

CHAPTER 9

The Computer and
Semiconductor Industries[1]

A former director of research at IBM has claimed that "the computer is the analogy in our time of the steam engine in its technical evolution and its revolutionary impact" (Gomory, 1983:577). Certainly, the computer is the most significant technological development of the second half of the twentieth century. Technical change in the computer and semiconductor industries has been associated with continuous and exceedingly rapid shifts in both scientific and technological frontiers. In contrast to the chemical industry (Chapter 8), in which engineers were largely responsible for both scientific and technical innovation, in the computer and semiconductor industries physicists and mathematicians also played important roles in advancing both knowledge and technology.

Also significant is the fact that the computer, semiconductor, and software industries were initially strongly nourished by the military and space programs. Much of the early exploratory research on computers was conducted by university-based researchers operating under government contract. And although the initial research on semiconductors was financed by the private sector, government procurement for military and space applications accounted for a high percentage of sales over the first decade of the industry's development. The research and development that led to the Internet were supported by the Defense Advanced Research Project Agency (DARPA) as a way for its contractors to more effectively communicate with each other. Even after commercial markets became well established substantial public resources continued to be allocated to research and education in support of the computer industry.

The development of computer technology has passed through at least four "generations," identified by reference to the technology of the basic components. The first generation of computers operated with vacuum tubes. These were followed, starting with the IBM 7000 series introduced in 1959, with machines that used transistors. A third generation with integrated circuits began with the IBM Series/370 machine in 1971. The fourth generation, which began in 1975, has involved

[1] I am indebted to William Carlson, Jason Cwik, Mark Jorgensen, Richard N. Langlois, Edwin T. Layton, Ian Maitland, Arthur Norberg, and Robert W. Seidel for comments on an earlier draft of this chapter.

very large-scale integration (VLSI). A fifth generation, now under way, will involves a change in architecture, from sequential to parallel processing, rather than in components.

I do not attempt in this chapter to provide a detailed history of the development of the computer and the transistor. Nor do I cover related developments in the electronics industry, information technology, or in communications and in industrial production made possible by the computer and the transistor. I do attempt to identify some of the major landmarks in the evolution and application of computer technology. A continuing theme that runs throughout this chapter is the consistent underestimation of latent demand by even the most optimistic scientists, engineers, entrepreneurs, and managers who developed the computer, semiconductor, and software industries.

FROM CALCULATORS TO COMPUTERS[2]

Electronic digital computers were preceded by a long history of the development of mechanical and electromechanical tabulating machines. In the latter decades of the nineteenth century numerous office machines—typewriters, adding machines, cash registers, mechanical calculators, and billing and accounting device—were introduced. During and immediately after World War II major efforts were made, with the support of the military and other branches of the government, to develop fully electronic computing machines.

Tabulators and Calculators

In 1886 Herman Hollerith, a statistician employed at the U.S. Census Office, designed and built an electrically run tabulator that used punched card inputs and electrical card reading. The Hollerith machine was able to process data in one-third the time it would have taken with handwritten tally sheets. Hollerith formed the Tabulating Machine Company in 1896. Following a merger in 1910 the firm was named the Computing–Tabulating–Recording Company. In 1924 the name of the company was changed to International Business Machines (IBM). Another Census Office employee, James Powers, invented an automatic card-punching machine and, in 1911, formed the Powers Tabulating Machine Company, which merged with Remington Rand in 1927.

These two firms would eventually become major players in the computer industry. The first fully automatic calculator was a product of collaboration between Harvard University and IBM. In 1937 Howard H. Aiken, then a graduate student at Harvard,

---

[2] In this section I draw primarily on Pugh (1984), Bashe et al. (1986), Katz and Phillips (1982), Shurkin (1984), Flamm (1987:42–93), Campbell-Kelly and Aspray (1996), and Mowery and Rosenberg, (1998: 135–151). Pugh (1984:301–312) contains a very useful "chronology."

prepared a memorandum on digital computation devices. The memorandum was brought to the attention of an IBM executive who in 1939 arranged for IBM to fund Aiken's project. The Automatic Sequence Controlled Calculator (Mark I) using standard off-the-shelf components was completed in 1944. The Mark I, an electromechanical machine, could add, subtract, multiply, divide, and table reference. Input data were entered on punched cards and the output was recorded either on punched cards or on an electric typewriter. Later, models were built for the Navy and the Air Force.

● **BOX 9.1**

THE ORIGIN OF THE COMPUTER

Historians of technology typically trace the origins of the modern automatic computer to Charles Babbage (1792–1871). Babbage was impressed by errors he discovered in astronomical tables and by the potential of instructing (programming) machines by the use of punched cards, such as those used with the Jacquard textile looms. Around 1820 Babbage conceived the idea of a "difference engine," which could progressively take first, second, third, and higher differences in successive numbers until a constant difference was found. It could then reverse the process (integrate) and produce the original numbers by successive additions. He initially designed a small calculator that could tabulate certain mathematical calculations to 12 decimals.

The engine's potential for reducing the enormous labor involved in producing accurate tables led to interest from Sir Humphrey Davies and the Royal Society and to financial support from the British Navy beginning in 1823. In the last 9 years of the grant period Babbage worked on an alternate concept, the "analytical engine." This machine continued the use of difference procedures. The operations were also to be controlled by Jacquard-type punch cards. However, the technology available to Babbage—cogs, wheels, and axles— was not adequate for such a project. In 1842 the government discontinued its support of Babbage's research.

Although Babbage failed to produce an operating device he identified the principal components of a digital computer. A calculator based on the Babbage difference engine concept was produced by a Swedish firm in 1855. Until recently, Babbage's work was generally believed to have been forgotten until it was rediscovered in the mid-1930s. It now seems clear, however, that it influenced Percy Ludgate's work on an analytical engine prior to World War I, Leonardo Torres y Quevedo's work on an electromagnetic arithmometer exhibited in 1920, and Vannevar Bush's work on a differential analyzer in the 1930s.

Sources: Adapted from Barbara Goody Katz and Almarin Phillips, "The Computer Industry." In *Government and Technical Progress: A Cross-Industry Analysis,* Richard R. Nelson, ed., New York: Pergamon Press, 1982:163, 164. For greater detail see Anthony Hyman, *Charles Babbage: Pioneer of the Computer,* Princeton: Princeton University Press, 1982, and Brian Randell, "From Analytical Engine to Electronic Digital Computer: The Contribution of Ludgate, Torres and Bush," *Annals of the History of Computing* 4 (October 1982):327–341.

Electronic Digital Computers

The first all-purpose, electronic digital computer was developed by John W. Mauchly and J. Prosper Eckert and associates at the University of Pennsylvania's Moore School of Electrical Engineering.[3] The project was funded by the Aberdeen Ballistics Research Laboratory. The Army was interested in a computer that could reduce the enormous labor involved in calculating artillery firing tables. The Mauchly–Eckert machine, called the Electronic Numerical Integrator and Calculator (ENIAC), was completed in 1946. It was capable of computing more than 1000 times faster than any then-available electromechanical machine. The successful completion of the ENIAC, by stimulating further military demand, provided a great impetus for the development of the computer industry, even though the original version had no immediate commercial applications.

A second project developed by the Moore School group, the Electronic Discrete Variable Computer (EDVAC), had an even more important impact on future computer development. It incorporated the concept of a stored program and sequential processing developed by Mauchly, Eckert, and Goldstine of the Moore group and the mathematician John von Neumann of Princeton University's Institute for Advanced Study (Princeton, NJ). In what came to be referred to as the von Neumann architecture, the processing unit of the computer fetches instructions from a central memory that stores both data and programs, operates on the data (for example, adds or subtracts), and returns the results to the central memory. Every computer system developed since the late 1940s has continued to be based on the von Neumann architecture in which both instructions and data reside in a common memory.

The role of the public sector in driving the development of the electronic computer can not be overemphasized. During and after World War II units of the military such as the Army Aberdeen Ballistics Research Laboratory, and the Office of Naval Research, as well as the National Bureau of Standards, the Bureau of Census, and the National Advisory Committee for Aeronautics, were active in mobilizing resources to improve

---

[3] The electronic digital computer was conceived by John V. Atanasoff of Iowa State University in 1937. In December 1940 he demonstrated a small prototype and in 1941 he published a paper on the theory and design. In 1941 Mauchly visited Iowa State University to examine the computer, read the technical papers, and discuss his work with Atanasoff. Iowa State failed to patent the Atanasoff design. Although the issue remains controversial, most historians of computing now credit Atanasoff rather than Mauchly and Eckert as the inventor of the electronic digital computer (Shurkin, 1984:114–116).

computational capabilities. Several universities initiated programs to develop stored-program machines [for example, the University of California–Berkeley (CALDIC), the University of Illinois (ILLIAC), and the University of Michigan (MIDIAC)]. Although the cadre of people working on computer development came from universities, government departments, and industry, funding came almost entirely from the federal government (Flamm, 1988).[4]

Commercial Development

In the postwar period there was a rapid formation and consolidation of firms formed to exploit the new technology. Eckert and Mauchly formed the Electric Control Company in June 1946 and the Eckert–Mauchly Computer Corporation in 1947. Because they had difficulty raising sufficient capital to complete their development work, Eckert and Mauchly accepted an offer to be acquired by Remington Rand in 1950. They brought with them several contracts, including one with the Bureau of the Census to develop an EDVAC-type computer called UNIVAC. Personnel from the Naval Communications Supplementary Activity, who had been involved in developing computers in support of the Navy's work in cryptology, formed Engineering Research Associates (ERA) in St. Paul, Minnesota in 1946. ERA also ran into financial difficulties and agreed to be acquired by Remington Rand in 1952. With its Eckert–Mauchly and ERA operations, Remington Rand controlled a significant fraction of the total computer engineering capacity in the United States (Tomash and Cohen, 1979).

Both Eckert–Mauchly and the ERA group were disappointed by Remington Rand's lack of enthusiasm for commercial computer development. This lack of enthusiasm was shared by other office equipment firms. In 1950 IBM president Thomas Watson Sr. asserted that the one Selective Sequence Electronic Calculator (SSEC) developed by IBM and on display at the IBM headquarters in New York City was sufficient to "solve all the important scientific problems in the world involving scientific calculations" (Katz and Phillips, 1982:171). And he saw only limited commercial possibilities for computers.

It was the Korean War that led to a decision by IBM to test the market for commercial computers. Armed with 30 letters of intent from government agencies and defense-related firms, IBM initiated the Defense Calculator project in early 1951. When the prospective rental price of $15,000 per month was announced all

---

[4] In spite of the apparent openness of communication in the early years of computer development, bitter tensions arose over priority in invention and intellectual property rights. Much of the controversy centers on von Neumann's June 30, 1945 memorandum, "First Draft of a Report to the EDVAC," which had the effect of weakening the attempts by Eckert and Mauchly to maintain intellectual property rights in later litigation. In 1946 Eckert and Mauchly became involved in a dispute over patent rights with the administration at the University of Pennsylvania and were forced to resign. For a highly personal account of these and related controversies, see Shurkin (1984).

but six clients withdrew (Katz and Phillips, 1982:177). IBM decided, however, to go ahead with development of the machines, to be renamed the IBM 701. "The IBM 701 was formally dedicated on April 7, 1953. Its replacement of the SSEC as the show piece of IBM's computer capability signaled IBM's transition to a new era of postwar electronic computer technology" (Pugh, 1984:32). IBM was not alone, however. ERA announced the most advanced machine commercially available, the ERA 1103 (later renamed the UNIVAC 1103), in February 1953. In response, IBM decided to produce an improved model, the IBM 650 Magnetic Drum Calculator. The 650, released in 1954, could originally output only 111 scientific or 291 commercial operations per second. It was, however, very flexible in its uses, carried a relatively low price, was reliable, was easy to install and maintain, and used punched-card input and output. Over time the 650 was upgraded by adding alphabetic capacity, a printer, and other features. "The 650 was the 'Model T' of computers" (Katz and Phillips, 1982:178). Almost two thousand were eventually produced.

Government contracts played a critical role in the development of IBM's capacity to market a fully transistorized commercial computer, the IBM 7090 (Usselman, 1993). In the early 1950s IBM became involved in a U.S.–Canadian cooperative effort to build a computerized air defense system, the Semi-Automatic Ground Environment (SAGE). SAGE was designed to detect alien aircraft, select appropriate interceptor aircraft, and determine antiaircraft missile trajectories. The system had to store and process large amounts of information and coordinate several computers in real-time mode. The success of the SAGE project led to a number of important developments that resulted in lower costs and improved performance.[5]

In 1952 the Justice Department filed an antitrust suit against IBM over its policy of only leasing its tabulating machines, monopolization of the punch card market, and price discrimination in punch card sales. But government policy, by also supporting IBM research and development, was operating at cross purposes. IBM president Thomas J. Watson Jr. agreed to a consent decree resolving the antitrust suit in 1956. His strategy was to forego dominance in the mature tabulating equipment and card

---

[5] The SAGE project has been characterized as one of the major learning experiences in technological history (Hughes, 1998:15–67). The innovations made in connection with the SAGE project at IBM and MIT included (1) techniques to manufacture ferrite core memory rapidly, inexpensively, and reliably, (2) computer-to-computer telecommunications, (3) real-time simultaneous use by many operators, (4) keyboard terminals for man–machine interaction, (5) simultaneous use of two linked computers, (6) ability to devolve certain functions to remote locations without interfering with the dual processors, (7) use of display options independently of dual processors, (8) inclusion of an interrupt system, diagnostic programming, and maintenance warning techniques, and (9) associative memory development (Katz and Phillips, 1982:185). Other IBM 7090 innovations included (1) radically new parallel architecture, permitting several operations to be performed simultaneously, (2) standard modular systems component technology, (3) printed circuit cards and improved back-panel wiring, (4) an 8-bit byte, (5) greatly improved transistors and the means for manufacturing them, (6) a common mode for attaching peripherals, (7) a combination of decimal and binary arithmetic, and (8) combined fixed and variable word length operations (Katz and Phillips, 1982:189).

markets and pursue dominance in the computer market. The contracts with the Air Force and Atomic Energy Commission contributed substantially to the realization of Watson's strategy (Jorgensen, 1996).

IBM SETS THE MAINFRAME STANDARD

By the mid-1950s IBM accounted for over two-thirds of the world sales of computers. Its experience in the production of mechanical office equipment was important to its success in manufacturing computer peripherals such as printers, tape drives, and magnetic drums. But IBM's market dominance rested more on its reputation for strong customer service in the office equipment field than on the technical superiority of its machines. IBM faced several difficult problems in the early 1960s. It was producing six different lines of computers, all of which had incompatible operating systems. Competitors were beginning to make inroads into IBM's market share. Software was accounting for a greater proportion of the cost of computer systems. Users were increasingly reluctant to pay for the higher costs of upgrading their software in order to adopt newer, more powerful machines (Fransman, 1995:139).

Many of these difficulties were resolved with the introduction of the IBM System/360 in 1965. The 360 family of computers used integrated circuits rather than transistors. They had large ferrite core memories with fast access times, multiprogramming, which allowed many programs to run simultaneously,[6] and an improved disk memory that allowed the machines to store more information in secondary memory than had previously been thought possible. The 360 machines ranged across a variety of customer requirements. Yet, no matter what size, all contained the same solid-state circuits and would respond to the same set of instructions. IBM had traditionally purchased the components for its office machines and computers from outside suppliers. In producing the 360 line IBM integrated further backward into component production, although it continued to purchase its integrated circuits. As it came on line the System/360 platform rapidly became the industry standard for the rest of the 1960s and the 1970s (Bresnahan, 1999:227–228).

The decision by IBM to commit to the System 360 line had not been easy. It required an enormous technical and financial commitment. The 360s, although more advanced than IBM's 8000 line that was already in the development stage, would not reach the market until the mid-1960s. In the meantime it was anticipated that General Electric and perhaps several other firms would bring a more advanced machine to the market. "IBM literally 'bet the company' on its 360 decision" (Katz and Phillips, 1982:218).

---

[6] Development of reliable, high-speed ferrite core memories that could be mass produced at low cost was probably the most important innovation that made stored-program computers a practical commercial reality" (Pugh, 1984:ix).

"System/360 was a runaway success and made IBM the powerhouse in mainframe computers for the next thirty years" (Gates, 1995:38).[7] Before the 360, IBM computer designs were intentionally incompatible with those from other companies. The goal was to make it difficult and expensive for customers to switch to a different brand. This changed in 1970 when Eugene Amdahl, who had been a senior engineer at IBM, formed a new company, also named Amdahl, and built computers that were fully compatible with the IBM 360 software. Soon other firms were also building machines that were compatible with IBM software. "By the mid 1970s the only mainframe companies doing well were those whose hardware could run on IBM's operating systems" (Gates, 1995:34).

In spite of its commercial success, the IBM System/360 was technically obsolete almost as soon as the first model was delivered. The limits to ferrite core memory were already apparent to technical managers both within IBM and the computer industry generally (Pugh, 1984:253). In June 1972, IBM introduced the System/370 Model 145, the world's first commercial computer with an all semiconductor main memory. By the end of the 1970s the memory market, which had been dominated for two decades by ferrite cores, was dominated by semiconductors chip memories.

Because of the importance of semiconductors in the development of the computer industry since the early 1970s, I discuss in the next section the development of the transistor, the integrated circuit, and the microprocessor.

THE TRANSISTOR REVOLUTION[8]

It was understood even in the 1940s that the speed, reliability, physical size, and heat-generating properties of the vacuum tubes used for memory drives would become a major technical constraint on electronic switching. A number of alternative technologies, including gas tubes (thyratons and trionodes) and magnetic amplifiers,

---

[7] In 1965 the U.S. computer industry was composed of IBM and the "seven dwarfs." The composition (Shurkin, 1984:261) was as follows:

Rank	Company	Share of Sales
1	IBM	65.3
2	Sperry Rand	12.1
3	Control Data	5.4
4	Honeywell	3.8
5	Burroughs	3.5
6	General Electric	3.4
7	RCA	2.9
8	NCR	2.9

By the mid-1990s only IBM was still active in the computer industry under its 1965 corporate identity.

[8] In this section I draw heavily on Nelson (1962), Levin (1982), Katz and Phillips (1982), Mowery (1983:183–197), Riordan and Hoddeson (1997), and Mowery and Rosenberg (1998:124–135, 151–152). For a discussion of the scientific and engineering aspects of semiconductors, including circuit design, engineering, and fabrication, see Warner (1965).

were developed and tested before the transistor was universally adopted in the late 1950s.

The Point-Contact Transistor

The transistor emerged out of research led by William Shockley of the Bell Telephone Laboratories solid-state research group. The group both advanced the theory of semiconductors and made important advances in transistor technology. Shockley had joined Bell Laboratories in 1936 after receiving his Ph.D. in physics from MIT. Shortly after Shockley joined Bell Laboratories Dr. Mervin Kelly, Director of Research, emphasized to Shockley his interest in developing electronic switching, in which metal contacts would be replaced by electronic devices, in the telephone system. By the late 1930s Shockley began to consider the possibility of an approach based on solid-state physics rather than vacuum tubes. During World War II Shockley, on leave from Bell, worked first on radar and later on operations research for the Navy and Air Force. After the war Bell formed a Solid-State Department to develop new knowledge that could be used in the development of completely new and improved components and apparatus for communications systems. A subgroup, in which Shockley participated, was selected to work on semiconductors (Box 9.2).

Shockley had proposed a semiconductor amplifier, a prototype of what was later called a field-effect transistor (FET), in 1939. In attempting to understand why Shockley's prototype failed, two colleagues, John Bardeen and Walter Brattain, produced the first working transistor (the point-contact design) on December 15, 1947 following a month of highly charged creative activity—"the magic month." Their work led to Shockley's effort to design a third type of transistor—the "junction" or "bipolar" transistor. A satisfactory design was not achieved, however, until the spring of 1950. Advances in process engineering, particularly the development of techniques for producing germanium and silicon crystals, were required before production of the junction transistor would become commercially feasible.[9]

Although the transistor is sometimes cited as an example of a "science push" invention, a clear demand-side need for such a device was apparent at Bell Laboratories. The motives of Bell Telephone Laboratories in establishing the solid-state physics group were that major advances in the field were likely to be fruitful in improving communications technology. Shockley's own interests embraced both the prospect of advancing semiconductor theory and of developing a solid-state amplifier.[10] The

---

[9] See particularly Shockley (1976:597–620) and Teal (1976:621–639).

[10] "Motivations were of a mixed variety—both practical and scientific. . . . What actually went on was a mixture which fits into the pattern of 'creative-failure methodology' . . . that some years later I analyzed and defined as *respect for the scientific aspects of practical problems*. . . . The attempt to make a semiconductor amplifier was blocked by a practical problem. . . . Our research on the science related to surface states led to new experimental conditions and to new observations. Then the breakthrough observations of 17 November 1947 showed at long last how to overcome the blocking effect of the surface states. Thus new possibility motivated the "will to think" phenomena that led to the peak of creativity that followed immediately

approach that Shockley and his associates at Bell undertook was to make an electric amplifier of semiconductor material. This approach involved advancing the understanding of electron flow in semiconductor materials. Although the research by Shockley, Bardeen, and Brattain was directed to the solution of an immensely important engineering problem, it was regarded as sufficiently fundamental that they received the Nobel Prize for Physics in 1956 for their research on semiconductors and discovery of the transistor effect.

Integrated Circuits

Until the late 1950s transistors were discrete devices—each transistor had to be connected to other transistors on a circuit board. In 1952 G. W. A. Dummer, a British physicist, had suggested that the next logical step beyond the transistor was electrical equipment built in a solid block with no connecting wires. Research on integrated circuits during the 1950s was stimulated very largely by military demand for modular circuit designs that could reduce the number and complexity of interfaces with missile guidance and detection devices. In the mid-1950s Texas Instruments, then the leader in silicon transistor production, initiated a research program under the direction of Jack Kilby to repackage the semiconductor products (transistors, resistors, and capacitors) as single components to reduce circuit interconnections. In 1958 Kilby developed a first very crude integrated circuit. The costs of assembling the separate components of Kilby's device by hand were too expensive for commercial application. At about the same time, however, Robert Noyce and Gordon Moore at Fairchild Semiconductor independently invented the integrated circuit. The invention involved incorporating very small transistors and resistors on a small sliver of silicon and adding microscopic wires to interconnected adjacent components. This "planar" process made it possible to produce an integrated circuit on a single semiconductor—a "chip." Initially this "contact printing" process used in fabrication produced imperfections that resulted in a low yield of usable chips. It was not until the late 1970s that the optical instrument company Perkin-Elmer, working in cooperation with Raytheon, developed a photolithography fabrication process that produced a high yield—in the 90% range—of usable chips. This development occurred just in time for these low cost chips, made by Intel, to be used in the first IBM PCs.

The Microprocessor

The third major innovation in the development of the semiconductor industry was the microprocessor. There are two types of integrated circuits that were critical in the

---

thereafter" (Shockley, 1976:618, 619). The development of the transistor has also been cited as a classic example of the impact of technology on science. Before the advent of the transistor in 1948, solid-state physics was an obscure subdiscipline. The invention of the transistor induced both universities and the private sector to devote substantial new resources to the field (Rosenberg, 1994, Chapter 2).

development of computers. One, a memory chip, allows the computer to temporarily remember programs and other information. The other is the microprocessor that processes information rather than storing it (Box 9.2).

Technical progress in the integrated circuit era has moved along a trajectory toward increasing the density of circuit elements per chip (Figure 9.1). The first microprocessor was developed by Intel in 1969–1970 (Chapter 3). At that time Intel was a leader in the design and production of memory chips. It had invented the first dynamic random-access memory (DRAM) chip a year earlier. In 1969 Intel was contacted by Busicom, a Japanese manufacturer of hand-held calculators, about developing memory chips for its machines. Marcian (Ted) Hoff, the Intel engineer assigned to the job, proposed an elegant solution to the problem of meeting the requirements of Busicom. Hoff put the central processing unit (CPU), the "brain," on a single silicon chip and attached two memory chips, one to move data in and out of the CPU and the other to provide the program to drive the CPU. In effect this meant that a simple computer was created on a single chip (Fransman, 1995:168). Instead of designing chips for different applications it was now possible for a single microprocessor chip to be used for many different applications.[11] Demand for microprocessors developed rather slowly, though, with initial applications in consumer electronics and instrumentations, until the potential market for the minicomputer and the microcomputer became apparent in the mid and late 1970s.

● **BOX 9.2**

SEMICONDUCTORS AND INTEGRATED CIRCUITS DEFINED

Semiconductors

A semiconductor is an electric circuit component, such as a transistor (or chip), that is fabricated from a material that is neither a good conductor of electricity nor a good insulator. Pure silicon is a poor conductor of electricity. But by a process called "doping" a number of atoms of another substance can be introduced into a silicon crystal to alter its electrical properties. By applying different voltages to each of the doped regions current flowing through a transistor can be used to amplify or switch signals. The device that switches signals is called a digital device because it turns the flow of current on or off in response to a signal. Because of this quality digital devices are able to perform the logical operations within a computer. A transistor is made of three layers of

---

[11] For a more personal account, see Moore (1996:55–80). See also Chapter 4.

silicon. Each layer is doped with impurities in such a way that electric current passing through the transistor can be influenced by the much smaller current applied to the middle layer.

Integrated Circuit

An integrated circuit is a single chip that has more than one active device on it, such as transistors, diodes, resistors, or capacitors, as part of an electric circuit, which are inseparably associated with a continuous base material (substrate). The first integrated circuits, developed by Jack Kilby at Texas Instruments, required the connections between the circuit elements to be made by hand. Robert Noyce and Gordon Moore at Fairchild developed a technique (the planar process) that allowed the metallic connections to be incorporated on a silicon surface in a batch process. Integrated circuits are classified according to the number of transistors per integrated circuits:

	Transistors/Circuit
Small-scale integration (SSI)	$< 10^2$
Medium-scale integration (MSI)	$10^2 – 10^3$
Large-scale integration (LSI)	$10^3 – 10^5$
Very large-scale integration (VLSI)	$10^5 – 10^6$
Ultralarge-scale integration (ULSI)	$> 10^6$

There are three main types of integrated circuits: (1) memory chips, (2) microprocessors, and (3) microcomponents. Random-access memories (RAMs) temporarily store data or information. Dynamic random-access memories (DRAMs) are designed to store large amounts of data. Static memories (SRAMs) are faster but hold less information. Read-only memories (ROMs) store data more permanently than RAMs. Erasable programmable read-only memories (EPROMs) allow data programs to be easily erased and reprogrammed. Microprocessors, computers on a chip, are the central processing units in computers. They provide the instructions (logic) for processing information. Microcontrollers are somewhat simpler and less powerful than microprocessors and have their main applications in automotive, automation, and processing machinery.

Source: Adapted from Harald Gruber, *Learning and Strategic Product Innovation: Theory and Evidence for the Semiconductor Industry,* Amsterdam: North Holland, 1994:143–161 and Jeffrey T. Macher, David C. Mowery, and David A. Hodges, "Semiconductors." In *U.S. Industry in 2000: Studies in Competitive Performance*, David C. Mowery, ed., pp. 245–285. Washington, DC: National Academy Press, 1999.

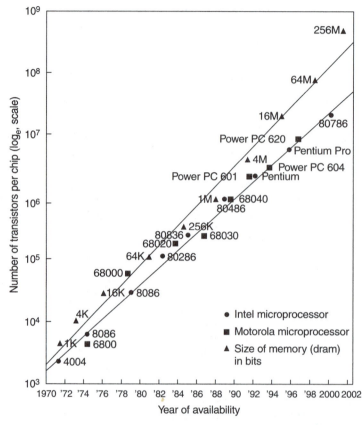

Figure 9.1 Transistor densities on micro processors and memory chips. (*Source:* Adapted from G. Dan Hutchinison and Jerry D. Hutcheson, *Technology and Economics in the Semiconductor Industry*, Scientific American 274 (January 1996:61).

Diffusion of Semiconductor Production[12]

During the 1950s and early 1960s AT&T, including Bell Laboratories, its research arm, and Western Electric, its manufacturing arm, was the source of a disproportionately large share of major semiconductor product and process inventions. AT&T was enjoined by a 1966 antitrust decree from selling semiconductors in the commercial market. It was restricted to production for the military and space market and for its own needs. Partly as a consequence it adopted a liberal licensing policy and a permissive attitude toward the movement of personnel to other firms, two decisions that would greatly influence the development of the computer industry.

---

[12] In this section I draw heavily on Tilton (1971).

Firms that were already producing receiving tubes, such as General Electric, RCA, and Sylvania, comprised a second group of semiconductor producers. These firms moved quickly into the production of transistors, even though semiconductor technology threatened the economic viability of their receiving tube operations. These firms also became important sources of technical innovation well into the late 1960s. By the mid-1950s all eight producers of receiving tubes were manufacturing transistors.

A third group of semiconductor firms was new to the industry. They included several large diversified firms, such as IBM, Motorola, Hughes, and Texas Instruments, that were engaged in other branches of the electronics industry at the time they entered the semiconductor industry. In another subgroup were companies established specifically to manufacture semiconductors. Many were start-up companies founded by scientists and engineers who had left Bell Laboratories or other established firms.

The margins between these several groups were somewhat porous. For example, William Shockley left Bell Laboratories and joined Raytheon, then left to found his own company, Shockley Laboratories. He recruited a group of very talented young scientists and engineers from industry and universities, and embarked on an effort to develop and manufacture new semiconductors. In 1967 several Shockley scientists and engineers left to start their own firm. They received initial financial assistance from Fairchild Camera and Instruments, which received an option, which it exercised in 1968, to buy the new firm. By the early 1970s a number of other firms had been started by alumni of Fairchild. These spin-offs were encouraged by the military procurement policy of "second sourcing" to avoid becoming dependent on a single supplier. Dosi argues that spin-offs were possible because "the American industry as a whole was already on the technological frontier. Scientists and managers, in leaving their previous companies, were doing so in order to exploit commercially, on their own, the cumulated experience of previous successes and failures acquired in established research laboratories and institutions or in their previous companies" (Dosi, 1984:42).

By the mid-1960s there were over 50 firms actively engaged in semiconductor production in the United States. Although Western Electric accounted for less than 10% of the market share in the mid-1950s, it, together with Bell Laboratories, accounted for over 40% of semiconductor patents awarded to U.S. firms. The receiving tube firms accounted for 25% of market share and about 40% of patents. In contrast, the new firms, which accounted for about two-thirds of the market share, accounted for less than 50% of patents.

Most innovations were initially introduced by the larger, well-established firms. However, new firms, most of them located in California's Silicon Valley, were mainly responsible for diffusion of the innovations. But why were the new firms relatively underrepresented in terms of invention? One reason is that the founders of many of the start-up firms "brought their technology with them" when they left their previous employers. Their entrepreneurial efforts left them with little time and fewer resources for R&D. Several new firms—Texas Instruments, Motorola, and Fairchild—did, however, emerge as leaders in both market share and in research.

The U.S. semiconductor industry quickly developed a distinctive organization. It consisted of two large computer producers, IBM and Remington Rand, and a large number of "merchant" companies. The U.S. antitrust environment worked to the disadvantage of integrated producers. AT&T was limited by the 1956 consent degree that restricted it to produce transistors only for its own use. IBM, sensitive to potential antitrust action, also produced only for its own internal use. The entry of new firms was greatly facilitated by the availability at low cost of AT&T's technological information, the ease with which technical personnel could move from the established companies, and the availability of venture capital. In the 1960s and 1970s new firms that specialized in production of semiconductors grew rapidly. Even so, in the early 1970s the eight largest merchant firms still accounted for 67% of industry shipments (Tyson, 1992:89, 90).

Demand for semiconductors was initially dominated by procurement for military and aerospace applications (Table 9.1). Since the 1970s the direction of spillover has been reversed. The military market has become increasingly dependent on developments in commercial technology. The development of integrated circuits has had the effect of increasing the fixed costs of innovation, which became a barrier to the entry of new firms into the industry. In the 1970s U.S. producers shifted substantial assembly capacity to low-wage developing countries, particularly Mexico, Taiwan, Singapore, Malaysia, and Korea. By the late 1970s over 80% of the semiconductors produced by U.S. firms were assembled and tested in low-wage locations overseas. By the early 1980s Japanese semiconductor makers were turning out memory chips of much higher quality for lower prices than even the leading U.S. producers such as Intel. Apparently the American industrial structure, which had earlier been so conducive to product innovation, was highly vulnerable to competition from a Japanese industry that was even more highly integrated. By the late 1980s Intel had withdrawn from memory chip production to concentrate on the production of microprocessors.

Writing in the early 1980s, Mowery (1983) drew a number of important inferences from the history of the semiconductor industry. Initial developments took place in an environment insulated from the forces of market demand—to meet the internal needs of the Bell Telecommunications system and the highly specific performance and technological requirements of the military market. He argues that neither a demand pull nor a supply push perspective provides an adequate understanding of subsequent evolution of the semiconductor industry. Rather, its evolution has reflected a logic internal to the technology itself—a "technical trajectory." My own perception is somewhat different than that of Mowery. The developments that led to the transistor and to the semiconductor were induced by the perception at Bell Laboratories in the 1930s that the vacuum tube was becoming a serious technical constrain on electronic switching. It was this perception that led to the establishment of the solid-state physics group, directed by Shockley, at Bell Laboratories and to the development of the transistor and the semiconductor.

Table 9.1 Distribution of U.S. Semiconductor Sales by End Use

End Use	Percentage of Total Semiconductor Sales in Year								
	1960	1965	1968	1972	1972	1974	1974	1979	1985
Computers	30	24	35	27	28	32	29	30	20
Consumer products (calculators, watches, automobiles, etc.)	5	14	10	18	22	22	24	28	25
Industrial products (process controls, test equipment, office and telecommunications equipment)	15	26	20	30	26	30	33	37	48
Military/aerospace	50	36	35	25	24	16	14	10	7

Source: Years 1960–1979 from Richard C. Levin, "The Semiconductor Industry," in *Government and Technical Progress: A Cross-Industry Analysis*, Richard R. Nelson, ed., New York: Pergamen Press, 1987:19. Year 1985 from Richard N. Langlois, Thomas A. Pugel, Carmela S. Haklisch, Richard R. Nelson, and William G. Egelhoff, *Microelectronics: An Industry in Transition*, Boston: Unwin Hyman, 1988:33.

MINICOMPUTERS AND MICROCOMPUTERS

By the late 1950s progress in semiconductor development was beginning to open up the possibility of designing smaller and less expensive computers. In 1957 Kenneth Olson, a former IBM employee, and Harlan Anderson founded Digital Equipment Corporation (DEC) with $70,000 in venture capital funding. Olson was committed to a vision of computers that were smaller, easier to operate, and much less expensive than the IBM mainframe. In December 1959 DEC demonstrated a prototype of the Programmed Data Processor (Rifkin and Harrar, 1988).

"The first DEC computer, the PDP-1 sold for $120,000, contained 4K bytes of memory, was the size of a refrigerator, and included a cathode ray television-like video display built into the console" (Langlois, 1992:7). DEC's first great commercial successes came with the introduction of the PDP-6, the first time-sharing computer, in 1964 and a powerful but inexpensive minicomputer, the PDP-8, in 1965. The PDP-8 was the first computer to use integrated circuits. It could be rented for $525 a month, less than 10% of the cost of IBM's smallest System 1360. The initial success of the PDP-8 encouraged the entry of other firms such as Data General, Scientific Data Systems, Hewlett-Packard, and Wang to enter the minicomputer market. By the late 1960s IBM itself was forced to put a minicomputer on the market.

From a longer term perspective the significance of the minicomputer is that it represented a first step in the displacement of the mainframe dinosaurs and the centralized computer centers established to operate and manage them. By sacrificing speed to achieve lower cost the market for computers was broadened to include a much wider range of scientific, engineering, and business applications. Incorporation of the adaptable and open UNIX™ operating system developed by Bell Laboratories contributed to the emergence of a community of programmers independent of both hardware manufacturers and the large centralized computer operations. They contributed to the development of an environment among both programmers and users that facilitated the development and diffusion of the "microcomputer" (Rochlin, 1997:2021).[13]

The transition to the microcomputer had to await Intel's 1969 development of the programmable chip (described earlier). The development of the microcomputer dates from the announcement in the January 1975 issue of *Popular Electronics* of the Atari 8800. The Atari was little more than a box with an Intel microprocessor in it. Its only input/output devices were lights and toggle switches on the front panel. It possessed a number of "slots" that allowed for additional memory and input/output devices. These slots hooked onto the microprocessor by a system of wires called a "bus." The Atari bus, termed the S-100 because of its 100-line structure, became the early industry standard. In spite of Atari's "impoverished capabilities" it gave rise to the growth of third-party suppliers of add-ons and stimulated the organization of hobbyists who shared information and software (Langlois, 1992:11).

Apple in the Lead

The Homebrew Computer Club of northern California became a seedbed for both the technical advances and commercial development of the new generation of computers. Bill Millard, who helped develop the first Atari clone, founded Computerland, a franchise chain of computer stores. William Gates and Paul Allen, who later founded Microsoft, wrote a programming language, Beginner's All-Purpose Symbolic Instruction Code (BASIC), for the Atari. Stephen Wozniac, who was employed at Hewlett-Packard, and Steven Jobs, who worked for Atari, formed Apple Computer. Industry leadership failed to recognize the market potential of the microcomputer even when it was staring them in the face. When Steve Wozniac attempted to interest his employer, Hewlett-Packard, in providing financial support he was rebuffed with the remark—"HP doesn't want to be in that kind of market" (Langlois, 1992:14).

Jobs and Wozniac started assembling circuit boards in Jobs' parents' garage. While Wozniac worked to refine the design, Jobs persuaded a hobbyist friend and owner of the Byte Shop to order 50 of the first Apple. The Apple II, demonstrated first at the West Coast Computer Fair in the spring of 1977, was the first commercially successful microcomputer. "Sales began to take off. The company took in $750,000 by the end of fiscal 1977; almost $8 million in 1978; $48 million in 1979; $117 million in 1980 (when the firm went public); $355 million in 1981; $583 million in 1982; and $983 million in 1983" (Langlois, 1992:15).

---

[13] I do not, in this chapter, attempt to cover the development of specialized workstations for graphics and other design applications, or the web servers that act as intermediaries in linking personal computers. The major server producers are Compaq, IBM, Hewlett-Packard, and DEC.

What accounted for the Apple II's phenomenal success? Some observers have argued that the Apple II was technologically inferior to the Commodore PET and the Tandy TRS-80 Model I introduced at about the same time. In one respect, however, it did have technological superiority. Wozniak designed a wholly novel approach of encoding data on a disk and a vastly simplified controller circuit.

> In the end, however, what made the Apple II so successful was its compromise between technology and marketing. Under Jobs' influence the machine was compact, attractive, and professional in appearance. Under Wozniak's influence, it was elegantly designed, easy to both use and to manufacture. . . . Yet thanks to Wozniak's slots, it was also still a system, able to draw on the large crop of external suppliers of software and add-ons that quickly sprang up. (Langlois, 1992:16)

A second factor was that VisiCalc, the first spreadsheet program, was adopted by Apple in 1979 and for a full year was marketed only for the Apple II.

By the early 1980s the shape of the microcomputer had become more clearly defined. The WordStar processor with capacity almost equivalent to the more expensive stand-alone word processor was introduced. By 1981 a microcomputer

> was a system comprising a number of more-or-less standard elements: a microprocessor unit with 64K bytes of RAM memory; a keyboard, usually built into the system unit; one or two disk drives; a monitor and a printer. The machine ran operating-system software and applications programs like word processors, spreadsheets, and database managers. The market was no longer primarily hobbyists but increasingly comprised businesses and professionals. (Langlois, 1992:19)

The result was a series of inexpensive laptop portable machines, such as the Osborne I and the Kaypro I, designed as a single package that users could simply plug in "like a toaster."

IBM Forges Ahead

The event that established the pattern for computer development in the 1980s was not, however, the bundled portables. It was the IBM PC. Like the Osborn and the Kaypro, the PC was not at the technical frontier. But unlike the bundled portables, it was an open system that was designed to accommodate reconfiguration, expansion, and upgrading.

The development of the PC required a complete departure from IBM's traditional approach to computer development. In July 1980 William Lowe was charged by the IBM Corporate Management Committee with getting IBM into the market for desktop computers. Lowe insisted that if he were to succeed he would need complete autonomy from the IBM bureaucracy. "The only way we can get into the personal computer business is to go out and buy part of a computer company, or buy the central processing unit (CPU) and software from people like Apple or Atari—because we can't do this within the culture of IBM" (Chposky and Leonois, 1988:9). The Management

Committee was unwilling to put IBM's name on someone else's computer; they gave Lowe the mandate he had asked for. "Lowe hand-picked a dozen engineers and within a month they had produced a prototype. The Committee approved and gave Lowe a deadline of one year to market" (Langlois, 1992:21).

To achieve the desired autonomy Lowe moved the project to Boca Raton, Florida. Philip Estridge, who succeeded Lowe, was allowed to operate as if the project were an independent start-up company. He relied heavily on outside vendors for parts and software. The one technical advance was the choice of the Intel 8088 microprocessor. Choosing the Intel 16-bit chip meant that the IBM PC could not use existing operating systems designed for 8-bit chips. IBM turned to Microsoft, which in turn bought an operating system for the Intel 8088 created by a local software house, put the finishing touches on it, and sold it to IBM as MS-DOS (microsoft-disk operating system).

Estridge also departed from IBM tradition in fabrication. All parts were put up for competitive bids from outside suppliers. Internal IBM divisions were told that they could submit bids like anyone else. Another radical departure from IBM tradition was in the marketing of the PC. The president of IBM's Office Products Division objected to pushing the PC off on his sales force! The PC group turned to retail outlets such as Computerland and Sears Business Centers, which they insisted could handle the new machine more effectively than the IBM Product Centers.

The IBM PC was an instant success. Sales exceeded forecasts by several multiples. The 13,533 machines it shipped in the first 4 months of 1981 lagged far behind demand. Order backlogs accumulated. By 1983 the PC had captured 26% of the market (Langlois, 1992:23). But by 1988 the market share of IBM and IBM-compatible computers had fallen to less than 25% from a 65% share in 1986. Part of the explanation was that after 1983, when Estridge was promoted to head the Entry Systems Division, the Boca Raton operation began to lose much of its earlier autonomy. Without the autonomy to adapt its technology and marketing strategies to changes in the market, its early advantages were dissipated. Constrained by the traditional IBM culture, many of the engineers who had participated in the development of the PC left IBM. A series of successor machines encountered technological difficulties and either floundered in the market or were discontinued.[14]

Apple Falls

While IBM was becoming the dominant force in the personal computer market in the early 1980s, Apple was floundering. After the initial success of Apple II, Jobs felt that Apple should develop a new machine with more capacities so as to capture a higher share of the business market. Over the objections of Wozniak, Jobs pushed a strategy that was the opposite of the IBM strategy. Apple attempted to develop its

---

[14] For a highly personal account of IBM's initial success in the development of the PC and of the subsequent mismanagement that led to its loss of market share in the personal computer field, see Chposky and Leonois (1988).

own disk drive for Apple III. It tried to write the bulk of its software in-house. Jobs insisted that all circuitry fit on one board. The Apple III was designed as a closed rather than an open system. Almost all of the first units shipped in 1980 failed and had to be returned.

Jobs' restricted conception of computer architecture also plagued the introduction of the Lisa in 1983 and the first Macintosh in 1984. The Lisa did contain an important innovation that eventually enabled Apple to again assume a leadership role. During a visit to the Xerox Palo Alto Research Center, which was developing advanced ideas for microcomputers in 1979, Jobs was introduced to bit-mapped graphics, overlapping windows, and a pointing control device called the mouse. These developments were incorporated into the Lisa. The Lisa had major deficiencies—it lacked software, it was slow, it was expensive, and it had limited commercial success. In 1985 John Scully, who had been brought into Apple in 1983, replaced Jobs as president. Over the next several years Scully managed to upgrade the Macintosh into a more capable business machine, capitalize on its desktop publishing and graphics capabilities, and challenge IBM for market share. By the mid-1990s Apple was again in trouble. Jobs was brought back to replace Scully. In 1998 Macintosh introduced a redesigned model, the I-Mac, that again began to reclaim market share.

As the Macintosh became a more open modular machine, IBM adopted a windows-type software and word-processing software features similar to those of the Macintosh. Since the mid-1980s, however, no company has been able to achieve as large a share of the world market share as Apple in the early 1980s or IBM in 1985 (Table 9.2). By the late 1990s Apple's market share had declined to less than 5%. IBM's market share had fallen to below 10%.

The Silverlake Project

At the same time that IBM was stumbling so badly in realizing its PC's market potential, it had underway in Rochester, Minnesota, almost unnoticed by its senior executives in Armonk, New York, a development that would lead to IBM dominance in the mid-range computers.[15] In 1956 IBM, in a move to achieve greater geographic diversification, located a facility to produce punch card readers in Rochester. Over the next decade the facility evolved into the site of an IBM "development laboratory" in which engineers and programmers began designing, building, and manufacturing a line of computers for small-to medium-sized business.

Rochester's first computer, the IBM System/3, came onto the market in 1969. It began offering a range of ready-to-use software applications for tasks such as manufacturing, management, construction planning, transportation scheduling, office administration, and other applications. Successor machines—System/32 in 1975, System/34 in 1977, and System/36 in 1983—each brought more capabilities and power to its users. In 1978 Rochester introduced a new machine, the System/38,

---

[15] In this section I draw heavily on Bauer et al. (1992), Boyett et al. (1993), and Soltis (1996).

Table 9.2 Worldwide Market Share of Personal Computers by Company, 1980–1997

Company[a]	1980	1985	1990	1997	1999
Compaq	0.0	1.5	3.9	13.9	14.4
IBM	0.0	16.1	11.9	9.9	9.0
Dell	0.0	0.0	0.6	6.3	10.9
Hewlett-Packard	1.3	1.1	1.2	6.2	6.4
Packard-Bell-NEC	4.6	4.1	7.8	5.3	4.9
Gateway	0.0	0.0	na	3.7	—
Fijitsu	0.0	2.4	2.6	3.5	—
Toshiba	0.8	0.8	3.7	3.3	—
Acer	0.0	0.0	0.7	3.2	—
Apple	13.9	7.9	7.5	2.6	—
Other	79.4	66.1	62.1	42.1	—
Total	100.0	100.0	100.0	100.0	100.0

[a]The firms listed are the 10 firms with leading market shares in the fourth quarter of 1997 as reported by Mathew Rose and Brandon Mitchener, "Siemens to Quite PC Market, Sell Plants to Acer," *Wall Street Journal* (April 24, 1998):A13. Data for 1980, 1985, and 1990 are from Richard N. Langlois, "External Economies and Economic Progress: The Case of the Microcomputer industry," *Business History Review* (Spring 1992):34–35. Langlois obtained the 1980, 1985, and 1990 data from Dataquest. I have not been successful in obtaining data from Dataquest. Data for 1999 are from Dwight Silverman, "Direct Competition: Compaq Tries to Regain Lost Momentum," *Huston Chronicle*, (September 18, 1999):B1.

developed by a team led by Frank Soltis, that embodied a number of new functions. It was also much easier to program. But its software was incompatible with the System/3 line, and it achieved only limited market penetration. By the early 1980s the Rochester operation was losing market share. Digital Equipment Corporation (DEC), which had earlier developed minicomputers for scientific, engineering, and other technical applications, began making mid-range computers for commercial business. Hewlett-Packard, Wang Laboratories, Data General, Tandem, and National Cash Register (NCR) as well as Olivetti (Italy), Nixdorf (Germany), and Fujitsu (Japan) also began to capture market share. Between the late 1970s and the mid-1980s IBM dropped from approximately a third to less than 10% of the global market share for mid-range computers.

Word began spreading in the computer industry and among customers that IBM was withdrawing from the mid-range computer market. Questions were being raised in Rochester about IBM's long-term commitment to the mid-range computer. "There were predictions that the mid-range computer would go the way of the dodo, squeezed into extinction by the shrinkage in size and price of mainframes and the explosion in the power and popularity of personal computers" (Bauer et al., 1992:157). But on July 21, 1988, IBM unveiled a new mid-range computer, the AS/400. The AS/400 was the most successful new computer introduction in IBM history. By January 1990 over 100,000 AS/400s had been sold. If IBM–Rochester had been a separate company it would have been the second largest computer firm in the world—second only to the rest of IBM.

What happened between 1975 and 1988? The first step was that the IBM staff at Rochester accepted the fact that unless something changed rapidly Rochester was on the way out. The second step was that Pat Hansen, an experienced engineer–programmer–entrepreneur at Rochester, insisted that the route to salvation had to be a hybrid of the System/36 and System/38 machines. In spite of substantial opposition he got permission to set up his own "skunk works"—a small five-person team to explore his proposal. The project was named Silverlake after the small reservoir below the Rochester power plant. The third step was a decision by IBM headquarters in 1986 to transfer Tom Fury to Rochester to head the development laboratory. His appointment reflected IBM's commitment to remain in the mid-range market. If it did not, it could not fulfill its strategy of providing a top-to-bottom product line—from mainframes down to personal computers.

After several months spent acquainting himself with the Rochester laboratory, Fury set up a task force to reorganize the laboratory with the object of developing a structure that would be able to deliver a new family of computers to IBM customers in little more than 2 years—as compared to the traditional 4 to 5 years it took for IBM to launch a new product. He was able to introduce a market-driven, in contrast to the traditional product- or technology-driven, orientation to the development group. He supervised the development of software programs to assist in making research and development and priority-setting and resource-allocation decisions. A sequential development cycle was replaced by a parallel development cycle, which was reinforced by the concept of "getting it right the first time." Customers from around the world were involved in both the development and the launching of the new AS400 series. At its launching the AS400 family consisted of five models ranging in price from $15,000 to $1.0 million. It was manufactured in the United States, Europe, and Japan with components supplied from 37 locations. Its software included 2500 applications available in 27 languages and dialects. By 1990 IBM Rochester was no longer the "nice little business" it had been in 1980.

The development of the AS400 illustrates a new style of industrial entrepreneurship. It is substantially different than the role played by individual inventors, engineers, and scientists who developed the early computers, and it is even further removed from the heroic leaders who contributed to the early technological development in the electric light and power (Chapter 7) and chemical (Chapter 8) industries. Over 2500 engineers and programmers were involved in designing and developing the AS400. There were heros, but their skills were more conceptual and organizational than technological. In 1990 IBM Rochester received the Malcolm Baldridge National Quality Award.[16]

---

[16] The Malcolm Baldridge National Quality Award was established in 1987 by the U.S. Congress in response to concern in the United States about competition with Japan. There was particular concern that one of the main factors leading to the emergence of Japan as an economic power was the quality of its industrial exports (Bauer et al., 1992:179–202). For IBM Rochester's 1990 Malcolm Baldridge National Quality Award application see Boyett et al. (1993:205–342). See also Chapter 11.

THE SOFTWARE INDUSTRY

Prior to the 1960s computer software hardly existed as a distinct technology or industry. "Software was effectively born with the development by von Neumann of his conceptual architecture for computers. . . . But even after the von Neumann scheme became dominant . . . software remained closely bound to hardware. During the 1950's, the organization designing the hardware generally designed the software as well" (Langlois and Mowery, 1996:55–56). A comprehensive treatment of the computer software (and services) industry would require a separate chapter. But because of its intimate relationship to the development and diffusion of the computer—computer hardware cannot be used without software—it will be useful to identify some of the main developments and structural characteristics of the software industry.[17]

These events were induced by several very special economic characteristics of software production. Software development is very labor intensive. But the cost of reproduction of software is very low or negligible relative to the cost of software development.[18] Furthermore, as software uses expanded to meet the needs of the complex U.S. economy, the ability of computers producers to understand and solve the specific software problems faced by the variety of industries that use information technology is limited. Thus the growth of an independent software industry contributed to the growth in demand for computers.

Three events in the mid and late 1960s contributed to the "disintegration" of the computer and software industries (Steinmueller, 1996:24–26). One was the introduction of the IBM System 360 family of computers beginning in 1964. The System 360 gave independent software service companies and vendors an opportunity to develop and market the same product to a variety of users. A second event was the decision by IBM in 1969 to unbundle the sale of hardware and software. This enabled independent software developers to develop software compatible with IBM products. The third important event was the development of the minicomputer industry. Minicomputers made it possible for small organizations to begin to purchase and use their own computers. Each of the many different uses of minicomputers—"as primary computers in smaller organizations, as 'front ends' for mainframes, in data communication systems, and in process central systems—required very different software" (Steinmueller, 1996:28).

During the 1970s the computer software industry grew at about the same rate as the computer industry. The event that led to explosive growth of the software industry in the United States since the early 1980s was the success of the personal computer. Software development for the personal computer began with the development of

---

[17] In this section I draw primarily on Mowery (1996), Steinmueller (1996:15–52), and Mowery and Rosenberg (1998:1953–1966).

[18] This characteristic is also responsible for the extreme concern about intellectual property protection on the part of the software industry. Software "piracy" has the effect of driving the price of software to the low marginal cost of its reproduction—too low to cover the costs of software development (Steinmueller, 1996:17).

Beginners All-Purpose Instruction Code (BASIC) at Dartmouth College—and its adaptation by Bill Gates and Paul Allen for the Atari 8800 in 1975. Microsoft, the company started by Gates and Allen, also provided the BASIC programming language for Apple, Commodore, and Radio Shack. Users could write their own applications in BASIC rather than buying packaged applications. "Microsoft's strategy was to get computer companies to buy licenses to include our software with the personal computers they sold and pay us a royalty" (Gates, 1995:11). By 1979, Microsoft BASIC had become the industry standard. The firm concentrated on writing programming languages for the profusion of new machines that were appearing (Gates, 1995:43, 44).

When IBM finally became committed to building a personal computer in 1980 it decided, as noted earlier, to buy its microprocessors from Intel and to license its operating system from Microsoft rather than creating software itself. Microsoft in turn bought an operating system for the Intel 8088 16-bit microprocessor from another Seattle software company and hired its top engineer, Tim Patterson. After substantial modification it became the Microsoft Disk Operating System (MS-DOS). IBM called the system PC-DOS. "We gave IBM a fabulous deal—a low, one-time fee that granted the company the right to use Microsoft's operating system on as many computers as it could sell. This offered IBM an incentive to push MS-DOS and to sell it inexpensively. . . . Our goal was not to make money directly from IBM, but to profit from licensing MS-DOS to computer companies that wanted to offer machines more or less compatible with the IBM-PC" (Gates, 1995:49). Within a few years almost all the competing standards for personal computers disappeared. The only successful exceptions were Apple II and Macintosh.

Mowery (1996:9–11) has argued that the U.S. software industry represents a classic case of "lock-in" resulting from the interaction of industry standards and "network externalities" (Chapter 4).[19] Once "first-mover" advantage was established by Microsoft, consumer choice among competing producers was influenced by the number of other adopters. The emergence of the IBM PC architecture as a "dominant design" further reinforced Microsoft's dominance as a supplier of PC operating systems. Mowery also argues that first-mover network externalities were a primary reason for continued segmentation of the software industry structure. It has been difficult for firms that have achieved dominance in one specific industry segment (such as spreadsheets) to successfully enter other segments (such as word processing or databases). By the late 1990s, however, it appeared that Microsoft

---

[19] The structure of the U.S. software industry has been quite different from the structure of the European or Japanese. The European markets are highly fragmented. Most firms tend to specialize in custom software for domestic markets. There are only weak links between industry and universities. It is possible that the development of a more homogeneous European market and common European standards will result in a more international competitive software industry (Malerba and Torrisi, 1996:165–196). The development of the software industry in Japan has been hampered by the fact that the computer industry has not unified around a dominant design, by the Japanese ideographic written language, by a small venture capital market, and by the slow (compared to the U.S.) diffusion of personal computers. The industry is, however, internationally competitive in a number of areas and is dominant in some, such as game software (Baba et al., 1996:104–127).

might be in the process of breaking this historical pattern. As this chapter was being completed Microsoft was under attack by the Justice Department for a broad pattern of anticompetitive behavior. The Federal Trade Commission was also preparing a case against Intel for anticompetitive practices designed to ensure its dominance of the high-end microprocessor market.

Defense-related support has contributed importantly to development of the software industry. Its support has, however, differed substantially from Department of Defense support for computer and semiconductor development. In the case of computers and semiconductors, defense support occurred primarily through procurement. "In software, by contrast, defense related R&D funded computer science in much of the 1950s and 1960s . . . was directed to facilitating advances in fundamental knowledge of computer architecture, software languages and design that found application in both the civilian and defense sectors. . . . Military-civilian spillovers in software occurred as a result of defense-related R&D spending rather than from procurement" (Langlois and Mowery, 1996:14; see also Flamm, 1987:42–92; Norberg and O'Neill, 1996).

At the time this book was written a highly fragmented software industry, fueled both by continuing hardware development and by expanding access to the Internet, was in the process of rapid evolution. The Internet itself involved the transformation of a computer network (ARPANET) established in the 1960s by DARPA (Box 9.3). A primary goal of the transformation was to enable the system to better survive a nuclear attack by removing it points of vulnerability, the central switching stations. Computer architecture was radically redesigned so that computers could function more autonomously with individual machines making decisions about how to reroute a message through an increasingly vast network. This technology was developed over a period of about 15 years and by 1983 the Internet was in place. For its first decade the Internet was conceived primarily as a way for scientific workers to exchange data and work closely together without leaving their laboratories (Norberg and O'Neill, 1996). By the late 1990s, however, the Internet was becoming clogged from recreational use and e-mail. Concern was being expressed that its effectiveness for scientific collaboration was being eroded. New rationing and pricing systems were being proposed (Chapter 13). Both the private sector and the government are attempting to achieve control, for commercial and security purposes, of a system that was originally designed to be uncontrollable (Saco, 1996; Hughes, 1998:255–300).

● BOX 9.3

INVENTING THE INTERNET

The Internet, to which millions of desktop computer users are connected, owes its origin to a project funded by the Defense Deparment Advanced Research Project Agency (ARPA). The initial objective of the ARPANET project, initiated in 1969, was to enable big computers of different design to "speak to each other." In October, 1972, at the first International Conference of Computer Communication in Washington, DC, the ARPANET project team displayed computers made by different manufactures communicating with each other at different sites across the country.

The decision to support the development of ARPANET followed several earlier successful Defense Department efforts in the field of computer communication. The Whirlwind computer developed in the early 1950s for the SAGE air defense system enable people to interact with the information being processed and displayed on a computer screen. Operators could select and highlight desired real time information from the other information being fed into the computer from radar and other sources. The military was interested in the development of a more sophisticated system that could ensure survival of the communications system following an attack that might disable any single control station.

The decision also reflected the pesonal interest of Joseph Licklider, who headed the ARPA Information Processing Techniques Office (IPTO) in the early 1960s, in man–machine interaction. Licklider was impatient with the "batch process" used to process data. To solve a problem using a computer, the researcher had to first formulate the problem; then he or she had to turn to a professional programmer to program the problem for the computer, after that the problem written in computer language was submitted to the operator of a centraly housed computer who placed the program in a queue; and, finally the computer processed the information and printed out the results (Hughes, 1998:261). Licklider visualized a system of "time sharing" in which a single computer located at a central location would be accessed a number of users with individual terminals connected to the central computer by telephone lines.

In 1966 Robert Raylor succeeded Licklider as IPTO head. Taylor secured the services of Lawrence Roberts, an MIT Lincoln Laboratory researcher who had already connected a Lincoln Laboratory computer to one at the RAND Corporation in Santa Monica, to head the ARPANET project to interconnect time sharing computers at seventeen academic, industrial, and government computer centers funded by ARPA. At a planning session it was suggested that if the host mainframe computers were interconnected by small interface computers, the host computers with different characteristics, would be able to interact through the interface computers.

The proposal was resisted by several principle investigators who wanted to develop their own software. Taylor proceeded, however, to award a contract for the development of an interface computer to Bolt Beranek and Newman (BBN) a high-technology firm located near MIT in the Cambridge area. BBN organized a small team to design an Interface Message Processor (IMP). Both the development of the software, which would route message blocks of "packages" through alternative connections, and the engineering design problems turned out to be much more difficult than anticipated.

But the "IMP guys" succeeded in completing development of the basic elements of the Internet nine months after the contract had been let.

In his assessment of the accomplishments of the "IMP boys" Thomas Hughes argued: "Future historians, fully aware of the remarkable development of the worldwide Internet, following hard upon the path-breaking ARPANET, may some day compare the inventive success of the small BBN group to the achievement of Thomas Edison and his small band of associates who invented the electric lighting system" (Hughes, 1998:278). As in the case of Edison's research at Menlo Park there was an intense dialectical interaction between advances in science and technology. Sometimes invention was informed by science and at other times invention came first followed by scientific insight.

Hughes also regards the flat management structure of the ARPANET project as an important institutional innovation. It stood in sharp contrast to the "command and control" structure employed so successfully by the military in the development of earlier air defense and ballistic missile projects. Interaction among the widely dispersed ARPANET engineers and scientists were collegial and meritocratic. Decisions were reached by consensus. Management and work styles were similar to those associated with the small start-up firms in the personal computer and software industries. Hughes also considers the ARPANET project an outstanding model of how the federal government can successfully interact with academic engineers and scientists in a misson-oriented context. And he raised the rather disturbing question: If government leadership and funding is needed to sustain the revolutionary development of computing, and if public leadership and support are still needed to generate other technological revolutions in the future, where will the leadership and the funding come from (Hughes, 1998:256)?

The demonstration of the Internet at the 1972 International Conference on Computer Communication was the defining moment in the diffusion of use of the Internet. It could no longer be considered simply a potential defense application or a research tool. Although its potential capacity as a communications utility was apparent, neither the Defense Department sponors of the research nor the members of the design team anticipated that its primary use would be for personal e-mail rather than for transmitting data or research collaboration.

Source: In this Box I draw primarily on T. P. Hughes, *Rescuing Prometheus*, New York: Random House, 1998:255–300. See also A. L. Norberg and J. E. O'Neill (with K. J. Freedman), *Transforming Computer Technology: Information Processing for the Pentagon, 1962–1968*, Baltimore, MD: Johns Hopkins University Press, 1996; and D. Saco, "Colonizing Cyberspace: National Security and the Internet," Minneapolis, MN: University of Minnesota Department of Political Science, 1996 (mimeo). For a highly personal account see K. Hafner and M. Lyon, *Where Wizards Stay Up Late: The Origins of the Internet.* New York: Simon and Schuster, 1996.

INTERNATIONAL DIFFUSION[20]

The development of the computer and semiconductor industries followed quite different paths in Western Europe and Japan than in the United States. From the initial inventions at Bell Laboratories in the mid-1940s to the late 1960s, most of the new semiconductor technology was developed and introduced by a half dozen U.S. companies. This new technology, however, was transferred in a remarkably short time to firms in Western Europe and Japan. In the 1950s much of the production by European firms was based on licenses with Western Electric covering the strategic Bell Laboratories patents. After the development of integrated circuits European firms found it necessary to make licensing agreements with Fairchild or Texas Instruments. Texas Instruments was particularly active in licensing its technology. It assumed that with technology advancing so rapidly new technology would be obsolete in a year or two and licensing would maximize returns from new technology development.

The patterns of diffusion were somewhat different in the several countries. In Western Europe, established receiving tube firms played a much more dominant role than in the United States (Tilton, 1971; Flamm, 1987:125–172, 1996:24–27). A number of the established receiving tube firms were subsidiaries of U.S. firms. Direct investment by U.S. producers to serve the European market was stimulated by tariff and nontariff barriers that effectively blocked imported semiconductors. The objective was to encourage production in Europe regardless of ownership. Direct foreign investment was encouraged as a substitute for imports. By the 1980s European companies were acting primarily as manufacturing subcontractors or as marketing and distribution arms of American and Japanese companies (Ferguson and Morris, 1993:10). Siemens, however, did emerge as one of the world's major semiconductor firms. Its growth in the 1980s was further stimulated by a U.S.–Japan trade agreement that pushed up the prices of DRAMs. In 1990 Siemens and Toshiba entered into an R&D agreement with IBM for a joint venture to produce 16M DRAMs.

In Japan new firms played a much more important role and foreign subsidiaries a much smaller role in technology transfer than in Western Europe. The lack of foreign subsidiaries in Japan was due to legislation that required government approval of direct investment by foreigners. In the computer and semiconductor industries the government routinely turned down all requests for establishment of joint ventures in which the foreign firm would hold over 50% of the equity. In this section I give primary attention to the diffusion of the computer and semiconductor industries to Japan. The Japanese experience is illustrative of large costs involved in an aggressive national program of technology transfer. As a result of its effort Japan emerged in the 1980s with the capacity to challenge U.S. dominance in the computer and semiconductor industries.

---

[20] In this section I draw heavily on Anchordoguy (1989), Tilton (1971), Fransman (1990), Usselman (1993), and Bresnahan and Malerba (1999).

Computers

Prior to 1960, information technology research in Japan was primarily conducted within government research laboratories, such as those of the Ministry of Trade and Industry Electrochemical Laboratory (MITI/ECL) and the National Telegraph and Telephone Electrical Communication Laboratories (NTT/ECL), and in universities. In this respect Japanese efforts in the 1950s resembled U.S. efforts in the 1940s (Fransman, 1990:13–23).

This changed in 1960, when the Japanese government designated computers as a "strategic industry"—critical to the future development of the country. By that time much of the institutional and industrial infrastructure needed to support the development of a computer industry was already in place. There was an agency—the Ministry of Trade and Industry (MITI)—to coordinate industrial policy, government-controlled investment banks, and the legal authority to control foreign exchange, investment, and imports. Japan had a strong industrial base that included a number of diversified companies already active in consumer-electronics, telecommunications, and heavy electronic equipment.[21] As in other sectors, Japanese firms in the electronics industries were organized into closely linked *keiretsu* that tend to be responsive to government policy.[22] In spite of these advantages, it took over a quarter of a century of substantial government support for Japan to develop a computer industry that was fully competitive with the U.S. industry (Anchordoguy, 1989:19–22).

Government support was not hard to come by. MITI saw the development of computers as consistent with Japanese factor endowments.

> Computers had the characteristics MITI considered important to the nation's long-term economic development—high value added, little raw material or energy input, high skilled labor component, and close linkages with many already established industries. The National Telegraph and Telephone Company (NIT), a national monopoly, would play a role as a promoter and purchaser similar to the military in the U.S. It was precluded by law from manufacturing its own equipment and was interested in encouraging the growth of domestic suppliers. The Ministry of Finance (MOF) was a reluctant supporter because "they knew it would require a lot of money." (Anchordoguy, 1989:20)

MITI viewed IBM as the main threat to the development of a domestic computer industry. IBM had been in Japan since the mid-1920s. After the war it acted quickly to

---

[21] Fransman points out that "the leading Japanese computer companies all have substantial technical competence in telecommunications while none of the U.S. companies have such competencies" (Fransman, 1995:132).

[22] The *keiretsu* groups consist of large vertically integrated firms linked by close buyer–supplier relationships, mutual shareholdings, personnel exchanges, and common ties to a major bank. Each member firm has independent management and is in principle free to operate as it chooses. However, since they own each others shares, have overlapping membership on their boards, and depend on the same bank for finances, there is also a strong tendency for close supplier–customer relationships among members (Anchordoguy, 1989:32–33).

establish a subsidiary in Japan, just prior to the passage of legislation that would have required it to form a joint venture with a Japanese partner. The Japanese government was, however, able to delay IBM plans to produce in Japan until IBM agreed to license all its computer technology to Japanese computer producers. Although IBM was allowed to function as a wholly owned subsidiary, it was forced to operate under severe constraints, including a requirement that it export 60% of its production and that the government approve the introduction of new models. A 25% duty on imported computers, including computers produced in Japan by IBM, was imposed. MITI encouraged Sperry Rand to form a Japanese partnership and market imported UNIVAC machines to counter IBM market power.

Once access to IBM patents was obtained, seven Japanese companies started producing computers. All of the major firms found it useful, in spite of MITI's reluctance to grant approval, to make arrangements with U.S. firms for technical backstopping. Nippon Electric Company (NEC) linked up with Honeywell, Hitachi with RCA, Toshiba with General Electric, Mitsubishi with TRW, and Oki Electric with Sperry Rand. Fujitsu was unsuccessful in working out a technical agreement with IBM. The opportunity to acquire IBM technology came in 1970. The Amdahl Corporation, founded by the designer of the IBM Series/360 machine, was having difficulty raising resources to put its own machine on the market. Fujitsu eagerly entered into a partnership with Amdahl, and by the 1980s had become Japan's most successful computer firm.

One of the most important institutional innovations of the 1960s was MITI's establishment of the Japan Electronic Computer Company (JEEC), which purchased computers from manufacturers and then leased them to users at competitive rates. JEEC was subsidized by low-interest loans from government-controlled banks. The advantage of the arrangement was that computer manufacturers received payment up front rather than having to depend on slower cash flow from rental payments. In exchange for this advantage, JEEC exerted pressure on the manufacturers to continuously upgrade by requiring that they stand ready to buy back, at book value, any machines that users wanted to return.

The Japanese computer industry underwent a severe crisis in the early 1970s. The precipitating event was IBM's introduction of its Series/370 computers, but other factors also played a part. The arrangement that gave Japanese firms access to IBM patents was scheduled to expire at the end of 1970, and stood little chance of being renewed. When Japan joined the General Agreement on Tariffs and Trade (GATT) in 1964 it had committed itself to liberalizing its trade regime. Under pressure from the United States Japan agreed to remove quantitative restrictions on peripheral equipment in 1972 and on the import of mainframe computers by the end of 1975.

The initial MITI strategy had not been to get ahead of IBM, but rather to match IBM as soon as possible. When IBM introduced its integrated circuit Series/360 machines in 1965, it took the Japanese firms 3 years to place comparable machines on the market. When IBM introduced its Series/370 in 1970, it took 5 years to catch up. The introduction of the IBM Series/370 also precipitated a shakeout in the U.S. computer industry. General Electric and RCA withdrew from mainframe computer production, which caused additional problems for the Japanese firms that had technology agreements with them.

In the late 1970s, MITI launched a series of projects designed to push the Japanese computer industry into leapfrogging IBM by developing machines to compete with yet unannounced fourth-generation IBM machines. Even before this program was launched it had become clear to leaders in the computer industry, in both Japan and the United States, that

> more highly integrated circuits was the path that computer advances would take. As the number of transistors on a chip increases, memory capacity and processing speed for a given size computer increase. Since the production costs per wafer [are] about the same no matter how many chips on each wafer, technology that could get more chips on each wafer and more transistors on each chip was critical to being competitive. The denser the chip, the smaller the computer size, the greater the processing speed, and the lower its production cost. (Anchordoguy, 1989:138)

The series of projects that began in the late 1970s were supported by substantial financial aid from the government and NTT. The MITI system, developed in earlier projects, coordinated participating companies' research efforts by assigning them nonoverlapping research areas. Resources were concentrated on NEC, Hitachi, and Fujitsu. These companies had already achieved parity in technical performance with a group of "subfrontier" American mainframe producers—Data General, Digital Equipment Corporation, General Electric, Honeywell, Radio Corporation of America (RCA), and Scientific Data Systems. By the early 1980s, they had achieved parity with the three frontier commercial mainframe producers—IBM, Control Data, and Amdahl (Figure 9.2). Sales by Fujitsu and IBM in the Japanese market were roughly equivalent. By 1983 the Japanese firms participating in the project introduced a generation of supercomputers that approached the performance of those produced by the leading producers of supercomputers used for scientific purposes such as Cray Research (Afuah and Utterback, 1991:315–328). In spite of the fact that the three leading Japanese firms ranked among the top 10 in the global computer market, about 80% of their sales were accounted for by the Japanese market.[23]

---

[23] Failure of Japanese firms to achieve higher levels of market penetration was not due to performance deficiencies. In 1997 Cray Research (then a division of Silicon Graphics) resorted to charges of "dumping" before the U.S. Court of International Trade to prevent the U.S. National Center for Atmospheric Research (NCAR) from purchasing a higher capacity and less expensive NEC computer for use in climate modeling weather simulation. The contract between NCAR and NEC would have been the first purchase of a Japanese supercomputer by a U.S. government agency (Williams, 1997:A14). In 1999 the U.S. National Research Council reported that lack of access to the world's fastest computers meant that U.S. climate modelers had fallen behind modelers in other advanced countries in their ability to achieve greater precision in modeling the effects of global climate change (Kerr, 1999).

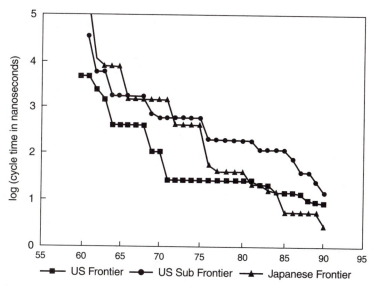

Figure 9.2 Mainframe computer technology frontiers. (*Source:* Reprinted from Taron Khanna, "Racing Behavior: Technological Evolution in the High-End Computer Industry," *Research Policy* 24 (1995):933–58. Copyright © 1995, with permission from Elsevier Science.)

Semiconductors

The development of the semiconductor industry followed a similar path. By the early 1950s engineers at MITI/ETL were sensitive to the potential impact of the transistor for computer development. Initially, the Japanese industry produced transistors for use in consumer electronics products. This was followed by the substitution of semiconductors for such uses. As late as 1968 60% of all Japanese semiconductor production went to consumer electronic products (Tyson, 1992:93, 95).

In 1964 Texas Instruments, which at that time accounted for about one-third of the world semiconductor market, applied to MITI to establish a wholly owned subsidiary in Japan. MITI initially rejected the application. After a protracted series of negotiations MITI specified "three conditions for entering Japan: creating a 50–50 joint venture with Sony; 'voluntarily' holding the volume of its integrated-circuit (IC) production to no more than 10 percent of Japan's total IC production for the first three years; and granting Japanese companies access to its patents for a reasonable price" (Anchordoguy, 1989:28). In 1972 Texas Instruments was allowed to buy out Sony's interest in the joint venture after threatening a patent infringement lawsuit against any Japanese exporter of consumer electronics using its technology. But MITI had accomplished its purpose; by delaying Texas Instruments' entry MITI gave the Japanese semiconductor firms an opportunity to achieve economies of scale before facing foreign competition (Anchordoguy, 1989:28: Flamm, 1996:68–77).

Increasingly, U.S. companies could penetrate the Japanese market only with advanced product innovations not yet produced by Japanese firms. As Japanese suppliers became increasingly competent in the production of more advanced devices, U.S. suppliers saw their share of the Japanese market level off or decline (Tyson, 1992:97, 98). By the late 1970s the relative position of U.S. and Japanese semiconductor firms had changed dramatically from a decade earlier. In 1977, Japanese exports of total semiconductors to the United States surpassed U.S. exports to Japan for the first time. In 1978, integrated circuit imports from Japan exceeded exports to Japan. And in 1979, U.S. imports of metal oxide semiconductors (MOS) exceeded exports to Japan. By the early 1980s all but two U.S. companies, Texas Instruments and Motorola, had withdrawn from the production of DRAMs. The development of high-quality integrated circuits enabled Japanese computer manufactures to increase their sales in domestic and international markets.

An intriguing puzzle is why Japanese producers of semiconductors failed to dominate the microprocessor market in the same way that they came to dominate the memory (DRAM) market. In April 1972, just 5 months after Intel announced its first microprocessor (the 4004), NEC produced Japan's first microprocessor (the PD700). Fransman (1995:167–182) argues that a major reason for the increased dominance by the United States was the different structure of the computer and semiconductor markets in the United States and Japan. In the United States computers and microprocessors were largely produced by different firms. When the IBM team that developed the PC decided to go outside for microprocessors it chose the Intel 8088. The growth of IBM clones created a rapidly expanding market for Intel microprocessors. In Japan the consumer electronics, communication, computer, and semiconductor industries are highly integrated. Microprocessors developed with only the PC in mind would not necessarily be optimal for other consumer products. (NEC, using its own microprocessors, did eventually come to dominate the Japanese PC market. It designed and produced its own microprocessor, designed its own operating system, and produced and marketed its own PC.)

The effect of these differences in market structure was that in Japan the market for memories has been relatively homogeneous, thus creating large markets for "commoditized" standard memories. This has in turn led to rapidly decreasing costs (Moore's law) and the capture of large shares of the memory markets both in Japan and abroad. The proprietary nature of the computers produced in Japan and the relatively slower diffusion of PCs in Japan have resulted in a more fragmented market for microprocessors. In contrast, in the United States Intel's microprocessors have become the market standard—"Intel Inside"—creating a large and rapidly growing market that has enabled Intel to achieve the lower costs associated with scale economies. By the late 1990s Intel had established a near monopoly on PC microprocessors and was engaged in an active program of diversification.

The Landscape Shifts

Beginning in the early 1980s the Japanese computer industry entered a new period of uncertainty very different from the crisis of the early 1970s. During the earlier catch-up period, the primary source of uncertainty was whether Japanese producers could master the existing technology fast enough to catch up with IBM mainframe technology and, at the same time, earn a rate of return that was sufficient to enable them to remain in the game. Once Japanese technology had reached the frontier, however, the Japanese computer and semiconductor industries faced an entirely new level of uncertainty. This uncertainty related to the future direction of technical change itself.

New research projects were initiated in the early 1980s in an attempt to "out-IBM" IBM (Fransman, 1990:269). But by the early 1990s the landscape had changed. The global computer industry was involved in a transition from the dominant vision of how information should be processed that began with von Neumann's sequential processing architecture of the mid-1940s. In Fransman's terminology,

> the first vision resembles a large continent consisting of a number of mainframe computers surrounded by smaller and less influential islands of smaller computers, first minicomputers and then personal computers. In the second vision the continent of mainframes has shrunk considerably in size relative to the islands, which have become more numerous. Each island is now more powerful, both in absolute terms and relative to the mainland, than it was before. And the islands are now increasingly connected to one another by huge quantities of information rapidly and cheaply. (Fransman, 1995:130)

In this new vision computing is seen as a network of decentralized information processors. In this new environment there was much less assurance of success.[24]

Some observers have viewed the more recent MITI and NTT efforts as evidence of the failure of Japanese industrial policy. It had cost the Japanese government very substantial resources to achieve its early 1960s objective of developing a world class computer industry. Anchordoguy (1989) estimates that during the "catch-up" period

---

[24] These changes in the computer landscape also had important structural and locational impacts within the United States. As late as the mid-1980s, Minnesota was, along with the Northeast and Pacific coast, a leading center of mainframe production. IBM began producing the System/3 minicomputer in Rochester in 1969 and has continued to produce new generations of minicomputers there. But Unisys, Honeywell, Control Data, and Cray Research, all once located in the Minneapolis/St. Paul area, have relocated or discontinued computer production. Although Honeywell's Federal Systems Division continued to manufacture computers into the early 1990s, it discontinued mainframe computer production. Unisys, with a genealogy that traces back to the early industry leader, Remington-Rand (becoming Sperry Rand in 1955 as a result of a merger with Sperry), continues in mainframe production, but not in Minnesota. Control Data was dissolved into a series of successor companies (Ceridion, Seagate Technology, Control Data Systems, and several smaller firms). Cray Research, the leading producer of supercomputers, was acquired by Silicon Graphics, a leading workstation and software firm in 1996, and moved its operation to Denver. By the early 1990s the Minnesota computer industry was evolving into an industry dominated by software.

the Japanese government provided in the neighborhood of $18 billion in subsidies and tax benefits and $4.4 billion in loans in support of the computer and semiconductor industries. Well over half of the entire amount was spent in support of the Very Large-Scale Integration (VLSI) Project of the late 1970s that enabled Japanese manufacturers to briefly "leapfrog" the anticipated fifth-generation IBM computers.

Although the Japanese were not successful in creating a fifth-generation machine, they were successful in the broader sense of providing leading researchers with experience in areas such as massive parallel processing, advanced software development, and more intensive interaction with the international research community. In 1991 MITI initiated a 10-year sixth-generation project that focuses on massive parallel processing. In 1995 a new super advanced electronic technology program was being planned. The new project, planned to cost approximately $1.0 billion, will focus on basic materials and techniques rather than on particular projects. In these and other future oriented projects technology policy has shifted toward promoting important areas of generic knowledge rather than specific projects. This reflects a general consensus that Japan must complement its capacity in manufacturing and development with greater capacity in technical and scientific research (Pollack, 1995a).

The Late-Late Developers[25]

As early as the mid-1960s U.S. semiconductor producers, consistent with the product cycle model (Chapter 5), were engaging in "offshore procurement." It is technically feasible for the several stages in semiconductor production—design, wafer fabrication, assembly, and final testing—to take place in different countries. Fairchild initiated offshore assembly in Hong Kong in 1963 and in South Korea in 1964. Other semiconductor companies rapidly followed the Fairchild example.

There were substantial cost advantages to locating in East and Southeast Asia. "Wages in the important host countries (except for Mexico) have been one fifth (or less) as high as wages in the United States. . . . Assemblers can be taught the basic techniques in one day and become proficient in less than two weeks" (Langlois et al., 1988:53). Furthermore, assembled devices reimported into the United States were initially subject to duties only on the foreign value added; in April 1985 the U.S. tariff rate on semiconductors was reduced to zero. As a result an estimated 40% of American semiconductor production was assembled abroad by 1969 and close to 80% in 1981 (Langlois et al., 1988:56). Japanese and Western European semiconductor firms engaged in substantially less offshore procurement than U.S. firms primarily because of less favorable tariff treatment by their home countries.

Offshore procurement of semiconductors was accompanied by increasingly complex arrangements—through foreign subsidiaries, licensing arrangements, joint

---

[25] In this section I draw on Levy and Kuo (1991:363–374), and Hobday (1994:333–361).

ventures, and equity ownership arrangements. During the 1980s several semiconductor firms in the newly developing East Asian countries had established an independent role as semiconductor producers. The three leading Korean firms, Samsung, Goldstar, and Hyundai, established complex technology alliances with Japanese, German, and U.S. manufacturers. They also established U.S. subsidiaries in order to gain more direct access to U.S. technology and personnel. By the early 1990s the Korean firms ranked among the world leaders in semiconductor memory production (Chen and Sewell, 1996:759–783).

Taiwan also acquired substantial capacity in computer and component production, but the strategy used to acquire personal computer technology has been quite different than in South Korea. South Korean firms followed a large-scale "assembly" strategy. Taiwan followed a small-scale "bootstrap" strategy. In the case of keyboard production, for example, Korean firms used joint ventures with Japanese firms to achieve high volume, even in start-up production. The high returns enabled them to move rapidly down the learning curve, increasing productivity and lowering costs as experience accumulated. This required substantial initial investment and the capacity to finance and absorb very large initial investment losses. This was possible because the Korean microelectronics industry was already dominated by large conglomerates. They were able to initiate keyboard production as integrated manufacturers of keyboard components. In contrast, Taiwanese firms relied on subcontractors to supply and assemble a significant proportion of keyboard components. Sales were initially limited to overseas assemblers of PCs. Taiwan has also become an important producer of private label computers marketed by developed country firms (AT&T, Unisys, Siemens). One Taiwanese firm, Acer, ranked among the top 15 manufacturers of personal computers in the mid-1990s.

Since the early 1980s there has also been substantial diffusion of software production in developing countries. One of the more dramatic developments has been the growth of the software industry in south India. The government of India has a long history of attempting to promote both the computer and software industries. These efforts were initially frustrated by excessive state intervention (Subramanian, 1992). In the mid-1980s cautious liberalization that emphasized greater access to computer imports and the promotion of software exports was initiated. This was followed by more complete liberalization in 1991 (McDowell, 1995).

India had a number of important potential advantages for software development. It had a strong industrial base and a large domestic market. Well-trained technical manpower, capable of working in English, was available at wages less than one-fifth those in the United States. This advantage began to attract international firms, beginning with Texas Instruments, in 1986. Texas Instruments was followed by other leading multinationals who set up their own operations or established joint ventures with Indian companies. The southern city of Bangalore, the home of the Indian Institute of Science, the Indian Space Research Organization, and a number of high technology industries, rapidly developed as the center of the software industry.

Initially the foreign multinationals used Indian software engineers primarily for programming and testing. Because of the availability of cadres of highly skilled and well-educated software engineers and technical workers, a number of Indian companies were set up as training and employment agencies who contracted with leading computer companies in the United States and Western Europe to supply software workers on short-term contracts. This learning-by-doing experience has fed back into the Indian labor force. Even longer term migration began to be seen not so much in terms of a "brain drain" but as a global diaspora that facilitates business contacts and communication in the software industry.

By the mid-1990s Indian-based software firms were accounting for a larger share of software exports from India. Exports to the United States exceeded $500 million. An interesting case of the development of an Indian firm is presented in Box 9.4. The India experience is particularly interesting because it had traditionally been assumed that software development capacity was dependent on strong domestic hardware industry. In contrast to India, Japan's strength in computer hardware has not been translated into strength in traded software (Mowery and Rosenberg, 1998:162).

● BOX 9.4
KALE CONSULTANTS

Kale Consultants began in 1980 with a staff of only two people. It did domestic work only until 1988. A significant part of its early business was generated from developing on-line hotel management software for the Taj Group of hotels. It then diversified into on-line hospital management information systems and consulting services to the banking industry. It began gaining experience in using UNIX systems for on-line commercial applications in 1981 and in 1985 made a commitment to focus on UNIX-based software.

Rather than execute several disparate projects on an ad hoc basis, the firm has focused on offering turn-key "solutions" to clients in specific domestic market segments. In 1987 Kale became the first software company in India to be selected for venture capital funding by the Technology Development and Information Company of India. After spending a considerable amount of time and resources on software services and automation for banks, it produced and marketed its own bank management system.

Kale's first export project, in 1988, was a collaboration with Nixdorf Computers for the development of a banking software system. The first phase of the project was completed within a year. It was followed by consulting and software development projects in other countries, such as Malaysia, where Nixdorf has an installed computer base. Its exports are largely on-line integrated commercial systems for hospitals and bank branches. It was Kale's domestic experience and expertise that led to its successful export venture.

Source: Adapted from Robert Schware, "Software Industry Entry Strategies for Developing Countries: A 'Walking on Two Legs' Proposition," *World Development* 20 (1992):143–164.

INDUSTRIAL POLICY

The computer, semiconductor, and software industries have been uniquely influenced by public policy. The first computers were developed at universities with financial support from the military. The semiconductor industry was born out of the U.S. effort to develop more sophisticated military equipment. The DOD and NSF supported fundamental research and graduate education to speed the development of the software industry. The internet was developed by the Defense Advanced Project Agency (DARPA).

Falling Behind

The Japanese government, through its MITI and NTT, played an active entrepreneurial role in the transfer of computer and semiconductor technology to Japan. European governments also devoted major resources to the development of the computer and software industries in their countries, though generally less successfully. Beginning in the late 1970s the issue of competitive advantage in the semiconductor industry emerged as a major area of conflict between the U.S. and Japanese governments. Activists, pointing to the apparent success of Japanese industrial policy, urged the U.S. government to take a more aggressive role in opening up Japanese markets and strengthening U.S. technological leadership, particularly in semiconductors. By the mid-1990s critics were pointing to the ineffectiveness of both Japanese and U.S. policy initiatives in support of the computer and semiconductor industries (Maitland, 1995).

In contrast to the United States, in which government support was primarily based on a national security rationale, the Japanese, the Europeans, and the governments of several newly industrializing countries have focused on commercial significance in their support of the semiconductor industry. The economic benefits they visualized were more productive, higher paying jobs for their workers, increased exports and a higher share of world markets, as well as spillover benefits in related industries such as consumer electronics, computers, and telecommunications. In contrast, the United States, through its antitrust policies, acted to inhibit the competitive position of its dominant firms—Bell in telecommunications and IBM in office equipment. These constraints left the United States in a weakened position when the industry began to mature in the 1970s and economies of scale began to play an important role in semiconductor development.

A crisis atmosphere resulting from the surge of imports of Japanese semiconductor devices in the early 1980s induced a search for a new politically acceptable industrial policy. This challenge from Japanese chip producers came at a time when the United States was undergoing a loss of confidence in its leadership in a number of industries—in steel, in automobiles, and in consumer electronics. "The semiconductor industry seemed to mirror what was 'wrong' in general: an industry that the United States had dominated in research and sales since its postwar inception was struggling to compete against Japanese producers buoyed by government subsidies and perceived unfair trade practices" (Dick, 1996:68). The Defense Department was concerned about the potential loss of a "strategic" industry. Computer chips were more important than potato chips! But the U.S. military and space programs could no longer be depended on as a covert form of industrial policy. And the dominance of a conservative political ideology in Washington inhibited open debate about a coherent post-Cold War industrial policy.

The move toward the development of an ad hoc policy in support of the semiconductor industry proceeded along several fronts. One was the negotiation of several semiconductor trade accords (STCA) with Japan. A second was the formation of Sematech, a research consortium to advance semiconductor manufacturing technology. In 1984 Congress passed the National Cooperative Research Act, which loosened antitrust restrictions on collaborative R&D.

Semiconductor Trade Accords[26]

Political support for a semiconductor trade accord was mobilized by the Semiconductor Industry Association.[27] Its initial successes included lobbying for the elimination of all semiconductor duties in the United States and Japan and the passage of the Semiconductor Chip Protection Act, which provides intellectual property rights to chip designers in the United States. The association also initiated a petition against unfair Japanese trading practices and a series of antidumping petitions accusing Japanese firms of dumping memory devices (Box 9.2). These actions provided sufficient motivation for Japan to enter into negotiations that led to an accord on semiconductor trade in August 1986.

---

[26] In this section I draw heavily on Tyson (1992), Irwin (1996), Flamm (1996), and Macher et al. (1999).

[27] The Semiconductor Industry Association (SIAS) was formed in 1977 by the five leading merchant producers (AMD, Intel, Fairchild, National Semiconductor, and Motorola). In 1982 it broadened its membership to include vertically integrated captive producers such as IBM, Hewlett-Packard, Digital Equipment (DEC), and AT&T. Broadening the membership gave SIA greater clout in Washington but also had the effect of moderating its trade policy stance because the merchants' interest in higher prices was not shared by the captive producers. Achieving industry consensus was also hampered by industry cross-ownership. Aggressive lobbying by firms without Japanese ties such as Motorola and Micron were muted by Intel which had numerous second sourcing agreements with Japanese producers (Dick, 1996:69).

The 1986 semiconductor trade accord addressed both access to the Japanese market and dumping by Japanese firms in the U.S. market. According to its terms, the dumping suit and the unfair trade practices case were suspended in return for stipulated actions to improve market access for U.S. companies and to terminate dumping by Japanese firms. With respect to market access the Japanese government agreed to provide assistance to U.S. and other foreign companies selling in Japan, and, in a side letter to the agreement, to encourage a doubling of the foreign share of the Japanese market. A dumping criteria formula was also agreed on (Tyson, 1992:109, 110).

As the SCTA came up for renewal in 1991 it became clear that the U.S. computer industry would oppose the antidumping provisions that had driven up the price of DRAMs. Evidence on dumping was inconclusive and the semiconductor industry was willing to see the antidumping provisions relaxed in exchange for a stronger commitment to market access. A new 5-year agreement was signed in the summer of 1991. By the end of 1995 the U.S. share of the Japanese semiconductor market had reached 22.9%. The SCTA comes up for renewal again in 1996. The Japanese Electronic Industries Association has urged that since foreign chip manufacturers are now firmly established in the Japanese market, the agreement should be allowed to expire (Pollack, 1995c:D4).

But what, if any, role did the agreement have on this reversal in market shares? There was a concerted effort on the part of Japanese semiconductor companies to increase the foreign share of their own purchases. U.S. firms made an effort to become more active in the Japanese market. Motorola expanded both its domestic production and its joint venture with Toshiba in Japan. Several Japanese firms located facilities in the United States.

There were also negative effects. In 1987 the Semiconductor Industry Association became convinced that the Japanese were violating the dumping provisions of the SCTA in third markets and failing to increase purchases from U.S. producers. In response the United States imposed sanctions in the form of 100% tariffs on certain Japanese computer and semiconductor products. The effect was a sharp rise in the prices of 256K DRAMS, higher costs for those products on the part of U.S. component manufacturers, and higher profits by Japanese producers. As an unintended consequence, the sanctions provided a short-term shield for the penetration of third country producers, particularly Korean and German, in the world market.

Some critics have argued that SCTA was a complete failure when evaluated against a free market alternative. Tyson (1992) supports the access provisions, arguing that the relevant alternative was not free trade but "manipulated" trade and that the "managed trade" regime was at least a qualified success. The share of U.S. and other foreign companies in the Japanese market did increase. The world market is more competitive than if the growing power of Japanese firms had remained unchecked. Tyson is much less enthusiastic, however, about the effects of the antidumping provisions.

If the goal of American policy had been, as it should have been, the preservation of a competitive global DRAM market, a temporary subsidy to deter the exit of at least some American suppliers in 1986 or to encourage their reentry in 1987 or 1988 would have been a more effective remedy. For considerably less than the $4 billion ultimately transferred to the Japanese companies in the form of bubble profits, the United States might have been able to secure more competitive markets and maintain a strong domestic DRAM capacity at the same time. (Tyson, 1992:141)

Sematech

Sematech grew out of industry and government concern that the Japanese semiconductor companies were outspending and outperforming their U.S. competitors in manufacturing, in process R&D, and in capital investment. A National Science Foundation study found that the level of R&D in at least 10 Japanese firms exceeded that of all but two U.S. firms. In 1987 the government, primarily the DOD/ARPA, agreed to match the contributions of private firms in sponsoring the formation of a consortium to be called Sematech. Sematech was incorporated in August 1987. It included 14 U.S. semiconductor companies, among them IBM, AT&T, and all of the major merchant suppliers. It also included most of the major semiconductor equipment manufacturers. It was designed to help improve U.S. semiconductor production technology, but not to design or produce semiconductors. Substantial support was provided for the development of lithography technology, which is used to print microscopic circuit patterns on silicon wafers.

How successful has Sematech been in enhancing the technology of member firms? It has been criticized for generating few benefits. One of the most heavily supported developers of lithographic technology failed to become commercially viable (Randazzese, 1996:46–49). Three firms that have left the consortium have criticized Sematech for moving away from in-house development work to making research grants to members. An attempt to quantify the impact of Sematech suggests that one effect was to reduce R&D research spending from resources owned by Sematech members (Irwin and Klenoweu, 1994:20). There is evidence, however, that Sematech has contributed to the revitalization of some segments of the semiconductor industry. Motorola and Intel have both increased their equipment purchases from U.S. producers. And the U.S. share of the global market for semiconductor equipment has experienced a modest growth in the 1990s. A 1991 survey of executives of Sematech members indicated general satisfaction with their participation and a belief that payoffs within their own firms were just beginning.

By the mid-1990s the semiconductor industry has emerged as a global oligopoly in which a relatively small number of firms, headquartered in the United States, Japan, Europe, and Korea, produce, invest, and sell throughout the world. In the semiconductor industry, for example, the IBM–Toshiba–Siemens memory chip development partnership was, in 1995, joined by Motorola. The objective of the new consortium was the development of a 1 billion bit memory chip. Motorola already had a joint venture with Toshiba to manufacture a 16-megabyte chip. But to move to the next generation Motorola would have had to license the technology from the alliance.

Instead it decided to buy into the alliance at a cost of several hundred million dollars (Pollack, 1995b:D5).

The personal computer industry is also characterized by increasingly complex alliances. In 1995 the Japanese NEC Corporation, which accounted for 43% of the personal computer market in Japan, purchased a 19.99% interest in Packard Bell, which, in 1995, led in personal computer sales in the United States with a market share of over 12%. Group Bull, the French computer company, had acquired 19.9% of Packard Bell in 1993. NEC, in turn, owns a 17% stake in Group Bull. Group Bull also owns U.S.-based Zenith Data Systems. This arrangement gave NEC, the only Japanese personal computer manufacturer that had not adopted an IBM PC design, access to the broader IBM-compatible market (Pollack, 1995c:D3).

Long-term competitive advantage in the computer industry can not yet be taken for granted. With each technical revolution here has been a substantial relocation of industrial leadership. Within the United States initial advantage in mainframe platforms was located in New York (and to a lesser extent in the Upper Midwest) region. The development of minicomputers was associated with the emergence of technical leadership in the Boston area. With the development of the microcomputer the advantage in hardware production moved to Silicon Valley (California). Beginning in the 1990s there was a major relocation in the production of computer hardware—devices, components, and systems—to East Asia (Bresnahan, 1999). As this book was being completed the computer industry appeared to be entering another revolution in its technical base and industrial organization. The emergence of network computing threatens to induce changes in both the structure and location of the industry. Microsoft appears to be attempting to impose a new vertically integrated structure on the Silocon Valley system of disintegrated specialty technoogy firms. It is doubtful, however, that current efforts to anticipate either the direction of the technology or the organization of the industry will be more successful than such efforts have been in the past.

COMPUTERS AND ECONOMIC GROWTH

The economic return from the allocation of public resources to the computer and semiconductor industries was, as long as the Cold War persisted, rarely questioned. The prospect for commercial application was not an important consideration in determining the level of government support. Indeed, most of the scientists, engineers, and managers in the computer industry, right up to the development of the microcomputer, consistently failed to anticipate the dramatic rate of growth of the commercial market, almost 20 percent per year since 1960, and in the consumer market of almost 50 percent per years since 1980 (Jorgenson and Stiroh, 1999).

But by the early 1980s questions were being raised about the productivity effects of the information revolution. In those industries in which computer use was most intense the impact was not being captured in either profitability or productivity indicators. The productivity surge that many observers anticipated as a result of more intense use of computers and related information technology had failed to materialize—at least in the official productivity series. In the service sector, where adoption was most rapid, there has been a negative relationship between increase in information technology capital investment and measured growth in labor productivity in the 1980s (Attewell, 1994:13–53; Landauer, 1995:13–77; Stiroh, 1998). Paul David (1990), drawing on the experience of the electric utility industry, argued that it was premature to expect substantial productivity impact from the rapid diffusion of computer technology. The diffusion of electricity did not have a significant impact on productivity in manufacturing until after adoption had passed the inflection point on the diffusion curve (Chapters 5 and 7).

In the early 1990s, however, there was a new burst of enthusiasm about the productivity impact of computers and related information technology.[28] *Business Week*, for example, reported that "Thanks to corporate America's restructuring and high-tech investment, the long-term trend of productivity is on a path not seen since the 1960s" (Cooper, 1994:62) and "after years of costly struggle, U.S. business is finally making the information revolution pay off" (Glickman et al., 1995:57). The *Wall Street Journal* reported that the payoff had become so obvious that many companies had simply quit trying to evaluate the return on investment in information technology. "Computer based information systems are so thoroughly intertwined with operations that the impact is impossible to evaluate" (King, 1994:R18). Other observers have identified this attitude on the part of information executives as a source of low productivity and low profits in computer-intensive firms (Strassmann, 1997:23–40).

There is no question that the rate of technical change and of productivity growth in the computer and semiconductor industries has been high by any standard. A modern personal computer costing less than $2000 has more memory and faster speed than a mainframe computer costing a million dollars or more as recently as the mid-1970s. The capacity of the memory chips and microprocessors that account for much of the increase in computer performance has risen dramatically (Figure 9.1). But it was not until December 1985 that the U.S. Department of Commerce Bureau of Economic Analysis (BEA) introduced a constant quality hedonic price index for computers.[29] Drawing on BEA data Jorgenson and Stiroh (1999, 2000) constructed price and quantity indexes for computer investment, capital stock, and services for computers used by business and consumers (Table 9.3). During 1990–1996, after 30 years of dramatic price declines, the price of computers used in business was still declining at

---

[28] Waves of enthusiasm in the business press about the productivity and growth impact of computers have appeared periodically since the late 1950s (Sichel, 1997:128–131).

[29] The basic premise in construction of hedonic price indexes is that price differences are due mainly to quality differences that can be measured in terms of some common attributes or characteristics. In the BEA price index for computers the characteristics are (1) the speed with which instructions are executed and (2) the capacity of the main memory. The application of the hedonic technique to develop a price index for computers and its use in deflating components of GNP were described in three articles in the *Survey of Current Business* in 1986 (Triplett, Cole et al., and Cartwright). For a review and response to criticisms of the BEA methodology, see Young (1989:108–115).

an annual rate of 16.6% per year. The prices of computer services were declining at 18.7 percent per year. The price of computers purchased by consumers declined even more rapidly.

The debate about why the rapid adoption of computers has not shown up in aggregate productivity measures, or even in the growth of productivity in the service industries that have adopted computers most intensively, has taken longer to resolve (Oliner and Sichel, 1994:273–334; Jorgenson, 1996; Oliner and Wascher, 1995:18–30; Filardo, 1995:41–59; Sichel, 1997; Stiroh, 1998; Jorgenson and Stiroh, 1999). By the late 1990s it was clear that the rapid diffusion of computers was largely induced by the dramatic declines in the price of computers and computer services. The growth in computer use represented primarily factor substitution, induced by declining prices, rather than a productivity-enhancing shift in the production function in computer-using industries (see Appendix to Chapter 2). Computer costs have fallen so fast and so far that they are often being used for purposes that have only a marginal impact on productivity.

Attempts have been made to use growth-accounting methods to capture the effects of the diffusion of computers on economy-wide economic growth (Oliner and Sichel, 1994:273–334; Sichel, 1997:75–112; Jorgenson and Stiroh, 1999). The Jorgenson–Stiroh results are presented in Table 9.4. Until at least the early 1970 investment in computer and related information technology was so small, as a share of producers' durable equipment investment, that it could not be expected to have a significant impact on economic growth. By 1990–1996, however, computers were accounting for over 16% of output growth. During this same period computers accounted for nearly 20% of the contribution of consumer durable services to growth (Table 9.4).

It seems clear that none of the quantitative studies that are available has been able to capture the full impact of the diffusion of computers on economic growth (Lohr, 1999). One reason is the spillover of knowledge and equipment from the computer and semiconductor industries to other industries such as telecommunications and transformation (Griliches, 1992:529–547). A generalization that can be made with some assurance is that the low rate of total factor productivity that began in the 1970s would have been even lower in the absence of rapid growth of the computer and semiconductor industries.

My own judgment is that even the best estimates concerning the contribution of computers and semiconductors have failed to fully capture the new income streams, or even more broadly, the full utility generated by the adoption of computers. Producers of computers have been forced by the market to share the new income streams generated by productivity growth in the computer and semiconductor industries with consumers. There has been a public goods aspect to the rapid productivity gains generated by the computer and semiconductor industries. Social rates of return have exceeded private rates of return generated by technical change in the computer industry. This does not negate, of course, the view that even larger gains may be realized from the diffusion of computers into the early decades of the twenty-first century (David, 1990:355–361; Sichel, 1997:100–107). There seem to be little doubt

Table 9.3 Computers as Business Capital and as a Consumer Durable: Investment, Stock, and Services Quantity and Price Indexes

	Computers as a Business Investment					
	Investment		Capital Stock		Capital Sales	
Year	Price	Quantity	Price	Quantity	Price	Quantity
1960	339.416	0.001	339.416	0.001	372.259	0.000
1961	262.479	0.001	262.479	0.002	290.514	0.000
1962	179.473	0.002	179.473	0.003	208.272	0.001
1963	134.285	0.006	134.285	0.008	140.629	0.001
1964	112.329	0.009	112.329	0.014	115.437	0.003
1965	92.825	0.013	92.825	0.023	98.848	0.006
1966	65.020	0.027	65.020	0.043	73.236	0.009
1967	52.812	0.037	52.812	0.067	57.646	0.017
1968	45.033	0.044	45.033	0.090	48.815	0.027
1969	40.819	0.062	40.819	0.124	41.779	0.036
1970	36.665	0.077	36.665	0.162	39.025	0.050
1971	27.923	0.104	27.923	0.215	31.910	0.065
1972	22.614	0.159	22.614	0.306	24.037	0.087
1973	21.444	0.170	21.444	0.379	21.380	0.124
1974	17.507	0.224	17.507	0.484	17.490	0.153
1975	16.196	0.229	16.196	0.560	15.954	0.196
1976	13.526	0.336	13.526	0.719	13.399	0.228
1977	11.771	0.496	11.771	0.989	11.478	0.293
1978	7.962	0.947	7.962	1.624	8.090	0.403
1979	6.597	1.579	6.597	2.692	6.266	0.661
1980	5.149	2.504	5.149	4.348	4.853	1.094
1981	4.525	3.892	4.525	6.871	4.294	1.766
1982	4.049	4.856	4.049	9.562	3.545	2.790
1983	3.376	7.393	3.376	13.943	3.049	3.882
1984	2.731	12.147	2.731	21.698	2.607	5.661
1985	2.322	15.209	2.322	30.072	2.177	8.812
1986	2.000	17.440	2.000	38.040	1.824	12.214
1987	1.704	21.963	1.704	48.021	1.736	15.450
1988	1.583	25.113	1.583	58.007	1.587	19.504
1989	1.470	30.781	1.470	70.516	1.469	23.557
1990	1.322	30.761	1.322	79.064	1.315	28.638
1991	1.174	34.053	1.174	88.212	1.167	32.107
1992	1.000	46.076	1.000	106.501	1.000	35.823
1993	0.867	59.153	0.867	132.106	0.877	43.243
1994	0.771	70.338	0.771	160.831	0.794	53.638
1995	0.638	106.428	0.638	216.597	0.678	65.318
1996	0.490	168.221	0.490	316.602	0.537	88.000
1960–96	−18.17	34.84	−18.17	36.47	−18.17	42.00
1980–96	−14.70	26.30	−14.70	26.80	−13.76	27.42
1990–96	−16.55	28.32	−16.55	23.12	−14.94	18.71

Source: The data in this table are a revised and updated version of data from Dale W. Jorgenson and Kevin J. Stiroh, *Computers and Growth*, Harvard University Institute of Economic Growth, Discussion Paper 1707, December 1994. Revised data provided by Kevin Stiroh, February 10, 1999.

Table 9.4 The Role of Computers in U.S. Economic Growth, 1948–1996

Measure	1948–1973	1973–1990	1990–1996
Output growth[a]	4.020	2.857	2.363
Contribution of noncomputer outputs	3.978	2.650	1.980
Contribution of computer outputs	0.042	0.207	0.384
Investment goods (I_c)	0.042	0.171	0.258
Consumption goods (C_c)	0.000	0.024	0.086
Consumers' durable Services (S_c)	0.000	0.012	0.040
Contribution of capital services (K)	1.073	0.954	0.632
Noncomputers (K_n)	1.049	0.845	0.510
Computers (K_c)	0.025	0.109	0.123
Contribution of consumers' durable services (D)	0.550	0.426	0.282
Noncomputers (D_n)	0.550	0.414	0.242
Computers (D_c)	0.000	0.012	0.040
Contribution of labor input (L)	1.006	1.145	1.219
Aggregate total factor productivity	1.391	0.335	0.231

[a]Contributions of inputs and outputs are real growth rates weighted by average, nominal shares.

Source: Dale W. Jorgenson and Kevin J. Stiroh, "Information Technology and Growth," *American Economic Review* 89 (1999):109–115.

that the rate of return on public investment in development of the computer and software industries has been high, in the 50–70% range, compared to most other public investments (Flamm, 1987:36–39). And it is simply not credible to assume that the market could have developed anywhere near as rapidly in the absence of the large public support that began in the mid-1940s.

What about other countries? Did the subsidies in support of development of the computer, semiconductor, and software industries, which were undertaken primarily for commercial purposes, have a favorable return when evaluated against other possible uses of public resources? There is a presumption, because of the limited success in the development of a commercially viable computer industry in Western Europe, against a return to public research support anywhere near the U.S. range. But what about Japan, which has developed computer and semiconductor industries that have challenged U.S. dominance? Baldwin and Krugman (1988:172–197) argue, somewhat tentatively, that the policies pursued by Japan to gain market share in the 16K DRAM market resulted in a welfare loss to the Japanese economy—that the returns were less than their opportunity cost. Their analysis failed, however, to account for the spillover effects of the 16K DRAM development on the computer, telecommunication, and related electronic industries. The definitive evaluation for Japan has yet to be written.

What about the presently less developed countries? India, as noted earlier, has made substantial public investments in an attempt to support the development of domestic computer and semiconductor industries. When recalling the large investments made by Japan and the large amount of time it took to approach parity with the U.S., there is a presumption that at least in the short-run, the most effective strategy in even the technically more sophisticated developing countries is to supply labor-intensive components to the larger U.S., Japanese, and European firms and to import the computers that are used as intermediate inputs.

COMPUTERS AND SOCIETY

There are three levels at which we might attempt to assess the economic and social impacts of computers (Rochlin, 1997:12). One is the direct effects of the introduction and diffusion of computers. As indicated in the last section, considerable research attention has been focused on this level. But the impact of computers on rates of return at the firm level, the impact of their use on productivity at the industry level, and the contribution of their use to economic growth remain controversial.

A second level of assessment is the ways in which the new capacities and opportunities opened up by technical change in the computer industry have interacted with the broader social and economic environment. It is quite clear that the initial scientific and technical effort to develop both computers and semiconductors was induced by forces operating on the demand side—in both the defense and civilian economies. It is also apparent that the rate and direction of technical change in the computer and semiconductor industries have been conditioned by trajectories inherent in the nature of the technology itself. As computer technology has progressed it has in turn contributed to reshaping research and development agendas in other fields. Little effort has yet been made to trace the spillover effects of technical change in the computer industry on the pace of scientific and technical change in other fields. Without computers, for example, it would be hard to imagine the pace of recent advances in biotechnology research and development.

A third level of assessment is the longer term societal and cultural impacts of the computer. This issue has been the subject of much speculation in both the popular and the professional press. But there is little analysis that goes beyond personal observation and thoughtful introspection. And there are few models on which researchers can rely in even attempting to respond to this concern. We do not yet have answers to similar questions about the social impact of earlier communication technologies such as the telephone (Fischer, 1985:284–299). Articles written in the early and mid-1980s, or even before the dramatic growth in the use of the Internet since the mid-1990s, on the social impact of the microelectronic and information revolution already have a somewhat archaic ring (Forester, 1981, 1985; Fallows, 1996).

It is clear that computers are a cultural artifact that has penetrated deeply into our economic, educational, leisure, and household life. But they have not yet fully lived up to the more extravagant promises made on their behalf—in the factory, in the office, or in the home. It is doubtful if they ever will—even as more and more people enjoy using them.

REFERENCES

Afuah, A. N., and J. M. Utterback. "The Emergence of a New Supercomputer Architecture." *Technological Forecasting and Social Change* 40 (1991:315–328).

Anchordoguy, M. *Computers Inc.: Japan's Challenge to IBM.* Cambridge, MA: Harvard University Press, 1989.

Attewell, P. "Information Technology and the Productivity Paradox." In *Organizational Linkages: Understanding the Productivity Paradox,* Douglas H. Harris, ed., pp. 13-53. Washington, DC: National Academy Press, 1994.

Baba, Y., S. Taki, and Y. Mizuto. "The User Driven Evolution of the Japanese Software Industry: The Case of Customized Software for Mainframes." In *The International Computer Software Industry: A Comparative Study of Industry Evolution and Structure,* D. C. Mowery, ed., pp. 104–130. New York: Oxford University Press, 1996.

Baldwin, R. E., and P. R. Krugman. "Market Access and International Competition: A Simulation Study of 16K Random Access Memories." In *Empirical Methods for International Trade,* R. C. Feenstra, ed., pp. 171–197. Cambridge, MA: MIT Press, 1988.

Bashe, C. J., L. R. Johnson, J. H. Palmer, and E. W. Pugh. *IBM's Early Computers.* Cambridge, MA: MIT Press, 1986.

Bauer, R. A., E. Caller, and V. Tang (with J. Wind and P. Houston). *The Silverlake Project: Transformation at IBM.* New York: Oxford University Press, 1992.

Boyett, J. H., S. Schwartz, L. Osterwise, and R. Bauer. *The Quality Journey: How Winning the Baldridge Sparked IBM.* New York: Dutton-Penguin, 1993.

Bresnahan, T. F. "Computing." In *U.S. Industry in 2000: Studies in Competitive Performance,* D. C. Mowery, ed., pp. 215–244. Washington, DC: National Academy Press. 1999.

Bresnahan, T. F. "Indusrial Dynamics and Evolution of Firms' and Nations' Competitive Capabilities in the World Computer Industry." In *Sources of Industrial Leadership: Studies of Seven Industries.* D. C. Mowery and R. R. Nelson, eds., pp. 79–132. Cambridge, UK: Cambridge University Press, 1999.

Campbell-Kelly, M., and W. Aspray. *Computer: A History of the Information Machine.* New York: Basic Books, 1996.

Cartwright, D. W. "Improved Deflation of Purchased Computers." *Survey of Current Business* 66 (March 1986):7–9.

Chen, C., and F. G. Sewell. "Strategies for Technological Development in South Korea and Taiwan: The Case of Semiconductors." *Research Policy* 25 (1996):759–783.

Chposky, J., and T. Leonois. *Blue Magic: The People, Power and Politics Behind the IBM Personal Computer.* New York: Facts on File, 1988.

Cole, R., Y. C. Chen, J. A. Barquin-Stolleman, E. Dulberger, N. Helvcian, and J. H. Hodge. "Quality-Adjusted Price Indexes for Computer Processors and Selected Peripheral Equipment." *Survey of Cement Business* 66 (January 1986):41–50.

Cooper, J. C. "The New Golden Age of Productivity." *Business Week,* September 26,1994:62.

David, P. A. "The Dynamo and the Computer: An Historical Perspective on the Modern Productivity Paradox." *American Economic Review* 80 (May 1990):355–361.

Dick, A. R. "Comment." In *The Political Economy of American Trade Policy,* A. O. Krueger, ed., pp. 66–71. Chicago: University of Chicago Press, 1996.

Dosi, G. *Technical Change and Industrial Transformation.* New York: St. Martins Press, 1984.

Fallows, J. "Caught in the Web." *New York Review* (February 14, 1996):14–18.

Ferguson, C. H., and C. R. Morris. *Computer Wars: How the West Can Win in a Post-IBM World.* New York: Times Books, 1993.

Filardo, A. J. "Has the Productivity Trend Steepened in the 1990s?" *Federal Reserve Bank of Kansas City Economic Review* (Fourth Quarter 1995):41–59.

Fischer, C. S. "Studying Technology and Social Life." In *High Technology, Space and Society*, Manuel Castels, ed., pp. 284–300. Beverly Hills, CA: Sage Publications, 1985.

Flamm, K. *Targeting the Computer: Government Support and International Competition.* Washington, DC: Brookings Institution Press, 1987.

Flamm, K. *Creating the Computer.* Washington, DC: Brookings Institution Press, 1988.

Flamm, K. *Mismanaged Trade: Strategic Policy and the Semiconductor Industry.* Washington, DC: Brookings Institution Press, 1996.

Forester, T., ed. *The Microelectronic Revolution: The Complete Guide to the New Technology and Its Impact on Society.* Cambridge, MA: MIT Press, 1981.

Forester, T., ed. *The Information Technology Revolution.* Cambridge, MA: MIT Press, 1985.

Fransman, M. *The Market and Beyond: Cooperation and Competition in Information Technology Development in the Japanese System.* Cambridge, UK: Cambridge University Press, 1990.

Fransman, M. *Japanese Computer and Communications Industry: The Evolution of Industrial Giants and Global Competitiveness.* Oxford, UK: Oxford University Press, 1995.

Gates, B. *The Road Ahead.* New York: Viking Penguin, 1995.

Glickman, H., et al. "The Technology Pay Off." *Business Week* (August 14, 1995):57–68.

Gomory, R. E. "Technology Development." *Science* 220 (May 6, 1983):576–580.

Gordon, R. J. "The Postwar Evolution of Computer Prices." In *Technology and Capital Formation,* D. W. Jorgenson and R. Landau, eds., pp. 77–125. Cambridge, MA: MIT Press, 1989.

Griliches, Z. "The Search for R&D Spillovers." *Scandinavian Journal of Economics* 945 (1992):29–47.

Hobday, M. "Export-Led Technology Development in the Four Dragons: The Case of Electronics." *Development and Change* 25 (April 1994):333–361.

Hughes, T. P. *Rescuing Prometheus.* New York: Random House, 1998.

Hutcheson, G. D., and J. D. Hutcheson. "Technology and Economics of the Semiconductor Industry." *Scientific American* 274 (January 1996):54–62.

Irwin, D. A. "Trade Politics and the Semiconductor Industry." In *The Political Economy of American Trade Policy,* A. O. Krueger, ed., pp. 11–71. Chicago, IL: University of Chicago Press, 1996.

Irwin, D. A., and P. J. Klenow. "High Tech R&D Subsidies: Estimating the Effects of Sematech." Cambridge, MA: National Bureau of Economic Research Working Paper No. 4974, 1994.

Jorgensen, M. R. "Monopoly and Markets in the U.S. Computer Industry to 1970: IBM and U.S. Government Technology and Antitrust Policy." University of Minnesota, Department of Sociology, 1996, mimeo.

Jorgenson, D. W., and K. J. Stiroh. *Raising the Speed Limit: U.S. Economic Growth in the Information Age.* Cambridge, MA: Harvard University, Department of Economics, May 1, 2000, mimeo.

Jorgenson, D. W., and K. J. Stiroh. "Information Technology and Growth." *American Economic Review* 89 (1999):109–115.

Katz, B. G., and A. Phillips. "The Computer Industry." In *Government and Technical Progress: A Cross-Industry Analysis*, R. R. Nelson, ed., pp. 162–232. New York: Pergamon Press, 1982.

Kenney, M. and U. von Burg. "Paths and Regions: The Creation an growth of Silicon Valley." In *Path-Dependence and Creation*, R. Garud and P. Karnoe, eds. Mahawah, NJ: Lawerence Erlbaum Associates (in press).

Kerr, R. A. "Research Council Says U.S. Climate Models Can't Keep Up." *Science* 283 (February 5, 1999):766–767.

King, Ralph T., Jr. "Magic Formula." *Wall Street Journal* 14 (1994):R18–19.

Landauer, T. K. *The Trouble with Computers.* Cambridge, MA: MIT Press, 1995.

Langolis, R. N. "External Economies and Economic Progress: The Case of the Microcomputer Industry." *Business History Review* (Spring 1992):1–50.

Langlois, R. N., and D. C. Mowery. "The Federal Government's Role in the Development of the U.S. Software Industry." In *The International Computer Software Industry: A Comparative Study of Industry Evolution and Structure,* D. C. Mowery, ed., pp. 53–85. New York: Oxford University Press, 1996.

Langolis, R. N., T. A. Pugel, C. S. Haklisch, R. R. Nelson, and W. G. Egelhoff. *Microelectronics: An Industry in Transition.* Winchester, MA: Unwin Hyman, 1988.

Levin, R. C. "The Semiconductor Industry." In *Government and Technical Progress: A Cross-Industry Analysis,* R. Nelson, ed., pp. 7–100. New York: Pergamon Press, 1982.

Levy, B., and W.-J. Kuo. "The Strategic Orientation of Firms and the Performance of Korea and Taiwan in Frontier Industries: Lessons from Comparative Case Studies of Keyboard and Personal Computer Assembly." *World Development* 19 (April 1991):361–374.

Lohr, S. "Computer Age Gains Respect of Economists." *New York Times* (April 4, 1999):A1, C14.

Macher, J. T., D. C. Mowery, and D. A. Hodges. "Semiconductors." In *U.S. Industry in 2000: Studies in Competitive Performance*, D. C. Mowery, ed., pp. 245–286. Washington, DC: National Academy Press, 1999.

Maitland, I. "Who Won the Industrial Policy Debate." *Business and the Contemporary World*, 1 (1995):83–95.

Malerba, F., and S. Torrisi. "The Dynamics of Market Structure and Innovation in the Western European Software Industry." In *The International Computer Software Industry: A Comparative Study of Industry Evolution and Structure,* D. C. Mowery, ed., pp. 165–196. New York: Oxford University Press, 1996.

McDowell, S. D. "The Decline of the License Raj: Indian Software Export Policies." *Journal Communication* 45 (1995):25–50.

Moore, G. E. "Intel-Memories and the Microprocessor." *Daedalus* 125 (Spring 1996):55–80.

Mowery, D. C. "Innovation, Market Structure, and Government Policy in the American Semiconductor Electronic Industry: A Survey." *Research Policy* 12 (1983):183–197.

Mowery, D. C., ed. *The International Computer Software Industry: A Comparative Study of Industry Evolution and Structure.* New York: Oxford University Press, 1996.

Mowery, D. C., ed. *U.S. Industry in 2000: Studies in Competitive Performance.* Washington, DC: National Academy Press, 1999.

Mowery, D. C., and N. Rosenberg. *Paths of Innovation: Technological Cane in 20th Century America.* Cambridge, UK: Cambridge University Press, 1998.

Nelson, R. R. "The Transistor." In *The Rate and Direction of Inventive Activity: Economic and Social Factors,* R. R. Nelson, ed., pp. 549–583. Princeton, NJ: Princeton University Press, 1962.

Norberg, A. L., and J. E. O'Neill (with K. J. Freedman). *Transforming Computer Technology: Information Processing for the Pentagon, 1962–1986.* Baltimore, MD: Johns Hopkins University Press, 1996.

Oliner, S. D., and D. E. Sichel. "Computers and Output Growth: How Big Is the Puzzle?" *Brookings Papers on Economic Activity* 2 (1994):273–334.

Oliner, S. D., and W. L. Wascher. "Is a Productivity Revolution Underway in the United States?" *Challenge* (November/December 1995):18–29.

Pollack, A. "In Japan Aid for Developing Chip of Future." *New York Times* (October 16, 1995a):D3.

Pollack, A. "Motorola Joins Competitors in International Chip Alliance." *New York Times* (October 19, 1995b):D5.

Pollack, A. "Japanese Seek to End Semiconductor Pact with U.S." *New York Times* (November 3, 1995c):D4.

Pugh, E. W. *Memories That Shaped an Industry: Decisions Leading to IBM System 1360.* Cambridge, MA: MIT Press, 1984.

Randazzese, L. P. "Semiconductor Subsidies." *Scientific American* (June 1996):46–49.

Rifkin, G., and G. Harrar. *The Ultimate Entrepreneur: The Story of Ken Olson and Digital Equipment Corporation.* Chicago, IL: Contemporary Books, 1988.

Riordan, M., and L. Hoddeson. *Crystal Fire: The Birth of the Information Age.* New York: W. W. Norton, 1977.

Rochlin, G. I. *Trapped in the Net: The Unanticipated Consequences of Computerization.* Princeton, NJ: Princeton University Press, 1997.

Rosenberg, N. *Exploring the Black Box: Technology, Economics and History.* Cambridge, UK: Cambridge University Press, 1994.

Saco, D. "Colonizing Cyberspace: 'National Security' and the Internet." Minneapolis: University of Minnesota, Department of Political Science, 1996.

Schware, R. "Software Industry Entry Strategies for Developing Countries: A 'Walking on Two Legs' Propositions." *World Development* 20 (1992):143–164.

Shockley, W. "The Path to the Conception of the Junction Transistor." *IEEE Transactions on Electronic Devices* ED-23 (July 1976):597–620.

Shurkin, J. *Engines of the Mind: A History of the Computer.* New York: W. W. Norton, 1984.

Sichel, D. E. *The Computer Revolution: An Economic Perspective.* Washington, DC: Brookings Institution Press, 1997.

Soltis, F. G. *Inside the AS/400.* Lowland, CO: Duke Communications International, 1996.

Steinmueller, W. E. "The U.S. Software Industry: An Analysis and Interpretive History." In *The International Computer Software Industry: A Comparative Study of Industry Evolution and Structure,* D. C. Mowery, ed., pp. 15–52. New York: Oxford University Press, 1996.

Stiroh, K. J. "Computers, Productivity and Input Substitution." *Economic Inquiry* 36 (1998): 175–191.

Strassmann, P. A. *The Squandered Computer: Evaluating the Business Alignment of Information Technologies.* New Canaan, CT: The Information Economics Press, 1997.

Subramanian, C. R. *India and the Computer: A Study of Planned Development.* Bombay, India: Oxford University Press, 1992.

Teal, G. K. "Single Crystals of Germanium and Silicon—Basic to the Transistor and Integrated Circuit." *IEEE Transactions on Electron Devices* ED-23 (July 1976):621–639.

Tilton, J. E. *International Diffusion of Technology: The Case of Semiconductors.* Washington, DC: Brookings Institution Press, 1971.

Triplett, J. E. "The Economic Interpretation of Hedonic Methods." *Survey of Current Business* 66 (January 1986):36–40.

Tomash, E. and A. A. Cohen. "The Birth of ERA: Engineering Research Associates, Inc., 1946–1955." *Annals of the History of Computing* 1 (October 1979):83–97.

Tyson, L. D'A. *Who's Bashing Whom? Trade Conflict in High Technology Industries.* Washington, DC: Institute for International Economics, 1992.

Usselman, S. W. "IBM and Its Imitators: Organizational Capabilities and the Emergence of the International Computer Industry." *Business and Economic History* 222 (1993):1–35.

Warner, R. M., ed. *Integrated Circuits: Design Principles and Fabrication.* New York, McGraw-Hill, 1965.

Williams, M. "NEC Seeks to Settle Supercomputer Case." *The Wall Street Journal* (September 15, 1997):A14.

Young, H. "BEA's Measurement of Computer Output." *Survey of Current Business* 69 (July 1989):108–115.

CHAPTER 10

The Biotechnology Industries[1]

The biotechnology industries are believed by many to be positioned to replace the computer and information industries as the dynamic growth industries of the first half of the twenty-first century. Biotechnology has been hailed as the "next strategic technology" after microelectronics. Concerns about the impact of new biotechnologies on human health and the environment have provoked intense public debate.

But what is biotechnology? Biotechnology is not an industry or a sector. It is instead a generic set of biochemical and bioengineering techniques. Traditionally the term biotechnology has been applied to any technique that uses living organisms to make or modify products, to improve plants and animals, or to develop and use microorganisms in pharmaceuticals, food processing, or other industrial uses. In the United States the term has been applied much more narrowly, since the early 1970s, to refer to the use of a new set of biochemical and bioengineering techniques that has emerged from recent advances in biology. In this chapter I use the term biological technology to refer to the older technologies that had evolved out of centuries of practice and from advances in the biological sciences in the nineteenth and first half of the twentieth century. I first review the development of the old biological technology, particularly its role in the agricultural and pharmaceutical industries. I then turn to the contribution of biotechnology to the further advancement of technology in the agricultural, pharmaceutical, and food industries.

A primary reason for including a chapter on biotechnology is that the biotechnologies are unique in the close articulation between advances in science and advances in technology. The power of the new biotechnologies lies in their ability to manipulate and modify genes and cells in a targeted fashion. This has made it possible to "engineer" a wide spectrum of organisms that are important in the agricultural, food, and health industries. Many of the new entrepreneurs in the biotechnology industries are the same scientists who were the source of the scientific advances on which the new biotechnologies are based. The power to manipulate and, potentially, to create

---

[1] I am indebted to John H. Barton, Richard Caldecott, Donald Duvick, Keith Fuglie, Robert Goodman, Lovell Jarvis, Nicholas Kalaitzandonakes, Maureen McKelvey, Ronald Phillips, Terry Roe, Pamela Smith, Burt Sundquist, Gary Toenniessen, and Garrison Wilkes for comments on an earlier draft of this chapter.

life forms has been the source of continuing concern in the scientific community and among the general public. There has been substantial resistance to both the conduct of research in biotechnology and to the development and adoption of transgenic technologies and products.

In examining the sources of technical change in the diverse industries affected by biotechnology I draw on the perspectives offered by the induced technical change, evolutionary theory, and path dependence models (Chapter 4). In biotechnology differences in resource endowments are themselves reflected in (1) the historical development of national chemical, pharmaceutical, and agricultural industries, (2) the quality of government, university, and industrial research systems, and (3) the scientific and technical capacity of a nation's human capital, particularly in science and technology. Differences in institutional endowments are also important. In the case of biotechnology these include (1) incentives, constraints, and protections offered by relevant regulatory regimes, (2) the ability of a nation's intellectual property rights system to provide incentives for the development of new biotechnologies, and (3) the evolution of market structures in the industries that are the suppliers and users of the new sources of technology (Callan, 1995:105–109).

FROM BIOLOGICAL TECHNOLOGY TO BIOTECHNOLOGY

The term biotechnology was first introduced by the Hungarian agricultural engineer, Karl Ereky, in 1919. It was used to describe the processes by which industrial products were produced from agricultural raw materials with the aid of living organisms. The most important applications at that time were the fermentation technologies used in brewing. As late as 1900 the value of beer produced in Germany was approximately the same as the value of the steel industry (Bud, 1993:6–50). During the 1930s biological technology acquired a more philosophical connotation. Lewis Mumford, in his influential *Technics and Civilization* (1934), advanced a vision of a world about to make a major transition from a past dominated by mechanical technology to a "biotechnic" future. New engineering curricula that placed greater emphasis on the interfaces between engineering, human agents, and the natural world were developed at MIT, UCLA, and elsewhere.

In the late 1930s the term molecular biology was being used by Warren Weaver, Director for Natural Sciences at the Rockefeller Foundation, to describe a program of research in fundamental biology below the cellular level.[2] In its modern use, the term biotechnology refers to techniques that emerged from advances in molecular biology and that use living organisms to make or modify products, improve plants and animals, and develop microorganisms for specific uses (Office of Technology Assessment,

---

[2] In the annual report of the Rockefeller Foundation for 1938 Weaver reported that among the studies to which the Foundation is giving support is a new branch of science—molecular biology—which is beginning to uncover many secrets concerning the ultimate units of the living cell (Weaver, 1938:203).

1984). In this section I discuss the advances in the older biological technology in (1) genetics and plant breeding, (2) fermentation processes, and (3) the production of pharmaceuticals. These were also the fields in which the new biotechnologies found their initial applications. My motivation is to emphasize the continuity and continuing complementarity between the "old" biological technology and the "new" biotechnology.

Genetics and Plant Breeding

The technology of crop improvement began when the first neolithic men and women began to save and plant the seeds of wild plants (Harlan, 1992). Many of today's cultivated plants originated in rather limited "centers of origin"—wheat in Asia Minor, maize in Central America, soybeans in North China, and potatoes in the Andean highlands. The term "landrace" is used to describe the cultivated varieties that have emerged as a result of seed selection by indigenous farmers over long periods of time. Differences in ecological conditions, cultivation practices, and crop usage resulted in selection for diverse traits, leading to great genetic diversity of landraces. For example, maize was adapted throughout the tropical and temperate Americas in the form of distinct landraces long before Columbus arrived.

During the nineteenth century the selection process became much more highly institutionalized. Plant exploration missions were sent throughout the world to identify and bring back potentially useful crop varieties. Great botanical gardens, such as the Royal Botanic Garden at Kew outside of London, were established as plant introduction stations. Plant breeders sought new sources of genetic variation for crop and animal improvement (Goodman et al., 1987; Harlan, 1992).

During the first half of the twentieth century advances in the technology of plant breeding drew more directly on the emerging science of genetics (Box 10.1) The rediscovery of Mendel's work marked the beginning of several decades in which there were rapid advances in knowledge. The nature of the gene, the basic unit of heredity, was clarified. The possibility of mutation, or sudden, permanent changes in the character of the gene, was recognized. In 1910, the intensive study of the genetics of the fruit fly led to an understanding of the role of linked genes, which are genes that reside on the same chromosome and are transmitted together. This paved the way for advances in understanding the mechanism of heredity. As late as the early 1950s, however, the gene itself remained an "invisible, formal and abstract unit" (Stent, 1969:16). The mechanism that enables the gene to cause the synthesis of another structure like itself, in which even mutations are copied, remained a mystery.

An example of the process of development of new crop varieties using the principles of classical Mendelian crop breeding has been discussed in Chapter 3 (see also Duvick, 1996). The impact of economic factors on the rate and direction of new technology in agriculture was discussed in Chapter 4, the diffusion of agricultural technology in Chapter 5, and biological technology in the process of agricultural development in Chapter 6. I now turn to a brief discussion of the relationship between advances in the older biological technologies and the development of the pharmaceutical industry prior to a discussion of the impact of the new biotechnologies in the agricultural and pharmaceutical industries.

● **BOX 10.1**

GREGOR JOHANN MENDEL

Gregor Johann Mendel was the first person to formulate the basic laws of inheritance in the form of simple statistical probability.

Mendel was born in Heinzendorf, Silesia (then part of Austria) on July 22, 1822. He entered the Augustinian monastery at Brünn, Moravia (now Brno in Czechoslovakia) in 1843. He was ordained a priest in 1847. After acting as a substitute teacher in Greek and Latin in the local high school for several years, he took, and failed, the examination for certification as a regular teacher. His lowest marks were in biology and geology. Mendel was then sent by his abbot to the university of Vienna where he studied physics, chemistry, mathematics, zoology, and botany. In 1854 he returned to Brünn and taught natural science in the technical high school until 1868.

The experiments that led to his discovery of the basic principles of heredity and to the science of genetics were begun in a small monastery garden in 1856. He crossed varieties of garden peas that he determined had maintained stable differences in characteristics such as tallness and dwarfness, presence or absence of color in the blossoms, seed color, seed shape, position of the flowers, and form of the pods. Through his crossing experiments Mendel determined that these characteristics obeyed simple statistical laws of inheritance. From these statistical results Mendel inferred that the hereditary characteristics are carried and passed on to the progeny as discrete units. Each plant carries a homologous pair of such units, of which one is selected at random for transmission to individual progeny.

Mendel's first law, the principle of independent segregation, accounts for the result that single pairs of alternative traits, such as blossom color, are transmitted through several generations. Mendel's second law, the principle of independent assortment, accounts for the result that when several pairs of alternative traits are observed, such as blossom color and height, the several pairs of traits enter into all possible combinations of the progeny in a manner that can be described by precise statistical laws. Mendel theorized that the occurrences of the visible alternative traits of the plants, in the constant varieties and their offspring, is due to paired elementary units of heredity known as genes.

The theory and the experimental results consistent with the theory were presented in a paper, "Experiments on Plant Hybrids," before the Brünn Natural Science Society in 1865 and published in the transactions of the society in 1866.

It is apparent that his colleagues, perhaps because of the mathematical presentation of his results, did not understand or appreciate the implications of Mendel's research. Between 1869, when he published a second paper, and 1900, there was only a single reference in the biological literature to Mendel's research. In 1881 a work was published in Berlin entitled *Die Eflanzenmischlinge* by W. O. Focke, which indicated that Mendel "believed he had found constant numerical ratios among the types produced by hybridization" (Iltis, 1932:285). In 1900 three plant breeders—Hugo de Vries in Holland, Carl Corren in Germany, and Erich Tschermak in Austria—independently rediscovered the reference by Focke and recognized the significance of Mendel's work to their own plant-breeding experiments. Following this rediscovery the fundamental techniques that continue to serve as a basis for most crop improvement research were developed.

Sources: In this box I draw on the article on Gregor Johann Mendel in *The New Encyclopedia Britannica*, Macropaedia, Vol. 11, Chicago: Encyclopedia Britannica, Inc., 1974:898–899; Hugo Iltis, *Life of Mendel*, London: George Allen and Unwin, 1932 (translated from the 1924 German edition); and Vítězslav Orel, *Gregor Mendel: The First Geneticist*, Oxford, UK: Oxford University Press, 1996. The elegant exposition of Mendel's thought by Curt Stern in "The Continuity of Genetics," *Daedalus* 99 (4, 1970):882–907, is particularly valuable. Mendel's two papers and the papers by de Vries, Corren, and Tschermak, and other key papers on the rediscovery of Mendel's work, have been collected in Curt Stern and Eva R Sherwood's *The Origin of Genetics: A Mendel Source Book*, San Francisco: W. H. Freeman, 1966.

Fermentation and Pharmaceuticals

The close link between biological technology and advances in basic biology began in the nineteenth century.[3] Initially the flow of knowledge was primarily from technology to science. For example, while studying fermentation to improve brewing and wine making in the 1860s, Louis Pasteur demonstrated that microorganisms cause fermentation. Penicillin was the first modern fermentation product to be adopted by the pharmaceutical industry. The antibiotic properties of *Penicillium* mold had been described by Alexander Flemming in 1928. But it was not until the late 1930s that a group of British scientists at Oxford University was successful in isolating the drug "penicillin," in establishing the protocols for its evaluation, in producing small quantities, and in using it to cure a few patients with potentially fatal infections.

Because of wartime resource constraints the Oxford group found it necessary to turn to the United States for the expertise, organization, and resources to achieve large-scale production. The expertise in fermentation technology at the U.S. Department of Agriculture (USDA) Northern Research Laboratory in Peoria (Illinois) enabled it to scale up the microbiological process developed in Britain. The USDA agricultural

---

[3] In this section I draw heavily on Bud (1993:103–107).

engineers had already built a new large-scale fermentator that allowed submerged mold culture using corn steep liquor as a feedstock. The Peoria technology raised penicillin production per liter of feedstock by 30-fold. The USDA research team also identified, on a Peoria cantaloupe, a mold that would raise the penicillin yield by another order of magnitude. Engineers at U.S. and British firms furthered the process technology and developed another antibiotic, streptomycin. In the years after World War II the fermentation industry experienced rapid growth as penicillin and streptomycin were followed by a growing list of antibiotics effective against a broad range of bacterial diseases (Rasmussen, 1999).

Although the development of antibiotics initially grew out of research and development in Britain and the United States, by the early 1960s it was Japan that emerged as the leader in the fermentation industry. A large number of traditional Japanese foods and beverages, such as tofu, soy sauce, and saki, are based on fermentation processes (National Research Council Board on Science and Technology for International Development, 1992). In the early post-World War II period the Japanese fermentation industry drew on the scientific and technical advances that had occurred in Britain and the United States and indigenous knowledge of fermentation technology to develop the penicillin industry. By the early 1960s Japan held a dominant position worldwide in the production of antibiotics as well as a variety of other pharmaceutical products based on fermentation technology.

The development of new industries for the production of antibiotics, amino acids enzymes, high fructose corn syrup, ethanol, and other fermentation products gave rise to the new field of biochemical engineering with roots in both chemical engineering and microbiology. Courses in biochemical engineering began to appear in college catalogues in the mid-1940s. A new professional journal, the *Journal of Microbiological and Biochemical Engineering and Technology* (later renamed *Biotechnology and Bioengineering)* was launched in 1958. But the field remained rooted in existing technologies. As late as the mid-1980s a text on the economics of the biotechnology industries focused almost entirely on the established fermentation-based technologies with only brief discussion of the new biotechnologies based on the post-World War II advances in molecular biology (Hocking, 1986).

MOLECULAR BIOLOGY AND BIOTECHNOLOGY

Four major advances in molecular biology were essential for the transition from the old biological technology to the new biotechnology.[4] The *first* was the 1938 identification, by Max Delbruck at the California Institute of Technology, of DNA

---

[4] For excellent and very accessible accounts see Stent (1968:390–395) and Watson (1968). For more technical accounts see Brock (1990), Cairns et al. (1992), and Cohen et al. (1973: 3240–3244). Stent refers to the periods in which these advances were made as the romantic phase, the dynamic phase, and the academic phase. See the Appendix for definitions of scientific and technical terms used in this chapter.

(deoxyribonucleic acid) as the physical carrier of genetic information. This was followed by the demonstration that microbes could exchange genetic information. The *second* was the discovery by James Watson and Francis Crick of the double helical structure of DNA in 1953 (Figure 10.1). Their discovery was followed by intensive research aimed at understanding the mechanism by which DNA transferred its encoded information to the cell. Increasing numbers of biochemists and physicists were attracted to molecular genetics. Departments of immunology, virology, and microbiology were colonized by molecular biologists. The *third* critical breakthrough occurred in 1973 when Stanley Cohen (Stanford) and Herbert Boyer (University of California at San Francisco) and their associates demonstrated a method for stably inserting genes from a foreign organism into a host genome. The invention of the Cohen–Boyer "gene splicing" technique opened up the possibility of "engineering" the genetics of a cell to induce it to produce a specific protein that might, for example, have pharmaceutical or agronomic value. The *fourth* breakthrough occurred in 1975 when Cesar Milstein and Georges J. F. Köehler invented hybridoma (fusion) technology. The Milstein–Köehler technique involves formation of a hybrid cell with nuclei and cytoplasm from different cells to combine the desirable characteristics from the different cells (Schmeck, 1981:A1, C2).

These breakthroughs were followed by the early development of a series of important biotechnology techniques. Plant and animal *cell and tissue culture techniques*, initially developed in the 1930s and 1940s, were the earliest of the new biotechnologies to be applied (Goodman et al., 1987). These techniques involve regenerating entire organisms from protoplasts, single cells, or plant parts. The *recombinant DNA* (rDNA) *technique*, invented by Cohen and Boyer, led to the production of hybrid gene material by joining pieces of DNA from different organisms together *in vitro* and then cutting the DNA into segments that contain specific sequences of nucleotides. *Cell fusion technology* involves fusing a myeloma cell and a lymphocyte to produce a cell line or clone (*hybridoma*) that combines the characteristics of both the original cells. The hybridomas are used to produce monoclonal antibodies, which, because of their high specificity and variety, are useful tools in diagnostic and therapeutic processes involving the recognition of particular molecules (specific proteins, for example). A fourth important technology, *protein engineering*, is used to introduce precise changes in the structure of a protein to create new proteins having specific catalytic or therapeutic properties. The potential for commercial development of these technologies opened up a period of both wild optimism about commercial opportunities and deep anxiety about the risks from application of the new biotechnologies. It also raised fears that genetically engineered microorganisms could become a source of new and more virulent disease if released into the environment.

Concern about DNA

In July 1974 a group of 10 eminent molecular biologists, headed by Paul Berg of Stanford University, published a letter in *Science* suggesting that the consequences

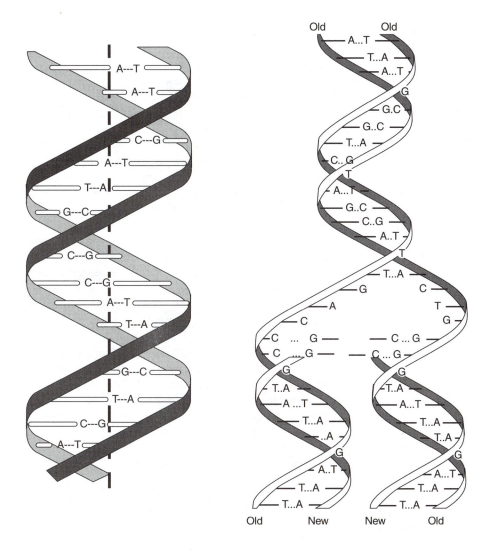

Figure 10.1 A schematic diagram of the DNA double helix and its replication. The DNA molecule is a double helix composed of two chains. There are four nitrogenous bases in DNA. Adenine (A) pairs with thymidine (T); guanine (G) pairs with cytosine (C). When DNA replicates, the double helix splits lengthwise to create two single helices. Each single helix then joins a new partner to create another double helix. (*Source:* Office of Technology Assessment. *Impacts of Applied Genetics: Micro-Organisms, Plants and Animals.* Washington, DC: U.S. Government Printing Office (OTA-HR-132), April 1981:36–37.)

inherent in bacteria and viruses containing recombinant DNA were potentially so destructive that a moratorium should be called on certain types of experiments until the issue could be explored in greater depth (Berg et al., 1974:303).[5] In February 1975 Berg, Maxine Singer, and their colleagues convened an international meeting of prominent biologists at Asilomar on California's Monterey Peninsula to assess the new technology and establish the conditions under which research could or should proceed (Krimsky, 1982:99). The outcome of the conference was a recommendation, unprecedented in science, that "there are certain experiments in which the potential risks are of such serious nature that they ought not be done with presently available containment facilities" (Berg et al., 1975:992). The conference recommended that a moratorium be placed on such experiments until more secure facilities were built, and appropriate protocols and regulations could be developed.[6]

The publicity given to the Asilomar conference also increased public sensitivity to the advances being made in molecular biology and raised fears of the epidemics that might be caused by organisms resulting from recombinant DNA research. As the National Institutes of Health (NIH) guidelines were being developed in 1976 the public debate was becoming highly politicized (Wade, 1977). The most dramatic example was a resolution by the Cambridge, Massachusetts, City Council calling on Harvard University to justify its decision to construct a genetic engineering containment facility. Other state and local governments throughout the United States also began to establish committees to oversee recombinant DNA research. Hearings were held in the U.S. Congress and legislation was drafted that would have made the NIH guidelines mandatory for all rDNA research (Kenney, 1986:24–26). In the late 1970s and early 1980s the guidelines were substantially revised. The NIH Recombinant DNA Molecule Program Advisory Committee was enlarged and appointment of public members with interests and expertise in public health and the environment was required. Institutional Biosafety Committees at universities and other research institutions that would include members not affiliated with the institution were also mandated.

At the same time the safety guidelines were relaxed in recognition that the anticipated hazards had not yet materialized. In 1980 the Senate held hearings that focused not on biosafety, but on how the government might facilitate the development

---

[5] Even prior to the Cohen–Boyer experiment microbiologists who were conducting research on cancer became concerned about the possibility that experiments involving the use of a tumor virus to transfer a cancer gene into the bacterium *Escherichia coli*, a normal inhabitant of the human gut, might carry the tumor virus into a human population. For a detailed account of the early controversies and the evolution of policy over the scientific use, development, and application of gene-transplantation research see Krimsky (1982) and Wright (1994).

[6] "The emergence of atomic energy came at a time when science was hostage to the threat of fascism. . . . Wartime imperatives legitimized government coverups of radiation hazards in atomic technology programs. . . . There are also important differences between the early development of synthetic organic chemicals and the creation of genetically engineered life-forms. . . . [In] the early development of industrial organic chemistry . . . no warnings were issued by the scientific community about the potential injurious effects of thousands of synthetic organic compounds" (Krimsky, 1991:15).

of biotechnology in industry. The effect of this series of incremental changes was to produce a reversal of the legacy of the Asilomar Conference and to open the entire spectrum of living things to genetic manipulation with controls remaining for only limited classes of experiments (Wright, 1994:256–278). In reviewing the early history of the regulation of biotechnology and its commercialization, Kenney noted, "it is quite remarkable how quickly doubts about its safety receded once it appeared that profits could be made from this new technology" (Kenney, 1986:27). There continued, however, to be considerable concern about the possible effects of introducing transgenic crops on the genetic integrity of closely related wild species, and on the emergence of new and more troublesome weeds and other pests and pathogens (Brill, 1985; Colwell et al., 1995; Snow and Palma, 1997).

THE UNIVERSITY–INDUSTRIAL COMPLEX

Prior to the mid-1970s almost all research in molecular biology and biotechnology had been conducted by universities and by the federal government. An important motivation for the very substantial growth in federal funding of research in molecular genetics was its potential contribution to solving health problems.[7] Solving health problems through biological research was more consistent with American political philosophy than a more direct attack on the social and institutional sources of ill health.

When the prospects for commercial exploitation of biotechnology became apparent, it also became obvious that the capacity to conduct the necessary research and development resided almost entirely in the universities and in a few federal laboratories. In the late 1970s and early 1980s there was a period of intense entrepreneurial activity in the formation of new university–industry relationships. The pioneers in molecular biology were thrust into a role they had not anticipated—the role of entrepreneurs in the new biotechnology industries.

Science Entrepreneurs

Many of the early genetic engineering companies were founded or cofounded by academic researchers. The commercially oriented research was initially undertaken in university laboratories. Even when the new start-up companies were able to provide their own laboratory space many entrepreneur–scientists preferred, and were permitted, to retain their university appointments.[8]

---

[7] In the fiscal year 1993, federal government support for biotechnology research amounted to approximately $90 billion. Of this $29 billion was by the National Institutes of Health (Federal Coordinating Council for Science, Engineering and Technology, 1992).

[8] The traditional practice in universities is that faculty members are authorized to spend up to one day a week consulting. Because of the highly decentralized nature of university administration and the frequent complementary relationship between consulting activity and sponsored university research consulting activity is typically monitored rather loosely.

> Genetic engineering as a commercial venture began in 1976 when Robert Swanson, a venture capitalist, . . . convinced Herbert Boyer, one of the inventors of the Cohen–Boyer gene splicing process, to form a company to commercialize new recombinant DNA techniques. . . . A new company, Genentech, was . . . started on Boyer's consulting time while he was a professor at the UCSF Medical Center. . . . In the early days Genentech did not have a laboratory so Boyer's campus laboratories were used. This was facilitated by a $200,000 grant to Boyer from Genentech. (Kenney, 1986:94, 95)

As the biotechnology industry has matured, the role of academic researchers as entrepreneurs has receeded.

The problem faced by Genentech, and every other genetic engineering start-up company, was how to secure sufficient income during the early years to maintain its research program. Genentech attempted to solve this problem by contracting to perform research and development services for major drug companies. The first contract that Genentech entered into was to provide genetically engineered insulin-producing bacteria to Eli Lilly, the leading producer of insulin. Under the contract with Lilly, Genentech was paid to conduct the research and was granted a royalty on all sales of Lilly's bacterially produced insulin. Lilly received exclusive worldwide rights to manufacture and market the insulin.

During the early 1980s Genentech entered into a number of other contracts with pharmaceutical companies under varying contract arrangements. With each successive arrangement Genentech sought to obtain greater control over the marketing of products that it developed. It attempted to avoid selling its technical know-how (by selling prepared bacteria, for example, rather than the knowledge or technology to produce the bacteria).[9]

The pattern followed by Genentech was repeated many times. The potential analogy with the dramatic profits realized by early start-up firms in the computer and software industries (Chapter 9) became an almost irresistible lure for venture capitalists. Three important ingredients for starting a biotechnology firm in the late 1970s were a university scientist who had command of the knowledge and techniques, an entrepreneur with good connections in the academic and financial communities, and financial backers who could be convinced that the business would develop a successful commercial product within 5 to 7 years. It was also helpful if one or two Nobel awardees in the field of molecular genetics could be attracted to the board of the new company. It is hard to escape the conclusion that a few "delusion genes" were also important!

The boom in the formation of new biotechnology companies continued into the late 1980s (Figure 10.2). Companies that had been founded prior to the discovery of recombinant DNA technology shifted their emphasis to genetic engineering. By

---

[9] For an account of the experience of a number of other biotechnology start-up firms in the early 1980s, see Kenney (1986:158–179).

the late 1980s seven biotechnology-based human therapeutics had been approved for marketing in the United States. Yet not a single biotechnology company had realized any profit from the manufacture and sale of a product based on rDNA technology (Krimsky, 1991:28). As late as the mid-1990s there were still fewer than 30 biotechnology therapeutics and vaccines on the market. Since the mid-1990s the rate of growth of new product approvals has exploded. Profitability and sustainability remained problematic, however, for most of the companies producing these new products.

In retrospect, it seems clear that well into the second decade of the biotechnology revolution the close articulation between advances in molecular biology and biotechnology was giving rise to considerable confusion, and often excessive promotion, regarding the implications of advances in scientific understanding and advances in the capacity to intervene in areas such as human health, plant and animal protection and improvement, and food safety and quality. Identification of a gene or a gene sequence responsible for a human disease, such as Alzheimer's or prostrate cancer, or of a plant pathogen such as a virus, has often been announced as if it would lead directly to an intervention in human health or plant protection. But advances in understanding above the cellular level are usually required to design successful intervention technologies. Furthermore, the scaling up of laboratory methods for commercial production can be both time consuming and expensive. The long delays in bringing new products to market, combined with the inherent uncertain results of R&D effort, slowed the formation of new biotechnology start-up companies after 1987.

Industrial Organization

By the early 1980s a new pattern of relationships involving the establishment of formal institutional arrangements between universities, research institutes, and multinational pharmaceutical and chemical companies emerged. This new pattern represented an effort by large pharmaceutical companies to obtain access to capacity in the field of molecular genetics that they did not have in their own laboratories. This close linkage between scientific advances and commercially useful innovations made prompt acquisition of such capacity an important source of competitive advantage. These new arrangements were sought by universities because of a perception that public funding would be much more difficult to come by than in the past. They were favored by faculty who were not unhappy to be relieved of the burden of continuous grant seeking. In these arrangements the funding corporation obtained access to not only the research skills of the principal investigator but, in some cases, to an entire laboratory or department, including assistant professors, postdoctoral researchers, and graduate students.

During the early 1980s large university–industry biotechnology research contracts were entered into by a number of major universities and research institutes and corporations. The first of these, and a model for several others, was between Massachusetts General Hospital, the primary teaching and research hospital for Harvard Medical

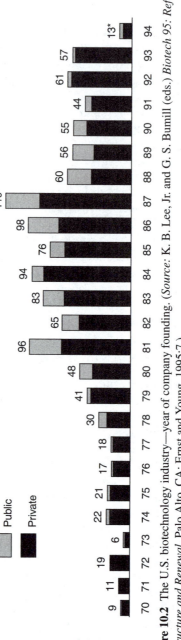

Figure 10.2 The U.S. biotechnology industry—year of company founding. (*Source:* K. B. Lee, Jr. and G. S. Burrill (eds.) *Biotech 95: Reform, Restructure and Renewal*, Palo Alto, CA: Ernst and Young, 1995:7.)

School, and Hoechst, a German-based multinational chemical company (Table 10.1). The details of the proposed arrangements between Hoechst and Harvard became public when Congressman Albert Gore raised questions about the propriety of "selling" the research investment, paid for by American taxpayers, to a foreign company. The final contract was rewritten to take into account some of the objections raised by Gore, particularly the coupling of federal and private funds. It is clear that Hoechst purchased more than "a window on the technology." It purchased the opportunity to build a cadre of researchers trained in a first rate laboratory in "state-of-the-art genetic engineering techniques" (Kenney, 1986:63).

A 1982 contract between Washington University (St. Louis) and Monsanto raised even more questions than the Harvard–Hoechst contract. The Washington University–Monsanto contract provided Monsanto with access to the entire Washington University Medical School. Its primary emphasis was on the development of new products with potential commercial value. The contract provided that the financial gains from the project would accrue not to the individual investigator, but rather to the institution, the particular department in the Medical School, and to the specific laboratory responsible for the creative effort.

Table 10.1   Summary of Large University–Industry Biotechnology Research Grants in the Early 1980s

Year	University	Company	Amount ($ million)	Duration (years)	Investigator	Area of Research
1981	Massachusetts General Hospital	Hoechst	70.0	10	H. Goodman	Genetics
1981	Harvard Medical School	Du Pont	6.0	5	P. Leder	Genetics
1981	UC Davis	Allied	2.5	3	R. Valentine	Nitroen fixation
1981	Scripps Clinic & Research Foundation	Johnson & Johnson	30.0	—	—	Synthetic vaccines
1981	Washington University	Mallinkrodt	3.8	5	J. Davie	Hybridomas
1981	Yale	Celanese	1.1	3	N. Ornston	Enzymes
1982	Johns Hopkins	Johnson & Johnson	1.0	—	—	Biology
1982	Rockefeller University	Monsanto	4.0	5	N. Chua	Photosynthesis
1982	Washington University	Monsanto	23.5	5	—	Biomedical
1982	MIT	W. R. Grace	8.0	5	P. Thilly	Amino acids
1982	Yale	Bristol-Myers	3.0	5	—	Anticancer drugs
1982	Cold Spring Harbor	Exxon	7.5	5	—	Molecular genetics
1983	Rochester	Kodak	0.45	—	—	DNA
1983	Medical University of South Carolina	Chugai	0.5	3	A. Strelkauskas	Monoclonal antibodies
1983	University of Illinois	Sohio	2.0	5	—	Plant molecular genetics
1983	Columbia	Bristol-Myers	2.3	6	A. Elstratiadis	Gene structure

Source: Martin Kenney. *Biotechnology: The University-Industrial Complex.* New Haven, CT: Yale University Press, 1986:56.

By the mid-1980s the system of industrial organization in the biotechnology industries had changed very substantially from a decade earlier, when almost all drug-related R&D had been conducted in-house by the major pharmaceutical and agrochemical companies.[10] The innovation process now depended on three types of agents: the universities, small- and medium-sized biotechnology firms, and large pharmaceutical and agrochemical companies. Two factors have led to an intimate and complex set of relationships among these agents. The first is that in biotechnology the relationship between scientific advances and technical development often has been relatively direct. The second is that even the largest pharmaceutical and agrochemical firms found it difficult or excessively expensive to internalize all the resources necessary to invent and develop new biotechnologies.

The major assets of the new biotechnology firms were their close articulation with university basic research in molecular biology, their tacit know-how in applied laboratory research, and the enthusiasm and energy of their scientific entrepreneurs. The product of this research is typically highly specific—a new protein obtained from a genetically engineered organism, for example. The synthesis of a new protein, however, does not complete the process. Engineering know-how is required to scale up from the laboratory bench to manufacturing. Familiarity with clinical testing procedures and with the regulatory process is also essential (Box 10.2). Finally, an extensive distribution network is necessary to successfully bring new products to the market. These are capacities that universities and new biotechnology firms did not have and that are very costly to acquire. Cooperative relations between universities, the new biotechnology firms, and the larger pharmaceutical and agrochemical firms proved to be advantageous for the development and commercialization of new biotechnology products.

Because there are substantial spillovers, and hence difficulty in appropriating the bulk of the benefits from scientific research, the major pharmaceutical and agrochemical companies entered into research agreements with universities in the hope of obtaining immediate access to advances in basic knowledge and any new discoveries that might have commercial potential. The scientific staff of the new biotechnology firms, because of their earlier university research experience and their continuing basic research, often had closer collegial relationships with university scientists than the scientific staff of the larger companies.

The reasons that larger firms typically enter into agreements with biotechnology firms are, however, somewhat different than their reasons for establishing linkages with universities. Linkages with new biotechnology firms are more likely to provide access to new processes and products than new scientific knowledge. They often invest in biotechnology start-ups to monitor the internal research activities of the start-ups and obtain an option on the results of the research generated by the start-up firm. These relationships are sometimes followed by acquisition of the smaller firms. In

---

[10] In the next several paragraphs I draw heavily on Arora and Gambardella (1990, 1994).

some cases the scientific entrepreneurs who start the new biotechnology companies consciously direct their research programs to make themselves attractive buy-out candidates. The apparent diseconomies of scale in scientific research and in the initial stage of product development are not inconsistent with findings of economies of scope in the pharmaceutical industry (Hendersen and Cockburn, 1996). The widening of scope through new product introduction economizes on the firm's capacity in clinical testing, product engineering, manufacture, and distribution.

● **BOX 10.2**

Stages in the Development of New Drugs

Before clinical trials, firms in the United States have to apply to the Food and Drug Administration (FDA) for an Investigational New Drug Exemption (IND). The FDA can reject IND applications if there is insufficient evidence that the new compounds can be safely tested in human beings.

Clinical trials comprise three stages (Figure 10.3). Going from stage I to stage III, a new compound is administrated to an increasing number of patients. Whereas stage I focuses on the toxicity of the product, stages II and III focus on its effectiveness. Typically, stage II and especially stage III involve a large number of patients, and they take place over a long period. This is to prepare an accurate profile of the drug, define its dosage, and evaluate side effects that occur with small probabilities or that reveal themselves only after several months.

In the United States, once a new compound has passed the clinical tests, companies have to present a formal request to the FDA to market the drug—the New Drug Application (NDA). The FDA can accept or reject the application or, alternatively, require the new medicine undergo further clinical tests to assess more carefully its safety and effectiveness. The average time from initial synthesis to NDA approval is approximately 100 months. Once a drug is approved for marketing, it is still kept under surveillance by the firm and the FDA. Market diffusion may reveal information that was not anticipated during clinical trials (learning by using). When a drug shows unanticipated side effects, the FDA may require that companies add warnings on the package or, if the side effects are severe, withdraw the product from the market.

Source: A. Gambardella, *Science and Innovation: The U.S. Pharmaceutical Industry During the 1980s*, Cambridge, MA: Cambridge University Press, 1995:18–20.

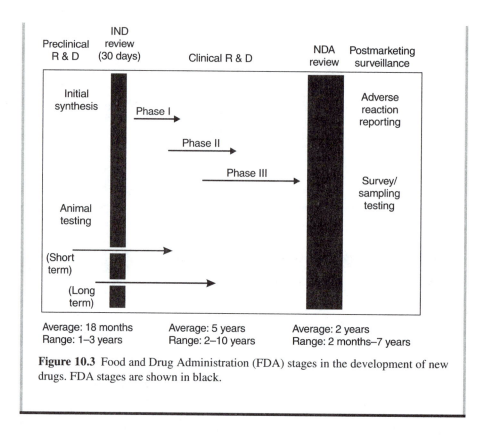

Average: 18 months Average: 5 years   Average: 2 years
Range: 1–3 years   Range: 2–10 years   Range: 2 months–7 years

Figure 10.3 Food and Drug Administration (FDA) stages in the development of new drugs. FDA stages are shown in black.

It has been argued that this set of relationships has emerged because the three organizations play highly complementary rather than competitive roles. At the basic end of the spectrum universities provide access to fundamental knowledge that is not being developed by the new biotechnology firms. The new biotechnology firms, in turn, command specialized knowledge and applied research techniques directed to product development. And the multinational pharmaceutical and agrochemical companies provide economies of scope through access to international distribution channels (Arora and Gambardella, 1990:366; Rausser, 1999).

INSTITUTIONAL INNOVATION

The drive to realize the commercial potential of advances in molecular biology and biotechnology has induced a series of institutional innovations. I have discussed earlier in this chapter the impact of biotechnology on university–industry relationships and the entrepreneurial behavior of university faculty, and have referred to the development of regulations concerning genetic engineering experiments. In this section I discuss the design of regulatory regimes for transgenic crops, the extension of patent rights to include life forms, and the changes in federal policy regarding intellectual property rights in technologies resulting from federally financed research.

Regulatory Regimes

The 1975 Asilomar conference, as noted earlier, contributed to both professional and public concern about biosafety. Such concerns led governments to regulate the field testing and release of transgenic crops. As in the case of biotechnology directed to pharmaceutical product development, there was a good deal of controversy about the appropriate degree of regulation for transgenic crops. Agronomists and plant breeders tended to view the protocols followed in conventional plant breeding as adequate for transgenic crops. Biologists and ecologists were more concerned about unanticipated gene exchange with wild relatives and weeds and favored the development of a more stringent regulatory regime. The United States and Canada employed a vertical or product-based regulatory system that defines the risk characteristics of the crops that require them to be regulated without requiring that every product developed using transgenic processes be regulated. European countries have, in contrast, generally developed a horizontal or process-based regulatory system that requires all plants produced by transgenic techniques to be regulated. A number of the more advanced developing countries (Argentina, India, Mexico, and Thailand, for example) have also developed regulatory regimes and many more are in the process of doing so. However, capacity to effectively monitor the implementation of field testing regulations in less developed countries is often lacking.

Regulations often require independent approval from more than one regulator agency. In the United States, for example, the Agricultural Plant Health Inspection Service (APHIS) issues permits for field trials and for environmental release. Any crop containing a gene for pest control also requires approval from the Environmental Protection Agency (EPA). If a product from a transgenic crop is for food use, the Food and Drug Administration (FDA) is also involved in approval. Approval may also be required from individual state agencies that often have more rigorous requirements than the federal agencies. Regulatory regimes have, however, been modified as a result of favorable experience. In 1993, APHIS introduced a modified notification system for the six transgenic crops with which the agency already had extensive experience (corn, tomato, soybean, potato, cotton, and tobacco). The notification system does not obligate applicants to acquire a permit and allows the conduct of field trials if there is no objection by APHIS.

Patenting Life

Intellectual property rights in the area of biological technology developed more slowly than in the traditional areas of industrial technology (Chapter 14). Patent protection for plants did not become available in the United States until 1930.[11] The Plant Protection Act of 1930 extended patenting rights to breeders of a number of "new and distinct" asexually reproduced plant varieties. In the 1960s a number of European countries enacted plant variety registration that provided protection of "breeders rights" for development of new varieties that were sexually propagated. The United States passed similar legislation in the 1970s. The "breeders rights" protected by crop variety registration differed from patents in that they allowed the protected varieties to be freely used by other breeders and to be reproduced by farmers for their own use (Ruttan, 1982:192–199).

The issue of plant variety registration remained controversial in the United States. Public sector plant breeders and the smaller seed companies were concerned that extending patent or patent-like protection to new crop varieties would inhibit the free exchange of genetic materials and access to public varieties and lead to excessive concentration in the seed industry. This opposition reflected the development of close institutional linkages between the university-based breeders of "public seeds," the private seed industry, and state-level seed-certification agencies. In Minnesota, for example, the Agricultural Experiment Station, operated by the University of Minnesota, supported a substantial crop variety research and development program. When the performance of a new variety of soybeans, developed by a university plant breeder, warranted seed multiplication and release to farmers, "breeder seed" was released to the Minnesota Crop Improvement Association for multiplication. The Crop Improvement Association, a nonprofit corporation whose owners were mostly farmers and small seed companies, also was designated by the state legislature as the official seed-certification agency in Minnesota. Rights to produce and market the public seeds were licensed to members of the Association. The seed-certification program was designed to ensure the purity and quality of seed sold by both the producers of public and private seeds. Similar associations had been organized in most other states (Ruttan, 1982:194).

In 1970 the U.S. Congress passed a Plant Variety Protection Act that had been developed by a committee of the American Seed Trade Association. The Act, administered by the U.S. Department of Agriculture, provided "patent-like" protection to novel varieties of plants that reproduced sexually. The Act was later amended to bring it into conformity with the provisions of the 1961 International Convention for the Protection of New Varieties of Plants (UPOV) that had earlier been established in Europe to ensure consistency among national plant registration laws.

In 1980 a judicial decision by the Supreme Court, the Diamond versus Chakrabarty ruling, extended patent protection to new microorganisms. In 1972 Ananda M. Chakrabarty, then a research scientist with General Electric, developed a strain of bacteria that would degrade four of the major components of crude oil. The new bacterium was designed to be placed on an oil spill to break down the oil into

---

[11] In this section I draw heavily on Office of Technology Assessment (1981:237–254); see also Ruttan (1982:192–199)

harmless products, use those products for food, and then disappear when the oil was gone.

Because anyone could acquire and reproduce the microbe once it was used, Chakrabarty applied for a patent on his invention. The U.S. Patent and Trademark Office granted a patent on the process by which the bacterium was developed, but refused to grant patent protection on the bacterium itself on the basis that living organisms, other than plants, were not patentable under existing law. On appeal the Court of Customs and Patent Appeals held that the inventor of a genetically engineered microorganism whose invention otherwise met the legal requirements for obtaining a patent could not be denied a patent solely because the invention was a living organism. The Supreme Court concurred. The majority ruled "the patentee has produced a new bacterium with markedly different characteristics from any found in nature and one having potential for significant utility. His discovery is not nature's handiwork, but his own; accordingly it is patentable" (quoted from Office of Technology Assessment, 1981:240).[12] The decision has been interpreted as extending not only to products of genetic engineering, but to any microorganism that is found in nature but whose useful properties depend on human intervention (such as the isolation of a pure culture of a microbial strain). The Patent Office approved patent authorization for plants and plant parts in 1985, and for nonhuman animals in 1987.

Since the early 1990s the patenting of genetic material has become increasingly controversial. In 1991 Craig Venter, a biologist at the U.S. National Institutes of Health (NIH), filed a patent application for 350 unique clones of human genes. The NIH action was apparently taken as a preemptive action, even though the functions of the genes were unknown, in order to prevent the private sector from establishing property rights in NIH gene sequence and databases. Nevertheless, it generated an intense reaction from the European collaborators in the Human Genome Project.[13] The most controversial action has been the claim by Agracetus

---

[12] The minority opinion argued that Congress did not intend the general patent provision of the Constitution to include living things. It noted that Congress had passed separate legislation to make agricultural inventions patentable but had not extended the law outside this limited area to other life forms. There continues to be substantial controversy on how broadly life forms can be patented. At the time this chapter was written there was intense concern about a plan by Abbott Laboratories and Genset, a French biotechnology firm, to patent human genetic markers. Alan Williamson, vice president for research at Merck, indicated that Merck opposed the patenting of genetic data. He indicated that Merck had become accustomed to paying royalties on the many small patents that went into each pharmaceutical product but that recently "royalty claims were stacking up" on each product to an unacceptable degree (Marshall, 1997b:1763). For a debate about whether the granting of broad patent claims in the area of genomic technology will have the effect of inhibiting research and dampening competition, see Doll (1998) and Heller and Eisenberg (1998).

[13] The Human Genome Project (HGP) is an international coordinated program initiated in 1990 to map the entire human genome. The program was initially headed by James D. Watson, who (with Francis Crick) discovered the double helix structure of DNA in 1953. It is funded in the United States primarily by the National Institutes of Health (NIH) and the Department of Energy (DOE). The initial plan envisaged the development of a complete human DNA library by 2005 at a cost of about $300 million. Watson resigned in the spring of 1992 over a dispute with NIH leadership over the patenting of gene fragments. Gene mapping technology has advanced so rapidly that in 1998 the nonprofit Institute of Genomic Research, directed by

to patent protection for all genetically engineered cotton regardless of the method used (Rosendal, 1995:453–477).[14]

As noted earlier most of the work leading to the development rDNA techniques was performed at Stanford University and the University of California at San Francisco (UCSF) under National Institute of Health (NIH) grants. Stanford University filed a patent application on the process developed by Cohen and Boyer in 1974. It was not until 1980 that a process patent and until 1984 that a product patent was granted (Reimers, 1984). In May 1977 the University of California applied for the first insulin gene patent, based on research by William Rutter and Howard Goodman. Information had been shared among the UC researchers and researchers at Genentech and Eli Lilly. It was not until 1997 that the dispute over patent rights was resolved (Marshall, 1997a).

Prior to 1980 there had been no comprehensive government-wide policy regarding ownership of patents on federally funded inventions. Although the Department of Health and Human Services (DHHS) permitted nonprofit institutional grantees to patent inventions resulting from research that it funded, most agencies retained title to such patents, making them available to anyone for development and commercialization through nonexclusive licenses. This arrangement had been criticized by some industry sectors for not providing sufficient incentive to take the risk of developing the invention into a viable commercial product. Beginning in 1980 Congress passed a series of acts designed to promote the utilization of inventions developed under federally supported R&D projects conducted by universities and other nonprofit organizations.[15] These acts, combined with the earlier Chakrabarty opinion, have been associated with a dramatic increase in the patenting of inventions by scientists at universities and government laboratories, particularly in the area of biotechnology.

Craig Venter, and the Perkin-Elmer Corporation, a leading producer of equipment of the biotechnology industry, proposed a joint venture that would decipher the entire gene code in 3 years, using a robotic machine developed by Perkin-Elmer rather than the more labor-intensive system employed in the HGP. The proposal generated an intense controversy over the quality of the results that would be obtained using the Perkin-Elmer technology and the economic and ethical issues involved in private patenting of genomic information. The HGP is not cutting edge science. The objective is to make the information in gene maps available as a source of technical advances in medicine, agriculture, and other areas of biotechnology (Speaker and Lindee, 1993; Carey, 1998).

[14] These developments have been opposed by a number of interest groups concerned about ecological implications, animal welfare and rights, loss of genetic diversity, the interests of smaller farmers, and the rights of less developed countries in maintaining control of their genetic resources (Raeburn, 1995; Kling, 1996). Another concern is that patents granted may be so broad that critics have argued that they will block or restrain scientific and technical progress (Merges and Nelson, 1990; Barton, 1997; Nelson and Mazzoleni, 1998; Doll, 1998; Heller and Eisenberg, 1998).

[15] These acts included The 1980 Stevenson–Wydler Act that allowed federal agencies to grant exclusive licenses for federally-owned patents; the 1980 Bayh–Dole Act that allowed institutions to patent technologies developed from federally-funded research; the 1984 National Cooperative Research Act that provided exemptions for private participation in research consortia; and the 1986 Federal Technology Transfer Act that established rules for federal–private cooperative research and development agreements (National Academy of Sciences, 1992; Chapter 13).

COMMERCIAL BIOTECHNOLOGY

In this section I discuss the development of those industries that have been most successful in realizing the commercial potential of the new biotechnologies. In the mid-1990s total sales of biotechnology products in the United States were estimated at slightly above $25 billion. Pharmaceuticals, which include human therapeutic and human diagnostic applications, accounted for over 90% of total sales. Agrochemical and agricultural biochemical products, which include animal health, plant protection, and transgenic plants, comprised the most rapidly growing sector. Specialties, defined to include a wide range of alternative techniques for the synthesis and production of products such as industrial enzymes, food additives, and specialty and fine chemicals, were also growing rapidly. A fourth area, nonmedical diagnostics, which included use of biosensors and nucleic acid probes and related techniques to detect chemicals, pathogens, and other contaminants in the food supply and in the environment, was also a rapidly growing subsector.[16] In this section I give primary attention to the process of commercial development in the pharmaceutical, agricultural, and food industries. I also focus primarily on U.S. firms since the development of the biotechnology industries initially occurred primarily in the United States.

The Pharmaceutical Industry

The pharmaceutical industry was the first industry to achieve commercial success in the development of new processes and products based on biotechnology. This was in part due to the fact that medical scientists played an important role in the development of molecular biology and genetic engineering techniques.[17] The effect was to shift the pharmaceutical industry onto a new technological trajectory.

During the 1980s, in its search for new drugs, the pharmaceutical industry underwent a major transition from a technology based primarily on the science of chemistry to a technology based on molecular biology. The chemical approach to discovery of new compounds involved systematic assays of many molecules in laboratory and clinical tests to find a few promising candidates. The biological approach was based on rational understanding of the functions of the human body, and new understanding of the biological and chemical mechanisms of diseases and drugs. These advances enabled R&D teams to design synthetic drug molecules with structural properties that interact in predictable ways with target receptors in the human body. Genetic engineering was making it possible to replace hard-to-isolate natural human immunogens and to use mutant organisms with desired therapeutic properties. Although large firm size is still

---

[16] This classification is based on product characteristics. Biotechnology firms can also be classified in terms of their technology focus: vaccines, rDNA and monoclonal antibodies, synthetics, cell therapy, diagnostic and biosensor, delivery and formulation, gene therapy and genomics (Cohen, 1997:767–772).

[17] The definitive analysis of the early commercialization of the biotechnology industry is Office of Technology Assessment (1984). For a more recent perspective, see Office of Technology Assessment (1991), Krimsky (1991), and Krimsky and Wrubel (1996).

important for testing molecules and for clinical trials, drug research now also requires a solid understanding of molecular actions and pathologies (Gambardella, 1995:162; Carr, 1998; Cockburn et al., 1999).

Pharmaceutical firms began to develop more effective articulation with the external scientific community as the innovation trajectory shifted in the direction of molecular genetics and biotechnology. University and research institute laboratories have typically focused their efforts on isolating genes, identifying their protein structures, and understanding gene functions. Problems in these areas are scientifically the most intriguing and the payoffs for academic scientists in terms of reputation and mobility are the greatest. As basic researchers isolate new genes or identify new receptor structures, pharmaceutical companies compete to exploit the new discoveries. The larger companies that have substantial internal research capacity may conduct research to clarify the function of receptors, discover new receptors, and design new drugs. The shift in trajectory has forced the larger drug companies to develop more open relationships with universities and with smaller biotechnology companies. They have also been forced to provide greater autonomy for the directors and staff of their own research laboratories (Gambardella, 1995:97).

Three distinctive techniques have been employed in the development of new biotechnology applications. One has involved the use of genetic engineering to manufacture proteins whose therapeutic qualities were already well understood. The human growth hormone case discussed in this section is an example. A second technique has involved the development of transgenic plants or other life forms. The herbicide resistant soybean case discussed below is an example. The third technique has been the design of synthetic drugs. The bovine growth hormone, also discussed below, is an example.

HUMAN GROWTH HORMONE[18]

The development of human growth hormone is of interest for several reasons. It was the second commercially successful pharmaceutical product (after insulin) developed using genetic engineering technology. It involved close scientific and technical collaboration between a U.S. biotechnology firm, Genentech, and a publicly owned Swedish pharmaceutical company, KabiVitrum. The product was important in Genentech's strategy to use its capacity in biotechnology to become an integrated pharmaceutical company, rather than specializing in contract R&D for major pharmaceutical companies.

At the time the collaboration began Kabi was the world's leading supplier of human growth hormone (hGH), used to treat severe (hypopituitary) dwarfism. The raw material, from human pituitary glands, was obtained through arrangements with

---

[18] In this section I draw heavily from the exceedingly useful case study by Maureen D. McKelvey (1996). McKelvey gives much more attention to the development of the regulatory system for genetically engineered products than I am able to cover in this section.

morgues throughout the world. Kabi was interested in obtaining an alternative source since the current supply was sufficient to treat only the most severe cases of dwarfism. Genetic engineering offered the possibility of overcoming the supply constraints associated with use of hGH extracted from pituitary glands. If successful, the protein would be produced by rapidly multiplying bacteria.

At that time Kabi had no competence in molecular biology. It did have technical and engineering experience with complex proteins and with the fermentation processes used in the production of penicillin. It also had a small research team working on the complex of proteins released by the pituitary gland and the hypothalamus and that monitored research in related areas. And it assumed that it could transfer the knowledge, techniques, and equipment developed for other biological processes to produce products developed through genetic engineering.

During 1977 and 1978 research on human growth hormone and insulin was proceeding along parallel and overlapping paths. At the UCSF there was considerable competition between the Baxter–Goodman and Boyer groups. At the same time that Kabi was exploring the possibility of an alternative source of supply for hGH, Eli Lilly was exploring the possibility of an alternative source of supply for insulin. In 1978 Lilly began supporting research by Baxter and Goodman on both insulin and hGH. In an effort to hedge its bets Lilly also contracted with Genentech for the development of insulin. The complexity of these relationships subsequently became a source of extensive litigation over patent rights to genetically engineered insulin (McKelvey, 1996:148–166; Marshall, 1997a:1028–1030).

The arrangements that Genentech worked out with Kabi and Lilly were quite different. The differences reflected both the greater economic clout that Lilly had in dealing with Genentech and Genentech's own ambition to become an integrated pharmaceutical firm. Under the contract with Lilly signed on August 24, 1978, "Genentech agreed to provide Lilly with recombinant DNA micro-organisms capable of producing insulin, related patent rights, trade secrets, technology and know-how in return for research fees and continuing royalty payments of 8% of Lilly's insulin sales" (quoted from McKelvey, 1996:138). "Genentech agreed to transfer all the knowledge, techniques, and secrets that Lilly needed to know about insulin-producing bacteria. The contract also limited the extent to which Lilly could use the genetic engineering knowledge for purposes other than insulin" (McKelvey, 1996:138). Genentech did not want to transmit knowledge, techniques, and biological materials that would become public knowledge. It wanted to sell them to Lilly solely for production of insulin.

In its contract with Genentech, Kabi committed in the neighborhood of $1 million to the development of hGH. It also agreed to pay an undisclosed percentage of sales to Genentech, which would in turn be divided with UCSF and City of Hope Hospital. Kabi retained exclusive world market rights outside the United States. Genentech initially obtained semiexclusive rights to the U.S. market, amended later to give Genentech exclusive U.S. rights. Kabi also obtained rights to any improvements that Genentech might make and was entitled to send its scientists to Genentech to learn about the bacteria expression (production) system.

Originally Genentech had not intended to produce hGH itself. However, as commercialization began to appear realistic and as Genentech's longer term strategy evolved it began to explore the idea of manufacturing hGH. It saw production of hGH as an opportunity to develop the necessary component technologies to support a production system based on genetically engineered products. It would also enable Genentech to gain experience and competence both in getting FDA approval and in marketing a pharmaceutical product and it would advance its ambition to become a major pharmaceutical firm.

Both Kabi and Genentech faced very substantial scientific and technical challenges. Although Kabi had experience with biological process technology, neither they nor any other firm had previously worked with genetically engineered bacteria on a commercial scale. They also needed to acquire capacity in genetic engineering. Genentech, on its part, had to acquire a capacity to integrate genetic engineering into a production system. Although Kabi was adding scientific capacity, Genentech was adding staff with industrial experience. Kabi also needed to secure additional funding to support its collaboration with Genentech. It established, with additional funding from the Swedish government biotechnology subsidiary, KabiGen.

The relationship between Kabi and Genentech was not always smooth. Genentech valued its molecular biology and genetic engineering knowledge very highly. This led some Kabi people to see Genentech as too self-assured and too focused on their basic science achievements. Kabi, on the other hand, valued their knowledge of proteins and purification processes and their experience in dealing with regulatory agencies to obtain approval for new pharmaceutical products.

Genentech was able to come up with an initial bacteria expression system in only 7 months after its contract with Kabi was signed. In April 1979 "the bacteria was ready and it made hGH" (McKelvey, 1996:180). But the problems involved in large-scale production (illustrated in Figure 10.4) had not been solved and the question of cost and whether it could be produced in economical quantities had yet to be resolved.

One of the problems that had to be confronted was that the hGH produced in bacteria had 192-amino acids instead of the 191 in the hGH produced in the human body. It was generally assumed in the medical community that the "natural" pituitary hGH was superior to the artificial 192-amino acid rDNA hGH. This assumption was refuted, however, when a fatal medical risk with pituitary hGH (Creutzfeld–Jacob disease) was discovered in 1985. This left the hGH market wide open for producing hGH with genetic engineering techniques. Genentech was able to respond immediately to the growth in demand in the U.S. market. In 1986 Genentech sales of hGH, the first pharmaceutical product it had produced, reached $41 million (McKelvey, 1996:253). The situation at KabiGen was more complicated than at Genentech. Taking pituitary hGH, sold under the name of Crescormer, off the international market would result in a large financial loss. Nevertheless, KabiGen did remove Crescormer from the market and replaced it with a new brand that did not carry the extra amino acid.

On April 25, 1983 Genentech filed for an American patent for a new bacteria expression system that produced hGH with 191 amino acids, like that produced in the body. Both Genentech and Kabi were already partially locked into a technological

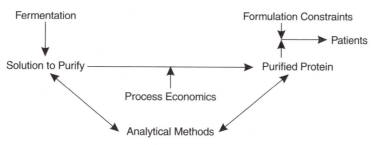

Figure 10-4 Relationships in a biological production scheme. The typical steps of a biotechnology production system are shown, from fermentation on the upper left to patients on the upper right. The fermentation process results in a liquid solution (solution to purify). This solution is composed of a number of elements, such as the desired protein, the nutrients, other proteins, and a number of contaminants. The goal is to purify out the protein (purified protein) and formulate it as a pharmaceutical (formulation constraints, patients). Doing so requires the use of analytical methods to test alternatives and consideration of costs (process economics). (*Source:* Maureen D. McKelvey, *Evolutionary Innovations: The Business of Biotechnology,* Oxford, UK: Oxford University Press, 1996:175.)

trajectory based on the 192-amino acid version. They had been working on that version for 4 years. They had invested within the firms to develop a functioning production system and had invested in collaboration with doctors and government regulatory agencies to negotiate legitimate use through clinical testing. Genentech–Kabi felt they could not drop the old hGH until they had developed a functioning production system for the new. This might take a couple of years during which time they needed to be able to sell the 192 amino acid hGH (McKelvey, 1996:238). After considerable internal debate and consultation both Genentech and Kabi decided to proceed with both versions.

Eli Lilly was pursuing the development of a 191-amino acid hGH at the same time as Genentech and Kabi. In the spring of 1987 both Kabi and Lily received approval to market the new hGH. In the United States, however, the effort by Genentech to place its version of (met-less) rDNA hGH on the market was blocked by the FDA. Under a program designed to provide a limited time monopoly for new pharmaceuticals intended for a small number of patients (orphan drugs), Genentech had been granted a monopoly on sales of the hGH containing the extra amino acid. To encourage competition the FDA granted a monopoly on the 191-amino acid hGH to Eli Lilly in 1987. In spite of this constraint Genentech was able, by 1995, to capture 75% of the U.S. hGH market and was planning to enter the international market when its agreement with Kabi expired. By the mid-1990s Kabi accounted for between 55 and 60% of the world market for hGH outside of the United States. In 1996 Kabi merged into Pharmacia and Upjohn. At the time of the merger human growth hormone was still its leading product. In addition to their remarkable market success insulin and human growth hormone have been subject to strong market competition and extensive patent litigation. Regulatory and intellectual property rights regimes have both been important factors in commercial success.

Agricultural Biotechnology

The opportunities that biotechnology opened up in the field of agriculture occurred several years later than in pharmaceuticals. The close link between advances in molecular biology and advances in the health sciences had not been matched in the agricultural sciences. The dramatic successes that had been achieved by plant breeders since the 1930s, drawing on the concepts of "classical" Mendelian genetics, encouraged initial skepticism about the claims of the molecular biologists. Progress was also inhibited by lack of knowledge on the part of plant breeders about plant gene transfer mechanisms and by an acute shortage of plant molecular biologists (Duvick, 1996).

In the early 1980s it seemed to some that the initial advances in agriculture would likely occur with the use of plant tissue culture. The development of *in vitro* tissue and cell culture techniques, which were occurring in parallel with monoclonal antibody and rDNA techniques, would make possible the regeneration of whole plants from a single cell or small piece of tissue, or the *in vitro* fertilization of livestock embryos. Early progress was also expected in the use of growth hormones to improve animal health and feed efficiency. In traditional plant breeding, only closely related species can be cross-bred. If no varieties are naturally resistant to a particular pest or pathogen, there is no way to create resistance. In the area of crop agriculture it was anticipated that the next series of advances would overcome this constraint through introduction or manipulation of genes from other species that would confer resistance to pests and pathogens. It was expected that the contribution of biotechnology to the improvement of animal breeds or the development of new crop varieties, processes that would require multigene expression, would occur further into the future.

By the late 1980s it appeared that some of the early projections had been overly enthusiastic. However, by the mid-1990s, it seemed clear that a transition to increased reliance on transgenic technology in both crop and animal production was well underway in developed countries and in several developing countries. The Republic of China introduced the first commercially successful transgenic crop, a virus-resistant tobacco, in the early 1990s. Monsanto placed recombinant bovine somatotropin (rbST), a genetically engineered hormone designed to enhance milk production, on the market in 1994. The Calgene Flavr Savr™ tomato, introduced (unsuccessfully) in 1994, was the first genetically altered whole food to be placed on the market. Progress had also been made in transgenic approaches to the development of herbicide resistance, insect resistance, and disease resistance in crops. The use of DNA marker technology was being employed to locate important chromosomal regions affecting a given trait in order to track and manipulate desirable gene linkages with greater speed and precision (Lee, 1995; Duvick, 1996; James, 1997).

Beginning in the mid-1990s the area devoted to transgenic crops began to expand rapidly (Table 10.2). As of the end of 1997, transgenic crop field trials had been conducted on 60 crops in over 40 countries and 48 transgenic crop products had been approved for commercialization in at least one country. In the United States 12 biotechnology products had been approved by the Animal and Plant Health and Inspection Service (APHIS) as no longer subject to regulation. During the late 1990s there was an important shift in emphasis from agronomic (or input) traits to quality (or output) traits, such as specialized nutritional food and feed products (James, 1998). Many of these developments have been surrounded by substantial controversy.[19] In this section I review the development of herbicide-resistant soybeans and bovine growth hormone.

HERBICIDE-RESISTANT SOYBEANS

During the 1960s and 1970s use of herbicides had largely replaced mechanical control of weeds in crop production. The ideal herbicide kills a broad spectrum of weeds found in a crop field while not affecting the growth of the crop. This differential activity against weeds but not crops, termed selectivity, is usually not perfect. Thus a common approach is to apply the herbicide prior to planting or before plant emergence to avoid killing the crop plants. The possibility of developing herbicide-resistant crops was potentially very attractive to the agrochemical and plant-breeding industries since it would be possible to use a broad-spectrum

Table 10.2 Global Area of Transgenic Crops in 1996–1998: By Country and By Trait

	1996 (Ha)[a]	1997 (Ha)[a]	1998 (Ha)[a]
	Country		
United States	1.5	8.1	20.5
Argentina	0.1	1.4	4.3
Canada	0.1	1.3	2.8
Other	<0.1	0.2	0.2
Total	1.7	11.0	27.8
	Trait		
Herbicide tolerance	0.6	6.9	19.8
Insect resistance	1.1	4.0	7.7
Other	<0.1	0.1	0.3
Total	1.7	11.0	27.8

[a]Millions of hectares.

Source: James Clive, *Global Status of Transgenic Crops*, Ithaca, NY: The International Service for the Acquisition of Agri-Biotech Applications, 1997, 1998.

---

[19] Among the major concerns were possible gene flows between crop plants and wild relatives, the ecological effects of release of plants encoding rival sequences, the effects of plant-produced insecticides on unintended targets, and the human health effects of genetically modified food (Kendall et al., 1997).

postemergence herbicide without damaging the crop plant endowed with herbicide resistance.

Monsanto is both a leading producer of herbicides and a leading contributor to the development of herbicide-resistant field crops.[20] Monsanto's Roundup, a broad-spectrum herbicide in which glyphosate is the active ingredient, was the world's largest selling herbicide in the mid-1990s. Its patent had expired in most foreign markets and was due to expire in the United States in 2000. If it could develop Roundup-resistant soybean and corn varieties Monsanto might be able to continue to dominate the market for broad-spectrum herbicides. In May 1995 the EPA approved a marketing label for Monsanto for glyphosate-resistant soybean, which had been developed in cooperation with Asgrow Seed Company. Monsanto licenses its technology to seed companies, which incorporate it into their soybean seeds, which are marketed under the label Roundup Ready. The use of Roundup Ready seed facilitates a change in weed management from several applications of several active ingredients to a single application of one broad-spectrum herbicide. The technology lowers weed control expenditures but slightly increases seed costs.[21]

Herbicide resistance became controversial even before the Monsanto–Asgrow variety was placed on the market (Snow and Palma, 1997:86–96). Environmental and alternative agriculture groups have been reluctantly supportive of the development of genetically engineered crops that would reduce the use of pesticides. But they have been severely critical of the development of herbicide-resistant crop plants. They viewed such development as evidence that the agrochemical companies engaged in such research are willing to sacrifice the long-term sustainability of agriculture for short-term profit. In contrast defenders of herbicides note that use of herbicides contributes to lower soil erosion by reducing the mechanical cultivation needed to control weeds and contributes to the economic viability of no-till and minimum-till farming systems. Monsanto also points out that Roundup has more desirable toxicological characteristics than the older widely used herbicides: it is relatively nontoxic to animals and is more readily degraded by soil microorganisms so that it is less likely to leach into groundwater or accumulate in the soil. The point is also made that Roundup, when applied on a resistant variety of soybeans, fits more effectively into integrated pest management programs than preemergence herbicides since it does not need to be applied until the level of weed infestation reaches an economic threshold (Chapter 6).

---

[20] For a discussion of Monsanto's introduction of genetically modified soybeans, cotton, and maize, see Carter and Goldberg (1996).

[21] In addition to its herbicidal activity, Roundup has health and environmental advantages. Many herbicides are persistent in the soil and may move into groundwater. Many soil-applied herbicides have carcinogenic activity. Roundup is neither persistent nor strongly carcinogenic. Farmers who use the new Roundup-Ready soybeans must sign a contract not to save their own seed and use approved herbicide practices. In effect they are sublicensing the technology from Monsanto. In addition to the cost of seed Monsanto charges a licensing fee of $5.00 per acre. Use of Roundup-Ready soybean seed reduced estimated weed control costs from $25–30 per acre for conventional herbicide treatment to $18 per acre ($13 for Roundup and $5.00 for the technology fee (Carlson et al., 1997:32).

RESISTANCE TO INTRODUCTION AND DIFFUSION

The health effects of herbicides and of transgenic crops have also been an important area of controversy. Most herbicides have little or no acute toxicity to humans and wildlife. But little is known about the health effects of low-level chronic exposure. Regulatory concerns, based on potential health problems, have caused some chemical companies to discontinue the development of herbicide-resistant crops.

In the mid-1990s a dispute broke out between the U.S. exporters of soybeans and the European Economic Community (EEC) over the export of transgenic soybeans to Europe. European environmental and consumer groups protested the mixing of transgenic soybeans with other soybeans in shipments to Europe (Ibrahim, 1996:B1). Attempts have also been made to prevent the introduction of transgenic crop plants in developing countries. In 1996 a European–U.S.–Philippines research team succeeded in producing, by particle bombardment with a gene from *Bacillus thuringiensis* (Bt), a transformed rice plant that was highly resistant to yellow and striped stem borer, a major insect pest of rice. In April 1995 a shipment of 100 grams of seed to the International Rice Research Institute in the Philippines, intended for field testing, was intercepted and impounded by Greenpeace. Disagreements between the United States and members of the EEC continued into the late 1990s. In February 1999 the United States, Canada, Australia, Chile, Argentina, and Uruguay refused to sign a proposed international treaty that would have required a country to approve in advance any imports of agricultural commodities that have been genetically altered. The United States and the other commodity-exporting countries argued that the treaty should include only seeds, plants, animals, and microorganisms. The move to adopt the treaty was led by European commodity-importing countries and supported by most developing countries. The United States took the position that the treaty represented an effort to use ecological and environmental concerns as an excuse to erect trade barriers.

Consumer concerns about the potential health effects of genetically altered crops are not entirely without foundation. In 1992 Pioneer Hi-Bred International, the worlds largest seed company, transferred a gene from a Brazil nut to the soybean. The transferred gene caused a naturally occurring amino acid, methionine, to be expressed at elevated levels in the soybean. Soon after the field trials of Pioneer's methionine-enhanced soybean began, Pioneer became aware, through a literature search, that an allergic reaction to Brazil nuts had been observed. Allergy studies commissioned by Pioneer with an independent clinical laboratory confirmed that patients who had Brazil nut allergies also reacted to Pioneer's methionine-enhanced soybean. Pioneer announced the results to the appropriate regulatory agencies (USDA and FDA) and stopped research that was intended to lead to the development of a commercial variety. Critics of the development of transgenic crops used the case to point out the legitimacy of their fears regarding biotechnology and what they considered to be lax regulation of the commercialization of biotechnology products. Although Pioneer did not respond directly to the critics, supporters of biotechnology characterize Pioneer's behavior as highly responsible and an example of the precautions that ensure that biotechnology products that actually reach the market have an exceedingly low probability of having any dangerous health effects.

BOVINE GROWTH HORMONE[22]

The "most publicized, contentious, and complex debate pertaining to the introduction of a bioengineered product" has centered on recombinant bovine somatotropin (rbST), a genetically engineered hormone designed to enhance milk production per cow (Krimsky and Wrubel:166). Proponents have stressed its capacity to increase production. Opponents have argued that its adoption will drive thousands of dairy farmers out of business, add to the surplus of dairy products, cause a higher incidence of disease in dairy cattle, and expose consumers to new health risks from enhanced somatotropin in the milk.

Somatotropin is a hormone that is naturally synthesized in the anterior pituitary gland in cattle. The major biochemical and physiological function of bST is to partition nutrients; bST directs nutrients toward milk production and away from body tissue storage. The effect is to increase milk production rather than animal weight when feeding rates are increased (Krimsky and Wrubel, 1996:167).

The first reported large mammalian experiments with bST were done by a group of Russian scientists in 1937. They treated more than 500 lactating cows with bST obtained from slaughtered cattle. Substantial increases in milk yield were obtained. In the early 1980s an inexpensive method of microbial production of rbST through DNA techniques was developed at Cornell University. This resulted in a race among American Cyanamid, Upjohn, Eli Lilly, and Monsanto to put rbST on the market. After a decade of use on an experimental basis in the United States, and substantial commercial use in several other countries, rbST was approved for commercial use in the United States in 1993 (Krimsky and Wrubel, 1996:168). It was first made available for commercial use in February 1994 under the name of Prosilac by Monsanto.

Because rbST was the first major biologically engineered veterinary product to be introduced in the market its success had great economic and symbolic importance not only for Monsanto but for the entire veterinary drug industry. The several companies engaged in commercial development of bovine growth hormone had spent very large amounts on research, estimated in the range of $100–$500 million. Potential annual sales of rbST were estimated in the $500 million range in the United States and upward of $1.0 billion worldwide.

A major concern of the critics of rbST is that residue of the hormone might end up in the milk. This concern was rejected by the National Institutes of Health and the Food and Drug Administration. Gerald P. Guest, Director of the Center for Veterinary Medicine at the FDA, testified in 1993: "Since rbST is orally inactive and since rbST,

---

[22] In this section I draw very heavily on Krimsky and Wrubel (1996:166–190).

even when injected, has no biological activity in humans, the agency has no human concern for rbST residues in tissues or milk" (Krimsky and Wrubel, 1996:175).

A more serious concern is that use of rbST increases the rate at which cows contract mastitis, an infection of the udder, that can be treated by antibiotics. There has been considerable disagreement in the scientific literature on whether the use of rbST does increase the incidence of mastitis, and whether the use of antibiotics to treat mastitis, and other health problems, results in increased antibiotic residues in milk. Public health professionals have become increasingly concerned with the development of antibiotic-resistant strains of human pathogens. The question of whether any innovation in biotechnology should be permitted that might result in increased antibiotic use in milk production has not yet been answered to the satisfaction of the critics.

In the United States consumer concerns resulted in legislation in Wisconsin and some other states that permitted milk from cows that had not been treated to be labeled rbST free. A number of distributors did segregate and label their milk, but the higher price for the non-rbST milk encountered more consumer resistance in most states than anticipated. Opposition to use of rbST has been stronger in Western Europe than in the United States; in 1993 the European Community banned the use of rbST for 7 years. It was somewhat surprising that during the rbST debate little attention was given to the use of growth regulators that had earlier been approved for use in beef cattle. It was also somewhat surprising that Monsanto and the other companies had not been more sensitive to public concern about anything that might appear to threaten the "natural" character of the milk supply. In retrospect it seems obvious that a more appropriate strategy would have been to place a porcine growth hormone on the market prior to the bovine hormone. There is no pork price support program to create an image of surplus of pork chops.

Economic Impacts of Agricultural Biotechnology[23]

The economic impact of agricultural biotechnology can be evaluated at two levels. At the microeconomic level the question is whether cost reductions or increases in value-added are sufficient to induce producers to adopt the new technology. At the industry or sector level an important question is whether increases in production significantly impact commodity output and prices. There is also a question of whether output and price effects are sufficient to alter the structure, the location, or output and productivity growth at the sector level (see Chapter 6). At the time this chapter was written none of the new agricultural biotechnology products had been available to producers long enough to provide definitive answers to these questions. There has, however, been sufficient analysis of the potential impacts of rbST to provide some tentative answers.

---

[23] In this section I draw primarily on the excellent review and assessment of the impact of rbST on the world dairy industry by Jarvis (1996).

The economic incentive to adopt depends on the size of the difference between the value of the incremental milk production per cow and the incremental cost per cow from adopting the rbST technology. The percentage increase in milk yield from using rbST is typically higher for low-yielding cows. But the absolute increase is typically larger for high-yielding cows. Thus the profitability of adopting rbST is higher for herds with high average yields.

A 1990 Wisconsin study projected incremental costs, which included not only the cost of rbST, but also additional feed, labor, and related costs, at $201, incremental revenue at $2ll, and net incremental profit per cow of $10 per year. At the milk prices that prevailed at that time the authors concluded that this would be sufficient incentive to induce adoption by the typical Wisconsin farm, where herd size averaged about 50 cows. Other studies conducted in California, where herd size averaged about 500 cows and milk prices are somewhat higher than in Wisconsin, suggested an incremental profit in the neighborhood of $200 per cow per year. Most studies have concluded that the cost savings from adoption of rbST technology represent a strong incentive for dairy farmers having high initial milk yields, good management, and large herd size. They tend to be skeptical that it will be profitable for farmers with small herd size or initial low milk yields per cow to adopt the rbST technology. It appears likely, however, that as a result of "learning by doing," cost reductions and incentives to adopt by farmers with smaller herds may increase after rbST has been in use longer.

The second question is what effect will the increase in milk production have on milk prices? Will milk prices decline sufficiently to dampen incentives to adopt rbST before the diffusion process is complete? In the United States milk consumption per person is inelastic with respect to both income and price. In an unregulated market, a 2 or 3% increase in the production of milk could be expected to result in a decline in the price of milk in the neighborhood of 10%. Jarvis estimates that if the rbST technology is adopted by the 10% of dairy farms that produced 15% of U.S. milk prior to the adoption of rbST, milk output could increase by 2.3% and milk prices would fall by 7.5%. The productivity gains from adoption of rbST would be rapidly transmitted from milk producers to milk consumers. Adoption would continue to be profitable for larger farms, however, even if milk prices fell (Jarvis, 1996).

In the United States milk is not produced in an unregulated market, however. The U.S. Department of Agriculture administers a milk price support program, mandated by Congress. The program attempts to maintain the price of milk by purchasing processed dairy products (butter and cheese). The rapid adoption of the rbST technology would result in the accumulation of surplus dairy products. As the financial cost to the government of the program rises, however, Congress could be expected to modify the program to reduce the price support level. Jarvis anticipated that the longer run impact of the rbST technology on the structure of the dairy industry would be to accelerate the exit from the industry of milk producers with smaller or less productive dairy herds.

In California adoption of rbST has been even more rapid than anticipated. In Wisconsin, however, adoption was slower than anticipated. By mid-1994, less than

6 months after it became commercially available, approximately 20% of California milk producers were using rbST. Adoption of rbST in other developed countries such as Canada, countries in Western Europe, and Japan was, at the time of this writing, still prohibited. It seems likely that when prohibitions are removed it will be adopted rapidly.

In less developed countries (LDCs) it seems likely that adoption will be slower and less complete. Average milk yields per cow in Eastern Europe and in South and Southeast Asia are less than half the average yield in the United States; average yields in Latin America and Africa are less than 20% of U.S. yields. There are, however, substantial numbers of producers in countries such as Mexico, Brazil, the Philippines, South Africa, and Zambia who obtain relatively high yields and who could be expected to be early adopters of rbST. Rapid adoption even by producers with very small herds might occur where good veterinary services are available, as in the Bombay Milk Scheme in India. The negative price effects that could occur in the United States will be smaller in rapidly growing low-income countries in which the income elasticity of demand for milk is relatively high. Adoption rates in LDCs also would be stimulated if the producers of rbST make their product available at prices closer to incremental production costs to expand markets. It seems likely, however, that widespread adoption will not occur until after 2000 when current patents on the rbST technology expire.

The rbST case illustrates a more general principle. The reason that development and adoption of some new biotechnologies will not be economically viable in many LDCs for some time is because of the limited adoption of the old biological technologies. The short-run effect of rbST is to shift comparative advantage toward countries that have high cost but skilled labor, high quality, but costly feedstuffs, and a production environment that is sufficiently free of disease, parasites, and heat stress to enable dairy cattle to respond well to the rbST technology. Over the long run as adoption of older technologies generates higher milk yields, adoption of rbST can also be expected to occur in well-managed dairy herds in LDCs.

MARKET STRUCTURE

In the early 1980s the global pharmaceutical industry was characterized by a two-tier structure in which 25–30 established firms, out of a total of more than 5000, accounted for roughly half of world sales and most private sector R&D expenditures (Sapienza, 1989). Two factors were particularly important for the relatively stable structure of the industry. The first was the regulatory regime. Prescription drugs are the most heavily regulated of industrial products, and this regulation has increased both the time and the cost required to bring a new product to market (Box 10.2). The second factor was the method of marketing prescription drugs. It is the physician who writes the prescription and decides what drug(s) the patient will consume. Marketing drugs to individual physicians typically accounts for more than one-third of a major drug company's annual pharmaceutical revenue—far more than the approximately 10% spent on R&D. These two factors together have made it exceedingly difficult for a new firm to enter the top tier of pharmaceutical companies.

The Biotechnology Challenge

During the 1990s the market structure of the pharmaceutical industry underwent a major transformation. For much of the postwar period the industry had been composed of large, research-intensive, vertically integrated—from laboratory to distribution—firms. These firms, however, had largely ignored the revolution in molecular biology and genetic engineering of the 1960s and 1970s. By the mid-1990s there were, in addition, over 1200 small- to medium-size research-intensive dedicated biotechnology firms (DBFs) in the United States. The rise of biotechnology firms has dramatically altered the drug discovery process.

The drug development and commercialization process has, however, largely remained unchanged. Very substantial scientific and organizational capacities are still required to conduct clinical trials. Large size is important in scaling up production systems, and extended distribution networks are necessary to sell the new products. These capacities have remained in the hands of the established pharmaceutical companies, creating a formidable obstacle to the ambitions of the new small biotechnology companies to integrate forward into independent product development and distribution. Even Genentech has been unsuccessful in its effort to become a major independent drug company. In 1989 Genentech was forced to sell a minority interest to Hoffmann-LaRoche. By 1996, LaRoche had assumed majority control over Genentech.

Gambardella (1995:78–80) asks why the division of labor in innovation in the pharmaceutical industry that has emerged since the early 1980s did not occur earlier. His answer is that when drug company scientists had little knowledge about the human body or the action of drugs, the process of discovery depended primarily on extensive screening of molecules for pharmaceutically useful characteristics. The key assets for innovation were research laboratories capable of conducting fairly routine analysis and screening, and the ability to recognize the relatively more favorable result. With advances in molecular biology and genetic engineering drug innovation became dependent on fitting together pieces of knowledge:

> With suitable contracts and intellectual property rights relevant "fragments" of knowledge can be exchanged among specialized agents. A certain company or scientific institution can establish the structure of a family of receptors in the human body. Another party can clarify their biological activity. A third agent can determine the molecular action of a family of compounds that fit the receptor sites and counteract the undesired behavior of cells. The entire set of information can be brought to a fourth party who controls resources to carry out the long and costly clinical trials and market the product. (Gambardella, 1995:79)

The new, more scientific approach to drug development led to an explosion of new medicines to treat heart disease, ulcers, arthritis, depression, and other diseases. However, many of the drugs that were developed in the 1970s and 1980s, and that fueled drug company growth and profits in the 1980s and 1990s, are set to lose their patent protection. In an attempt to fill the "patent gap" the major drug companies turned to more intensive research collaboration and acquisition of biotechnology companies. The pressure to widen product lines also set off a new wave of mergers and acquisitions between the major drug companies and between the major and second-tier companies (Tanouye and Langreth, 1997; Carr, 1998).

Restructuring

It was widely anticipated, both by students of the biotechnology industry and by the new DBFs, that the technical challenge to the upper-tier pharmaceutical companies by the new DBFs would open up the structure of the industry and provide opportunities for at least some of the new DBFs to move into the upper tier (Sapienza, 1989). By the mid-1990s, however, it seemed clear that what was emerging was a complementary structure between the upper tier and the DBFs, the universities, and national health research institutes. The advantages of the traditional upper tier firms, particularly in marketing, were resulting in an even more concentrated industry at that level. Instead of new firms entering the upper tier, the international pharmaceutical industry is undergoing a series of mergers and acquisitions that is leading to even greater concentration (Table 10.3). At the same time, relationships between the larger pharmaceutical and agrochemical firms and the DBFs were becoming more complex. The pharmaceutical industry is increasingly composed of a few large marketing firms, many small knowledge intensive biotechnology and research-tool firms, associated university research laboratories, and foundations and government agencies that support biological, biochemical, and biotechnology research.

During the 1990s, consolidation proceeded even more rapidly in the agricultural biotechnology sector than in the pharmaceutical biotechnology sector.[24] The seed industry had experienced two waves of consolidation prior to the 1990s. In the 1970s a number of agrochemical companies, attracted by the high profit margins in hybrid seed and the potential synergy with their own products (such as fertilizer and pesticides), began to acquire seed companies. Sandoz acquired Northrup King, Ciba-Geigy acquired Funk Seeds, Upjohn acquired Asgrow, and Shell acquired Nickerson. In the 1980s several other agrochemical companies that were initiating biotechnology research anticipated that seed would become the delivery system for their biotechnology products and began acquiring seed companies.

Many of these consolidations turned out to be disappointing. It was difficult to harmonize the scientific and entrepreneurial cultures of the seed companies with the

---

[24] In this discussion of consolidation in the agricultural seed and biotechnology sector, I draw heavily on Sehgal (1996) and Hayenga (1998).

Table 10.3   Top 15 Ethical Pharmaceutical Firms in World Sales (early 1990s)

Company	Country	1986–1987 Sales ($ million)	1992–1993 Sales[a] ($ million)
Merck[b]	United States	3441.0	8214.5
Hoechst[b]	Germany	3042.6	6042.1
Ciba-Geigy[b]	Switzerland	2851.2	5192.0
Bayer[b]	Germany	2787.5	4669.9
American Home Products[b]	United States	2560.4	4589.3
Glaxo	United Kingdom	2536.7	7986.4
Pfizer[b]	United States	2203.0	4557.9
Sandoz[b]	Switzerland	2155.1	4885.5
Eli Lilly[b]	United States	2119.8	4536.5
Abbott	United States	2057.0	4025.0
Warner-Lambert[b]		2041.0	
Takeda		1997.4	
Bristol-Myers[b]		1961.7	
SmithKline Beecham[b]	United Kingdom	1896.0	5100.5
Upjohn[b]		1863.0	
BMS	United States		6313.0
Hoffman-La Roche	Switzerland		4896.9
Johnson & Johnson	United States		4340.0
Rhone Poulenc Rorer	United States		4095.9

[a]From "Leading Companies in 1992/1993," *Scrip Magazine* (January 1994):34–35.
[b]First appearing on list in 1981–1982.
Source: SCRIP, 1–6 January 1998:6. Reproduced with permission from PJB Publications Ltd.

bureaucratic cultures of the larger chemical companies. Since the mid-1990s, however, as genetically engineered products finally began to reach the market, biotechnology has become a major catalyst responsible for a second wave of consolidation in the chemical, pharmaceutical, and seed industries. Monsanto and DuPont have been particularly aggressive in this second round of acquisitions. Other leaders have been Hoechst-Shering (AgrEVO), Sandoz-CibaGeigy (Novartis), and Dow Elanco. Two factors seem to be driving the new wave of mergers and alliances. One is the consolidation of intellectual property rights. A second seems to be the development of new traits that enhance the value of food and feed end products. This wave of acquisitions and alliances appears to be leading to three or four large corporate groupings, each built around a major chemical or drug company, with ambitions to dominate crop biotechnology (Kalaitzandonakes and Maltsbarger, 1998).

Much of the motivation for this third wave of mergers and alliances is the difficulty that many firms experience in obtaining legal access to the technologies required to bring a new biotechnology product to the market. "For example, a transgenic insecticide tolerant plant may involve plant variety rights and plant patents, as well as several patents relating to transformation technology, the genetic markers employed in selection, the gene coding for the insecticide promotor and various elements and modifications needed to adequately express genes in plant cells" (Sehgal, 1996:16). The point emphasized by Sehgal with respect to the plant biotechnology sector also applies more broadly to the entire set of industries that draws on advances in biotechnology. Development of new biotechnology products depends on technologies on which other firms have intellectual property claims. It remains an open question at present whether the increasingly complex industry structure that emerged during the 1990s will continue. The process of acquisitions, mergers, and alliances is proceeding so rapidly that it is exceedingly difficult to keep track of the changing structure of the chemical–pharmaceutical–biotechnology seed industry complex. One clear trend has been the failure, during the 1990s, of the major German pharmaceutical–chemical companies, burdened by commitment to traditional methods of drug discovery and a political environment that was hostile to biotechnology, to retain the dominant position they had regained in the decades since World War II.

INDUSTRIAL POLICY AND INTERNATIONAL COMPETITION

There is probably no other industry in which as large a share of early research and development costs has been accounted for by the public sector. In contrast to the computer and semiconductor industries (Chapter 10), the federal government has funded molecular biology and genetic engineering research primarily in university settings. As the commercial potential of biotechnology became increasingly apparent in the 1980s federal support for basic and generic research expanded dramatically. The federal government has not, however, as in the computer and semiconductor industries, implemented any coordinated set of policies specifically directed to improving the international competitive position of the U.S. biotechnology industry.[25] It did, however, provide strong support, in the 1994 Uruguay Round of international trade negotiations, for an agreement on Trade-Related Aspects of Intellectual Property Rights (TRIPS). The agreement requires all World Trade Organization members to adopt strict minimum standards for protecting and enforcing intellectual property rights. These provisions are particulary important for the chemical, pharmaceutical, and biotechnology industries (Braga, 1996; Chapter 13).[26]

By the end of the 1970s systematic policies in support of biotechnology were being implemented in Japan and in Western Europe (Orsenigo, 1989:168–195; Henderson et al., 1999:267–311). In Germany the Ministry of Technological Research initiated a program for the development of industrial biotechnology in 1972. But it was not until

---

[25] For a more general discussion of national systems of technology development in the United States, Japan, and Germany, see Chapter 15.

[26] The issue of how to share in a fair and equitable manner the benefits arising from the exploitation of genetic resources with the indigenous populations, who have been responsible for conserving those resources, emerged in the 1990s as a major issue for those concerned with intellectual property rights and the preservation of biodiversity (Organization for Economic Cooperation and Development, 1996).

1997 that the parliament of the European Union (EU) passed legislation to permit patenting of genetically modified life forms (excepting plant and animal varieties and the products of human genetic manipulation). In Japan the Science and Technology Agency established a Committee for the Promotion of Life Sciences in 1973. In both Germany and Japan the programs attempted to maintain a technological trajectory that reflected the traditional interests of the food, pharmaceutical, and chemical industries in fermentation technologies. France, the United Kingdom, and Italy reacted more slowly to the potential possibilities of biotechnology; France took a relatively strong interventionist approach beginning in the early 1980s, whereas the United Kingdom and Italy moved even more slowly toward an active role in the promotion of biotechnologies. When Japan and the European countries began to increase their public support for the development of biotechnology capacity in the early 1980s, U.S. public expenditures exceeded the public expenditures of all other countries combined. As noted earlier, the decision by Hoechst to enter into a research collaboration with Massachusetts General Hospital reflected a lack of genetic engineering capacity, not only in its own laboratories but also in German universities.

A Japanese Challenge?

In the early 1980s there was a good deal of concern in the United States that lack of an interventionist industrial policy, coupled with a more activist Japanese policy, would lead, as it had in the computer and semiconductor industries, to rapid catch-up on the part of Japan. The fragmentation of the U.S. industry, with so much of its innovative activity concentrated in weakly financed biotechnology start-up firms, was regarded as a severe weakness in the U.S. industrial structure.

The U.S. industry included, in addition to the large pharmaceutical companies, numerous small companies focused on novel product generation. Several of the leading European biotechnology companies, such as Transgene, Immunotech, and Bioeurope, were not independent start-ups but rather companies established by the large pharmaceutical companies to explore technical possibilities and economic potential. As of the mid-1990s there were no Japanese independent start-ups.[27] Japanese companies entered biotechnology from a completely different institutional environment. They were fewer, well established, and less interested in developing new products than in pursuing biotechnology applications in fields such as chemicals, agriculture, food, and energy. With their strong base in fermentation technology Japanese firms placed

---

[27] I draw heavily on Callan (1995, 1996) for my discussion of U.S.–Japanese competition in the biotechnology industry. "The American system of innovation pushes researchers to think about biotechnology for the creation of novel products. Production engineering problems, though important, are secondary. Small biotechnology firms share in the 'basic science' culture of their university colleagues. In addition, the pressures of continuously securing funding from venture capitalists, the stock market, and strategic alliances push American biotechnology firms to concentrate on new product generation because patents, and later new drug applications, signal to the market the value of a corporation. Production problems will be solved later, when large scale production becomes an issue" (Callan, 1996:16).

greater emphasis on process technology. Japanese pharmaceutical and chemical companies did not have a history of innovative product development. And they were not in a position to exploit academic research, because in the Japanese academic community there were few incentives for scientists to direct their efforts to the development of new products. University–industry contract research arrangements were actively discouraged.

The Japanese government, however, considered biotechnology, along with new materials and microelectronics, as a "Next Generation Basic Industrial Technology." But the government did not put large financial resources into biotechnology development. Rather, it encouraged the development of biotechnology research associations to facilitate collaboration among private firms in the area of biotechnology research. It was not until the mid-1990s that Japan began to substantially increase its expenditures on basic research related to biotechnology.

Japanese companies that became involved in biotechnology were almost all vertically integrated with investments in a wide range of industries. Financing of small start-up firms is extremely difficult in the Japanese economic environment. Japan does not allow companies that have not had 5 years of profit to post initial public stock offerings on the Tokyo Stock Exchange. Venture capitalists are, as a result, reluctant to invest in start-ups. The banking sector has also been reluctant to invest in new ventures. There are few tax credits for research and development. Japanese universities are still producing relatively few Ph.D.s in molecular biology and Japanese biotechnology firms have few Ph.D.s in their laboratories. As a result no true start-ups have emerged to translate basic research in the public sector, or from abroad, into commercial possibilities.

In view of these constraints Japanese firms have adopted three tactics to strengthen their capacity in biotechnology: (1) they sourced and licensed technology from abroad; (2) they strengthened their expertise in production technology; and (3) they sought to develop stronger in-house capacity in biotechnology. They have been relatively successful in the first. Technology was easily available from many financially strained U.S. start-up firms. Japanese partners were attractive because they were willing to let the American firms retain U.S. marketing rights. American universities and hospitals also contracted with Japanese firms. "From 1985–1989 a majority of the biotechnology strategic alliances struck by Japanese companies involved an American partner, and in eighty percent of these alliances the flow of technology was from the American to the Japanese company" (Callan, 1996:25).

In the mid-1980s it was widely assumed, both in Japan and in the United States, that the strategy adopted by Japan would, as in the case of computers and semiconductors, enable Japan to emerge as a major player in the biotechnology industries. The same skills that enabled Japan to dominate in important areas of the old biological technologies would, it was anticipated, apply to the new biotechnologies. As of the late 1990s, however, the skills in production engineering had not enabled Japanese firms to achieve the success that had earlier been anticipated. Biotechnology has no "key technology" such as the semiconductor, which automatically unlocks the door to a wide range of applications. Access to advances in basic science remains critical to the development of new products in biotechnology. And this access is available only to other scientists, whether in universities, government research institutes, or the private sector, who are themselves doing science at the most advanced level. The close linkages between the universities and the biotechnology industries that had generated so much concern in the 1980s has turned out to be a major source of competitive advantage for the U.S. biotechnology industries.

The prospect for the Japanese biotechnology industries thus appears less certain from the perspective of the late 1990s than it did in the mid-1980s. In contrast, there were signs of renewed vitality in Western Europe. In 1997 the European Parliament approved legislation liberalizing Europe's biotechnology patent system. Although the European biotechnology industries were beginning to experience more rapid economic growth, the industry was still only about one-fourth as large as in the United States (Williams, 1997).

Developing Countries

What about the prospects for biotechnology in the developing world?[28] In many tropical countries substantial opportunities exist for improving traditional fermentation-based food products (National Research Council, 1992). It is possible that some biotechnologies, such as genetically modified pest resistance and control technologies, will have a greater impact on both agricultural productivity and health in many tropical developing countries than in more temperate countries. In the mid-1990s four major efforts by the U.S. Agency for International Development (USAID), The Netherlands Directorate General for International Cooperation, the Rockefeller Foundation, and the McKnight Foundation were providing major support for research on plant biotechnology in developing countries. The AID program is targeted at crop pest control, the Netherlands program focuses on cassava, the Rockefeller Foundation program supports biotechnology applicable to rice production, and the McKnight program is directed at strengthening research capacity on food crops in developing countries. In addition several of the international agricultural research institutes supported by the CGIAR have modest biotechnology research programs, often carried out in cooperation with developed country's laboratories. The total annual support for these programs probably amounts to less than $50 million (Kendall et al., 1997).

Substantial progress has been made by national programs in several Asian countries, particularly China, India, Korea, and Philippines, to institutionalize biotechnology research capacity (Box 10.3). Cell tissue and other culture techniques for crop improvement have been widely diffused. Genetic marker techniques are also being used in plant breeding in many developing countries. In Latin America, Brazil, Cuba, and Mexico were making significant investments in biotechnology research. It seems unlikely, however, that any of these countries, other than Cuba, were becoming important

---

[28] For very useful reviews, see Altman and Watanabe (1995) and Brenner (1996).

new sources of knowledge and technology in biotechnology.[29] The emerging structure of the biotechnology industries, discussed earlier in this chapter, will make entry by firms based in developing countries more difficult. Furthermore, the provisions of the World Trade Organization Trade Related Intellectual Property Rights agreements may render any technology they do develop more vulnerable to challenges by multinational pharmaceutical and agrochemical companies.

Most developing countries will, however, be confronted with the problem of how to most effectively utilize the new biotechnologies being developed by the international firms in the pharmaceutical and the agrobiotechnology industries. Biopesticides, based on the transformation of crop plants such as cotton and rice with the gene that produces a toxin from the naturally occurring bacterium *Bacillus thuringiensis* (Bt), are already being used in a number of developing countries. Insect-resistant transgenic plants such as cotton and tobacco are also being diffused in developing countries (Krattiger, 1997). Genetic marker technologies are being used by plant breeders in developing countries. Substantial strengthening of scientific and technical capacity will be required if developing countries are to manage the diffusion of these technologies effectively. Modification will be required in delivery systems for many of the new pharmaceutical products. Economic choices will have to be made about health priorities. In the case of agrobiotechnologies, health, environmental, and economic assessments will be required.

● BOX 10.3

PLANT BIOTECHNOLOGY IN CHINA AND INDIA

Carl Pray, Department of Agricultural Economics and
Marketing, Rutgers University

The two major impacts of plant biotechnology on plant breeding have been through using genetic markers to improve conventional breeding and through transforming plants by introducing genes from other crops or species. China is considerably ahead of India in the use of both of these techniques. However, it is still too early to tell whether China will make better commercial use of these techniques.

In China there are at least three centers of strength in rice biotechnology—at Huazhong Agricultural University, at South China Agricultural University in Guangzhou and at Zhejiang Agricultural University, and the China National

---

[29] During the 1990s Cuba created a world class biotechnology research center in Havana. By the late 1990s several products, including hepatitis B vaccine, meningitis B vaccine, tick vaccine, and monoclonal antibodies for kidney transplants had been developed and introduced (Kaiser, 1998).

Rice Research Institute. The Chinese government supports a national project to map the rice genome, and both the Chinese Academy of Science and the Shanghai government are making major investments in a laboratory in Shanghai. China is clearly the most advanced country in the world in terms of using genetic markers in rice breeding. China is also ahead in the testing and commercialization of transgenic plants. It was the first to commercialize transgenic plants, having started growing transgenic virus-resistant tobacco commercially in 1992. China is estimated to be growing transgenic crops, mainly tobacco, on more than 2,500,000 hectares. By the late 1990s there had been about 60 field trials of transgenic varieties in China.

In India leading centers are located in Hyderabad, at Tamil Nadu Agricultural University in Coimbatore, through a combination of the Directorate of Rice Research, Osmania University, and the University of Hyderabad, and in Bangalore through a combination of the University of Agricultural Sciences, the Indian Institute of Science, and the Tata Institute Center for Biological Sciences. In contrast to China, India still did not have any commercial transgenic crops in the field and as of December 1996 only 16 field trials had been approved. The field trial data probably underestimate research activity in both countries since some government and commercial scientists in both countries have conducted field trials without getting official permission.

Why the difference? It appears to be a combination of higher levels of investment in China and weaker levels of regulation. The governments of both countries have proclaimed that biotechnology is a major investment priority, but in agriculture the Chinese government has invested more resources. Another difference between the two countries is that India has a vocal minority of intellectuals and activists who are opposed to biotechnology because of health and environmental concerns. If similar groups exist in China, they have not been able to generate much public support. This opposition may have influenced the amount of money invested in biotechnology research.

The regulatory climate primarily affects transgenic plants, not the use of markers. India clearly had more regulation of transgenic crops until 1996 when China passed new tough regulations. Before 1996 transgenic varieties in China had to go through the regular testing procedures for new varieties, which require new varieties to have higher yields or better quality characteristics than existing varieties, but there were no special regulations on the testing and release of transgenic crops. In India there was informal regulation of transgenic varieties in the early 1990s. These regulations were formalized in 1994. The existence of regulations and the organized opposition to biotech account for some of the differences in utilization.

Will China continue to stay ahead? The answer to this is unclear. In crops in which self-pollinated varieties are the primary type of seed, China will probably stay ahead because their public sector seems to have a major lead over India in the use of molecular markers. For transgenic crops the main uncertainty is how firmly the 1996 regulations will be implemented.

In commercial crops such as corn, sunflower, rapeseed, sorghum, cotton, and soybeans the Chinese have so far kept foreign seed and biotechnology companies out by giving provincial and county seed companies regional monopolies and by restricting joint ventures with foreign companies. In contrast India has liberalized seed sector controls to permit the major international seed and chemical firms that are active in plant biotechnology in the West to establish subsidiaries or joint ventures in India. Thus, for technology developed elsewhere that could be transferred, India may have an advantage in making biotechnology products available to its farmers through the transfer of technology from developed countries.

The uncertainty that remains for transgenic varieties is whether India will start approving them for commercial use and whether the new Chinese biosafety regulations and industrial policy on the seed industry will slow down the commercialization of transgenic varieties.

_____

Material in this box draws on Sachin Chaturvedi, "Biosafety Policy and Implications in India," *Biotechnology and Development Monitor* 30 (March 1997):10–13; Clive James and Anatole P. Krattiger, "Global Review of the Field Testing and Commercialization of Transgenic Plants, 1986 to 1995: The First Decade of Crop Biotechnology," *ISAAA Briefs* No. 1, Ithaca, NY: ISAAA, 1996; Gary Toenniessen, "Rice Biotechnology Capacity Building in Asia," *Agricultural Biotechnology in International Development*, C. Ives and B. Bedford, eds., Bedford, MA: CAB International (1998); Carl E. Pray, "Public and Private Collaboration on Plant Biotechnology in China," *AgBioForum* 2 (1999):48–53.

BIOTECHNOLOGY AND THE FOOD INDUSTRIES

The impact of the biotechnology revolution on the food industry has occurred even more slowly than on agriculture. In the mid-980s enthusiasts were heralding a future in which the food industry would become completely decoupled from an unstable climate and a limited agricultural resource base (Rogoff and Rawlins, 1987).

The techniques of growing and fermenting bacteria already being used in the production of alcoholic beverages, cheese, and bread, combined with new techniques of cell culture, can be used to transform the production of many agricultural products into industrial processes (National Research Council, 1992). In principle any commodity that is consumed in an undifferentiated form could be produced in this manner. Tissue culture techniques could, for example, be used to produce edible "look-alike" plant parts. Food industry leaders anticipated substantial spillover from the advances being made in the use of genetic engineering techniques in the pharmaceutical and agricultural industries. They began to make modest investments in research capacity to monitor the new and emerging developments in biotechnology.

In 1990 the FDA approved rDNA rennin, an enzyme that had traditionally been extracted from the stomach of calves, for use in the production of cheese, yogurt, and other dairy products. A number of major companies and new biotechnology companies have used *in vitro* approaches to create substitutes for natural fruit flavors, mint oil, quinine, and saffron. Work was in progress using *in vitro* processes to produce substitutes for coffee and cocoa.

As this chapter was being completed food industry spokesmen were still anticipating dramatic advances in the biotechnology and genetic engineering opportunities that would lead to the development of novel neutraceuticals—food or food ingredients that provide medical or health benefits (Adelaja and Schilling, 1999). Several of the companies that had led in the integration of the pharmaceutical, biotechnology, and seed industry (such as Monsanto, Du Pont, and Novartis) had merged or formed alliances with firms in the feed and food industries. At the same time industry leaders were warning of an increased incidence and heightened public concern about food safety from food-borne disease and from pesticide and animal drug residues and environmental contaminants. Some observers anticipate that progress in use of rDNA techniques in attacking food-borne illnesses will be more rapid than the development of neutraceuticals for the consumer market.

The bovine growth hormone and herbicide-resistant soybean cases, discussed earlier, do illustrate several challenges in the sociopolitical environment, not only in the United States but also in other high-income countries. One is that some consumer concerns run deeper than immediate health implications. This reflects concern over widespread use of new technologies about which consumers have little information and over which they feel they have little control (Killman and Cooper, 1999; Kershen, 1999). It also reflects a growing skepticism about official assurances regarding public health implications of new technologies. It is a major source of debate over efforts to regulate trade in biotechnology products such as agricultural commodities and processed foods. And it is a major reason why, in the United States and Western Europe, organic foods are the most rapidly growing sector of the retail food industry (Murphy, 1997). These are issues that have important implications for both the suppliers of technology and the food industry.

Substantial changes in the marketing system will be required to meet more diverse customer requirements. When transgenic crops with quality-enhanced (or differentiated) traits are placed in the market, identity will have to be preserved from farm through processing, transportation, and distribution to the consumer. This will mean a transition from a high-volume low margin to a low-volume high value-added system.

BIOTECHNOLOGY IN THE TWENTY-FIRST CENTURY

Biotechnology is only now beginning to live up to the expectations of the scientific entrepreneurs and venture capitalists who established the first biotechnology firms. In some respects the stage of development of biotechnology, in the late 1990s, is similar to that of the computer industry in the late 1950 when semiconductors were beginning to replace vacuum tubes (Chapter 10).

It is hard to avoid a conclusion, however, that the biotechnology industries are poised for dramatic growth in the first decades of the twenty-first century. In the late 1990s there was an explosive growth in the number of biotechnology therapeutics and vaccines brought to the market and in advanced stages of clinical development. Agricultural biotechnology appears to have overcome its initial development lag and was, in the late 1990s, the most rapidly growing, and potentially the largest, sector of the industry. Bioengineered fruits and vegetables are beginning to appear on supermarket shelves. And the food industry is developing more applications of biotechnology in food processing, storage, and distribution.[30]

There are, however, reasons for questioning the more optimistic projections. Advances have come more slowly than anticipated by those who authorize and prepare the news releases announcing the "genetic discovery of the week." Only a few biotechnology firms have been able to generate a succession of profitable new products. The sector of the industry that generates most of the important scientific and technical innovations, firms other than the major pharmaceutical and chemical companies, continues to operate at a loss. All but a few firms are dependent on infusions of new venture capital to maintain their research and development activities.

Data on earnings from biotechnology products are not available for the larger firms. External evidence suggests that their biotechnology units are at least marginally profitable. Monsanto has divested itself of its older heavy chemical businesses and is concentrating its resources in pharmaceutical and agricultural applications of biotechnology. In both the United States and in Western Europe, pharmaceutical and agrochemical companies are continuing to acquire smaller biotechnology firms with strong research staffs and promising product lines at what some observers consider to be inflated prices.

Acceptance of biotechnology products continues to present a mixed picture. Even as new agricultural and food applications come on stream consumers, particularly in Western Europe, are becoming increasingly militant about process regulation, product approval, and labeling. Whereas some consumer groups express militant concerns about food safety, other consumer groups press the Food and Drug Administration to ease procedures for ensuring the safety and efficacy of new drugs designed to treat cancer and AIDS.

Serious questions continue to be raised about the social and ethical implications of biotechnology and genetic engineering (Rifkin, 1998). Some critics are concerned that biotechnology, particularly the emergence of "life-style" as well as therapeutic drugs, will become a major source of social and economic change in the twenty-first century. These concerns were heightened by the birth of the first cloned mammal, a sheep named Dolly, in Scotland in 1998. Engineered crops are seen by some critics as the instrument by which international agribusiness will finally impose its will on farmers and gain control over the world food supply (Rifkin, 1998). A more

---

[30] For details on biotechnology applications in the pipeline, see Feldbaum (1996).

immanent issue is whether genetic engineering techniques are enhancing the capacity to develop new bioweapons—more dangerous than any existing in nature.[31] I suspect, when we look back at the end of the first quarter of the twenty-first century, that most of these concerns will seem rather exaggerated. But we should not rule out surprise. Both benefits and costs in terms of agricultural production, human health, and environmental integrity will probably exceed our expectations.

The driving forces behind the biotechnology revolution remain complex (Walsh, 1993). It would be easy, but misleading, to interpret the development of the biotechnology industries as an idealized example of the linear progression from curiosity-driven, investigator-initiated basic scientific research through technology development and commercialization. Even the earliest support for the development of the new discipline of molecular biology in the 1930s was motivated by a strong mission orientation. The support by the federal government of research in molecular biology under the impetus of the "War on Cancer" suggests a demand-induced interpretation. The initial focus of pharmaceutical biotechnology development on products such as insulin and human growth hormone, for which the market was constrained by the cost or availability of a natural raw material, suggests a factor-induced interpretation. And the new agrobiotechnology products, like the products of the old biological technology, have also been factor saving. The lag between exaggerated early expectation and realized technology development suggests that the stochastic processes emphasized in evolutionary models of technical innovation played an important role.

REFERENCES

Adelaja, A. O., and B. J. Schilling. "Neutraceuticals: Blurring the Line Between Food and Drugs in the Twenty-First Century." *Choices*, Fourth Quarter, 1999:35–39.

Altman, D. W., and K. N. Watanabe. *Plant Biotechnology Transfer to Developing Countries.* Austin, TX: R. G. Cordes, 1995.

Arora, A., and A. Gambardella. "Complementary and External Linkages: The Strategies of the Large Firms in Biotechnology." *Journal of Industrial Economics* 38 (June 1990):361–379.

Arora, A., and A. Gambardella. "Evaluating Technological Information and Utilizing It." *Journal of Economic Behavior and Organization* 24 (1994):91–114.

Barton, J. H.. "Patents and Antitrust: A Rethinking in Light of Patent Breadth and Sequential Innovation." *Antitrust Law Journal* 65 (1997):449–496.

Barton, J. H. *The Impact of Contemporary Patent Law on Biotechnology Research.* In *Global Genetic Resources: Access and Property Rights*, S. A. Eberhart, ed., pp. 85–97. Madison, WI: Crop Science Society of America, 1998.

Berg, P., et al. "Potential Biohazards of Recombinant DNA Molecules." *Science* 185 (July 26, 1974):303.

Berg, P., D. Baltimore, S. Brenner, R. O. Roblen, III, and M. F. Singer. "Asilomar Conference on Recombinant DNA Molecules." *Science* 188 (1975):991–994.

---

[31] The definitive authority on bioweapons is Sidell et al. (1997). See also Preston (1998).

Braga, P. "Trade Related Intellectual Property Issues: The Uruguay Round Agreement and Its Economic Implications." In *The Uruguay Round and the Developing Countries*, W. Marin and L. A. Winters, eds., pp. 341–379. Cambridge, UK: Cambridge University Press, 1996.

Brenner, C. *Integrating Biotechnology in Agriculture: Incentives, Constraints and Country Experiences.* Paris: Organization for Economic Cooperation and Development, 1996.

Brill, W. J. "Safety Concerns and Genetic Engineering in Agriculture." *Science* 227 (January 25, 1985):381–384.

Brock, T. D. *The Emergence of Bacterial Genetics.* Plainview, NY: Cold Spring Harbor Laboratory Press, 1990.

Bud, R. *The Uses of Life: A History of Biotechnology.* Cambridge, UK: Cambridge University Press, 1993.

Cairns, J., G. S. Stent, and J. D. Watson. *Phage and the Origins of Molecular Biology.* Plainview, NY: Cold Spring Harbor Laboratory Press, 1992.

Callan, B. *Who Gains from Genes? A Study of National Innovation Strategies in the Globalizing Biotechnology Markets.* Dissertation, University of California, 1995.

Callan, B. "Why Production Technology Is Not a Measure of Competitiveness in Biotechnologies." Berkeley, CA: Berkeley Roundtable on the International Economy Working Paper #86, April 1996, mimeo.

Carlson, G., M. Marra, and B. Hubbell. "The New Super Seeds: Transgenic Technology for Crop Production." *Choices* (Third Quarter, 1997):31–36.

Carey, J. "The Duo Jolting the Gene Business." *Business Week* (May 25, 1998):70–72.

Carr, G. "The Pharmaceutical Industry." *Economist* (February 21, 1998):S3–9, 12–18.

Carter, M, H., and R. A. Goldberg. *Monsanto Company: Licensing 21st Century Technology.* Cambridge, MA: Harvard Business School (N9–597-038), October 15, 1996.

Cockburn, I., R. Henderson, L. Orsenigo, and G. Pisano. "Pharmaceuticals and Biotechnology." In *U.S. Industry in 2000: Studies in Competitive Performance*, D. C. Mowery, ed., pp. 363–398. Washington, DC: National Academy Press, 1999.

Cohen, J. "The Genomics Gamble." *Science* 275 (February 7, 1997):767–772.

Cohen, S. N., A. C. Y. Chang, H. Boyer, and R. B. Helling. "Construction of Biologically Functional Bacterial Plasmids In Vitro." *Proceedings of the National Academy of Sciences U.S.A.* 70 (November 1973):3240–3244.

Colwell, R. K., E. A. Norse, D. Pimental, F. E. Sharples, D. Simberloff, W. Szbalski, and W. Brill. "Genetic Engineering in Agriculture." *Science* 229 (July 12, 1995):111–112.

Doll, J. J. "The Patenting of DNA." *Science* 280 (May 1, 1998):689–690.

Dubos, R. *Louis Pasteur.* Boston, MA: Little Brown, 1950.

Duvick, D. N. "Plant Breeding, An Evolutionary Concept." *Crop Science* 36 (1996):539–548.

Federal Coordinating Council on Science, Engineering and Technology. *Biotechnology for the 21st Century.* Washington, DC: US/GPO, February 1992.

Feldbaum, C. B. "Agricultural Biotechnology: The Future of the World's Food Supply." Biotechnology Industry Organization, Website—http://www.bio.org/bio/2usbio.html, January 1996.

Gambardella, A. *Science and Innovation: The U.S. Pharmaceutical Industry during the 1980s.* Cambridge, MA: Cambridge University Press, 1995.

Goodman, R. M., H. Hauptli, A. Crossway, and V. C. Knauf. "Gene Transfer in Crop Improvement." *Science* 236 (April 3, 1987):48–54.

Harlan, J. R. *Crops and Man,* 2nd ed. Madison, WI: American Society of Agronomy and Crop Science Society of America, 1992.

Hayenga, M. "Structural Change in the Biotech, Seed and Chemical Industrial Complex." *Ag Bio Forum* 1 (Fall 1998). (Retrieved from http://www.agbioforum.missouri.edu).

Heller, M. A., and R. S. Eisenberg. "Can Patents Deter Innovation? The Anticommons in Biomedical Research." *Science* 280 (May 1, 1998):698–699.

Henderson, R., and I. Cockburn. "Scale, Scope and Spillovers: The Determinants of Research Productivity in Drug Discovery." *RAND Journal of Economics* 27 (Spring 1996):32–59.

Henderson, R., L. Orsenigo, and G. P. Pisano. "The Pharmaceutical Industry and the Revolution in Molecular Biology: Interactions among Scientific, Institutional and Organizational Change." In *Sources of Industrial Leadership: Studies in Seven Industries*, D. E. Mowery and R. R. Nelson, eds., pp. 267–311, Cambridge, UK: Cambridge University Press, 1999.

Hocking, A. J. *Economic Aspects of Biotechnology.* Cambridge, UK: Cambridge University Press, 1986.

Ibrahim, J. M. "Genetic Soybeans Alarm Europeans." *New York Times,* November 7, 1996.

James, C. *Global Status of Transgenic Crops in 1998.* Ithaca, NY: The International Service for the Acquisition of Agri-Biotech Applications, 1998.

James, C., and A. F. Krattiger. *Global Review of the Field Testing and Commercialization of Transgenic Plants: 1986–1995.* Ithaca, NY: The International Service for the Acquisition of Agri-Biotech Applications, 1996.

Jarvis, L. S. *The Potential Effects of Two New Biotechnologies on the World Dairy Industry.* Boulder, CO: Westview Press, 1996.

Kaiser, J. "Cuba's Billion-Dollar Biotech Gamble." *Science* 282 (1998):1626–1628.

Kalaitzandonakes, N., and R. Maltsbarger. "Biotechnology and Identity-Preserved Supply Chains." *Choices* (Fourth Quarter, 1998):15–18.

Kendall, H. W., R. Beachy, T. Eisner, F. Gould, R. Herdt, P. Raven, J. S. Schell, and M. S. Swaminathan. *Bioengineering of Crops: Report of the World Bank Panel on Transgenic Crops.* Washington, DC: The World Bank, 1997.

Kenney, M. *Biotechnology: The University-Industrial Complex.* New Haven, CT: Yale University Press, 1986.

Kershen, D. L. "Biotechnology: An Essay on the Academy, Cultural Attitudes and Public Policy." *Ag Bio Forum* 2 (1999):137–146. (Retrieved from http://www.agbioforum.missouri.edu.)

Killman, S., and H. Cooper. "Monsanto Falls Flat Trying to Sell Europe on Bioengineered Food." *Wall Street Journal* 103 (May 11, 1999):A10.

Kling, J. "Could Transgenic Supercrops One Day Breed Superweeds." *Science* 274 (1996):180–181.

Krattiger, A. *Insect Resistance in Crops: A Case Study of Bacillus thuringiensis (Bt) and Its Transfer to Developing Countries.* Ithaca, NY: The International Service for the Acquisition of Agri-Biotech Applications, 1997.

Krimsky, S. *Genetic Alchemy: The Social History of the Recombinant DNA Controversy.* Cambridge, MA: MIT Press, 1982.

Krimsky, S. *Biotechnics and Society: The Rise of Industrial Genetics.* New York: Praeger, 1991.

Krimsky, S., and R. Wrubel. *Agricultural Biotechnology and the Environment: Science, Policy and Social Issues.* Urbana, IL: University of Illinois Press, 1996.

Lee, M. "DNA Markers and Plant Breeding Programs." *Advances in Agronomy* 55 (1995): 265–344.

Marshall, E. "A Bitter Battle over Insulin Gene." *Science* 277 (1997a):1028–1030.

Marshall, E. "Snipping Away at Genome Patenting." *Science* 227 (September 19, 1997b):1752–1753.

McKelvey, M. D. *Evolutionary Innovations: The Business of Biotechnology.* Oxford, UK: Oxford University Press, 1996.

Merges, R. P. and R. R. Nelson. "On the Complex Economics of Patent Scope." *Columbia Law Review* 90 (May 1990):839–916.

Mumford, L. *Technics and Civilization.* New York, NY: Harcourt Brace, 1934.

Murphy, K. "There's Big Green in Organic Food." *Business Week* (October 6, 1997), 170.

National Research Council Board on Science and Technology for International Development. *Applications of Biotechnology to Traditional Fermented Foods.* Washington, DC: National Academy Press, 1992.

Nelson, R. R., and R. Mazzoleni. *The Benefits and Costs of Strong Patent Protection: A Contribution to the Current Debate.* New York: Columbia University School of International and Public Affairs, 1998.

Office of Technology Assessment. *Impacts of Applied Genetics: Micro-Organisms, Plants, and Animals.* Washington, DC: U.S. Government Printing Office (OTA-HR-132), April 1981.

Office of Technology Assessment. *Commercial Biotechnology: An International Analysis.* Washington, DC: U.S. Government Printing Office (OTA-BA-218), January 1984.

Office of Technology Assessment. *Biotechnology in a Global Economy.* Washington, DC: U.S. Government Printing Office (OTA-BA-495), October 1991.

Organization for Economic Cooperation and Development. *Intellectual Property, Technology Transfer and Genetic Resources.* Paris: OECD, 1996.

Orsenigo, L. *The Emergence of Biotechnology: Institutions and Markets in Industrial Innovation.* New York: St. Martin's Press, 1989.

Preston, R. "The Bioweaponeers." *New Yorker* (March 9, 1998):52–65.

Raeburn, P. *The Lost Harvest.* New York: Simon and Schuster, 1995.

Rasmussen, N. "What's So New About Biotechnology? Tales of Life Science and Industry in 1930 and 40s America." Sidney, Australia: The University of New South Wales, School of Science and Technology Studies, February 2, 1999 (mimeo).

Rausser, G. "Public/Private Alliances." *AgBioForum* 2 (1999):5–10. Retrieved April 15, 1999 from the worldwide web: http://www.agbioforum.missouri.edu.

Reimers, N. "Tiger by the Tail." *Chemtech* 17 (1984):464–471.

Rifkin, J. *The Biotech Century: Harnessing the Gene and Remaking the World.* New York: Putnam, 1998.

Rogoff, M. H., and S. L. Rawlins. "Food Security: A Technological Alternative." *Bioscience* 37 (December 1987):800–807.

Rosendal, G. K. "The Politics of Patent Legislation in Biotechnology: An International View." In *Biotechnology Annual Review*, M. Raafat and El Gewely, eds., pp. 453–477. Amsterdam: Elsevier, 1995.

Ruttan, V. W. *Agricultural Research Policy.* Minneapolis, MN: University of Minnesota Press, 1982.

Sapienza, A. M. "R&D Collaboration as a Global Competitive Tactic—Biotechnology and the Ethical Pharmaceutical Industry." *R&D Management* 19 (1989):285–295.

Schmeck, H. M., Jr. "3 Immunology Investigators Win Nobel Prize in Medicine." *New York Times* (October 16, 1981):A1, C2.

Sehgal, S. "Biotechnology Heralds a Major Restructuring of the Global Seed Industry." *Diversity* 12 (1996):13–15.

Sidell, F. R., E. T. Takafuji, and D. R. Franz. *Medical Aspects of Chemical and Biological Warfare.* Falls Church, VA: Office of the Surgeon General, U.S. Army, 1997.

Snow, A. A., and P. M. Palma. "Commercialization of Transgenic Plants: Patented Ecological Risks." *BioScience* 47 (1997):86–96.

Speaker, S. L., and M. S. Lindee. *A Guide to the Human Genome Project: Technologies, People and Institutions.* Philadelphia, PA: Chemical Heritage Foundation, 1993.

Stent, G. S. "That Was the Molecular Biology That Was." *Science* 160 (April 26, 1968): 390–395.

Stent, G. S. *The Coming of the Golden Age: A View of the End of Progress.* Garden City, NY: American Museum of Natural History, 1969.

Tanouye, E., and R. Langreth. "With Patents Expiring on Big Prescriptions, Drug Industry Quakes." *Wall Street Journal* (August 12, 1997):A1.

Wade, N. "Gene-Splicing: At Grass-Roots Level a Hundred Flowers Bloom." *Science* 195 (February 1977):558–560.

Watson, J. D. *The Double Helix: A Personal Account of the Discovery and Structure of DNA.* New York: Athenium, 1968.

Weaver, W. "The Natural Sciences." Rockefeller Foundation *Annual Report*, New York (1938):203–221.

Williams, N. "European Parliament Backs New Biopatent Guidelines." *Science* 277 (July 25, 1997):472.

Wright, S. *Molecular Politics: Developing American and British Regulatory Policy for Genetic Engineering: 1972–1982.* Chicago, IL: University of Chicago Press, 1994.

APPENDIX

TERMS USED IN MOLECULAR BIOLOGY AND BIOTECHNOLOGY

The technical terms used in molecular biology and genetic engineering are not as familiar as those used in many other fields of technology. The following is a glossary of terms used in this chapter.

Amino acids: The building blocks of proteins. There are 20 common amino acids.

Antibiotic: A specific type of chemical substance that is administered to fight infections, usually bacterial infections, in humans or animals. Many antibiotics are produced by using microorganisms; others are produced synthetically.

Antigen: A substance, usually a protein or carbohydrate, which, when introduced in the body of a human or higher animal, stimulates the production of an antibody that will react specifically with it.

Bacteria: Any of a large group of microscopic organisms having round, rodlike, spiral, or filamentous unicellular or noncellular bodies that are often aggregated into colonies, are enclosed by a cell wall or membrane, and lack fully differentiated nuclei. Bacteria may exist as free-living organisms in soil, water, or organic matter, or as parasites in the live bodies of plants and animals.

Bacteriophage (or phage)/bacterial virus: A virus that multiplies in bacteria. Bacteriophage lambda is commonly used as a vector in recombinant DNA experiments.

Bioprocess: Any process that uses complete living cells or their components (e.g., enzymes, chloroplasts) to effect desired physical or chemical changes.

Bioprocess technology: Facilities the adaptation of biological methods of production to large-scale industrial use. Most industrial biological syntheses were initially carried out on a small-scale batch process using fermentation techniques.

Catalysis: A modification, especially an increase, in the rate of a chemical reaction induced by a material (e.g., enzyme) that is chemically unchanged at the end of the reaction.

Catalyst: A substance that induces catalysis; an agent that enables a chemical reaction to proceed under milder conditions (e.g., at a lower temperature) than otherwise possible. Biological catalysts are enzymes; some nonbiological catalysts include metallic complexes.

Cell: The smallest structural unit of living matter capable of functioning independently; a microscopic mass of protoplasm surrounded by a semipermeable membrane, usually including one or more nuclei and various nonliving products, capable alone, or interacting with other cells, of performing all the fundamental functions of life.

Cell fusion: The artificial joining of cells, combining the desirable characteristics of different types of cells into one cell. A single hybrid cell with nuclei and cytoplasm from different cells is formed. The cell from such a fusion (hybridoma) produces **monoclonal antibodies** (MAbs), which are the clones of a single hybridoma cell.

Chromosomes: The rodlike structures of a cell's nucleus that store and transmit genetic information; the physical structure that contains genes. Chromosomes are composed mostly of DNA and protein and contain most of the cell's DNA. Each species has a characteristic number of chromosomes.

Complementary DNA (cDNA): DNA that is complementary to messenger RNA; used for cloning or as a probe in DNA hybridization studies.

Deoxyribonucleic acid (DNA): A linear polymer, made up of deoxyribonucleotide repeating units, that is the carrier of genetic information; present in chromosomes and chromosomal material or cell organelles such as mitochondria and chloroplasts, and also present in some viruses. The genetic material found in all living organisms. Every inherited characteristic has its origin somewhere in the code of each individual's DNA.

DNA probe: A sequence of DNA that is used to detect the presence of a particular nucleotide sequence.

DNA sequence: The order of nucleotide bases in the DNA helix; the DNA sequence is essential to the storage of genetic information.

Enzymes: Any of a group of catalytic proteins that are produced by living cells and that mediate and promote the chemical processes of life without themselves being altered or destroyed. Their function in living systems is to catalyze the making and breaking of chemical bonds. They have been used commercially since the 1890s when fungal cell extracts were first added to brewing vats to facilitate the breakdown of starch into sugar. The enzyme market is dominated by two European companies, Noro Industries (Denmark) and Gist-Brocades, NV (Netherlands)—65% of market.

Escherichia coli (*E. coli*): A species of bacteria that inhabits the intestinal tract of most vertebrates. Some strains are pathogenic to humans and animals. Many nonpathogenic strains are used experimentally as hosts for recombinant DNA.

Fermentation: An anaerobic bioprocess. Fermentation is used in various industrial processes for the manufacture of products such as alcohols, acids, and cheese by the action of yeasts, molds, and bacteria.

Gene: The basic unit of heredity; an ordered sequence of nucleotide bases, comprising a segment of DNA. A gene contains the sequence of DNA that encodes one polypeptide chain (via RNA).

Gene expression: The mechanism whereby the genetic directions in any particular cell are decoded and processed into the final functioning product, usually a protein. See also **transcription** and **translation.**

Gene transfer: The use of genetic or physical manipulation to introduce foreign genes into host cells to achieve desired characteristics in progeny.

Genome: The total complement of genetic material in an organism or an individual.

Genomics: "Structural genomics" includes the mapping, sequencing, and analyzing of genomes. Functional genomics involves the development of experimental approaches to making use of the information and reagents provided by structural genomics.

Growth hormone (GH): A group of peptides involved in regulating growth in higher animals.

Hormone: A chemical messenger found in the circulation of higher organisms that transmits regulatory messages to cells.

Hybridoma: Product of fusion between myeloma cell (which divides continuously in culture and is "immortal") and lymphocyte (antibody-producing cell); the resulting cell grows in culture and produces monoclonal antibodies.

Immune response: The reaction of an organism to invasion by a foreign substance. Immune responses are often complex, and may involve the production of antibodies from special cells (lymphocytes), as well as the removal of the foreign substance by other cells.

Interferons (Ifns): A class of glycoproteins (proteins with sugar groups attached at specific locations) important in immune function and thought to inhibit viral infections.

Messenger RNA (mRNA): RNA that serves as the template for protein synthesis; it carries the transcribed genetic code from the DNA to the protein-synthesizing complex to direct protein synthesis.

Monoclonal antibodies (MAbs): Homogeneous antibodies derived from a single clone of cells; MAbs recognize only one chemical structure. MAbs are useful in a variety of industrial and medical capacities since they are easily produced in large quantities and have remarkable specificity.

Monoclonal antibody technology: The use of hybridomas that produce monoclonal antibodies for a variety of purposes. Hybridomas are maintained in cell culture or, on a larger scale, as tumors (ascites) in mice.

Neurotransmitters: Small molecules found at nerve junctions that transmit signals across those junctions.

Plant tissue culture: Techniques make it possible to regenerate exact replica plants (clones) from single plant cells. The tissue culture process itself gives rise to unique variations, that is, **somoclonal variation**.

Plasmid: An extrachromosomal, self-replicating, circular segment of DNA; plasmids (and some viruses) are used as "vectors" for cloning DNA in bacterial "host" cells.

Protoplast fusion: The joining of two cells in the laboratory to achieve desired results, such as increased viability of antibiotic-producing cells.

Recombinant DNA (rDNA): The hybrid DNA produced by joining pieces of DNA from different organisms together *in vitro*.

Recombinance DNA technology: The use of recombinant DNA for a specific purpose, such as the formation of a product or the study of a gene.

Recombinant DNA (rDNA) technology: Allows direct manipulation of genetic material of individual cells. It is used to develop microorganisms that produce new products, existing products more efficiently (insulin), large quantities of otherwise scarce products, and microorganisms that themselves are useful (microorganisms that degrade toxic wastes). The commercial success of specific individual applications of rDNA and cell fusion technologies depends on advances in bioprocess engineering.

Restriction enzymes: Bacterial enzymes that cut DNA at specific DNA sequences.

Steroid: A group of organic compounds, some of which act as hormones to stimulate cell growth in higher animals and humans.

Strain: A group of organisms of the same species having distinctive characteristics but not usually considered a separate breed or variety. A genetically homogeneous population of organisms at a subspecies level that can be differentiated by a biochemical, pathogenic, or other taxonomic feature.

Transcription: The synthesis of messenger RNA on a DNA template; the resulting RNA sequence is complementary to the DNA sequence. This is the first step in gene expression. See also **translation.**

Transformation: The introduction of new genetic information into a cell using naked DNA.

Translation: The process in which the genetic code contained in the nucleotide base sequence of messenger RNA directs the synthesis of a specific order of amino acids to produce a protein. This is the second step in gene expression. See also **transcription**.

Transposable element: Segment of DNA that moves from one location to another among or within chromosomes in possibly a predetermined fashion, causing genetic change; may be useful as a vector for manipulating DNA.

Virus: Any of a large group of submicroscopic agents infecting plants, animals, and bacteria and unable to reproduce outside the tissues of the host. A fully formed virus consists of nucleic acid (DNA or RNA) surrounded by a protein or protein and lipid coat.

PART IV

TECHNOLOGY POLICY

In the chapters in this final section I return to some of the issues posed in Part I. Is economic growth sustainable? As we enter the twenty-first century, confidence has weakened with respect to the role of technical change in the advanced industrial economies of the West. The former centrally planned economies have experienced a decline, in some cases a collapse, of their scientific and technical capacity. A number of formerly poor countries, particularly in East and Southeast Asia, have achieved remarkably high rates of productivity and income growth. At the same time a number of other poor countries, including most countries in Africa, seem to have been almost completely left behind.

In the past there were substantial differences among national systems of technology development. National governments played distinctively different roles in the promotion of science and technology (Chapter 11). Technology policy in the United States has, for example, been characterized as "mission oriented" and in Germany as "diffusion oriented." But is it still meaningful in a world characterized by multinational firms and open trading systems to talk about national systems of technical innovation? In the past science and technology policy has been effectively directed to catching up to the leaders—by Germany to catch up to Great Britain and by Japan to catch up to the United States. An important unresolved issue is whether the countries left behind in the economic development process can in the future successfully utilize science and technology policy to repeat the success of Japan and Germany?

In the 1960s the formula that had permitted the United States to move to a position of scientific and technical leadership in the world community was confronted by both an intellectual and a populist challenge (Chapter 12). A view emerged that the consequences of modern science and technology—reflected in the cataclysm of war, the degradation of the environment, and the psychological costs of rapid social change—were obviously dangerous to the modern world and the future of humankind. New regulatory regimes were introduced to manage formerly open-access public resources. Institutional innovation such as "constructed markets" were developed to replace older "command and control" approaches to environmental management.

In the United States the origins of the science and technology policies of today rest primarily on the institutional arrangements established in the 1940s for the mobilization of science and technology in support of the war effort (Chapter 13).

423

During the post-World War II era the relationship between the federal government and the scientific community and the universities was governed by an "implicit social contract." Government assumed responsibility for funding basic research and the scientific communities assured the government and society that a steady stream of scientific advances would be translated into new weapons, new medicine, new materials and products, and new jobs. The post–World War II social contract was initially challenged by the environmental and anti-Vietnam War movements of the 1970s and 1970s and has substantially eroded since the end of the Cold War. Society is no longer as clear about what it wants from its scientific and technical communities as it was during the Cold War. The architects of U.S. science and technology policy have not yet been able to articulate a fully coherent, or convincing rationale for a post-Cold War science and technology policy.

In a final chapter I return to the issue that was initially articulated in Chapter 1— the transition to sustainable development (Chapter 14). A continuation of the growth trajectory of the past two centuries will lead to a richer, but also to a dirtier world. A more pessimistic scenario is that a widening of income differences within and among countries will lead to both a dirtier and less secure world. A third possibility is that society will acquire the vision and the will to make the technical and institutional changes necessary to bring about convergence of levels of economic living among rich and poor countries and adopt patterns of production and consumption that reduce the flow of energy and materials through the economic system.

It is apparent that if humankind fails to successfully navigate the sustainability transition, the sources of failure will be found in the failure of institutional design rather than in the inherent constraints on the availability of natural resources or the capacity for technical innovation.

CHAPTER 11

Technical Innovation in Three Systems

s it meaningful in today's world to talk of national technical innovation systems? In the past, natural and human resources and institutional and cultural endowments have clearly influenced the rate and direction of technical change (Chapters 4, 6–10).[1] Some have argued that modern transportation and communication systems, coupled with lowered barriers to the movement of financial resources and commodities, have eroded the significance of differences in resource and cultural endowments, at least among industrial countries. Institutional innovations such as the transnational corporation have contributed to the rapid diffusion of technology and the weakening of commitments to the countries in which their home base is located. However, in this chapter I show that national differences in the capacity to develop, transfer, and absorb technology remain important. Differences in resource and cultural endowments, in investment in education and research, and in institutional structure influence the rate and direction of technical and institutional change.

During the first half of the nineteenth century Great Britain led the world in industrial technology. Leadership had passed to the United States by the early decades of the twentieth century. During the last half of the twentieth century U.S. leadership has been challenged by Japan and Germany. In this chapter I focus primarily on the development of national technical innovation systems in the United States, Japan, and Germany.[2]

I give particular attention to the development of the automobile industry and of science-based technology in the three countries. The automobile industry is the world's largest manufacturing industry. It played a dominant role in the emergence of U.S. technological leadership in the first quarter of the twentieth century and an important role in Japanese and German industrial revival after World War II. During the last quarter of the twentieth century science-based high-technology industry emerged as a major focus of competitive advantage among major industrial countries.

---

[1] I am indebted to Yujiro Hayami and Richard Nelson for comments on an earlier draft of this chapter.

[2] I do not attempt to address the issue of British industrial decline. There is a very large literature on this subject. See, for example, Edbaum and Lanzonick (1986), and Weiner (1981).

AMERICAN SYSTEMS OF TECHNICAL INNOVATION

In 1800 the manufacturing sector accounted for less than 10% of U.S. commodity production. By the end of the century it accounted for over 50%. A unifying theme of this dramatic growth in the manufacturing sector was what came to be referred to as "The American System of Manufacturing" (Hounshell, 1984:331–336).

Interchangeable Parts

Economic historians have traditionally characterized the American System as the assembly of complex products from mass-produced interchangeable individual parts (Rosenberg, 1972:87–116). The system which had gradually evolved since the 1820s, first came to prominence in firearms manufacturing.[3]

The significance of interchangeability can best be understood when compared to the handicraft technology used in British gun making into the 1850s. Handicraft gun making involves precisely fitting together, primarily by hand filing, individual components produced by a large number of craftsmen. Substantial skill and patience were required for tasks such as filing and recessing the gunstock to properly accommodate the lock and barrel and correctly arranging the pins and screws. In contrast, the system of interchangeability required little skill, and thus vastly simplified gun production, repair, and maintenance. It also meant that an army in the field no longer had to be accompanied by armorers to repair a broken part or fit a new part (Mokyr, 1990:136, 137).

The large-scale production that would typify the American system was quite limited prior to 1840. Only the Army was in a position to subsidize the high cost of moving materials to remote manufacturing locations such as Springfield and Harpers Ferry and then shipping the finished firearms to the posts at which they were to be used. In the late 1840s and 1850s, however, as cheap coal became available and transportation and communication improved, volume production by the fabrication and assembling of standardized parts became common, not only in firearms, but also in locks, watches, clocks, sewing machines, and other wood and metal working industries.

During the second half of the nineteenth century "armory practice" slowly defused to other branches of manufacturing, usually by the movement of skilled machinists from the New England arms factories to other industries and regions. The sewing machine industry was the first to adopt armory techniques. At the Wheeler and Wilson

---

[3] In the early and mid-1850s a number of industrial commissions from Great Britain and other European countries traveled to the United States to report on the machine processes used in American manufacturing and to purchase tools and equipment. During a visit to the Army Ordnance Department armory in Springfield, Massachusetts, one such committee selected 10 muskets, each made in a different year between 1844 and 1858, "which they caused to be taken to pieces in their presence, and the parts placed in a row of boxes, mixed up together. They then requested the workman, whose duty it is to 'assemble' the arms to put them together, which he did—the Committee handing him the parts, taken at hazard—with the use of a turnscrew only, and as quickly as though they had been English muskets, whose parts had carefully been kept separated" (Rosenberg, 1972:92).

Manufacturing Company (Bridgeport, Connecticut), the armory system was adapted to the production of sewing machines in 1857 by former employees of the Colt and Springfield armories. In contrast, the Singer Manufacturing Company, which began operations in New York City in 1852, adopted the European practice, involving a few general purpose machines and a great deal of hand labor. In spite of higher labor costs and prices, Singer was able to achieve a dominant position in the industry because of its reputation for high quality, its aggressive advertising, and its efficient distribution system (Hounshell, 1981). It did not make the transition to full armory practice until it opened a new factory at Elizabethport, New Jersey, in 1873.

The evolution of the American system was closely associated with the emergence of the machine tool industry (Rosenberg, 1963). In 1820 there was no separate identifiable machinery-producing sector. Machinery-producing establishments made their first appearance as adjuncts to factories specializing in the production of final products, especially textiles and firearms. As the capacity of such shops expanded they began to sell machines, first to other firms in their own industry and then to firms in other industries. With the continued growth in demand for an increasing array of specialized machines, machine tool production emerged as a separate industry consisting of a large number of firms, many of which focused their efforts on a single type of machine tool. The makers of machine tools worked with manufacturers in various industries to overcome production problems relating to the cutting, planing, boring, and shaping of metal parts. As each problem was solved the new knowledge was fed back to the machine tool firms, which then applied the knowledge to solving similar problems in other industries (Hounshell, 1984:4).

Steady improvements in machine speeds, power transmission, lubrication, gearing mechanisms, precision metal cutting, and many other dimensions of performance were applied in one industrial setting after another. Industries such as textiles, arms, sewing machines, farm machinery, locks, clocks, boots and shoes, and locomotives were unrelated from the point of view of final product, yet very closely related from a technical perspective. Because it dealt with processes common to a number of industries, the specialized machine tool industry became a source of rapid diffusion of machine technology across the whole range of metal-using industries (Nelson and Wright, 1992).

The question of why, by the end of the nineteenth century, American machine technology had come to occupy an increasingly dominant position has been intensely debated by economic historians. Ames and Rosenberg (1968) suggest an induced technical change interpretation. At least part of the explanation lies in relative factor prices—particularly the prices of raw materials (wood and metal) and the wages of highly skilled machinists relative to other skilled laborers. They also emphasize demand-side factors such as a more stable American arms procurement policy, and differences in nonmilitary demand—inexpensive utilitarian firearms in the United States versus fine sporting arms in Britain. Other observers have emphasized cultural factors— "military rationalism," "Yankee Ingenuity," "eager resort to machinery," and an open social order uniquely favorable to innovation and entrepreneurship (Sawyer, 1954).

During the third quarter of the nineteenth century the American System, broadly defined as the mass production of precision metal components by a sequence of specialized machines, was adapted to an ever-widening range of products. The development of this new machine technology depended on a high order of mechanical skill as well as ingenuity in conception and design. Increasingly the advances were the product of a specialized machine tool industry; they were not the product of institutionalized research and development, nor did they draw in any substantial way on recent advances in scientific knowledge.[4] But, in the terminology of Usher's model of invention and innovation (Chapter 3), the advances in machine making and machine using identified with the American System "set the stage" for the emergence of "mass production."

Mass Production[5]

By the end of the nineteenth century a number of American industries had achieved high volume production—what later came to be termed "mass production." Mass production was made possible by advances in machine technology; mass marketing was made possible by the development of national rail and telegraph networks and the large domestic market. These industries included new branded and packaged consumer products (cigarettes, canned goods, flour and grain products, beer, dairy products, soaps, and drugs) and light machinery (sewing machines, typewriters, cameras, electrical equipment, and standardized industrial machinery). Although most of these products were initially developed for the domestic market many—including industrial machinery, farm equipment, and other engineering and producer goods—they came to dominate international markets (Chandler, 1977:240–286).

These turn-of-the-century achievements have been attributed to the confluence of two technological streams: (1) the continuing advance of mechanical and metal working skills and their application to high-volume production of standardized commodities; and (2) the exploration, development, and use of the U.S. economy's mineral resource base (Nelson and Wright, 1992:1938). Mineral discovery and extraction and advances in metallurgy drew on, stimulated, and induced some of the most advanced engineering developments of the time.[6] The oft-noted complementarity between

---

[4] "The period beginning in 1859 was one of remarkable scientific progress. If one had to choose any fifteen-year period in history on the basis of density of scientific breakthroughs that took place, it would be difficult to find one that exceeded 1859–74" (Mowery and Rosenberg, 1989:22). But these advances in science were only loosely coupled with advances in technology. "Relatively little of the American performance during this era was based on science, nor even on advanced technical education. American technology was practical, shop-floor oriented, and built on experience" (Nelson and Wright, 1992:1940).

[5] In this section I draw very heavily on Hounshell (1984:189–302).

[6] The development of the mineral industries represented an early example of the contribution of public support for science to technology development in the United States. The U.S. Geological Survey, under the leadership of Major John Wesley Powell, was the most ambitious and successful government science project of the nineteenth century. Under Powell's leadership the United States achieved world leadership in the training of mining engineers and in mining practice (Nelson and Wright, 1992:1938).

capital and natural resources in that era was not merely an exogenous technical relationship, but was induced by a combination of natural resource abundance and rising industrial wage rates (Cain and Patterson, 1981). This meant that although American products were often competitive on world markets, the technology employed in their production was often inappropriate to economies with different resource endowments, or to economies in which a mass market had not yet developed (Chapter 2).

The American system of "mass production" emerged in its most highly developed form at the Ford Motor Company in the first decade of the twentieth century. Early bicycle production, however, represented a transitional technology between the American System that emerged out of New England armory practice and the era of mass production.[7] The bicycle industry was responsible for a number of important technical innovations that set the stage for the automobile industry, including the use of ball-bearings and pneumatic tires. The most important innovation, however, was the adoption and development of sheet steel stampings to replace drop forging and machining. In New England armory practice, drop forging and machining were the principal processes used in metal fabrication. Western Wheel Works broke from this tradition by adopting stamping technology to produce frame joints previously imported from Germany. The metal-stamping equipment developed by Western Wheel's toolmakers enabled it to extend the stamping technology to almost every part of the cycle and to reduce machining to a bare minimum.

The contributions of the bicycle industry to the automobile industry were not only technical. The bicycle revealed a latent demand on the part of the American public for an effective means of personal transport. It remained for the automobile industry, however, to resolve the problem of assembly that would make possible low-cost mass production of a means of personal transportation.[8]

The stage had also been set for the automobile industry by the remarkable growth of the U.S. economy in the later half of the nineteenth century. The growth continued through the first three decades of the twentieth century. From 1903, the year in which the Ford Motor Company was organized, to 1926, when the last Model T rolled off the Ford assembly line, net national product grew at a rate of over 7% per year—comparable to the rates of growth achieved by the East Asian "miracle countries" from

---

[7] The manufacture of bicycles in the United States began in 1878 when Albert A. Pope, a Boston merchant who had been importing English high-wheel bicycles, contracted with the Weed Sewing Machine Company of Hartford, Connecticut, to manufacture an American version. By the time the safety bicycle was introduced from England in 1887, Pope and several smaller firms had produced in the neighborhood of 250,000 high wheelers. Introduction of the safety bicycle set off a new wave of enthusiasm for the bicycle that reached its peak in the mid-1890s when the industry produced 1.2 million machines. In 1896 production by the Pope firm was exceeded by Western Wheel Works of Chicago (Hounshell, 1984:189–215).

[8] "The question of who built the first automobile is still a matter of dispute, but the Germans Karl Benz and Gottlieb Daimler were probably the first, with their gasoline-powered vehicle of 1885. Later Armand Peugeot built a workable car in France, and by the 1890s the European auto industry had begun. . . . In the United States, the auto era dates from September 21, 1893, when the brothers Duryea of Springfield , Massachusetts, who were bicycle mechanics, . . . built a carriage driven by a one-cylinder motor. By 1899 about thirty American companies had built some 2,500 automobiles for sale" (McCraw, 1996:6–7).

the 1960s into the early 1990s. It was this growth in consumer income, combined with the large decline in the real price of the automobile, that made the rapid growth in automobile ownership possible (Hughes, 1986:285).

The Ford Motor Company was established in 1903 following two earlier unsuccessful attempts by Henry Ford to enter automobile production.[9] When Ford achieved control of the company in 1907 he set out to realize an objective he had enunciated a year earlier. "The greatest need today is a light, low priced car with an up-to-date engine of ample horsepower, and built of the very best materials. . . . It must be powerful enough for American roads and capable of carrying its passengers anywhere that a horse-drawn vehicle will go without the driver being afraid of ruining his car" (Hounshell, 1984:189–215).

THE MODEL T IDEA

Mass production at the Ford Motor Company was a product of Ford's commitment to simplicity in design and efficiency in manufacturing. The transition from production in a poorly equipped job shop to mass production was accomplished by substantial experimentation. Ford himself was the classic mechanic. He had remarkable insight about how machines worked and could be made to work better. He brought together a talented team of young engineers and executives, and encouraged experimentation with fresh ideas for gauging, fixture design, machine tool design, factory layout, quality control, and material handling. Ford production engineers tested and adapted what they found useful from New England armory practice, particularly interchangeable parts, and from "western practice," such as pressed steel parts, and added a continuous stream of their own innovations. A first step toward mass production began with eliminating "static assembly" by rearranging machine tools according to the sequence of manufacturing operations rather than by type of machine. A second step was the construction of a new factory at Highland Park designed to facilitate the handling of materials.

THE HIGHLAND PARK FACTORY

In 1906, before the design of the Model T had been completed, Ford purchased a 60-acre tract on the northern edge of Detroit on which to build a new factory. The new factory, designed by Albert Kahn, was a "daylight factory" with extensive windows set in reinforced concrete.

> The principle structure at Highland Park consisted of a four-story building 865 feet in length and 75 feet in width with some fifty thousand square feet of glass (roughly 75 percent of the wall area). Khan placed beside this structure a single-story building with a sawtooth glass roof, 840 by 140 feet, which served as the principal machine

---

[9] For an exceedingly useful account of Ford's early background and the personality and cultural and economic factors that contributed to his early success and later failures, see Hughes (1986:274–355).

shop. Kahn connected these buildings with an impressive glass enclosed craneway on all floors so materials could be moved with ease from one building to the other through the craneway. This craneway would serve as the major distribution point for all the raw material that made up the Model T. (Hounshell, 1984:226–227)

Power was distributed through the plant by electric motors, which drove units connected by line shafts and belting (Chapter 7).

The Assembly Line

The move to the new Highland Park factory was simplified when Ford made a decision in 1909 that the Ford Motor Company would produce only the Model T with identical chassis for its several variants (runabout, touring car, town car, and delivery car). Workers distributed the necessary parts to each workstation and timed their delivery so that they reached the station just before they were needed. Assembly teams moved from station to station to perform specialized tasks. Even before the assembly line was introduced the Highland Park plant was regarded as a showplace of technical efficiency. "A complete Model T emerged from the factory every forty seconds of the working day. Five trains of forty cars left the factory daily, loaded with finished automobiles" (Hounshell, 1984:228).[10] The Model T itself represented the ultimate standardized machine. It was small, light, and strong, and contained a minimum of moving parts.

The first Ford assembly lines for components, such as the magneto coil, were installed in the spring of 1913. Within a year virtually every assembly operation at Ford had been put on a moving line basis. The impact on labor productivity was dramatic. Within a year adjustments in the height of the line and the development of a continuous chain to move the magnetos along the line had reduced the assembly time from one every 20 minutes to about one every 5 minutes per person (Hounshell, 1984:248). In December 1913 a line on which the car was carried along an endless chain during final assembly was introduced. By April 1914 the time required for assembly had been reduced from approximately 12.5 man-hours the previous August to just 1.5 man-hours. These productivity increases were accompanied by a vast number of related technical innovations including special purpose machine tools, fast drying paints, improved glassmaking, pneumatic tools, metal stamping machines, and others. The gains in productivity were reflected in a dramatic price decline of more than two-thirds. The advances in process technology that led to the gains in labor productivity and the decline in price were not accompanied, however, by comparable improvements in product technology. Some critics have argued that the first Model T to roll off the assembly line was technically obsolete and that few improvements were made thereafter.

---

[10] In describing the Highland Park Plant and its technology Hounshell draws very heavily on a series of articles by Fred Colvin published, beginning in 1913, in the *American Machinist* (Hounshell, 1984:392).

In a retrospective article in the *Encyclopedia Britannica*, Henry Ford (1926:821–823) articulated the principles of mass production. To Ford (or his ghost writer) mass production was the method by which "great quantities of a single standardized commodity are manufactured. Mass production is not merely quantity production, for this may be had with none of the requisites of mass production. Nor is it merely machine production, which also may exist without any resemblance to mass production" (Ford, 1926:821). According to Ford the essential principles were (1) the orderly progression of the commodity through the shop, (2) the delivery of parts to the worker, and (3) an analysis of operations into their constituent parts. "Every part must be produced to fit at once into the design for which it is made. In mass production there are no fitters" (Ford, 1926:822). It is doubtful that the machine tool industry could have met the standard that Ford articulated prior to 1913 (Hounshell, 1984:233).[11]

MANAGING MEN, MACHINES, AND WORK

The New England Armory System of the mid-1800s had induced a number of institutional changes in the management of men and machines. The development of mass production resulted in even more dramatic changes in the relationship among men, machines, and work.

The inside contract system was one of the early managerial innovations associated with the American System. The management of various operations or departments was "put-out" to independent contractors. An early example was the arrangement for production of gunstocks at the Springfield armory. In 1819 Thomas Blanchard invented the first lathe that could reproduce the irregular shape of a gunstock (or any other irregularly shaped wooden object such as an ax handle or a shoe last). The Springfield armory agreed to provide Blanchard with shop space, free use of materials and machinery, water power, and the necessary raw materials for producing gun stocks. Blanchard contributed the use of his patented machinery and received a contract price of 37 cents per gunstock (Hounshell, 1984:38).

The inside contract arrangement rapidly became a distinguishing characteristic of the New England Armory System. As factory size expanded it simplified the management of labor and materials and provided an incentive for innovation. The contractor hired, managed, and fired his own workmen. But as factory operations became more complex, as in the sewing machine industry, the insider contract system began to be viewed as an obstacle to innovation and to coordination among departments. In 1878 the sewing machine department at Brown and Sharp replaced the inside contract system with a piecework system, which resulted in a 47% savings in labor costs. After a good deal of internal stress the Singer Company likewise decided to eliminate the inside contract system. This effort by Singer and other manufacturers

---

[11] Ford engineers were not, of course, the first to achieve success in mechanical material handling. In 1890 Westinghouse Airbrake began mechanizing some of its foundry operations. The Ford engineers were familiar with the "disassembly" lines used by Chicago meat packers and with the mechanical conveying systems used in grain handling and flour milling (Hounshell, 1984:239–244).

to obtain control over the shop floor by breaking up the power of the craft workers was realized even more completely with the introduction of the assembly line. The assembly line's initial effect was to enhance efficiency. Its long-term effect, though, has been to deprive American mass production industry of the creative contributions— "of the learning by doing"—of the machine operators and mechanics, the very workers whose creativity gave rise to the American System.

A second managerial innovation instituted at Brown and Sharp was the development of operations sheets on which all operations were listed along with all the necessary tools, jigs, fixtures, and gauges. The purpose was to ensure that the work could be more closely followed by the foreman and that materials could be moved more smoothly in proper sequence (Hounshell, 1984:82). In the mid-1880s Singer introduced a similar "blue book" for its Elizabethtown factory that delineated all of the machining operations and work flow routes for the Improved Family sewing machine. The codification of Singer production operations was the last step in the company's transition from the internal contract system to a system of management in which complete control of the shop floor had passed to professional engineers and managers.

When Ford initiated production of the Model T at its new Highland Park factory it followed Brown and Sharp and Singer in instituting operations sheets. Ford production managers detailed the manufacturing operations for various parts, the necessary tools, fixtures, and gauges (all of which were numbered and referenced to drawings of parts), and suggestions for the layout of sequential operations. Operation sheets were maintained for each subassembly and major assembly, and were continuously updated as improvements were made in operating procedures. When production quotas were raised, the engineering machine tool procurers referred to operations sheets and ordered the appropriate tools from Ford's own tool department or from outside suppliers. When a new machine tool arrived at the factory, the engineering department attached a brass tag with its inventory number and transported it immediately to its prepared site. Hounshell points out that the Ford Motor Company not only kept impressive records but used its records quite creatively to increase efficiency (Hounshell, 1984:271).

At the same time that Ford's Highland Park factory was being built and equipped, Frederick W. Taylor published his now classic treatise, *Principles of Scientific Management* (1911). Taylor advocated the rationalization of factory operations through the careful analysis of work (time and motion studies) to eliminate wasteful motions, and the "scientific" selection of workmen for prescribed tasks. It was widely assumed that Taylor's work influenced the Ford engineers who designed the Highland Park factory. As early as 1912 or 1913 Ford had established a time study department that attempted to establish work standards, a task that "is the very heart of Taylorism" (Hounshell, 1984:250).

It is doubtful how much Taylor's ideas contributed to the design of the Highland Park assembly system, however. Henry Ford was skeptical of any systematic theory of organization or administration, including Taylor's scientific management. In the *Encyclopedia Britannica* Ford ridiculed Taylor's example of how his system had contributed to productivity in the hand loading of pig iron (Ford, 1926:821). Taylor took the technology as given and sought improvements in work methods and organization. Ford engineers would have asked why pig iron should be hand loaded at all. They were concerned with shifting the production function rather than simply reducing inefficiency!

The system of mass production that became characteristic of many manufacturing industries during the first quarter of the twentieth century emphasized the division of labor into very narrow, relatively unskilled tasks, each of which was performed repeatedly by a single worker who was closely supervised by lower level managers. Workers lost their earlier responsibility for the organization and pace of the work process, or for assurance of product quality. This system encountered resistance from workers, which they initially expressed by high turnover rates and later by efforts at unionization. Ford responded by instituting the widely heralded $5.00 a day wage rate—up from the $2.50 range for unskilled labor. The $5.00 wage represented, in effect, a social contract between Ford and his assembly line workers. They would discontinue unionization efforts and accept the assembly line in exchange for the highest wages for unskilled workers in American manufacturing.[12]

When the last Model T rolled off the assembly line in 1927, 15 million had been produced.[13] The Model T was the only revolutionary automobile of the twentieth century. Its design and mass production made people want an automobile. Ford had made the automobile a powerful instrument of social change in America. "Any man who owned a car was on equal terms with any other. And virtually anyone could afford to own a car. . . . Ford liberated the American man (and woman) on a greater scale than any hero in history" (Hughes, 1986:294). The era of "classical" mass production ended at Ford in 1926 when Ford was forced to abandon the Model T and follow

---

[12] Even the $5.00 wage met a mixed reception. Ford's workers hated him and his organization. The wife of a Ford assembly line worker wrote (anonymously) to Henry Ford: "the chain system you have is a *slave driver*! My God!, Mr. Ford. My husband has come home and thrown himself down & won't eat his supper—so done out! Cant it be remedied? . . . That $5.00 day is a blessing—a bigger one than you know but *oh* they earn it" (quoted from Hounshell, 1984:259). "The Ford system in application resulted in fantastic economic efficiency and the most appalling industrial relations in American history" (Hughes, 1986:297). For a more complete discussion of the social and cultural implications of mass production from a 1920s and 1930s perspective, see Hounshell (1984:303–330).

[13] By the end of the Model T Era, Ford had established manufacturing facilities in four other countries (Australia, Canada, England, and Ireland) and assembly operations in an additional 14 countries (Argentina, Brazil, Chile, Denmark, France, Germany, India, Italy, Japan, Malaya, Mexico, South Africa, Spain, and Uruguay). Although it did not establish a Ford plant in the U.S.S.R., it did play an important role in the development of the U.S.S.R. automobile, truck, and tractor industries. The Communist regime in the U.S.S.R. embraced Ford's mass production and labor system (Fordism) with great enthusiasm. Ford began shipping cars, trucks, and tractors to the U.S.S.R. in the early 1920s. A Ford delegation visited the U.S.S.R. in 1926 and began to provide technical assistance in the late 1920s. In 1929 Albert Kahn, who had designed the Ford Highland Park factory, was delegated by Henry Ford to assist in the design of the new U.S.S.R. automotive production complex at Nizhni Novogorad. Frank Bennett, a Ford production manager, spent 1930 and part of 1931 in Nizhni Novogorad to oversee plant construction and the setting up of the assembly line. Ford supplied the plant with a large quantity of tools, dies, jigs, and fixtures that became available as Ford was retooling to make the shift from the Model A to the V8 (Wilkins and Hill, 1964:208–227, 434–437).

General Motors into the new era of "flexible mass production," characterized by annual model changes.

THE ANNUAL MODEL CHANGE

Annual model change, introduced at General Motors under the leadership of Alfred P. Sloan, Jr., was the other major revolution in American automobile technology (Hounshell, 1984:278). In a less groundbreaking, but still significant innovation, General Motors developed a product line with a clear status hierarchy. The buyer could move up the status and price hierarchy through Chevrolet, Pontiac, Buick, and Oldsmobile to Cadillac. Annual styling changes were also introduced. "Every September a group of 'all new' General Motors' cars would make their much-publicized appearance, presumably sowing discontent among millions of drivers whose own cars had sunk deeper into obsolescence" (Volti, 1996:671). To make sure that the price did not represent too large an obstacle General Motors created the General Motors Acceptance Corporation to facilitate purchase on credit.[14]

By the late 1940s the American automobile industry had fully adopted the Ford–Sloan production system that it would continue to pursue for the next 40 years. The industry assumed that consumers preferred variety as long as it did not cost too much. Cosmetic styling had become the main method of product differentiation. This permitted the continuation of low-cost, large-scale production for the major mechanical components, such as engines and transmissions, that were hidden under the sheet metal. "Hang on" options such as air conditioning, power steering, and paint and trim options could be added with an annual model change while engines and transmissions stayed the same.

Industry changes encompassed more than just the product. Job simplification along the lines pioneered by Ford was extended from the shop floor to engineering and management. Design team members knew little about manufacturing and financial officers knew little about either. Cyclical fluctuations in demand were handled by a policy of "hire and fire." The social contract with unionized workers was maintained through a strict seniority system governing who would be fired and rehired. This system offered little incentive for investment in training programs to upgrade the skills of most production workers. The heavy capital investments in automation reduced production flexibility and required even longer product runs with single-purpose dedicated machines to amortize capital investment (Hounshell, 1995).

For the first 20 years after World War II labor productivity in the North American motor vehicle industry grew at 5% per year—well above the average rate in U.S.

---

[14] For the early history of General Motors, including its founding by William C. Durant and its relationship with the DuPont Company, see Chandler (1962:114–162). The transition to the Sloan system was exceedingly difficult at Ford. By the late 1920s, Ford himself had become a vindictive recluse rather than the mechanical genius of his first two decades. The trauma associated with the design and retooling for the introduction of the Ford Model A in 1928 and the V8 in 1932 has been described by Hounshell (1984:280–301).

manufacturing. After 1965, it slowed to around 2.5%. And importantly, much of the American technological impetus that had led to mass production had disappeared. With the exception of the automatic transmission, introduced in 1949, virtually every significant postwar advance in automotive technology adopted in the production of automobiles in the United States first appeared in other countries. These included fuel injection, disk brakes, independent rear suspension, overhead camshaft engines, front wheel drive, and radial tires. In the 1920s Ford lost market share to General Motors because, while obsessively pursuing technological change in manufacturing, it failed to pursue technical change in the cars that it produced. In the post-World War II period the U.S. automobile industry fell behind in both manufacturing technology and in product technology. In retrospect it is hard to escape a conclusion that the ascendancy of a new business school trained managerial elite, with no experience and little appreciation of manufacturing and process technology, was an important source of the loss of U.S. competitive leadership in the automobile industry. The stage had been set for the European and Japanese challenges to the supremacy of the U.S. automobile industry.

Science-Based Technology[15]

Neither the New England Armory System nor the system of mass production drew directly on contemporary scientific advances in making improvements in machine tools or processes. In the United States, well into the age of mass production, industrial innovation drew only lightly on recent advances in science. U.S. resource endowments favored the development of machines for the agricultural, manufacturing, raw material, and transport sectors. Advances in the design of machine tools, of machine processes, and of systems of production drew largely on principles developed out of practice (Layton, 1971:562–580). These advances were made almost entirely by mechanics, machinists, and engineers through the process of learning by doing and learning by using.

During the first decades of the twentieth century, however, a much closer articulation began to emerge between advances in science and technology. The critical institutional innovations that supported the emergence of science-based technology were the agricultural experiment station, the industrial research laboratory, and the research university (Chapter 3). By the turn of the century the precedents of science-based agricultural and industrial research, in industry and in universities and technical schools, had already been established in Germany (this chapter).

In the United States a number of industrial research laboratories had been established in the nineteenth century. Most of them, however, were testing or engineering laboratories in which engineers or scientists were employed to ensure quality and

---

[15] In this section I draw heavily on Mowery and Rosenberg (1989), Nelson (1993), Nelson and Wright (1992), and Mowery (1998).

efficiency in production rather than to conduct research. Even Thomas Edison's laboratories, which drew on nineteenth century advances in theoretical and experimental physics to design a system of electric lighting, did not attempt to contribute to those advances[16] (Chapter 7).

The first U.S. industrial research laboratories were not established until the turn of the century. General Electric organized the General Electric Research Laboratory in 1900 (Chapter 8). After several abortive attempts to institutionalize research, AT&T established a Research Branch within the Western Electric Company's Engineering Department. It was not until 1925, however, that research was consolidated in Bell Telephone Laboratories, established as a wholly owned subsidiary of AT&T and Western Electric (Chapter 7). In 1927 DuPont established a central laboratory dedicated to "filling in the gaps of knowledge affecting important chemical processes" (Chapter 8). Employment of engineers and scientists in industrial research in manufacturing rose from roughly 3000 in 1921 to nearly 46,000 at the end of World War II (Mowery and Rosenberg, 1993:33, 34).[17]

Developments in higher education in the United States in the late nineteenth and early twentieth centuries also helped establish the institutional foundation for the emergence of a science-based technology. In the 1890s the ratio of university students to primary students was several times that of any other country. By 1900 the system of public universities established by the Morrill Act of 1862 had resulted in the location in every state of colleges offering degrees in the agricultural sciences and engineering. After 1900, programs in enrollment in the applied sciences and engineering grew rapidly. Graduate programs in fields such as agronomy, electrical engineering, and chemical engineering were developed. As these programs were developed they were closely articulated, particularly in the public universities, with opportunities in the industries in which graduates were expected to find employment. The public universities were under continuous pressure to demonstrate the practical benefits of their education and research. Although this pressure has been criticized for subordinating educational objectives to vocational objectives, it was essential to the development of the human capital necessary for the emergence of science-based technology.

In the interwar period the U.S. economy maintained, and in some cases enhanced, its dominant position in the mass production industries relative to Western Europe. In 1929 the United States accounted for over 80%, and in 1938 for almost 70%, of world

---

[16] Edison's work did indirectly lay certain conceptual foundations. His attempts in 1883 to improve the incandescent lamp led him to observe the flow of electricity inside the lamp, across a gap separating a hot filament from a metal wire. Edison had observed the existence of electrons before their existence had even been postulated. Although Edison did not appreciate the significance of his observation at the time, the Edison Effect formed a basis for much twentieth century science (Nelson and Rosenberg, 1993:7, 8).

[17] Both Markham and Mowery have argued that the increasingly strict application of the Sherman Antitrust Act of 1890, which made agreements among competing firms to control prices and output subject to prosecution, contributed to both the merger movement of 1895–1904 and the establishment of central research facilities (Markham, 1966:293–294; Mowery, 1990:346).

motor car production (Hoffman and Kaplinsky, 1988:80). The electrical and chemical industries combined science-based technical innovation and mass production of the new products developed in their laboratories. It was not, however, until after World War II that the United States achieved clear dominance in the "high-technology" industrial sectors. The skills and experience needed to advance technology in these new science-based industries were not acquired in the process of learning by doing, as in the wood and metal working industries of the nineteenth century, or even the mass production industries that emerged during the first half of the twentieth century. The industries in which the United States forged ahead after World War II required organized R&D, in addition to experience and specialized training, for the effective advancement of technology. These industries included, in addition to the agricultural, electrical, chemical, aircraft, and defense industries, completely new industries such as the computer, semiconductor, and biotechnology industries (Chapters 6–10). Employment in industrial research grew from around 40,000 just before World War II to approximately 300,000 in the early 1960s.

These science-based industries were complemented by the emergence of a system of research universities that, by the mid-1950s, were clearly working closer to the frontiers, across a broad spectrum of science, engineering, agricultural, and health research, than universities in the rest of the world. Public funding of university research was provided by a set of new institutions, such as the National Science Foundation and the National Institutes of Health, as well as mission-oriented agencies such as the Department of Defense, the Atomic Energy Agency, the National Aeronautics and Space Agency, and the Department of Agriculture. Corporate research related to national defense and space also received substantial public support. In the mid-1960s government funds accounted for about half of private sector R&D (Chapter 13).

Another distinctive feature of the American system in the post-World War II period has been the importance of small start-up firms in the initial exploitation of science-based technology. Such firms have been characteristic in the microelectronics, computer software, and biotechnology industries (Chapters 9 and 10). Several factors have contributed to the prominence of new firms in the postwar science-based industries. Large basic research units in universities, government, and industry have served as "incubators" for the development of the knowledge and skills that have "walked out the door" with the scientists and engineers who went on to start new firms. A second factor has been the development of a sophisticated financial system, including the rise of venture capital firms, as well as equity investment by established firms in start-up firms whose research and product development efforts were complementary to their own. A third factor was an intellectual property regime, reinforced by antitrust considerations, that encouraged cross-licensing rather than litigation. Military procurement policies also provided important opportunities for smaller firms in fields such as microelectronics and computers.

The success of military applications of science-based technology during World War II created a positive political environment for the public support of science-based technology in the postwar period. American investment in the development of military technology during World War II and in the first two decades after the war resulted in substantial spillovers of knowledge and technology into the civilian sector (Chapters 7–9). By the 1970s, however, the spillover was shifting in the opposite direction. And by the 1980s it became increasingly difficult to make the argument that investment in the development of military technology could even be partially defended in terms of spinoff to civilian technology (Nelson and Wright, 1992:1959). Some critics have insisted that the demands on fiscal resources and on scientific capacity, combined with the distortion of incentives to defense and space oriented R&D, had a negative impact on the development of civilian technology (Solo, 1962; Chapter 13).

In the mid-1960s American dominance in the new high-technology industries was widely assumed in the United States and acknowledged, with substantial concern, in the rest of the world. Jean Jacques Servan-Schreiber, in his acclaimed book, *The American Challenge* (1968), both acknowledged this dominance and issued an alarm about its consequences. By the early 1980s, however, the United States was no longer confident of its leadership in either the older mass production industries of the "rust belt" or in its newer science-based industries. There was increasing concern about the disarticulation of scientific research, technology development, and improvement in manufacturing process (Florida and Kenney, 1990). An important symbol of this disarticulation was the break-up and decline in emphasis in basic research at Bell Laboratories.[18] In the mid-1980s a group of leading MIT scientists, engineers, and economists launched a landmark research effort to explore the reasons for American industrial malaise (Dertouzos et al., 1989).

By the late 1990s confidence in U.S. technical and industrial leadership had revived. The United States had experienced almost a decade of continuous economic growth. Industrial reorganization had resulted in higher rates of productivity growth and lower costs of production. The United States dominated the information revolution (Chapter 9). Loss of confidence had been replaced by complacency. It will be some time before it is possible to assess whether this complacency is well founded. What is clear is that since the early 1990s there have been a number of important structural changes in the U.S. system of technical innovation. These include (1) greater reliance by U.S. firms on research conducted outside their own laboratories, through consortia and collaboration with federal laboratories and universities and with other firms; (2) increased location of R&D facilities in other countries and expansion of R&D in the United States by foreign firms; (3) greater reliance by U.S. universities on industrial

---

[18] At the time of the AT&T dissolution in 1984 Bell Laboratories was the greatest U.S. industrial research center. Part of Bell Laboratories was spun off to form a new firm, Bell Communications Research, to perform research for the seven regional operating companies formed following the dissolution of AT&T. In 1996, following further reorganization, AT&T's part of Bell Laboratories was retained as AT&T Laboratories and the larger part was spun off as part of Lucient Technologies. These changes were accompanied by a reduction in resources devoted to basic research, a deemphasis on research in the physical sciences, an increased emphasis on product development, and substantial staff reductions (Heppenheimer, 1996; Service, 1996).

funding, by U.S. and foreign firms, and expanded efforts to realize, through patenting licensing or other arrangement, financial returns from commercially oriented research (Mowery, 1998:646). I return to these issues in Chapter 13.

THE JAPANESE SYSTEM

Japan was the first nonwestern country to successfully challenge the dominance of Western European and North American industrial technology.[19] Technology has been central to Japanese national development policies since "the opening up of the country" (*kaikoku*) in the middle of the nineteenth century. From the arrival of Admiral Perry's "black ships" in the Kyoto harbor in 1854 until World War II, Japan's system of technical innovation was driven by efforts to enhance its political and economic autonomy—by what has come to be termed a military industrial technonationalism. Cotton, steel, and ships are examples of goods that were initially promoted primarily for strategic reasons but later became central to Japan's domestic commercial and international trade policies.

The stage had been set by the progress of indigenous technology during the previous several centuries.[20] In many areas the level of technology practiced in Japan was not far behind that in the West. In 1850 the level of literacy and numeracy in Japan exceeded that in any western country. By almost any measure, however, its per capita income was substantially lower than that of western economies at the beginning of their industrialization.

In 1858, 4 years after Admiral Perry's arrival, the Tokugawa government was forced to sign a treaty with the United States, the United Kingdom, the Netherlands, France, and Russia that granted the western powers extraterritorial rights and limited Japanese tariffs on imports. As a result of the unequal treaties, the Tokugawa government, already weakened by political ineptitude and fiscal insolvency, was seen as no longer able to defend the national interest. After a brief military struggle in 1867–1868, a revolt deposed the Tokugawa Shogun, restored the emperor to the throne, and initiated a program of military and economic reform. The emperor, in his first address to the nation, committed Japan to seek knowledge from abroad.

---

[19] In the next several paragraphs I draw heavily on Odagiri and Goto (1993), Howe (1996), and Samuels (1994).

[20] The role of military technology was particularly noteworthy. Firearms were introduced in Kyushu in the early 1540s by Dutch and Portuguese merchants. When the Dutch and Portuguese arrived in Japan, they were confronted by a militaristic society that already possessed a highly sophisticated armaments industry. Japanese swords and armor, regarded as the finest in the world, were exported in large numbers throughout East Asia. The Tokugawa Shogunate (1603–1868), which had seized power from the emperor during the civil wars of the late sixteenth century, tried to seclude the country from outside contact. Trade with the West was confined to a Dutch post on an island in the Nagasaki harbor. Although the production of guns was banned, there was a resurgence of arms manufacture in the early nineteenth century as control of the Shogunate over the country weakened. The mastery of gun manufacture and gun powder production established a technical base for the production of other mechanical and chemical inventions (Samuels, 1994:79–83).

During its initial years, the Meiji government played a very direct role in both military-related and other industries. It invested heavily in the development of the physical infrastructure required for industrial development—in transportation, communication, and utilities. It also acted to improve the institutional infrastructure—education, public finance, and property rights. These reforms were led by a group of young military bureaucrats from the samurai class that had led the revolt against the Shogunate. By the 1880s and 1890s they had been joined by a new class of industrialists, financiers, and public officials recruited not only from among the samurai ranks but also from the more prosperous families of the merchant and agricultural classes.

By the 1880s the Japanese economy had achieved a "take-off" into sustained economic growth (Chapter 2). Much of Japan's success has been attributed to the latecomer's advantage of benefitting from the transfer of technology from more advanced countries. The Japanese government initiated a very successful campaign to acquire technology from abroad. But Japan's success was also based on a remarkable capacity to adapt the borrowed technology to its own particular resource endowments and economic environment.[21]

Cotton Textiles

The close link between the government and private sectors in Japanese industrial development is illustrated in the development of the textile industry, which has repeatedly played the role of a "leading sector" in the initial stage of industrial development.[22] The Japanese government began importing equipment from England for several small spinning mills in 1865 and, with the assistance of English advisors, erected the Kagoshima Spinning mill in 1867 and the Sakai Spinning Mill in 1870. In 1878 the central government established two more mills. It also imported spinning machinery for sale to private firms on favorable credit terms and subsidized the establishment of other private firms. The publicly owned firms had great difficulty in achieving profitable operation and were later sold to private firms.

Japanese textile producers immediately began adapting the English system to meet the needs of the Japanese economic environment and resource endowments. Many of these modifications were induced by an effort to substitute low-cost Japanese labor for expensive English textile machinery. One of the first was to introduce two 11-hour shifts instead of one shift per day. Introduction of new machinery in the late 1880s

---

[21] An important issue not directly addressed in this chapter has been the role of natural resource constraints on Japanese economic development. In the case of agriculture, limited land resource endowments induced technical change in a land-saving direction (Chapter 6). Constraints on minerals and energy resources have also induced Japanese industrial development in a natural resource-saving and human capital-intensive direction (Johnson, 1999:1–9).

[22] "In . . . the first round of industrialization (1783 to 1873) Britain led the way with the textile leading sector complex" (Rostow, 1990:196). Rostow dates the "take off" for Japan as 1878–1900. In this discussion of the origins of the Japanese textile industry I rely heavily on the very careful study by Otsuka et al. (1988).

facilitated the use of less skilled workers. By adding workers, mainly young women, to tie broken yarns the machinery could be run at even higher speed. The high-speed equipment was, however, not as well suited to the short staple Japanese and Chinese cotton. This problem was solved by mixing the short staple cotton with longer staple Indian and American cotton. The effectiveness of the policy of introducing technical changes designed to facilitate the substitution of low-cost labor for capital is confirmed by the decline in the number of spindles tended per worker from 24.8 in 1886–1890 to 13.9 in 1891–1895 (Otsuka et al., 1988:21).[23]

The importation of power looms and the factory production of cloth began around 1900. The adoption of power looms was encouraged by removing the 5% duty on raw cotton imports while retaining the 5% duty on yarn and cloth. Since the raw material makes up over 75% of the cost of producing yarn, this represented a substantial increase in effective protection. The large military demand during the Russo-Japanese War of 1904–1905 provided a further impetus for rapid adoption of power looms. Between 1905 and the beginning of World War I, production of cotton fabrics more than doubled and exports, primarily to Korea and China, more than quadruped. During World War I Japan took advantage of British withdrawal from world markets to expand the production of higher quality cotton fabrics.[24] By the mid-1930s Japan had forged ahead of Britain in the production and exports of both yarn and cotton piece goods.

The importation of English spinning machinery was quickly followed by the establishment of repair and maintenance shops. By the early 1890s these shops were producing parts for the imported machinery, and by the early 1900s domestically produced spindles and looms were beginning to replace imported equipment. The automatic loom had been invented in the United States in the 1890s, but by the early 1920s the American models were being replaced by looms produced by Toyoda and other Japanese manufacturers. By the early 1930s Japan had become a major exporter of textile equipment.

The development of the Japanese textile industry illustrates four important continuing elements of Japan's national technology system: (1) aggressive identification and transfer of technology from abroad, (2) strong public support for the adoption and diffusion of the new technology, (3) rapid adaptation of imported technology consistent with Japanese factor endowments and demand, and (4) development of the

---

[23] For a more detailed discussion of the role of indigenous technical change in facilitating the substitution of labor for capital during the labor-surplus phase of Japanese economic development, see Blumenthal (1980:547–559, 1981:845–848) and Fei and Ranis (1981:841–844).

[24] The failure of other countries characterized by low labor costs to emerge as dominant players in the world textile industry has been a continuing puzzle and source of controversy to economic historians. It is generally agreed that there was a strong positive relationship between labor productivity and wage rates across countries. The puzzle is why India was not successful in converting its low-wage rates into a cost and profit advantage through higher output per worker (see Clark, 1987:141–173; Wilkins, 1987:981–983; Clark, 1988:143–148; Hanson, 1988:660–672; Clark, 1989:706–714, 1992). In his initial work Clark argued that the low labor productivity in Indian textile production, in spite of equipment comparable to that in the United Kingdom, reflected low levels of labor productivity throughout the Indian economy—a weak intersector labor market.

capacity to innovate and manufacture (Samuels 1994:33). During the early decades of the twentieth century, these same principles were applied in a number of heavy industry sectors such as iron and steel, chemicals, and machinery. The development of the capacity to narrow the gap between European innovation and Japanese adoption of new technology in the iron and steel industry during the latter years of the nineteenth century is illustrated in Table 11.1.

Japan as Number One[25]

From the time of the Meiji restoration Japanese economic policies have been characterized by what economist historians have referred to as the "development state." In the economic arena this has meant policies that have encouraged high rates of savings and investment and have discouraged consumption. A second element has been a set of policies characterized as "technonationalism." Technonationalism is based on "the belief that technology is a fundamental element in national security and that it must be indiginized, diffused and nurtured by the government in order to make a nation rich and strong" (Samuels, 1994: x). Commitment to technonationalism led to an explicit linkage and interdiffusion between military and civilian technology. A national consensus in support of techno-nationalism was central to the emergence of Japan as an important economic and military power between the Meiji restoration and World War II.

After World War II, an initial objective of the U.S. military government was the complete demilitarization of the Japanese economy. The Cold War, however, lead to a relaxation of these constraints. During the Korean War (1950–52) Japanese industry became a major supplier of war materiel to the U.S. operations in Korea. U.S. military

Table 11.1   Japanese–European Technology Gaps in Metallurgy, 1858–1909

Technique	European Innovation	Japanese Adoption	Place	Gap (years)
Charcoal-fired furnace	ca. 1700	1858	Kamaishi	160+
Coke-fired furnace (Darby)	1717	1894	Tanaka works	177
Crucible steel (Huntsman)	1740	1882	Tsukuji arsenal	142
Reverberatory furnace (Smeaton)	1766	1850–1852	Saga ironworks	86
Puddling method (Cort)	1784	1875	Kamaishi	91
Hot power bellows (Neilson)	1828	1875	Kamaishi	47
Air-blown steel converter (Bessemer)	1856	1901	Yawata steelworks	45
Open hearth process (Siemens-Martin)	1863	1890	Osaka arsenal	17
Stassano electric arc furnace	1899	1909	Dobashi electric steelworks	10

Source: Christopher Howe, *The Origins of Japanese Trade Supremacy: Development and Technology in Asia from 1540 to the Pacific War*, Chicago, IL: University of Chicago Press, 1996:249.

---

[25] The title of this section is from Vogel (1979).

procurement accounted for approximately 70% of Japanese exports. As much as three-quarters of Japan's industrial capacity was related to the defense industry. U.S. procurement in effect paid for the rehabilitation of the Japanese economy.

As the Korean War ended, an intense debate occurred in Japan about the future of the arms industry. Would Japan revert to the prewar system of technonationalism? The Ministry of Finance and the Keidanren, the major Japanese industrial federation, took the position that Japan should not depend on the defense industry to sustain economic growth and technology development. During the negotiations that led to the U.S.–Japan Mutual Security Agreement in 1954, the United States agreed to provide technical assistance for the reconstruction of Japanese industry and Japan agreed to accept the guarantee of its security by the United States. The Agreement ensured that the Japanese defense bureaucracy and arms industry would remain subordinated to the civil bureaucracy, and that priority would be given to technology for commercial application. But technology would remain central to the Japanese continuing concern with national security—now defined primarily in economic terms.

In many areas of economic activity the operational implications of Japan's drive for security were expressed in terms of a national effort to catch up with or surpass the West. I have discussed how this drive has played out in the computer (Chapter 9) and biotechnology (Chapter 10) industries. Earlier in this chapter I traced the emergence of the Japanese textile industry. I now trace the successful effort of the Japanese automobile industry to overcome and surpass its U.S. counterpart.

The Automobile Industry[26]

Beginning in 1903 there were several abortive attempts to assemble or produce automobiles in Japan. After World War I, the army began a small program to subsidize domestic production. In the 1920s a number of companies responded by entering the market to produce motorcycles, three wheel vehicles, and cars. Toyoda, already established in the textile machinery industry, was one of the more successful. It sent engineers to Detroit to study the Ford assembly plant and to order equipment. It reverse engineered a Chevrolet and purchased parts from GM and Ford, which had established assembly plants in Japan. The Nissan Zaibatsu established Nissan motors and began producing automobiles using Harley–Davidson motors and with the guidance of American engineers. Dihatsu, Mazda, and Isuzu were also survivors of the initial "shake out." Beginning in 1936 the government restricted production to licensed companies and placed a ceiling on production by Ford and General motors. Licenses were granted to Toyota (Toyoda's brand name), Nissan, and Isuzu. By 1939 Toyota and Nissan were each producing around 15,000, and Isuzu about

---

[26] The best single account of the Japanese system of automobile production is a book reporting the results of research by MIT International Motor Vehicle Program (Womack et al., 1991). See also Cusumano (1985). For a highly personal discussion of the issues and personalities involved in the development of the Japanese automobile industry and the decline of the U.S. automotive industry in the post-World War II period, see Halberstam (1986).

7500, units per year, although most were sold to the military and quality continued to be poor.

By the end of the 1930s Japanese engineers had mastered American truck technology. In the immediate post-World War II period Japanese cars were built using small truck engines, frames, and chasses. During the 1950s, they incorporated small-car technology from Great Britain, France, and Germany. In 1970 truck production in Japan exceeded that in the United States and automobile production was approaching half that of the U.S. (Table 11.2). The two leading Japanese firms, Nissan and Toyota, had surpassed U.S. productivity levels. More important than mere quantity, these small cars compared favorably in quality, performance, and price with European automobiles. By the early 1980s they had achieved levels of productivity well above the levels in the United States and Europe and were viewed as a threat to the viability of the European and U.S. motor vehicle industries.

Japanese automobile manufacturers employed two technology transfer modes in learning how to design and manufacture automobiles (Chapter 6). The *direct technology transfer* mode employed by Nissan (and by Isuzu, Hino, and Mitsubishi) involved formal tie-ups with foreign automobile producers and parts manufacturers and direct assistance from foreign engineers. The second approach, *indirect technology transfer*, involved the importation and reverse engineering of automotive designs and manufacturing technology. Toyota (and Honda, Fuji, Suzuki, Prince, Daihatsu, and Mazda) relied primarily on indirect technology transfer (Cusumano, 1985:375). Out of a somewhat chaotic process of learning by doing rather than any grand design Toyota developed and perfected, over a 20-year period, a new system of "flexible" or "lean" production. The system involved four key principles: "a new conception of the market, a new approach to production management, a new way to think about human resources, and new way of organizing work based on teams and groups (Womack, 1989:19)

TECHNOLOGY

In the late 1940s the Japanese motor vehicle market was small and fragmented. Industry needed large trucks. Farmers needed small trucks. Business executives and government officials wanted large cars. The general public wanted small cars. High gasoline taxes acted to induce a demand for smaller automobiles with higher gas mileage. In response to these competing demands, Japanese motor vehicle producers sought ways to produce at a low cost and at low volume and to shift competition to other factors such as product quality. This called for a new approach to production machinery. The Japanese solution was to develop flexible machinery, which could be rapidly switched from one product to another. The Japanese, for example, used one set of stamping presses to make a wide range of parts rather than dedicating a press to a single part as in the U.S. system. This meant changing the press dies frequently and rapidly.[27]

---

[27] It is somewhat ironic that the idea of rapid set-up was based on U.S. technology. Ono Taiichi, then a production manager at Toyota, observed the operation of Danley stamping presses with rapid die change

Table 11.2   Passenger Automobile[a] and Truck and Bus[b] Production: Selected Countries (Thousand Units)

	1970	1980	1985	1989	1990	1991	1992	1993	1994
				Passenger automobiles					
Japan	3,179	7,038	7,645	8,370	9,948	9,756	9,374	8,682	8,014
United States	6,547	6,400	8,022	6,808	6,052	5,407	5,684	5,936	6,614
Germany	3,655	3,689	4,375	4,861	4,618	4,270	4,866	3,926	4,223
Spain	455	1,048	1,217	1,638	1,679	1,774	1,795	1,506	1,758
South Korea	NA[c]	58	262	846	956	1,132	1,294	1,528	1,756
United Kingdom	1,641	924	1,048	1,300	1,296	1,278	1,291	1,375	1,466
Italy	1,720	1,455	1,354	1,970	1,873	1,627	1,475	1,118	1,407
Mexico[d]	137	316	286	455	614	733	788	848	831
Russia[e]	257	1,166	1,165	NA	1,103	1,030	963	956	798
Brazil	255	652	460	313	268	293	331	363	395
China	NA	NA	NA	NA	NA	NA	NA	230	250
				Trucks and buses					
United States	1,692	1,667	3,358	4,062	3,720	3,372	4,042	4,776	5,649
Japan	2,126	4,006	4,711	4,010	3,550	3,498	3,106	2,730	2,764
Brazil	161	516	508	725	672	684	749	1,092	1,115
China	70	136	269	379	305	403	440	935	998
Canada	236	528	856	949	808	790	901	856	NA
Russia	35	55[f]	60[f]	NA	764	746	678	655	NA
France	292	505	460	509	551	476	506	342	401
Germany	345	420	341	247	349	390	365	271	290
United Kingdom[g]	458	389	266	338	274	222	240	196	232
Spain	77	146	157	319	302	220	232	152	167

[a]Factory sales. Starting in 1980 excluding passenger vans.

[b]Unless otherwise indicated, data are for light and heavy trucks, wheeled tractors for road haulage, special vehicles, and buses.

[c]NA, not available.

[d]Including vehicles assembled from imported parts.

[e]Excluding production for the armed forces.

[f]Bus production only, truck production unavailable.

[g]Data include complete units exported for assembly.

Source: S. C. Davis, *Transportation Energy Data Book: Edition 17*, Oak Ridge, TN: Oak Ridge National Laboratory (for U.S. Department of Energy), August 1997, Tables 87, 88.

features on a trip to the United States during the mid-1950s. Japanese workers changed the dies in the Danley machines three or four times as fast as U.S. workers. Ono concluded that because of longer model runs, U.S. workers were not under the same time pressure as Japanese workers. To produce a variety of models Japanese automobile manufacturers had to make frequent changes on assembly runs (Cusamano, 1985:285). By the late 1980s Japan had replaced the United States as the worlds largest producer and exporter of machine tools (Mazzoleni, 1999:169–216).

By the 1970s Japanese companies, led by Toyota, had reduced the time it took to change dies to approximately 5 minutes, as compared to the American standard of 8 to 24 hours. Frequent changes of dies and production of parts in small batches resulted in fewer faulty parts. The same workers who operated the machine were also responsible for changing the dies and for routine maintenance and repair. Inspection systems were installed so that the production of defective parts could be spotted immediately and the machines could be reprogrammed. This, in turn, enabled manufacturers to maintain low inventories. To make this approach to production machinery workable, a new approach to production management was required. This involved perfect first time quality, elimination of waste, and continuous improvement of the production process. This was in contrast to the American system, which involved reworking of defective products at the end of the assembly line.

INSTITUTIONS

The Japanese system also required a different approach to human resources and to the social organization of work. The larger Japanese firms had adopted "lifetime" employment guarantees after World War II as a response to the organizing drive of a Marxist-led labor movement. This made labor a fixed rather than a variable cost, which in turn induced Japanese firms to invest in enhancing workers' skills. Because workers could not be released in response to fluctuations in demand it was in the employer's interest to continuously improve workers' skills and, once they were highly skilled, to hold onto them through steep wage progression linked to age and seniority. A revolution in process technology was induced, at least in part, by an institutional innovation in labor relations.

A second institutional innovation was the organization of production around groups. The Japanese system is based on the premise that work can be done more efficiently if workers and even whole organizations are grouped in teams. The grouping in Japanese motor vehicle production occurred at four levels—the work team in the plant, the product development team, the component supply group, and the conglomerate group.

A third institutional innovation was the system of "total quality control" introduced to Japan by the American statistician–management consultant W. Edwards Deming in the late 1940s (Box 11.1). The lowest level of organization, the work team, which consisted of a small number of workers and a team leader, was given the assignment of accomplishing a given number of manufacturing steps. Instead of giving each worker a specific assignment and charging the leader (foreman) with enforcing standards (the American mass production approach), the Japanese management gave the team as a whole the set of tasks and directed the team members to decide just how to do them. The tasks included quality control, machine maintenance, parts stocking, and housekeeping managed by quality circles *(kaizen)* in addition to actual manufacturing. "The quality control department and the industrial engineers were still part of this system, but now as consultants to the work team. Exact standardization of work tasks was still performed . . . but by the work team and in a manner enabling each member of the work team to do any of the team's tasks. This meant that the work teams were capable of responding effectively to changes in product mix and work flow" (Womack, 1991:22, 23).

At the next level, Japanese automobile producers introduced product development teams that included product planners, product engineers, process engineers, and manufacturing plant staff. The teams included product and process engineers from suppliers as well as from the assembler. The product development team was kept together from the beginning of the product concept phase until well into actual manufacturing. The objective was to cut development time, reduce development effort, and produce a better product. In the 1970s the product cycle phase at Toyota was about 4 years, compared to 6 years at General Motors. By 1996 Toyota product development had been condensed to 16 months (*Business Week*, April 7, 1997:104–114).

One of the reasons it was possible to achieve the level of cooperation required in the successful product development teams was because of the close grouping of suppliers and assembler in a component supply group. In the late 1980s, for example, the Toyota Group consisted of Toyota Motor Corporation and about 225 suppliers of component parts, process machinery, and services. The groups involve cross-equity holdings, loans of machinery and personnel, design collaboration, and a general commitment to a shared destiny. But they generally do not involve equity control, exclusive sales to one assembler, or sole sourcing.

● BOX 11.1

W. EDWARDS DEMING AND TOTAL QUALITY CONTROL

The name and message of W. Edwards Deming were first brought to the attention of U.S. managers when a group of Detroit automobile executives made a trip to Japan in 1978 in an attempt to discover why Japanese automobile manufacturers were outperforming their U.S. counterparts in quality, design, and productivity. The Japanese had been familiar with Deming's message for over 30 years. He initially went to Japan in 1947, at the behest of General Douglas MacArthur's military government, to help organize a census and to assess the problem of industrial reconstruction. His impact on Japanese management was so dramatic that in 1951 the Japanese government created an award, the Deming Prize, to recognize outstanding performance in "total quality management."

While still a student, Deming worked two summers at Western Electric's Hawthorne plant in Chicago. The Hawthorne plant was the location of a series of industrial experiments by Elton Mayo, professor of industrial research at the Harvard Business School, conducted from 1924 to 1932. They indicated that output improves when trust and cooperation between workers and supervisors are fostered, when fear in the workplace is eliminated, and when monitoring is reduced. The study also showed that paying workers according to a piecework system was counterproductive. Workers felt that if they demonstrated a higher rate of production their piecework rates would be lowered. The findings of the Hawthorne studies appeared to be so inconsistent with the American system of mass production that they were initially ignored by American management (Gabor, 1990:41, 42).

Deming's reputation in Japan was initially based on his adaptation of statistical quality control. His innovation was to distinguish between sources of variation in quality—between "special" unique causes and "common" or systemic causes. The special causes are the result of a temporary problem— the malfunction of a single machine, for example, that can usually be readily recognized and corrected at the shop level. The common or systems causes, such as the use of inferior materials or an inferior design, are typically created by management and can be improved only by management.

While lecturing at the USDA Graduate School in the 1930s, Deming brought attention to the work Walter Schwhert of Bell Laboratories had done on statistical quality control. Schwhert was the first to show that variability was an inescapable aspect of industrial production and that it could be understood and managed with the use of statistical methods. During World War II, Deming helped organize a program of short courses on statistical quality control for executives and engineers who were engaged in war production. This wartime experience was the basis for the lectures on quality control he was invited to give to Japanese industrialists in 1949. The Japanese Keidannen (Japanese Federation of Economic Organizations) was so impressed with his methods that he was asked to return to Japan to lecture annually in the 1950s.

The model that Japanese industry developed, based on Deming's lectures, involved "the harnessing of all business processes involving people, machines, and customer needs; to translate those needs into production strategies; and to constantly improve both the product and the process" (Gabor, 1990:56). In his work in Japan and later in the United States, Deming stressed 14 simple, and almost obvious points.

- Create constancy of purpose toward improvement of product and service.
- Adopt the new philosophy of Total Quality Management.
- Cease dependence on inspection to achieve quality. Eliminate the need for inspection.
- End the practice of awarding business on the basis of price. Move toward a single supplier for each item based on a long-term relationship of loyalty and trust.

- Improve constantly the system of production and service to improve quality and productivity and to decrease costs.
- Institute training on the job for both workers and management.
- Develop leadership. Leaders must know the work they supervise.
- Drive out fear, so that everyone may work effectively for the company.
- Break down barriers between departments. People in research, design, sales, and production must work as a team.
- Eliminate slogans, exhortations, and targets for the work force. The bulk of the causes of low quality and low productivity are a fault of the system and thus lie beyond the power of the work force.
- Eliminate work standards (quotas) on the factory floor. Eliminate management by objective. Eliminate management by numerical goals. Substitute leadership.
- Remove barriers that rob the hourly worker of his right to pride of workmanship. Remove barriers that rob people in engineering and management of their right to pride of workmanship.
- Institute a vigorous program of education and self-improvement.
- Put everybody in the company to work to accomplish the transformation. The transformation is everybody's job.

Total quality control (*kaizen*) was a central feature of the Deming system. In the 1950s total quality control (TQC) referred primarily to the application of the Deming approach to production problems. By the 1970s Japanese managers had adapted it to virtually all functions of the firm. *Kaizen* called for continuous improvement of every process, product, and strategy in an organization. It involved systematic and continuous feedback from customers and to suppliers. The purpose of consumer research was not how to convince consumers that they wanted what industry produced but to produce what consumers wanted.

Deming's work helped redefine the interaction of blue-collar workers and management in manufacturing. His theories provided an intellectual rationale for reenlisting the knowledge and skills of production workers to solve production problems. "Learning by doing" was recognized as a source of productivity growth. But Deming also stressed that the performance of individual workers, and the fate of the enterprise, is at the mercy of the quality of the decisions made by management.

Whereas Deming and his process-oriented approach to quality management were embraced in Japan, in the U.S. postwar economy, quality control became unfashionable. It was only in the 1980s, when American automobile executives discovered that Japanese firms such as Toyota were producing higher quality vehicles, and achieving levels of labor productivity double the levels of the best

General Motors and Ford plants in the United States, that Deming's methods were reintroduced into the United States. As TQC was increasingly adopted in the United States, the approach was made less rigid and adapted to specific situational environments under the rubric of total quality management (TQM).

In 1987 the U.S. Congress established the Malcolm Baldridge National Quality Awards, named after the Secretary of Commerce in the first Reagan Administration, modeled after the Deming Prize in Japan. The competition is managed by the U.S. National Institute of Science and Technology (NIST).

Sources: Adapted from Andrea Gabor, *The Man Who Discovered Quality,* New York: Random House, 1990; William W. Schenkenbach, *The Deming Route to Quality and Productivity: Roadmaps and Roadblocks,* Washington, DC: Cree Press, 1986. See also Rafael Aguayo, *Dr. Deming the American Who Taught the Japanese about Quality,* New York: Simon and Schuster, 1991; W. Edward Deming, *Out of the Crisis,* Cambridge, MA: Massachusetts Institute of Technology Center for Advanced Engineering Study, 1982. For a more technical treatment of quality control practice, see J. M. Juran, *Quality Planning and Analyses: From Product Development through Use,* New York: McGraw-Hill, 1980. For a critical perspective, see Sam B. Sitkin, Kathleen M. Sutcliffe, and Roger G. Schroeder, "Distinguishing Control from Management: A Contingency Perspective," *Academy of Management Review* 19 (1994):537–564.

At the highest level in the Japanese system is the conglomerate group, the *keiretsu.* This usually consists of the assembler, a bank, a trading company, an insurance company, materials-processing companies, and a number of manufacturing companies in other sectors.

DIFFUSION

Japanese automobiles were first exported to the United States by Toyota and Nissan in 1958. Initially, they did not compete well with the smaller European imports such as Volkswagen. The Japanese imports were not only small, but underpowered for their size. By the late 1960s and early 1970s, a second wave of more powerful, more attractively styled Japanese imports began to enter the U.S. and European markets and established a new standard for low maintenance and reliability. Their acceptance was enhanced by a lowering of tariff and nontariff barriers in both the United States and Western Europe. The oil price increases of 1973 and 1978 (Chapter 8) further enhanced the attractiveness of the fuel-efficient Japanese cars. Between 1970 and 1980 Japanese imports rose from 4.2 to 22% of the U.S. market share. During this same period, European imports fell from 10.5 to 5.4% of the U.S. market share (Hoffman and Kaplinsky, 1988:79–82).

As Japanese penetration of the U.S. and European markets rose, these markets instituted protectionist measures. Beginning in 1975 the Western European countries responded to the "Japanese Challenge" by negotiating so-called voluntary export restrictions (VERs). A U.S.–Japanese VER was negotiated in April 1981. The Japanese response to this new protectionism was to leapfrog national borders by establishing production capacity in Western Europe and the United States. In 1981 Honda opened a new plant in Ohio with a capacity to produce 150,000 Accords per year. The early move by Honda reflected both its greater export dependence and its less successful effort to fully implement the flexible manufacturing system. Toyota and Nissan were more cautious in entering the U.S. market because they were concerned about the difficulty of introducing the lean production system in the U.S. labor market. Between the early 1980s and 1990s, however, Japanese firms had built a new automobile industry in the U.S. Midwest that was larger than that of Great Britain, Italy, or Spain and almost the size of the French industry (Womack et al., 1991:240–242). Studies conducted in the late 1980s indicated that productivity levels achieved in U.S. "transplants" tended to run in the neighborhood of 30% below productivity levels in the parent plants in Japan. In strictly economic terms, it would have been more profitable if the Japanese firms had produced the automobile in Japan and exported to the United States (Abo, 1994:238–245).

Among U.S. automobile firms, Ford was the first to embrace the Japanese lean production system. Confronted by a crisis in loss of market share in the early 1980s both management and labor were more open to the changes needed to implement major elements, particularly in labor and supplier relationship, of the lean production system. By the mid-1990s, some Ford plants were achieving productivity levels comparable to the most productive plants in Japan (Figure 11.1a and 11.1b); Chrysler and General Motors moved more slowly than Ford. Productivity gains were achieved by closing their worst plants. Even in the late 1990s General Motors had not yet fully committed itself to lean production. In 1998 *Business Week* (June 29, 1998:36, 38) titled a story about productivity in the automobile industry "If Ford Can Do It Why Can't GM?"

Science-Based Technology

Since the beginning of the twentieth century Japanese producers have successfully challenged global leadership in a series of industries. Japan achieved a dominant position in the world textile industry between World War I and World War II. In the 1960s it became a leading exporter of steel and ships, in the 1970s of consumer electronics products, and in the 1980s of automobiles and machine tools. Japan caught up in several areas of computer and semiconductor technology in the 1980s (Chapter 9) and made strides, albeit less successfully, in the pharmaceutical and biotechnology industries (Chapter 10).

The emphasis on process technology and efficiency in production that Japanese firms employed first in the textile industry and later in the automobile industry was characteristic of the pattern used in steel, ship building, consumer electronics, and computers. This process involved the targeting, under the leadership of the Ministry of Trade and Industry (MITI), of a succession of industries followed by an attempt to catch up with the technological leaders. Japanese firms were able to move to the

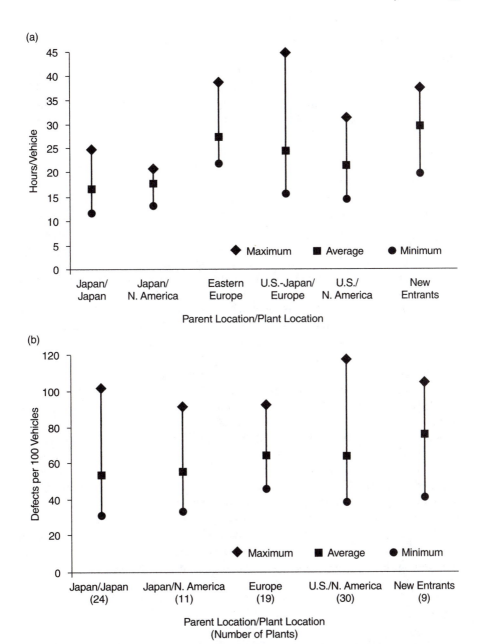

Figure 11.1 (a) Productivity and (b) quality performance of automobile manufacturing plants within and across regional groups, 1994. (*Source:* Charles H. Fine and Richard St. Clair, *The U.S. Automobile Manufacturing Industry*, Washington, DC: U.S. Department of Commerce, Office of Technology Policy, December 1996.)

technical frontier and then draw on their traditional advantage in process technology innovation to produce the products of the targeted industry at lower cost.

The MITI system worked so effectively that it was viewed by many observers in other advanced countries as a model for industry policy in the high-technology industries. Japanese semiconductor firms, organized into consortia in which R&D was partially subsidized by MITI, had displaced U.S. merchant producers of dynamic random-access memory (DRAM) chips in the United States and in other world markets in the early 1980s. Japanese computer firms, also organized into an R&D consortia, was able to achieve parity with the leading U.S. mainframe computer firms—IBM, Control Data, and Cray (Chapter 9). But the Supercomputer consortium organized by MITI in 1982 failed to achieve significant industry participation. The Fifth-Generation Consortium, designed to advance fundamental knowledge in artificial intelligence and other building blocks for the "thinking machines" of the future, was even less successful in gaining support from the computer industry. By the early 1990s it was apparent that the MITI system was in disarray.

By the early 1980s Japan had emerged from a nation that had been forced to play "catch-up" with other western economies to become a leading technology-driven economy. It had successfully navigated the two oil shocks of the 1970s by shifting from energy-intensive heavy industries toward higher value-added more knowledge-intensive industries. The size of its economy was exceeded only by that of the United States. By why did MITI effectiveness erode just as it had achieved such apparent success? Scott Callon argues that it was the structural transformation in the Japanese economy was responsible. Japan's emergence as a technological and economic giant in the 1980s destroyed MITI's ability to carry out an effective industrial policy (Callon, 1995:146).

As Japanese firms became increasingly confident, they became increasingly independent of MITI technological leadership and refused to contribute funds to its consortia. As the MITI technology budget shrank relative to the rapidly growing R&D budgets of private firms, its leverage declined. The transition from a strategy of technology catch-up to a strategy that would depend increasingly on science-based technology—and on scientific leadership—seemed beyond MITI's capacity. Finally, external political pressures, particularly from the United States, have acted to constrain the flexibility of Japanese industrial policy. These pressures have been initiated in an effort to counter Japan's competitive advantage in fields such as automobiles and consumer electronics.

Perspective

Since World War II, the development of science and technology (S&T) policy in Japan has gone through three main phases. From the late 1940s until well into the 1960s, the focus of Japanese technology policy was on rebuilding the capacity of its heavy industrial sectors. Substantial resources were devoted to the transfer and enhancement of imported technologies. The Japanese government assisted this catch-up phase by adopting policies that both encouraged exports and protected Japanese firms from foreign competition. During this catch-up phase, total factor productivity grew at almost 5.0% per year and gross domestic product (GDP) in the 9% per year range. These were the growth rates that led to the labeling of Japanese economic performance as a "miracle."

The energy crisis of the 1970s and growing concern about the environmental impacts of the growth of heavy industry induced a transition away from heavy industry in the 1970s and 1980s. Scientific and technical resources were devoted to strengthening the infrastructure for advanced research and development. Industry made a successful transition toward production and export of the higher value products of the consumer electronics and communications industries. The automobile industry expanded its capacity both at home and abroad. During this second stage there was, however, a substantial slowing of economic growth. Growth in total productivity declined to the 1.0% per year range and GNP to the 4.0% per year range (Katz, 1998:137).

In the third period, Japanese S&T policy shifted toward greater emphasis on the development of science-based technologies. During the 1990s, Japan invested over 2.5% of GDP in research to enhance commercial technology development. These investments reflected a concern that the strategy of focusing scientific and technical effort on specific areas in order to catch up with and then surpass foreign firms operating on the technical frontier was no longer viable. It was also clear that this new strategy would have a much slower payoff in terms of economic growth than the strategy of the earlier catch-up stages. The dramatic slowing of economic growth in the Japanese economy in the 1990s is sometimes interpreted as evidence that the new S&T policy has not worked. It would be more correct to interpret the slowing of growth to a series of economic policy failures (Katz, 1998:75–235). It is hard to believe, however, that Japanese industry will not maintain, or even enhance, its competitive advantage in the early decades of the twenty-first century.

Several institutional changes will be required, in addition to changes in S&T policy, if Japan is to realize the benefits form its scientific and technical capacity. In the short term it will be necessary to modernize its financial institutions. Japan has been less successful in transforming its financial institutions than in transforming its manufacturing industries. A second, and more difficult institutional change will be the transition from a developmental economy to a liberal market economy phase (Hayami, 1995). In its development phase, like Germany 100 years earlier, Japan adopted policies to suppress domestic consumption and promote investment. It had adopted trade policies that protected its less efficient industries and export enhancement policies for industries that it hoped could compete in international markets. But during the 1980s and 1990s the continuation of the policies that were appropriate during the developmental stage were no longer effective at home and were generating a strong political reaction on the part of the older industrial countries (Prestowitz, 1988, 1994; Fallows, 1989; Katz, 1998; Porter and Takeuchi, 1999). The post-World War II economic success of Japan has rested on its success in improving both the process technology and product quality, while continuing to borrow the basic ideas and technical concepts from abroad. But Japan's supremacy in the mass manufacture of high-quality products has been undermined as this approach has been adopted by other East and Southeast Asian economies. To sustain growth it will be necessary for Japan to make the transition from being a borrower of innovative ideas and concepts to a source of scientific and technical innovation (Hayami and Ogasawara, 1999). In the early 1990s the Japanese economy entered a decade-long recession. By the late 1990s, it had, however, begun to make a number of the institutional reforms that could lead to a revitalization of its economy in the first decade of the twenty-first century.

GERMAN SYSTEMS OF TECHNICAL INNOVATION

Germany is the classic example of a backward economy that invested in science, technology, and education to catch up with more advanced countries.[28] In the early nineteenth century, France was the world leader in advancing science and in scientific education. The industrial revolution was well under way in Great Britain. But German industry relied on other countries, primarily Great Britain, both for machinery and for skilled workers to install and operate it.

This backwardness was reversed, however, with a highly significant German institutional innovation: the modern research university. The traditional European university was devoted to education in the classical professions such as theology, medicine, and law. The founding of the Friedrich-Wilhelm-Universität (now Humboldt Universitätae) in Berlin by Wilhelm von Humboldt and his associates in 1809 represented the beginning of a new type of university. von Humboldt's objective was to create a university that could nurture the development of new laboratory-based sciences such as chemistry, physics, and biology. The university mission also included the practical application of scientific knowledge. By mid-century Justus von Liebig had demonstrated the importance of organic chemistry to the understanding of plant nutrition and to advances in crop production. The first publicly supported agricultural experiment station was organized, with von Liebig's support, in Germany in 1852 to develop "methods of applying science to agriculture" (Chapter 6).

von Liebig's effort to reform the teaching of chemistry by combining the pursuit of pure knowledge with laboratory research in the training of students met with substantial resistance on the part of the academic establishment. His approach, which was designed to advance technology as well as scientific knowledge, was criticized for undermining the purposes of the university. By the 1870s, however, his laboratory approach had diffused widely both in Germany and abroad. Research collaboration between industrial firms such as Hoechst and BASF and the directors of university laboratories had become an established practice. Chemical companies also moved to establish their own internal research laboratories (Lenior, 1998). The commercial

---

[28] In this section I draw heavily on Keck (1993).

success of a number of German firms such as Bayer, Agfa, and Siemens rested directly on the results obtained in their laboratories. The science-based technology emerging from German firms in the chemical, electrical, and pharmaceutical industries enabled firms in these industries to establish dominant positions in world markets (Reich, 1985:12–41; Chapters 7 and 8).

By the beginning of the twentieth century, Germany had established a sophisticated system for education in scientific, technical, and commercial fields ranging from elementary school to the doctoral level. The system included universities, technical universities (Technische Hochschulen), and middle-level technical schools. Dozens of foundations were founded, often affiliated with universities or Technische Hochschulen, for support of technical and scientific research. There were close connections between the different levels and a flow of knowledge in most areas of specialization. There were also close links between the education system and industrial firms, not only through the supply of trained personnel but through consulting by engineering professors in areas of applied science (Chapter 8). The German educational infrastructure for science and technology was distinguished from that of other countries both by the high quality of its institutions and by the large number of students enrolled. At each level, a higher proportion of the population was enrolled than in any other country.

Science-Based Technology

In Germany, unlike the United States, science-based technical innovation preceded mass production (Chapter 8). The first major science-based industry was the beet sugar industry. But it was in the synthetic dyestuffs industry that scientific research first became a fully institutionalized function separate from production (Chapter 8). By 1913 Germany produced over three-quarters of the world output of synthetic dyes. It also occupied a dominant position in the heavy chemical industry and in pharmaceuticals. In electrical machinery Germany accounted for 35% of world production compared to 30% for the United States and 16% for Great Britain. Transfer of technology from Great Britain and the United States, particularly in the cotton textile and the machine industries, contributed to Germany's rapid industrialization. It was not, however, the advantage of technical backwardness that enabled Germany to catch up and in many areas surpass Great Britain and the United States. Rather, it was the establishment of new institutional arrangements—in education, in research, and in industrial organization—that enabled German firms to quickly follow up advances in technical and scientific knowledge with new product opportunities or new process technologies.

The advances that Germany had achieved during the previous 50 years were severely compromised as a result of World War I, economic crises in the 1920s and 1930s, the rise of Hitler's National Socialist (Nazi) government in the 1930s, and World War II. World War I cut German industry off from its main export markets. It also stimulated efforts by the United States, France, Great Britain, and other countries to substitute domestic production for German imports. The World War I peace treaty involved the expropriation of German patents in critical areas such as chemistry and pharmaceuticals and imposed a heavy war reparation burden on the economy.

The accession to power of Hitler's National Socialist government in 1933 resulted in a further weakening of educational and research institutions. Many leading scientists and engineers were purged from their positions. During World War II large parts of the industrial infrastructure were destroyed. After World War II subsidiaries of German firms located in the allied countries were separated from their parent companies and expropriated along with their intellectual property rights. Some factories were dismantled and removed as reparations. Each of the allied powers engaged in a race to capture and gain access to scientists and engineers engaged in defense-related research (Keck, 1993:130).

The allied powers prohibited R&D for military technology, as well as for several areas of civilian technology related to military capacity, such as nuclear technology, aeronautics, rocket propulsion, marine propulsion, radar, and remote and automatic control. Special permission was required for work on things such as electronic valves, ball and roller bearings, synthetic rubber, synthetic oil, and radioactivity. The allies deconstructed the chemical and steel industries, and abolished the economic planning structures of the National Socialist government (Keck, 1993:133–137). These restrictions, which remained in force until 1955, effectively eliminated German capacity in the military and aeronautic industries and prevented several other industries from operating near the technological frontier.

During the 1950s the basic institutions of the German technical innovation system were reconstructed and expanded. A system of public and semipublic research institutions was designed to complement and bridge the R&D activities of both the universities and industry.[29] The Max Planck Society (MPG) is the major institution performing basic and long-term applied research in physics, biology, and chemistry. The Helmholtz Centers conduct research on long-term national priority problems that involve large facility investments and entail considerable economic risk, such as nuclear energy research, aerospace, health, and environment. The centers are funded primarily with public money, but an attempt has been made in recent years to increase the share of research that is relevant to industry by reducing institutional support in favor of project support.

The Fraunhofer Society (FhG), established after World War II to manage government industrial projects, had emerged by the 1990s as the major German nonprofit organization in the area of applied research. Its research has a strong commercial orientation. Only 20–30% of the FhG's budget is in the form of institutional support from the government, and even that funding is linked directly to the FhG's success in doing contract research for public and private clients. A close relationship between the FhG and the German universities is institutionalized through the appointment

---

[29] In the next several paragraphs I draw heavily on Abramson et al. (1997:246–250).

of FhG directors as regular university professors. There has been no institution in the United States comparable to the Fraunhofer Society, although there is some similarity with the new programs initiated by the U.S. National Institutes of Science and Technology (NIST) in the 1980s such as the Advanced Technology Program (ATP) and the Manufacturing Technology Extension Centers (Chapter 13).

The German universities remain the weakest link in the German national innovation system. They have not, in the post-World War II era, achieved the research capacity or international stature that they held earlier. German university linkages with the industrial sector remain less intensive than in the United States. The linkages are largely through collaboration, contract research, consulting conferences, and the training of technical and scientific personnel. In contrast to the United States, there is little transfer of personnel between the universities and industry. The number of faculty positions has not expanded to accommodate the increased number of students. A combination of decline in quality and overcrowding has lengthened the time to complete a "diploma" degree from 4 to 6.5 years. German doctoral programs have very long matriculation time with low completion rates. German industrial firms consider training at the polytechnic institutions (Fachhochschulen) more relevant to their needs than training at the university level (National Science Foundation, 1996:25–32). Although steps have been initiated to reform the university system, it will be some time before German universities can become a source of the innovations in science-based high-technology industries, comparable to the role that U.S. universities have played in biotechnology (Chapter 10).

During the post-World War II period, the West German economy made a remarkable recovery. Its rate of growth in output and productivity has exceeded that of any other Western country and was only slightly lower than that of Japan (Table 2.1). It is rather striking, however, that the largest and most successful firms were, with few exceptions, those that had achieved success during the period of German technological leadership before World War I (Patel and Pavitt, 1997). In a careful assessment of the German technical innovation system Kleck argued that when the German innovation system of the 1980s is put into historical perspective "it reflects mainly the momentum of organizations that have existed for a long time, have survived the period of wars and crises, and then have grown in size. In the reconstruction period after World War II, each organization primarily looked after itself, and the system as such fell into oblivion" (Kleck, 1993:145). He goes on to argue that German industry's ability to maintain it capacity in traditional areas, while unable to extend its innovative capacity into new areas, has reflected a lack of central leadership in science, technology, and education.[30]

---

[30] During most of the post-World War II period, the most important source of the public R&D research funding has been the Ministry of Education, Science, Research and Technology. In the early 1980s the Ministry was split into a Federal Ministry for Research and Technology and a Federal Ministry of Education and Science. This had the effect of diluting the role of the federal government in articulating a coherent S&T policy (Kleck).

Fordism and Beyond

The German automobile industry was a major exception to the generalization that German industrial success was built on its early development of science-based industry. Although German inventors (Karl Benz, Gottlieb Daimler) played an important role in the early development of the automobile, Germany did not begin to produce a significant number of automobiles until the mid-1920s. In the early 1920s German and other European automobile manufactures visited Detroit to study the Ford mass production system. "Their public response was that European craftsmen would never agree to work under such conditions . . . and that Europe should pursue a different strategy. Then they went home and immediately attempted to duplicate the Ford system" (Womack, 1991:18).

Although European producers were successful in copying the Ford production methods, they were not as successful in producing an inexpensive automobile. The European automobile market was highly fragmented. No standardized "European car" emerged to dominate the market in the way the Model T had dominated the U.S. market. This resulted in a range of products, particularly small cars, that became attractive to U.S. consumers after World War II. Although British cars dominated the European export market in the immediate post-World War II years, they quickly lost market share to German imports, largely because of quality considerations. The most successful of the European exports was the German Volkswagen (VW).

The Volkswagen originated as a project inspired by Adolf Hitler. While in prison in 1924, Hitler read Henry Ford's autobiography. When he came to power in 1933, he made the production of an automobile that would be affordable for German workers a policy priority. The only manufacturer to come up with a model in the acceptable price range was Opel, the German subsidiary of General Motors. Hitler was unwilling to accept that his promise of a "peoples car"—a Volkswagen—could be met only by a foreign-owned firm. In 1937 he assigned the Volkswagen project to the German Labor Front, the Nazi labor organization. The Labor Front settled on a design similar to one originally submitted by Porsche—a car with a rear-mounted, air-cooled engine, torsion bar suspension, and seats for four in a streamlined steel body. In 1938 the Labor Front began construction of a huge new parts and assembly complex, modeled on the Ford River Rouge plant, in Wolfsburg, east of Hannover. When war broke out in September 1939, construction of the factory had not been completed. During World War II, the factory produced a military version of the Volkswagen to serve the same purpose as the U.S. Jeep (Laux, 1992:115, 116).

At the end of World War II no one was quite sure what to do about the huge Volkswagen facility. The Labor Front had been disbanded. The plant, located in the zone occupied by the British army, had not experienced significant damage from wartime bombing. An American industrial inspection team characterized it as the most modern automobile manufacturing facility in the world (Abelshauser, 1995:282). The British administrators took control of the plant, made essential repairs, and began producing small numbers of the original VW cars. Through 1947 the plant supplied a total of 20,000 cars to occupation forces and to German officials. In 1949 the British turned the plant over to the new West German Government. In 1950 Volkswagen production exceeded 90,000 vehicles. The plant's director, Heinz Nordhoff, reportedly remarked, "By one of those ironic jokes history is sometime tempted to produce, it was the Occupation Powers who, after unconditional surrender, brought Hitler's dream into reality" (Laux, 1992:170).

Since the end of World War II, Volkswagen has remained the largest German auto firm. In addition to its low price, it established a reputation for quality and reliability and dominated the low cost end of the German car market in the early postwar period. It gradually installed larger engines, better brakes, and more sophisticated transmissions. In 1953 VW began a determined effort to penetrate the U.S. market. By 1959 it accounted for one-fourth of the over 600,000 cars imported into the United States. It filled a niche that U.S. manufacturers had neglected. It promoted itself with unusually clever advertising, claiming that it was an honest car and that one had to look under the hood to see its annual improvement rather than to its styling (Laux, 1992:185, 186)

In effect Volkswagen held closely to the system Ford had pioneered with the Model T throughout the 1950s. It restricted production to a single model, the Beetle. It developed a strong dealer and service network both in Germany and abroad. But it departed from the Ford system in two important respects. It systematically emphasized technical improvements "under the hood" as well as technical advances in production. And it developed a cooperative rather than adversarial relationship with its trade unions. Unlike the Ford system, a division of power in the workplace between management and labor was assumed. Volkswagen also remained committed to the classical German approach to industrial relations by combining the traditions of craftsmanship and mass production (Abelshauser, 1995:282–289).[31]

But Volkswagen's advantage, and that of other European exporters of small cars such as Fiat, lasted only as long as European currencies remained weak relative to the dollar and until the Japanese chose to compete in the U.S. and European market. The Japanese cars were less expensive, superior in quality and reliability, and more innovative in styling. The Datsun 510, introduced in 1968, embodied the best of European engineering and Japanese manufacturing. It was mass produced, sporty, and inexpensive. By 1975 Toyota exceeded Volkswagen in exports to the United States.

The German response was to focus on a new class of luxury cars that were smaller, more powerful, and more reliable than U.S. luxury cars. This strategy effectively countered the success of Japanese imports to Western Europe and the United States while the three mass market producers (Volkswagen, Ford, and Opel) experienced declining or stagnant production and sales. During the late 1970s and early 1980s

---

[31] Volkswagen gradually phased out its "Beetle" model in Germany in the 1970s. In 1978, when the last one was produced at its Emden plant, it had produced 19.3 million units, of which some 5 million had been sold in the United States. Production of the Beetle continued, however, in Nigeria, Brazil, and Mexico (Laux, 1992:230). In 1998 it introduced a redesigned Beetle for the U.S. market.

the three producers that occupied the upper end of the market (Daimler-Benz, BMW, and Audi) continued to experience growth in production and sales. By the mid-1980s Germany had captured almost the entire U.S. luxury car market. Though the number of German automobiles exported to the United States declined, the value of the German exports continued to rise (Womack, 1989:18).

By the mid-1990s, however, German dominance of the luxury cars market was being challenged by Japanese producers of luxury cars. Japanese producers were able to place luxury cars of superior quality on the market at lower prices than the German (or other European) luxury car producers. During the 1980s Japanese producers had learned to apply lean production methods that could compete effectively with German "craft" producers. When MIT International Motor Vehicle Program researchers visited a German luxury car assembly plant they found, at the end of the assembly line, an enormous rework and retrification area "where technicians in white laboratory jackets labored to bring the finished product up to the company's fabled quality standard" (Womack et al., 1991:90). A third of the total assembly labor occurred in this area. It required more craft labor to correct problems that had been created in assembly than Japanese luxury car plants required to produce a comparable car.

Toward Revival

Writing in the late 1980s, Michael Porter emphasized a number of institutional constraints on German technological leadership (Porter, 1990:715–719). German workers, the highest paid in the Western world, have elected to take the benefits of productivity growth in the entirely understandable form of a shorter work week, longer vacations, and greater job security. Environmental regulations, which made it difficult to conduct research and introduce new products in biotechnology, had led German pharmaceutical companies to relocate R&D facilities abroad. Company leaders with training in finance began replacing executives with training and experience in production. Conservative credit institutions inhibited the development of a vigorous venture capital market. A culture of competition was replaced by industrial cooperation and consolidation.

It is difficult to evaluate the importance of Porter's observations. It is clear, however, that Germany possesses a number of advantages that should enable it to move toward a revival of industrial dynamism. It still has, for its size, one of the strongest S&T bases in the Western world. In the mid-1990s German and U.S. R&D spending as a share of GDP was quite comparable—with Germany spending 2.3% of GDP on R&D and the U.S. spending 2.5%. In the United States, however, the public sector accounted for a much larger share of R&D spending primarily because of the heavy concentration of U.S. R&D in the areas of defense and space. Germany had, by the late 1990s, succeeded, at very high cost, in absorbing the former East Germany into its national economic system. A major constraint limiting the impact of German R&D on economic growth has been the small size of its domestic market (Eaton et al., 1998). If its leadership in the formation of the European monetary union is followed by continued progress toward a more open European market the effect should be more vigorous intra-European competition and, as a consequence, stronger international competitive advantage, not only for Germany but for the entire European Union.

SYSTEMS OF TECHNICAL INNOVATION

In two seminal papers published in the late 1980s Henry Ergas presented a framework designed to aid in interpreting the development of the three innovation systems discussed in this chapter (Ergas, 1987a; 1987b). Ergas characterized the contemporary U.S. innovation system as primarily mission oriented, the German system as diffusion oriented, and the Japanese system as both mission oriented and diffusion oriented.

In characterizing the U.S. system as mission oriented Ergas was referring to the U.S. tendency to concentrate science-based technology development efforts on a limited number of industries. In the post-World War II period these technologies have been closely related to national security (atomic energy, space, computers) and health (biotechnology).

The term diffusion oriented applies to countries such as Germany in which public sector support is directed to the development of broad-based capacity for applying advances in technology throughout the industrial system. Ergas argues that the capacity to pursue a diffusion-oriented approach depends on both the depth and breadth of investment in human capital. In Germany this took the form of a high-quality university system, an extensive system of vocational education, and a comprehensive system of secondary education that effectively streams students into both the vocational and the university system.

The Japanese system has been mission oriented in that at each stage in its development it has concentrated its technical effort on a few sectors important to national military or economic strategy. The chosen sectors have shifted over time—first textiles, then steel and shipbuilding, followed by automobiles, and now electronics and computers. At the same time, Japan has developed institutional arrangements, including its educational system and a system of intraindustry cooperation, that have resulted in rapid diffusion of technology and institutions.

Ergas has employed the concept of technological trajectories (Chapter 4) to illustrate both the strengths and weaknesses of the three systems. A trajectory has three phases— an emergence phase, a consolidation phase, and a maturity phase (Figure 11.2). Success in the *emergence phase* requires the capacity to carry on sophisticated R&D across a broad front and financial institutions that are flexible enough to respond to promising but uncertain new opportunities. The system must also be capable of generating a continuous series of new technical innovations that give rise to new technical trajectories. Success in the *consolidation stage* depends on the capacity to exploit the results of successive new trajectories without having been actively involved in the R&D that gave rise them. It also requires the capacity to transfer resources from one trajectory to another as earlier trajectories mature. Success in exploiting technological trajectories at the *maturity stage* requires a highly skilled labor force and production engineering. Ergas argues that in the post-World War II era the comparative advantages have been in the emergence stage for the United States; in the consolidation stage for Japan; and in the maturity stage for Germany. The automobile industry as described in this chapter clearly fits the Ergas topology.

Concentration of technological capacity in any one stage can carry severe penalties. Success in the emergence stage is inadequate to ensure rapid growth in productivity and income across a broad industrial front. Success in the consolidation phase depends on a capacity to shift rapidly from an older trajectory to a new trajectory that is just reaching the emergence phase. In the consolidation phase productivity growth is harder to come by. Firms in this phase are continuously vulnerable to firms that are able to move from the consolidation to the maturity stage along their own trajectory.

Each of the three national technology development systems reviewed in this chapter will face severe problems in the early decades of the twenty-first century. Each country's educational and technology development systems support its existing technology trajectories (Table 11.3). The United States has, in the post-World War II period, been less successful in achieving the efficiency and productivity necessary to move through the consolidation phase and into the maturity phase. This is because even, as noted above, a dynamic high-technology sector has not translated into rapid growth in high-technology employment. Throughout most of the post-World War II period employment in the high-technology R&D-intensive industries was heavily concentrated on the defense-dependent industries. Since the early 1980s increases in employment in R&D-intensive non-defense-related industries has largely been offset by declines in employment in defense-related industries. In 1996 employment in R&D-intensive manufacturing amounted to less than one-third of the 18.5 million workers employed in manufacturing and less than 5% of total employment of 127 million (Luker and Lyons, 1998; Riche et al., 1983).

For Germany an important issue is whether it can move into the consolidation and emergence stages of new trajectories more effectively than in the post-World War II era. By concentrating its technological capacity on the maturity phase it becomes vulnerable to countries such as Japan, which have gained capacity to follow their trajectories into the maturity phase in industries such as machine tools and automobiles. Japan's test is whether its technology development systems can become more effective in the emergence phase.

During the 1960s and 1970s Japanese firms established world standards in process technology—in enhancing productivity and in improving quality. The technical challenge Japan now faces is to become as innovative in product technology as in process technology. But the major challenge Japan faces in its efforts to recover from the stagnation of the 1990s is institutional rather than scientific or technical. Japan has sought to shelter its inefficient domestic industries, wholesale trade, financial services, and agriculture, from both domestic and international competition. During the period of rapid expansion of its more efficient export industries, the costs of supporting these inefficient sectors remained hidden. With the slowing of economic

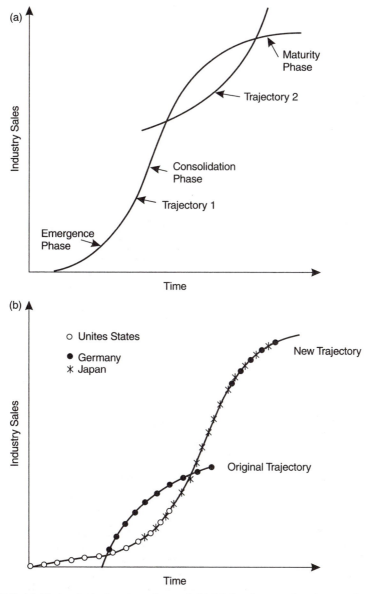

Figure 11.2 (a) Technological trajectories and (b) National strengths along technological trajectories. (*Source:* Adapted from Henry Ergas, "Does Technology Policy Matter?" In *Technology and Global Industry: Companies and Nations in the World Economy*, B. R. Guile and H. Brooks, eds., Washington, DC: National Academic Press, National Academy of Sciences, 1987:226, 231.)

Table 11.3 Indicators of Technology Development Systems in the United States, Germany, and Japan in the mid-1980s.

	United States	Germany	Japan
Share of defense-related R&D on total government expenditures on R&D (1981)	54	9	2
Proportion of total national public R&D funding by type of industry (1980)			
High technical industry	88	67	21
Medium technical industry	8	23	12
Low technical industry	4	10	67
Share of government-funded R&D performed in the government sector (early 1980s)	26	32	
Research scientists and engineers per 1000 workers in the labor force (1981)	6.2	4.7	5.4
Diplomas gaining access to higher education as proportion of age group (early 1980s)	72	26	87

Source: H. Ergas, "Does Technology Policy Matter?" In *Technology and Global Industry: Companies and Nations in the World Economy*, B. R. Guile and H. Brooks, eds., Washington, DC: National Academic Press, National Academy of Sciences, 1987.

growth in the 1980s and 1990s the costs of low productivity in those industries that had been protected from competition became an increasing burden on economic growth. A series of reforms in structure will be required to open the Japanese internal market to both domestic and international competition (Katz, 1998; Porter and Takeuchi, 1999).

Why, particularly in the post-World War II era, have U.S. firms been relatively ineffective in pursuing technology development into the consolidation and maturity phases? Nathan Rosenberg and Edward Steinmueller (1988) posed this question in a slightly different way. Why are American firms such poor imitators? And why have Japanese firms been so much better at imitation than American firms? Japan has several advantages. One is, of course, that, at last until recently, the entire history of modern Japanese development has been built on a culture of creative imitation. A second, closely related answer is that Japanese technology development places a stronger emphasis on process than on product development. Mansfield (1988) observes that among Japanese firms that he studied only one-third of their R&D budgets was devoted to improved product technologies; the other two-thirds went to process technology. Furthermore, much of the focus of product technology was devoted to incremental improvement rather than breakthrough technologies.

Until at least the early 1980s most American firms were not aware that there was much in Japanese industry that was worth imitating. In the 1980s U.S. firms did become aware that Japanese firms were achieving high levels of productivity and capturing market share in the electrical, electronic, transportation, and machinery fields, where sophisticated manufacturing skills and technology were of central importance. What was worth imitating on the Japanese side, though, was not hardware but the much less subtle and less visible ways in which production activities are carried out. These included close articulation of research and manufacturing and of design and development, and long-term relational contracts with suppliers, for example (Kenney and Florida, 1993).

It is time to return to the question that began this chapter. Have advances in transportation and communication and increased mobility of financial resources, technology, and goods eroded the significance of national technical innovational systems? Is it true that we are approaching a time when there will no longer be German or Japanese or American companies—"only successful ones"? In automobiles, for example, firms headquartered in one nation have plants or cooperative manufacturing arrangements throughout the world. There has been a narrowing of productivity and quality differentials among plants located in North America, Europe, and Japan. American, and to a lesser extent, European automobile producers began to adopt Japanese production methods and supplier relationships (Shimokawa, 1997). There remain major differences between automobile plants in each region.[32] There are also wide differences in quality within each region. But the differences among the best plants in the three regions are quite small (Figure 11.1). The 1998 merger of Daimler-Benz and Chrysler raised questions about the longer term structure of the automobile industry. Would the future bring a world automobile industry with perhaps three to six global firms plus a few "niche" producers (*Business Week*, May 18, 1998:40–43). As attention is shifted to the newly industrializing countries, the formerly centrally planned economies, and the least developed countries it is apparent that national systems remain important in facilitating (or dampening) technical and economic development.

Even with convergence, substantial differences remain among national systems (Patel and Pavitt, 1997). Although R&D as a share of national income is comparable for the United States, Japan, and Germany, the United States continues to allocate a much higher share of public sector R&D support to defense and space-related research. The United States also spends a much higher share of non-defense-related R&D on basic biology and health-related research (Chapter 13). German industrial research continues to be heavily concentrated in those traditional manufacturing industries in which German firms have long excelled, such as the automotive, machinery, electronic and communication equipment, and industrial chemical sectors. Neither Japan nor the United States has an industry-oriented applied research system comparable to the German Fraunhofer Society; similarly, there is no counterpart in either Germany or Japan to the prominent role that venture capital firms and start-up companies perform in commercializing new technology in the United States.

---

[32] A *Business Week* article (June 29, 1998:36–38) raised the question "If Ford Can Do It Why Can't GM?" The answer by *Business Week* was in terms of GM's dismal record of labor relations. The article failed to mention Ford's success in adopting lean production.

TECHNOLOGY, TRADE, AND COMPETITIVENESS

In the half century since the end of World War II U.S. technological leadership has been severely eroded in a number of important industries. Japan and Germany, in particular, were remarkably successful in narrowing the gaps in productivity and in income that prevailed in the early postwar period (Chapter 2). In addition, a number of newly industrializing countries such as Korea and Mexico became important suppliers of manufactured products to the United States. The decline in the U.S. trade balance for high-technology products, an area in which the United States had assumed it could remain preeminent, was particularly difficult to accept.

The dramatic rise in the U.S. trade deficit in the 1980s, and the rapid shift of the United States from the world's largest creditor to its largest debtor, served to focus both popular and professional attention on the problem of U.S. competitiveness in global markets. This, in turn, generated a massive literature on the reasons for the loss of U.S. competitiveness. The literature is characterized by three broad perspectives on the sources of the decline in U.S. technological leadership and of the emergence of a challenge to that leadership by other industrialized countries.[33]

One view is that the U.S. lead was inherently transient. It was partly attributable to the later start of industrial development by other presently advanced economies and partly to the destruction of our major industrial rivals during World War II. A second view sees not convergence but U.S. industrial decline. The United States is failing, as England failed a century ago, to exploit technical opportunities and to organize economic activity. A third interpretation regards the U.S. relative decline as a consequence of the emergence of a new global economy in which national borders and national systems of technology play a less decisive role as centers of technological leadership emerge in newly developing countries (Nelson and Wright, 1992:1933). Each of these explanations is at least partially correct.

Much has been written on how the United States might regain technological leadership and become more competitive in the world economy. One response has emphasized macroeconomic policy reform to correct the slow rate of capital formation in the United States. It was argued that technical change, rather than being disembodied as implied in much of the growth-accounting literature (Chapter 3), is largely embodied in the form of new capital equipment. Thus, whereas Japanese steel producers were expanding capacity and investment in the new basic oxygen and continuous casting technology, their U.S. counterparts were investing in the maintenance and repair of outmoded steel facilities. In the United States a combination of low saving rates and high capital costs forced U.S. industry to scale back on investment and employ a short-run planning horizon in considering capital investment. The United States was urged to adopt fiscal and monetary policies that would avoid subsidies to consumption and encourage higher rates of saving and capital formation (Hatsopoulas et al., 1988).

---

[33] In the following paragraphs I draw heavily on Nelson and Wright (1992). See also Krugman (1990, 1991, 1997).

A second response has been the advocacy of "strategic" or "managed" trade policy. It is argued that rather than the natural resource endowments that determined comparative advantage in traditional trade theory, "constructed" or "created" advantage resulting from technical change is now a major source of comparative advantage. An initial technological lead may be converted into a self-reinforcing comparative advantage due to technical and/or pecuniary external economies (Chapter 4). Thus the reason for U.S. dominance in jet passenger aircraft production should not be sought in the nation's natural resource endowments but rather in the historical circumstances that gave the United States a head start in the industry (Krugman, 1997:129). Similarly, support by the Japanese government for development of the computer industry is viewed as necessary to enable Japanese firms to overcome the initial advantages enjoyed by IBM (Chapter 9). The strategic trade perspective represents a new and more sophisticated version of the older infant industry argument. It provides an intellectually respectable case for a more aggressive trade policy in support of new high-technology industries.

A third response has been a call for more explicit U.S. policy of public and private sector support for commercial technology development. An underlying premise was that the defense orientation of the industrial policy of the United States during World War II delayed the translation of scientific and technical knowledge into commercial process and product technology. Industrial leaders were highly critical of U.S. industry for giving inadequate attention to manufacturing, in contrast to Germany and Japan, in which manufacturing technology remained a high priority. "One reason why U.S. manufacturers did not capture the greatest part of the profits from the development of color TV, for which RCA was primarily responsible, is that RCA and its U.S. licensees were not competitive at manufacturing" (Teese, 1987:91). The proponents of technology policy argued that the United States should adopt a more active role in advancing the "encompassing" or general purpose technologies that would become the source of future growth in high wage employment and export earnings.

As the dialogue about technology, trade, and competitiveness has progressed the weight of opinion has shifted rather strongly toward concern about efficiency and productivity growth in the domestic economy and away from those analysts who place their major focus on the gains (or losses) from trade (Krugman, 1991:811–815). Until recently the discussion often ignored the effects of technical change and international trade on income distribution. Changes in technology often have significant effects on the distribution of income among skilled and unskilled workers within countries and these changes in income distribution are often a much more significant source of political tension among the proponents and critics of more liberal trade policy than the efficiency or productivity effects of trade (Box 11.2).

During the 1980s and 1990s the United States became a world leader in the global trend toward greater inequality. The wages of management professionals and skilled workers rose as the wages of unskilled workers declined. Similar but less extreme divergence occurred in other developed and even in several newly industrializing countries. These changes have stimulated a vigorous debate among labor economists and trade economists about the sources of divergence in wage rates. Labor economists have tended to attribute the divergence to the effects of trade liberalization. Trade economists have tended to give greatest weight to the effects of technical change on the demand for skilled and unskilled workers (Box 11.2).

● BOX 11.2

GLOBALIZATION, TECHNOLOGY, AND INCOME DISTRIBUTION

Traditional trade theory provides very clear implications for trade liberalization's effect on income distribution. In its simplest form the Stolper–Samuelson theorem states that in a hypothetical, open economy providing two tradable goods, if the price of one of these goods falls, then the factor of production used relatively intensively in the production of this good will experience a fall in its factor rental (or wage) while the price of the factor used in the production of the other good will rise. If we think of the factor used most intensively in the production of one industry (say electronics) as skilled labor and the factor used most intensively in the production of the industry whose price has fallen (say textiles) as unskilled labor, then the real wage of skilled labor can be expected to rise and the real wage of unskilled labor can be expected to fall. The reason for this is that resources (both skilled and unskilled labor) will be drawn out of the textile industry and into the electronics industry. But since electronic production requires a smaller proportion of unskilled labor, the demand for unskilled labor will decline and the wage rate for unskilled labor will fall.

The analysis can be extended to the effects of trade on income distribution within countries. Imagine a trading system composed of a high-income country named North and a low-income country named South. North produces electronics, an industry that employs a high ratio of skilled to unskilled workers. South produces textiles, an industry that employs a low ratio of skilled to unskilled workers. North imposes a tariff on imports of textiles.

Now suppose that the tariff is removed as a result of a North–South trade agreement. Textiles become available at a lower price to consumers in the North. International trade in textiles expands. The effects on income distribution in North would be similar to that in the single country case—real wages of skilled workers rise and of unskilled workers fall. In South, however, the model suggests that the wages of unskilled workers will rise relative to the wages of skilled workers. This is expected because the expanded trade in textiles would, at least in the short run, drive up the price of textiles. This would, in turn, drive up the wages of unskilled workers and narrow the wage differential between skilled and unskilled workers in South.

Apparently the real world is somewhat more complex than assumed in the Stolper–Samuelson model. In North the expected widening of income differentials, as predicted by the model, has occurred. In the United States the distribution of income has widened, dividing society into an increasingly prosperous group of high-wage high-skilled workers and an increasingly disadvantaged group of low-paid less-skilled workers. Similar, but less extreme changes are occurring in other developed countries. The surprise is that scattered evidence indicates a widening rather than the expected narrowing of the wage differentials even in newly industrializing economies.

One possible explanation is technical change. There is substantial evidence that skilled labor and capital are complements, and unskilled labor and capital are substitutes, in North. The effect of technical change in North is to increase the complementarity between capital and skilled labor. Thus the widening of the wage differential in North is due, at least in part, to technical change in addition to any effect of a decline in the prices of labor-intensive commodities imported from South.

If capital-intensive technology is transformed directly from North to South in the form of turn-key plants, it is possible that this may account for a widening of the wage differential between skilled and unskilled workers, particularly if South is experiencing rapid industrialization. Will it be possible for South to minimize the effects of capital–labor complementarity, and thus avoid what has been termed "immizering" growth, by acquiring the research, development, and design capacity that will enable it to invent or adapt technology in a manner consistent with its own factor endowments rather than simply importing turn-key plants from North? The issue can also be stated more broadly. Are the rapid advances in advanced technology creating a new class structure, in both developed and developing countries—with one class whose skills are primarily the manipulation of ideas and symbols and a second class whose skills lie primarily in the manipulation of materials?

Source: Adapted from John S. Chipman, "Globalization, Technology, and Income Distribution," paper presented to the conference on "International Economic Justice: Theory and Policy," Minneapolis, Hubert H. Humphrey Institute of Public Affairs, November 14, 1997 (mimeo). See also Per Krusell, Lee E. Ohanian, José-Victor Rios-Rull, and Giovanni L. Violante, "Capital-Skill Complementarity and Inequality: A Macroeconomic Analysis," Minneapolis, MN: Federal Reserve Bank of Minneapolis Research Department, Staff Report 239, September 1997.

PERSPECTIVE

Discussion of science and technology policy has often focused on two closely related propositions. One is that the science-based industries represent leading sectors that tend to drive and shape technical change and economic growth across a broad front.

The second is that the ability of a high-wage economy to compete in international markets is increasingly dependent on the science-based industries and that government direction and assistance are warranted to ensure that such industries emerge and thrive. Both assertions must be qualified (Nelson, 1984). An industry can play the role of a leading sector without being closely articulated with recent scientific advances. The automobile industry, first in the United States, and then in Germany and Japan, is an example. Conversely a nation can be a leading source of new knowledge in science and technology and yet be relatively unsuccessful in realizing economic benefits from such an investment in the form of productivity or per capita income growth (Broadberry, 1994).

One conclusion that does emerge with considerable force, both in this chapter and in earlier chapters, is that general strength in scientific education and research is a prerequisite for innovation capacity in the newer science-based industries. It is also essential for the adaptation and diffusion of industrial and agricultural technologies in countries in which resource endowment or the stage of economic development differs substantially from that in which the technology was initially developed. The preeminence of the United States in science and engineering enabled it to emerge as the leading source of new science-based industries in the period since World War II. Its weaknesses in intermediate technical education and in industrial management have at times acted as a constraint to fully realizing the gains from scientific and technical innovation. Germany has developed exceptional quality in its technical education and in the skills of its labor force. The capacity of Japan to achieve dramatic success in manufacturing process technology and to move toward the frontier in a number of technical and scientific fields has been associated with its population's high level of both general education and technical training. Japan has been able to challenge Germany in the area of product quality as well as in process technology. A major problem for Japan will be to more effectively challenge the United States in terms of innovation in the science-based industries.

The slowing of economic growth in Japan (and East Asia) and in Germany (and Western Europe) and the rise in the U.S. economic growth rate since the early 1990s have caused the financial press and even some analysts to conclude that concerns about U.S. competitiveness are no longer relevant—"Wall Street Won" (Murray, 1997). The United States has reasserted its leadership in a number of high-technology and skill-intensive industries such as semiconductors and software. Meanwhile, Japan has experienced a slowing of economic growth and other countries in East Asia have experienced severe financial crises. Germany has been plagued by high levels of unemployment since assuming responsibility for the integration of the former East Germany. By the end of the 1980s, it appeared that the process of productivity convergence among the United States, Japan, Germany, and the other OECD countries had slowed (Figure 2.1).

As the United States was completing the longest period of sustained growth since World War II, a number of observers were proclaiming a new era of U.S. technological and economic dominance. Mortimer Zuckerman, editor of *U.S. News and World*

Report, announced America's economy is better suited for today's rapidly changing knowledge-based economy than it was for the mass production industrial economy (Zuckerman, 1998:23). Paul Krugman stated that "the current sense that the United States is on top of the world, is based on a huge exaggeration of the implications of a few bad years elsewhere" (Krugman, 1998:45).

My own sense is that each of the three national systems discussed in this chapter will face enormous difficulties in achieving rapid sustained growth in productivity and income in the early decades of the twenty-first century. The United States will be forced to confront the enormous gap in income distribution and the large deficit in the quality of its education and health services that emerged during the last quarter of the twentieth century, and it will be forced to complete the restructuring of its science and technology innovation systems to meet the needs of a post-Cold War environment. The reforms in education and health to enhance the human capital accumulation necessary to sustain growth in productivity remain to be made (Van Opstal, 1998/99). Japan will be forced to modernize its largely traditional service economy, particularly its financial markets, to sustain its world-class manufacturing capacity, and its political system will be forced to accommodate the transition of its economic policies from those appropriate for a "development state" to a liberal political and economic order. Germany (and Europe more generally) will be faced with completing the economic and political integration involved in a European Union that will expand to include the former centrally planned economies of Central Europe if the energies and capacities of its sophisticated technology are to be released.

Given the uncertainty involved in navigating these enormous challenges, it would hardly be surprising if, by the second decade of the twenty-first century, much of what is written today about the trajectories of the national innovational systems of the United States, Japan, and Germany will appear both premature and naive. It is much easier to rationalize the past than to anticipate the future.

REFERENCES

Abelshauser, W. "Two Kinds of Fordism: On the Differing Roles of the Industry in the Development of the Two German States." In *Fordism Transformed: The Development of Production Methods in the Automobile Industry,* H. Shiomi and K. Wada, eds., pp. 269–296. Oxford, UK: Oxford University Press, 1995.

Abo, T., ed. *Hybrid Factory: The Japanese Production System in the United States.* New York: Oxford University Press, 1994.

Abramson, H. N., J. Encarnação, P. Reid, and U. Schmoch, eds. *Technology Transfer Systems in the United States and Germany.* Washington, DC: National Academy Press, 1997.

Ames, E., and N. Rosenberg. "The Enfield Arsenal in Theory and History." *Economic Journal* 78 (1968):827–842.

Blumenthal, T. "Factor Proportions and Choice of Technology: The Japanese Experience." *Economic Development and Cultural Change* 28 (April 1980):547–559.

Blumenthal, T. "Factor Proportions and Choice of Technology: The Japanese Experience: Reply." *Economic Development and Cultural Change* 29 (July, 1981):845–848.

Broadberry, S. N. "Technological Leadership and Productivity Leadership in Manufacturing Since the Industrial Revolution: Implications for the Convergence Debate." *Economic Journal* 104 (1994):291–302.

Cain, L. P., and D. G. Patterson. "Factor Bias and Technical Change in Manufacturing: The American System." *Journal of Economic History* 41 (June 1981):341–360.

Callon, S. *Divided Sun: MITI and the Breakdown of Japanese High-Tech Industrial Policy, 1975–1993.* Stanford, CA: Stanford University Press, 1995.

Chandler, A. D., Jr. *Strategy and Structure: Chapters in the History of the Industrial Enterprise.* Cambridge, MA: MIT Press, 1962.

Chandler, A. D., Jr. *The Visible Head: The Managerial Revolution in American Business.* Cambridge, MA: Harvard University Press, 1977.

Clark, G. "Why Isn't the Whole World Developed? Lessons from the Cotton Mills." *Journal of Economic History* 47 (March 1987):141–173.

Clark, G. "Can Management Develop the World: Reply to Wilkins." *Journal of Economic History* 48 (March 1988):143–148.

Clark, G. "Why Isn't the Whole World Developed? A Reply to Hanson." *Journal of Economic History* 49 (September 1989):707–714.

Clark, G. "Textile History as World History: Labor Organization as World History: Labor Organization and Productivity in England, the USA, India and Japan." Davis, CA: University of California, Department of Economics, March 1992 (mimeo).

Cusumano, M. A. *The Japanese Automobile Industry: Technology, and Management at Nissan and Toyota.* Cambridge, MA: Harvard University Press, 1985.

Detouzos, M. L., R. K. Lester, and R. M. Solow. *Made in America: Regaining the Productive Edge.* Cambridge, MA: The MIT Press, 1989.

Eaton, J., E. Gutierrez, and S. Kortum. *European Technology Policy.* Cambridge, MA: National Bureau of Economic Research, 1998.

Edbaum, B., and W. Lanzonick, eds. *The Decline of the British Economy.* Oxford, UK: Oxford University Press, 1986.

Ergas, H. "Does Technology Policy Matter?" In *Technologies and Global Industry: Companies and Nations in the World Economy,* B. R. Guile and H. Brooks, eds., pp. 191–245. Washington, DC: National Academy Press, 1987a.

Ergas, H. "The Importance of Technology Policy." In *Economic Policy and Technology Performance,* P. Dasgupta and P. Stoneman, eds., pp. 51–96. Cambridge, MA: Cambridge University Press, 1987b.

Fallows, J. "Containing Japan." *The Atlantic* 263 (1989):40–54.

Fei, J. C. H., and G. Ranis. "Factor Proportions and Choice of Technology: The Japanese Experience: Comment." *Economic Development and Cultural Change* 29 (July, 1981): 841–844.

Florida, R., and M. Kenney. *The Breakthrough Illusion: Corporate America's Failure to Move from Innovation to Mass Production.* New York: Harper Collins, 1990.

Ford, H. "Mass Production." *Encyclopedia Britannica,* 13th ed., Supplement Vol. 2, 1926:821–823.

Halberstam, D. *The Reckoning.* New York: William Morrow, 1986.

Hanson, J. R. II. "Why Isn't the Whole World Developed? A Traditional View." *Journal of Economic History* 48 (September 1988):668–672.

Hatsopoulos, G. N., P. Krugman, and L. Summers. "U.S. Competitiveness: Beyond the Trade Deficit." *Science* 241 (July 15, 1988):299–307.

Hayami, Y. "Japan in the New World Confrontation: A Historical Perspective." *The Japanese Economic Review* 46 (1995):351–357.

Hayami, Y., and J. Ogasawara. "Changes in the Sources of Modern Economic Growth: Japan Compared with the United States." *Journal of the Japanese and International Economics* 13 (1999):1–21.

Heppenheimer, T. A. "What Made Bell Labs Great." *Invention and Technology* 12 (1996):46–56.

Hoffman, K., and R. Kaplinsky. *Driving Force: The Global Restructuring of Technology, Labor and Investment in the Automobile and Components Industries.* Boulder, CO: Westview Press, 1988.

Howe, C. *The Origins of Japanese Trade Supremacy: Development and Technology in Asia from 1540 to the Pacific War.* Chicago, IL: University of Chicago Press, 1996.

Hounshell, D. A. "The System: Theory and Practice." In *Yankee Enterprise: The Rise of the American System of Manufacturers*, O. Mayer and R. C. Post, eds., pp. 127–152. Washington, DC: Smithsonian Institution Press, 1981.

Hounshell, D. A. *From the American System to Mass Production, 1800–1932.* Baltimore, MD: Johns Hopkins University Press, 1984.

Hounshell, D. A. "Planning and Executing 'Automation' at Ford Motor company, 1945–65: The Cleveland Engine Plant and Its Consequences." In *Fordism Transformed: The Development of Production Methods in the Automobile Industry,* H. Shiomi and K. Wada, eds., pp. 49–86. Oxford, UK: Oxford University Press, 1995.

Hughes, J. *The Vital Few: The Entrepreneur and American Economic Progress.* New York: Oxford University Press, 1986.

Johnson, B. *We Were Burning: Japanese Entrepreneurs and the Forging of the Electronic Age.* Boulder, CO: Westview Press, 1999.

Katz, R. *Japan: The System that Soured: The Rise and the Fall of the Japanese Economic Miracle*, Armonk; NY: M. E. Sharp, 1998.

Kleck, O. "The National System for Technical Innovation in Germany." In *National Innovation Systems: A Comparative Analysis,* R. R. Nelson, ed., pp. 115–157. New York: Oxford University Press, 1993.

Kenney, M., and R. Florida. *Beyond Mass Production: The Japanese System and Its Transfer to the U.S.* Oxford, UK: Oxford University Press, 1993.

Krugman, P. A. *Rethinking International Trade.* Cambridge, MA: MIT Press, 1990.

Krugman, P. A. "Myths and Realities of U.S. Competitiveness." *Science* 254 (November 8, 1991):811–815.

Krugman, P. A. *The Age of Diminished Expectations: U.S. Economic Policy in the 1990s*, 3rd ed. Cambridge, MA: MIT Press, 1997.

Krugman, P. A. "American the Boastful." *Foreign Affairs* 77 (May/June 1998):32–45.

Laux, J. M. *The European Automobile Industry.* New York: Twane Publishers, 1992.

Layton, E. "Mirror Image Twins: The Communities of Science and Technology in 19th Century America." *Technology and Culture* 12 (1971):562–580.

Lenoir, T. "Revolution from Above: The Role of the State in Creating the German Research System, 1810–1910." *American Economic Review* 88 (1998):22–27.

Luker, W., Jr., and D. Lyons. "Employment Shifts in High technology Industries, 1988–96." *Monthly Labor Review* 120 (June 1998):12–25.

Mansfield, E. "Industrial R&D in Japan and the United States: A Comparative Study." *American Economic Review* 78 (May 1988):223–228.

Markham, J. W. "The Joint Effect of Antitrust and Patent Law Upon Innovation." *American Economic Review* 56 (May 1966):291–300.

Mazzoleni, R. "Innovation in the Machine Tool Industry: A Historical Perspective on Comparative Advantage." In D. C. Mowery and R. R. Nelson, eds., pp. 169–216. Cambridge, UK: Cambridge University Press, 1999.

McCraw, T. K. "Henry Ford and Alfred Sloan." In *Management Past and Present: A Casebook on the History of American Business,* A. D. Chandler, Jr., T. K. McCraw, and R. S. Tedlow, eds., pp. 6-6–6-30. Cincinnati, OH: Southwestern College Publishing, 1996.

Mokyr, J. *The Lever of Riches: Technological Creativity and Economic Progress.* New York: Oxford University Press, 1990.

Mowery, D. C. "The Development of Industrial Research in U.S. Manufacturing." *American Economic Review* 80 (May 1990):345–349.

Mowery, D. C. "The Changing Structure of the U.S. National Innovation System: Implications for International Conflict and Cooperation in R&D." *Research Policy* 27 (1998):639–654.

Mowery, D. C., and N. Rosenberg. *Technology and the Pursuit of Economic Growth.* New York: Oxford University Press, 1989.

Mowery, D. C., and N. Rosenberg. "The U.S. National Innovation System." In *National Innovation Systems: A Comparative Analysis*, Richard Nelson, ed., pp. 29–75. New York: Oxford University Press, 1993.

Murray, A. "New Economic Models Fail While American, Inc. Keeps Rolling: Why?" *Wall Street Journal*, Dec. 8, 1997:1, 13.

National Science Foundation. *Human Resources for Science and Technology: The European Region.* Arlington, VA: NSF Special Report 96–316, 1996.

Nelson, R.R., ed. *National Innovation Systems: A Comparative Analysis.* New York: Oxford University Press, 1993.

Nelson, R. R., and N. Rosenberg. "The U.S. National Innovation System." In *National Innovation Systems: A Comparative Analysis,* Richard Nelson, ed., pp. 3–21. New York: Oxford University Press, 1993.

Nelson, R. R., and G. Wright. "The Rise and Fall of American Technological Leadership: The Postwar Era in Historical Perspective." *The Journal of Economic Literature* 23 (December 1992):1931–1964.

Odagiri, H., and A. Goto. "The Japanese System of Innovation: Past, Present, and Future." In *National Innovation Systems: A Comparative Analysis,* R. Nelson, ed., pp. 76–114. New York: Oxford University Press, 1993.

Otsuka, K., G. Ranis, and G. Saxonhouse. *Comparative Technology Choice in Development: The Indian and Japanese Cotton Textile Industries.* New York: St. Martin's Press, 1988.

Patel, P., and K. Pavitt. "The Technological Competencies of the World's Largest Firms: Complex and Path-Dependent, But Not Much Variety." *Research Policy* 26 (1997):141–166.

Porter, M. E. *The Competitive Advantage of Nations.* New York: Free Press, 1990.

Porter, M. E., and H. Takeuchi. "Fixing What Really Ails Japan." *Foreign Affairs* 78 (May/June 1999):66–81.

Prestowitz, C. V., Jr. *Trading Places: How We Allowed Japan to Take the Lead.* New York: Basic Books, 1988.

Prestowitz, C. V., Jr. "Playing to Win." *Foreign Affairs* (July/August 1994):186–189.

Reich, L. S. *The Making of American Industrial Research: Science and Business at GE and Bell, 1876–1926.* Cambridge, UK: Cambridge University Press, 1985.

Riche, R. W., D. E. Hecker, and J. U. Burgan. "High Technology Today and Tomorrow: A Small Slice of the Employment Pie." *Monthly Labor Review* 106 (November 1983):50–58.

Rosenberg, N. "Technological Change in the Machine Tool Industry, 1840–1910." *Journal of Economic History* 23 (1963):414–443.

Rosenberg, N. *Technology and American Economic Growth.* New York: Harper & Row, 1972.

Rosenberg, N., and W. E. Steinmueller. "Why Are Americans Such Poor Imitators?" *American Economic Review* 78 (May 1988):229–234.

Rostow, W. W. *The Stages of Economic Growth: A Non Communist Manifesto,* 3rd ed. Cambridge, UK: Cambridge University Press, 1990.

Samuels, R. J. *Rich Nation, Strong Army: National Security and the Technological Transformation of Japan.* Ithaca, NY: Cornell University Press, 1994.

Sawyer, J. E. "The Social Basis of the American System of Manufacturing." *Journal of Economic History* 14 (1954):361–379.

Servan-Schreiber, J. J. *The American Challenge.* New York: Avon, 1971.

Service, R. F. "Relaunching Bell Labs." *Science* 272 (1996):638–639.

Shimokawa, K. *The Ever Changing Competition between the Japanese and U.S. Auto Industry.* Tokyo, Japan: Jiji Tsushin Sha, 1997 (in Japanese).

Taylor, F. W. *The Principles of Scientific Management.* New York: Harper and Brothers, 1911.

Teese, P. J. "Capturing Value from Technological Innovation: Integration, Strategic Partnering and Licensing Decisions." In *Technology and Global Industry,* B. R. Guile and H. Brooks, eds., pp. 65–95. Washington, DC: National Academy of Engineering Press, 1987.

Vogel, E. F. *Japan as Number 1: Lessons for America.* New York: Harper & Row, 1979.

Volti, R. "A Century of Automobility." *Technology and Culture* 37 (October 1996):663–685.

Von Opstal. "The New Competitive Landscape." *Issues in Science and Technology* 15 (Winter 1998/99):47–54.

Weiner, M. J. *English Culture and the Decline of the Industrial Spirit: 1850–1980.* London: Cambridge University Press, 1981.

Wilkins, M. "Efficiency and Management: A Comment on Gregory Clark's 'Why Isn't the Whole World Developed?' " *Journal of Economic History* 47 (December 1987):981–983.

Wilkins, M., and F. E. Hill. *American Business Abroad: Ford on Six Continents.* Detroit, MI: Wayne State University Press, 1964.

Womack, J. P. "The U.S. Automobile Industry in an Era of International Competition: Performance and Prospects." In *Working Papers of the MIT Commission on Industrial Productivity, Vol. 1,* pp. 1–51. Cambridge, MA: MIT Press, 1989.

Womack, J. P., D. T. Jones, and D. Roos. *The Machine that Changed the World.* New York: Harper Collins, 1991.

Zuckerman, M. B. "A Second American Century." *Foreign Affairs* 77 (May/June 1998):18–31.

CHAPTER 12

Technology, Resources, and Environment

A belief that the application of science to the solution of practical problems represented a sure foundation for human progress has been a persistent theme in American intellectual and economic history. During the first two decades following World War II this belief was seemingly confirmed by the dramatic association between the progress of science and technology and rapid economic growth. The technological revolution in American agriculture, the growth of industrial productivity, the contributions of science to military and space technology, and the virtual elimination of the business cycle seemed to reinforce this perspective.[1]

Beginning in the mid-1960s, however, the formula that had permitted the United States to move into a position of scientific and technical leadership in the world community was faced with both an intellectual and a populist challenge. A view emerged that the potential consequences of modern science and technology—reflected in the cataclysm of war, degradation of the environment, and psychological cost of rapid social change—were obviously dangerous to the modern world and to the future of humankind. The result was to seriously question the significance for human welfare of scientific progress, technical change, and economic growth.

A central issue in this chapter is the relationship between changing resource endowments and technical and institutional change (Chapter 5). The externalities and spillovers associated with agricultural and industrial intensification have dramatically enhanced the value of formerly open-access natural resources. Since the beginning of the industrial revolution increases in the price of labor relative to raw materials and capital have been a powerful force inducing technical change. During the latter half of the twentieth century, increases in the value of open-access natural resources have become a powerful force inducing both technical and institutional change. The value of these resources—including water, air, and natural environments—has been inadequately reflected in economic markets. Efforts have been made to design institutional innovations that limit the distortions in economic incentives associated

[1] I am indebted to Sandra Archibald, Jay S. Coggins, William K, Easter, Arnulf Grubler, Frances R. Homans, Robert W. Kates, Joseph V. Kennedy, Allan V. Kneese, Stephen Polasky, C. Ford Runge, James R. Roumasset, Lore M. Ruttan, V. Kerry Smith, Robert N. Stavins, Douglas A. Tiffany, and Iddo Wernick for comments on an earlier draft of this chapter. Many of the issues covered in this chapter are discussed in a survey article by Dasgupta and Mäler (1995).

with externalities. The first phase of institutional innovations involved new regulations designed to limit the disposal of residuals into the environment. Beginning in the 1980s, regulations have been supplemented with economic incentives to correct the distortions associated with the earlier "command-and-control" approaches. An example, discussed later in this chapter, is the tradable permit designed to limit sulfur dioxide emissions from coal-fired electricity generators.

THREE WAVES OF CONCERN

The United States has experienced three major waves of concern about the adequacy of natural resources to sustain economic growth since World War II (Bennett, 1949).

Resource Requirements for Growth

During the late 1940s and early 1950s there was intense speculation about the future development and availability of the earth's natural resources. This first postwar wave of concern focused primarily on the quantitative relations between resource availability and growth—the adequacy of land, water, energy, minerals, and other natural resources to sustain growth. In 1952 the President's Materials Policy (Paley) Commission concluded that "in the U.S. the supplies of the evident, the cheap, the accessible are running out." In the half century since the Paley report there has been a decline in the resource component of national output and both an absolute and relative decline in employment in the resource sectors (Barnett and Morse, 1963; Ausubel and Sladovich, 1989). If the Materials Policy Commission were writing today, it would have to conclude that there have been abundant examples "of the nonevident becoming evident; the expensive, cheap; and the inaccessible, accessible" (Ruttan, 1971:708). A stretch of high prices has seldom failed to induce successful efforts to locate new deposits, exploit old ones, and promote substitution of more abundant for relatively scarce resources.

Demand for Environmental Services

In the second postwar wave of natural resource policy, traditional concern with the ability of the natural resource base to sustain growth was supplemented by concern with the capacity of the environment to assimilate pollution generated by growth. An intense conflict emerged between two sources of demand for environmental services. One was the rising demand for the traditional environmental service of assimilating the residuals derived from growth in commodity production and consumption— chemicals in our water, asbestos in our insulation, pesticides in our food, smog in the air, and radioactive wastes in the biosphere. The second was the rapid growth in consumer demand for environmental amenities, such as clean water and clean air, due to growth in population and in per capita income. Competition between the demand for environmental services for disposal of residuals and the demand for resource amenities was associated with a dramatic rise in the value that society placed on these environmental amenities formerly regarded as free goods (Ayres and Kneese, 1969). These concerns precipitated a vigorous debate about the limits to economic growth—whether environmental quality was consistent with economic growth (Ehrlich and Ehrlich, 1970; Meadows et al., 1972; Nordhaus, 1973b). The response to these concerns, still incomplete, was to design institutions to induce individual firms and other organizations to bear the costs arising from the externalities generated by commodity production.

Global Change

Since the late 1980s earlier concerns about resources and the environment have been supplemented by a third. These newer concerns center around environmental changes that are occurring on a transnational scale, such as global warming, ozone depletion, acid rain, pollution of international waters, and others (Committee on Global Change, 1990; Committee on Science, Engineering and Public Policy, 1991).[2] The institutional innovations needed to respond to these problems are more difficult to design. They will, like the sources of change, need to be transnational or international. Experience with attempts to design incentive-compatible transnational institutional innovations, even the relatively successful Montreal Protocol on reduction of ozone-depleting chemical emissions, suggests the difficulty of resolving free-rider and distributional equity issues when there is still substantial uncertainty about the scale and implications of environmental change (Lambright, 1995). These difficulties impose severe constraints on how rapidly effective transnational regimes to resolve concerns such as global climate change can be designed and implemented (Ruttan, 1994a:9, 10).

There has also been a change in focus from the "limits-to-growth" concerns of the late 1960s and early 1970s to a concern for both enhancing environmental quality and sustaining economic growth. This new focus reflects the impossibility of convincing the rich nations that they should curb their economic growth, and of convincing the poor nations that they should not try to catch up. Attention has shifted to how growth could be achieved in a sustainable manner (Pearce and Warford, 1993:7; National Research Council, 1999).

RESOURCE ECONOMICS

The conservation movement and the environmental movement draw on very different popular and intellectual roots.

---

[2] Global change has been defined as "transformation processes that operate at a truly planetary scale plus processes that operate at smaller scales but that are so ubiquitous and pervasive as to assume global importance" (Grübler, 1998:3). An example of the first type of global change is global warming. An example of the second type is urban air pollution.

> The conservation movement has been technologically optimistic and chiefly con-
> cerned with the efficient use of resources. It has sought to avoid waste by promot-
> ing the rational and efficient use of nature's wealth. Moreover, the leaders of the
> conservation movement have generally not questioned, but rather have attempted
> to inform the system of political authority about the consequences of alternative
> resource and environmental problems. The environmental movement, in contrast,
> has been more normative in orientation. It has attempted to demonstrate that the
> unintended negative impacts of human economic activities on the environment are
> often excessive. (Marcus, 1993:413)

In this and several following sections I discuss the subject matter and the concepts
employed in the subfields of resource, environmental, and ecological economics.[3] In
spite of somewhat different subject matter, a central analytical and policy concern of
the three subfields is the externalities generated by human activity.[4] I first consider
the role of technical change in enhancing, degrading, or exhausting natural resource
endowments within the framework of traditional resource economics. In discussing
these issues it is useful to consider the principles that apply to the use of nonrenewable
and renewable resources separately.

Nonrenewable Resources

One distinguishing feature of a nonrenewable resource is that it is used up when
employed as an input in production. A second is that its total stock is determined by
nature. New deposits or reserves can be discovered. But the sum of all "proven" and
undiscovered reserves must be taken as given, at least for economically meaningful
geologic time. This holds even if the resource is recycled after it has been used. It
is not technically feasible or economically viable to recover the entire quantity used.
For example, it is not possible to recover an entire ton of secondary copper from a
ton of primary copper after it has been used, nor an entire ton of secondary copper
after it has been used. There will be leakage during every round of recycling.

Ensuring a supply of a nonrenewable natural resource for the future is more difficult
than maintaining reproducible capital such as plant and equipment.[5] Even if almost the

---

[3] For a very useful review of the development of the field of resource economics, see Kneese (1995).
For a useful introductory discussion of many of the issues discussed on this and subsequent sections, see
Oates (1999).

[4] An externality exists whenever the welfare of one agent, either a firm or a household, depends on the
activities of some other agent. The term *external diseconomy* refers to a situation in which the affected
party is damaged by actions of the other agent. Smoke pollution generated by coal-burning power plants
is an example of an external diseconomy. *External economy* refers to a situation in which the affected
party benefits from the externality. The benefits from research and development that are not captured by
the firm that conducts the research are examples of an external economy. Markets that are characterized by
externalities cannot be relied on to realize efficient resource allocation. External economies or diseconomies
occur as a consequence of "market failure" (Scitovsky, 1954; Tietenberg, 1992:51–54).

[5] It may, of course, be possible to extend the availability of a natural resource by energy-intensive
technologies that facilitate extraction from lower quality deposits. In the case of copper, the solvent

entire stock of reproducible capital were destroyed it could be replaced over time—sometimes quite rapidly as in the case of Germany and Japan after World War II. In contrast, if the world's stock of fossil fuel were destroyed, it could not be recreated (Common, 1975:8). The basic rule for sustaining consumption in a simple economy (that is not experiencing technical change in resource extraction) is that investment in reproducible capital, both physical and human, must be equivalent to the economic depletion of the nonrenewable resource. In effect, reductions in natural capital must be offset by increases in other forms of capital to maintain the level of consumption. This implies that whether productive capital should be transmitted across generations in the form of mineral deposits or reproducible capital is more a matter of efficiency than of intergenerational equity (Hartwick, 1977:972–974; Solow, 1986:143).

Since nonrenewable natural resource stocks provide no service by being held in undeveloped form, owners must be compensated for holding them instead of depleting them as fast as possible. Harold Hotelling (1931) was the first to demonstrate that under extremely simplified conditions—constant marginal extraction costs, a competitive market for the resource product, an accurate knowledge of reserves—the price of an extractive resource product would have to rise as least as fast as the return that could be obtained by holding some other reasonably secure asset such as a U.S. treasury bill (Pindyck, 1978; Berck, 1995).

In a more complex world the Hotelling rule must be modified.[6] The effect of a change in extraction costs is to widen the wedge between the price of resource stocks and the price of resource products. If costs rise as extraction is extended to more marginal deposits, the price can be expected to rise more rapidly than the market rate of interest or the discount rate. If the cost of extraction declines due, for example, to technical change, the price may decline. Thus in a more complex economy resource rents (the value of the resource in the ground) and the most profitable rate of resource extraction will depend on both the cost of holding the resource and the cost of extraction.[7]

In a study conducted in the early 1960s, Barnett and Morse (1963) drew on the Hotelling analysis to determine whether resources were becoming increasingly scarce. Traditionally geologists and policy analysts had used potential reserves of natural resources as measures of resource scarcity (Figure 12.1). Barnett and Morse insisted that an appropriate indicator of scarcity should reflect the terms on which resources became available to users—"the sacrifice made, direct and indirect, to obtain a unit of the resource" (Fisher, 1979:252). Two scarcity indexes were developed. One, which

---

extraction–electric winning process (Sx-Ew) has enabled producers to recover commercial quantities of copper from waste dumps that were abandoned as a result of earlier less efficient methods of extraction (Tilton and Landsberg, 1999).

[6] Much of the theoretical research on the economics of exhaustible resources since the renewal of interest in Hotelling's work in the 1960s has involved attempts to elaborate the Hotelling model to incorporate more realistic assumptions about extraction costs, depletion costs, technical change, and uncertainty (Hartwick 1977; Solow, 1974; Fisher, 1979; Smith, 1979, 1980; Farzin, 1995).

[7] The existence of two interconnected markets, for resource deposits and for resource commodities, has the effect of dampening tendencies for disequilibrium in either the resource market or the commodity market (Solow, 1974).

they termed the weak test, was based on the unit cost of extraction. A second, which they termed the strong test, was based on the price of natural resource products relative to an index of the prices of goods produced in other sectors. The strong test meets the Fisher criteria that both direct and indirect sacrifices should be reflected in the scarcity measure.[8]

Barnett and Morse (1963) found, to the surprise of most observers, that (1) for almost all extractive products, the average private cost of extraction, in constant prices, fell over the period 1870–1960; and (2) for almost all extractive products, prices fell slightly in real terms during this period. The one exception was for forest stumpage (standing timber) prices. In a 1979 reanalysis, using a longer data series, Barnett concluded that their results were broadly in agreement with their earlier analysis (Barnett, 1979:186). By the late 1970s it was generally accepted by economists that

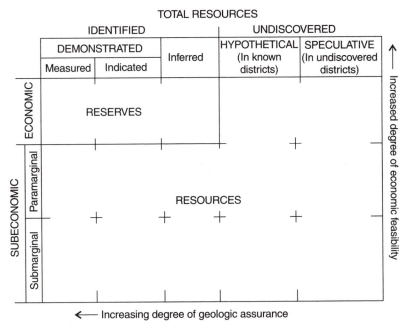

Figure 12.1 U.S. Geological Survey's classification system (McKelvey Box). (*Source:* V. Kerry Smith, "The Evaluation of National Resource Adequacy: Elusive Quest on Frontier of Economic Analysis," *Land Economics* (August, 1980):266.)

---

[8] The unit cost measure employed by Barnett and Morse is, in effect, an index of the input requirements per unit of extractive output (Smith, 1980). Smith characterizes the unit cost test as classical and the price test as neoclassical. The Barnett–Morse tests had been anticipated by Theodore W. Schultz (1951) in a study that indicated that the contribution of land to agricultural production relative to labor and capital in the United States and the United Kingdom had declined (1951). In poor countries the services of natural resources continue to account for a relatively high share of the inputs into production and consumption.

the price system provided the most effective available indicator of resource scarcity. A secular decline in the real price of a resource product (of crude oil or wheat, for example) relative to the general price level could be regarded as a reasonably accurate measure of a reduction in resource scarcity. Similarly, a secular increase in the price of a resource product relative to the general price level could be regarded as a reasonably accurate indicator of an increase in resource scarcity.

A number of theoretical objections have been raised regarding the reliability of the Barnett–Morse formulation (Dasgupta and Heal, 1979:464–469; Berck, 1995; Farzin, 1995). One is that the price of the raw material itself can rarely be observed. Only the price of the processed raw material can typically be observed. The price of the processed raw material may, depending on factors such as the capital intensity of the process technology and imperfections in the market for the *in situ* raw material, represent a biased measure of scarcity. The market price may not, for example, capture the spillover effects on the environment from mining operations. Much of the theoretical argument has centered around the effects of lower extraction costs on the rate of depletion. If lower extraction costs lead to more rapid depletion, resource rents may rise faster than in the absence of technical change (Farzin, 1995).

A reworking of the historical data, using more sophisticated statistical methods, has also raised questions about the Barnett–Morse conclusions. In studies completed in the late 1970s Kerry Smith, a colleague of Barnett's at Resources for the Future, found the evidence insufficient to support the Barnett–Morse conclusion that resource scarcity had declined (Smith, 1979, 1980). A few years later Margaret Slade presented a reanalysis that suggested a U-shaped time path for the real prices of most exhaustible resource products (Slade, 1982). Slade argued that the U-shaped curve reflects initial dominance of resource discoveries and productivity improvements over resource depletion and extraction costs followed by the dominance of depletion and extraction costs in the later stages of extraction. The Slade results were tested again, and confirmed, a decade later by Moazzami and Anderson (1994). The long-term implications of the criticisms advanced in the late 1970s and early 1980s seem less compelling today than they did at that time. During the 1980s and 1990s the real prices of energy resources resumed their downward trend. The real prices of most minerals also declined (Nordhaus, 1992; Simpson, 1999).

The most frequently suggested factors in explaining the apparent resiliency of modern production activities in the face of apparent narrowing of the resource base are (1) the substitution of other inputs for nonrenewable resources, and (2) technical changes induced by resource scarcity. Empirical estimates of the short-run elasticity of substitution between resource inputs and other factors, at existing levels of technology, are generally less than unity (Binswanger and Ruttan, 1978:235–239; Smith, 1980; Thompson and Taylor, 1995). In the absence of resource-augmenting technical change, if the elasticity of substitution between capital and natural resources is less than unity, consumption must ultimately decline to zero (Smith and Krutilla, 1984). Thus the impact of substitution, in the absence of resource-saving technical change, is primarily to slow the tendency of resource prices to rise.

The second possibility, of induced technical change biased in a resource-saving direction, would seem to carry more weight as a source of declining real prices of exhaustible resources. Research by Jorgenson and Fraumeni (1981) indicates that from 1957 to 1974 technical change in 29 of 36 industries studied was material saving and energy using. The effect of resource-saving technical change is to widen the possibility of substitution. Apparently the decline of energy prices relative to other raw material prices during the period studied induced changes in technology that led to the substitution of energy for raw materials in extraction, processing, and use (Chapter 7).

The issue of induced technical change is closely linked to the availability of back-stop technology.[9] Investment in technology development and exploitation of backstop technology typically lag until either physical or economic indicators of scarcity become apparent. Substantial technical effort is often required to make backstop technology economically viable. For example, it was not until the Minnesota Mesabi iron range's high-quality ore approached exhaustion that the steel companies and researchers at the University of Minnesota directed research effort toward the development of technologies for exploiting the enormous deposits of low-grade taconite. Similarly, U.S. copper producers were induced by the exhaustion of high-grade deposits and foreign competition to search for more efficient extraction processes (Slade, 1982; Tilton and Landsberg, 1999).

My sense is that a combination of induced technical change in resource exploration, in the development and use of backstop technology, and in raw material utilization makes the issue of inadequate nonrenewable resources less urgent than seemed apparent at the time of the President's Materials Policy Commission report (1952) or the resource assessment studies of the 1970s (National Commission on Materials Policy, 1973; National Commission on Supplies and Shortages, 1976).

There have, however, been major limitations in much of the literature on nonrenewable resources. Much of the literature has been narrowly focused on the direct use of material resources as raw material inputs for production and consumption. The spillover effects of the residuals generated by the extraction processing and use of these materials—air and water pollution, for example—were given little attention in the traditional resource economics literature. The services provided by the whole range of open-access environmental services as inputs into production of resource commodities were neglected in both the modeling and in empirical research.[10]

Renewable Resources

In contrast to nonrenewable resources, renewable resources can provide a continuous flow of services as long as the environment in which they are nurtured remains

---

[9] A backstop technology can provide large quantities of substitutes for a depleted resource at a reasonably close cost. The backstop technology ensures the existence of a "choke price" equal to the marginal cost of the backstop technology. Lower grade ore, as in the case of copper cited above by Slade, is an example of a backstop technology.

[10] See Krutilla (1972), Howe (1979:256–329), and Smith and Krutilla (1979).

favorable. Thus soil resources, if carefully managed, can provide a constant flow of services over time. Atmospheric pollutants, particulates, and gases are dispersed by wind and rain, and, if pollution is reduced sufficiently, air quality in a particular airshed can be maintained at acceptable levels over long periods of time. The flow of resource services from a renewable resource may be diminished or enhanced depending on the management of the resource.

The basic principles for sustaining consumption of a renewable resource over time, even in a very simple economy, are more complicated than for an exhaustible resource. Many renewable resources, even after substantial depletion or degradation, are capable of self-renewal. Water, for example, generally undergoes a self-cleansing process. But this process depends on the rate at which pollutants are deposited. If the rate of deposition of pollutants is unduly high over a period of years it may take a very long time, even after the rate of pollution is reduced to a sustainable level, for regeneration to occur. In the case of fish and other wildlife, if depletion is carried too far, the viability of a species may be endangered or the capacity for regeneration may be destroyed.

Sustaining the yield of a renewable resource will often depend on whether the resource is exploited under an open-access, communal, private, or state property regime. The distinction between open-access and communal property was initially advanced by Ciriacy-Wantrup and Bishop (1975). In a communal property regime, a relatively stable structure of norms and conventions governs rights to the common resources. Examples range from Swiss village communities' management of members' rights to graze animals on the Alpine pastures held in common by the village to cooperation among Indonesian villagers to defend access to and regulate the harvesting of mother-of-pearl shell (Netting, 1972, 1976; Ruttan, 1998). In contrast, in an open-access regime there are no enforceable rules regarding individual use. When access is governed by an open-access regime, exploitation will continue to the point that the resource is not capable of recovery without a change in property regime or, in some extreme cases, is unable to recover at all.[11] It is important to distinguish between open access and common property for appropriate policy design. The problems of open access arise from unrestricted entry. These problems arise in a number of structurally similar cases such as fishing, extraction of oil and natural gas, depletion of underground water aquifers, and depletion or degradation of air and water resources (Runge, 1981).

In the case of fisheries, how far a species may be driven toward extinction is influenced by the cost of operating fishing vessels relative to the price at which the fish is marketed. The lower the cost of operating the fishing vessel, the more

---

[11] Several important early works in the field of resource and environmental economics used the term common property to refer to both open-access and communal property (Hardin, 1968; Dasgupta and Heal, 1979; Baumol and Oates, 1975). Open access is the absence of property rights with no restraint on entry or exit; under communal property access rights are restricted to an identifiable group of users. The Hardin article has been the subject of extended controversy. For a useful review see Feeny et al. (1996). For a useful analytical treatment see Runge (1981).

likely the catch will be driven toward exhaustion. As the technology of harvesting improves, larger trawling vessels and more efficient nets, for example, the cost of harvesting declines. This trend speeds the rate at which populations approach the critical minimum level that permits regeneration. But why do firms not anticipate the effects of more intensive exploitation and limit their catch, as in the case of a nonrenewable resource? The traditional answer is that firms may not understand the population dynamics of the species being exploited in a particular catchment area. There may be no natural indicator that enables firms to know that exploitation has proceeded beyond the point of regeneration.

Dasgupta and Heal (1979) have argued that for a pure open-access regime, optimal policy involves two alternative measures. One is a tax on each unit of the species that is removed from the catchment area. This corrects for the fact that the species, in its natural environment, has a positive "shadow price" or value that the exploiting firms avoid in an unregulated open-access regime. A second is a tax on each vessel that operates in the catchment area. This partly corrects for the fact that as long as the catchment area is managed as an unregulated common property the firms that operate vessels do not bear the cost of the damage that entry of an additional vessel imposes on operators of vessels already operating in the catchment area. It is possible, of course, that the management of the resource, including the imposition of fees on the catch and the vessel, could be operated by a group or cooperative with or without the support of government. At present, however, many of the world's major fisheries operate under what might be termed "regulated open access." In regulated open-access fisheries participants are free to enter but are subject to regulations such as gear restrictions, access to fishing grounds, and restrictions on the length of the fishing season. Homans and Wilen (1997) have argued that the regulations are most appropriately viewed as endogenously determined. They are induced by the biological dynamics of the fisheries population, the economic behavior of the fishing industry, and changes in fishing technology. The effect has been to transform formerly open-access fisheries resources into a quasicommon property system.

ENVIRONMENTAL ECONOMICS

The materials that enter into production and consumption must eventually emerge as residuals into the environment.[12] The focus of environmental economics is the regulation of the flow of the residuals (or pollutants) generated by production and consumption and the valuation of environmental amenities. This is in contrast to resource economics, which focuses on the exploitation and processing of the flow of raw materials into the production process (Figure 12.2).

---

[12] This insight was initially introduced into economics by Kneese (1964) and elaborated by Ayres and Kneese (1969), Kneese et al. (1970), and Mäler (1974). The results of the Resources for the Future program on residual management directed by Kneese are summarized in Kneese and Bower (1979).

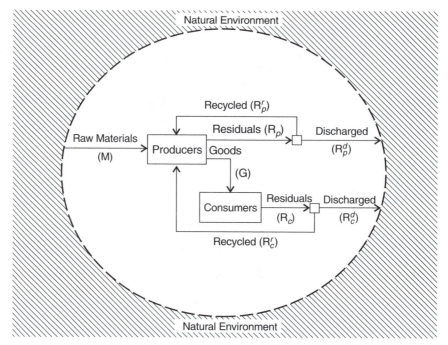

Figure 12.2 A materials balance view of the environment and the economy. (*Source:* Barry C. Field, *Environmental Economics: An Introduction*, 1994, New York: McGraw-Hill, p. 24. Reproduced with permission of The McGraw-Hill Companies.)

One can imagine that in many preindustrial societies there was a reasonable balance between human society and the environment. Plants and animals were harvested to meet human needs and waste materials were recycled back into the environment. But even in primitive and ancient society both technology and energy limited the capacity of communities to dispose of the residuals generated by human activity. Since the beginning of the industrial revolution, the large-scale extraction of raw materials and the exploitation of fossil fuels have intensified the problem of how to manage the residuals resulting from human activity in a manner that does not threaten the sustainability of human society. Among the industries studied earlier in this book the agricultural (Chapter 6), energy (Chapter 7), and chemical (Chapter 8) industries have been particularly important sources of environmental degradation.

During the second half of the twentieth century industrial economies have been confronted by rising demands for environmental services pressing against an inelastic supply.[13] This rising demand is the result of conflict between (1) the traditional demands on the environment to assimilate residuals derived from commodity production

---

[13] For a more detailed discussion of environmental or ecosystem services see Daily (1997). Daily uses the term ecosystem services to include (1) ecosystem goods such as the material products of natural environments, (2) life support functions such as cleansing, recycling, and renewal, and (3) the aesthetic and cultural amenities derived from natural environments.

and consumption and (2) the rising consumer demand for environmental amenities—for the direct consumption of environmental services—arising out of the rapid growth in per capita incomes and a high-income elasticity of demand for environmental services such as freedom from environmental hazards and access to natural environments. By the closing years of the twentieth century, as more formerly poor countries experienced both rapid industrialization and growth in per capita incomes, these concerns were no longer confined to the most affluent societies.

Externalities

A central issue of environmental economics centers around how to manage the externalities generated by production and consumption. The problem of externalities arises in rapidly growing modern and modernizing societies because open-access resources such as water, air, and natural environments continue to be undervalued for purposes of market transactions even as their economic value has risen. This is referred to in the economics literature as market failure.

Production theory implies that if the market price of a factor input is zero (or close to zero) that factor input will be used until the value to the firm of its marginal product approaches zero. This will occur even though the marginal social product may be negative. In an environment characterized by rapid technological change the effect of pricing open-access environmental resources at below their marginal social value will be to bias the direction of technical change and accelerate the growth in demand for the resources that are priced at or below their marginal social value. The demand will grow even more rapidly than in situations in which substitution possibilities occur only along a given production surface or within the constraints of existing technology (Chapter 6; Ruttan, 1971; Smith, 1972). As a result an open-access resource will undergo stress or degradation more rapidly than in a world characterized by static technology or even by neutral technical change (Chapter 2, Appendix). The effect is to accelerate the wedge between the private and social costs of environmental services. In contrast, if institutions can be designed to more adequately reflect the value of the open-access resources the effect will be to induce technical changes that reduce the discharge of residuals into the environment (Chapter 4).

Discussion by economists of how to design policies and institutions in response to the problem of externalities began with suggestions by Pigou, in his classic *The Economics of Welfare* (1932:172–205), that the problem of externalities could be resolved by an appropriate mix of taxes and subsidies. There was a tendency among economists, however, to regard externalities as an aberration. Pigou's suggestion remained largely neglected, except in the literature in market socialism, until the 1960s when the concern about the degradation of natural environments generated an intense debate about the appropriateness of the Pigovian prescriptions.[14]

---

[14] The best single review of these debates is Baumol (1972). See also Mishan (1971), Ruttan (1971), Mäler (1974), Baumol and Oates (1975), and Dasgupta and Mähler (1995:2414–2421). In the market socialism

Professional debate during the 1960s and early 1970s focused on the need and appropriate form of public intervention to manage the generation and disposal of residuals. An argument was advanced by Coase (1960) that there was no need for government intervention since both the perpetuators and the victims of pollution have incentives to directly negotiate reductions in pollution-producing activities. A criticism of the Coase argument was that excessive transaction costs would be incurred in negotiations involving large numbers of perpetuators and victims. Baumol (1972) responded to the Coase argument by showing, under highly simplified conditions, that imposing a Pigovian tax on the source of pollution—making the polluter pay—could represent an optimum solution. Mäler (1974) went on to show that if environmental managers had access to the appropriate information the same environmental objectives could be obtained at the same social cost by imposing either environmental standards or charges. The results would differ only in their distribution effects. Neither Baumol nor Mähler incorporated technical change in their models. In a dynamic model, in which technical change is taken into account, an effluent tax can be shown to be more effective than environmental standards in inducing technical change in an effluent-abatement direction (Magat, 1978).

Mäler also argued that effluent charges would impose less demanding information requirements on the resource planning and management agency. Either option, effluent charges or effluent standards, would require the monitoring of effluent discharges. In many cases, particularly for "nonpoint" sources of pollution, such monitoring is prohibitively expensive. This problem has led to a search for "second best" combinations of standards, charges, subsidies, and refunds that are operationally feasible to administer. One example is an extension of the "safe minimum standard" principle, initially proposed by Ciriacy-Wantrup (1952)[15] for the management of renewable resources, to problems of the disposal of residuals. Another example is the imposition of a tax on the production of products that, after their use, create hazardous waste combined with a refund if the product is delivered to an approved waste-collection site.

Valuation

The technique most commonly used by resource and environmental economists to assess the social benefits and costs associated with a resource development or conservation project or the implementation of resource use and environmental regulations is termed benefit–cost analysis. Benefit–cost analysis involves application of the principles of neoclassical welfare economics to generate information relevant to

---

literature, it was argued that it would be easier for a socialist economy than a capitalist economy to solve the Pigovian problem of externalities (Lange, 1938).

[15] Baumol notes that the safe minimum standard is analogous to "the approach employed in the formulation of stabilization policy, where it is decided that an employment rate exceeding w percent and an inflationary rate exceeding v percent are unacceptable and fiscal and monetary policy are then designed accordingly" (Baumol, 1972:318).

public decisions. The measures that are used in estimating costs and benefits must be consistent with the formal properties of microeconomic welfare theory if the benefit–cost estimates are to be taken seriously.[16] One property is that it is only the marginal (or incremental) changes in costs and benefits associated with a project or regulation that is considered. The total value of the environment resource or service is not relevant. A second is that the values assigned to the benefits should reflect the willingness of the public to pay for the benefits—either in the market or in the form of taxes. The third is that the costs should include the opportunity costs, including both direct expenditures and the cost of foregone alternatives (Farrow and Toman, 1999:12–15, 33–38). The purpose of considering opportunity costs is to avoid selecting projects or regulations that have lower benefit–cost ratios relative to other opportunities when confronted by budget or other resource constraints.

Since many of the values involved in estimating benefits and costs are not adequately accounted for in market transactions, resource and environmental economists have devoted considerable effort to developing methods to measure nonmarket values. Some benefits are expressed in the form of healthier lives, reduced illness, and lowered mortality. Other benefits may be primarily aesthetic such as the value of a unique natural resource. Placing values on the preservation of biological diversity poses a particularly difficult challenge.

In some cases market behavior can provide information about the economic benefits from improvements, or loss, of environmental quality. The environmental effects of the odors and possible water pollution from a large hog production facility on surrounding property values can be estimated by comparing changes in home prices with similar changes in a comparable area (Palmquist et al., 1997). In other instances researchers have used "contingent valuation" methods in which they ask respondents to estimate their support for specified improvements in the environment. Although contingent valuation has generated considerable controversy (Hanemann, 1994:19–43; Diamond and Hausmann, 1994:45–69), there has been substantial progress in the methodology used to elicit usable responses from such inquiries (Smith and Osborne, 1996).

The use of benefit–cost analysis has been criticized on both empirical and theoretical grounds. The empirical criticisms typically focus on the difficulty and integrity of measuring the nonmarkets costs and benefits. Supporters of benefit–cost analysis insist that by explicitly identifying costs and benefits biases and uncertainties can be identified and taken into consideration. The more difficult conceptual problems center on the issue of contemporary and intergenerational income distribution. It is incorrect to argue that benefit–cost analysis must necessarily ignore the income distribution effects. When conducted skillfully it can help clarify the impact of costs and benefits on income distributions across individuals and groups. The more difficult

---

[16] For an early exposition of benefit-cost methodology see Eckstein (1958). See also Freeman (1993) and several of the papers in Oates (1992). For an excellent nontechnical introduction see Farrow and Toman (1999:12–15; 33–38).

problem is the problem of the intergenerational impact. The issue of sustainability is, in effect, a question of intergenerational equity—the fair division of benefits and costs across generations. The issue of intergenerational equity is a central issue in the newer subdiscipline of ecological economics.

ECOLOGICAL ECONOMICS

To many social scientists and ecologists, the analysis of environmental spillovers employed by economists working within the framework of neoclassical economics has seemed excessively confining (Gowdy, 1997). In the late 1980s a new subfield, ecological economics, became differentiated from the older fields of resource economics and environmental economics. Although there are wide differences among those who identified themselves as ecological economists, a common concern has been with the optimal scale of human activity. A basic organizing principle is that economic and ecological systems depend on maintaining the integrity of the ecosystem—protecting the ecosystem from the negative externalities associated with ever expanding human activity. The distinction between the concerns of resource and environmental economists and ecological economists can be illustrated by their differing approaches to valuing biodiversity. It is conventional for resource and environmental economists to conceptualize the value of preserving biodiversity as a way of holding a diverse portfolio of assets, which might in the future have useful agricultural or pharmaceutical applications, but with uncertain payoffs. Ecologists and ecological economists would extend attempts to value biodiversity to its contribution to maintaining life support systems such as the basic biogeochemical cycles that are essential to life on earth (Dasgupta and Mäler, 1995:2377).

Much of the stimulus for the development of the field of ecological economics as a separate subdiscipline can be traced to a series of articles and a book by Herman Daly (1968, 1974, 1977). Ecological economists also trace their intellectual ancestry to S. V. Ciriacy-Wantrup (1952) for the concept of safe minimum standards and threshold effects, to Nicholas Georgescue-Roegen (1971) for drawing the attention of economists to the thermodynamic consequences of the dissipative use of energy and materials (entropy), to Kenneth Boulding (1966) for advancing the concept of "spaceship earth" as a metaphor for the significance of closed systems in relation to environmental concerns, and to John Krutilla (1967) for his demonstration that it may be optimal to permanently preserve some natural resources whose current value for development, as reflected in conventional benefit–cost analysis, is greater than the current return to preservation.

There are several ways in which the research agenda of ecological economics differs from that of resource economics and environmental economics. One is in choice of problems. Among the issues most closely identified with ecological economics are those of appropriate policies toward unique natural environments, endangered species, and biological diversity. What are the considerations involved when unique natural environments are threatened by economic development—the construction of a hydroelectric facility or a mining operation? How do we evaluate the increasingly valuable amenities provided by unique natural environments, such as Hells Canyon on the Colombia River or the Serengeti Plain (in Kenya)? Some ecological economists continue to employ the tools of neoclassical microeconomics and welfare economics such as benefit–cost analysis to address these issues.

A second school of ecological economists embraces a methodological agenda that contemplates the development of a new economics that would replace the use of methodologies based on neoclassical economics. Pretensions of value neutrality would be abandoned—that the consumer tastes of the present generation must, for example, be taken as given (Norton et al., 1998). Allowance must be made for the coevolution of tastes, technology, and ecosystems. Consideration should be given not only to the equitable distribution of resources between present and future generations of humans but also among human and nonhuman species and life forms.

The difference between these two schools can be illustrated by an attempt by a group of economists and ecologists to value the world ecosystem's natural capital and services (Costanza et al., 1997). An attempt was made to build on the idiosyncratic data that are available from microeconomic studies to estimate the per-hectare economic value of each of 17 ecosystem services in 16 biomes, and then to aggregate the values into a global total. For the entire biosphere, the estimate of the annual value of ecosystem services was valued at U.S. $33 trillion (with a range between $16 and $50 trillion). This compares to a global gross national product total of around $18 trillion per year.

There has been a broad consensus that the treatment of natural resources in national income accounts has been inadequate.[17] But the Costanza report has been severely criticized by resource economists on both methodological and empirical grounds (Smith, 1997; Pearce, 1998). The methodological criticism is that it violates the incremental benefit and cost calculus and the "willingness to pay" criteria employed in the neoclassical economics-based benefit–cost analysis: "If . . . the world's GNP is 18 trillion dollars, the world's population does not have 33 trillion dollars to spend annually" (Bockstael et al., 1998). The empirical criticism is that it is incorrect to aggregate individual microlevel value estimates.[18] The approach used in the Costanza

---

[17] Robert Eisner, the leading scholar in the field of national income accounts, agrees that conventional handling of natural resources in national income accounting systems is inadequate. "We should take account of deterioration of our natural wealth or its associated flow of services. But then we should note as well investment to maintain or increase that wealth. And to the extent that the wealth is increased by discoveries or technological change we should recognize that accumulation, perhaps as capital gains or evaluations" (Eisner, 1989:86). For further discussion of ecosystem services valuation, see Goulder and Kennedy (1997).

[18] When the value of one element of an ecosystem is valued, it is assumed that other elements remain unchanged. "For example, we might compute the value lost from the elimination of one specific wetland while leaving another in its natural state. In a second analysis the value lost from elimination of the second wetland might be estimated assuming the first remained in its natural state. But it is not valid to add the two values" (Bockstael et al., 1998:6).

study has also been criticized by ecologists. Gretchen Daily, while insisting that the decisions facing society require that the marginal value of the loss, or the benefits, of preserving a given amount or quality of nature's services should be estimated as a contribution to the environmental policy process, also argued that "there exists no absolute value of ecosystem services to be discovered by members of the intellectual community" (Daily, 1997:7).

The problem of how to value ecological resources that are not direct or indirect inputs into either production or consumption remains intellectually intractable. The ecological economics research agenda of measuring the value of all natural things as a basis for policy decisions is not achievable (Goulder and Kennedy, 1997). It is possible to measure the impact of human activity on natural environments. But methods for the assignment of economic value to the intrinsic rights of natural things are not available. Decisions about safe minimum standards involve political decisions that must be made with little contribution from either economic or political theory.

In the next sections I turn first to a discussion of the environmental impacts of consumption and production. I then discuss the design of institutional innovations to manage two major environmental threats—acid rain and global climate change.

ENVIRONMENTAL IMPACTS OF PRODUCTION

Prior to the industrial revolution, the primary sources of environmental pollution were human and animal wastes. Agriculture had also been an important source of environmental degradation in some regions. The impacts on the environment and on human health were, however, largely local. With the industrial revolution, energy production and the mining and transformation of raw materials became major sources of environmental change. The impacts on the environment and on human health became regional and global.

Material Flows

Evaluating the environmental impacts of technical change requires a capacity to trace the materials flows and the transformation of raw materials and energy used in agricultural and industrial production. A general equilibrium *materials balance* approach was developed in the 1970s.[19] The approach helped to clarify the systemwide implications of the interrelationships among production, consumption, and disposal.

Technologies for processing or purifying one type of waste discharge do not destroy the residuals generated by production and consumption, but only alter their

---

[19] The materials balance approach was first outlined in Ayres and Kneese (1969). See also Kneese et al. (1970) and Ayres (1978). More recently the materials balance approach has been discussed under the rubric of industrial metabolism (Ayres and Simonis, 1994). The term *industrial ecology,* introduced by Frosch (1992, 1997), has been used to describe the life cycle planning of industrial products for durability, reuse, and recyclability (Socolow et al. 1994). For a retrospective discussion, see Kneese (1998).

form. Given the technology available, the choices are to recycle the materials into productive use or discharge them into the environment. Advances in technology may make it possible to reduce the flow of materials between extraction and use.[20] Many undesirable residuals can, with sufficient energy, be recovered and transformed, reused, or disposed of in solid form. Analysis of the disposal of residuals from a materials balance perspective reveals the interconnections among air, water, and land pollution. Narrowly conceived environmental policies have often ignored these interconnections and at times have simply shifted residuals from one medium to another without significantly reducing the total. Technologies designed to reduce land or water pollution, the combustion of solid wastes, for example, have often contributed to air pollution.

The materials balance approach has also served to reveal the size of the disposal problem. The weight of the materials disposed into the environment must be equal to the weight of the raw materials entering the system, plus the weight added by reactions with the atmosphere (sulfur and nitrous oxides, for example). It was apparent even in the 1970s that the assimilative capacity of the environment had been exceeded in many areas as a result of using the environment as a cheap source of waste disposal.

Considerable effort has been devoted to measuring the burden of materials flows into the environment. In the mid-1960s the weight of annual materials use (production plus imports) in the UnitedStates was estimated to amount to 2492 million tons (Ayres and Kneese, 1969:286). Of this amount fuels accounted for 58%, other minerals for 23%, agriculture and fisheries for 16%, and forestry for 7%. Construction and structural materials such as stone, sand, and gravel were excluded in the calculations. Mine tailings and soil loss were also excluded since the use of these materials involved little more than moving them from one location to another. It would, however, be appropriate to include some of these materials in a classification in which aesthetic considerations carry more weight.

● BOX 12.1

INDUSTRIAL ECOLOGY AND ENVIRONMENTAL TECHNOLOGY

The passage of major environmental legislation in the early 1970s provided an impetus for a new growth industry—the environmental technology industry. By the late 1990s, over $150 million was being invested annually in the

[20] The literature on economics of technical change gives inadequate attention to advances in knowledge in materials science and technology. Advances in materials science and technology have been particularly important in technical change in each of the industries discussed earlier in this book (Larson et al. 1986). The technologies used to reduce the flow of materials are classified as (1) dematerialization, (2) material substitution, (3) recycling, and (4) waste mining (Larson et al., 1986; Rohatgi et al., 1998).

United States, and over $300 million internationally, in pollution control. Two new U.S. trade associations, the Environmental Technology Council and the Council for a Sustainable Energy Future, joined forces with mainstream environmental groups to lobby for stronger environmental regulation. The Business Council For Sustainable Development, organized by Stephan Schmidheiny of Switzerland, has publicized efforts by international firms to develop technologies that reduce "leakages" from production processes and product disposal into the environment.

A number of early efforts to reduce environmental impacts of production were initiated in anticipation of more stringent environmental regulation. Minnesota Mining and Manufacturing (3M), for example, shifted the focus of pollution prevention from end-of-pipe technology to process technology in the mid-1970s. By the mid-1980s, 3M was devoting substantial research effort to the design of new products that both reduced pollution and improved product quality. A broad range of industries in both developed and developing countries instituted cleaner process technology, cleaner product design, and less polluting resource exploitation (Schmidheiny, 1992).

In spite of such early examples of corporate good citizenship, the driving force behind the growth of the environmental technology industry has been regulation or threat of regulation. Firms that have been traditionally opposed to environmental regulation now direct substantial effort toward influencing how environmental laws and regulations are written. Although they often support regulations that are in the public interest they are not unmindful of securing competitive advantage. Du Pont, for example, strongly supported the 1987 Montreal Protocol to curb the use of ozone-depleting chlorofluorocarbons (CFCs). But Du Pont was, at the same time, in a position to dominate the market for CFC substitutes for refrigerants, foam plastics, and aerosols. Much of the difficulty in negotiating the Protocol stemmed less from debate over the environmental impact of CFCs than from concern that the agreement would strengthen Du Pont's competitive advantage. Similarly, General Electric has been a major beneficiary of the Clean Air Act. It became a leader in the development of both clean coal scrubber technology and gas turbine technology.

The emergence of the environmental technology supply industry has coincided with the emergence of a new field of industrial engineering, industrial ecology, which involves a systems approach to the study of material and energy flows in industrial and consumer activities. The roots of industrial ecology are located in the older fields of materials balance, industrial metabolism, and mass-flow analysis. The total flow of materials is tracked through the industrial system, from raw material production through final use and disposal. Ideally, the material flow analysis is combined with an analysis of the human health and environmental risks associated with the material flows. Industrial ecology focuses on life cycle planning of products for durability, reuse, and recycling, and aims for near complete recycling of materials back into the production system at the time of disposal.

The contribution of the industrial ecology approach can be illustrated by a comparative study of the health effects of two uses of lead in automobiles— lead in gasoline and lead in batteries (Socolow and Thomas, 1977). The use of lead as a gasoline additive is a dissipative use. When the lead leaves the tailpipe it disperses in the air. People are exposed not only by inhaling but also by consuming food produced on soil in which lead has been deposited. The environmental and health impacts can be controlled only by phasing out the use of lead in gasoline. In contrast, lead in batteries for electric vehicles does not dissipate into the environment, and is recyclable. Clean recycling requires that all batteries go to secondary smelters at the end of their useful life, and that secondary smelters and battery-manufacturing plants meet exacting, but feasible, environmental and occupational health standards.

The industrial ecology movement has been criticized from several perspectives. Populist critics have argued that efforts to publicize the greening of industry represents little more than establishment appropriation of sustainability rhetoric. They are skeptical about claims of change in corporate culture (Greer and Bruno, 1996). Environmental economists have argued that an almost exclusive focus on firm behavior has been associated with a lack of constructive dialogue with government about the policies that must be put in place to remove the biases in incentives—price distortions, depletion allowances, tax benefits, and subsidies for mineral and fuel exploitation—that encourage excessive energy and raw material use (Kneese, 1998).

Sources: Robert Socolow and Valerie Thomas, "The Industrial Ecology of Lead and Electric Vehicle," *Journal of Industrial Ecology* 1 (1, 1977):13–36; Stephan Schmidheiny, *Changing Course: A Global Business Perspective on Development and the Environment,* Cambridge, MA: MIT Press, 1992; R. Socolow, C Andrews, F. Berkhout, and V. Thomas, *Industrial Ecology and Global Change*, Cambridge, UK: Cambridge University Press, 1994; "How to Make Lots of Money and Save the Planet Too," *Economist*, June 3, 1995:65–66; Jed Greer and Kenny Bruno, *Greenwash: the Reality Behind Corporate Environmentalism,* New York: Apex Press, 1996; James K. Hammitt and Kimberly Thompson, "Protecting the Ozone Layer," In *The Greening of Industry: A Risk Management Approach,* John D. Graham and Jennifer Kassalow Hartwell eds., Cambridge, MA: Harvard University Press, 1997:43–92.

A more comprehensive effort to track material flows was made by the World Resources Institute (WRI) in the mid-1990s (Adriaanse et al., 1997; see also Wernick and Ausubel, 1995). The WRI study employed a broader definition that includes (1) the direct material inputs that enter the industrial economy, and (2) the hidden or intermediate materials that are part of the process of providing those direct material inputs (Table 12.1). The study found that for the United States, total material requirements (TMR) amounted to 21,237 million metric tons in 1991. This amounted to 84 kilograms—enough to fill 300 shopping bags, per capita. In contrast, per capita TMR in Japan was only 46 kilograms in 1991.[21] In the United States, however, TMR has been declining, whereas in Japan and Germany it has been rising since the mid-1970s (Figure 12.3).

There has been a long-term decline in material intensity in the United States (Figure 12.3). This decline has resulted from several approaches to enhancing productivity in the use of material resources. These include (1) dematerialization, such as reductions in the weight of automobiles, (2) material substitution, such as the replacement of cast iron or copper water pipes by plastic pipes, (3) recycling, such as recovery of mercury from fluorescent lights, and (4) waste mining, such as recovery of elemental sulfur from oil and gas refineries (Ayres and Ayres, 1996:7–17). The pattern has, however, been rather complex (Figure 12.4). Material intensity—material input per dollar of GNP—has been declining for lumber since at least the beginning of the twentieth century, and for steel and other heavy materials since mid-century. For some materials, particularly light weight materials such as plastics and aluminum, material

Table 12.1 Material Flows in Three Industrial Countries, 1991 (Million Metric Tons)

	United States	Japan	Germany
Total domestic commodities[a]	4,581	1,424	1,367
Total foreign commodities	568	710	406
Grand total commodities	5,149	2,133	1,773
Grand total commodity per capita	20	17	22
Domestic hidden flows[b]	15,494	1,143	2,961
Foreign hidden flows	594	2,439	2,030
Total hidden flows	16,088	3,583	4,991
Total flows (commodities + hidden flows)	21,237	5,716	6,764
Total flows/capita	84	46	86

[a]*Commodities* are the flow of natural resource materials that enter the economy for further processing. This category includes grains used by food processors, petroleum sent to a refinery, metals used by a manufacturer, and logs taken to a mill.

[b]*Hidden flow* is the portion of the total material requirement that does not directly enter the industrial economy. It is comprised of two components: (1) *ancillary flows* include the materials that must be removed from the environment along with the desired material such as the portion of an ore that is processed and discarded to concentrate the ore and the forest biomass that is removed from the land and separated from the logs before processing into wood products; (2) *excavated and /or disturbed material flow* is material moved or disturbed to obtain a natural resource or to create and maintain an infrastructure. This would include, for example, the overburden that must be removed to permit access to an ore body, the soil erosion from agriculture, and material moved in construction of infrastructure.

Source: Albert T. Adriaanse, Stefan Bringezu, Allan Hammond, Yuichi Moriguchi, Eric Rodenberg, Donald Rogich, and Helmut Schütz, *Resource Flows: The Material Basis of Industrial Economies*, Washington, DC: World Resources Institute, 1997. Copyright © 1997 World Resources Institute. All rights reserved.

---

[21] The term total material requirement is somewhat misleading. It carries an implication of a technical input–output relationship. TMR is, in fact, substantially influenced by economic factors. The OECD has adopted as a long-range goal a reduction of material intensity by a factor of 10 in the industrial countries—a target that can hardly be regarded as realistic in the foreseeable future (Adriaanse et al., 1997:2).

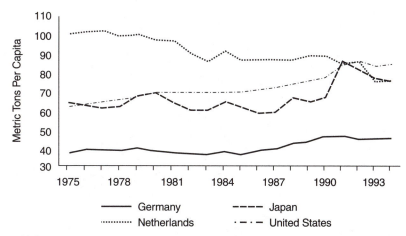

Figure 12.3 Total material annual flows per capita. (*Source:* Albert Adriaanse, Stefan Bringezu, Allan Hammond, Yuichi Moriguchi, Eric Rodenberg, Donald Rogich, and Helmut Schütz, *Resource Flows: The Material Basis of Industrial Economies*, Washington, DC: World Resources Institute, 1997:12. Copyright © 1997 World Resources Institute. All rights reserved.)

intensity has risen. The general pattern of production for each material seems to follow a common pattern. Its production initially exceeds the rate of economic growth as new uses are discovered. As demand for older materials matures and substitute materials are developed, growth declines relative to the rest of the materials sector (Goeller and Weinberg, 1976; Ayres and Simonis, 1994; Wernick, 1996). Decline in material intensity does not, however, translate directly into a decline in aggregate material use. With rapid growth of GNP, there may be substantial growth in the use of particular materials even though use per unit of GNP is declining.

Improved estimates of material flows are highly important. But the totals have little significance until interpreted in terms of environmental impact. The materials released into the atmosphere, dissipated into water systems, or disposed of on land differ widely in their environmental and health impacts. Environmental impacts are not proportional to volume or weight; moving one thousand tons of sand or gravel will result in much less environmental damage than widely dispersing a few kilograms of heavy metals. Materials that are biodegradable generally have less harmful long-term effects than materials that have been chemically transformed. Filling in a small wetland may have little national or global environmental significance, but may impinge significantly on quality of life at the local level. While emphasizing the uncertainty involved in determining which flows will be environmentally damaging, the WRI report estimates that in the United States about 17% of material flows have high potential for harm. The report does not, however, present a comprehensive assessment of the risks to human health and the environment resulting from the material flows.

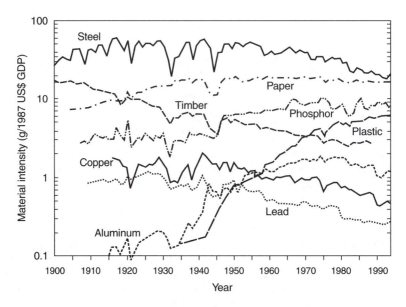

Isolines of decreasing materials intensity at the rate of GDP
growth of 3% per year (= constant absolute materials use)

Figure 12.4 Materials intensity of the U.S. economy (grams per constant 1987 US$ GDP) since 1990. (*Source:* Iddo K. Wernick, "Consuming Materials: The American Way," *Technological Forecasting and Social Change*, 53 (1996):114, adapted by Arnulf Grübler, *Technology and Global Change*, International Institute for Applied Systems Analysis, Laxenburg, Austria; Cambridge, UK: Cambridge University Press, 1998:240.)

Impact of Material Flows

The production of waste materials with direct implications for environmental degradation and human health is concentrated in relatively few sectors.[22] Impacts on health and the environment might be characterized in several ways. One way would be to identify the effects of spillovers from material flows on (1) human health, (2) agricultural and industrial production, and (3) environmental services. Another would be to classify the impacts in terms of the media in which the pollution occurs. This would include (1) water pollution, (2) air pollution, (3) soil degradation, (4) waste disposal, (5) deforestation and decertification, and (6) loss of biodiversity.

The only comprehensive effort to identify the sources of environmental impact that I have been able to find is more than a decade old (Holdren, 1987, 1992). These

---

[22] For a comprehensive source of information on the effects of hazardous material on human health, see Sullivan and Krieger (1992).

studies attempted to estimate the effects of industrial and traditional energy, and of agricultural and manufacturing energy, on the global environment (Table 12.2). The results are highly subjective.[23] But it is clear that the environmental effects of producing electricity from fossil fuel and nuclear energy sources are very large. Attempts to estimate the size of the health hazards from electric power generation are very uncertain. Estimates of health hazards from indoor air pollution from traditional fuels, which is a major health hazard in rural households in developing countries, are more reliable. "About 80 percent of global exposure to particulate air pollution occurs indoors in developing countries; and the smoke inhaled is heavily laden with carcinogenic genzpyrene and other dangerous hydrocarbons. A disproportionate share of this enormous burden is borne, moreover, by women and small children" (Holdren, 1992:17).

The U.S. EPA has employed comparative risk assessment (CRA) methods to rank perceptions of the importance of several sources of pollution for human and environmental and ecological health (Figure 12.5). There is very little correspondence between the CRA rankings and either the media attention given to the sources of risk or EPA expenditures on the risk areas (Davies and Mazurek, 1998:101–122). The two top rated health risks—radon and indoor air pollution—receive minimal funding. Nonpoint water pollution sources, such as runoff from farms and roads, pose the major environmental problem, but resources are allocated primarily to point sources.

Agriculture is heavily impacted by environmental change—most agricultural activities are carried on outdoors in intimate contact with both natural and constructed environments (Chapter 6). Agricultural intensification is itself a major source of health-related hazards and environmental change (Runge, 1997a, 1997b:200–216). Farming activities are a particularly important source of water quality problems. Soil erosion, pesticide and fertilizer use, and animal waste disposal all have negative impacts on water quality. Agricultural production is also a source of greenhouse gases, particularly nitrous oxide from nitrogen fertilizer and methane from rice fields and ruminant animals. Consumers have become increasingly sensitive to food safety issues associated with agricultural- and food-processing practices. Much of the concern centers around the use of insecticides and herbicides in crop production and the use of antibiotics as prophylactics in animal production. On a larger scale, pressures on the landscape from conversion of grasslands, wetlands, and forest land to more intensive agricultural uses contribute to loss of biodiversity. Loss of biodiversity represents both a threat to the integrity of natural environments and a loss of germplasm with potential value for improved commercial crops, new crops, and materials with pharmaceutical value.

---

[23] For an attempt to develop a more rigorous approach to the quantification of hazards and risks, see Hohenemser et al. (1983:379). "Hazards are threats to humans and what they value, whereas risks are quantitative measures of hazard consequences that can be expressed as conditional probabilities. Thus exposure to toxic materials is a hazard; the risk is the probability of exposure on human or nonhuman mortality" (Kates, 1985:51).

Table 12.2 Contributions to Global Environmental Impacts[a]

Indicator of Impact	Natural Baseline	Human Disruption Index	Share of Human Disruption Caused by			
			Industrial Energy Supply	Traditional Energy Supply	Agriculture	Manufacturing, Other
Lead emissions to atmosphere	25,000 tonnes/yr	15	63% (fossil fuel burning, including additives)	Small	Small	37% (metal processing, manufacturing, refuse burning)
Oil added to oceans	500,000 tonnes/yr	10	60% (oil harvesting, processing, transport)	Negligible	Negligible	40% (disposal of oil wastes)
Cadmium emissions to atmosphere	1,000 tonnes/yr	8	13% (fossil fuel burning)	5% (burning traditional fuels)	12% (agricultural burning)	70% (metals processing, manufacturing, refuse burning)
Sulfur dioxide emissions to atmosphere	50 million tonnes/yr (S content)	1.4	85% (fossil fuel burning)	0.5% (burning traditional fuels)	1% (agricultural burning)	13% (smelting, refuse burning)
Methane stock in atmosphere	800 parts per billion	1.1	20% (fossil fuel harvesting and processing)	3% (burning traditional fuels)	62% (rice paddies, domestic animals, land clearing)	15% landfills
Mercury emissions to atmosphere	25,000 tonnes/yr	0.7	20% (fossil fuel burning)	1% (burning traditional fuels)	2% (agricultural burning)	77% (metals processing, manufacturing, refuse burning)
Land use or conversion	135 million km^2 ice-free land	0.5	0.2% (occupied by energy facilities)	6% (to supply fuelwood use sustainably)	88% (grazing, cultivation, cumulative desertification)	6% (lumbering, towns, transport systems)
Nitrogen fixation (as NO_2, NH_4)	200 million tonnes/yr	0.5	30% (fossil fuel burning)	2% (burning traditional fuels)	67% (fertilizer, agricultural burning)	1% (refuse burning)

Nitrous oxide flows to atmosphere	7 million tonnes/yr (N content)	0.4	12% (fossil fuel burning)	4% (burning traditional fuels)	84% (fertilizer, land clearing aquifer disruption)	Small
Carbon dioxide stock in atmosphere	280 parts per million	0.25	75% (fossil fuel burning)	3% (net deforestation for fuelwood)	15% (net deforestation for land clearing)	7% (net deforestation for lumber, cement manufacturing)
Particulate emissions to atmosphere	500 million tonnes/yr	0.25	35% (fossil fuel burning)	10% (burning traditional fuels)	40% (agricultural burning, wheat handling)	15% (smelting, nonagricultural, land clearing, refuse)
Ionizing radiation dose to humans	800 million person-rem per year (300 from whole-body equivalent of radon lung dose)	0.20	1% (half from nuclear energy, half from radon in coal)	Unquantified extra radon release from soil disturbance	Unquantified extra radon from soil disturbance	99% (medical X-rays, fallout, air travel)
Nonmethane hydrocarbon emissions to atmosphere	800 million tonnes/yr	0.13	35% (fossil fuel processing and burning)	5% (burning traditional fuels)	35% (agricultural burning)	20% (nonagricultural land clearing, refuse burning)

[a]Some impacts are most appropriately characterized as alterations of natural inventories, or stocks, and others as alterations of natural flows. The Human Disruption Index is the ratio of the size of the human alteration to the size of the undisturbed stock or flow, denoted the "natural baseline." The figures for the shares of human disruption accounted for by different classes of activities are based on current conditions. Estimates are the author's based on a variety of sources and are very approximate; see, e.g., Holdren (1987), Lashof and Tirpak (1989), Graedel and Crutzen (1989), Intergovernmental Panel on Climate Change (1990), and World Resources Institute (1990).

Source: John Holdren, "The Transition to Costlier Energy," in *Energy Efficiency and Human Activity: Past Trends, Future Prospects*, L. Schipper and S. Meyers (with R. B. Howarth and R. Steiner), eds., Cambridge, UK: Cambridge University Press, 1992:18, 19.

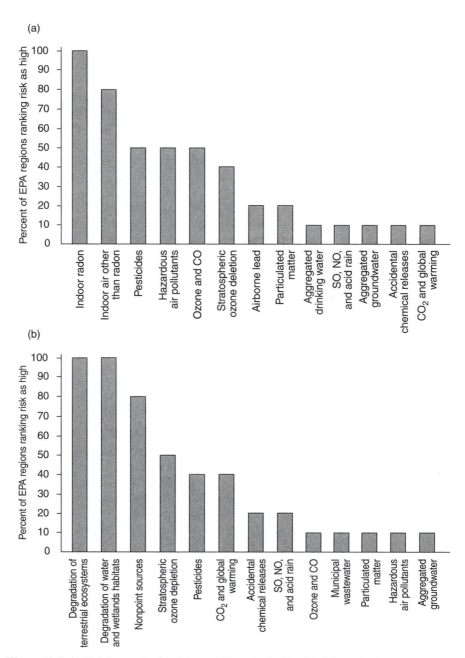

Figure 12.5 (a) U.S. human health risks and (b) ecological health risks ranked as high by EPA regions.(*Source:* J. Clarence Davies and Jan Mazurek, *Pollution Control in the United States: Evaluating the System*, Washington, DC: Resources for the Future, 1998:115, 116.)

In contrast with the industrial sector, few significant environmental controls have been placed on agricultural practices. This is partly because the environmental impacts arise from widely diffuse nonpoint sources (Ervin et al., 1998). In the past these nonpoint sources were difficult to trace. However, increasing analytic and environmental engineering sophistication coupled with increased public perception of the health and environmental impact of agricultural intensification are blurring the distinction between point and nonpoint sources of pollution. Although there remains considerable scientific uncertainty, there is general agreement that pesticides are the main nonpoint source of pollution. The health risks associated with direct exposure to pesticides are well documented. Additionally, pesticides can affect distant nontarget organisms through a number of channels, such as ground and surface water contamination and concentration in the food chain. The epidemiological evidence on which to base regulation of low-level pesticide exposure in food and water is, however, much weaker than for direct exposure.

ENVIRONMENTAL IMPACTS OF CONSUMPTION[24]

The environmental stresses associated with energy production, the use of raw materials, and agricultural production arise out of population and income growth. It has been conventional for environmentalists in developed countries to point to the burgeoning population in developing countries as a source of environmental degradation. Other environmentalists have pointed to the consumption habits of affluent consumers in developed countries as a primary source of resource drains and environmental damage.[25]

In popular discussion, environmental impact of consumption appears to reflect everything that people do, including increasing their numbers, that may harm the environment.

> The images implied by the term include dumps filled with disposable products, plastics and consumer packaging waste; freeways clogged with traffic that pollutes the air but barely moves; automobiles and appliances junked when they might have been repaired; tracts of large, single-family houses with few occupants, but

---

[24] In this section I draw heavily on Stern (1997). See also the exchange between Myers (1997) and Vincent and Panayotou (1997:53–56).

[25] In an attempt to capture the effects of population and human activity on the environment, Ehrlich and Holdren (1971) advanced what has been termed the IPAT formulation:

$$I = P \times A \times T$$

in which I represents environmental impact, P represents population, A represents output per capita, and T represents the environmental impact per unit of output. T should be interpreted as representing not only technology but also culture and social organization. As originally stated the equation is an identity rather than a functional relationship. For an attempt to formalize and estimate the IPAT model, see Dietz and Rosa (1994, 1997).

centrally air-conditioned and with heated or cooled swimming pools; advertisements for products that no one seemed to want a few years ago but that soon everyone will need; air-conditioned shopping malls surrounded by acres of asphalt; and trash lined streets and highways. The images portray excesses of resource use, waste, and material acquisitiveness. (Stern, 1997:10)

This stands in sharp contrast to the poor societies of South Asia or Africa, in which the material components of consumption are used and reused.

Stern has attempted to capture the implications of these images in a coherent definition: "Consumption consists of human and human-induced transformation of materials and energy. Consumption is environmentally important to the extent that it makes materials or energy less available for future use; moves a biophysical system toward a different state, or, through its effects on those systems, threatens human health, welfare or other things people value" (Stern, 1997:20). This definition encompasses the environmental impacts of both production and consumption. It is not inconsistent, however, with the view that population and income growth are the ultimate sources of demand for the transformation of energy and materials, and of the residuals—the environmental pollution—that results from such transformation.

In a presidential address to the American Agricultural Economics Association, I argued that

in high-income economies the income elasticity of demand for commodities and services related to sustenance is low and declines as income continues to rise, while the income elasticity of demand for more effective disposal of residuals and for environmental amenities is high and continues to rise. This is in sharp contrast to the situation in poor countries where the income elasticity of demand is high for sustenance and low for environmental amenities. (Ruttan 1971:707–708)

It was not until well into the 1990s that empirical tests of what has been termed the "environmental transition hypothesis" became available (World Bank, 1992:9–11; Shafik and Bandyopadhyay, 1992; Antle and Heidebrink, 1995; Grossman and Krueger, 1995; Lucas, 1996; Hauer, 1997). Several of these studies found, for an important group of air and water quality indicators, that the relationship between per capita income and pollution resembles an inverted U.[26] It was also found that countries with higher population densities control pollution at lower income levels than countries with low population densities (Hauer, 1997:101–119). A similar relationship was found between per capita income and two classes of environmental amenities: (1) total area of parks in a country and (2) the average annual rate of afforestation (the opposite of deforestation) (Antle and Heidebrink, 1995). These studies suggest that when per capita incomes are very low, economic growth is likely to be accompanied by

---

[26] For critical reviews of these and related studies, see Arrow et al. (1995), Dasgupta and Mäler (1995), Stern et al. (1996), and Ezzati et al. (1998).

environmental degradation. As per capita income rises into the $8,000–10,000 range, levels now being achieved by middle-income countries, the demand for environmental protection tends to increase—leading to a development path characterized by both economic growth and environmental quality improvements. It would be premature, of course, to accept these generalizations as applying to all forms of negative spillovers from production and consumption.[27]

The World Bank studies (Shafik and Bandyopadhay, 1992) suggest several stages in the relationship between per capita income and environmental degradation (Figure 12.6). The two upper panels in Figure 12.6 indicate strong demand for safe water and waste disposal even at relatively low income levels. The middle panels are consistent with the inverted **U** hypothesis. A rise in income into even the lower middle-income range results in a rise in demand for cleaner air, which induces governments to intervene to reduce the concentration of air pollutants. The two lower panels suggest that even at relatively high-income levels governments have been slow to intervene effectively to reduce the material waste associated with high levels of consumption. Failure to intervene to slow per capita CO_2 emissions reflects a combination of several factors. One is that recognition of the threat of global climate change from CO_2 emissions is relatively recent. Another is the continuing rapid growth in demand for electricity and personal transportation. A third is skepticism about the efficacy of control of CO_2 at the local or national level in the absence of a comprehensive international agreement. I return to this issue later in this chapter.

● BOX 12.2
DEFINITIONS OF CONSUMPTION

Consumption has fairly precise, but different, meanings in the several scientific communities. These meanings are in common use in their respective disciplines, whose adherents often have them in mind when discussing the "environmental impacts of consumption."

The Physicists' Meaning

According to the First Law of Thermodynamics, consumption is impossible: matter/energy can be neither produced nor consumed. So for physicists, consumption must be translated as *transformations* of matter/energy. According to the Second Law (the Entropy Law) of Thermodynamics, such transformations increase entropy, and this increase in entropy, to the extent that it takes the form

---

[27] For qualifications, see Dasgupta and Mäler (1995:2384–2388) and Ezzati et al. (1998).

of pollution or of a decrease in the usefulness of the transformed resource, is an important aspect of what is meant by environmental impacts of consumption. It is the physical basis on which methodologies such as material balance and industrial ecology rests.

The Ecologists' Meaning

Green plants are a primary source of the products on which consumption by humans and other animals depends. Ecologists define production, or net primary productivity (NPP), in terms of photosynthesis. NPP is the amount of energy left after subtracting the respiration of primary producers (mostly plants) from the total amount of energy (mostly solar) that is fixed biologically. In this meaning, any organism that obtains its energy by eating is a consumer. NPP is not a valid measure of the global environmental impact of human consumption. Human activity also transforms ecosystems, substituting species that are more efficient in meeting human needs for those that are less efficient. In this process some species become more prevalent, and, in some cases, increase productivity.

The Sociologist's Meaning

Consumption also has sociological meanings that are reflected in terms such as consumerism and conspicuous consumption. In this usage, consumption includes what individuals and households do when they use their incomes to purchase goods designed to increase social status. In some American subcultures, status can be increased by building an all-solar house that conspicuously consumes financial resources (for architectural design, solar panels, and so forth) but that may reduce environmental impact if it decreases fossil and nuclear energy consumption enough to compensate for the additional materials in the house. Similarly, a late-model luxury car may cost more money, provide more status, and yet consume less fuel and steel than an old pickup truck. Thus the sociological definition does not distinguish environmentally benign from environmentally destructive consumption.

The Economists' Meaning

Economists distinguish the consumption of goods and services from their production and distribution. Consumption is defined as total spending on consumer goods and services. Economic activity also involves investment in capital goods. In neither of these senses does the economists' usage conform to what is meant in the phrase "environmental impacts of consumption." Investment also has environmental impacts. Most economists might prefer to translate the environmental impact of consumption as the environmental impact of *economic activity*. From an economic perspective it is not appropriate to treat an increase in consumer spending as if it automatically indicates a proportional increase in environmental impact.

Source: Adapted from Paul C. Stern, Thomas Dietz, Vernon W. Ruttan, Robert H. Socolow, and James L. Sweeney, eds., *Environmentally Significant Consumption: Research Directions.* Washington, DC: National Academy Press, 1997.

The apparent optimism about an "environmental transition" driven by income growth should be tempered by several qualifications. As noted earlier (Chapter 2) there is little evidence that per capita income levels in the poorest countries are converging toward the levels of the high-income countries, or even of the more successful middle-income countries. Many low-income countries remain trapped at per capita incomes below $1000. A second qualification is that the forms of environmental degradation and enhancement that were studied are largely amenable to the environmental regulations of regional and national governments. The inverted U relationship appears to hold primarily for pollutants that have readily observable local effects. There is room for substantial skepticism whether similar results would be obtained for environmental indicators that require international or transnational agreements for their implementation. A third qualification is that there has been little attention, in the studies reviewed above, to analysis of the negative feedbacks of environmental change on economic growth (Lopez, 1994). A final qualification is that many decisions about the transformation of materials and energy are made not by consumers but, as emphasized in the industrial ecology literature, by firms engaged in the transformation activities. Decisions by firms engaged in the transformation of material and energy resources may be only weakly influenced by changes in consumer income. Decisions are also made by public agencies, at the local and national levels, that may be only weakly responsive to environmental policy. In the United States, the laboratories of the Department of Defense and the Department of Energy (and its predecessors, the Atomic Energy Commission and the Energy Research and Development Administration) have been among the worst offenders.

The promise of the materials balance approach, and its recent extension such as industrial metabolism and industrial ecology, of identifying the resource, environmental, and health impacts of production has yet to be fully realized. A recent World Resources Institute study concluded that in view of the uncertainties about environmental impacts of production and consumption, needed institutional innovations should include more intensive monitoring capacity, consistently enforced regulations to protect workers from environmental hazards, enhanced research capacity in agricultural–environmental interactions and in sanitary and phytosanitary issues, and public health investments to provide epidemiological monitoring and health interventions (Runge et al., 1997:43). It is important to note that in responding to these environmental challenges low-income countries today have access to information and

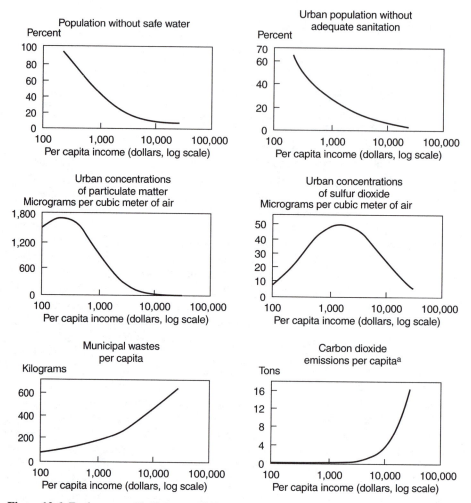

Figure 12.6 Environmental indicators at different country income levels. (*Source:* World Bank, *World Development Report, 1992: Development and the Environment,* New York: Oxford University Press, 1992; adapted from a Shafik and Bandyopadhyay Background Paper, 1992; reprinted by permission of Oxford University Press, Inc.)

technology unavailable to the presently developed countries at the time in their history when they were navigating the steep part of the inverted **U** curve.

The view that the environmental Kuznets curve is structurally determined and is an almost inevitable consequence of economic growth provides considerable comfort to those who would prefer to focus attention on economic growth and avoid responding to concerns about loss of environmental resources and services. The evidence suggests that the environmental Kuznets curve is a valid empirical generalization but that it is not structurally determined. Appropriate environmental policies such as those based on a safe minimal standard will be necessary to enable presently developing countries to avoid the worst environmental health hazards or excessive degradation of environmental resources.

EMISSIONS TRADING

One of the clear implications of the earlier discussion is that continued access to the material sources of production and reduction of the environmental impacts of economic activity will require the design of incentive-compatible institutions. The theory of induced institutional innovation does not assume that these innovations will occur as a simple response to the "invisible hand" of the market (Chapter 4). It does assume that changes in both relative prices, as expressed in economic markets, and in the values placed on public goods, as expressed through political markets, will induce institutional change. If market prices do not accurately reflect relative scarcities, substantial institutional rents can be generated, which in turn will induce both technical and institutional change.

In this section I discuss the emergence of emissions trading as an example of a public sector institutional innovation—a "constructed market"—induced by the rising economic value of formerly open-access resources. The development of a "constructed market" for emissions trading has been one of the most successful institutional innovations in the field of environmental management in the 1980s and 1990s. The concept is relatively simple. It is based on the realization that the behavioral sources of the pollution problem can be traced, to a substantial degree, to poorly defined property rights in environmental resources such as air and water.

The policy mechanisms available to control environmental pollution can be classed under three broad categories. These include "*market based approaches* such as emission taxes, subsidies or tradeable emission permits, *performance standards*, such as requirements that firms not emit more than specified amounts of pollutants per unit of economic activity; and *technology standards* such as requirements that particular industrial equipment and processes be employed" (Jaffe and Stavins, 1995:5–45). Both performance standards and technology standards are often discussed under the rubric of "command and control." Technology-based standards usually identify particular equipment that must be used to comply with regulation. For example, utilities may be required to install flue gas scrubbers to control sulfur dioxide emissions or electrostatic precipitators to remove harmful particulates. Performance standards, in contrast, typically identify a specific goal, such as maximum units of a pollutant emitted per unit of time. The performance standards approach typically does not specify the choice of technology and hence provides opportunities for greater flexibility in technology adoption and stronger incentives for technology development than technology-based standards. Market-based approaches can be even more effective in inducing the development, adoption, and diffusion of technology for achieving a particular level of environmental protection (Plott, 1983:106–127; Keohane et al., 1998; Chapter 4).

In focusing on a market-oriented approach, such as the SO_2 emissions allowance trading system, I do not intend to imply that market-based approaches are always superior to performance- or technology-based standards. Emissions allowance trading may not always be the most efficient or the most equitable way of meeting performance standards. And when the transaction costs of monitoring and enforcement are particularly burdensome neither performance standards nor market-based approaches may be cost effective. Transaction costs may be lowest for technology or performance standards that focus on the inputs to production systems, such as controlling the lead content of gasoline or the carbon or sulfur content of fossil fuels. Emissions trading permits represent a first step toward greater sophistication but may also involve substantially greater transaction costs. Additional steps in sophistication include ambient or concentrate permit trading, exposure trading, and risk trading (Stavins, 1995; Roumasset and Smith, 1990). The SO_2 emission trading case was selected because of the insight it provides to the design of an important institutional innovation in the field of environmental policy.[28]

The appeal of market-based systems to manage air pollution can be understood to a substantial degree in terms of the deficiencies of the "command-and-control" regulatory system established after the passage of the 1970 Clean Air Act. The objective of the Act was to "protect and enhance the quality of the nation's air" (Chapter 8). EPA in response to the Act defined air quality standards to be implemented by the individual states. Emission standards were established for each emitter based on what could be achieved by the use of "best practice" or best available technology.[29] Any emissions above these standards placed the emitter in noncompliance and subject to sanctions. In principle the Clean Air Act regulatory approach involved the specification of emission standards or legal ceilings on all major emission sources at specific emission points—stacks, vents, storage tanks, and others.

A system of property rights and tradable permits for the management of pollution was first proposed in the late 1960s (Crocker, 1966; Dales, 1968a, 1968b). As in the

---

[28] Stavins (1998) points out that although there are several alternative market-based instruments available, U.S. experience has been dominated by "grandfathered" trading permits in spite of the fiscal advantages to the government of emission taxes or auctioned permits. One explanation is that both environmental advocates and politicians have a strong incentive to avoid policy instruments that make the costs of environmental protection highly visible to consumers and voters. A second is that industry prefers grandfathered permits because they minimize the cost of compliance for existing firms (Keohane et al., 1998).

[29] The 1970 Clean Air Act recognized two main types of air pollutants. *Criteria pollutants* are relatively ubiquitous substances. They included sulfur dioxide, suspended particulates, carbon monoxide, nitrogen oxides, hydrocarbons, ozone, and lead. "Criteria documents" that summarized the existing research on the health and environmental effects associated with these pollutant were required as a step in the formulation of emission standards. *Hazardous pollutants* included a number of airborne substances, particularly heavy metals, that had been implicated in cancer or other serious health effects. The Act required the EPA to list and regulate any pollutants that fit this description. These included asbestos, beryllium, mercury, vinyl chloride, benzene, radio nuclides, and arsenic (Tietenberg, 1985:2, 3).

case of technical inventions discussed in earlier chapters, this institutional innovation did not emerge from its inventors in a fully operational form. The early proposals were followed by a large theoretical and empirical literature (Bohm and Russell, 1985). Implementation has involved an extended process of "learning by doing" and "learning by using" (Chapter 4).

A proposal by President Johnson for effluent fees and by President Nixon for a tax on lead in gasoline had been dismissed as impractical and characterized by environmental activists as a "license to pollute." Beginning in the mid-1980s, however, a series of events conspired to make a more market-oriented approach to reducing SO_2 emissions politically feasible (Taylor, 1989:28–34; Hahn and Stavins, 1991, Stavins, 1998). One was President Bush's predilection in favor of a market-oriented approach to environmental policy. Another was the enthusiasm of EPA administrator William K. Reilly and a number of key staff members in the Executive Office for validating President Bush's desire to be known as "the environmental president." Congress also provided high-profile, bipartisan support for a variety of market-based approaches, including SO_2 allowance trading.

Within the environmental community, the Environmental Defense Fund (EDF) began to support market-based approaches as early as the mid-1980s. In 1989 the EDF worked closely with the White House staff in drafting an early version of proposed legislation. The credibility of the effort was enhanced by the fact that EPA Administrator Reilly, formerly president of The Conservation Foundation, was a "card-carrying" environmentalist. The business community displayed a curious ambiguity toward the emissions trading proposal. Executives of several major corporations, influenced by subtle lobbying by the EDF, commented favorably on the emissions trading proposal. At the same time, lobbyists representing several of the major business associations opposed the proposed reforms.

The design of the SO_2 emissions trading system under the Clean Air Act 1990 Amendment drew on earlier EPA experience. The EPA began experimenting with emission trading permits in 1974. The early programs included the elimination of lead in gasoline, the phase-out of chlorofluorocarbons and halons in refrigeration, and reduction of water pollution from nonpoint sources. The early programs had a mixed record. They were typically grafted onto existing command-and-control programs. Converting from command-and-control requirements into tradable emissions programs encountered substantial transaction costs. These experiences did, however, provide important lessons for the development of more market-oriented trading programs in the 1990s.

The Clean Air Act created a national market for SO_2 allowances for coal-burning electrical utilities. The commodity exchanged in the SO_2 emissions trading program is a property right to emit SO_2 that was created by EPA and allocated to individual firms. A firm can make allowances that had been issued to it available to be traded to other firms by reducing its own emissions of the pollutant below the baseline level.

In 1995, the program's first year, 110 of the nations dirtiest coal-burning plants were included. The affected plants were allowed to emit 2.5 pounds of SO_2 for each million

British thermal units (Btu) of energy that they generated. During Phase II, scheduled to begin in 2000, almost all coal-burning electric power plants will be included and allowances for each plant will be reduced to 1.2 pounds per million Btu. Utilities that "overcomply" by reducing their emissions more than required may sell their excess allowances. Utilities that find it more difficult, or expensive, to meet the requirement may purchase allowances from other utilities.

The evidence available suggests that emission trading has been even more cost effective than initially anticipated.[30] Prior to initiation of the program the utility industry had complained that reducing SO_2 in amounts sufficient to meet the projected target (down from about 19 million tons in 1980 to 8.95 million tons in 2000) might cost as much as $1500 per ton. By the mid-1990s allowances were being sold in the $100–125 range. The decline in the cost of abatement has been due in part to technical changes in coal mining and deregulation of rail transport that have lowered the cost of low-sulfur coal. It has also been due to technical changes in fuel blending and SO_2 scrubbing technology induced by the introduction of performance-based allowance trading. Benefits have exceeded early estimates (Coggins and Swinton, 1996; Schmalensee et al., 1998; Stavins, 1998).

As of the late 1990s other emissions trading programs were being implemented. One of the most ambitious was the RECLAIM program developed by the South Coast Air Quality Management District in the Los Angeles area. Emitters of sulfur and nitrogen oxides were issued annual allowances that were scheduled to decline each year. Any new emission sources must be accommodated within the cap by acquiring allowances from existing emitters. Some oil refiners have met part of their obligations by purchasing and junking pre-1971 automobiles. In 1998 a group of 12 northeastern states was considering an emission trading system for reducing ozone levels. The Chicago Board of Trade was exploring the possibility of a futures market in carbon dioxide emission certificates (Fialka, 1997). In the spring of 1998 the EPA proposed an emission trading program, modeled on the SO_2 program, to reduce emissions of nitrous oxides.

The successful experience with SO_2 emissions trading illustrates a very important principle in inventing new property rights institutions to manage access to formerly open-access resources. In a now-classic paper Coase (1960) argued that when only a few decision makers are involved in the generation of externalities and only a few consumers are affected by the externality, the two parties, if left to themselves, will be induced to voluntarily negotiate a set of payments (or bribes) that results in a reduction of the externalities to an acceptable level. However important analytically, the Coase theorem has little relevance to most externality problems. The important externality problems that concern society today, such as SO_2 pollution, typically involve large numbers of polluters and even larger numbers of persons affected by

---

[30] The original motivation of the acid rain control program was to reduce acidification of forest and aquatic ecosystems. However, the bulk of the benefits have resulted from reduced human risk of premature mortality through reduced exposure to sulfates (Stavins, 1998:71).

the externalities. Direct negotiation would involve unacceptably large transaction costs. In 1968 Dales argued that "there exists no economically optimum division between amenity and pollution uses of water" (1968a:799). Regardless of political or economic considerations the decision must be arbitrary. An implication is that in contrast to a "natural" market the government must make the decision to establish the conditions necessary for a "constructed" market to function.[31] In the SO_2 case it was necessary for an outside principle, the U.S. Congress, to define the size (or the boundaries) of the private resource, in this case the maximum tons of SO_2 emissions, and to establish trading rules. In the absence of public intervention there would have been no private market in emissions.

GLOBAL CLIMATE CHANGE

The possibility that burning coal could result in enough accumulated carbon dioxide (CO_2) in the atmosphere to induce global warming was first advanced by the Swedish geochemist Svante Arrhenius in 1896. During the 1960s and 1970s it became increasingly clear that the level of CO_2 in the atmosphere had increased by somewhere in the neighborhood of 25% since the beginning of the industrial revolution. By the late 1980s climate change was emerging from the status of scientific speculation to an issue of worldwide concern.

As concerns about global climate change have moved onto the policy agenda, a number of observers have pointed to an offsetting trend. Since well before Arrhenius made his observations, the carbon intensity of energy use—the average ratio of carbon to hydrogen—has been declining at about 0.3% per year (Ausubel et al., 1988; Nakicenovic, 1997). This decline has been associated with important structural changes in energy use—from biomass to coal and from coal to petroleum, natural gas, and nuclear energy (Figures 7.1–7.3). There has also been a decline in primary energy intensity—energy input per unit of output—in industrialized and some developing countries. Yet in both industrialized and developing countries energy use and carbon emissions, associated with economic growth, have continued to rise. Furthermore, the economic models that are available do not provide an adequate interpretation of the structural changes in energy use that have led to the trend in decarbonization.

The international community has responded to the possibility of human-induced global climate change by adopting, at the UN Conference on Environment and Development (UNCED) in June 1992, in Rio de Janeiro, Brazil, a framework convention on climate change. The convention advanced as its objective the stabilization of greenhouse gas concentrations in the atmosphere at a level that would prevent dangerous human-induced changes in the climate system. Signatories agreed to undertake national policies to limit greenhouse gas emissions to 1990 levels. A subsequent

---

[31] For the distinction between natural and constructed markets, see Coggins and Ruttan (1999).

conference in Kyoto in 1997 reached an agreement that a group of 24 rich country members of the OECD and the European countries of the former Soviet Union would reduce their CO_2 and other greenhouse gases 6–8% from 1990 levels over the period from 2008 to 2012 (Bolin, 1998:330, 331).[32] In the fall of 1998 a conference was held in Buenos Aires to discuss the implementation of the Kyoto accords.

Human Forcing

During the past century global average temperature has risen somewhere in the neighborhood of 0.5°C. In 1996 the Second Assessment Report by the UN Intergovernmental Panel on Climate Change (IPCC) concluded that a "significant change" in global mean temperature can now be detected, that "the observed warming trend is unlikely to be entirely natural in origin," and that "the balance of evidence suggests there is a discernible human influence on global climate" (Houghton et al., 1996:44–45).[33]

The authors of the Second Assessment Report also concluded that by the year 2100 human activities are likely to raise the mean global temperature from 1.0 to 3.5°C (1.8 to 6.3°F) above its 1990 level. They found general agreement among model simulations that the effects will include late autumn and winter warming in high northern latitudes, reduced sea ice and snow cover, a reduction in the diurnal (daytime) temperature range, changes in the global hydrological cycle, and increased precipitation and soil moisture in high latitudes in winter (Houghton et al., 1996:47–48). They also expect dryer summers in the continental interiors in the northern hemisphere and a rise in sea level (in the range of 15–95 centimeters by 2100). The 1995 report is more conservative than earlier reports in its projections of the rate of increase in CO_2 accumulation, the rate of increase in global average temperature, and the rate of sea level rise. More greenhouse gases were incorporated explicitly in the models and greater attention was given to the still uncertain impact of aerosols (windblown soil and dust, particles from the combustion of fossil fuels and ash, and soot from forest and agricultural burning). A major limitation continues to be the resolution level of climate change projections. The computers available to climate modelers were not capable of achieving resolution below the 300 square kilometer range—an area roughly the size of Oregon.

---

[32] CO_2 accounts for about two-thirds of "radiative forcing"—the tendency to raise atmospheric temperature. The other important greenhouse gasses include methane (CH_4), nitrous oxides (N_2O), and chlorofluorocarbons (CFCs). The 1992 and 1998 conventions did not cover CFCs since they had already been covered by the Montreal Protocol of 1987 (and 1990 amendments) in which major CFC-producing countries agreed to eliminate CFC production and consumption by 2000. CFCs were widely used for refrigerants, insulation, cleaning solvents, and in aerosols. In addition to greenhouse effects they were identified as responsible for depletion of ozone over Antarctica.

[33] The Second Assessment Report is published in three volumes (Houghton et al., 1996; Watson et al., 1996; Bruce et al., 1996). For review and evaluation, see Clark and Jaeger (1997:23–28), Kates (1997:29–33), and O'Riordan (1997:34–39). The suggestion that a discernible human effect on global climate had become apparent has generated a strong critical reaction in the congress, among a group of skeptic scientists, and in the conservative press. For a review and response to the skeptics, see Ehrlich and Ehrlich (1996) and Brown (1997).

Impact

What will be the impact of climate change in the ranges projected? Impacts can be expected on most natural ecological systems, on socioeconomic systems, and on human health. It also seems clear that the largest negative impacts can be expected in those systems that are already most seriously stressed and that have the least capacity to adapt. Thus, the impact will be much greater on people in poor countries that remain highly dependent on agriculture than in rich countries such as the United States, where less than 2% of the labor force is engaged in farming. But the impacts will be quite complex. For example, higher concentrations of greenhouse gases in the atmosphere may lead to global warming, but the higher concentration may also increase plant growth through nitrogen fertilization and reduced water demand for many plants. There are four areas in which vulnerability to climate change will be most significant: forest ecosystems, coastal zones and small islands, human health, and agriculture (Kates, 1997:30).

Two alternative policy approaches, characterized as *preventionist* and *adaptationist,* have been advanced for dealing with the threat of global warming. Preventionist argue that the accumulation of greenhouse gases may have a catastrophic impact on nature and humankind and that action should be taken immediately to drastically reduce the rate of increase in CO_2 accumulation in the atmosphere. In contrast, adaptationists argue that climate change will occur slowly and that nature and human society can adapt. These two schools have been reluctant to engage each other in constructive dialogue. "The preservationists fear that research on adaptation will weaken society's willingness to reduce greenhouse gas emissions and thus play into the hands of those who argue that any action is premature. Many adapationists, on the other hand, see no need to study adaptation in a systematic way because they trust the invisible hand of either natural selection or market forces to bring it about" (Kates, 1997:32).

Economists and other social scientists have, however, devoted substantial effort to projecting the comparative costs and benefits of mitigation and adaptation strategies.[34] A number of studies carried out in the early 1990s attempted to estimate the cost of abatement (Manne and Richels, 1990; Jorgenson and Wilcoxen, 1992). These studies typically estimated a cost in the range of 2% of GNP in the United States for a reduction in carbon emissions of 50% by 2050. A major limitation in the early studies was their insensitivity to the effects of abatement efforts on the rate and direction of technical change. Technology was usually taken as "given" or assumptions about technical change inserted exogenously—"by hand."

A second set of studies attempted to compare the economic damage from global warming with abatement costs (Cline, 1992; Nordhaus, 1991, 1994). The Cline study was exceedingly ambitious. Impacts of global warming and the costs and benefits of

---

[34] See, in particular, Committee on Science, Engineering and Public Policy (1991), Stern et al. (1992), Kaya et al., (1993), Nakićenović et al. (1994), and Nakićenović et al. (1996). See also the collection of papers in Tietenberg (1997).

abatement were projected to 2275. The overall pattern that emerged from this analysis is an initial phase of low carbon reductions, followed by a period when costs rise to 3.5% of world GDP, and then taper off to 2.5%. On the benefit side, the pattern is one of initial small benefits (because of the long lag of warming behind emissions) followed by a steady rise. Benefit–cost comparisons were made for high-, medium-, and low-benefit scenarios. After several decades (depending on the scenario) benefits begin to exceed costs. If policymakers are assumed to be risk averse even an aggressive mitigation policy generates a favorable benefit–cost estimate.

Models constructed by Nordhaus (1994) in the early 1990s attempted to go beyond the calculation of benefit–cost estimates for alternative abatement scenarios to construct an optimum path of greenhouse gas abatement. The Nordhaus model (the DICE model) is a one sector neoclassical model for the world economy that integrated a production model for world output, a model of intertemporal choice based on utility maximization by a representative customer, and a model of the impact of climate change on productivity. Economic activity, primarily the combustion of fossil fuels, generates climate change. Climate change feeds back into economic activity by reducing productivity. A carbon tax partially internalizes the externality associated with CO_2 emissions. The model provides a sophisticated version of cost–benefit analysis to determine the optimal path of greenhouse gas emission reduction. To evaluate the impact of policy to control climate change by limiting emissions Nordhaus carried out two simulations—one with no-controls and a second with optimal control on the emissions. The difference between the two simulations is, unexpectedly, quite small. The optimal reduction in greenhouse gas emissions, compared to the no-control scenario, is 9% and gradually rises to 14% by the year 2100. The optimal policy can be implemented by a carbon tax that rises from $5 per ton to $20 per ton by the end of the twenty-first century. The Nordhaus DICE model implies that an abatement policy far less aggressive than the abatement policy of the Cline scenarios would be optimal.

The evidence reviewed in Chapter 7 suggested that technical change in the energy sector has been powerfully induced by changes in the price of energy relative to other factors (Jorgenson and Fraumeni, 1981; Jorgenson and Wilcoxon, 1993; Schipper and Myers, 1992). A third round of energy climate models has been constructed in which technical change is induced, at least in part, by economic factors rather than being incorporated exogenously. In a modified DICE model (the R&DICE model), technical change is partially induced by letting the rate of energy-efficiency improvement vary in proportion to the additional research invested in the energy sector (Nordhaus, 1997). Carbon abatement accrues as a result of both energy-efficiency improving R&D and substitution of capital inputs for energy inputs. In the R&DICE model the inducement effect is quite small because of the high opportunity cost of research resources allocated to the development of technical change to reduce carbon emissions.

Partial induced technical change models with endogenous substitution among resources and an exogenously declining cost trend for the backstop technology, similar in concept to the R&DICE model, have been conventional for some time (International Institute for Applied Systems Analysis and World Energy Council,

1995). An example is a modified Nordhaus model employed to assess the effects of anticipated declines in the costs of photovoltaic technology (Chakravorty et al., 1997:1201–1234). The model incorporates endogenous substitution among energy sources (coal, oil, natural gas, and photovoltaic) with an exogenous decline in the price of electricity generated by photovoltaic technology at the rate of the past several decades. In these simulations carbon emissions continue to increase through the first quarter of the twenty-first century, but then decline sharply as energy generation shifts from coal, oil, and natural gas to photovoltaic (or other solar) technology.[35]

Beginning with a seminal article by Grubb et al. (1996) a number of suggestions have been made about how to fully endogenize the rate and direction of technical change in energy–climate models.[36] In models in which technical change is treated as exogenous, delay in instituting abatement policies has often appeared justified because of the long delay in realizing the benefits. Furthermore, it has been assumed that the cost of abatement would decline in the future as costs of carbon abatement and energy conservation technologies declined. With induced technical change it seems apparent that greater near-term abatement efforts would become economically more attractive. Grubb and associates insist that although the system has substantial inertia because of long-lived capital equipment, imposition of even a modest carbon tax in a model with induced technical change would act as a powerful inducement to bias technology in an energy (and carbon)-saving direction. Policies that strengthen market incentives for abatement have the effect of generating more market opportunities, strengthening expectations, and enhancing cash flows in support of technical change and learning by doing in a carbon-saving direction across a broad technological front.[37]

An important potential advantage of incorporating induced technical change into energy climate models would be to reduce the perceived tension between mitigation and adaptation. Induced technical change reduces the cost of mitigation and widens the possibilities of adaptation. But there have been substantial analytical difficulties in formalizing models that fully incorporate induced or endogenous technical change. Research currently underway promises to overcome many of these difficulties. Until these newer models have been implemented, it is important to recognize that technical

---

[35] The substantial declines in energy-related R&D in the developed countries (except Japan) since the mid-1980s suggests that the development of alternative power sources such as grid-connected photovoltaic systems may be slower than anticipated (Dooley, 1998:551).

[36] These studies are reviewed by Weyant (1997) and Weyant and Olavson (1998). Several were presented at the June 1997 IIASA International Workshop on Induced Technical Change and the Environment.

[37] The presence of induced technological change generally lowers the cost of achieving a given abatement target. At the same time, the costs of a given carbon tax are generally higher in the presence of induced technological change than in its absence. In the presence of induced technological change, the economy responds more "elastically" to the carbon tax. The greater costs are a reflection of the greater amounts of emissions abatement. However, even when it gives rise to greater costs, induced technological change raises the attractiveness of CO_2 abatement policies by generating larger benefits from a given tax. It is possible, though, that induced technical change can reduce the costs of a carbon tax if, prior to its imposition, R&D had been substantially biased toward the fossil fuel industries (Goulder and Schneider, 1998; Goulder and Mathai, 1998; Weyant and Olavson, 1998).

change is more endogenous than implied in the conventional models. Furthermore these models suggest that although early investment may be expensive, promising low zero carbon technologies can dramatically reduce the cost of CO_2 mitigation (Weyant and Olavson, 1998; Grübler and Gritseuzkii, 1998).

Institutional Design

The rich country signatories to the 1997 Kyoto Framework Convention on Climate Change (FCCO) committed themselves to achieving a set of binding emission targets for each of the six greenhouse gases over a 5-year period centered on 2010.[38] The Kyoto agreement provides opportunities for the industrial countries to trade rights to emit greenhouse gases with each other. They may also invest in clean development projects in the developing world and use these projects' emission reductions toward meeting their own targets. In addition, countries can count reduced CO_2 levels from changes in land use and new forest technology that remove greenhouse gases from the atmosphere toward meeting their commitments. However, the Kyoto signatories did not adequately address the institutional arrangements that must be put in place to induce the development and adoption of energy-saving and lower carbon-emitting technologies. President Clinton has indicated that he did not intend to submit the Kyoto agreement for ratification by the U.S. Senate until there is meaningful participation by several of the larger developing countries.

There are widely varying assessments of the accomplishments of the Kyoto Protocol on Climate Change (Cooper, 1998:66–79; Jacoby et al., 1998:54–66). A number of informed observers fear that the Kyoto agreement accomplished little more than postponing the serious actions that will be necessary if atmospheric concentrations of greenhouse gases are to be stabilized or reduced. There is fairly broad agreement that progress must be made in at least three dimensions. First, a substantial reduction in global emissions will require worldwide participation. Even a total ban on the use of fossil fuels by the presently industrialized countries would be inadequate. To achieve sufficiently broad participation, the rich countries must be prepared to transfer resources to poor countries that cannot bear the costs of emission control. A second essential requirement is research leading to the development of technologies that will reduce emissions or lower the cost of emission control. The technical options include increasing reliance on nuclear power, using solar power to produce electricity, and converting fossil fuels to hydrogen fuel and storing the by-product CO_2 (underground or in the deep ocean). The third and most difficult task will be the creation of the institutional infrastructure for monitoring and enforcing any agreed on policies.

Richard Cooper, a leading scholar in the field of international economic treaties, has argued for a common emission tax (Cooper, 1998:74).[39] The Intergovernmental

---

[38] For a useful discussion of the U.S. position at the Kyoto Framework Convention, see U.S. Council of Economic Advisors (1998:155–194, 1999:205–210).

[39] As yet, inadequate attention has been given to the equity implication of alternative tax or permit systems. In the case of a tax, for example, there are important income distribution effects depending on whether

Panel on Climate Change (Bruce et al., 1996:356–439) has argued, however, that a tradable permit system for CO_2 emissions is the only cost-effective way of achieving an acceptable level of emissions. The Clinton administration took a strong position in favor of a tradable emission permit system at the Kyoto meeting. Although controversial, the concept of emissions trading was accepted in principle (Bolin, 1998). The Kyoto Protocol also included a provision, based on a proposal by Brazil, for a Clean Development Mechanism (CDM). The CDM would provide a credit to OECD countries for investments in projects to abate emission in developing countries.

Regardless of what form of performance standards are inherently most efficient (or most equitable), it is clear that few national governments have the institutional capacity to effectively implement either a system of pollution taxes or tradable emission permits. It is also clear that no global organization has, or is likely to have in the near future, the capacity to administer, monitor, and enforce a set of international agreements capable of achieving the objectives set out in the Kyoto agreements (Stavins, 1997:293–329). It will require a strong sense of urgency to induce the national and international institutional innovations that will be necessary if greenhouse gas emissions are to be stabilized at anywhere near present levels. This is a task that will require decades rather than years to accomplish. It is difficult to visualize ratification of a proposal for either a carbon tax or a tradable permit system in the near future. The Congress has repeatedly demonstrated apathy to carbon or energy taxes. A tradable permit system would involve very large transfers of financial resources, variously estimated in the $130 billion per year range, to countries of the former Soviet Union and to developing countries.

An effective international response to the threat of global climate change means that the global community must confront several important issues with greater candor than in the past. First, it will be at least several decades before the technical and institutional changes necessary to reduce global greenhouse gas emissions can or will be put in place. Policies must be designed to both mitigate and adapt to climate change. Second, substantial transfer of resources from rich to poor countries will be necessary if the poor countries are to be induced to restrain or curtail emissions. Even large countries cannot be expected to divert large resources from meeting current development objectives to achieve climate change benefits that will be realized only in the distant future.[40] The political resolve to make such a transfer will, however, not come easily or quickly in the rich countries. A third, and more optimistic, consideration is that the cost of controlling their own emissions and the transfer to poor countries will not bulk large when measured against the anticipated growth in per capita incomes of the rich countries over the next 50 years (Schelling, 1997).

---

the tax is placed on the production or consumption of fossil fuels traded in international markets. Taxes on production would be collected by the producing country, whereas taxes on consumption would be collected by the consuming country (McKibbin, 1998).

[40] The equity and efficiency implications of alternative marketable permits for CO_2 emissions have been examined by Rose and Stevens (1993). They show that permit trading systems can be designed that would generate very large efficiency gains and transfer substantial resources to developing countries such as Indonesia and Brazil that could more than offset abatement costs.

PERSPECTIVE

In this concluding section I return to the issues raised at the beginning of the chapter. Should technology be viewed as an important threat to the life support system of the planet? Or can technical change be relied on to rescue modern economies from the threats of resource scarcity and environmental stress? My response is both and neither!

Progress in capturing the benefits of economic growth requires that we also acknowledge the hazards associated with technical change. Technical change in each of the industries discussed earlier in this book has improved human welfare. Yet change has also generated technical externalities that are hazardous to human health and the environment. In some cases it has been possible to limit the hazards associated with technical change by more technical change—by technological fixes. This is the promise, for example, of the students of material balance and industrial ecology. In other cases it has been possible to reduce the hazard by designing of institutional innovations that modify behavior. This is the promise of students of institutional innovation and design.

At the analytical level the challenge is to advance our capacity to understand and model the process of induced or endogenous technical and institutional change. But it will not be sufficient to advance our knowledge and anticipate the consequences of technical and institutional change. Advances in knowledge will have to be accompanied by advances in capacity, in both the private and public sectors, to engage in the coordinated design of new technologies and institutions.

This capacity is not yet available. This means that it will be necessary to continue to rely very heavily on tacit as well as formal knowledge in the design of technical and institutional institutions. Learning by doing and learning by using will continue to be important sources of technical and institutional change. To some this may bear an unfortunate analogy to driving down a four-lane highway while looking out the rear view mirror rather than cruising on a new highway with electronic controls.

New technology will continue to be the source of unanticipated impacts on human health and the environment. Neither public nor private institutions can be expected to accurately produce the results anticipated by designers. This limitation means that we will continue, in the future as in the past, to be confronted by unanticipated technical and institutional shocks or surprises. The emergence of global climate change as a major issue in international relations was completely unanticipated only a quarter century ago. The end of the Cold War, the major institutional change of the last quarter century, was not anticipated even in the mid-1980s.

REFERENCES

Adriaanse, A., S. Bringezu, A. Hammond, Y. Moriguchi, E. Rodenberg, D. Rogich, and H. Schutz. *Resource Flows: The Material Basis of Industrial Economies.* Washington, DC: World Resources Institute, 1997.

Antle, J. M., and G. Heidenbrink. "Environment and Development: Theory and International Evidence." *Economic Development and Cultural Change* 43 (April 1995):603–626.

Arrow, K., B. Bolin, R. Costanza, P. Dasgupta, C. Folke, C. S. Holling, B. Jansson, S. Levin, K. Maler, C. Perrings, and D. Pimentel. "Economic Growth, Carrying Capacity and the Environment." *Science* 168 (1995):520–521.

Ausubel, J., and H. E. Sladovich, eds. *Technology and the Environment*. Washington, DC: National Academy Press, 1989.

Ausubel, J. H., A. Grübler, and N. Nakicenovic. "Carbon Dioxide Emissions in a Methane Economy." *Climatic Change* 12 (1988):245–263.

Ayres, R. U. *Resources, Environment and Economics: Applications of the Materials/Energy Balance Principle*. New York: John Wiley & Sons, 1978.

Ayres, R. U., and A. V. Kneese. "Production, Consumption and Externalities." *American Economic Review* 59 (June 1969):282–297.

Ayres, R. U., and U. E. Simonis. *Industrial Metabolism: Restructuring for Sustainable Development*. New York: United Nations University Press, 1994.

Barnett, H. J. "Scarcity and Growth Revisited." In *Scarcity and Growth Reconsidered*, V. K. Smith, ed., pp. 162–217. Baltimore, MD: Johns Hopkins University Press, 1979.

Barnett, H. J., and C. Morse. *Scarcity and Growth: The Economics of Natural Resource Availability*. Baltimore, MD: Johns Hopkins University Press, 1963.

Baumol, W. J. "On Taxation and Control of Externalities." *American Economic Review* 62 (June 1972):307–322.

Baumol, W. J., and W. E. Oates (with V. S. Bawa and David Bradford). *The Theory of Environmental Policy: Externalities, Public Outlays and the Quality of Life*. Englewood Cliffs, NJ: Prentice-Hall, 1975.

Bennett, M. K. "Population and Food Supply: The Current Scare." *Scientific Monthly* 68 (1949):17–26.

Berck, P. "Empirical Consequences of the Hotelling Principle." *Handbook of Environmental Economics*, D. W. Bromley, ed., pp. 202–221. Oxford, UK: Blackwell Publishers, 1995.

Binswanger, H. P., and V. W. Ruttan. *Induced Innovation: Technology, Institutions and Development*. Baltimore: Johns Hopkins University Press, 1978.

Bockstael, N. E., A. M. Freeman III, R. J. Kopp, P. R. Portney and V. K. Smith. "On Valuing Nature." College Brook, MD: University of Maryland Department of Agricultural and Resource Economics, 1998 (mimeo).

Bohm, P., and Russell. "Comparative Analysis of Alternative Policy Instruments." In *Handbook of Natural Resource and Energy Economics, Vol. I*, A. V. Kneese and J. Sweeney, eds., pp. 395–460. Amsterdam: North Holland, 1985.

Bolin, B. "The Kyoto Negotiations on Climate Change: A Science Perspective." *Science* 279 (January 16, 1998):330, 331.

Boulding, K. E. "The Economics of the Coming Spaceship Earth." In *Environmental Quality in a Growing Economy*, Henry Jarrett, ed., pp. 3–14. Baltimore, MD: Johns Hopkins University Press, 1966.

Bromley, D., ed. *Handbook of Environmental* Economics. Oxford, UK: Blackwell Publishers, 1995.

Brown, G. E. "Environmental Science Under Siege in the U.S. Congress." *Environment* 39 (March 1979):13–20, 29–31.

Bruce, J. P., H. Lee, and E. F. Haites, eds. *Climate Change 1995: Economic and Social*

Dimensions of Climate Change. Contribution of Working Group III to the Second Intergovernmental Panel on Climate Change. New York: Cambridge University Press, 1996.

Burtraw, D. "The SO_2 Emissions Trading Program: Cost Savings without Allowance Trades." *Contemporary Economic Policy* 14 (April 1996):79–94.

Carlson, R. *Silent Spring.* Boston, MA: Houghton Mifflin, 1962.

Carson, R. T. "Valuation of Tropical Rainforests: Philosophical and Practical Issues in the Use of Contingent Valuation." *Ecological Economics* 24 (1998):15–29.

Chakravorty, U., J. Roumasset, and K. Tse. "Endogenous Substitution among Energy Resources and Global Warming." *Journal of Political Economy* 105 (1997):1201–1233.

Ciriacy-Wantrup, S. V. *Resource Conservation: Economics and Policies.* Berkeley, CA: University of California Press, 1952.

Ciriacy-Wantrup, S. V., and R. C. Bishop. "Common Property as a Concept in Natural Resource Management." *Natural Resources Journal* 15 (1975):713–727.

Clark, W. C., and J. Jaeger. "Climate Change 1995: The Science of Climate Change." *Environment* 39 (November 1997):23–28.

Cline, W. R. *The Economics of Global Warming.* Washington, DC: Institute for International Economics, 1992.

Coase, R. H. "The Problem of Social Cost." *Journal of Law and Economics* 3 (October 1960):1–44.

Coggins, J. S., and J. R. Swinton. "The Price of Pollution: A Dual Approach to Valuing SO_2 Allowances." *Journal of Environmental Economics and Management* 30 (1996):58–72.

Coggins, J. S., and V. W. Ruttan. "U.S. Emission Permit System." *Science* 284 (1999):263, 264.

Committee on Global Change of the Commission on Geoscience, Environment, and Resources. *Research Strategies for the U.S. Global Change Research Program.* Washington, DC: National Academy Press. 1990.

Committee on Science, Engineering and Public Policy. *Policy Implications of Greenhouse Warming.* Washington DC: National Academy Press, 1991.

Common, M. "Comments on Papers by Robinson, Sumay and Page." In *The Economics of Natural Resources Depletion,* D. W. Pearce, ed., pp. 74–80. London: MacMillan, 1975.

Cooper, R. N. *Environment and Resource Policies for the World Economy.* Washington, DC: The Brookings Institution Press, 1994.

Cooper, R. N. "Toward a Real Global Warming Treaty." *Foreign Affairs* 77 (March/April 1998):66–79.

Costanza, R., R. d'Arge, R. de Groot, S. Farber, M. Grasso, B. Hannon, K. Limburg, S. Naeem, R. V. Oneill, J. Parueto, R. Raskin, P. Sutton, and M. van den Belt. "The Value of the World's Ecosystem Services and Natural Capital." *Nature* 387 (May 15, 1997): 253–260.

Costanza, R., C. Perrings, and C. J. Cleveland. *The Development of Ecological Economics.* Cheltenham, UK: Edward Elgar, 1997.

Crocker, T. D. "The Structure of Atmospheric Pollution Control Systems." In *The Economics of Air Pollution,* H. Wolozin, ed., pp. 61–86. New York: W. W. Norton, 1966.

Daily, G. C. *Natures Services: Societal Dependence on Natural Ecosystems.* Washington, DC: Island Press, 1997.

Dales, J. H. "Land, Water and Ownership." *Canadian Journal of Economics* 1 (November, 1968a):791–804.

Dales, J. H. *Pollution, Property and Prices.* Toronto: University of Toronto Press, 1968b.

Daly, H. E. "On Economics as a Life Science." *Journal of Political Economy* 76 (1968):392–406.

Daly, H. E. "The Economics of the Steady State." *American Economic Review* (May 1974):15–21.

Daly, H. E. *Steady State Economics.* San Francisco, CA: W. H. Freeman, 1977.

Daly, H. E. "From Empty World Economics to Full World Economics: Recognizing an Historical Development." In *Environmentally Sustainable Economic Development: Building on Bruntland*, R. Goodland, H. Daly, and S. El Serafy, eds., pp. 18–26. World Bank Environment Working Paper 46, Washington, DC: World Bank, 1991.

Dasgupta, P., and G. Heal. *Economic Theory and Exhaustible Resources.* Cambridge, UK: Cambridge University Press, 1979.

Dasgupta, P., and K.-G. Mäler. "Poverty, Institutions, and the Environmental Resource Base." In *Handbook of Development Economics*, J. Behrman and T. N. Srinivasan, eds., pp. 2370–2463. Amsterdam, The Netherlands: Elsevier Science B. V., III A 1995.

Davies, J. C., and J. Mazurek. *Pollution Control in the United States: Evaluating the System.* Washington, DC: Resources for the Future, 1998.

Demsetz, H. "Toward a Theory of Property Rights." *American Economic Review* 57 (1967): 347–359.

Diamond, P. A., and J. A. Hausmann. "Contingent Valuation: Is Some Number Better Than No Number?" *The Journal of Economic Perspectives* 8 (1994):45–64.

Dietz, T., and E. A. Rosa. "Rethinking the Environmental Impacts of Population, Affluence and Technology." *Human Ecology Review* 1 (1994):277–300.

Dietz, T., and E. Rosa. "Environmental Impacts of Population and Consumption." In *Environmentally Significant Consumption: Research Directions*, P. C. Stern et al., eds., pp. 92–99. Washington, DC: National Academy Press, 1997.

Dooley, J. J. "Unintended Consequences: Energy R&D in a Deregulated Energy Market." *Energy Policy* 26 (1998):547–555.

Eckstein, O. *Water Resource Development: The Economics of Project Evaluation.* Cambridge, MA: Harvard University Press, 1958.

Ehrlich, P. R., and A. H. Ehrlich. *Population Resources, Environment: Issues in Human Ecology.* San Francisco, CA: W. H. Freeman, 1970.

Ehrlich, P. R., and A. H. Ehrlich. *Betrayal of Science and Reason: How Anti-Environmental Rhetoric Threatens Our Future.* Washington, DC: Island Press, 1996.

Ehrlich, P. R., and J. P. Holdren. "Impact of Population Growth." *Science* 121 (1971):1212–1217.

Eisner, R. *The Total Incomes System of Accounts.* Chicago, IL: The University of Chicago Press, 1989.

Ervin, D. E., C. F. Runge, E. A. Graffy, W. E. Anthony, S. S. Batie, P. Faith, T. Penny, and T. Warman. "Agriculture and the Environment: A New Strategic Vision." *Environment* 40(July/August 1998):8–15, 35–40.

Ezzati, M., B. Singer, and D. Kammen. *Toward an Integrated Framework for Development Policy: The Dynamics of Environmental Kuznets Curves.* Princeton, NJ: Princeton University Center for Environmental Studies Report PUICEES No 315, 1999.

Farrow, S. and M. Toman. "Using Benefit-Cost Analysis to Improve Environmental Regulation." *Environment* 41 (March 1999):12–15, 33–38.

Farzin, Y. H. "Technological Change and the Dynamics of Resource Scarcity Measures." *Journal of Environmental Economics and Management* 29 (1995):105–120.

Feeny, D., S. Hanna and A. F. McEvoy. "Questioning the Assumptions of the 'Tragedy of the Commons' Model of Fisheries." *Land Economics* 72 (May 1966):187–205.

Fialka, J. J. "Breathing Easy: Clear Skies Are Goal as Pollution Is Turned into a Commodity." *Wall Street Journal* (October 3, 1997):A1, A5.

Fisher, A. C. "Measures of Natural Resource Scarcity." In *Scarcity and Growth Reconsidered,* K. Smith, ed., pp. 249–275. Baltimore, MD: Johns Hopkins University Press, 1979.

Freeman, A. M. *The Measurement of Environmental and Resource Values: Theory and Methods.* Washington, DC: Resources for the Future, 1993.

Frosch, R. A. "Industrial Ecology: A Philosophical Introduction." *Proceedings of the National Academy of Sciences of the United States of America* 89 (1992):800–803.

Frosch, R. A. "Toward the End of Waste: Reflections on a New Ecology of Industry." In *Technology Trajectories and the Human Environment,* J. H. Ausubel and H. Dale Langford, eds., pp. 157–167. Washington, DC: National Academy Press, 1997.

Georgescue-Roegen, N. *The Entropy Law and the Economic* Process. Cambridge, MA: Harvard University Press, 1971.

Goeller, H. E., and A. M. Weinberg. "The Age of Substitutability." *Science* 191 (1976):683–689.

Goulder, L. H. "Induced Technical Change, Crowding Out, and the Attractiveness of CO_2 Emissions Abatement." Palo Alto, CA: Stanford University Department of Economics, January 1998 (mimeo).

Goulder, L. H., and D. Kennedy. "Valuing Ecosystem Services: Philosophical Bases and Empirical Methods." In *Nature's Services: Societal Dependence on Natural Ecosystems,* G. C. Daily, ed., pp. 23–47. Washington, DC: Island Press, 1997.

Goulder, L. H., and K. Mathai. "Optimal CO_2 Abatement in the Presence of Induced Technical Change." Palo Alto, CA: Stanford University Department of Economics, February 1998 (mimeo).

Gowdy, J. M. "The Value of Biodiversity: Markets, Society and Ecosystems." *Land Economics* 73 (February, 1997):25–41.

Grossman, G. M., and A. B. Krueger. "Economic Growth and the Environment." *Quarterly Journal of Economics* (May, 1995):353–377.

Grubb, M., J. Chapius, and M. Ha Duong, "The Economies of Changing Course." *Energy Policy* 23 (1996):1–14.

Grubb, M. "Technologies, Energy Systems, and the Timing of CO_2 Emissions Abatement: An Overview of Economic Issues." In *Climate Change: Integrating Science, Economics, and Policy,* N. Nakicenovic, W. D. Nordhaus, R. Richels, and F. L. Toth, eds., pp. 249–270. Laxenburg, Austria: International Institute of Applied Systems Analysis, 1996.

Grübler, A. *Technology and Global Change.* Cambridge, UK: Cambridge University Press, 1998.

Grübler, A., and A. Gritseuzkii. "A Model of Endogenous Technological Change through Uncertain Returns on Learning (R&D and Investments)." Laxenburg, Austria: International Institute for Applied Systems Analysis, 1998 (draft).

Hahn, R. W., and R. N. Stavins. "Incentive Based Environmental Regulation: A New Era from an Old Idea?" *Ecology Law Quarterly* 18 (1, 1991):1–42.

Hanemann, W. M. "Valuing the Environment through Contingent Valuation." *The Journal of Economic Perspectives* 8 (1994):19–43.

Hartwick, J. M. "Intergenerational Equity and the Investing of Rents from Exhaustible Resources." *American Economic Review* 67 (1977):972–977.

Hauer, G. K. *International Pollution Externalities: Public Bads with Multiple Jurisdictions.* Ph.D. thesis, Minneapolis, MN: University of Minnesota, 1997.

Hayami, Y., and M. Kikuchi. *Asian Village Economy at the Crossroads: An Economic Approach to Institutional Change.* Tokyo: University of Tokyo Press; Baltimore, MD: The Johns Hopkins University Press, 1981.

Hayami, Y., and V. W. Ruttan. "Factor Prices and Technical Change in Agricultural Development: The United States and Japan, 1880–1960." *Journal of Political Economy* 78 (1970):1115–1141.

Hayami, Y., and V. W. Ruttan. *Agricultural Development: An International Perspective.* Baltimore, MD: Johns Hopkins University Press, 1971, 1985.

Herman, R., S. A. Ardekani, and J. H. Ausubel. "Dematerialization." In *Technology and Environment,* J. H. Ausubel and H. E. Sladovich, eds., pp. 50–69. Washington, DC: National Academy Press, 1989.

Hicks, J. R. *The Theory of Wages.* London: Macmillan, 1932.

Hohenemser, C., R. W. Kates, and P. Slovic. "The Nature of Technological Hazard." *Science* 220 (April 22, 1983):378–384.

Holdren, J. P. "Global Environmental Issues Related to Energy Supply: The Environmental Case for Increased Efficiency of Energy Use." *Energy* 12 (10/11, 1987):975–992.

Holdren, J. P. "The Transition to Costlier Energy." In *Energy Efficiency and Human Activity: Past Trends, Future Prospects,* L. Schipper and S. Meyers (with R. B. Howarth and R. Steiner), eds. Cambridge, UK: Cambridge University Press, 1992:1–51.

Homans, F. R. and J. E. Wilen. "A Model of Regulated Open Access Resource Use." *Journal of Environmental Economics and Management* 32 (1997):1–21.

Hotelling, H. "The Economics of Exhaustable Resources." *Journal of Political Economy* 39 (April 1931):137–75.

Houghton, J. T. et al., eds. *Climate Change 1995: The Science of Climate Change.* Contribution of Working Group I to the Second Assessment Report of the Intergovernmental Panel on Climate Change. New York: Cambridge University Press, 1996.

Howe, C. W. *Natural Resource Economics: Issues, Analysis and Policy.* New York: John Wiley & Sons, 1979.

International Institute for Applied Systems Analysis and World Energy Council (IIASA-WEC). *Global Energy Perspectives to 2050 and Beyond.* London: World Energy Council, 1995.

Jacoby, H. D., R. G. Prinn, and R. Schmalensee. "Kyoto's Unfinished Business." *Foreign Affairs* 77 (July/August 1998):54–66.

Jaffe, A. B., and R. N. Stavins. "Dynamic Incentives of Environmental Regulations: The Effects of Alternative Policy Instruments on Technology Diffusion." *Journal of Environmental Economic and Management* 29 (1995):S93-S63.

James, D. E., P. Nijkamp, and J. B. Opschoor. "Ecological Sustainability in Economic Development." In *Economy and Ecology: Toward Sustainable Development,* F. Archibugi and P. Nijkamp, eds., pp. 27–48. The Netherlands: Kluwer, Dordrecht, 1989.

Jorgenson, D. W., and B. M. Fraumeni. "Relative Prices and Technical Change." In *Modeling and Measuring Natural Resource Substitution,* E. R. Berndt and B. Field, eds., pp. 17–47. Cambridge, MA: MIT Press, 1981.

Jorgenson, D. W., and P. J. Wilcoxen. "Reducing U.S. Carbon Dioxide Emissions: The Cost of Different Goals." In *Advances in the Economics of Energy and Resources,* Vol. 7, J. R. Moroney, ed., pp. 125–158. Greenwich, CT: JAI Press, 1992.

Jorgenson, D. W., and P. J Wilcoxen. "Energy, the Environment and Economic Growth." In *Handbook of Natural Resource and Energy Economics*, Vol. III, A. V. Kneese and J. L. Sweeney, eds., pp. 1267–1349. Amsterdam: North Holland, 1993.

Kasperson, J. X., R. E. Kasperson, and B. L. Turner, II. *Regions at Risk: Comparisons of Threatened Environments*. New York: United Nations University Press, 1995.

Kates, R. W. "Success, Strain and Surprise." *Issues in Science and Technology* 2 (1, 1985):46–58.

Kates, R. W. "Climate Change 1995: Impacts, Adaptations and Mitigation." *Environment* 39 (November 1997):29–33.

Kaya, Y., N. Nakicenovic, W. D. Nordhaus, and F. L. Toth, eds. *Costs, Impacts, and Benefits of CO_2 Mitigation*. Laxenberg, Austria: International Institute for Systems Analysis, 1993.

Keohane, N. O., R. L. Revesz, and R. N. Stavins. "The Positive Political Economy of Instrument Choice in Environmental Policy." *Harvard Environmental Law Review* 22 (1998):313–367.

Kikuchi, M., and Y. Hayami. "Inducements to Institutional Innovations in an Agrarian Community." *Economic Development and Cultural Change* 29 (1980):21–36.

Klaasen, G. *Acid Rain and Environmental Degradation: The Economics of Emission Trading*. Cheltenham, UK: Edward Elgar, 1996.

Kneese, A. V. *The Economics of Regional Water Quality Management*. Baltimore, MD: Johns Hopkins University Press, 1964.

Kneese, A. V. "The Economics of Natural Resources." In *Natural Resource Economics: Selected Papers of Allen V. Kneese*, pp. 281–309. Aldershot, UK: Edward Elgar, 1995.

Kneese, A. V. "Industrial Ecology and Getting the Prices Right." *Resources* 130 (Winter 1998):10–13.

Kneese, A. V., and B. T. Bower. *Environmental Quality and Residuals Management*. Baltimore, MD: Johns Hopkins University Press, 1979.

Kneese, A. V., R. U. Ayres, and R. C. D'Arge. *Economics and the Environment: A Materials Balance Approach*. Baltimore, MD: Johns Hopkins University Press, 1970.

Krutilla, J. V. "Conservation Reconsidered." *American Economic Review* 57 (June 1967): 767–786.

Krutilla, J. V., ed. *Natural Environments: Studies in Theoretical and Applied Analysis*. Baltimore, MD: Johns Hopkins University Press, 1972.

Lambright, W. H., "NASSA, Ozone, and Policy Relevant Science." *Research Policy* 24 (1995):747–760.

Lange, O. "On the Economic Theory of Socialism." In *On the Economic Theory of Socialism*, B. E. Lippincott, ed., pp. 57–129. Minneapolis, MN: University of Minnesota Press, 1938.

Larson, E.D., H. M. Ross, and R. H. Williams, "Beyond the Era of Materials" *Scientific American* 254 (6, 1986): 34–41.

Lipton, M. "Accelerated Resource Degradation by Third World Agriculture: Created in the Commons, in the West, or in Bed?" In *Agricultural Sustainability, Growth and Poverty Alleviation: Issues and Policies,* S. Vosti, T. Reardon, and W. von Urff, eds., pp. 213–241. Washington, DC: International Food Policy Research Institute, 1991.

Loehman, E., and D. M. Kilgour, eds. *Designing Institutions for Environment and Resource Management*. Aldershot, UK: Edward Elgar, 1998.

Lopez, R. "The Environment as a Factor of Production: The Effects of Economic Growth and Trade Liberalization." *Journal of Environmental Economics and Management* 27 (1994): 163–184.

Lucas, R. E. B. "International Environmental Indicators: Trade, Income and Endowments." In *Agriculture, Trade and Environment: Discovering and Measuring the Critical Linkages*, M. E. Bredahl, N. Ballinger, J. C. Dunmore, and T. L. Roe, eds., pp. 243–277. Boulder, CO: Westview Press, 1996.

Magat, W. A. "Pollution Control and Technological Advance: A Dynamic Model of the Firm." *Journal of Environmental Economics and Management* 5 (1978):1–25.

Mäler, K.-G. *Environmental Economics: A Theoretical Inquiry*. Baltimore, MD: Johns Hopkins University Press, 1974.

Manne, A. S., and R. G. Richels. *Buying Greenhouse Insurance*. Cambridge, MA: MIT Press, 1992.

Marcus, A. *Business and Society: Ethics, Government and the World Economy*. Homewood, IL: Irwin, 1993.

Masood, E., and L. Garwin. "Costing the Earth: When Ecology Meets Economics." *Nature* 395 (1998):426–427.

McKibbin, W. J. "Greenhouse Abatement Policy: Insights from the G-cubed Multi-country Model." *Australian Journal of Agricultural and Resource Economics* 42 (1998): 99–113.

Meadows, D. H., and D. L. Meadows, with J. Randers and W. W. Behrens III. *The Limits to Growth*. New York: Universe Books, 1972 (Limits I).

Meadows, D. H., D. L. Meadows, and J. Randers. *Beyond the Limits*. Post Mills, VT: Chelsia Green Publishing Company, 1992 (Limits II).

Mishan, E. J. *Technology and Growth: The Price We Pay*. New York: Praeger, 1970.

Mishan, E. J. "The Postwar Literature on Externalities: An Interpretive Essay." *Journal of Economic Literature* 9 (March 1971):1–28.

Moazzami, B., and F. J. Anderson. Modeling Natural-Resource Scarcity Using the Error-Correction Approach." *Canadian Journal of Economics* 17 (1994):801–812.

Musgrave, R. A. *The Theory of Public Finance*. New York: McGraw-Hill, 1959.

Myers, N. "Consumption: Challenge to Development." *Science* 276 (April 4, 1997):53–55.

National Commission on Materials Policy. *Materials Needs and the Environment Today*. Washington, DC: U.S. Government Printing Office, 1973.

National Commission on Supplies and Shortages. *Government and the Nation's Resources*. Washington, DC: U.S. Government Printing Office, 1976.

National Research Council. *Our Common Journey: A Transition Toward Sustainability*. Washington, DC: National Academy Press, 1999.

Netting, R. M. "Of Men and Meadows: Strategies of Alpine Land Use." *Anthropological Quarterly* 45 (1972):132–144.

Netting, R. M. "What Alpine Peasants Have in Common: Observations on Communal Tenure in a Swiss Village." *Human Ecology* (4, 1976):135–146.

Nakićenović, N. "Freeing Energy from Carbon." In *Technological Trajectories and the Human Environment*, J. H. Ausubel and H. D. Langford, eds., pp. 74–88. Washington, DC: National Academy Press, 1997.

Nakićenović, N., W. D. Nordhaus, R. Richels and F. L. Toth, eds. *Integrative Assessment of Mitigation, Impacts, and Adaptations to Climate Change*. Laxenberg, Austria: International Institute for Systems Analysis, 1994.

Nakićenović, N., W. D. Nordhaus, R. Richels, and F. L. Toth, eds. *Climate Change: Integrating Science, Economics, and Policy*. Laxenberg, Austria: International Institute for Applied Systems Analysis, 1996.

Nordhaus, W. D. "The Allocation of Energy Resources." *Brookings Papers on Economic Activity* 3 (1973a):22–26.

Nordhaus, W. D. "World Dynamics: Measurement without Data." *Economic Journal* 83 (1973b):1156–1183.

Nordhaus, W. D. "To Slow or Not to Slow: The Economics of the Greenhouse Effect." *Economic Journal* 101 (July, 1991):920–937.

Nordhaus, W. D. "Lethal Model 2: The Limits to Growth Revisited." *Brookings Papers on Economic Activity* (#2, 1992):1–59.

Nordhaus, W. D. *Managing the Global Commons: The Economics of Climate Change*. Cambridge, MA: MIT Press, 1994.

Nordhaus, W. D. "Modeling Induced Innovation in Climate-Change Policy." New Haven, CT: Yale University Department of Economics, 1997 (mimeo).

Norton, B., R. Costanza, and R. C. Bishop. "The Evolution of Preferences: Why 'Sovereign' Preferences May Not Lead to Sustainable Policies and What to Do about It." *Ecological Economics* 24 (2&3, 1998):193–211.

Oates, W. E., ed. *The Economics of the Environment*. Aldershot, UK: Edward Elgar, 1992.

Oates, W. E., ed. *The RFF Reader in Environmental and Resource Management*. Washington, DC: Resources for the Future, 1999.

O'Riordan, T. "Climate Change 1995: Economic and Social Dimensions." *Environment* 39 (November 1997):34–39.

Ostrom, E. *Governing the Commons: The Evolution of Instruments for Collective Action*. Cambridge, UK: Cambridge University Press, 1990.

Palmquist, R. B., F. M. Roka, and T. Vukina. "Hog Operations, Environmental Effects, and Residential Property Values." *Land Economics* 73 (February 1997):114–124.

Pearce, D., A. Markandya, and E. B. Barbier. *Blueprint for a Green Economy*. London: Earthscan, 1989.

Pearce, D. "Auditing the Earth: The Value of the World's Ecosystem Services and Natural Capital." *Environment* 40 (March 1998):23–28.

Pearce, D. W., and J. J. Warford. *World without End: Economics, Environment, and Sustainable Development*. New York: Oxford University Press, 1993.

Pigou, A. C. *The Economics of Welfare*. London, UK:Macmillan, 1948.

Pindyck, R. S. "The Optimal Exploration and Production of Nonrenewable Resources." *Journal of Political Economy* 86 (October 1978):841–862.

Pizer, W. A. "Optimal Choice of Policy Instruments and Stringency Under Uncertainty: The Case of Climate Change." Resources for the Future Policy Paper, Washington, DC: Resources for the Future (March 1997):57–17.

Plott, C. "Externalities and Corrective Policies in Experimental Markets." *Economic Journal* 93 (1983):106–127.

President's Materials Policy Commission. *Resources for Freedom. A* Report to the President by the President's Materials Policy Commission, Washington, DC, 1952.

President's Water Resources Policy Commission. *A Water Policy for the American People*. The Report of the President's Water Policy Commission, Vol. 1, Washington, DC, 1950.

Repetto, R., W. Magrath, M. Wells, C. Beer, and F. Rossini. "Wasting Assets: Natural Resources in the National Income Accounts." In *The Earthscan Reader in Environmental Economics,* A. Markandys and J. Richardson, eds., pp. 364–388. London: Earthscan Publications, 1992.

Rohatgi, P., K. Rohatgi, and R. U. Ayres. "Materials Future: Pollution Prevention, Recycling, and Improved Functionality." In *Eco-restructuring: Implications for Sustainable Development*, R. U. Ayres and P.M. Weaver, eds., pp. 109–148. New York: United Nations University Press, 1998.

Rose, A., and B. Stevens. "The Efficiency and Equity of Marketable Permits for CO_2 Emissions." *Resource and Energy Economics* 15 (1993):117–146.

Roumasset, J. A., and K. R. Smith. "Exposure Trading: An Approach to More Efficient Air Pollution Control." *Journal of Environmental Economics and Management* 18 (1990):276–291.

Runge, C. F. "Common Property Externalities: Isolation, Assurance, and Resource Depletion in a Traditional Grazing Context." *American Journal of Agricultural Economics* 63 (November 1981):595–606.

Runge, C. F. "Common Property and Collective Action in Economic Development." *World Development* 14 (5, 1986):623–625.

Runge, C. F. "Induced Agricultural Innovation and Environmental Quality: The Case of Groundwater Regulation." *Land Economics* 63 (1987):249–258.

Runge, C. F. "Environmental Protection from Farm to Market." In *Thinking Ecologically: The Generation of Environmental Policy*, M. R. Chertow and D. C. Esty, eds., pp. 200–216. New Haven, CT: Yale University Press, 1997.

Runge, C. F., E. Cap, P. Faeth, P. McGinnis, D. Papageorgiou, J. Toby, and R. Houseman. *Sustainable Trade Expansion in Latin America and the Caribbean: Analysis and Assessment*. Washington, DC: World Resources Institute, 1997.

Ruttan, L. M. "Closing the Commons: Cooperation for Gain or Restraint." *Human Ecology* 26 (1998):43–66.

Ruttan, V. W. "Technology and the Environment." *American Journal of Agricultural Economics* 63 (December 1971):707–717 (Presidential address).

Ruttan, V. W., ed. *Agriculture, Environment and Health: Sustainable Development in the 21st Century*. Minneapolis, MN: University of Minnesota Press, 1994a.

Ruttan, V. W. "Constraints on the Design of Sustainable Systems of Agricultural Production." *Ecological Economics* 10 (1994b):209–219.

Schelling, T. C. "The Cost of Combating Global Warming: Facing the Tradeoffs." *Foreign Affairs* 76 (November/December 1997):8–14.

Schipper, L. "Lifestyles and the Environment: The Case of Energy." In *Technology Trajectories and the Human Environment*, J. H. Ausubel and D. Langford, eds., pp. 89–109. Washington, DC: National Academy Press, 1997.

Schipper, L. and S. Myers (with J. B. Shoven, R. Howarth, and R. Steiner). *Energy Efficiency and Human Activity: Past Trends, Future Prospects*. Cambridge, UK: Cambridge University Press, 1992.

Schmalensee, R., D. L. Joskow, A. D. Ellerman, J. P. Montero, and E. M. Bailey. "An Interim Evaluation of Sulfur Dioxide Emissions Trading." *Journal of Economic Perspectives* 12 (1998):53–68.

Schultz, T. W. "The Declining Importance of Agricultural Land." *Economic Journal* 61 (1951):725–740.

Scitovsky, T. "Two Concepts of External Economics." *Journal of Political Economy* 62 (April 1954):143–151.

Shafik, N., and S. Bandyopadhyay. "Economic Growth and Environmental Quality: Time

Series and Cross-Country Evidence." In *World Development Report: Environment and Development.* Washington, DC: World Bank, 1992.

Simpson, D., ed. *Productivity in Natural Resource Industries.* Washington, DC: Resources for the Future, 1999.

Slade, M. E. "Trends in Natural -Resources Commodity Prices.*" Journal of Environmental Economics and Management* (1982):122–137.

Smith, V. K. "The Implications of Common Property Resources for Technical Change." *European Economic Review* 3 (1972):469–479.

Smith, V. K. *Scarcity and Growth Reconsidered.* Baltimore, MD: Johns Hopkins University Press, 1979.

Smith, V. K. "The Evaluation of Natural Resource Adequacy: Elusive Quest or Frontier of Economic Analysis." *Land Economics* 56 (August 1980):257–298.

Smith, V. K. "Mispriced Planet." *Regulation* 3 (Summer, 1997): 325–334.

Smith, V. K., and J. V. Krutilla. "Resources and Environmental Constraints to Growth." *American Journal of Agricultural Economics* 61 (August, 1979):395–408.

Smith, V. K., and J. V. Krutilla. "Economic Growth, Resource Availability and Environmental Quality." *American Economic Review* 74 (1984):226–230.

Smith, V. K., and L. L. Osborne. "Do Contingent Valuation Estimates Pass a 'Scope' Test? A Meta-analysis." *Journal of Environmental Economics and Management* 31 (1996):287–301.

Socolow, R., C. Andrews, F. Berkhout and V. Thomas, eds. *Industrial Ecology and Global Change.* Cambridge, UK: Cambridge University Press, 1994.

Solow, R. M. "The Economics of Resources or the Resources of Economics." *American Economic Review* 64 (1974):1–14.

Solow, R. M. "On the Intergenerational Allocation of Natural Resources." *Scandinavian Journal of Economics* 88 (1986):141–149.

Solow, R. M. *An Almost Practical Step Toward Sustainability.* Washington, DC: Resources for the Future, 1992.

Stavins, R. N. "Transaction Costs and Tradeable Permits." *Journal of Environmental Economics and Management* 29 (1995):133–148.

Stavins, R. N. "Policy Instruments for Climate Change: How Can National Governments Address a Global Problem." *University of Chicago Legal Forum* (1997):293–329.

Stavins, R. N. "What Can We Learn from the Grand Policy Experiment? Lessons from SO_2 Allowances Trading." *Journal of Economic Perspectives,* 12 (1998):69–88.

Stern, D. I., M. S. Common, and E. B. Barbier. "Economic Growth and Environmental Degradation: The Environmental Kuznets Curve and Sustainable Development." *World Development* 24 (1996):1151–1160.

Stern, P. C. "Toward a Working Definition of Consumption for Environmental Research and Policy." In *Environmentally Significant Consumption: Research Directions,* P. C. Stern, T. Dietz, V. W. Ruttan, R. H. Socolow, and J. L. Sweeney, eds., pp. 12–16. Washington, DC: National Academy Press, 1997.

Stern, P. C., O. R. Young, and D. Druckman, eds. *Global Environmental Change: Understanding the Human Dimensions.* Washington, DC: National Academy Press, 1992.

Sullivan, J. B., Jr., and G. R. Krieger. *Hazardous Materials Toxicology: Clinical Principles of Environmental Health.* Baltimore, MD: Williams & Wilkins, 1992.

Sullivan, J. B., Jr., M. Gonzales, G. R. Krieger, and C. F. Runge. "Health-Related Hazards of Agriculture." In *Hazardous Materials Toxicology: Clinical Principles of Environmental*

Health, J. B. Sullivan, Jr. and G. R. Krieger, eds., pp. 642–666. Baltimore, MD: Williams & Wilkins, 1992.

Taylor, R. E. *Ahead of the Curve: Shaping New Solutions to Environmental Problems*. New York: Environmental Defense Fund, 1989.

Thompson, P., and T. G. Taylor. "The Capital-Energy Substitutability Debate: A New Look." *Review of Economics and Statistics* 77 (1995):565–569.

Tietenberg, T. H. "Transferable Discharge Permits and the Control of Stationary Source Pollution: A Survey and Synthesis." *Land Economics* 56 (November 1980):391–357.

Tietenberg, T. H. *Emissions Trading: An Exercise in Reforming Pollution Policy*. Washington, DC: Resources for the Future, 1985.

Tietenberg, T. H. *Environmental and Natural Resource Economics*, 3rd ed. New York: Harper Collins, 1992.

Tietenberg, T. H. "Design Lessons from Existing Air Pollution Control Systems: The United States." In *Property Rights in a Social and Ecological Context,* S. Hanna and M. Munasinghe, eds., pp. 15–32. Washington, DC: The World Bank, 1995.

Tietenberg, T. H., ed. *The Economics of Global Warming*. Cheltenham, UK: Edward Elgar, 1997.

Tilton, J., and H. Lansberg. "Innovation in the Copper Industry." In *Productivity in Natural Resource Industries,* D. Simpson, ed., pp. 109–139. Washington, DC: Resources for the Future, 1999.

Tripp, J. T. B., and D. J. Dudek. "Institutional Guidelines for Designing Successful Transferable Rights Programs." *Yale Journal on Regulation* 6 (1989):369–391.

U.S. Council of Economic Advisors. *Annual Report of the Council of Economic Advisors*. Washington, DC: U.S. Government Printing Office, 1998, 1999.

Vincent, J. R., and T. Panayotou. "Consumption: Challenge to Development or Distraction?" *Science* 276 (April 4, 1977):53, 55–57.

Watson, R. T., M. C. Zinyowere, and R. H. Moss, eds. *Climate Change 1995: Impacts, Adaptations and Mitigation of Climate Change—Scientific-Technical Analyses*. Contribution of Working Group II to the Second Assessment Report of the Intergovernmental Panel on Climate Change. New York: Cambridge University Press, 1996.

Wernick, I. K. "Consuming Materials: The American Way.*" Technological Forecasting and Social Change* 53 (1996):11–122.

Wernick, I. K., and J. H. Ausubel. "National Materials Flows and the Environment." *Annual Review of Energy and the Environment* 20 (1995):463–452.

Wernick, I., R. Herman, S. Govind, and J. Ausubel. "Materialization and Dematerialization: Measures and Trends." In *Technological Trajectories and the Human Environment,* J. H. Ausubel, eds., pp. 135–156. Washington, DC: National Academy Press, 1977.

Weyant, J. P. "Technological Change and Climate Policy Modeling." Paper prepared for the Workshop on Induced Technical Change and the Environment, International Institute for Systems Analysis, Laxenberg, Austria, June 1997.

Weyant, J. P., and T. Olavson. "Induced Technological Change in Climate Policy Modeling." Energy Modeling Forum Working Paper 14.6. Stanford, CA: Stanford University, April 1998.

World Bank. *World Development Report, 1992: Development and the Environment*. New York: Oxford University Press, 1992.

World Commission on Environment and Development. *Our Common Future*. The Bruntland Report. New York: Oxford University Press, 1987.

CHAPTER 13

Science and Technology Policy[1]

F or 50 years World War II and the Cold War provided the political and fiscal context for public investment in science and technology in the United States. In the United States the origins of today's R&D policies, as well as the political principles on which they are based, rest primarily on the institutional arrangements established in the 1940's for the mobilization of science and technology in support of the war effort. As noted earlier (Chapter 3), Vannevar Bush, then president of the Carnegie Institution in Washington and a former dean of engineering at MIT, persuaded President Franklin Roosevelt in the summer of 1940 that the university science and engineering communities should be mobilized in support of the development of the new military technologies that would be needed to defeat Germany and Japan. Roosevelt responded by establishing the National Defense Research Committee (later the Office of Scientific Research and Development).

As the war was ending, Bush prepared, at Roosevelt's request, a report, *Science: The Endless Frontier* (1945), that established the charter for U.S. postwar science policy (Dickson, 1988:25; Bush, 1970:26–68). The Bush report insisted that basic research not only contributes to national security but also generates new processes, new products, new industries, and new jobs, and this should be encouraged through government policy (Chapter 3). For most of U.S. history, however, science policy had been derivative of technology policy. The agricultural and industrial preeminence achieved by the United States in the late nineteenth and early twentieth centuries was not a product of science-based technology. Rather the advances in technology associated with the exploitation of natural resources and advances in labor productivity were primarily the results of incremental advances in knowledge and technology associated with improvements in practice.

It was only after World War II that science policy and technology policy emerged as distinct fields (Salomon, 1977).[2] The success of science in advancing military

---

[1] I am indebted to C. Eugene Allen, Irwin Feller, Keith Fuglie, Daniel M. Kammen, Kenneth Keller, Edward Layton, Pamela Smith, and Peter Stenberg for comments on an earlier draft of this chapter.

[2] There is an unfortunate tendency to employ the term science policy to include both science and technology policy. For example: "By science policy we mean here the collective measures taken by a government in order, . . . , to encourage the development of scientific and technical research and, . . . , to exploit the results of this research for general political objectives" (Salomon, 1977:45). In earlier work I have preferred to discuss science and technology policy under the rubric of research policy (Ruttan, 1982).

technology during the war created a presumption that advances in scientific knowledge could, in the postwar world, become a major source of economic growth and human welfare. The flow of vastly greater resources into scientific and technological research and training opened the question of how resources should be allocated among basic research, applied research, and technology development, and concern over commercialization and diffusion within the several fields of science and technology.

The primary purpose of this chapter is to trace how public policy has shaped the institutions that generate, sustain, and direct scientific and technical change in the United States. I first discuss the principles of science and technology policy. I then turn to the role of two traditional policy instruments, patents and military procurement, in advancing science and technology. I then trace the evolution of the public policy instruments used to direct and manage federal science and technology policy.[3] In the final sections I discuss some continuing debates about U.S. science and technology policy.

PRINCIPLES OF SCIENCE AND TECHNOLOGY POLICY

The institutional foundations for public support of science and technology were established during the nineteenth century. The primary instruments of technology policy were the support and development of internal improvements, the patent system, and military procurement. The Geological Survey, established in 1879, became the federal government's first great scientific bureau (Dupree, 1957:195–214). In the 1880s Congress legislated the establishment of several additional scientific research bureaus and provided support for the establishment of state agricultural experiment stations (Chapter 6). Congress later supported the development of the commercial aircraft industry, beginning in 1919, through the National Advisory Committee on Aeronautics (Mowery and Rosenberg; 1982:128–130).

Doing Science and Doing Technology

Whether the motivation, even the integrity, of scientific and technological research are so different that they are guided by a different logic is a long-standing issue. In the traditional view, "Science was . . . aristocratic, speculative, intellectual in intent; technology was lower-class, empirical, action oriented" (White, 1968:79). Science was about understanding nature. Technology was about controlling nature (Chapter 3). It has been argued that this traditional distinction is no longer apt, that "The distinction between science and technology is not between the abstract functions of knowing and doing" (Layton, 1977:209). The distinction is based on differing social attitudes toward knowledge. "There are today two broad *social organizations*—we

---

[3] I do not, in this chapter, discuss science and technology policy for national security. For an introduction, see Skolnikoff (1993:49–92).

may call them science and technology—that are moved by distinct attitudes toward the output of research. Science, as a social organization, views knowledge as a *public consumption good*, whereas technology regards it as a *private capital good* (Dasgupta, 1987:10).

One problem that arises within this structure is how to reward scientists for producing public knowledge. Dasgupta maintains that the "rule of priority" in scientific discovery addresses this problem. The priority rule serves two purposes: (1) it establishes a contest for priority in scientific discovery. A scientist is thus rewarded not for his or her efforts or good intentions, but for achievement. (2) It serves as an incentive for public disclosure of new knowledge. Disclosure is required to ensure scientific integrity. And without disclosure there is no reward.

In technology the rewards are in this idealized view, quite different. Members of the technology community are motivated by the economic rents that can be earned from their findings. Integrity requires the incorporation of knowledge into a product that is technically and economically viable. The rewards that motivate the technologist (engineer, agronomist, clinician) are linked to the rents that can be appropriated from the production of knowledge. The patent system, in principle, allows individuals and firms, by disclosing their findings, to assert ownership of new knowledge and establish a claim on the rents from its use. Thus a patented invention shares a fundamental feature of the reward structure of the scientific community by providing a reward to the first inventor (Stephan, 1996).

The functional distinction between doing science and doing technology began to break down in the late nineteenth century. "Engineers, for example, adopted the experimental and theoretical methods of physics to their own use. To do this they needed new institutions which were analogous to those in physics; the scientific professional society, the research journal and the research laboratory" (Layton, 1977:209). A result was the growth and proliferation of technological sciences in fields such as engineering, medicine, and agriculture.

The traditional distinction between "doing science" and "doing technology" has broken down most completely in those fields in which advances in science and advances in technology are closely articulated (Narin and Noma, 1985:369–381). For example, the key personnel on the Manhattan Project, which produced the atomic bomb, were scientists functioning as engineers "because only scientists possessed the fundamental knowledge necessary for the engineering effort" (Dresch, 1995:179). The development of the transistor by Shockley and his colleagues at Bell Telephone has been viewed as a technological development rather than a scientific discovery. Many of the same biochemists and geneticists have been involved in both developing knowledge in genomics and advancing the techniques employed in biotechnology (Chapter 10). The "star scientists" who have been involved in the patenting and commercialization of their research have often remained more productive in advancing scientific knowledge than their less involved colleagues (Dasgupta and David, 1994; Zucker and Darby, 1998).

By the 1980s a much more complex interpretation of the relationship between scientific research and technology development than implied by the linear or assembly line model had emerged (Chapter 3, Figure 3.6; McKelvey, 1997; Stokes, 1997: 58–89).[4] Figure 13.1 illustrates the impact of the institutional environment in which science and technology is conducted on the relationship between advances in science and technology.

The lower right hand quadrant of Figure 13.1, curiosity-inspired basic research, has been termed Bohr's Quadrant after the great Danish physicist, Niels Bohr. Bohr's search for a model atomic structure was a case of pure curiosity-driven science, even though his ideas later became the source of dramatic technical developments in the field of atomic energy. Support for curiosity-driven research may be provided by private foundations, universities, or government. But regardless of motivation "the defining quality of basic research is that it seeks to widen the understanding of the phenomena of a scientific field" (Stokes, 1997:7).

The upper left hand quadrant of Figure 13.1, applied research and industry-sponsored technology development, has been termed Edison's Quadrant. The research in Edison's Menlo Park laboratory was self-consciously focused on the development

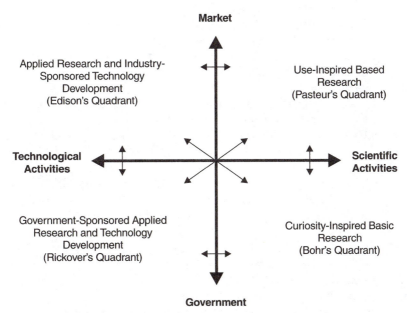

Figure 13.1 Quadrant model of organization of scientific research and technology development. (*Sources:* Adapted from Donald E. Stokes, *Pasteur's Quadrant: Basic Science and Technological Innovation*, Washington, DC: Brookings Institution, 1997; Maureen McKelvey, "Emerging Environments in Biotechnology," in *Universities and the Global Knowledge Economy*, Henry Etzkowitz and Loet Leydesdorff, eds., London: Pinter, 1997:63.)

---

[4] In an iconoclastic work Terence Kealey (1996) argues (1) that advances in scientific knowledge are more often induced by technical change than the reverse and (2) that public support for scientific research is not only less productive than private support but also displaces private support.

of commercial technology (Box 3.1). It was designed to meet the tests of both technical and economic viability. It drew on but did not contribute to scientific knowledge. Support for the research was provided entirely by the private sector—by the profits from Edison's earlier research and the expectation of future profits.

The upper right hand quadrant of Figure 13.1, use-inspired basic research, is referred to by Stokes as Pasteur's Quadrant. Pasteur's early basic research on fermentation was devoted to solving the difficult problems involved in using beets to produce alcohol. He identified the microorganisms responsible for fermentation and showed how they produced the alcohol resulting from fermentation by separating the oxygen from the sugar molecules in the fermenting juice. His later work on the development of vaccines continued to reflect an approach that involved advancing scientific knowledge to solve problems of economic or social significance.

I have termed the lower left hand quadrant of Figure 13.1, government-sponsored applied research and technology development, Rickover's Quadrant. It refers to research directed to technology development in areas in which market institutions are too weak to induce private investment: Admiral Hyman Rickover organized the effort, involving the Atomic Energy Commission Oak Ridge, Los Alamos, and Livermore laboratories and the Westinghouse and General Electric laboratories, to develop the power plants for the first nuclear submarines. Much of the federal- and state-funded agricultural research that was the source of productivity growth in U.S. agriculture during the twentieth century and much of the public sector support for research in the field of material science and technology also falls in this Rickover Quadrant.

It should be clear that the several quadrants are not self-contained. The arrow in Figure 13.1 connecting Bohr's Quadrant with Edison's Quadrant is, in effect, the Vannever Bush linear model. But there are other vertical and horizontal linkages as well that are captured in more detail for the agricultural sciences and technology in Table 6.2.

The rapid expansion of "big science" during World War II and during the early decades of the Cold War resulted in large flows of scientific, technical, and financial resources into activities located in Rickover's quadrant. The more active role that universities have played in research directed to commercial technology development in the 1980s and 1990s has also expanded the flow of scientific, technical, and financial resources in the same quadrant. Modern societies have asked scientists not only to advance understanding of the natural world but to participate in the advancement of technology—and to the amelioration of the unintended consequences of technical change. These developments have raised serious questions about the integrity of the scientific enterprise. The policies associated with these developments are discussed later in this chapter (see "Big Science" and "Commercial Technology").

The Underinvestment Rationale

It was not until the late 1950s and early 1960s that a clear economic rationale for public support of scientific research was articulated. In seminal articles published in the late 1950s and early 1960s Richard Nelson (1959:297–306) and Kenneth Arrow (1962:609–625) argued that the social returns to research investment exceeded the private returns realized by the individual firm.[5] Thus, scientific and technical knowledge possess a "public goods" dimension. The benefits from advances in science and technology "spill over" to other firms and consumers. A conclusion was that the private sector could be expected to underinvest in scientific research and that public investment would be necessary to achieve a socially optimal level of research.

This market failure argument was initially applied to basic research. However, it was increasingly found relevant to applied research and technology development as well. Social rates of return for publicly supported agricultural research, across a broad range of commodities and at the sector level, were several multiples the average rate of return on conventional private sector investment (Evenson and Kislev, 1999; Chapter 6). In a wide range of industries, social rates of return to investment in research appear to be significantly higher than private rates of return (Mansfield et al., 1977:144–166; 1986; Scherer, 1982; Griliches, 1992, 1995; Jones and Williams, 1998). The more productive private research programs typically have combined long-term sustained support by a firm with a sufficiently broad product line to capture the benefits of a major in-house research program. Public sector academic research has also demonstrated rates of return comparable to the high rates of return in publicly funded agricultural research (Mansfield, 1991:11–12).

These microeconomic studies, combined with the more macroeconomic studies of the sources of productivity growth (Chapter 2), led to a view that underinvestment in civilian R&D has represented a serious constraint on U.S. economic growth (Jones and Williams, 1998). The policy implication of this underinvestment was to expand public support to correct the private sector's underinvestment in research. This conclusion was qualified, however, by the ambiguous results of attempts to measure the private rates of return to firms that conduct publicly funded R&D. A large number of studies since the early 1970s have failed to find a consistent pattern of positive rates of return to the firms that conduct federally sponsored R&D. The problem may be that a high percentage of federally funded industrial research has been in the defense and space-related industries. Since neither the R&D nor the products produced by the performing industries are subject to normal market tests, it may be unrealistic to evaluate the returns to such research against economic criteria (Hall, 1996:148–155; Moore et al., 1995:112–118).[6]

By the early 1990s the underinvestment rationale for public sector support was being supplemented by several new analytical developments (Feller, 1992:119–131).

---

[5] The book, *The Rate and Direction of Inventive Activity*, based on a National Bureau of Economic Research conference held at the University of Minnesota in 1959 (Nelson, 1962), represented the landmark of early postwar thought on the economics of R&D. Most of the papers in the book still retain their currency. For a retrospective view, see Nelson (1997).

[6] There is some evidence that by the mid-1990s the new incentives introduced to encourage technology transfer by federal laboratories were having a positive impact on patenting activity (Jaffe and Lerner, 1999).

One line of argument, associated with the work of Arthur and David, suggests that the economies of scale realized by firms that are first to introduce a new technology may result in a "lock-in" of the initial technological trajectory, even though an alternative path of technological developments might be more efficient (Chapter 4). A second line of argument, based on strategic trade theory, is that in an industry in which the optimum scale limits the number of low-cost producers, wide-bodied aircraft for example, subsidization of R&D may determine which firms can remain economically viable. Both the increasing returns argument and the strategic trade arguments suggest that government support may be necessary to stimulate the optimal level of private sector R&D. Critics argue, however, that the information necessary to fine tune subsidies to meet the implicit criteria of the two arguments is rarely available to the government (Cohen and Noll, 1991).

A third argument emphasizes the institutional constraints on the utilization and diffusion of knowledge. Much of the literature on U.S. industry's loss of international competitiveness emphasized that although the United States led in making new scientific and technical discoveries and inventions, it lagged behind foreign rivals in commercial development. The tacit knowledge associated with the development and utilization of new technology is difficult and expensive to transfer. In this view it is insufficient for government to support the generation, of new knowledge and technology—greater weight should be given to more effective institutional arrangements for the transfer of technology. This third argument was the basis for many of the new federal and state commercial technology development and transfer programs initiated in the 1970s and 1980s.

It is somewhat ironic that the underinvestment argument, which was initially developed as a rationale for public support of fundamental or basic research, has found its primary application in the evaluation of the returns for public and private research directed to commercial technology development. In the meantime, efforts by the scientific community to develop operational criteria for the allocation of resources to scientific research have foundered.

The difficulty that the scientific community has experienced in confronting the issue of research resource allocation arises from a fundamental contradiction in the ideology (the dogma) of post-World War II science policy. This contradiction was reflected with particular force and conviction in the Bush report. As noted earlier, the Bush report advanced an investment rationale for federal support of scientific research, coupled with a profoundly agnostic view toward using the investment rationale for the allocation of research resources. The report insisted that "basic research is performed without thought of practical ends" (Bush, 1945:18) and that "Important and highly useful discoveries will result from some fraction of the undertakings in basic sciences but the results of any one investigation can not be predicted with accuracy" (Bush, 1945:19).

It is useful, in attempting to think about the criteria for the allocation of resources to basic research, to remind ourselves of what can reasonably be expected from basic research. Basic research can be viewed as an intermediate input that enhances the productivity of applied research and technology development. If applied research can be thought of as a process of sampling from a distribution of potential processes or products, as in the Nelson–Winter evolutionary model (Chapter 3), basic research can be thought of as expanding the distribution of attributes within which the sampling occurs (Evenson and Kislev, 1975:140–155). By expanding the distribution basic research increases the probability of discovering technically and economically viable research outcomes and of reducing the cost of the search process.

This view leads to what might be termed a "double derived demand" model of the demand for basic research. The demand for technical change is derived primarily from the demand for commodities and services. The demand for advances in knowledge is in turn derived from the demand for technical and institutional change. But how can this model be employed in the development of criteria for research resource allocation if, in fact, the process of search and discovery in basic science—the supply of fundamental knowledge—is governed by a stochastic process?

Alvin Weinberg, then Director of Oak Ridge National Laboratory, attempted to respond to this question in addressing the future of "big science" in the early 1960s (Weinberg, 1961:161–164, 1964:42–48). Weinberg's first step was to insist on the legitimacy of both internal and external criteria in the allocation of research resources. There are two important internal criteria: "(1) Is the field ready for exploitation? (2) Are the scientists in the field really competent?" (Weinberg, 1964:44). These criteria typically carry the most weight in peer reviews of investigator-initiated project proposals. External criteria are generated outside of the scientific field. They attempt to determine why and how intensively a field of science should be pursued. Weinberg insisted that whether a field has scientific merit cannot be answered within the field itself: "That field has the most scientific merit which contributes most heavily and illuminates most brightly its neighboring scientific disciplines" (Weinberg, 1964:45).

A similar argument has been made by David et al. (1992:73–90). They reject conventional cost–benefit or rate of return analysis as a basis for resource allocation to or within basic research. Like Weinberg, they regard basic research as an intermediate input that enhances the productivity of scientific effort in closely related fields, and of applied research and technology development. But "the channels through which basic research yields economic payoffs are so complex, and the assumptions necessary to develop estimates of the returns on an investment in basic research are so fragile and unrealistic, that this exercise is of little use in guiding actual policy decisions" (David et al., 1992:87).[7]

---

[7] David et al. note that basic research can also yield important additional externalities. (1) Basic research, when conducted in academic institutions, serves as a vehicle for the education and advanced training of scientists. (2) Basic research projects create social networks through which information that has not yet been reviewed and published diffuses rapidly. (3) Basic research projects induce advances in the technology of research, in both techniques and instrumentation, that reduce the cost and enhance the productivity of research effort. They also note that these characteristics are shared by applied research and technology development (David et al., 1992:75).

Like Weinberg, David et al. emphasize that the "number and richness of links between the knowledge generated by basic scientific projects . . . are important determinants of the potential economic returns from discoveries in a specific discipline" (1992:84). These links may involve simple parametric mapping of the results of one field into a closely related field—of the results obtained from model organisms to other organisms (Chapter 3). Or they may involve analogic links based on physical regularities across fields as in chemistry and physics. They also worry that the absence of such obvious linkages may result in underinvestment in basic research, particularly if the costs of research are exceedingly high as in high-energy particle physics.

The issues discussed in this section have emerged as an increasingly important focus in national science and technology research policy during the last decade. During the Cold War era an abundant flow of federal funds in support of science and technology acted to obscure the contradictions in science and technology policy. With the end of the Cold War and the decline in federal funding for research, the issues of research resource allocation have acquired a new urgency. I will return to this issue in a later section on science and technology policy. In the next two sections I discuss the patent system and military procurement—the two traditional areas through which the U.S. federal government stimulated technology development.

THE PATENT SYSTEM

Few institutions have stirred as much controversy for such a long time as the patent system (Scherer, 1980:439). The patent system has traditionally been the primary policy instrument employed by the United States to induce invention and innovation.[8] The U.S. Constitution provides that "The Congress shall have the power . . . to promote the progress of science and the useful arts, by securing for limited times to authors and inventors the exclusive rights to their respective writings and discoveries." Congress responded by passing a patent act in 1790. Although the legal provisions and administrative rules that make up the U.S. system of intellectual property rights— particularly the "patent system" and the "copyright system"—have changed considerably since then, they appear remarkably resistant to rapid or radical reform (David, 1993:23).[9]

A patent application has two main parts. The first, a specification of the invention, is written like a brief science or engineering article describing the problems the inventor faced, the steps that were taken to solve them, and the "best mode" known to the inventor for solving the problem. An important function served by this provision is

---

[8] In this section I draw heavily on the excellent reviews by Scherer (1980:439–458, 1990:613–660), Siebeck (1990), and David (1993:19–61).

[9] For a brief history of the evolution of intellectual property law since its origins in medieval and Renaissance Europe, see David (1993:43–54). Modern intellectual property law falls into five major classes: patents, plant breeders' rights, copyrights, trademarks, and trade secrets (Lesser, 1990). For discussion of the controversy about the extension of patents on life forms, see Chapter 10.

to provide access to the knowledge involved in developing the invention. The second part of the patent application is a set of claims that defines what the inventor considers to be the invention. This section has the function of providing the inventor with the exclusive right to make, use or sell a product based on the invention (Merges and Nelson, 1990:844).

To meet the U.S. Patent Office requirements for patentability, an invention must meet the tests of novelty, nonobviousness, and utility. Patents are governed by the laws of the nation in which an invention is patented. Thus a patent issued by the U.S. Patent and Trademark Office provides protection only within the territory of the United States. A U.S. company doing business in another country must obtain a patent in that country.

There have been a number of inconsistencies among national patent laws. One is that several countries, including Germany, Japan, and Brazil, issue short-term utility patents (or "petty patents") for incremental improvements. A second is that the United States has followed a "first-to-invent" ownership rule and permitted an inventor a grace period of 1 year between announcing a discovery at a scientific or technical meeting and filing for a patent. Other nations follow a "first-to-file" ownership rule and do not permit disclosure before filing a patent application. The Boyer–Cohen recombinant DNA technique, for example, was granted patent protection before the patent was filed in the United States but not in Europe (Chapter 10). Other national differences in patent laws include (1) term of coverage, (2) extent of coverage, (3) examination procedures, (4) transferability of rights, (5) compulsory licensing, and (6) enforcement. For example, some countries, such as India, have been reluctant to patent inventions that have health implications. Some have examination procedures that require very little disclosure of sensitive information. Other have compulsory licensing arrangements that require the transfer of technology to a local firm if the foreign patent holder does not exploit the technology in the local market for a number of years. Many low-income countries have strong patent laws but weak enforcement capacity.

Controversy about Patents

From the perspective of the individual inventor or firm there are a number of reasons why it is advantageous to patent (Scherer, 1980:444). The most obvious, of course, is to strengthen the advantage of being the first to develop a new process or product. The advantage of being first is greatest when there are a large number of potential innovators or when development costs are high. Another advantage is to guard against being foreclosed from a field of technology by another firm exercising parallel patent rights. A third is to preclude potential competitors from introducing an identical or closely related substitute without incurring development costs. When Du Pont scientists "invented" nylon, for instance, they "systematically investigated and patented the whole array of molecular variations with properties potentially similar to nylon in an attempt to prevent other firms from developing an effective substitute. The effort was, however, only partly successful. I. G. Farben and other companies invented competitive fibers using polyester and polyolefin molecules" (Scherer, 1990:624).[10]

From the perspective of the broader society, the purpose of the patent is not to reward the inventor but to provide an incentive to develop and commercialize inventions (Bush, 1970:196). Many economists have remained skeptical of the role of patents as a stimulus to invention. "It is only when the barriers to widespread and rapid imitation are weak, or when the advantages of competitive leadership are modest, or when the profit potential of the innovation is small, or when there is some adverse combination of the three, that patent protection becomes an important stimulus" (Scherer, 1980:447). There is, however, a broad consensus that although patents may provide only weak encouragement to research, it is more effective in encouraging diffusion, including the innovation and investment included in bringing a product to market (Barton, 1995:614).

Nor are patents always a very effective protection against imitation (Mansfield et al., 1981). Barton (1993:256–283) argues that in the "normal" pattern patents are used primarily as a basis for cross-license arrangements. This was the approach followed by General Electric and Westinghouse as the two firms moved toward a mature technology in electric generation and lighting (Chapter 7). The system rewards the inventor while avoiding expensive litigation, except in cases in which there is serious disagreement about the value of one or both parties' claims. Barton notes that there are two major exceptions to the "normal" pattern. One is in those industries, for example the chemical and pharmaceutical industries, in which individual patents are the basis of specific products, each of which has substantial market potential. Each product is, in effect, a market monopoly developed and marketed independently of similar products developed by competitors. In the medical biotechnology industry, for example, firms introduce only a small number of new products each year. Each involves very large front-end research and regulatory investment and each is likely to have a substantial lifetime and can be readily imitated (Chapter 10). A period of monopoly usually is essential to recover front-end fixed costs. Because of this, firms are willing to engage in substantial litigation to protect their patents from infringement (Barton, 1993:279).

Another exception to the general pattern occurs when an industry is going through a period of dynamic technical change. "Communications firms, computer firms and

---

[10] In the mid-1960s Jesse Markham suggested that in the United States, industrial R&D and patenting have been stimulated by antitrust policy. "In the United States the patent laws have for 175 years made invention and its attendant innovational activity an open road to monopoly gain; contrariwise, antitrust statutes enacted over the past 75 years have gradually foreclosed most of the remaining more obvious means for attaining such gains. Accordingly . . . the two policies have reinforced each other in stimulating innovational activity (Markham, 1966:293–294). Barton notes, however, that the United States has since replaced the earlier pattern of weak patent law and strong antitrust law with a pattern of strong patent law and weak antitrust law. In 1983 the creation of a centralized appellate court with responsibility for all patent-related appeals, and with judges drawn predominantly from the patent law bar, greatly strengthened the presumption of patent validity and scope (Barton, 1993).

software firms are all vying for additional influence and control and are seeking to assert whatever intellectual property rights they can or have been able to define" (Barton, 1993:280). Barton's comments apply equally to the biotechnology industries (Chapter 10). When the technology of these industries matures, the normal cross-licensing pattern is likely to become the dominant mode of settling intellectual property conflicts.

Students of patent policy have traditionally been even more skeptical of the advantages of a patent system for less developed countries (LDCs) (Gould and Gruben, 1996). It was generally believed that since the amount of domestic inventive activity was small, the benefits of a patent system would be small relative to the social costs of granting foreigners patent protection. The least developed countries were advised that it was to their advantage to "beg, borrow or steal" the intellectual property (including not only patented inventions but also trade secrets and copyrighted materials) developed in the more advanced countries. It was widely held that a patent system did not represent an effective method of inducing significant inventive activity in LDC's nor was it effective in enhancing the transfer of technology to LDCs from abroad. The only reason for LDCs to follow international intellectual property was to respond to political pressure from developed countries (Greer, 1973:223–266).

New Perspectives

During the 1980s and 1990s perspectives on the contribution of patent and other intellectual property rights institutions to economic growth in both developed and developing countries have shifted substantially. Scientific and technical changes, occurring rapidly and across a broad spectrum of "high-technology" industries, resulted in unprecedented pressure for the "harmonization" of intellectual property rights institutions among developed and developing countries. This demand has been strengthened by the increasing globalization and diffusion of science and technology advanced by the development of a more open international trading system and by the transition from statist to more market-driven national economies.

There is now relatively widespread agreement that a well-developed patent system serves to facilitate the successful transfer and commercial application of new scientific and technical knowledge in developing countries. A regime of strong intellectual property protection in the recipient country provides an incentive for the transfer of the tacit knowledge needed for the profitable operation of industrial processes on the part of multinational firms (Arora, 1992:141, 189). Strong patent rights may, however, reduce incentives for national firms to transfer technology by copying or adapting technology developed by firms in developed countries (Smith, 1999). If an intellectual property rights (IPR) system can be viewed as a productive investment in a country's institutional infrastructure, the issue becomes what form a country's IPR system should take and what the level of public investment in the development and maintenance of the national IPR system should be.

A consensus has not yet emerged, even within the research community, on the benefits to developing countries from a uniform framework for intellectual property rights (Lanjouw, 1977). Does, for example, a strong system stimulate—or a weak system inhibit—economic growth? This is an exceedingly important issue but one on which empirical research provides little objective evidence. Huffman and Evenson have developed a classification of countries according to their stages of scientific and technological development and have related the capacity of IPRs to stimulate inventive activity and technology transfer to the several levels in the classification (Table 6.2). Most Stage 1 countries have such limited R&D and inventive capacity that they have little capacity to develop technology that would benefit from protection. Countries in stages 2b and 2c do have capacity to reverse engineer and pirate more complex technologies. As this capacity is developed they also acquire the capacity to advance technology. As this point, the gains from a national IPR system that meets international standards may begin to exceed the gains from unrestricted imitation. An implication is that intellectual property policy is endogenous—the development of intellectual property institutions is induced when scientific and technical capacity reaches a level that national firms begin to develop technology that is worth protecting.

This perception has been reinforced since the completion of the Uruguay Round of Multilateral trade negotiations in 1994. The Uruguay Round led to the creation of a World Trade Organization (WTO) to replace the General Agreement on Tariffs and Trade (GATT). The creation of the WTO involved a comprehensive agreement on trade-related intellectual property rights (TRIPS) (Maskus, 1998). The TRIPS agreement, for the first time, sets minimum standards for all forms of intellectual property: patents copyright, trademarks, service marks, geographic indications, industrial design, design for integrated circuits, and trade secrets. The United States committed itself to adopting the standards agreed to by the other OECD countries, including extending the life of patents from 17 to 20 years from application date. The provisions of the TRIPS became applicable to the developed country signatories in 1996. The more advanced developing countries were granted an additional 5-year transition period and the least developed countries an additional 10-years transition period for product patents not protected before 1996 (including pharmaceutical patents) (World Bank, 1999:33–36). But for the poorest countries TRIPS may still be a premature institutional innovation.

A clear inference from the economics literature is that an effective intellectual property regime, while a useful component of a nation's institutional infrastructure, is hardly a sufficient instrument for inducing either innovative activity or successful commercialization of new technology. In a modern economy, more proactive policies are necessary both to protect existing advantage and to narrow the gap between advanced and lagging countries. There is substantial evidence that stronger intellectual property rights are associated with higher economic growth. The advantages of strong intellectual property rights appear to be greatest in relatively open economies and weaker in countries in which domestic firms are protected from foreign competition (Gould and Gruben, 1996). And in both developed and developing countries rethinking and reform of intellectual property rights systems—particularly in the areas characterized by "network" or "system externalities"—such as biological and information technology will be necessary if the existing intellectual property rights system is not to become a burden on technology development and diffusion.

MILITARY PROCUREMENT

It is hard to overemphasize the historical role that military procurement has played in the process of technology development (Roland, 1985).[11] Knowledge acquired in making weapons was an important source of the industrial revolution. To bore the condenser cylinders for his steam engines "Watt had to turn to John Wilkinson, a cannon-borer, who had invented the one machine in all England that could drill through a block of cast iron with accuracy" (Kaempffert, 1941:435). An important impetus for the development of the Haber–Bosh process for nitrogen fixation was to relieve the German military from dependence on foreign sources of nitrogen (Chapter 7). In the United States what came to be termed the American system of manufacturing emerged from the New England system of gun manufacture (Chapter 11). In the nineteenth century the military was often the only reliable consumer of new technical products. In Great Britain an assured market for cannon contributed importantly to the establishment of coal-fired blast furnaces in the remote regions of Wales and Scotland. In France the navy provided the market that enabled French entrepreneurs with an opportunity to catch up with British advances in ferrous metallurgy (McNeill, 1982:177, 211–212).[12]

Spin-off, Spin-away, and Spin-on

In the United States, it was only in the half century between World War II and the end of the Cold War that the defense establishment came to dominate research and development (R&D) expenditures. For 50 years the Cold War provided the political and fiscal context for public investment in science and technology (Mowery and Rosenberg, 1989:123–168; Gibbons, 1995:119). During much of this period over half of the federal R&D budget was devoted to the advancement of defense technology (Table 13.1). Nondefense research in space exploration, energy R&D, and even fundamental mathematics and in the physical, biological, and social sciences was

[11] Nef (1950) has argued, however, that this creates a false impression of progress, which is, in fact, achieved by the intensification of military production based on the accumulated advances in science and technology of the past.

[12] Edgerton argues that until well into the post-World War II period the relationship among science, technology, and war was badly neglected by historians. This myopic perspective led to "a historiography of science–state–war relationships written almost exclusively in terms of state funded civil science and technology" (Edgerton, 1996:37). Similarly Samuels notes, with some surprise, how little attention leading economic theorists have given to the interdependence of the military and civilian economies (Samuels, 1994:4–14).

Table 13.1   Federal Expenditures for Research and Development by Function, 1960–1999 (in Current Dollars)

Year		Total	Cold War				Civilian Technology							
			Defense	Space	Atomic Science	Total	National Science Foundation	Energy	Transportation	Health	Agriculture	Natural Resources	Other	Total
1960	Amount	7,322	5,937	330	183	6,450	57	159	77	277	107	68	127	872
	Percent	100.0	81.1	4.5	2.5	88.1	0.8	2.2	1.1	3.8	1.4	0.9	1.7	11.9
1970	Amount	15,153	8,021	3,518	393	11,932	292	491	407	1,073	246	301	451	3,221
	Percent	100.0	52.9	23.2	2.6	78.4	1.9	3.2	2.7	7.1	1.6	2.0	3.0	21.6
1980	Amount	30,235	14,643	4,262	345	19,250	838	3,289	861	3,682	563	951	801	10,985
	Percent	100.0	48.4	14.1	1.1	63.7	2.8	10.9	2.8	12.1	1.9	3.1	2.6	36.3
1990	Amount	63,810	41,078	5,624	784	47,486	1,520	2,342	973	8,253	937	1,220	1,081	16,324
	Percent	100.0	64.4	8.8	1.2	74.4	2.4	3.7	1.5	12.9	1.5	1.9	1.4	25.6
1995	Amount	68,432	32,699	8,243	700	46,642	1,894	3,152	1,353	11,260	1,126	1,602	1,283	21,790
	Percent	100.0	55.1	12.1	1.0	68.2	2.8	4.6	1.9	16.4	1.7	2.4	1.9	31.8
1996	Amount	68,439	39,428	6,963	705	47,096	2,077	2,938	1,654	10,498	1,168	1,610	1,398	21,343
	Percent	100.0	57.6	10.2	1.0	68.8	3.0	4.3	2.4	15.3	1.7	2.4	2.0	31.2
1997	Amount	71,073	40,177	8,137	703	49,017	2,015	2,641	1,782	11,458	1,178	1,590	1,392	22,054
	Percent	100.0	56.5	11.5	1.0	69.0	2.8	3.7	2.5	16.2	1.7	2.2	2.0	31.0
1998	Amount	71,379	39,024	7,975	1,438	48,437	2,111	1,527	1,920	13,069	1,228	1,734	1,353	22,942
	Percent	100.0	54.7	11.2	2.0	67.8	3.0	2.1	2.7	18.3	1.7	2.4	1.9	32.2
1999	Amount	73,704	39,417	7,880	1,234	49,031	2,360	4,573	2,255	14,087	1,247	1,985	1,366	24,673
	Percent	100.0	53.4	10.7	2.4	66.5	3.2	2.1	3.0	19.1	1.7	2.4	1.8	33.5

Source: Adapted table from data assembled by Keith Fuglie, Staff Economist, Council of Economic Advisors, February 1998. Data from D. C. Mowery and N. Rosenberg, *Technology and the Pursuit of Economic Growth*, Cambridge, UK: Cambridge University Press, 1989, Table 6.12; *Budget of the United States Government, Fiscal Year 1999: Historical Tables* (1999 data are preliminary).

supported because of its historical connection and potential relevance to national security (Cohen and Noll, 1996:306). There has been a continuing argument about the impact this emphasis in defense has had on the vitality of civilian technology and on economic growth (Cowan and Foray, 1995:851–868). Richard Samuels has discussed these arguments in terms of *spin-off*, *spin-away*, and *spin-on* (Samuels, 1994:18).

The concept of *spin-off* rests on a view that military R&D represents a pervasive source of civilian technology. The requirements of technically sophisticated military systems contribute to the scientific and technical capacity of supplier firms. These firms in turn become a source of technologies that diffuse throughout the industrial system. Commonly cited products include jet engines and airframes, insecticides, microwave ovens, satellites (for telecommunication, navigation, or weather forecasting), robotics, medical diagnostic equipment, lasers, digital displays, kevlar, fire-resistant clothing, integrated circuits, and nuclear power (Samuels, 1994:18). Spin-off also involves process technology developed to meet the technically sophisticated performance requirements of military-related technology and of institutional innovations developed for the management of complex systems (Box 13.1). There can be little doubt that support for R&D and procurement from the military and space programs have had a significant impact on the focus of scientific effort and on direction and diffusion of technical change. But military R&D also carries an opportunity cost—the civilian technology developments that may be foregone as a result of investment in military and space technology. Whether investment in military and space technology has represented a net benefit or burden on the pace of technical change and productivity growth in the post-World War II period is problematic.

● **BOX 13.1**

THE SPIN-OFF OF AN INSTITUTIONAL INNOVATION: THE SYSTEMS APPROACH

The military–industrial–university complex was a source of both technical and institutional innovations. The case of the systems approach illustrates both the potential power and the difficulties faced in the transfer of institutional innovations. The systems approach to project management evolved out of efforts to manage the very large-scale complex defense and space projects during and immediately after World War II. The Atlas project of the 1950s, which produced the first intercontinental ballistic missile, evolved a mode of management that became known as systems engineering. The approach first diffused throughout the military space agencies and then into nondefense industry and to civilian government agencies (Hughes, 1998:4).

Efforts to transfer the systems approach to the nondefense industrial and government sectors were undertaken with great enthusiasm. Simon Ramo, of the Ramo–Wooldridge Corporation (later TRW), a major defense and space contractor, thought the new management tools would narrow the gap between rapid technical progress and lagging social institutions. Systems analysis and planning offices involving multidisciplinary teams of engineers and behavioral scientists (economists, sociologists, psychologists) were established. President Lyndon Johnson issued an executive order requiring all federal government technical departments and agencies to institute planning, programming, and budgeting system (PPB) procedures based on systems analysis principles.

In 1968 Bernard Schriver, who had established a brilliant record as head of the Intercontinental Ballistic Missile Program, left the government to form a consulting firm established to transfer systems approaches to the nondefense sectors. He visualized the development of public interest partnerships between government and industry that would use systems analyses "to solve problems in the public interest on a profit basis" (Hughes, 1998:172). When the firm he established closed its doors in March 1969, Schriver attributed the failure to "lack of clearly understood goals among government officials, general resistance to innovation, and the role of political pressures in shaping economic policy" (Hughes, 1998:174). In effect, Schriver had concluded that the institutional innovations that had proven so effective in managing the military–industrial–university projects in the Cold War environment were ineffective in public and private sector environments that were not conducive to command-and-control organizational structures.

By the early 1980s many of the managerial innovations that had been spun-off form the systems engineering approach were in disarray. Operations research units that had been established in industry were downgraded from the managerial level to more specific applications. Academic operations research departments were being closed or merged into other units. In federal and state agencies the PPB approach to planning, programming, and budgeting had largely been abandoned. This should not be taken to imply, however, that the impact of the systems approach on the management of large organizations and large projects had disappeared. Many of the formal analytical approaches relevant to a command-and-control environment have been abandoned. But "systems thinking" and more open systems approaches remain pervasive. The integrated assessment models employed to assess the impact of global climate change (Chapter 12) are a recent example of use of the systems approach.

Sources: I draw primarily on C. West Churchman, *The Systems Approach*, New York: Delacorte Press, 1968; Thomas P. Hughes, *Rescuing Prometheus*, New York: Random House-Pantheon Books, 1998; Russell L. Ackoff, "The Future of Operational Research Is Past," *Journal of the Operational Research Society* 30 (1979):93–104.

The concept of *spin-away* refers to the progressive lack of articulation between technical change in the defense industries and the civilian economy. By the 1960s defense and space-related R&D came to be viewed as a burden on productivity growth. "Military and space research, by drawing scientific and technological capacity away from civilian application, slowed the advance of industrial technologies and reduced the rate of economic growth" (Solo, 1962:49–60). In addition, U.S. industry often failed to take advantage of the technology transfer opportunities that did exist. Defense contractors often insulated their defense R&D from nondefense R&D. These concerns became increasingly prominent in the 1970s when the slowdown in U.S. productivity growth became much more evident (Chapter 2). By the 1980s a perspective that the technological lead previously enjoyed by military technology was passing to the civilian economy became pervasive.

Spin-on is Samuels' term for the transfer of off-the-shelf technologies from civilian to military applications. Historically, spin-on has always been an important source of military technology. The most important innovations in microelectronics—Bell Laboratories' transistor, Texas Instruments' integrated circuits, Fairchilds' planar process, and Intel's microprocessor—were all the products of research directed to civilian applications but which found immediate use in military applications (Chapter 9). Not only is an increasing share of military procurement in the United States based on products initially developed for use in the civilian sector but an increasing share of these products is sourced internationally. "The Patriot missile deployed in the Gulf War of 1991 used technologically advanced components produced by Japanese subcontractors and developed initially for commercial markets" (Samuels,1994:28).

There are three reasons for the shift toward spin-on. One is the higher performance that is increasingly required in civilian markets. In the mid-1990s the microprocessors in Nintendo games were more sophisticated than in some of the latest military equipment. Another is the large and increasing development costs for new technologies. Third is that the product life cycles in commercial markets are generally shorter than for military systems. As a result the technological sophistication of commercial products was increasingly running ahead of military requirements (Samuels, 1994:28). By the late 1990s a number of technology-oriented defense contractors had discontinued their defense R&D activities (Chen, 1999).

The Defense–Industrial Base

A consequence of these developments is a much more complex relationship between the military and civilian economies in the United States than prevailed during the first several decades after World War II. The United States has shifted more toward Japan's historical pattern. Japan's industrial development in the late nineteenth and early twentieth century was motivated by the "rich nation, strong army" metaphor— civilian technology should have important military spin-on implications. Thus in the 1930s the motor vehicle industry emphasized the production of trucks rather than automobiles. In the post-World War II period, with the size of the military limited by the "one percent rule," Japanese practice has continued to emphasize those strengths in the civilian economy that would provide the foundation for a strong military (Chapter 11).

One solution for the United States, advocated by a series of official and unofficial commission and study groups, is for the military to move toward a procurement system that would encourage closer integration of civilian and military technology development to create a stronger defense industrial base. In 1986 the Presidential Commission on Defense Management (The Packard Commission) recommended that the Pentagon pursue the cost savings and quality improvements that could be realized through applications of civilian technology and the relaxation of functionally irrelevant performance requirements (Samuels, 1994:27). The Carnegie Commission on Science Technology and Government noted that the strengthening of the global technology base, particularly in Western Europe and East Asia, has two implications for U.S. defense technology policy. "First, DOD needs to draw upon the much larger commercial technology base for technologies that are not unique to defense. Second, the nation's economy as a whole needs to benefit from DOD's still large expenditure on technology" (May 1993:14). This implies reducing the bureaucratic barriers to technology sharing between the commercial and defense sectors. Budgetary stringency has forced some progress toward these objectives. But when the next national commission is appointed to study reform of miliary procurement, it is almost certain that the recommendations of the Packard and Carnegie Commissions will remain apt.

POLITICS OF SCIENCE AND TECHNOLOGY POLICY

A principal expression of a nation's science and technology policy is how it allocates its research resources. Some countries, France, for example, have central research or science and technology ministries that manage and conduct much of the nation's publicly funded research. The United States does not have such a central agency. Instead, a relatively high share of federally supported R&D is performed by university research laboratories and private defense contractors than in other OECD countries (Figure 13.2).

From its earliest day there have been efforts in the United States to establish a central agency responsible for research and development. A national university to be located in the District of Columbia was proposed by President Washington. The debates about establishing the Smithsonian Institution and the National Academy of Sciences during the mid-nineteenth century reflected the same concern. The establishment of a Science Advisory Board in the 1930s, the National Defense Research Committee in 1940, and the National Research Council as a research arm of the National Academy of Sciences during World War II, all reflected a concern, particularly during times of emergency, that a central planning and coordinating mechanism for federal science and technology policy was needed (Dupree, 1985:ix, x).

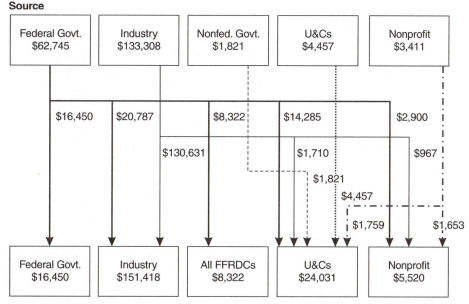

Figure 13.2 U.S. research and development expenditure by source of funds and performer: 1997. U&Cs, universities and colleges; FFRDCs federally funded research and development centers. (*Source:* National Science Board, *Science and Engineering Indicators: 1998*, Appendix table 4–5.)

In 1942 an Office of Science and Technology Mobilization that would link scientific research more directly with economic development was proposed by Senator Harley M. Kilgore (D, West Virginia). It would provide institutional grants to the nation's research universities, somewhat in the manner in which the federal government supported the state agricultural experiment stations (Chapter 6). A proposal was advanced in the Bush report, *Science: The Endless Frontier* (1945), to establish a National Research Foundation that would support primarily basic research. The outcome was the establishment in 1950 of the National Science Foundation (NSF), governed by a National Science Board made up of an independent committee of scientists appointed by the President. Bush had been able to mobilize the science community, which feared centralized control of science by nonscientists; the business community, which objected to direct involvement of the federal government in technology development; and the defense establishment, which objected to greater civilian control over military science and technology development against the Kilgore proposal.[13]

---

[13] For an excellent account of the political struggle over the framework for post-war science and technology policy, see Kleinman (1995:75–144). The National Science Foundation remained a junior partner in the

Prior to the establishment of the NSF, the Departments of Agriculture, Interior, Labor, and Commerce each had research programs related to their missions. While Congress was busy debating the establishment of a National Science Foundation, the research program of the National Institutes of Health was undergoing rapid expansion and the Atomic Energy Commission was assuming control of R&D for nuclear weapons and nuclear power. For almost a decade after World War II the Office of Naval Research was the principal source of support for basic scientific research in the physical sciences at universities. None of these agencies, or their constituencies, was anxious to have their research activities absorbed by a central science agency. The NSF, with a budget of less than $10M even in the mid-1950's, was forced to confine its efforts to supporting basic research and related educational activities. The launch of Sputnik by the Soviet Union in 1957 led to immediate efforts to strengthen U.S. science and technology (S&T) research and related science education. Within months of the Sputnik launch, the National Aeronautics and Space Administration (NASA) and the Department of Defense Advanced Research Projects Agency (ARPA) were established.

The pluralistic approach to S&T policy that has evolved in the United States means that there is no single S&T priority setting agency. The process by which the budgets for R&D are established in the several departments and agencies is highly decentralized. It involves the several executive departments and agencies, the authorization and appropriation committees of the House and the Senate, and at the level of the Executive Office of the President, the Office of Management and Budget (OMB), the Office of Science and Technology Policy (OSTP), and the National Science and Technology Council (NSTC) (Figure 13.3). The flow of research resources from the federal government to its own research laboratories, to the private sector, and to universities is exceedingly complex (Figure 13.2). In the next sections I discuss the development of institutional capacity to advise the President and the Congress on S&T policy.

Stages in Research and Development Policy

Since the end of World War II, federal government support for R&D has experienced four major shifts (Figure 13.4, Table 13.1). In the first two postwar decades support for R&D was initially based primarily on its potential for advancing military technology and nuclear power. By the 1960s the objectives had been expanded to include the conquest of space. During the 1960s research expenditure, particularly for defense and space expanded rapidly.

This was followed by a decade, roughly corresponding to the Johnson and Nixon administrations, in which an effort was made to shift R&D research resources to areas

---

funding of even basic research until well into the 1960s (Kleinman, 1995:145–170). It has consistently resisted attempts by the Congress and the president to expand its support of applied science and engineering (Belanger, 1998).

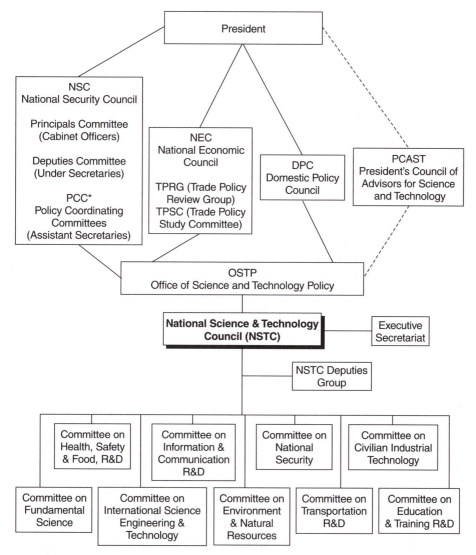

Figure 13.3 Federal science and technology policy organization. (*Source:* OSTP, the White House, 1997.)

deemed more relevant to social needs. President Johnson called on the scientific community to redirect its efforts from basic research in the physical sciences to areas of science and technology more relevant to his War on Poverty. President Nixon urged the research community to focus on clean energy, control of natural disasters, transportation, and drug control. Congress authorized a "war on cancer" to

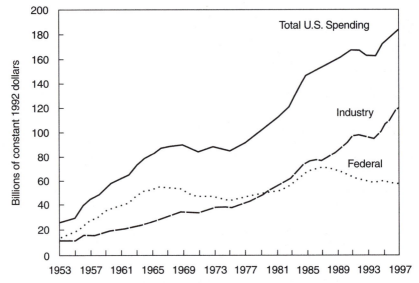

Figure 13.4 U.S. R&D spending: 1953–1997. (Adapted from United States General Accounting Office, *Measuring Performance: Strengths and Weakness of Research Indicators*, Washington, DC: GAO/RCED - 97 - 91, March 1997:30 from National Science Foundation, Science Resources Studies Division. *Source: NSF/ SRS, National Patterns of R&D Resources: 1997*, Table 7, Arlington, VA.)

demonstrate that the same focusing of scientific capacity that led to man's landing on the moon could also result in a cure for cancer. During the Johnson and Nixon administrations federal R&D expenditures declined and did not recover to their 1967 level until well into the Ford administration. Contributing to the decline was a vigorous criticism of the science community for its contribution to the technology employed in the Vietnam War and the technology associated with the degradation of the environment.

Large increases in energy R&D during the 1970s were followed by a rapid decline in the 1980s. In the 1980s public support for R&D was again refocused on the development of military technology. Between 1980 and 1990 the military-related proportion of the federal R&D budget rose from 48 to 64%. The Reagan administration was, except in the area of military technology, ideologically committed to reducing federal support of applied research and technology development. However, it vigorously promoted other incentives, such as tax credits, for private sector R&D (Day and Ruttan, 1991:32–40).

The end of the Cold War resulted in a slowing during the Bush administration, and a decline during the Clinton administrations, of total federal support for R&D, defense, and space-related R&D in particular. Commitment to a balanced budget, one of the few areas of broad agreement between President Clinton and his Republican opponents, placed the research community in competition with other discretionary components of the federal budget. Efforts by the science bureaucracy to find something new to be afraid of in order to advance their budgetary agendas, reflected in rhetorical capsules such as "environmental security" and "global competitiveness," were unsuccessful in developing a sufficient political constituency to sustain the federal science and technology budget. The Department of Defense and the Department of Energy, the agencies whose research budgets had benefited most from Cold War tensions, experienced substantial real dollar reductions in their R&D budgets during the 1990s. Expenditure for health research rose consistently since 1960 to reach almost 20% of the federal R&D budget by the late 1990s. As budget pressure relaxed during the late 1990s, almost all of the nondefense S&T agencies realized substantial budget increases.

Science in the White House

Institutional arrangements for providing science advice to the President are a relatively recent development.[14] They emerged primarily out of the demands of war and national defense. The appointment of Vannevar Bush by President Roosevelt to head an Office of Scientific Research and Development (OSRD) in 1941 was the first formal introduction of a scientific adviser into a presidential advisory system.[15]

In assessing the success of OSRD several institutional elements were of particular importance. One was the fact that Bush reported directly to a president who sought the counsel of his scientific advisor. A second was that OSRD was established with its own budget. A third consideration was that the overwhelming imperative of winning the war created a political environment that was supportive of a centralized planning mechanism. Subsequent science advisors have not been so fortunate.

During the 1950s the structure of advice to the president on science and technology went through several reorganizations. Its primary function continued, however, to be to provide advice on matters related to scientific research and technology development in areas of defense and national security. In the early 1960s the science and technology advisory structure was given more formal status as a result of an initiative to bring the office under congressional oversight. In March 1962 President Kennedy formally established the Office of Science and Technology (OST) in the Executive Office of the President. Responsibility for long-term S&T planning was shifted from the National Science Foundation, where it had never been adequately fulfilled, to OST. The Science Advisor's portfolio was broadened to include health, environment, and other areas of civilian science and technology.

---

[14] In this section I draw on a number of books and articles by former scientific advisors to the White House. See particularly Bush (1970), Burger (1980), and Barfield (1982). See also Carnegie Commission on Science, Technology and Government (October 1988, September 1991a).

[15] For an account of attempts during the 1930s to institutionalize science advisory capacity to the President, see Auerbach (1965:458–482).

After his reelection in 1972, President Nixon abolished both OST and the President's Science Advisory Council (PSAC). Nixon's actions were the result of three political concerns. There was a growing tension between the White House and the academic community over the Vietnam War and Nixon felt that this view was shared by most members of PSAC. When he abolished PSAC, Nixon moved the duties of the Science Advisor from the Executive Office of the President and added them to the Director of the National Science Foundation. This was correctly interpreted by the S&T community as a substantial demotion.

In 1976, Congress mandated that the executive branch coordinate and oversee all federal R&D activities. In addition to the President's science adviser, ad hoc panels of scientists and engineers from universities and the private sector were convened for advice on military, space, environmental, and other issues. During the Reagan administration, the Advisor's office again became more heavily engaged in military and space issues than in issues of civilian technology.[16]

In response to growing evidence of the erosion of U.S. technical leadership in a number of industries, technology policy assumed an increasingly important role in the Bush and Clinton administrations. In 1990 D. Allan Bromley, Director of OSTP in the Bush administration, issued a report that attempted, for the first time, to articulate a federal government technology policy. The report, *U.S. Technology Policy* (Bromley, 1990; 1994:122–141), represented a remarkable political achievement. It required substantial input and the mobilization of support from the mission-oriented S&T agencies that composed the membership of Federal Coordinating Council on Science, Engineering and Technology (FCCSET). And it involved the finessing of a White House staff that regarded "industrial policy" as a dirty word. His success was due, at least in part, to the fact that the report confined itself to the articulation of very broad principles rather than advocating specific reallocations of the S&T budget or particular technology initiatives. The recommendations of the Bromley report were hardly controversial (Box 13.2). But the report did provide a platform on which future OSTP Directors might stand in battles within the federal government and with the Congress in efforts to develop new initiatives or to defend the role of the federal government in technology development and diffusion.

In February 1993, shortly after assuming office, President Clinton and Vice President Gore issued a second federal government technology policy report, *Technology for America's Economic Growth: A New Direction to Build Economic Strengths* (1993). The Clinton–Gore report shared with the Bromley report a commitment to emphasize technology development commercialization and transfer relative to support for basic science. It was also somewhat more explicit than the Bromley report in its emphasis on (1) technology to protect the environment, (2) support for

---

[16] Several other offices and policy councils in the Executive Office of the President have also played an important role in S&T policy. The most powerful are the Office of Management and Budget (OMB) and the National Security Council (NSC). Others include the Chief-of-Staff in the White House Office, the National Economic Council (NEC), the Domestic Policy Council (DPC), and the U.S. Trade Representative.

the National Institute for Standards and Technology Advanced Technology Program (NIST/ATP), and (3) support for the development of an information technology infrastructure.

The underlying principle that informed the Clinton–Gore policy was to reinforce the direction of S&T policy, already underway during the Bush administration, away from those area of science and technology intended to serve the missions assigned to the federal government during the Cold war, particularly in the defense, space, and nuclear fields, and toward areas of nondefense technology that would enhance U.S. competitiveness in world markets. Congress responded by significantly increasing the funding for civilian technology in the 1994 and 1995 budgets. Agencies and programs such as the National Science Foundation (NSF), the National Institute of Technology Advanced Technology Program (NIST/ATP), and the National Institute of Health (NIH) received substantial budget increases. It appeared that the administration's goal of achieving a 50–50 split between the budgets for military and civilian technology would be achieved before the end of the decade.

● BOX 13.2

STRATEGY TO IMPLEMENT U.S. TECHNOLOGY POLICY

Government Incentives for the Private Sector:

- Incorporate technology policy concerns into formulation of related policies (e.g., fiscal, monetary, trade, environmental).
- Encourage private technology-related investment through federal monetary and fiscal policies (e.g., capital gains tax and tax credit for research).
- Provide an appropriate legal environment (antitrust, stable regulatory environment).
- Improve opportunities to commercialize technologies resulting from government contracts.
- Encourage multilateral standardization efforts.
- Better international protection of intellectual property.

Education and Training:

- Revitalize education at all levels.
- Develop a framework for federal coordination and cooperation on mathematics, science, engineering, and technology education.
- Encourage continuing education and training.

Federal R&D Responsibilities:

- Increase federal investment in support of basic research.
- Participate with the private sector in precompetitive research in generic technologies.
- Continue the federal government's development of products and processes for which it is the major consumer.
- Maintain a strong defense technology base.
- Encourage international cooperation in science and technology.

Transfer of Federally Funded Technology

Source: D. Allan Bromley, *U.S. Technology Policy*, Washington, DC: Executive Office of the President, Office of Science & Technology Policy, September 26, 1990.

As this effort was getting underway it was confronted with severe financial constraints associated with efforts by Congress and the Administration to move toward a balanced budget. A reporter for the *Washington Post* noted: "The budget bills pending in Congress leave the Clinton administration's ambitious science and technology agenda looking as if it were zapped by one of those space based x-ray lasers from the Strategic Defense Initiative that never quite got built. The destruction is near total. Never have a sitting president's programs promising new public-private partnerships for innovation been so throughly extirpated so soon after launch" (Schrage, 1995:F3).

Science Advice to the Congress

Congress has acted more hesitantly than the President in establishing formal institutional arrangements to provide itself with scientific and technical information and advice.[17] But by the last quarter of the twentieth century it had become apparent that the strengthening of such arrangements had become imperative. Members of the House and Senate found themselves debating issues such as throw weights of ballistic missiles, stratospheric ozone depletion, and the AIDS epidemic. Scientific and technical information became essential not only for members of committees that consider science and technology policy issues such as the establishment and funding of R&D, it also became an important input in policy debates about a broad range of economic, social, and ethical issues. The Carnegie Commission on Science, Technology and Government found that "it is difficult to identify a single

---

[17] In this section I draw heavily on three reports by the Carnegie Commission on Science, Technology and Government (February 1991, October 1991, and January 1994).

congressional committee that does not make policy decisions that influence or are influenced by science and technology" (February 1991:13). The Congress could, and does, draw on scientific and technical capacity within the executive agencies of government for scientific and technical information and advice. But over time Congress has established institutional capacity to provide at least part of its own needs for information and analysis.

The only organization created explicitly to meet congressional needs for information and analysis in the area of S&T policy was the Office of Technology Assessment (OTA), created in 1973. The OTA assessments were widely used and well regarded by members of Congress and their staffs and by the science and technology community outside of Congress. In its report on *Science, Technology and Congress* the Carnegie Commission (October 1991) urged that the OTA be strengthened to include additional analytical capacity to more effectively integrate economic analysis with other assessment activities and to give greater attention to international science and technology issues. But neither the quality of its work nor its effective working relationship with the Congressional leadership served to protect the OTA from the fiscal revolutionaries elected to Congress in 1994. Neither its small size (115 professional staff) and budget ($22 million in 1994) nor the support of senior members of Congress was sufficient to protect it from assassination (Bimber, 1996:69–77).

Advice from Nongovernmental Organizations

In addition to the official advisory mechanisms, advice on science and technology is provided by a broad range of nongovernmental research and advocacy organizations (NGOs). These range from broad-spectrum scientific and technical groups, such as the National Academy complex (National Academy of Science, National Academy of Engineering, Institute of Medicine, and National Research Council) and the American Association for the Advancement of Science, to an extensive array of discipline-specific societies, such as the American Physical Society, public policy think tanks such as the Rand Corporation and the Brookings Institution, and various left- and right-wing policy advocacy groups. The National Academy complex is uniquely influential (Carnegie Commission, 1993).

The National Academy of Science (NAS), established in 1863, is a self-governing private, nonprofit organization charged by Congress with furthering the advancement of knowledge and providing independent advice to the federal government. The National Research Council (NRC), established in 1916, serves as the operating arm of the NAS, the National Academy of Engineering (founded in 1964) and the Institute of Medicine (founded in 1970).[18] It enlists professionals in science, technology, and the policy sciences for study committees and related advisory activities.

---

[18] The two sister academies were founded largely because it was felt that the NAS did not adequately represent, in its membership, the contributions of applied scientists and engineers. When the agricultural science community raised similar concerns in the early 1980s the Academy formed a Board on Agriculture.

The close relationship between the NAS–NAE–IOM–NRC complex and the federal government has both advantages and disadvantages.[19] In the neighborhood of 75% of the complex's budget comes from federal agencies (the rest from endowment and private sources). Although studies are often initiated by the Congress or the White House, the funds are typically channeled through the agency whose program is being evaluated—through NASA for an evaluation of a proposed Earth Observing System or through the NSF to evaluate its system of awarding research grants. Because of its dependence on external resources, the NRC staff is under continuous pressure to develop new projects, often on rather mundane topics, to generate the resources needed to maintain committee staff. At times some committee members have felt that the primary purpose of a study was to keep the staff employed even if the study topic was relatively prosaic, such as the efficacy of waterproofing membranes on concrete bridge decks.

There is no question that the work of the NRC is highly valued. Its reputation for independence and objectivity is unmatched by any other organization. With the demise of the OTA it remains the only organization capable of drawing on the range and depth of knowledge needed to address major science and technology policy issues. At times the NAS has been willing to address issues that were too controversial for any government agency to address. When the Reagan Administration refused to make a major commitment to AIDS research, the NRC drew on its own endowment money to conduct the first comprehensive study of the controversial disease. That study helped prod the government into action (Lawler, 1997:900–904).[20]

In this section I have given major attention to the National Academy complex. If space permitted, I would discuss several other institutions in similar detail. One of the most important has been the Carnegie Corporation of New York. Between 1991 and 1994 the Carnegie Commission on Science, Technology and Government produced a series of 19 highly regarded reports on issues of science and technology policy. The Brookings Institution is also a regular contributor of studies and reports on S&T policy. The operations-oriented research of the RAND corporation has evolved from issues of primary concern to the Air Force to broad social and economic policy issues (Smith, 1966). There is also a very large population of think tanks and foundations, many located in Washington, D.C., that have research agendas directed to sectoral interests such as natural resource policy. Some have been founded to pursue ideologically oriented research agendas. The advise they provide often tends to be hortatory and polemic.

---

[19] In this section I draw heavily on the Carnegie Commission (January 1993). I also draw on my personal experience of service on several National Research Council Committees and Boards.

[20] In spite of the high regard in which the work of the NRC is held, it has recently come under considerable criticism. Members of Congress and representatives of some government agencies have commented that the Council takes too long to conduct and deliver its reports. The National Resources Defense Council and the Animal Legal Defense Fund have challenged the objectivity of study panels. Court rulings have been obtained that required the NRC to open most of their meetings to public participation. Perhaps the most serious challenge to the NRC is the tighter federal budgets for S&T during the past decade. Support by federal agencies for NRC studies has declined since the early 1990s (Lawler, 1996).

ISSUES IN SCIENCE AND TECHNOLOGY POLICY

An intense reexamination of science and technology policy has been underway in the United States since the late 1980s. Two factors have been particularly important in inducing this reexamination. One was the growing perception of the loss of U.S. leadership in a number of areas of commercial technology. A second was the winding down of the Cold War. This reexamination has occurred during a period of budget stringency. Between the mid-1980s and mid-1990s, the resources allocated for support of federal R&D declined by about 1% per year (Figures 13.4 and Table 13.1). Most of this decline was accounted for by a decline in defense related R&D. Both the President and the Congress initiated a series of reviews of S&T policy. They were joined in this effort by universities, private foundations, professional associations, and the business community. There is yet, however, no agreement on a federal S&T policy capable of replacing the Cold War consensus forged around national security (Smith and McGeary, 1997:37). In this section I discuss some of the issues that have received major attention during recent policy debates.

Policy Objectives

Frank Press, Science Advisor to President Carter, has noted that "there is no more powerful statement of government policy than budget decisions" (Press, 1995:1449). But budget decisions rarely reflect a coherent national policy. Convoluted Congressional decision processes make difficult direct trade-offs and transfers between R&D components of the federal research and development (FR&D) budget or between the FR&D budget and other national priorities. Although a FR&D budget can be "added up," it has never been allocated or managed as a coherent whole. It represents little more than the aggregation of the budgets of the individual departments and agencies that engage in R&D.

In 1995 the Senate Appropriations Committee asked the National Academy Complex to address "the criteria that should be used in judging the appropriate allocation of funds to research and development activities, the appropriate balance among differing types of institutions that conduct such research, and the means of assuring objectivity in the allocation process" (Committee on Criteria for Federal Support of Research and Development, 1995:v.). The Academy responded by establishing a Committee on Criteria for Federal Support of Research and Development, under the Chairmanship of Frank Press.

The Press Committee saw its charge as advising Congress on the entire federal science and technology (FS&T) research budget. It also adopted a perspective that science and technology were intimately related—"a complex relationship has evolved between basic and applied science and technology to the point that it is more appropriate to treat them as one interrelated FS&T enterprise" (Press, 1995:1449). But the committee avoided dealing with the research involved in technology commercialization and diffusion by restricting itself to "fundamental technology." More particularly the Press Committee attempted to focus its attention on that part of FR&D that could be labeled FS&T. Funds awarded by the Department of Defense to private industry for things such as testing and evaluation, setting up production lines for aircraft, and upgrading and modernization of weapons components and systems were ruled out as outside the "national science and technology base." Under this definition the FS&T budget accounted for only slightly more than half of the approximately $70 billion research and development budget in the mid-1990s. Federal laboratories accounted for 39%, academic institutions for 31%, industry for 21%, and nonprofit and other institutions for 9%.

The recommendations of the Press Committee (Box 13.3) have been the subject of both substantial acclaim and criticism. One critic has asked why the Committee was deemphasizing the federal role in support of precompetitive generic technology at a time when industry was turning more toward short-term research focused on product development (House Committee on Science, 1996:4, 5). Another has argued that Recommendation 4—"The President and Congress should ensure that the FS&T budget is sufficient to allow the United States to achieve preeminence in a select number of fields and to perform at a world-class level in the other major fields"— is inappropriate. The amount we spend on any area of S&T should be related not to our preeminence or lack thereof, but to the primary social goal to which the S&T is related. To view science as primarily a competitive activity in which relative international standing is more important than the value of the knowledge in realizing national goals is, in effect, to let the funding decisions of other nations determine U.S. priorities (Robinson, 1997).

Furthermore, preeminence in an area of science does not translate directly into effectiveness in achieving societal goals. For example, the United States is preeminent in almost every aspect of biomedical science, in both the underlying basic science and in clinical applications. But there is widespread dissatisfaction with the institutional arrangements for delivering health services. Many health indicators for the United States, such as infant mortality rates, rank well below similar health indicators for countries with much more limited biomedical research capacity.

The goals set out by the Press Committee, in spite of numerous caveats, both in the Commission report and in Congressional hearings, have not been able to avoid being interpreted as a defense of "science for scientists." Nor did the committee succeed in developing any operational criteria for allocating resources among fields of science and fundamental technology. In February 1997 House of Representative Speaker Newt Gingrich (R-GA) directed the House Science Committee to prepare a report that would help the Congress develop a long-range S&T policy. The study, prepared under the direction of the Committee Vice Chairman Vernon Ehlers (R-MI), was thoroughly conventional. The report did express concern that although federal support for research was becoming more basic, private sector industrial research was becoming more applied. Furthermore, it failed to address either health or defense R&D spending. Its principal recommendation in the area of commercial technology was to make the R&D tax credit permanent (House Committee on Science, 1998).

● BOX 13.3

PRINCIPLES FOR ALLOCATION OF FEDERAL FUNDS FOR SCIENCE AND TECHNOLOGY

Recommendation 1. The President should present an annual comprehensive FS&T budget, including areas of increased and reduced emphasis. The budget should be sufficient to serve national priorities and foster a world-class scientific and technical enterprise.

Recommendation 2. Departments and agencies should make FS&T allocation decisions based on clearly articulated criteria that are congruent with those used by the Executive Office of the President and by Congress.

Recommendation 3. Congress should create a process that examines the entire FS&T budget before the total federal budget is disaggregated into allocations to appropriations committees and subcommittees.

The United States Should Strive to Continue as the World Leader in Science and Technology. (*Recommendations 4 and 5*)

Recommendation 4. The President and Congress should ensure that the FS&T budget is sufficient to allow the United States to achieve preeminence in a select number of fields and to perform at a world-class level in the other major fields.

Recommendation 5. The United States should pursue international cooperation to share costs, to tap into the world's best science and technology, and to meet national goals.

Recommendation 6. Research and development conducted in federal laboratories should focus on the objectives of the sponsoring agency and not expand beyond the assigned missions of the laboratories. The size and activities of each laboratory should correspond to changes in mission requirements.

Recommendation 7. FS&T funding should generally favor academic institutions because of their flexibility and inherent quality control, and because they directly link research to education and training in science and engineering.

Recommendation 8. The federal government should encourage, but not directly fund, private-sector commercial technology development, with two limited exceptions:

- Development in pursuit of government missions, such as weapons development and spaceflight; or
- Development of new enabling, or broadly applicable, technologies for which government is the only funder available.

Recommendation 9. FS&T budget decisions should give preference to funding projects and people rather than institutions. That approach will increase the flexibility in responding to new opportunities and changing conditions.

Within the General Constraints Determined by National Priorities, the Selection of Individual Projects Must Reflect the Standards of the Scientific and Technical Community. (*Recommendations 10 and 11*)

Recommendation 10. Because competition for funding is vital to maintain the high quality of FS&T programs, competitive merit review, especially that involving external reviewers, should be the preferred way to make awards.

Recommendation 11. Evaluations of research and development programs and of those performing and sponsoring the work should incorporate the views of outside evaluators.

The Federal Government Must Implement a Structure Capable of Fostering, Not Hindering, the Management of Research and Development. (*Recommendations 12 and 13*)

Recommendation 12. Research and development should be well managed and accountable but should not be micromanaged or hobbled by rules and regulations that have little social benefit.

Recommendation 13. The federal government should retain the capacity to perform research and development within agencies whose missions require it. The nation should maintain is resulting flexible and pluralistic system of support. The executive and legislative branches should implement the procedures outlined in the committee's Recommendations 1 through 4 to ensure a more coherent FS&T budget process whether or not a Department of Science is established.

Source: Committee on Criteria for Federal Support of Research and Development, *Allocating Federal Funds for Science and Technology,* Washington, DC: National Academy Press, 1995:8–10.

Measuring and Evaluating

As budget constraints tightened in the early 1990s Congress became increasingly concerned about the lack of information on the relationship between the resources allocated to research and the effectiveness of research programs. These and related concerns lead in 1993 to the passage of a Government Performance and Results Act (GPRA). The Act attempts to shift the focus of federal management and accountability from a preoccupation with staffing, activity levels, and tasks completed to a focus on results. Implementation involves the preparation of strategic plans, annual performance plans, and the development of measures to show how well the annual plans are being met (General Accounting Office, 1997; Kostoff, 1997:651). In the case of research this means measuring the contribution of individual research projects to national goals such as security, health, and productivity. A major criticism of the GPRA process has been that it focuses too narrowly on projects rather than on evaluation of broad program areas.

As pressure by Congress for more objective output measures has intensified, the science and technology community has become increasingly concerned, about the implications. The Press Committee noted that most quantitative measures are incomplete—"mindless application can undermine the very functions such measures are intended to improve" (Committee on Criteria for Federal Support of Research and Development, 1995:27). A 1995 report of the National Science and Technology Council stressed the limited role that quantification could reasonably play in measuring the results of R&D. And a series of official reviews have found that quantitative indicators such as return on investment, patenting rates, and citation analysis fail to meet the needs of either the public or private sector research policymakers and managers (Office of Technology Assessment, 1986; General Accounting Office, 1997). In seeking budget increases, the science community has been quite willing to embrace the finding of economic research that suggests that the social rates of return to R&D are significantly above private rates of return (Griliches, 1992:S43). But it is reluctant to use the same methodologies to guide the allocation of resources to research.

Evaluation can occur at several levels and several stages. These range from the peer review of investigator-initiated project proposals at the time they are submitted to performance reviews of the program of a research institute or the research portfolio of a scientific agency. There is almost universal agreement within the science community that use of the peer review mechanism in the evaluation of project or program merit should be the primary method of determining priorities in the allocation of resources to research projects and programs (Committee on Criteria for Federal Support of Research and Development, 1995:25–27, 68).[21] This consensus is so strong that there

---

[21] The distinctive feature of the merit review process used by the National Science Foundation (NSF) is reliance on outside peer reviewers to evaluate research proposals. The evaluation criteria included (1) competence of the investigator and technical soundness of the approach, (2) intrinsic merit of the

is often an implicit judgment that unless research support is obtained through a peer review process "it can't be good science"! But what is the basis for the peer review consensus? Empirical evidence that it generates better science or technology than other methods, institutional support grants, for example, is lacking.

The Press Committee pointed out that there is benefit to having a variety of funding mechanisms because mission-oriented agencies have specialized applied research and technology development responsibilities that require more directed research. However, the Committee took the position that "fiscal constraints make it important to level the playing field. Competitive merit review should therefore be increased relative to other mechanisms for awarding FS&T funds" (Committee on Criteria for Federal Support of Research and Development, 1995:26).[22] My own sense is that the commitment of the academic science community to the system of peer review of investigator-initiated proposals as a basis for project funding is based at least as much on equity considerations—on maintaining a level playing field—as on considerations of research quality or productivity. It can also be viewed as a disguised attack on the legitimacy of mission-oriented research programs.[23]

There is much less consensus within both the science community and in the broader research community on how to evaluate research programs, institutes, or agencies.

---

research in advancing progress in science and engineering, (3) utility or relevance of the research in advancing technology or assisting in the solution of societal problems, and (4) effect of the research on the infrastructure of science. For an evaluation of the methods employed by the NSF in making major awards see the report by the Committee on Science, Engineering, and Public Policy (1994). The report was prompted by controversy over the award of a $60 million grant to build and operate a National High Magnetic Field Laboratory to a consortium headed by Florida State University rather than to the Massachusetts Institute of Technology. The committee concluded that "no clearly superior method of selecting research projects for support (than peer review) has been discovered" (31). Itako noted: "Peer reviewers often confine themselves to those criteria they are most qualified to judge, usually technical merit and capability of the proposers, and it is not always clear who is assessing the other criteria and how they are integrated by staff in the final decision" (71). The commission did not address the issue of the allocation of research resources among major NSF Directorates and Divisions or the initiation of new program areas. Both mandates from the Congress and pressure from the Executive Office of the President have played a role in new initiatives and in resource allocation. For further discussion see Chubin and Hackett (1990) and the literature on the controversy about the effectiveness of peer review in the mid and late 1970s (Stein, 1973:2–16; Bowers, 1975:624–626; Cole et al., 1977:34–41; Gustafson, 1975:1060–1066; Ling and Hand, 1980:1203–1207). I have reviewed this literature in the context of agricultural research (Ruttan, 1982:215–236; Fuglie and Ruttan, 1989:365–380).

[22] The Press Report notes that the system of formula grant allocation, such as that employed by the U.S. Department of Agriculture in providing partial funding to the state agricultural experiment stations, has not been given high marks for responsiveness or the quality of the resulting research (Committee on Criteria for Federal Support of Research and Development, 1995:26). This finding, which is attributed to a National Research Council study (1990), is somewhat puzzling given the carefully documented estimates of the high social rates of return to research conducted by the U.S. federal–state system of agricultural research (Echeverria, 1990; Evenson and Kislev, 1999; Chapter 6).

[23] A former Surgeon General, Dr. Jesse Stinfeld, in arguing for a more directed research program at the National Institutes of Health, commented somewhat facetiously, "If the space program had been conducted by NASA on an investigator-initiated project basis, we might now have 60,000 space scientists, each 80 miles on the way to the moon" (Burger, 1980:41). In 1997 both the NIH and the NSF announced modest changes in their peer review processes that would give greater weight to innovation and benefits to society in project evaluation.

It is at this higher level that the issue of relevance to broader social objectives becomes increasingly important—is the research worth doing no matter how well it is done? It is clear that at this level reliance on peer-reviewed investigator-initiated proposals becomes a less adequate basis for making decisions about research resource allocation. The Press Committee emphasizes the importance of the competitive peer review mechanism for the allocation of resources among projects but provides little guidance on methods that might be used in allocating research resources across programs and agencies. In spite of the strictures about "mindless application" of quantitative measures, rate of return analysis has, when applied with skill and insight, been exceedingly useful (Mansfield, 1991:1–12; Evenson and Kislev, 1999). There is also an appropriate role for methods such as citation and patent counts (Narin and Olivastro, 1992:237–249; Narin et al., 1997).

The difficulty the science community is having in confronting the problem of evaluation reflects a basic contradiction, noted earlier in the discussion of the Bush Report. The Report insisted that support for science should be viewed as an investment that contributes not only to national security but that also generates new products, new processes, new industries, and new jobs (Bush, 1945:17–19). The contradiction is that the report coupled this investment argument with the older humanistic view that insisted that "basic research is performed without thought of practical ends" (Bush, 1945:18). By these criteria very little scientific research would be conducted or funded.[24] During World War II and the Cold War an abundant flow of federal resources obscured this contradiction. It must, however, now be confronted.

There are two important questions that any research system or institution cannot avoid answering—either explicitly or implicitly:

- What are the possibilities of advancing knowledge or technology if resources are allocated to a particular researcher or research team, to a particular field of science or technology, or to accomplish a particular mission? Such a question can be answered with any degree of authority only by scientists or technologists who are on the leading edge of the field of research or problem being considered. The intuitive judgments of research administrators (even former scientists or engineers), planners, economists, and other social scientists are rarely adequate. Peer reviews are one appropriate way of generating such information.

---

[24] This is not to argue that there is not a strong basis for funding curiosity-driven science that is not directed to meeting any obvious economic or social purpose. Archeological research on the use of metal by the prehistoric peoples of the arctic need not be justified by the investment criteria but rather to enliven our understanding of the evolution of humankind's tool-making skills under adverse environmental conditions. Similarly the development of technology to permit the manned exploration of space can hardly be justified in terms of the investment criteria in any meaningful time horizon. But it is hard to believe that support for science and technology development would be more than a fraction of present levels if it relied primarily on the humanistic rational. Nor does it represent a challenge to the concept of freedom of inquiry. Freedom of inquiry requires that the result of scientific inquiry should not be influenced by factors extrinsic to science. But the freedom of inquiry does not require that society should place equal value on all fields of inquiry. It is not a limitation on freedom of inquiry for a poor society to place greater emphasis on advances in biotechnology related to food production then on biotechnology related to aging (Mohr, 1979).

- What will be the value to society of the new knowledge or the new technology if the research effort is successful? The answer to this question requires the use of formal analytical methods employed by planners, economists, and other social scientists. The intuitive insights of research scientists and technologists and of research administrators or political leaders are no more reliable in answering questions of value than are the intuitive insights of research planners, economists, and other social scientists in evaluating scientific or technical possibilities (Ruttan, 1982:363).

Each major mission-oriented public research organization should have a small unit devoted to testing and refining the analytical methods research managers use in making research resource allocation decisions and in demonstrating the value of the contributions of the organization's research program to agency administrators and congressional committees. A research institution that does not develop such capacity will have great difficulty in responding to its critics or arming its defenders.

Transforming the Technology Base

During World War II and the immediate postwar period, as noted earlier in this chapter, military support for R&D created a defense technology base that, in a number of fields, both led and contributed to commercial technology development. "In 1960 the Department of Defense (DOD) funded half of all U.S. R&D and the U.S. accounted for two-thirds of all the R&D in North America and Western Europe combined. Thirty years later, DOD supports just one-third of U.S. R&D and the U.S. share of the total has dropped off to one-half" (Carnegie Commission, 1991:15). These trends are not necessarily undesirable. A prosperous global economy requires that the technological base, particularly in less developed countries, expand relative to the United States and, more generally, relative to the richer OECD countries. And in the United States it is important that the commercial technical base continue to expand relative to the defense-related, technological base.

These changes have been the result of several developments: (1) the erosion of U.S. commercial dominance in several important industries such as steel, automobiles, and computers, (2) the increasing importance of commercial demands in determining R&D priorities, and (3) the advances in commercial R&D and its rigid separation from military R&D, even in firms that produce for both sectors (Carnegie Commission, September 1991:6).

The Carnegie Commission found no organizational mechanism at the Presidential level currently addressing the critical policy linkage between the defense technology base and the commercial technology base. The Commission recommended three institutional changes to respond to this deficiency. One was that the Defense Advanced Research Projects Agency (DARPA), which has a long history of support and collaboration with academic and industrial R&D institutions, be transformed into a National Advanced Research Projects Agency (NARPA). The responsibilities of

NARPA would be expanded to include support of dual-use technologies, particularly long-range, high-risk, and generic technologies with potentially high payoff. The Commission also recommended that the National Institute of Science and Technology (NIST), of the Department of Commerce, particularly the Advanced Technology Program (ATP), be given central responsibility for supporting generic and precompetitive industrial R&D that has potential commercial application over a range of industries and that does not fall within the mission or R&D programs of other departments and agencies. Finally the Commission recommended that the National Security Council (NSC) serve as the instrument for coordinating and integrating the various policy perspectives of the councils and offices in the Executive Office of the President on those issues that link national security, economic performance, and technological strength.

Big Science

Prior to World War II most science was "little science." The model of the individual scientist working in his (seldom her) laboratory with a few graduate students was a reasonably apt description of how science was done. Big engineering, however, was pervasive. It was epitomized by civil engineering works such as those of the Tennessee Valley Authority and the mass production of the automobile at Ford's River Rouge plant (Chapter 11). The success of wartime projects such as the Manhattan Project, which produced the atomic bomb, marked a decisive break in the conduct of science. It also became clear that the success of "Big Science" projects depended at least as much on big engineering as on science.[25]

The problems posed for science and technology policy by big science were articulated most elegantly by Alvin Weinberg, director of Oak Ridge National Laboratory in the early and mid-1960s (Weinberg, 1961:161–164, 1964:42–48, 1967). Weinberg noted that when history looks at the second half of the twentieth century "she will find in the monuments of Big Science—the huge rockets, the high-energy accelerators, the high-flux research reactors-symbols of our time just as surely as she finds in Notre Dame and Mont-Saint-Michel symbols of the Middle Ages" (Weinberg, 1961:161). Weinberg went on to address three questions that arise from the growth of Big Science: "First, is Big Science ruining science?; Second, is Big Science ruining us financially?; And third, should we divert a larger part of our effort toward scientific issues which bear more directly on human well-being than do such Big Science spectaculars as manned space travel and high energy physics?" (Weinberg, 1961:161). The support

---

[25] The "big science"–"little science" controversy emerged in the late 1950s and early 1960s. See, for example, Weinberg (1961:161–164, 1967), and Price (1963, 1986). Price noted: "Big science is so new that many of us can remember its beginnings. Big science is so large that many of us began to worry about the sheer mass of the monster we have created. Big science is so different from the former state of affairs that we can look back, perhaps nostalgically, at the little science that was once our way of life" (Price, 1986:2). Weinberg worried about the cost of Big Science: "A big research reactor or accelerator is very costly. Its operation keeps people employed and provides a convenient means for turning out scientific papers. To what extent has science suffered because scientists are understandably reluctant to junk a very expensive piece of apparatus?" (Weinberg, 1967:40).

for Big Science (and big technology) induced by Cold War tensions enabled the United States to avoid confronting the Weinberg questions for three decades. As we confront these issues it is worth reviewing how Weinberg responded to his own questions.

Weinberg's response to his first questions was that "Big Science is here to stay and we must learn to live with it. We must make Big Science flourish without, at the same time, allowing it to trample Little Science." (1961:162). Weinberg was particularly concerned with the bureaucratization of Big Science and the dangers of Big Science penetrating the universities and crowding out of little science. In response to his second question, Weinberg noted that federal research and development expenditures had been growing at about 10% per year. "At the present rate we shall be spending all of our money on science and technology in about 65 years" (1961:162). He suggested that we settle on some figure, less than 1% of gross national product, as the level of support for federally supported nondefense science.

Much of the recent concern about the future of Big Science centers on the national laboratories operated by the Department of Energy. Concern about the future of these laboratories (then operated by the Atomic Energy Commission) emerged as work on the first commercial pressurized water nuclear reactor electric power plant was completed. The laboratories were given a new lease on life as a result of the petroleum crisis of the 1970s (Chapter 7). But federal support for energy research and development eroded rapidly during the first Reagan Administration (Table 13.1). And by the late 1980s new questions were being raised about the viability of their missions in a post-Cold War era. A 1995 report for the DOE National Laboratories proposed shifting the management of the laboratories to a government owned corporation. Bills were introduced in Congress that would have established a laboratory-closure commission modeled after the Department of Defense's base closing commission. In 1995 the DOE established a Laboratory Operations Board, composed of DOE senior managers plus external members with broad experience in industry and government, to guide reforms at the laboratories.

As of the mid-1990s the DOE system was composed of nine large multiprogram laboratories and a number of specialized laboratories (Figure 13.5). The laboratories, although owned by the government, are operated by nongovernmental contractors. They had a total annual budget of more than $6 billion and employed some 30,000 scientists and engineers. In the neighborhood of $1.6 billion came from outside DOE, primarily from other federal agencies but also from private industry. There is no line item in the DOE budget for the individual laboratories. Program managers decide, with some congressional direction, how to allocate funds among missions, laboratories, and private firms. Managers in each program decide on the allocation of resources among the laboratories, universities, and industry in terms of the contribution to the several missions of the DOE: (1) national security, (2) science, (3) energy, and (4) environmental quality.[26]

---

[26] In the next several pages I draw heavily on Curtis et al. (1997).

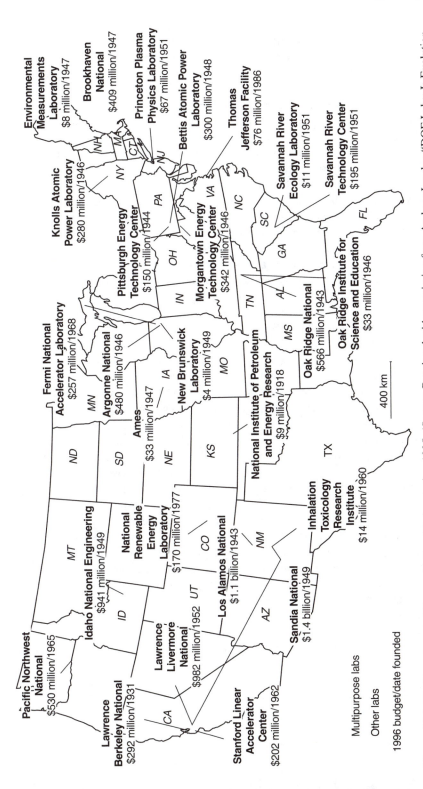

Figure 13.5 The Department of Energy National Laboratories, 1995. (*Source:* Reprinted with permission from Andrew Lawler, "DOE Labs: Is Evolution Enough?" *Science* 172 (June 14, 1996):1577. Copyright © 1995 American Association for the Advancement of Science.)

Environmental Measurements Laboratory
$8 million/1947

Brookhaven National
$409 million/1947

Princeton Plasma Physics Laboratory
$67 million/1951

Bettis Atomic Power Laboratory
$300 million/1948

Thomas Jefferson Facility
$76 million/1986

Knolls Atomic Power Laboratory
$280 million/1946

Savannah River Ecology Laboratory
$11 million/1951

Savannah River Technology Center
$195 million/1951

Pittsburgh Energy Technology Center
$150 million/1944

Morgantown Energy Technology Center
$342 million/1946

Fermi National Accelerator Laboratory
$257 million/1968

Argonne National
$480 million/1946

Ames
$33 million/1947

New Brunswick Laboratory
$4 million/1949

National Institute of Petroleum and Energy Research
$9 million/1918

Oak Ridge National
$566 million/1943

Oak Ridge Institute for Science and Education
$33 million/1946

Pacific Northwest National
$530 million/1965

Idaho National Engineering
$941 million/1949

National Renewable Energy Laboratory
$170 million/1977

Lawrence Berkeley National
$292 million/1931

Lawrence Livermore National
$982 million/1952

Los Alamos National
$1.1 billion/1943

Stanford Linear Accelerator Center
$202 million/1962

Sandia National
$1.4 billion/1949

Inhalation Toxicology Research Institute
$14 million/1960

400 km

Multipurpose labs

Other labs

1996 budget/date founded

NH
MA
CT
NY
NJ
PA
VA
NC
SC
GA
FL
OH
IN
TN
AL
MS
MO
KS
IA
NE
SD
ND
MN
MT
ID
CO
UT
AZ
NM
TX
CA

The primary goal of the *national security mission* is to maintain the safety and reliability of the nation's nuclear arsenal without nuclear weapons testing. The objective of the *science mission* is to provide national laboratory, university, and industry scientists with large-scale science facilities for research in the physical sciences. The *energy mission* focuses on the advancement of nuclear and other energy technology. The goal of the *environmental mission* is to clean up the environmental damage resulting from the nuclear weapons legacy of the security mission! This involves stabilizing, storing, or disposing of nuclear wastes, deactivating and decommissioning surplus facilities, and remediation of contaminated environment. Nearly all of the R&D for the national security mission is performed at the national laboratories. Seventy percent of the science mission is conducted at the laboratories and 25% goes to university performers. Fifty-eight percent of the energy mission is performed by industry. The environmental mission is carried out primarily by contractors. An attempt is being made to expand the role of universities in all four areas.

It is clear that we are now in a period when all Big Science R&D programs will be subject to increasingly critical review and reexamination. In decisions about their future, scientific merit will carry smaller weight than technical and economic criteria. An illustration of the point is the contrasting fate of the Global Climate Change program and the Superconducting Supercollider project. The purpose of the Global Climate Change program is to advance understanding of the science and impact of rising atmospheric levels of greenhouse gases (carbon dioxide, nitrous oxide, methane) and the consequent impact on global climate change (Chapter 12). Most of the funding is channeled through NASA and NOAA. It has been criticized for underfunding of research on the human dimensions of climate change. But the agencies involved have been successful in generating constituencies among the general science community, Congress, and the public for this program. Even though the efforts to model sources and impact lack precision and remain controversial, the program continues to be funded, although at a considerably lower level than in the early 1990s when it was budgeted at a level in excess of $1.5 billion.

The contrast with the Superconducting Supercollider project is quite striking. The primary purpose of that project was to advance scientific understanding in the field of high-energy physics. The project was initially located in Texas, after a national competition that involved a bidding contest among several states. The Texas state government agreed to commit $1 billion for construction (Walsh, 1988:248). Long-term benefits in the form of technology development were, however, never convincingly developed. The project received substantial funding for planning and initial construction over several years in the early 1990s. But in 1993, amid concerns about cost overruns and lack of international participation, and diversion of resources from other areas of science and technology development, Congress cut off the funding for the project.

Issues similar to those that led to the demise of the Superconductor Supercollider have also been raised in connection with fusion research. In 1977 the Department of Energy decided to close down the Princeton Plasma Physics Laboratory and to participate in a proposed International Thermonuclear Experimental Reactor (ITER) program. Supporters argue that significant participation in ITER is the only way that the United States can remain involved in the experimental investigation of the leading issues in plasma science. They also point to the potential for significant technological spinoffs. Critics have argued that the particular technology that would be pursued, known as Tokamak, has no possibility of becoming a source of energy that can compete with fission, fossil fuel, or even solar power in the foreseeable future. It is hard to escape a conclusion that fusion research should be demoted from a Big Science to a little science program until ideas that could lead, at least potentially, to economically and environmentally viable power generation emerge.[27]

John H. Gibbons, then assistant to the President for Science and Technology and Director of the Office of Science and Technology Policy, has noted the increasing difficulty any nation, even the United States, faces in going it alone on Big Science projects. "It has become more and more difficult, for instance, for one nation to justify projects such as mapping the human genome, developing fusion power, exploring space, rooting out the mysteries of particle physics, or global ecological problems, such as ozone depletion and climate change" (1995:122). Increasingly, such Big Science projects will be feasible only through international cooperation and partnerships.[28] Gibbons also notes an inherent tension between scientific cooperation and economic competition in an environment in which scientific and technical research are key prerequisites for economic growth.

My own sense is that the United States is unlikely, in the early years of the twenty-first century, to discover any sufficiently persuasive rationale to mobilize the political effort needed to initiate new Big Science projects of the magnitude of the early Cold War projects. And it will be exceedingly difficult to maintain the momentum of existing projects in areas such as space exploration and global climate change. At the same time, as the costs of instrumentation become larger most "little science" is becoming more like the Big Science of the past. The human genome project with its extensive international collaboration and sharing of data within the framework of an overall research plan may represent a model for "Big–Little Science" in the future (Chapter 10) (Speaker and Lindee, 1993; Chapter 10).

Commercial Technology

The United States has had great difficulty in defining an economically and politically viable policy to support commercial technology development. It has been difficult to transfer the institutional arrangements of the highly successful federal–state system

---

[27] For the controversy about fusion technology see the articles in the Summer 1997 issue of *Issues on Science and Technology* by Stacy (1997:53–59) and by Hirsch et al. (1997:60–64). See also the letters in the fall 1997 issue by Calvert et al., (1997:5–9).

[28] For a review of the rapid evolution of both informal and formal international collaboration in research, see Georghiou (1998:611–626).

of agricultural technology support to other sectors. Attempts that have been made have been short lived. For example, the State Technical Services Act of 1965, which provided support for universities to provide technical assistance to small and medium-sized businesses and to accelerate the diffusion of technology, was discontinued in 1972 as a result of Vietnam War budget pressures. Budget support for programs initiated by the Congress in the early 1980s to encourage technology transfer by the National Department of Energy laboratories was discontinued in the mid-1990s.

The energy crisis of the 1970s, concern about U.S. industrial competitiveness in the 1980s, and the winding down of the Cold War have, however, induced a proliferation of federal and state institutional innovations designed to support the development and extension of commercial technology for the private sector. Some observers have characterized the emergence of new federal and state institutional arrangements for the support of technology development as a third revolution in science policy—comparable to the Morrill Act of 1862 that established the land grant colleges to advance higher education in agriculture and the mechanic arts and to the 1945 Vannevar Bush report, *Science—The Endless Frontier*, that became the charter for post-World War II science policy.

FEDERAL POLICY

Historically the federal government has pursued two alternative strategies to support the development of commercial technology.[29] One has involved measures to increase the profitability of investments in R&D. The second has been an attempt to correct market failure through subsidization of research, development, and diffusion.

Policies designed to make technology development more profitable include making intellectual property rights more secure, providing tax subsidies such as the R&D tax credit, or permitting horizontal mergers to take advantage of potential R&D scale economies. These policies are often ineffective. Intellectual property rights have been discussed earlier in this chapter. It has been difficult to design a politically viable system of R&D tax credits that targets the areas of greatest private sector R&D underinvestment, and although R&D tax credits have involved very large "tax expenditures," particularly in the mid and late 1980s, it has been difficult to identify positive net impacts on R&D (Scherer, 1998).

Since the early 1980s there have been a series of institutional innovations in federal policy aiming to enhance commercial technology development (Table 13.2). These initiatives were prompted by a concern that inadequate effort was being made to commercialize the results of federally supported R&D. Research originally performed in the United States was being commercialized more rapidly by foreign countries than by U.S. firms. Among the most important of these innovations was the Bayh–Dole Act of 1980, which liberalized patent policies for inventions arising from federal grants

---

[29] In this section I draw heavily on Office of Technology Assessment (1991), Cohen and Noll (1991, 1992:223–265, 1996:72–214); Kelley (1997), and Johnson and Teske (1997:42–60). I have also drawn on the series of Congressional Research Service reports by Wendy H. Schact (1997a,b,c,d).

and contracts; the Stevenson–Wydler Technology Innovation Act of 1980, which provided a legislative basis for redirecting the activities of the federal laboratories toward a more commercial focus; and the Cooperative Research Act of 1984, which relaxed antitrust enforcement for research joint ventures.[30] The winding down of the Cold War tensions after the mid-1980s created additional opportunities to redirect resources toward commercial R&D in spite of a decline in total federal R&D spending (Figure 13.3). The federal laboratories, in a search for a nondefense mission, attempted to shift resources to assist in the development of commercial products and to intensify their "technology transfer" efforts.

Table 13.2   Federal Technology Transfer Initiatives: 1980–1993

Year	Legislative/Executive Initiatives	Highlights
1980	Bayh–Dole Act (PL 96-517)	Permitted universities, nonprofit firms, and small businesses to own title to inventions from research funded by the federal government so they may license these inventions to industry for commercialization
1980	Stevenson–Wydler Technology Innovation Act (PL 96-480)	Mandated federal laboratories to take an active role in technical cooperation with industry by establishing at each laboratory an Office of Research and Technology Application (ORTA)
1982	Small Business Innovation Development Act (PL 97-219)	Required federal agencies to provide special funds for small business R&D within the scope of their agency mission
1984	National Cooperative Research Act (PL 98-462)	Encouraged firms to enter into joint precompetitive R&D ventures without fear of antitrust laws and eliminated the treble damages standard of antitrust laws in litigation arising therefrom
1986	Federal Technology Transfer Act (PL 99-502)	Empowerd government-owned government-operated laboratories (GOGOs) directly to enter into cooperative R&D agreements (CRADA) with firms and established the Federal Laboratory Consortium (FLC) for Technology Transfer
1987	Executive Orders 12591 and 12618	Further articulated the Federal Technology Transfer Act for administrative purposes
1988	Omnibus Trade and Competitiveness Act (PL 100-418)	Designated the National Institute of Science and Technology (NIST) as lead agency to establish and administer Manufacturing Technology Centers (MTC)
1989	National Competitiveness Technology Transfer Act (PL 101-189)	Extended the CRADA authority to all government-owned contractor-operated federal labs (GOCOs)
1993	Defense Authorization Act (PL 103-160)	Directed the Advanced Research Projects Agency (ARPA) to promote dual-use technology via technology reinvestment

Source: Technology Transfer and Public Policy, Young S. Lee, ed. Copyright © 1997 by Young S. Lee. Reproduced with permission of Greenwood Publishing Group, Inc., Westport, CT.

---

[30] The texts of these three acts are reproduced in Lee (1997:225–273).

The federal agency with the greatest experience in contributing to the development of commercial industrial technology has been the Defense Advanced Research Projects Agency (DARPA). It was created in 1958 to "develop 'revolutionary' technologies that can make a significant impact on the future of the United States' defense posture to ensure that those technologies effectively enter the appropriate forces and supporting industrial base" (Office of Technology Assessment, 1996:106). DARPA funds were deployed in a highly flexible manner. Program managers have traditionally been given a high degree of program autonomy. Each manager typically creates a portfolio of mission-oriented research projects, such as the use of gallium-arsenide in microcircuitry development. Managers also have access to discretionary funds to explore ideas for future programs. DARPA-funded projects played an important role in the development of high-performance computing, advanced materials, and artificial intelligence. In the 1970s it funded the development of ARPANET, the forerunner of the Internet system. In the 1980s it provided support for the establishment of SEMATECH (Chapter 9).

For proponents of a more focused industrial policy DARPA provides the strongest evidence that given an appropriate institutional design, the federal government is capable of effective support for technology development at the sector level. In 1991 the Carnegie Commission recommended that DARPA be transformed into a national ARPA with authorization to move beyond its strategy of encouraging commercial technology spin-off from defense technology. The Clinton administration responded to the Carnegie Commission's recommendation by changing the name of the agency to ARPA and giving it a central role in its Technology Reinvestment Project (TRP). TRP was originally conceived as an instrument to assist firms, regions, and workers in the transition from defense to commercial markets. Funds were made available for three key areas: technology development, technology deployment, and support for manufacturing education and training (Kelley, 1997:313–328). The TRP program added about $500 million to the approximately $1.5 billion ARPA program. Unlike the traditional DARPA program the TRP program has been subject to considerable political pressure, particularly from states such as California and Texas, which faced substantial defense industry conversion problems (Cohen and Noll, 1992). The program was canceled in 1995 due to Congressional concern that it was diverting R&D resources away from the defense mission.

The most important program designed specifically for the development of commercial technology is the Advanced Technology Program (ATP) of the National Institute of Standards and Technology (NIST).[31] The ATP provides multiyear funding for projects involving cost sharing with individual companies or industry-led joint ventures to pursue high-risk R&D that is judged to have substantial commercial potential. Universities, federal laboratories, or independent nonprofit research organizations can participate as a member of a joint venture that involves several for-profit companies.

---

[31] See Cohen and Noll (1996:305–333), National Institutes for Standards and Technology (1994), United States General Accounting Office (1996), Kelley (1997:313–328), and Long (1999).

The rationale behind this approach is that the ATP projects can reduce the incidence of market failure by having industry rather than the government decide which technical option to pursue and by limiting federal financial participation (Cohen and Noll, 1992:243).

Projects are screened through a rigorously competitive process involving technical review by senior federal scientists and engineers and outside reviewers. No proposal is accepted unless it meets the criteria for scientific and technical merit regardless of its merits in the other criteria. Examples of projects supported by ATP in partnership with private industry include (1) transgenic cotton fiber with polyester qualities via biopolymer genes (Agracetus: $757 K; ATP: $1,131 K, 3 years), (2) computer-integrated total hip replacement (Integrated Surgical Systems, Inc. and IBM Corporation: $2,135 K; ATP: $2,051 K, 3 years), (3) advanced technologies for the manufacture of very high-power, single-chip, MOS-controlled solid-state switches (Advanced Power Technology: $3,380 K; ATP: $1,904 K, 2 years), and (4) manufacturing methods for vehicle composite frames (Budd Company: $1,312 K; ATP: $2,000 K, 3 years).

The Clinton Administration came into office viewing the ATP as a centerpiece of its effort to strengthen U.S. industrial competitiveness. The first Clinton Administration budget more than doubled the ATP budget, from $67.9 million in 1993 to $199.5 million in 1994. The ATP budget was doubled again in FY 1995 and was projected to almost double again in FY 1996. The Administration's ambitious plans for ATP were severely challenged following the 1994 mid-term elections that resulted in a Republican majority in both the House and the Senate. Concerns were raised in Congress about the appropriateness of funding technology development and whether the ATP projects would have been funded by the private sector if they had not received funding from the ATP.[32]

A second major federal program to advance commercial technology was the Cooperative Research and Development Agreements (CRADAs) between government-owned and operated laboratories and the private sector, authorized in 1986.[33] The research performed under a CRADA must be consistent with the government laboratory's mission. The laboratory may accept funds, personnel, services, and property from the collaborating party and may provide personnel, services, and property to the participating organization. The laboratory can cover overhead costs incurred in support of a CRADA, but is prohibited from providing direct funding to the industrial partner.

Inventions made solely by federal scientists remain federal property available to be licensed to the private sector partner for commercialization in exchange for reasonable

---

[32] See U.S. Congress, House of Representatives, Committee on Science (1995).

[33] A third and smaller program was the Engineering Research Centers (ERC) initiated by the National Science Foundation in 1986. The ERCs are located at universities. They receive funding, in addition to the NSF, from private companies, states, and the host universities. As of 1987 there were 29 ERCs (Abelson, 1997).

compensation. In cases of jointly developed technology arising under a CRADA, the collaborating firm has the right of first refusal of an exclusive license for a defined field of use. The program expanded rapidly after 1990 when the Department of Energy contractor-operated laboratories began to enter into such agreements. By the end of 1995 over 1000 CRADA agreements had been entered into between DOE laboratories and the private sector.

The operation of the CRADAs can be illustrated by an example of two closely related projects that led to the development of a technology for producing the anticancer drug Taxol. Research in the 1960s demonstrated that paclitaxel, a natural product found in extremely small quantities in the bark of the Pacific Yew, is a highly effective treatment for certain cancerous tumors. The development of an anticancer drug was complicated by two problems—obtaining enough paclitaxel for all the patients who might need treatment and funding a company to commercialize the drug. To address these problems the National Institutes of Health (NIH) entered into a CRADA with Bristol-Myers Squibb. NIH provided the preclinical animal studies, chemical data from its national chemical trials network, research agents, and enough isolated paclitaxel and yew tree bark to continue the chemical trials. Bristol-Myers Squibb developed improved procedures to increase the amount of paclitaxel that could be extracted from natural bark supplies. It also supported research on the development of an alternative plant tissue cell culture technology for making paclitaxel.

The plant tissue cell culture technique for producing paclitaxel was based on procedures for plant tissue cell culture developed at the Agricultural Research Service (ARS) of the U.S. Department of Agriculture. In 1990 the ARS signed a CRADA with Phyton, Inc., a biotechnology company started by three graduate students. The agreement gave Phyton an exclusive license to adapt laboratory-scale procedures to produce commercial quantities of Taxol. Phyton then entered into a contract to produce Taxol for Bristol-Myers Squibb. The effect of the two CRADAs was to overcome the supply constraint resulting from the limited supply of Pacific Yew. It enabled Bristol-Myers Squibb to add a new anticancer drug to its existing line of anticancer drugs. And it enabled Phyton to achieve commercial viability.

The 1988 Omnibus Trade and Competitiveness Act that created the ATP program also authorized the establishment of the Regional Manufacturing Technology Transfer Centers to assist companies in adopting and adapting technologies and manufacturing techniques generated by federal agencies in pursuit of their various missions (Kelley, 1997:313–328). In 1994 the program was combined with the NIST State Technology Extension Program, which provides states with grants to develop the infrastructure necessary to transfer technology from the federal government to the private sector. The combined program became the Manufacturing Extension Partnership (MED).

In a 1995 review of the (MED) program the GAO took the position that it was too soon to provide a definitive economic evaluation (General Accounting Office, 1995). The GAO did report, however, very positive evaluations from firms that had received technical assistance through the NIST programs. It also noted that 93% of all U.S. small- and medium-sized manufacturers had not yet received any services from the

NIST Manufacturing Extension Programs. When control of the Congress shifted to the Republican party in 1995 the NIST budget was cut and funding for support of CRADAs at the Department of Energy National Laboratories was sharply reduced.

STATE POLICY

Higher education has traditionally been the primary instrument for state contributions to the U.S. science and technology base. The Morrill Land Grant Act of 1862 initiated a federal–state partnership that established and sustained the development of the nation's great public universities. State tuition subsidies represented an important source of support for the development of the human capital that would contribute to technology development and transfer. More recently graduate education became an important instrument through which both public and private universities organized and enhanced their capacity for scientific and technical research. State support for commercial technology development and diffusion was initially organized through the establishment of agricultural experiment stations and extension services within the colleges of agriculture at the land grant colleges and universities (Chapter 6). State governments have also provided modest support, sometimes within state agencies and sometimes to the public universities, for research on natural resources, public health, energy, and transportation.[34]

During the 1980s state governments began to take a much more active role in investing in science and technology-based economic development. By the early 1990s most states had developed science and technology-based economic development programs. These programs involved the establishment of centers of advanced technology, research grant programs, and research parks and incubators. Several factors were behind this trend. The most important was that states began to view science and technology programs as potential solutions to the emerging problems associated with the decline of traditional heavy industry sectors. High technology rather than "smokestack industries" was viewed as the most promising source of growth in income and employment. States also began to compete vigorously for the location of federally supported facilities such as SEMATECH and the Supercollider Superconductor. A second reason was that as federal support for science and technology began to decline, university administrators, and even scientists and engineers, began to look more favorably on alternative sources of funding even if it meant bending research priorities in the direction of commercial development. States were also motivated by the failure to include state participation in the design of federal programs for commercial technology development.

The primary objective of state science and technology programs has been somewhat narrowly focused on the generation of new products and processes that could be used to launch new firms, enhance the competitiveness of existing firms, and create new

---

[34] The leading student of state technology policy is Irwin Feller. In this section I draw heavily on his work (Feller, 1991:68–71, 1997a:181–197; Feller and Anderson, 1994:127–140). See also Carnegie Commission (September 1992b), and Lambright and Rahm (1991:49–60).

and better jobs. The programs were administered by state science and technology offices or by departments of commerce and economic development. Support for research was often conditioned, like the federal programs, on university–industry cooperative arrangements. Both public and private universities have aggressively pursued the new opportunities opened up by the expansion of state support. They have also become much more aggressive in the effect to generate increased resources through the patenting and licensing of university-generated technology.

The strategic thrusts of the state technology development programs have included (1) research infrastructure and human capital development, (2) generic and precommercial research, and (3) product development and transfer. The research infrastructure model was characteristic of some of the earliest programs. In the 1950s North Carolina involved its three major universities—Duke, the University of North Carolina, and North Carolina State—in the development and support of Research Triangle Park. Other models have included the Massachusetts Route 128 development based on technology generated at Harvard and MIT and the Silicon Valley development based on technology generated at the University of California and Stanford.[35] The generic and precommercial model represents the most typical model of government–university–industry cooperation in the 1980s. The states typically employed a competitive mechanism to determine the location of centers. The proposals, in addition to university–industry cooperation, involved a consortium of universities and other educational institutions such as the more technically oriented community colleges. During the 1990s, as experience with state programs developed, there has been somewhat less emphasis on generic precommercial research. Some states have placed greater emphasis on strengthening the state technology base. In Maryland, a new University of Maryland Biotechnology Institute (UMBI) was established as an independent campus within the University of Maryland system. In Georgia, very large resources have been devoted to attracting world class scientists to a new vaccine research center located at Emory University. Other states are placing increased emphasis on technology transfer, technical assistance, technical training, and business practice and management skills.

State government support for R&D amounted to approximately $2.5 billion in 1995—a level substantially larger than expenditures by the National Science Foundation that same year (Battelle, 1998). During the 1990s as the early policy entrepreneurs left the stage and the programs lost some of their freshness, budgets have tended to level off or even decline. During this same period academic research expenditures were in the $17–18 billion range. But, "while not accounting for a very large share of total U.S. research investment in dollars, state technology programs are in many ways the thin edge of a very large wedge" (Carnegie Commission, September 1992b:40).

There has been considerable controversy about the benefits of the state programs. Critics have argued that universities would use state funds to further faculty research

---

[35] These and related efforts seem to have generated exaggerated perceptions of the potential entrepreneurial role of universities in regional development (Dorfman, 1983; Lowood, 1987). See also Stenberg (1998).

agendas rather than state economic development objectives and that the benefits, if any, could be expected to "spill over" into other political jurisdictions. A National Research Council study (1990) of the Ohio Thomas Edison Centers concluded that qualitative evaluations, using case studies and expert panels, were the only realistic approach to evaluation. Feller and Anderson (1994:127–140) have demonstrated, however, that a reasonably rigorous benefit–cost analysis of state programs can be conducted. Their study of New York State's Centers for Advanced Technology (CAT) program indicated that benefits have ranged between three and six times the state's direct investment in the program.

The states are in the process of establishing a new social contract with universities to supplement the now fractured contract between the federal government and the universities. How state-level science and technology investment can be most effective in generating state economic development has not yet, however, been fully sorted out or institutionalized. Although the level and durability of state commitments to industrial technology have continued to expand, the depth of commitment remains tentative in many states. My own perspective is that when the federal–state system commercial research and extension program becomes more fully institutionalized, it will look more like the older contract between the states and the universities, embodied in the land grant model of the public university, than the post-Cold War social contract between the universities and the federal government.

An Implicit Social Contract

The post-World War II relationship between the federal government, the scientific community, and the universities, where most basic research is conducted, has been governed by what some have termed an implicit social contract. "Government promises to fund the basic science that peer reviewers find most worthy of support, and scientists promise that the research will be performed well and honestly and will provide a steady stream of discoveries that can be translated into new products, medicines, or weapons" (Guston and Keniston, 1994b:2).

During the Cold War era the social contract has represented the central dogma of the appropriate relationship among the federal government, the scientific community, and the research universities. But it has never been practiced in its idealized form. The agencies that administer federal research support, including the National Science Foundation, have always found it necessary to designate the program areas that would receive funding and the amount of funding for each area.[36] Furthermore, federal funding of investigator-initiated peer-reviewed research has seldom accounted for as much as half of federal support for university research. Other support for university

---

[36] I have not, however, been able to find in the literature a discussion of the criteria used to allocate research resources to program areas at the National Science Foundation. Discussion with NSF staff suggests that the interplay between historical continuity and "targets of opportunity" governs research resource allocation among directorates.

research has been through formula funding of agricultural research and institutional support for military, space, and energy research. Much of the research conducted within government laboratories and larger university programs has been evaluated by "merit review" methods such as periodic site visits.

Even in the 1960s and 1970s there was increasing concern in Congress about the relevance of federally funded research. The 1970 Mansfield Amendment limited the ability of the Department of Defense to fund research unrelated to military application. In 1971 Congress earmarked funds for a Research Applied to National Needs (RANN) program at the NSF. Several sources of tension among the federal government, the universities, and the broader public community contributed to the erosion of the social contract between government and science over the past few decades. This erosion is reflected in a continuing decline in the federal share of support for university research since the late 1960s.

One issue was public concern about the ethical implications of research (Woolf, 1994:82–100). Highly publicized cases of fabrication, falsification, and plagiarism created a perception of widespread scientific misconduct (Chubin, 1990). Publicity about irresponsible research on human subjects and animals raised public concern about the sensitivity of the scientific community to human values. Controversies about environmental and health hazards, particularly in the areas of agricultural and biomedical research, raised the level of distrust.

A second source of tension between universities and Congress has been the rather arcane issue of indirect cost recovery for research (Likins and Teich, 1994:176–193). Research grants and contracts typically include overhead charges for services and facilities. These charges, which are intended to cover a share of overhead costs, for libraries for example, are typically aggregated into a "cost pool" to obtain an average overhead rate. In the late 1980s Representative John Dingle (D-MI) conducted hearings that focused on the inclusion of inappropriate items, such as a Stanford University luxury yacht, as a part of the overhead cost pool. Although the disputed items do not involve large amounts of money, they have the capacity to generate dramatic headlines—"Tax Dollars Buy Stanford Booze" (Likins and Teich, 1994:187).

A third source has been the growing effort by universities to bypass the federal peer and merit review systems. During the 1990s there has been a dramatic increase in academic earmarking by Congress. Universities have employed lobbyists to bring pressure on Congress to fund facilities construction and to provide support for institutes and programs. Federal research agencies have been confronted by earmarked budget items that divert funds from mission priorities. The effect of academic earmarking on the quality of research remains ambiguous (Office of Technology Assessment, 1991:Chapter 3). But it is clear that the pursuit of earmarked funding by universities has contributed to the erosion of the social contract.

Regardless of the weight that is placed on the several sources of erosion of the post-World War II social contract, the relationship among the federal government, the universities, and the broader public has been undergoing continuous alteration. During the 1980s and 1990s there was a ratcheting up in the matching fund and cost-sharing requirements by universities in federal agency research grant and contract awards (Feller, 1999b). Federal support for graduate training of scientists and engineers has shifted away from fellowships and toward research assistantships (Chubin, 1994:126). A larger share of federal funding for university research is predicated on cooperative relations with industry and state agencies. There is also increased concern that universities cost too much and have failed to increase productivity—if downsizing is conducive to efficiency in the private sector, why not in the university (Honan, 1998:33, 44, 46)? Although this concern may be exaggerated, there is little question that universities have had great difficulty, in restructuring their programs in response to changing scientific and technical opportunities. In response to this difficulty, new forms of university organization have emerged to deliver educational services.[37] At the end of World War II there were less than 50 U.S. universities that could properly be identified as research universities. By the end of the 1990s over 400 aspired to this status. Research resources were highly skewed. Fifty universities accounted for 51.0%, and 100 universities for 79.1%, of federal research funding. There was an intense ferment to retain elite status, to move up in the rankings, or to develop scientific or technological expertise in specialized areas (Feller, 1999a). It is hard to avoid a conclusion, given the constraints on federal funding anticipated in the early decades of the twenty-first century, that the number of higher education institutions that can be properly identified as research universities will decline.

EXPERIENCE WITH PUBLIC INVESTMENT

The most comprehensive effort to understand the history of government technology programs in the United States was organized by Richard Nelson in the early 1980s (Nelson, 1983; Nelson and Langlois, 1983:814–818). The inferences drawn by Nelson have retained their currency. They are generally consistent with those that I draw from the six sector studies (Chapters 5–10) in this book. They suggest three types of policies that have been relatively successful: (1) direct government support for technology development in areas in which the government itself has a strong involvement, (2) decentralized systems of government support in the "generic" area between basic

---

[37] A frequently cited example is the University of Phoenix. It has many of the core elements of a traditional university—students, teachers, classrooms, examinations, and degree-granting programs. Others are missing. There is no campus—its teaching is delivered through distance education and at numerous sites throughout the United States. Its professors are not tenured and are largely hired on part-time contracts. It conducts no research. In number of students registered, it ranks among the largest universities in the United States (Traub, 1997:114–122). The emergence of the University of Phoenix, and similar programs at traditional universities gives some credence to the vision articulated by Peter Drucker: "thirty years from now the big university campuses will be relics. Universities won't survive . . . already we are delivering more lectures and classes off campus via satellite on two-way radio at a fraction of the cost. The college won't survive as a residential institution. Today's buildings are hopelessly unsuited and totally unneeded" (1997).

and applied research, and (3) a decentralized system of clientele-oriented support for applied research and technology development. A fourth type of policy under which the government has attempted to "pick winners" was judged by Nelson and his colleagues to have been "a clear-cut failure." The reasons for success (or failure) differ among the several areas.

Procurement-Related Technology

In industries such as aviation, computers, and semiconductors the U.S. government itself has been an important user of the technology. This has had two important policy implications. The government, as a consumer of the technology, had knowledge of its own needs and also had the "in-house" technical capacity to communicate its requirements to the private sector suppliers. A second advantage is that public support of the government's mission—defense or space, for example—provides the legitimacy for government support of R&D. Such projects have often had important spillover benefits in the civilian economy. But the spillover effects did not provide the primary source of legitimacy for public support.[38]

Decentralized Generic Technology

Generic research (sometimes referred to as precommercial or precompetitive technology) falls between the basic disciplinary research typically favored in academic research and the kinds of development-oriented research favored by most corporate R&D laboratories. It is usually a step or two removed from commercial development but is directed to areas of potential application or social concern. It seeks to advance scientific and technical knowledge but does not require government administrators to make decisions involving commercial potential.

An early example was the research supported through the National Advisory Committee on Aeronautics (NACA), the forerunner of NASA. NACA research, though conducted in an industry rather than in an academic setting, focused on broad scientific and engineering problems related to aviation rather than on specific designs. More recent examples include biomedical and biotechnology research (Chapter 10). This research is conducted by scientists located in university settings, often in professional schools such as medicine and agriculture, but is largely funded by the National Institutes of Health with the objective of contributing to the improvement of health.

Client-Oriented Technology

Public support directed to technology development, other than in the area of procurement, poses exceptionally difficult information problems for program managers.

---

[38] For a similar conclusion based on Swedish experience, see Edquist (1995).

The political viability of such programs also requires effective mobilization of constituency support. The most successful example of a government program in support of technology development, other than in the area of procurement, has been in the area of agricultural research (Chapter 6; Ruttan, 1982; Huffman and Evenson, 1993). Much of the research in this area has been basic or generic, but even this support has been derived from a technology development mission—higher yielding crops, improvement in animal feed conversion, management of soil and water, and the economics of farm operation.[39]

Picking Winners

The failure of programs such as housing technology, supersonic transport, synthetic fuels, and other examples of attempts by the federal government to pick winners has led some to conclude that the results of efforts to develop particular technologies for a commercial market are "unequivocally negative" (Cohen and Noll, 1991). Nelson is not, however, so pessimistic. "There is certainly an argument that the government can be more forward looking than a private firm, supporting projects that are unpromising today but may be promising tomorrow. But the most effective way to perform such a next-generation function is not by competing in the commercial market place but by research of a more generic sort" (Nelson and Langlois, 1983:219).[40]

These conclusions informed many of the new federal and state efforts in the area of commercial technology development in the 1980s and 1990s. Cohen and Noll (1991), in reviewing this more recent experience, draw somewhat different conclusions. They argue that private control of research (that is, privately owned intellectual property rights) yields greater incentives to innovate and commercialize research results, that efficient technical choices for commercial products require that private participants, rather than government managers, strongly influence technical choices, and that cooperation among businesses can provide a basis for the efficient conduct of research activities but requires encouragement by government. Finally, government resources—most importantly, the laboratories and publicly supported universities—can play an important role in developing technology primarily for private use, rather

---

[39] A major question that has puzzled research policy analysts is why the agricultural research model has not been transferred to other industries organized along atomistic lines such as residential construction. Government efforts to develop housing research programs have been relatively unsuccessful in transferring technology to users or in sustaining political support. Two reasons have been advanced. One is that building codes are both pervasive and intractable. A second is that firms in the building supply industry, which is organized on a larger scale, have seen housing innovation as a threat to their market position.

[40] I am somewhat more positive, drawing on my experience in agricultural research, about the possibility of picking winners than some of the more extreme critics of government research policy. Much of the criticism appears to be guided at least as much by vested interest and ideology as by analysis. There seems to be, for example, a pervasive view that if it worked in agriculture it obviously cannot work in industry. Greater sensitivity to the institutional arrangements that have contributed to the success of public sector agricultural technology development would have enabled other programs to avoid their addition to the list of government failures.

than accidentally yielding commercial applications as essentially serendipitous spin-offs from government missions (Cohen and Noll, 1996:311).

In general the lessons about the effectiveness of public sector support for the development of commercial technology drawn by Cohen and Noll are less optimistic than those drawn by Nelson and his colleagues. This is in part because they employ a broader political economy perspective. They are highly skeptical that new programs can avoid the "pork barrel" problems that plagued the large-scale technology development projects of the past. They emphasize the inability of government agencies, operating under political pressure, to cut losses and cancel failed projects and programs.

What is clear is that neither federal nor state governments have been able to articulate a compelling vision of their role in post-Cold War commercial technology development. It is possible that the new programs initiated during the past two decades will lead to the emergence of a new social contract in the area of commercial technology development that will replace the post-war social contract.

PERSPECTIVE

There are a number of points that emerge rather clearly from this and earlier chapters.

1. Public sector investment has played an important role in the emergence of every U.S. industry that is competitive on a global scale. This ranges from the role of the public sector in providing the highway infrastructure for the automobile, to the use of military procurement for supporting the development of the computer, to the support for biomedical science that became the source of the biotechnology industries. It has also included the support for education and research at U.S. universities that produced the human capital employed in advancing science and technology.

2. The system of intellectual property rights that was originally developed to encourage the dissemination of technology is an essential component of the institutional infrastructure of any national science and technology policy. But it is not a sufficient instrument. It is more effective in providing incentives for the diffusion then the generation of technology. There is a fundamental conflict with the use of the intellectual property rights system to reward the inventor (the equity argument that everyone should have the rights to the fruits of his or her own labor) and the social objective of inducing more rapid diffusion of technology. There is concern, however, that the system of intellectual property rights will need to be reformed if it is not to become an obstacle to progress in newer areas such as biotechnology and to the electronic sharing of information.

3. During World War II and the initial years of the Cold War, massive investments in defense-related science and technology, particularly military procurement, nuclear energy, and space exploration, created a presumption that these investments could become a pervasive source of spin-off commercial technology. As the Cold War wound down and defense-related research began to decline, the weakness of this

perspective became increasingly clear. The United States has never been politically committed to a strong national R&D enterprise beyond national security concerns. It is now in the process of returning to the more traditional spin-on relationship between miliary and commercial technology in which military technology becomes increasingly dependent on civilian technology. Attempts to appeal to new concerns such as international competitiveness or environmental security have not succeeded in generating political commitment.

4. We have now entered a period of increased skepticism, in both the public and private sectors, that investments in S&T lead directly to commercial technology development. The postwar social contract between the scientific community and society, embodied in the linear or assembly line model of the relationship between science and technology, has been rapidly eroding since the end of the Cold War. We are entering a period in which investments in basic science "performed without thought of practical ends" (Bush, 1945:181) must be justified in terms of investment in advancing scientific culture rather than in terms of contributions to other social or economic objectives. My own sense is that those areas of science and technology for which identifiable benefits are not anticipated within a half century will have increasing difficulty in achieving the credibility needed to lay claim to substantial scientific and technical resources. This implies very significant constraints on the ability to generate funding for Big Science. Big Science investments will become increasingly dependent on trajectories opened up by little science.

There are several issues that I have not found a way to confront in this chapter. Among the most important is the question of whether the United States is investing too much (or too little) in scientific research. Those who argue the United States is investing more than an optimal level in scientific research (and in publicly supported technology development) have asked whether the United States is producing too many scientists. In almost all fields of science the distribution of output (measured by scientific publications) is highly skewed. Only slightly more than one-third of all research papers ever published are cited as much as twice. It has been argued, somewhat naively, that a reduction in the production of new scientists by 1%, or even 10%, would not have a measurable effect on the advancement of scientific knowledge (Dresch, 1995:176, 187). There is the common assumption that increasing returns to scale in R&D may be too optimistic (Segerstrom, 1998). There is substantial evidence, however, indicating that the resources devoted to R&D have been increasing more rapidly than growth in patentable inventions.

Questions are increasingly being raised about whether too much of the scientific knowledge produced in the United States is spilling over into the rest of the world. It has been argued that the United States is contributing more than its optimal share to the advancement of knowledge and technology development. One response to this argument are proposals to reduce access to U.S. universities, public laboratories, and private research by foreign students, scientists, and engineers. A second response is that the United States should "free ride" to a greater extent on research conducted elsewhere. Sixty percent of the world scientific literature is now generated outside of the United States. It seems likely that more than this amount of new technology is generated abroad. The investment in science and technology needed to appropriate the knowledge and technology generated elsewhere would be less than that required to generate it in the United States (Dresch, 1995:186).

There have been numerous calls for the development of a new social contract between science and society. One call has been for the allocation of public support to those areas of science and technology that are likely to provide broadly useful knowledge for commercial technology development (Nelson and Langlois, 1983). A second has been a call for the scientific community to focus its efforts on developing the knowledge needed to inform the decisions and implement the policies needed to ensure sustainable development (Lubchenko, 1998). Although there is wide disagreement on the content of a new social contract, there is a general rejection of the notion that basic research cannot and should not be targeted toward the solution of important national security, economic, and social priorities. Successful examples of targeted basic research, such as the support by the Department of Defense for basic research in electronics and of the National Institutes of Health for research in molecular biology (Chapters 9 and 10), are cited in support of a policy of targeted basic research. A sharp distinction is made between support of target basic research and generic technology and the more narrow policy of "picking winners" in technology development.

As we enter the twenty-first century, however, U.S. science and technology policy is still searching for a unifying intellectual foundation. The new programs that have emerged in the 1980s and 1990s were an array of ad hoc initiatives in which the relationship among program expenditures, national priorities, and political viability remains unclear. Neither the science community nor those responsible for science policy have yet been willing to confront the problem of research resource allocation. Yet a rate of growth of R&D expenditures that substantially exceeds the rate of growth of either labor productivity or of per capita income will not be sustainable over the long run.

REFERENCES

Abelson, P. H. "Global Technology Competition." *Science* 277 (1997):1587.

Arora, N. *The Transfer of Technological Know-How to Developing Countries; Technology Licensing, Tacit Knowledge, and the Acquisition of Technological Capability.* Stanford, CA: Ph.D. Thesis, Department of Economics, Stanford University, 1992.

Auerbach, L. E. "Scientists in the New Deal: A Pre-war Episode in the Relations Between Science and Government in the United States." *Minerva* 3 (1965):458–482.

Arrow, K. J. "Economic Welfare and the Allocation of Resources for Invention." In *The Rate and Direction of Inventive Activity: Economic and Social Factors,* R. R. Nelson, ed., pp. 609–625. Princeton, NJ: Princeton University Press, 1962.

Barfield, C. E. *Science Policy from Ford to Reagan: Change and Continuity.* Washington, DC: American Enterprise Institute, 1982.

Barton, J. H. "Adapting the Intellectual Property System to New Technologies." In *Global*

Dimensions of Intellectual Property Rights in Science and Technology, M. B. Wallerstein, M. E. Magee, and R. A. Schoen, eds., pp. 256–283. Washington, DC: National Academy Press, 1993.

Barton, J. H. "Patent Scope in Biotechnology." *International Review of Industrial Property and Copyright Law* 26 (1995):605–617.

Battelle Memorial Institute. *Survey of State Research and Development Expenditures: Fiscal Year 1995.* Columbus, OH, September 1998.

Belanger, D. O. *Enabling American Innovation: Engineering and The National Science Foundation.* West Lafayette, IN: Purdue University Press, 1998.

Bimber, B. *The Politics of Expertise in Congress: The Rise and Fall of the Office of Technology Assessment.* Albany, NY: State University of New York Press, 1996.

Bowers, R. "The Peer Review System on Trial." *American Scientist* 63 (1975):624–626.

Bromley, D. A. *U.S. Technology Policy.* Washington, DC: Executive Office of the President, Office of Science and Technology Policy, September 26, 1990.

Bromley, D. A. *The Presidents Scientists: Reminiscences of a White House Science Advisor.* New Haven, CT: Yale University Press, 1994.

Burger, E. J. *Science at the White House: A Political Liability.* Baltimore, MD: Johns Hopkins University Press, 1980.

Bush, V. *Pieces of the Action.* New York: William Morrow, 1970.

Bush, V. *Science: The Endless Frontier.* Washington, DC: U.S. Office of Scientific Research and Development, 1945. Reprint eds., National Science Foundation, 1960, 1980.

Carnegie Commission on Science, Technology and Government Reports[41]:

Science Technology and the President (October 1988).

E³: Organizing for Environment, Energy, and the Economy in the Executive Branch of the U.S. Government (April 1990).

New Thinking and American defense Technology (August 1990; May 1993).

Science, Technology, and Congress: Expert Advice and the Decision-Making Process (February 1991).

Technology and Economic Performance: Organizing the Executive Branch for a Stronger National Technology Base (September 1991a).

In the National Interest: The Federal Government in the Reform of K-12 Math and Science Education (September 1991b).

Science, Technology, and Congress: Analysis and Advice from the Congressional Support Agencies (October 1991).

Science and Technology in U.S. International Affairs (January 1992).

International Environmental Research and Assessment: Proposals for Better Organization and Decision Making (July 1992).

Enabling the Future: Linking Science and Technology to Societal Goals (September 1992a).

Science, Technology and the States in America's Third Century (September 1992b).

Environmental Research and Development: Strengthening the Federal Infrastructure (December 1992a).

Partnerships for Global Development: The Clearing Horizon (December 1992b).

---

[41] Copies of these reports are available from the Carnegie Commission on Science, Technology, and Government, 437 Madison Avenue, 27th Floor, New York, NY 10022 (Fax: 212–838-6019).

A Science and Technology Agenda for the Nation: Recommendations for the President and Congress (December 1992c).

Facing Toward Governments: Nongovernmental Organizations and Scientific and Technical Advice (January 1993).

Science and Technology in Judicial Decision Making: Creating Opportunities and Meeting Challenges (March 1993).

Science, Technology, and Government for a Changing World: The Concluding Report of the Carnegie Commission on Science, Technology and Government (April 1993).

Risk and the Environment: Improving Regulatory Decision Making (June 1993).

Science, Technology and Congress: Organizational and Procedural Reforms (January 1994).

Calvert, K., C. Starr, R. W. Bussard, S. O. Dean, W. E. Parkins and J. Adams. "Fusion: Pro and Con." *Issues in Science and Technology* 14 (1997):5–9.

Chen, K. "Pentagon Finds Fewer Firms Want to Do Military R&D." *Wall Street Journal,* October 22, 1999:A20.

Chubin, D. A. "Scientific Malpractice and the Contemporary Politics of Knowledge." In *Theories of Science and Society,* S. E. Cozzens and T. F. Gieryn, eds., pp. 144–233. Bloomington, IN: Indiana University Press, 1990.

Chubin, D. "How Large an R&D Enterprise?" In *University Science and the Federal Government,* D. H. Guston and K. Keniston, eds., pp. 118–144. Cambridge, MA: MIT Press, 1994.

Chubin, D. E., and E. J. Hackett. *Peerless Science: Peer Review and U.S. Science Policy.* Albany, NY: State University of New York Press, 1990.

Clinton, W. J., and A. Gore, Jr. *Technology for America's Growth: A New Direction to Build Economic Strengths.* Washington, DC: Executive Office of the President, February 22, 1993.

Clinton, W. J., and A. Gore, Jr. *Science in the National Interest.* Washington, DC: Executive Office of the President, 1994.

Coates, J. F. "The Role of Formal Models in Technology Assessment." *Technological Forecasting and Social Changes* 9 (1975):139–189.

Cohen, L. R., and R. G. Noll (eds.) *The Technology Pork Barrel.* Washington, DC: Brookings Institution Press, 1991.

Cohen, L. R., and R. G. Noll. "Research and Development." In *Privatizing Domestic Priorities: What Can Government Do?* H. J. Aaron and C. L. Schultze, eds., pp. 223–265. Washington, DC: Brookings Institution Press, 1992.

Cohen, L. R., and R. G. Noll. "Privatizing Public Research: The New Competitiveness Strategy." In *The Mosaic of Economic Growth,* R. Landau, T. Taylor, and G. Wright, eds., pp. 305–333. Stanford, CA: Stanford University Press, 1996.

Cole, S., L. E. Rubin, and J. R. Cole. "Peer Review and Support of Science." *Scientific American* 237 (October 1977):34–41.

Committee on Criteria for Federal Support of Research and Development. *Allocating Federal Funds for Science and Technology.* Washington, DC: National Academy Press, 1995 (The Press Report).

Committee on Science, Engineering and Public Policy. *Major Award Decision Making at the National Science Foundation.* Washington, DC: National Academy Press, 1994.

Cowan, R., and D. Foray. "Quandaries in the Economics of Dual Technologies and Spillovers from Military to Civilian Research and Development." *Research Policy* 24 (1995): 851–868.

Cowling, E. B., J. T. Sigman, and C. E. Putnam. "Maximizing Benefits from Research: Lessons from Medicine and Agriculture." *Issues in Science and Technology* 12 (1996): 29–32.

Curtis, C. B., J. P. McTague, and D. W. Cheney. "Fixing the National Laboratory System." *Issues in Science and Technology* 12 (1997):49–56.

Dasgupta, P. "The Economic Theory of Technology Policy: An Introduction." In *Economic Policy and Technological Performance*, P. Dasgupta and P. Stoneman, eds., pp. 1–6. Cambridge, UK: Cambridge University Press, 1987.

Dasgupta, P., and P. A. David. "Toward a New Economics of Science." *Research Policy* 23 (1994):487–521.

David, P. A. "Intellectual Property Institutions and the Pandora's Thumb: Patents, Copyrights, and Trade Secrets in Economic Theory and History." In *Global Dimensions of Intellectual Property Rights in Science and Technology,* M. B. Wallerstein, M. E. Mogee, and R. A. Schoen, eds., pp. 19–61. Washington, DC: National Academy Press, 1993.

David, P. A., D. Mowery, and W. E. Steinmueller. "Analyzing the Economic Payoffs from Basic Research." *Economics of Innovation and New Technology* 2 (1992):73–90.

Day, K., and V. W. Ruttan. "The Deficit in Natural Resources Research." *BioScience* 41 (1991):32–40.

Dickson, D. *The New Politics of Science*. Chicago, IL: University of Chicago Press. 1st ed., 1984; 2nd ed., 1988.

Dorfman, N. S. "Route 128: The Development of a Regional High Technology Economy." *Research Policy* 12 (1983):299–316.

Dresch, S. P. "The Economics of Fundamental Research." In *The Academy in Crisis: The Political Economy of Higher Education,* J. W. Sommer, ed., pp. 171–196. New Brunswick, NJ: Transaction Publishers, 1995.

Dupree, A. H. *Science in the Federal Government: A History of Policies and Activities to 1940.* Cambridge, MA: Harvard University Press, 1957, 1985.

Edquist, C. "Government Technology Procurement as an Instrument of Technology Policy." Linköping, Sweden: Linköping University Department of Technology and Social Change, September 1995.

Edgerton, E. E. H. "British Scientific Intellectuals and the Relations of Science, Technology and War." In *National Military Establishments and the Advancement of Science and Technology: Studies in 20th Century History*, P. Forman and J. M. Sanchez-Ron, eds., pp. 1–35. Dordrecht, The Netherlands: Kluwer Academic Publishers, 1996.

Evenson, R. E. "Intellectual Property Rights, R&D Inventions, Technology Purchase and Privacy in Economic Development: An International Comparative Study." In *Science and Technology: Lessons for Development Policy*, R. E. Evenson and G. Ranis, eds., pp. 325–355. Boulder, CO: Westview Press, 1990.

Evenson, R. E., and Y. Kislev. *Agricultural Research and Productivity*. New Haven, CT: Yale University Press, 1975.

Evenson, R. E., and Y. Kislev. "Research for Agriculture: Economic Evaluation." Paper presented at Zvi Griliches' Commemoration Symposium. National Bureau of Economic Research, March 5–6, 1999 (mimeo).

Evenson, R., P. E. Waggoner, and V. W. Ruttan, eds. "Economic Benefits from Research: An Example from Agriculture." *Science* 205 (1979):1101–1107.

Feller, I. "Manufacturing Technology Centers as Components of Regional Technology Infrastructures." *Regional Science and Urban Economics* 27 (1977):181–197.

Feller, I. "Universities as Engines of State Economic Growth: They Think They Can." *Research Policy* 19 (1990):335–348.

Feller, I. "Do State Programs on Technology Work." *Forum for Applied Research and Public Policy* 6 (1991):69–71.

Feller, I. "Recent Theoretical and Organizational Approaches to U.S. Technology Policy." In *Technology and U.S. Competitiveness: An Institutional Focus,* H. Lambright and D. Rahm, eds., pp. 119–131. New York: Greenwood Press, 1992.

Feller, I. "Manufacturing Technology Centers as Components of Regional Technology Infrastructures." *Regional Science and Urban Economics* 27 (1997a):181–197.

Feller, I. "Federal and State Government Roles in Science and Technology." *Economic Development Quarterly* 11 (1997b):283–295.

Feller, I. "Elite and Distributed Science: An Analytical Guide to Public Policy in the Distribution of Federal Academic R&D Funds." College Park, PA: Institute for Policy Research and Evaluation, 1999a (mimeo).

Feller, I. "University Experiences with Federal Agency Matching and Cost-Sharing Policies and Evaluation." College Park, PA: Institute for Policy Research and Evaluation, 1999b (mimeo).

Feller, I., and G. Anderson. "A Benefit-Cost Approach to the Evaluation of State Technology Development Programs." *Economic Development Quarterly* 8 (May 1994):127–140.

Fishel, W., ed. *Resource Allocation in Agricultural Research.* Minneapolis, MN: University of Minnesota Press, 1971.

Fuglie, K., and V. W. Ruttan. "Value of External Reviews of Research of the International Agricultural Research Centers." *Agricultural Economics* 3 (1989):365–380.

General Accounting Office. *Manufacturing Extension Programs: Manufactures Views of Services.* Washington, DC: GAO/GGO-95-216BR, August 1995.

General Accounting Office. *Measuring Performance: Strengths and Limitations of Research Indicators.* Washington, DC: GAO/RCED-97-91, March 1997.

Georghiou, L. "Global Cooperation in Research." *Research Policy* 27 (1998):611–626.

Gibbons, J. H. "Science and Technology in a Post-Cold War Era." *Forum for Applied Research and Public Policy* 10 (1995):119–122.

Gould, D. M., and W. C. Gruben. "The Role of Intellectual Property Rights in Economic Growth." *Journal of Development Economics* 48 (1996):323–350.

Greer, D. F. "The Case Against Patent Systems in Less-Developed Countries." *Journal of International Law and Economics* 8 (1973):223–266.

Griliches, Z. "The Search for R&D Spillovers." *Scandinavian Journal of Economics* 44 (1992):29–41.

Griliches, Z. "R&D Productivity: Econometric Results and Measurement Issues." In *Handbook of the Economics of Innovation and Technological Change*, P. Stoneman, ed., pp. 52–89. Oxford, UK: Basil Blackwell, 1995.

Gustafson. "The Controversy over Peer Review." *Science 190 (1975):1060–1066.*

Guston, D. H., and K. Keniston, eds. *The Fragile Contract: University Science and the Federal Government.* Cambridge, MA: MIT Press, 1994a.

Guston, D. H., and K. Keniston. "Introduction: The Social Contract for Science." In *The Fragile Contract: University Science and the Federal Government*, pp. 1–41. Cambridge, MA: MIT Press, 1994b.

Hall, B. H. "Private and Social Returns to Research and Development." In *Technology R&D*

and the Economy, B. R. Smith and C. E. Barfield, eds., pp. 148–155. Washington, DC: Brookings Institution Press, 1996.

Hirsch, R. L., G. Kulcinski, and R. Shanny. "Fusion Research with a Future." *Issues in Science and Technology* (1997):60–64.

Honan, W. H. "The Ivory Tower Under Siege." *New York Times*, January 4, 1998, Sec. 4A:33, 44, 46.

House Committee on Science. *Allocating Funds for Science and Technology*. Washington, DC: USGPO, 1996.

House Committee on Science. *Toward A New National Science Policy*. Washington, DC: September 24, 1998.

Huffman, W. C., and R. E. Evenson. *Science for Agriculture: A Long Term Perspective*. Ames, IA: Iowa State University Press, 1993.

Hughes, T. P. *Rescuing Prometheus*. New York: Random House-Pantheon Books, 1998.

Jaffe, A. B., and J. Lerner. *Privitizing R&D: Patent Policy and Commercialization of National Laboratory Technologies*. Cambridge, MA: National Bureau of Economic Research Working Paper 7064, April 1999.

Johnson, R. J., and P. Teske. "Toward an American Industrial Technology Policy." In *Technology Transfer and Public Policy*, Y. S. Lee, ed., pp. 42–60. Westport, CT: Quorum Books, 1997.

Jones, C. I. and J. C. Williams. "Measuring the Social Return to R&D." *The Quarterly Journal of Economics* (1998):1119–1135.

Kaempffert, W. "War and Technology." *The American Journal of Sociology* 46 (January 1941):431–444.

Kealey, T. *The Economic Laws of Scientific Research*. New York: St. Martins Press, 1996.

Kelley, M. R. "From Missions to Commercial Orientation: Perils and Possibilities for Federal Industrial Technology Policy." *Economic Development Quarterly* 11 (1997):313–328.

Kleinman, D. *Politics on the Endless Frontier: Postwar Research Policy in the United States*. Durham, NC: Duke University Press, 1995.

Kostoff, R. N. "Peer Review: The Appropriate GPRA Metric for Research." *Science* 277 (1997):651–652.

Lambright, W. H., and D. Rahm. "Science, Technology and the States." *Forum for Applied Research and Public Policy* 6 (Fall 1991):49–60.

Lanjouw, J. O. "Introduction of Pharmaceutical Product Patents in India: Heartless Exploitation of the Poor and Suffering." New Haven, CT: Yale University Economic Growth Center Paper 775, 1997.

Lawler, A. "OSTP: A Mixed Midterm Report." *Science* 268 (April 1995):192–194.

Lawler, A. "DOE Labs: Is Evolution Enough?" *Science* 272 (June 1996):1576–1578.

Lawler, A. "Is the NRC Ready for Reform." *Science* 276 (May 1997):900–904.

Layton, E. T. "Conditions of Technological Development." In *Science, Technology and Society: A Cross-Disciplinary Perspective*, I. Spiegel-Rosing and D. de Solla Price, eds., pp. 197–222. Beverly Hills, CA: Sage Publications, 1977.

Lee, Y. S., ed. *Technology Transfer and Public Policy*. Westport, CT: Quorum Books, 1997.

Lesser, W. "An Overview of Intellectual Property Systems." In *Strengthening Protection of Intellectual Property in Development Countries: A Survey of the Literature*, W. Siebeck, ed., pp. 5–15. Washington, DC: World Bank Discussion Paper 112, 1990.

Likins, P., and A. H. Teich. "Indirect Costs and Government-University Partnership." In *The*

Fragile Contract: University-Science and the Federal Government, D. H. Guston and K. Kenisten, eds., pp. 177–192. Cambridge, MA: MIT Press, 1994.

Ling, J. G., and Mary A. Hand. "Federal Funding in Materials Research." *Science* 201 (1980):1203–1207.

Long, W. F. *Advanced Technology Program: Performance of Completed Projects Status Report.* NIST Special Publication 950–1. Washington, DC: U.S. Government Printing Office, 1999.

Lowood, H. "Steeples of Excellence and Valley of Silicon: The Industrial Park and Industry Connection at Stanford." Stanford, CA: Stanford University Libraries, 1987 (mimeo).

Lubchenko, J. "Entering the Century of the Environment: A New Social Contract for Science." *Science* 279 (1998):491–497.

Mansfield, E. "Academic Research and Industrial Innovation." *Research Policy* 20 (1991): 1–12.

Mansfield, E., J. Rapoport, A. Romero, E. Villani, S. Wagner, and F. Husic. *The Production and Application of New Industrial Technology.* New York: Norton, 1977.

Mansfield, E., M. Schwartz, and S. Wagner. "Imitation Costs and Patents: An Empirical Study." *The Economic Journal* 91 (1981):907–918.

Markham, J. W. "The Joint Effect of Antitrust and Patent Laws Upon Innovation." *American Economic Review* 56 (1966):291–300.

Maskus, K. E. "The International Regulation of Intellectual Property." *Weltwirtschaftlichs Arch IV* 134 (1998):186–208.

McKelvey, M. D. "Emerging Environments in Biotechnology." In *Universities and the Global Knowledge Economy,* Henry Etzkowitz and Loet Leydesdorff, eds., pp. 60–70. London: Pinter, 1997.

McNeill, W. H. *The Pursuit of Power: Technology, Armed Forces and Society since A.D. 1000.* Chicago, IL: University of Chicago Press, 1982.

Merges, R. P., and R. R. Nelson. "On the Complex Economics of Patent Scope." *Columbia Law Review* 90 (1990):839–916.

Mohr, H. "The Ethics of Science." *Interdisciplinary Science Reviews* 4 (1979):45–53.

Moore, D., J. Sturrock, and P. Webre. "Can U.S. Support of Research Fuel Economic Gains?" *Forum for Applied Research and Public Policy* 10 (1995):112–118.

Mowery, D. C., and N. Rosenberg. "The Commercial Aircraft Industry." In *Government and Technical Progress: A Cross Industry Analysis,* R. R. Nelson, ed., pp. 101–161. New York: Pergamon Press, 1982.

Mowery, D. C., and N. Rosenberg. *Technology and the Pursuit of Economic Growth.* Cambridge, UK: Cambridge University Press, 1989.

Mowery, D. C., and N. Rosenberg. *Paths of Innovation: Technological Change in 20th Century America.* Cambridge, UK: Cambridge University Press, 1998.

Narin, F., K. S. Hamilton, and D. Olivastro. "The Increasing Linkage between U.S. Technology and Public Science." Hadden Heights, NJ: CHI Research, March 17, 1997 (mimeo).

Narin, F., and E. Noma. "Is Technology Becoming Science." *Scientometrica* 7 (1985):369–381.

Narin, F., and D. Olivastro. "Status Report: Linkage Between Technology and Science." *Research Policy* 21 (1992):237–249.

National Institutes for Standards and Technology. *National Institute of Standards and Technology Program: Proposal Preparation Kit.* Washington, DC: U.S. Department of Commerce, 1994.

National Research Council. *Ohio's Thomas Edison Centers: A 1990 Review.* Washington, DC: National Academy Press, 1990.

National Science and Technology Council. *Assessing Fundamental Science.* Washington, DC: National Academy Press, 1996.

Nef, J. U. *War and Human Progress.* Cambridge, MA: Harvard University Press, 1950.

Nelson, R. R. "The Simple Economics of Basic Scientific Research." *Journal of Political Economy* 67 (1959):297–306.

Nelson, R. R., ed. *The Rate and Direction of Inventive Activity: Economic and Social Factors.* Princeton, NJ: Princeton University Press, 1962.

Nelson, R. R., ed. *Government and Technical Progress: A Cross-Industry Analysis.* New York: Pergamon Press, 1983.

Nelson, R. R. *"Why Bush's 'Science: The Endless Frontier' Has Been a Hindrance to the Development of an Effective Civilian Technology Policy."* New York: Columbia University, School of International and Public Affairs, 1997.

Nelson, R. R., and R. N. Langlois. "Industrial Innovation Policy: Lessons from American History." *Science* 219 (1983):814–818.

Office of Technology Assessment. *Research Funding as an Investment: Can We Measure the Returns.* OTA-TM-SET 36, Washington, DC: Government Printing Office, April 1996.

Press, F. "Needed: Coherent Budgeting for Science and Technology." *Science* 270 (December 1, 1995):1448–49.

Price, D. J. de Solla. *Little Science, Big Science . . . And Beyond.* New York: Columbia University Press, 1986 (1st ed., 1963).

Robinson, D. Z. "Think Twice Before Overhauling Federal Budgeting." In *AAAS Science and Technology Policy Yearbook, 1996–97,* A. H. Teich, S. D. Nelson, and C. McEnany, eds., pp. 217–224. Washington, DC: American Association for the Advancement of Science, 1997.

Roland, A. "Technology and War: A Bibliographic Essay." In *Military Enterprise and Technological Change: Perspectives on the American Experience,* M. R. Smith, ed., pp. 347–379. Cambridge, MA: MIT Press, 1985.

Ruttan, V W. *Agricultural Research Policy.* Minneapolis, MN: University of Minnesota Press, 1982.

Saloman, J. J. "Science Policy Studies and the Development of Science Policy." In *Science Technology and Society: A Cross-Disciplinary Perspective,* I. Spiegel-Rösing and D. de Solla Price, eds., pp. 43–70. Beverly Hills, CA: Sage Publications, 1977.

Samuels, R. J. *Rich Nation, Strong Army: National Security and the Technological Transformation of Japan.* Ithaca, NY: Cornell University Press, 1994.

Schact, W. H. *Cooperative Research and Development Agreements (CRADA's).* Washington, DC: Congressional Research Service, Library of Congress, 95–150 SPR, January 10, 1997a.

Schact, W. H. "Technology Transfer: Use of Federally Funded Research and Development." Washington, DC: Congressional Research Service, March 4, 1997.

Schact, W. H. *The Advanced Technology Program.* Washington, DC: Congressional Research Service, Library of Congress, 95–36 SPR, July 28, 1997c.

Schact, W. H. *Manufacturing Extension Partnership Program: An Overview.* Washington, DC: Congressional Research Service, Library of Congress, 97–104 SPR, August 11, 1997d.

Scherer, F. M. "Inter-industry Technology Flows and Productivity Growth." *Review of Economics and Statistics* 64 (1982):627–634.

Scherer, F. M. *Industrial Market Structure and Economic Performance.* Chicago, IL: Rand McNally, 1980; rev. ed. 1990.

Scherer, F. M. *New Perspectives on Economic Growth and Technical Innovation.* Washington, DC: Brookings Institution Press, 1999.

Schrage, M. "The GOP Needs a Bit More R&D in Its Science and Technology Policy." *The Washington Post,* May 19, 1995:F3.

Siebeck, W., ed. *Strengthening Protection of Intellectual Property in Developing Countries: A Survey of the Literature.* Washington, DC: The World Bank, Discussion Paper 112, 1990.

Skolnikoff, E. B. *The Elusive Transformation: Science, Technology and the Evolution of International Politics.* Princeton, NJ: Princeton University Press, 1993.

Smith, B. L. R. *The RAND Corporation: Case Study of a Nonprofit Advisory Corporation.* Cambridge, MA: Harvard University Press, 1966.

Smith, P. J. "Intellectual Property Rights and Trade: Analysis of Biological Products, Medicinals and Botanicals, and Pharmaceuticals." St. Paul, MN: Department of Applied Economics, May 25, 1999 (mimeo).

Smith, P., and M. McGeary. "Don't Look Back: Science Funding for the Future." *Issues in Science and Technology* 13 (1997):33–40.

Solo, R. A. "Gearing Military R&D to Economic Growth." *Harvard Business Review* (1962):49–60.

Speaker, S. L., and M. S. Lindee. "A Guide to the Human Genome Project: Technologies, People and Institutions." Philadelphia, PA: Chemical Heritage Foundation, 1993.

Stacy, W. M. "The ITER Decision and U.S. Fusion R&D." *Issues in Science and Technology* 14 (Summer 1997):53–59.

Stein, B. R. "Public Accountability and the Project Grant Mechanism." *Research Policy* 2 (1973):2–16.

Stenberg, P. L. "The Growth of the Minneapolis-St. Paul Instrument Industry Cluster." Washington, DC: U.S. Department of Agriculture, Economic Research Service, 1998 (mimeo).

Stephan, P. E. "The Economics of Science." *Journal of Economic Literature* 34 (1996):1199–1235.

Stokes, D. E. *Pasteur's Quadrant: Basic Science and Technological Innovation.* Washington, DC: Brookings Institution Press, 1997.

Traub, J. "Drive-Thru U." *New Yorker,* October 20, 1997:114–122.

United States Congress, House of Representatives, Committee on Science. *FY 1996 TA/NIST Budget Authorization.* 104th Congress 1st Session, March 23, 1995. Washington, DC: Government Printing Office, 1995.

United States General Accounting Office. *Measuring Performance: The Advanced Technology Program and Private-Sector Funding.* Washington, DC: US/GAO/RCED-96–47, January 1996.

Wallerstein, M. B., M. E. Mogee, and R. A. Schoen, eds. *Global Dimensions of Intellectual Property Rights in Science and Technology.* Washington, DC: National Academy Press, 1993.

Walsh, J. "Texas Wins R&D Center." *Science* 239 (1988):248.

Weinberg, A. M. "Impact of Large Scale Science in the United States." *Science* 134 (1961): 161–164.

Weinberg, A. M. "Criteria for Scientific Choice." *Physics Today* 17 (March 1964):42–48.

Weinberg, A. M. *Reflections on Big Science*. Cambridge, MA: MIT Press, 1967.

White, L., Jr. *Machina Ex Deo: Essays in the Dynamics of Western Culture*. Cambridge, MA: MIT Press, 1968.

Woolf, P. "Integrity and Accountability in Research." In *The Fragile Contract: University Science and the Federal Government,* D. H. Guston and K. Kenisten, eds., pp. 177–192. Cambridge, MA: MIT Press, 1994.

World Bank, *Knowledge for Development: World Development Report, 1998/99*. New York: Oxford University Press, 1999.

Zucker, L. G., and M. R. Darby. "Entrepreneurs, Star Scientists, and Biotechnology." *NBER Reporter* (Fall, 1998):7–16.

The Transition to Sustainable Development[1]

The institutional and cultural foundations of the modern world began to emerge in the seventeenth and eighteenth centuries. The scientific and technical foundations were established with the agricultural and industrial revolutions of the eighteenth and nineteenth centuries. These institutional and technical changes combined to sustain unprecedented growth in population, in resource use, and in human welfare. Since 1950, global population has more than doubled, energy production has more than tripled, and economic output has increased by a factor of five.

But is this growth sustainable? In this chapter I turn to some of the challenges that must be addressed in our attempts to advance the knowledge and technology needed to sustain growth over the next half century.

WHAT HAVE WE LEARNED?

General Purpose Technologies

A succession of strategic or general purpose technologies has served as important vehicles for technical change across the agricultural, industrial, and service sectors. In the nineteenth century the steam engine was a dominant general purpose technology (Chapter 7). Steam powered the industrial revolution. In the twentieth century the electric generator—the dynamo—become a pervasive source of technical change throughout the economy. It is not possible to visualize twentieth-century technology—from mass production, to communication technology, to consumer electronics—without electric power. Advances in chemistry, and in chemical engineering, represent a third important general purpose technology (Chapter 8). The chemical industry has been a pervasive source of advances in both agricultural and military technology, of new fibers and new materials, and of new pharmaceutical products throughout the twentieth century. The computer and semiconductor industries became, during the second half of the twentieth century, major sources of technical change in both the manufacturing and service industries (Chapter 9). By the late twentieth century, biotechnology—a result of the merging of knowledge streams from physics,

---

[1] I am indebted to Robert W. Kates and Kai N. Lee for comments on an earlier draft of this chapter.

chemistry, and biology—was emerging as a source of dynamic new general purpose technologies (Chapter 10).

A consistent feature in the history of these general purpose technologies has been a lengthy period between their initial emergence and their impact (David, 1990; Lipsey et al., 1998). The steam engine underwent a century of modification and improvement before widespread adoption in industry and transportation in the first half of the nineteenth century. It was half a century from the time electric power was first introduced until it became a measurable source of growth in industrial productivity. Controversy about the impact of computers on productivity continued into the 1990s. And it seem likely that it will be well into the twenty-first century before biotechnology begins to exert a significant impact on agricultural production or on human health.

Induced Innovation

The rate and direction of technical change are powerfully influenced by changes in the economic environment, particularly the prices of products relative to prices of factors, and prices of factors relative to each other. In the short run the impact of economic forces on the rate and direction of technical change may be obscured by market imperfections and political intervention. Over the longer run, however, it is hard to imagine a more powerful device for directing scientific and technical effort than a rise in the price of labor relative to capital.

The rate and direction of technical change are also influenced by powerful autonomous forces. The internal logic of scientific discovery has repeatedly opened up opportunities for the advancement of knowledge and technology, recently, for example, in the field of molecular biology (Chapter 10). But even when technical development is science driven, the economic environment plays a powerful role in determining the direction of science-based technology development and in selecting which advances in knowledge will be most intensively exploited .

The economic forces that act to induce technical change operate through political as well as economic markets. During the second half of the twentieth century, the rising value of environmental resources and services, formerly regarded as free goods, has induced institutional innovations in both economic and political markets. Examples include both the "command and control" regulatory approaches and the design of "constructed markets" to manage sulfur dioxide (SO_2) emissions (Chapter 12).

The case of atomic energy represents an important example of the premature forcing, by the political system, of a science-based technical change (Chapter 7). It is possible that future changes in energy resource endowments and environmental concerns will induce the scientific and technical effort necessary to generate an economically viable and environmentally benign nuclear energy technology. But, at least in retrospect, it is difficult to argue that the time when this will occur has been advanced by the premature forcing of commercial development.

Government Role

Government has played an important role in technology development in almost every U.S. industry that has become competitive on a global scale. The government has supported agricultural technology through research, the automobile industry through the design and construction of the highway infrastructure, the development of the computer through military procurement, and the growth of the biotechnology industries through support for basic biological research.

Three types of public support have been successful. One is direct support of technology development in areas in which the government is strongly involved. A dramatic recent example is the Internet, which was initially developed by the Defense Department's Advanced Research Projects Agency (ARPA) to facilitate communication among its contractors and grantees. A second area in which government support has been successful is in the development of generic technology. A recent example has been the support for basic research in molecular biology and closely related research in biotechnology. A third category has been in the area of client-oriented technology. Agricultural research is a highly successful example. Most of the increases in plant and animal productivity of the last century have been the result of public sector agricultural research. An important element in the success of client-oriented public research is the close articulation between the public sector suppliers and the private sector users of knowledge and technology.

A second lesson that emerges from U.S. experience is the importance of a decentralized national research system. The structure of the U.S. national research system took its present form in the half century between 1880 and 1930. In this period we witnessed the formation of scientific and technical bureaus within the federal government, the establishment of industrial research laboratories, the formation and growth of public and private research universities, and the emergence of philanthropic foundations to support research and education. These institutions drew on each other for their leadership. Universities and small entrepreneurial firms conducted a much larger share of research, drawing on multiple sources of funding, than in other industrial countries. This decentralized structure has given the United States greater capacity to adjust to changing national and global priorities, and to direct research to the exploration of commercial opportunities, than in countries in which government-funded research is conducted primarily in national laboratories or research institutes only marginally linked with universities and in which private sector research is limited primarily to large firms (Mowery and Rosenberg, 1998:11–46).

Mature Industries

A fourth important lesson is that the productivity gains associated with advances in technology, particularly process technology, can be important sources of productivity growth and competitive advantage even in industries in which technology is relatively mature. The agricultural and automobile cases are particularly instructive. During much of the first half of the twentieth century gains in labor productivity in agriculture ran ahead of growth in the domestic demand for agricultural commodities. This enabled the agricultural sector to release labor to rapidly growing industries such as the automobile industry. During this same period the rapid growth of productivity, combined with rapid growth in per capita income in the U.S. economy, rapidly expanded the market for automobiles and opened up growth in well-paying jobs in the automobile industry. Leadership in manufacturing technology also enabled the U.S. automobile industry to dominate world markets.

The situation changed dramatically during the second half of the twentieth century. Agricultural employment declined to less than 2% of the labor force. But rapid productivity growth and the consequent decline in the real cost of production enabled the United States to achieve a dominant position in world markets for a number of major agricultural commodities. The contrast with the automobile industry was quite striking. During most of the post-World War II era the U.S. automobile industry lagged behind Japan and Germany in productivity growth (Chapter 11). The U.S. agricultural sector strengthened its position in world markets even while losing jobs. In contrast, the U.S. automobile industry lost both jobs and markets.

There are important implications for developing countries. Even while the automobile industry was becoming a mature industry in the United States, it became a dynamic source of economic growth in Western Europe and Japan. Other mature industries, such as textiles, steel, and shipbuilding, also played an important role in Japanese post-World War II growth. More recently, these same industries have become important leading sectors in the economic growth of several developing countries. In some cases the technology has been transferred to developing countries by direct foreign investment. In other cases, for example, in Korea and Taiwan, the technology has been transferred and adapted by local firms. Although policies that encourage import substitution through quota and tariffs have generally been discredited, as leading to substitution of inefficient or high-cost domestic production for lower cost imports, policies that support efficient technology transfer will continue to represent an important source of economic growth for developing countries.

Bending the Trajectory

An important path of technical change in western economies during the nineteenth and twentieth centuries was the development of processes for the conversion of low-value raw materials into commercially useful products. The steam engine transformed coal into a valued resource to power industry and transportation. The Haber–Bosch process converted atmospheric nitrogen into a substitute for natural fertilizers and increasingly scarce soil resources. Petroleum was transformed from a resource of modest value for illumination into a fuel for transportation and an industrial raw material. The electric arc furnace transformed bauxite from a mineral of little economic significance to a new metal (aluminum) with many new commercial uses. And the same technology converted scrapped automobiles into a low-cost source of steel to replace the dwindling domestic supplies of high grade iron ore (Mowery and Rosenberg, 1998:169–178).

During the second half of the twentieth century the trajectory of technological development in the United States began to shift toward a new postindustrial revolution path. Scientific and technical effort was developed and directed, through the allocation of federal resources, into those areas of science and technology that were seen as particularly relevant to the military and space missions of the government during the Cold War. The Cold War experience demonstrated that when supported by large flows of public resources over several decades, scientific and technical effort could produce revolutionary new "high-technology" industries in fields such as aerospace, electronics, communications, computing, and biotechnology.

By shortly after the middle of the twentieth century, the technical change trajectories associated with greater energy and material intensity and with high-technology military and space initiatives were under attack. The spillovers of residuals from agricultural and industrial production and consumption were increasingly viewed as a threat to human health and the environment. These perceptions stimulated substantial innovation in environmental policy and law in developed countries. Yet there continue to be deep divisions about the appropriate response to the changes associated with the growing impact of material and energy intensity. Optimists point to the advances already underway in dematerialization and decarbonization (Ausubel, 1989; Ausubel and Langford, 1997). Pessimists point to a more than doubling of material demands anticipated by the middle of the twenty-first century, and to the erosion of essential services from nature if recent trends continue (Daily, 1997). But the importance of the sustainability transition is indisputable. The disagreements are more about the pace of the transition to a sustainable trajectory rather than about whether such a transition is necessary.

Not every lesson from past experience will be useful as an attempt is made to navigate the transition to sustainable development. But there can be little question that as we enter the twenty-first century the rising value of a number of open-access resources—the services of nature—will become an increasingly important driving force for technical and institutional change. In meeting this challenge very substantial public sector investment in the generation of new knowledge and new technology will be required. The capacity to advance knowledge and technology represents the "reserve army" that will be required to deal with the surprises that will be confronted.

THE SUSTAINABILITY CRITIQUE

The major challenge of the twenty-first century will be to make the transition to sustainable prosperity in both presently developed and low-income countries. This will involve a transition to a stable global population. It will also involve a transition to a predominantly urban society. And it may involve a transition to a stable level of material consumption. Whether these transitions will be accompanied by material and energy consumption in presently poor countries comparable to the levels that have been achieved by the industrial countries is the subject of intense debate. How much land will be left to nature is even more problematical.

Before turning to the details of navigating the sustainability transition, it is useful to review the "sustainability critique" of technical change. During the last quarter of the twentieth century the conception of natural resources has expanded from the traditional categories of nonrenewable and renewable to include the social value of environmental and ecosystem services (Daily, 1997, Chapter 12). This broader concept of the value of natural resources has emerged in response to the presumed conflict between ecology and development and between the present and the future. The term sustainability was first advanced in 1980 in a report of the International Union for the Conservation of Nature and Natural Resources (Lele, 1991; Jamieson, 1998). Prior to the mid-1980s the concept of sustainable development had achieved its widest currency among critics of "industrial" approaches to agricultural development.

Three alternative definitions of sustainability have been proposed. For some sustainability is primarily an ecological issue. A system that "depletes, pollutes, or disrupts the ecological balance of natural systems is unsustainable and should be replaced by one which honors the longer-term biophysical constraints of nature" (Douglass, 1984:2). Among those advancing the ecological agenda there is a pervasive view that population levels are already too large to be sustained at present levels of per capita consumption (Ehrlich, 1968; Ehrlich and Ehrlich, 1970; Myers, 1994). A second group, primarily mainstream resource and agricultural economists, defines sustainability in technical and economic terms—the capacity to supply the expanding demand for resources and commodities on increasingly favorable terms (Chapter 12). A third group emphasizes sustaining not just the physical resource base, but a broad set of community values. Proponents have often viewed technical change as an assault, not only on the environment, but also on rural people and indigenous communities. This third group, by broadening the sustainability agenda from its initial agroecological origins, contributed to the emergence of an agenda that includes social and economic development (Ruttan, 1994a).

By the late 1980s the sustainability rhetoric was undergoing "establishment appropriation." The concept had diffused rapidly from the confines of its agroecological origins to include the entire development process. The Brundtland Commission defined sustainable development as "development that meets the needs of the present without compromising the ability of future generations to meet their own needs" (World Commission on Environment and Development, 1987:3). This definition represented a deliberate attempt to expand the concept of sustainability to take into account the growth in demand for natural resource-based commodities and environmental services arising out of economic growth.

The Brundtland Commission also raised the possibility that those who are alive today, particularly those living in more affluent societies, may have to curb their material consumption, both to accommodate increased consumption in less affluent societies and to avoid an even more drastic decline in the consumption levels of future generations. The issue of intergenerational resource transfers was not a welcome message to wealthy societies that have resisted the idea of transferring resources to reduce either domestic or international income disparities. Historical experience, at least in the West, often causes us to be skeptical about our obligations to future generations. "We have actually done quite well at the hands of our ancestors. Given how poor they were and how rich we are, they might properly have saved less and consumed more" (Solow, 1974:9).

Mainstream economists have generally interpreted the Brundtland definition as implying that a sustainable path of development gives future generations equal treatment with the present generation—each generation bequeaths to its successor whatever it takes to achieve a level of living at least as desirable as its own (Chichilinsky, 1997). In this view a sustainable path of development replaces whatever it takes from its natural and produced capital. But what matters is not the particular form that replacement takes, but only the capacity to produce the things that posterity will demand. This *weak sustainability* rule is not inconsistent with "running down" the stock of a particular form of natural capital, provided that the productivity of the aggregate capital stock, including constructed capital, remains intact (Solow, 1992). Much of the ecological literature denies the assumption of substitutability between constructed capital and at least some forms of natural capital, particularly the natural capital that is responsible for "life support" functions such as maintaining the hydrologic cycle, the carbon cycle, and the nitrogen cycle. The *strong sustainability* rule advanced by the ecological community, including many ecological economists, requires that the stock of natural capital, including important "life support" components, be held constant or enhanced (Pearce and Atkinson, 1995).[2]

Beginning in the 1980s international research programs were initiated to "describe and understand the interactive physical, chemical, and biological processes that regulate the Earth's unique environment—the changes that are occurring in the system and the manner in which they are influenced by human action" (National Research Council, 1983; 1992a, 1992b). Out of these initial efforts, some natural scientists became convinced that the effects of the exploding scale of human activity—particularly the intensification of agricultural and industrial activity with its concomitant use of fossil fuel and chemical transformation of raw materials—had thrust human society into a gigantic experiment. This experiment was transforming the basic interactive physical, chemical, and biological processes in a manner that might not be possible to reverse. Humankind, in this view, is engaged in a massive gamble with nature about the future of the earth—a gamble that nature would surly win even at the cost of humankind.

There is substantial disagreement—within the several physical, biological, and social science communities—about what should be sustained and what should be

---

[2] There has been considerable controversy among environmentalists, ecological economists, and resource economists over the relevance of both the strong and the weak sustainability rules for environmental policy. For the arguments advanced by one of the more vigorous critics, see Beckerman (1994, 1995).

developed, and the functional relationships between the two. There is even less agreement about the time horizons that are relevant in considering what is to be sustained and what is to be developed. It is clear, however, that a successful sustainability transition must include the enhancement of the level of material consumption of the vast majority of the people now living and that will be added to the global population over the next half century (National Research Council, 1999).

MODELING THE FUTURE[3]

One thing that we can be certain about is that the future will not be a linear extension of the past. One approach to the exploration of plausible futures is the construction of integrated assessment models. An early, and highly controversial, example was the Club of Rome's report, *Limits to Growth* (Meadows et al., 1972). The report depicted a world entering an "era of limits" in which even low rates of growth would no longer be sustainable. More recent integrated assessment models have emphasized the specification of more realistic model structures and parameter values. There has also been a tendency to shift away from prediction and toward the exploration of the sensitivity of outcomes to alternative parameter values and policy regimes (Wyant et al., 1996; Rottman and Dowlatabadi, 1998).

A second approach, which attempts to explore the future beyond the analytical constraints imposed by the more formal, integrated assessment models, has been to construct scenarios of alternative development paths. Scenarios are stories about the future told in the language of words as well as numbers. They draw on scientific and technical understanding of historical patterns, current conditions and physical processes. They may employ formal modeling to provide structure, discipline, and rigor, but they also draw on insight and imagination to provide accounts of potential institutional and cultural changes. Scenarios are not predictions or forecasts. Rather, they suggest how future events might unfold.

Both the integrated assessment and scenario approaches are subject to similar problems. No matter how sophisticated the method, assumptions must be made about the trajectories of exogenous variables. This leads to two sources of bias in the results. One is that analysts often find it exceedingly difficult to escape the heavy weight of conventional opinion. For example, almost all official petroleum price projections constructed between the mid-1970s and the early 1980s incorporated exogenous variables that led to the projection of higher future petroleum prices (Chapter 7). A second source of bias is a strong temptation, when efforts are made to break out of the bounds of conventional wisdom, to project catastrophe—what Wagar (1982) refers to as "terminal visions."

---

[3] In this section I draw on my participation in the work of the National Research Council Board on Sustainable Development (1999).

Recent global change scenarios include reports prepared for the World Resources Institute–Santa Fe Institute–Brookings Institution "2050 Project" (Hammond, 1998) and the Stockholm Environmental Institute (Raskin et al., 1996). Both reports present three basic scenarios—Conventional Worlds, Great Transitions, and Barbarization (Figure 14.1).

Conventional Worlds

The Conventional Worlds "Reference Scenario" assumes that economic trends will, with minor variations, continue along the historical trajectory of the twentieth century without fundamental changes in institutions or values. These trends

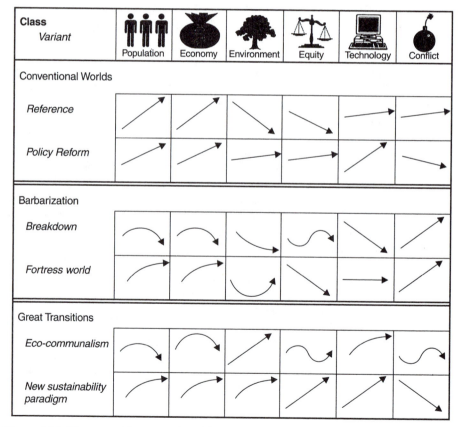

Figure 14.1 Three transition scenarios. (*Source:* G. C. Gallopin, A. Hammond, P. Raskin, and R. Swart, *Branch Points: Global Scenarios and Human Choice*, (Stockholm: Stockholm Environment Institute, 1997).

include markets, private investment, and competition as the fundamental engine for economic growth and wealth allocation: free trade and unrestricted capital and financial flows to foster globalization of product and labor markets; rapid industrialization and urbanization; possessive individualism as the motive of human agents and the basis of the "good life;" and the nation-state and liberal democracy as the appropriate form of governance in the modern era. The conventional development paradigm envisions the continuous unfolding of these interlinked processes without major social, technological, or natural surprises and disruptions. (Raskin et al., 1996:2–3)

The Reference Scenario assumes that population will increase from about 6 billion in 2000 to a peak of about 10 billion in 2050, with nearly all the increase in developing regions. The economies of the developing countries will grow more rapidly than those of the developed (OECD) countries—3.6 as compared with 2% per year. The ratio of average gross domestic product (GDP) in developing countries to that in OCED regions will decline from 20 in 1990 to 15 in 2050—but the absolute difference will continue to rise even as the ratio declines. The structural shift in economic activity—from agriculture to industry to services—will continue. The trends toward dematerialization and decarbonization will also continue. Although energy and water use will grow far less rapidly than GDP, due to structural and technological changes, the greater scale of human activities increasingly stresses the assimilative capacity of the air, water, and soil. Oil and gas resources will become increasingly scarce.

The world described by the Reference Scenario will be a richer but dirtier world than the one we live in at the beginning of the twenty-first century! The cumulative loads on earth's geochemical cycles and ecosystems could exceed natural assimilative capacities, heightened pressure on natural resources could lead to economic and social disruption or conflicts, and social and geopolitical stresses could threaten socioeconomic sustainability (Gallopin and Raskin, 1998:11; Homer-Dixon, 1994).

These concerns led to the construction of a "Policy Reform" variant of the Conventional Worlds Scenario. The Policy Reform variant assumes that within the context of current values and institutional structures, governments act vigorously to achieve rapid economic growth, greater distributional equity, and serious protection of environmental quality. The realization of the Policy Reform variant would require major institutional changes, including a larger transfer of resources from rich to poor countries as well as technical changes, leading to an even more rapid shift toward dematerialization and decarbonization than implied in the Reference Scenario. It would also require a stronger role of government in environmental management. The benefits would be realized in terms of improvements in environmental quality, greater equity, and a reduction in sociopolitical conflict (Figure 14.1).

Great Transformations

The Great Transformations scenario is intended to illustrate the implications of a more radical response to the sustainability challenge. It posits a society that is more protective of natural resources, that achieves higher levels of well-being with lower levels of material consumption, and that is characterized by more equitable distribution of income both within and among countries. In the New Sustainability variant, environmental technology along the lines advocated in the industrial ecology literature would result in dramatic reductions in the flow of energy and material through the economy (Chapter 12). Incomes in the poorer regions of the world converge toward those in developed countries. Cultural consumption emerges as a substitute for growth in material consumption.

The Ecocommunalism varient seeks to incorporate the "deep green" version of sustainable society—characterized by localism, face to face democracy, small-scale organization of production, and regional economic autonomy. It involves a planned retreat from large-scale industrial and agricultural production similar to that promoted by the "small is beautiful" and "appropriate technology" movements of the 1970s (Schumacher, 1973; Briggs and Clay, 1981). A local craft economy emerges to complement small-scale factories and farms. Large urban centers decline in response to reverse migration to smaller cities and towns linked by low-energy transportation systems and new communication technologies.

Barbarization

The Barbarization scenario contemplates a failure to achieve a sustainability transition. It is a possible consequence of failure to realize the institutional reforms necessary to achieve either the Conventional Worlds or Great Transition transformations. A combination of environmental degradation and a widening gap in income distribution both among and within countries results in an erosion of the institutions of governance and of civil society (Gallopin and Raskin, 1998:262).

The Breakdown version involves institutional disintegration, economic collapse, and intensified conflict along ethnic, religious, and ideological lines. The Fortress World varient involves an authoritarian response to the threat of internal breakdown in the more developed countries. These authoritarian governments achieve hegemony over resource-rich regions outside their own borders. And they manage to protect their borders against mass immigration from the poor regions of the world.

It is easy to underestimate the magnitude of the cultural and institutional changes that must occur if a successful transition toward sustainable development is to be achieved over the next half century. One way to characterize these changes, particularly in the presently developed countries, is by a shift from a material and energy-intensive to a service and cultural-intensive pattern of consumption. The sustainability scenarios reviewed in this chapter have been constructed, however, with little explicit reference to either the classical or modern growth theory literature (Chapters 1 and 2). In models based on economic growth theory steady-state growth can occur as a result of the continued advances in technology needed to sustain productivity growth.

The more optimistic sustainability scenarios posit continued technological change leading to decarbonization and dematerialization. But the effect of continued decarbonization and dematerialization will be a decline in the share of materials and energy as a percentage of personal or national income. This implies that a larger share of income must be consumed in the form of services. The two-sector classical model presented in Chapter 1 suggests that if the rate of growth in per capita consumption is not to fall to zero, the productivity gains in the service sector, including the production of cultural services, must account for a larger share of economic growth as the gains from the material-intensive sectors decline.

My own sense is that although the several scenarios provide valuable insight into plausible future development trajectories there will continue to be great diversity among countries and regions well beyond the middle of the twenty-first century. A substantial number of countries will fail to achieve a transition to either satisfactory levels of material consumption, substantial reduction in the stress on environmental services, or greater equity in income distribution. It seems unlikely that the conditions described in the New Sustainability variant will be more than partially realized, or that the conditions described in the Barbarization Scenario will be completely eliminated.

SUSTAINABILITY TRANSITIONS

The scientific and technical challenges that will be confronted as attempts are made to navigate the sustainability transition during the first half of the twenty-first century will be very different from the challenges of the nineteenth and twentieth centuries. Substantial progress has already been achieved in navigating a series of transitions that are most relevant to sustainability. Several of these transitions have progressed so far that their continuation can hardly be in doubt. One is the human settlement transition, from predominantly rural to predominantly urban. A second is the agricultural productivity transition from obtaining increases in agricultural production through expanding the area cultivated to increasing production through higher output per land unit, based on advances in knowledge and technology. A third is the demographic transition from high birth and death rates to low birth and death rates.

Several other transitions have progressed far enough to inspire some confidence that they will be sustained. These include the economic transition from a low to a high level of material and energy consumption and the educational transition from low to high levels of literacy and numeracy. Other transitions that are well underway include the transition from high to low levels of material and energy intensity—dematerialization and decarbonization—and the epidemiological transition from early death by infectious and parasitic disease to late death by cancer, heart attack, and stroke (National Research Council, 1999). The demographic transition and the educational transition are both occurring more rapidly than they occurred in presently developed countries, or than anticipated only a generation ago. Furthermore, our understanding of the processes and policies that have contributed to these transitions has advanced substantially over the past half century. We also can learn from the experience of countries such as Taiwan and South Korea that have achieved the economic, demographic, and educational transition over a period of approximately two generations, and of countries such as Brazil, China, and India that seem well on the way toward these same transitions.

But a measure of caution is in order. Progress in the material, energy, and epidemiological transitions are closely associated with the economic transition, which remains problematical for the poorest countries. In many middle and low-income countries, in spite of increasingly favorable demographic and education trends, economic growth continues to be constrained by the failure of institutional development. A "development state" capable of instituting the rule of law, maintaining a relatively low level of public consumption or diversion of public resources to private consumption, and of managing monetary and fiscal policy to avoid high levels of inflation and extreme fluctuations in economic activity will be required to make a rapid transition to high levels of material consumption (Barro, 1997). The epidemiological transition may be vulnerable to surprises that could reverse the direction of change. The resistance to treatment of older parasitic and infectious disease and the emergence and diffusion of newly recognized diseases may signal the emergence of even greater health threats in the future (Lederberg, 1996).

In many middle-income and most low-income countries the investments in scientific and technical effort necessary to continue the health transition and to advance the material and energy transitions necessary to achieve sustainable growth will be difficult to mobilize until substantial progress has been made in the economic, the demographic, and the educational transitions. If the challenges represented by the transition to sustainability are to be met, very substantial investments will have to be made in advancing scientific knowledge and technology development. If the technologies needed to sustain ecological viability in the low-income countries are to be economically viable they must be capable of lowering the real cost of achieving the demographic, educational, health, and energy transitions.

Private sector research and technology development can hardly be economically viable unless the product can be embodied in proprietary products. Nor can it be viable unless potential users of the technology have entitlement to the resources needed to obtain access to the technology. As public sector support for research and development in many traditional areas is transferred to the private sector it will be necessary, as noted earlier, to enlarge public support for technology development in a number of areas that are essential for the sustainability transition.

Equitable access to food, health, and environmental services are among the most difficult challenges that must be confronted over the next several decades (Chapters 6, 12). Meeting these challenges will pose particularly difficult problems for public policy and institutional design, as well as for scientific knowledge and technology development. The solutions will be closely linked to poverty reduction—to achieving higher levels and more equitable distribution of per capita income and material consumption. The scientific and technical challenges of meeting food, health, and environmental objectives will be particularly difficult. They will, as argued below, be confronted by biological systems that will challenge the sustainability of the gains from each advance in technology. The task will be further complicated because it is unlikely that private sector incentives will be adequate to generate the necessary knowledge and technology.

Food

The task of providing food for an additional 3–6 billion people over the next half century will represent a very difficult challenge. Growth in demand for food will rise in response to population growth, growth of per capita income, and attempts to reduce the undernutrition of the very poor. It seems likely that the world's farmers will be confronted by at least a doubling of food demand over the next half century. Food production will have to compete with nonfood uses of land and water. These uses include, in addition to traditional nonfood crops such as cotton and rubber, potential new uses such as biomass for energy production, the conversion of cropland for urban use, and environmental demands for water (Waggoner, 1994). These demands will impinge very unevenly in different parts of the world. In rich countries, a combination of slowing population growth and rapid productivity growth has, over the past half century, released substantial land for nonagricultural use. In much of Asia, agricultural productivity and slowing population growth have enabled agriculture to meet food demands in spite of severe constraints on land availability. In Latin America, a combination of expansion in area cultivated and rising productivity has begun to generate more rapid growth in agricultural production. But in a number of the poorest countries, particularly in Sub-Saharan Africa, but also in some of the poorer countries in Asia and Latin America, the capacity to expand production rapidly enough to meet future growth in demand has not yet been established.

The experience of the past half century has taught us that there are three institutional requirements for sustainable growth in agricultural production: (1) decentralized public and private agricultural research capacity, (2) local public and private capacity to make knowledge, technology, and materials available to producers, and (3) the schooling and informal education of farmers and farm workers (Chapter 6). Over the past several decades an international agricultural research system, under the auspices of the Consultative Group on International Research (CGIAR), has become an important source of new knowledge and new technology. The national research systems in a number of countries have acquired substantial capacity to borrow, adapt, and generate new knowledge and technology. Private sector agricultural research accounts for a higher share of new knowledge and technology in developed countries and is expanding rapidly in a number of the larger developing countries.

There are also substantial grounds for concern. Financial support for agricultural research in many developed countries, and support by developed country aid donors to both international and national agricultural research in developing countries, eroded during the 1990s . Institutional developments such as the consolidation of private sector agricultural research, particularly in the area of biotechnology, in a few multinational firms or alliances and the extension of exceedingly broad intellectual property rights to the new technologies raise the possibility of slowing both technical advance and diffusion.

The gains in agricultural productivity that will be needed to respond to the demands on the world's farmers will be more difficult to achieve than in the immediate past (Chapter 6). Agricultural scientists are now experiencing difficulty in raising yield ceilings, particularly for the major cereal crops, as rapidly as during the past half century. Expansion of irrigated land has become more costly and competition between food and nonfood crops and between food and animal feed uses seems likely to intensify. Soil loss and degradation have become important constraints on agricultural production in some areas. The spillover of pollutants from agricultural and industrial intensification has affected the productivity and suitability of food production on some agricultural lands. Pest control has become more difficult as a result of the evolution of resistance to both chemical and biological methods of control. Emerging advances in biotechnology will help producers realize the biological yield potential of existing crops and animals. But it remains unclear whether, or how soon, advances in biotechnology will raise yield ceilings—potential yields—above the levels achieved over the past several decades.

Health

A global health research system has emerged more slowly than a global agricultural research system. For most of the last century—since the time of Koch and Pasteur—health research has been thought of principally as laboratory-based biomedical research, seeking "silver bullets" against specific infections or diseases—new vaccines, new drugs, and new surgical techniques. This focus, plus the remarkable improvements in health in recent decades, led to the misperception that all the new knowledge and new technology needed to protect families and communities around the world from illness could be generated in the universities, research institutes, and pharmaceutical and biotechnology laboratories of the industrialized countries.[4]

This conception, which is clearly wrong, has been changing recently. Three gains in perception are especially important. The *first* is the recognition that health technologies, to be useful, must be applied in particular social settings. Achieving health improvements requires not only technology but also policies, organizations, and processes adapted to the varied economic, social, cultural, and historical circumstances among and within countries. Even vaccines, the simplest of technologies, cannot be applied in Lagos by the same means they are in Liverpool.

A *second* gain in perception is the recognition that the principal actors in improving health are individuals and families—the users and beneficiaries of advances in health technology. Preventing illness and promoting health depend first and foremost on the ability of families to use essential knowledge about nutrition, cleanliness, and

---

[4] In this section I draw on the papers in Ruttan (1994b, 1994c). See particularly the papers by Gunatilleke (1994) and Kaseje (1994) in Ruttan (1994c). See also Tendler (1994).

other health practices—and how and when to call on the help of health professionals. An effective health research system must be organized not simply to serve physicians, but to support the flow of health knowledge and technology to families and communities—and to provide for the reverse flow of information from families and communities to researchers about the actual nature of health problems and how they are changing.

Also significant is the recognition that the world's health research efforts are overwhelmingly concentrated in industrialized countries, seeking technologies to address the diseases of more affluent societies—particularly the diseases and afflictions characteristic of the later stages of the health transition. Less than 10% of global health research financing is directed to the major diseases and health problems of the developing countries, where more than 90% of the world's preventable deaths occur (Commission on Health Research for Development, 1990).

The resources families need to provide effective health services to their members, and to draw on health professionals when needed, are very similar to those farmers need to respond to the demands placed on them. The high-payoff health inputs include the following: (1) the capacity of the health research community to produce new knowledge and materials appropriate to the resource and cultural endowments of poor communities, (2) the capacity of national, regional, and local institutions to make the knowledge and the materials available to families, and (3) the formal schooling and informal education of families, particularly mothers, to make effective use of the knowledge available to them.

Failure to complement science-based health research with effective delivery and education are illustrated by the U.S. experience. The United States is preeminent in almost every aspect of biomedical science—in both the underlying basic science and in clinical applications. But there is pervasive dissatisfaction in the United States with the institutional arrangement for delivering health services. Many U.S. health indicators, such as infant mortality rates, rank well below similar health indicators for countries with much more limited biomedical research capacity. The health technologies needed to meet the needs of the poor and the institutional reforms necessary to enable the poor to lead more healthy lives continue to be neglected. In contrast, several very poor countries, faced with extremely limited resources to devote to health services, have to put into place some of the important elements outlined above. Sri Lanka has, for example, been able to achieve health indicators— a life expectancy of above 70 years and infant mortality below 20 per 1000 live births—comparable to the levels achieved by societies that are much more affluent.

Environment

The science base for the technical and institutional innovations that will be needed to make the transition to environmental sustainability—the science for environmental policy—is far less firmly established than the science base for agriculture and health policy. It is only about a decade and a half ago that the fundamental relationships among the biological, chemical, and geophysical processes of the biosphere were outlined (Bretherton, 1985). Knowledge about ecosystem processes and the role of biological diversity remain uncertain. There is as yet no coherent system in place to monitor the environmental changes that are most relevant to the sustainability transition.

It is now clear that the science needed to understand the global changes that are underway and to develop the technical and institutional innovations necessary to navigate the sustainability transition must be institutionalized at the regional and local levels. The START (SysTem for Analysis, Research, and Training) initiative of the International Geosphere–Biosphere Program, the World Climate Program, and the International Human Dimensions Program on Global Environmental Change represent examples of such an effort (National Research Council, 1999, Chapter 6). The NRC Board on Sustainable Development has identified four areas that will require more intensive research. These include (1) understanding and monitoring the transitions that are now underway, (2) identifying safety limits for the earth's life support and ecological systems, (3) understanding the process of learning about and adapting to the changes in the global environment, and (4) building capacity to design the technology and institutions that will be needed for a sustainability transition.

The serious mismatch between the scale of environmental change and the functional scales of the human institutions needed to respond effectively to these changes may be an ever more serious constraint on the transition to sustainability (Lee, 1993a). Very substantial institutional innovations, particularly the establishment of the property regimes capable of internalizing—within families, firms, and public jurisdictions—the external costs of environmental change will be required.

The global research system needed to support the sustainability transition will have many of the features of effective agricultural and health research systems. The behavior of the households, firms, and farms that contribute to local, regional, and global environmental changes will have to be recognized as central to the process of environmental change. The knowledge and the technology that will be needed to place factories, farms, and households in a position to mitigate, or adapt constructively to environmental change will depend on (1) the capacity of the global change research community to provide the knowledge, including the national and local research needed by factory, farm, and household decision makers, (2) the capacity of national, regional, and community institutions to transfer the knowledge and technology, and to create the appropriate incentives for those who make decisions about resource use, and (3) the depth of understanding possessed by factory, farm, and household decision makers about the consequences of their own actions and the actions of the economic and political institutions in which they participate.

INTELLECTUAL CHALLENGES

If the commitment to the sustainability transition is to be translated into an internally coherent reform agenda it will be necessary to confront a number of unresolved intellectual and analytical issues. These include (1) substitutability, (2) obligations toward the future, and (3) institutional design.

Substitutability

Our knowledge about the role of technology in widening the substitutability among natural resources and constructed capital is clearly inadequate. Economists and technologists have traditionally viewed technical change as widening the possibility of substitution among resources—of fiber optic cable for copper cable, for example. The sustainability community, as noted above, rejects the implications of the "age of substitutability" argument (Goeller and Weinberg, 1976). The loss of plant genetic resources is viewed as a permanent loss of capacity. The substitutability between natural factors and constructed factors is viewed as severely constrained. When considering the production of a particular commodity—for example, the substitution of fertilizer for land in the production of wheat—this is an argument over the form of the production function. But substitution also occurs through the production of a different product or process that performs the same function or fills the same need—of fuels with higher hydrogen to carbon ratios for coal, for example (Chapter 12).

The argument about substitutability is inherently an empirical issue. But the scientific and technical knowledge needed to resolve disagreements about the possibilities of substitution will always lie in the future. Yet the issue is exceedingly important. If a combination of capital investment and technical change can continuously widen opportunities for substitution, imposing constraints on resource and environmental exploitation could leave future generations less well off. If, on the other hand, real output per unit of natural resource or environmental input is narrowly bounded—if it cannot exceed some upper limit that is not too far from where we are now—the catastrophe is unavoidable.

Obligations Toward the Future

A second issue that has divided mainstream economists from the sustainability community is how to deal analytically with the obligations of the present generation toward future generations. The issue of intergenerational equity, as noted above, is at the center of the sustainability debate (Pearce et al., 1990:23–56; Page, 1991:58–74; Pearce and Atkinson, 1995; Solow, 1992). The conventional approach, employed by resource and other economists, involves calculating the "present value" of a resource development or protection project by discounting the cost and benefit stream by some "real" rate of interest. Critics insist that this approach results in a "dictatorship of the present" over the future. At conventional rates of interest, the present value of benefits 50 years into the future approaches zero. "Discounting can make molehills out of even the biggest mountain" (Batie, 1989:1092).

Traditional discounting is perfectly appropriate when comparing the costs and benefits of alternative near-term environmental projects—in determining the order of priority in which toxic waste disposal sites should be cleaned up, for example. For projects that are likely to benefit distant future generations, such as greenhouse gas abatement, the use of discounting is more questionable. Decisions about inter-generational transfers of income are similar in many respects to decisions about contemporary intercountry income transfers. In such decisions it is appropriate to compare the opportunity costs of direct investment in the economic improvement of the well-being of the people living in poor countries as compared with invest-ments that will enhance the well-being of people living several generations into the future. For societies that find it difficult to find principled reasons to devote resources to reducing contemporary inequity in income distribution, this is a diffi-cult trade-off.

It seems clear that in most countries efforts to achieve sustainable growth must in-volve some combination of (1) a high contemporary rate of saving—deferring present in favor of future consumption, (2) high investment in human capital formation, and (3) more rapid technical change—particularly the technical changes that will enhance resource productivity and widen the range of substitutability among resources. But will these ensure sustainability? For the next half century even the pattern of devel-opment associated with the Conventional Worlds scenarios seems sustainable. But over the very long run almost no scenario involving continuing economic growth appears sustainable. Extended indefinitely, even exceedingly low rates of growth in population, resource use, or per capita income appear to be unsustainable (National Research Council, 1999, Chapter 1). In the longer run it may be necessary to impose sumptuary regulations to constrain current consumption.

Institutional Design

A third area in which knowledge needs to be advanced is in the design of institutions that are capable of internalizing—within individual households, private firms, and public organizations—the costs of actions that generate the negative externalities that are the source of environmental stress. Under present institutional arrangements important elements of the physical and social environment continue to be undervalued. The dynamic consequences of failure to internalize spillover costs can be particularly severe. In an environment characterized by rapid economic growth and changing relative factor prices, failure to internalize resource and environmental costs will bias the direction of technical change along an inefficient trajectory. The demand for a resource that is priced below its social cost will grow more rapidly than if substitution possibilities are constrained by existing technology. As a result, "open-access" resources will undergo stress or depletion more rapidly than in a world characterized by static technology or even by neutral (unbiased) technical change (Chapter 12).

The design of incentive-compatible institutions—institutions capable of achieving compatibility among individual, organizational, and social objectives—remains at this stage an art rather than a science. The incentive-compatibility problem has not been solved even at the most abstract theoretical level.[5] Economists and other social scientists have made a good deal of progress in contributing the analysis needed for "course correction," but capacity to contribute to institutional design remains limited.

These unresolved analytical issues impose severe constraints on our ability to design widely accepted sustainability indicators. There is no coherent conceptual intellectual foundation for deciding what to develop and what to sustain and over what time period. As a result, sustainability indicators are often selected more for their political acceptability, or their consistency with ideological commitments, than on the basis of objective knowledge of the ecological or economic implications of the changes captured by the indicators. No single set of sustainability indicators to monitor social and environmental changes that might lead to irreversible damage has yet been designed (National Research Council, 1999, Chapter 5).

PERSPECTIVE

In concluding it may be worth reminding ourselves of several perspectives that are often overlooked in our concern about the difficulties that will be faced in navigating the sustainability transition.

First, humankind has throughout history been continuously challenged by the twin problems of how to provide itself with adequate sustenance and how to dispose of the residuals arising from production and consumption. Failure to make balanced progress along one or both of these fronts has at times imposed serious constraints on society's growth and development. Throughout history human society has been highly vulnerable to environmental hazards. Nature has not always been willing to accommodate the stress on the environment imposed by intensive human activity over long periods of time (Meyer et al., 1998).

Second, the advance of science and technology has enabled modern society to achieve a more productive and a better balanced relationship to the natural world than ancient civilization or the earlier stages of Western industrial civilization. Continued technical advance is essential for further improvements in both the material and cultural dimensions of civil life. The fundamental significance of technical change is that it permits the substitution of knowledge for resources, or of less expensive resources for more expensive resources, or that it releases the constraints on growth imposed by inelastic resource supplies.

---

[5] The concept of incentive compatibility was introduced by Hurwicz (1972, 1998), who showed that it was not possible to specify an informationally decentralized mechanism for resource allocation that simultaneously generated efficient resource allocation and incentives for consumers to honestly reveal their true preferences. For a survey of the state of knowledge in this area, see Groves et al. (1987). For a detailed discussion of the difficulties of achieving incentive compatibility in natural resource and environmental policy and management, see Young (1992).

Third, if humankind fails to successfully navigate the sustainability transition over the next century, the fault will more likely be found in the failure of institutional innovation, rather than in inherent constraints in resource supplies and the other services of nature. This is not an optimistic conclusion. At our present state of knowledge institutional design is analogous to driving down a four lane highway looking out the rear view mirror. Mankind has demonstrated greater skill at making course corrections after hitting the highway margin than in using foresight. Our vision of the future will continue to be limited by the opaqueness of the navigation instruments available to us. But we can design information systems that will increase our sensitivity to the location of the highway margins and we can develop greater technical and institutional capacity to respond to the uncertain events of the future.

Finally, the transition toward sustainability must be visualized not as a goal, but as a process of discovery (Lee, 1993b:185–201). The transition to sustainability will involve a search for an appropriate relationship between humankind and the natural order. It will also involve a search for the appropriate technologies and institutions to sustain the constructed order that humankind has built on this planet. It is unlikely that either will be resolved over the next half century. But it is not too much to anticipate that measurable progress will be achieved.

REFERENCES

Ausubel, J. H. "Regularities in Technological Development: An Environmental View." In *Technology and Environment,* J. H. Ausubel and H. E. Sladovich, eds., pp. 70–91. Washington, DC: National Academy Press, 1989.

Ausubel, J., and D. Langford, eds. *Technological Trajectories and the Human Environment.* Washington DC: National Academy Press, 1997.

Batie, S. "Sustainable Development: Challenges to the Profession of Agricultural Economics." *American Journal of Agricultural Economics* 71 (1989):1085–1101.

Barro, R. J. *Determinants of Economic Growth: A Cross-Country Empirical Study.* Cambridge, MA: MIT Press, 1997.

Beckerman, W. "Sustainable Development: Is It a Useful Concept?" *Environmental Values* 3 (1994):191–209.

Beckerman, W. "How Would you Like Your 'Sustainability,' Sir? Weak or Strong? A Reply to My Critics." *Environmental Values* 4 (1995):169–179.

Bretherton, F. "Earth System Science and Remote Sensing." *Proceedings of the IEEE* 73 (1985):1118–1127.

Briggs, S., and E. Clay. "Sources of Innovation in Agricultural Technology." *World Development* 9 (1981):321–336.

Chichilinsky, G. "What Is Sustainable Development?" *Land Economics* 73 (1997):467–491.

Commission on Health Research for Development. *Health Research: Essential Link to Equity in Development.* Oxford, UK: Oxford University Press, 1990.

Daily, G. C., ed. *Nature's Services: Societal Dependence on Natural Ecosystems.* Washington, DC: Island Press, 1997.

David, P. A. "Computer and Dynamo: A Historical Perspective on the Modern Productivity Paradox." *American Economic Review* 80 (1990):355–361.

Douglass, G. K., ed. *Agricultural Sustainability in a Changing World Order.* Boulder, CO: Westview Press, 1984.

Ehrlich, P. R. *The Population Bomb.* New York, NY: Ballentine Books, 1968.

Ehrlich, P. R., and A. H. Ehrlich. *Population, Resources, Environment: Issues in Human Ecology.* San Francisco, CA: W. H. Freeman, 1970.

Gallopin, A., A. Hammond, P. Raskin, and R. Swart. *Branch Points: Global Scenarios and Human Choice.* Stockholm, Sweden: Stockholm Environmental Institute, 1997.

Gallopin, G. C., and P. Raskin. "Windows on the Future: Global Scenarios and Sustainability." *Environment* 40 (3, April 1998):6–11, 26–31.

Goeller, H. E., and Alvin M. Weinberg. "The Age of Substitutability." *Science* 191 (1976):683–689.

Groves, T., R. Radner, and S. Reiter, eds. *Information, Incentives, and Economic Mechanisms.* Minneapolis, MN: University of Minnesota Press, 1987.

Gunatilleke, G. "Health Policy for Rural Areas: Sri Lanka." In *Agriculture, Environment, and Health: Sustainable Development in the 21st Century*, V. W. Ruttan, ed., pp. 208–234. Minneapolis, MN: University of Minnesota Press, 1994.

Hammond, A. *Which World? Scenarios for the 21st Century.* Washington, DC: Island Press, 1998.

Homer-Dixon, T. F. "Environmental Scarcities and Violent Conflict." *International Security* 19 (1994):5–40.

Hurwicz, L. "On Informationally Decentralized Systems." In *Decisions and Organization*, C. B. McGuire and R. Radner, eds., pp. 297–336. Amsterdam, Netherlands: North Holland, 1972.

Hurwicz, L. "Issues in the Design of Mechanisms and Institutions." In *Designing Institutions for Environmental and Resource Management*, E. T. Loehman and D. M. Kalgour, eds., pp. 29-56. Cheltenham, UK: Edward Elgar, 1998.

Jamieson, D. "Sustainability and Beyond." *Ecological Economics* 24 (1998):183–192.

Kaseje, Dan C. O. "Health Systems for Rural Areas: Kenya." In *Agriculture, Environment, and Health: Sustainable Development in the 21st Century*, V. W. Ruttan, ed., pp. 235–255. Minneapolis, MN: University of Minnesota Press, 1994.

Lederberg, J. "Infectious Disease: A Threat to Global Health Security." *Journal of the American Medical Association (JAMA)* 276 (1996):412–419.

Lee, K. M. "Greed, Scale, Mis-match and Learning." *Ecological Applications* 3 (1993a):560–564.

Lee, K. M. *Compass and Gyroscope: Integrating Science and Politics for the Environment.* Washington, DC: Island Press, 1993b.

Lele, S. M. "Sustainable Development: A Critical Review." *World Development* 19 (1991):607–621.

Lipsey, R. G., C. Bekar, and K. Conlaw. "What Requires Explanation?" In *General Purpose Technologies and Economic Growth*, E. Helpman, ed., pp. 16–54. Cambridge, MA: MIT Press, 1998.

Meadows, D. H., D. L. Meadows et al. *The Limits to Growth.* New York: Universe Books, 1972.

Meyer, W. B., K. W. Butzer, T. E. Downing, B. L. Turner, G. W. Wenzel, and J. L. Wescoat.

"Reasoning by Analogy." In *Human Choice and Climate Change, Vol III, The Tools for Policy Analysis,* S. Rayner and E. L. Malone, eds., pp. 217–289. Columbus, OH: Battle Press, 1998.

Mowery, D. C., and N. Rosenberg. *Paths of Innovation: Technological Change in the 20th Century America.* Cambridge, UK: Cambridge University Press, 1998.

Myers, N. "Pre-Debate Statement." In *Scarcity or Abundance? A Debate on the Environment,* N. Meyers and J. L. Simon, eds., pp. 69–109. New York: W. W. Norton, 1994.

National Research Council. *Changing Climate.* Washington, DC: National Academy Press, 1983a.

National Research Council. *Policy Implications of Greenhouse Warming: Mitigation, Adaptation and The Science Base.* Washington, DC: National Academy Press, 1983b.

National Research Council. *Global Environmental Change: Understanding Human Dimensions.* Washington, DC: National Academy Press, 1992.

National Research Council, Board on Sustainable Development. *Our Common Journey: Toward a Sustainability Transition.* Washington, DC: National Academy Press, 1999.

Page, T. "Sustainability and the Problem of Valuation." In *Ecological Economics: The Science and Management of Sustainability,* R. Costanza, ed., pp. 58–74. New York: Columbia University Press, 1991.

Pearce, D., and G. Atkinson. "Measuring Sustainable Development." In *The Handbook of Environmental Economics,* D. W. Bromley, ed., pp. 166–181. Oxford, UK: Blackwell Publishers, 1995.

Pearce, D., E. Barbier and A. Markandya. *Economics and Environment in the Third World.* London: Earthscan Publications, 1990.

Raskin, P., M. Chadwick, T. Jackson, and G. Leach. *The Sustainability Transition: Beyond Conventional Development.* Stockholm, Sweden: Stockholm Environment Institute, 1996.

Rottman, J., and H. Dowlatabadi. "Integrated Assessment Modeling." In *Human Choices and Climate Change, Vol. III, The Tools for Policy Analysis,* S. Rayner and E. L. Malone, eds., pp. 291–377. Columbus, OH: Battle Press 1998.

Ruttan, V. W. "Constraints on the Design of Sustainable Systems of Agricultural Production." *Ecological Economics* 120 (1994a):209–219.

Ruttan, V. W., ed. *Health and Sustainable Agricultural Development: Perspectives on Growth and Constraints.* Boulder, CO: Westview Press, 1994b.

Ruttan, V. W., ed. *Agriculture, Environment and Health: Sustainable Development in the 21st Century.* Minneapolis, MN: University of Minnesota Press, 1994c.

Schumacher, E. F. *Small is Beautiful: Economics as if People Mattered.* New York: Harper, 1973.

Solow, R. M. "The Economics of Resources and the Resources of Economists." *American Economic Review* 64 (1974):1–14.

Solow, R. *An Almost Practical Step Toward Sustainability.* Washington, DC: Resources for the Future, 1992.

Tendler, J. "Trust in a Rent-Seeking World: Health and Government Transformed in Northeast Brazil." *World Development* 22 (1994):1771–1791.

Wagar, W. W. *Terminal Visions: The Literature of Last Things.* Bloomington, IN: Indiana University Press, 1982.

Waggoner, P. E. "How Much Land Can Ten Billion People Spare for Nature?" In *Technological Trajectories and the Human Environment,* J. H. Ausubel and H. D. Langford, eds., pp. 56–73. Washington, DC: National Academy Press, 1994.

World Commission on Environment and Development. *Our Common Future*. New York: Oxford University Press, 1987 (The Brundtland Commission).

Wyant, J., W. Clive, S. Frankhauser et al. "Integrated Assessment of Climate Change: An Overview of Comparison of Approaches and Results." In *Climate Changes, 1995: Economic and Social Dimension of Climate Change,* J. P. Bruce, H. Lee, and E. F. Haites, eds., pp. 374–396. Contribution of Working Group III to the Second Assessment Report of the Intergovernmental Panel on Climate Change. New York, NY: Cambridge University Press, 1996.

Young, M. D. *Sustainable Investment and Resource Use: Equity, Environmental Integrity and Economic Efficiency*. Park Ridge, NJ: Parthenon, 1992.

Author Index

Subject Index